Measuring Patient Changes
in Mood, Anxiety, and Personality Disorders

Measuring Patient Changes

in Mood, Anxiety, and Personality Disorders

Toward a Core Battery

Edited by

Hans H. Strupp
Leonard M. Horowitz
Michael J. Lambert

AMERICAN PSYCHOLOGICAL ASSOCIATION

WASHINGTON, DC

Published by
American Psychological Association
750 First Street, NE
Washington, DC 20002

Copies may be ordered from
APA Order Department
P.O. Box 92984
Washington, DC 20090-2984

In the United Kingdom and Europe, copies may be ordered from
American Psychological Association
3 Henrietta Street
Covent Garden, London
WC2E 8LU England

Typeset in Minion by G & S Typesetters, Austin, TX

Printer: Braun-Brumfield, Inc., Ann Arbor, MI
Cover designer: Berg Design, Albany, NY
Technical/production editor: Valerie Montenegro

Library of Congress Cataloging-in-Publication Data
Measuring patient changes in mood, anxiety, and personality disorders : toward a core
    battery / edited by Hans H. Strupp, Leonard M. Horowitz, Michael J. Lambert.
        p.   cm.
    Includes bibliographical references and index.
    ISBN 1-55798-414-X (cb : acid-free paper)
    1. Personality change—Measurement—Congresses.   2. Outcome assessment (Medical
care)—Congresses.   3. Anxiety—Treatment—Evaluation—Congresses.   4. Affective
disorders—Treatment—Evaluation—Congresses.   5. Personality disorders—
Treatment—Evaluation—Congresses.   6. Personality tests—Congresses.   I. Strupp,
Hans H.   II. Horowitz, Leonard M.
    [DNLM: 1. Personality Tests—congresses.   2. Treatment Outcome—congresses.
3. Personality Disorders—diagnosis—congresses.   4. Affective Disorders—diagnosis—
congresses.   5. Anxiety Disorders—diagnosis—congresses.   BF 698.5 M484   1997]
RC480.5.M354   1997
616.85'2—dc21
DNLM/DLC
for Library of Congress   97-7469
                                                                                                          CIP

British Library Cataloguing-in-Publication Data
A CIP record is available from the British Library.

Printed in the United States of America
First edition

APA Science Volumes

As part of its continuing and expanding commitment to enhance the dissemination of scientific psychological knowledge, the Science Directorate of the APA established a Scientific Conferences Program. A series of volumes resulting from these conferences is produced jointly by the Science Directorate and the Office of Communications. A call for proposals is issued twice annually by the Scientific Directorate, which, collaboratively with the APA Board of Scientific Affairs, evaluates the proposals and selects several conferences for funding. This important effort has resulted in an exceptional series of meetings and scholarly volumes, each of which has contributed to the dissemination of research and dialogue in these topical areas.

The APA Science Directorate's conferences funding program has supported 47 conferences since its inception in 1988. To date, 32 volumes resulting from conferences have been published.

WILLIAM C. HOWELL, PhD
Executive Director

VIRGINIA E. HOLT
Assistant Executive Director

Contents

Contributors

Monica Ramirez Basco, University of Texas Southwestern Medical Center at Dallas

Larry E. Beutler, Graduate School of Education, University of California, Santa Barbara

Thomas D. Borkovec, Distinguished Professor of Psychology, Pennsylvania State University, University Park

Louis G. Castonguay, Pennsylvania State University, University Park

Mary Beth Connolly, Center for Psychotherapy Research, Department of Psychiatry, University of Pennsylvania, Philadelphia

Paul Crits-Christoph, Center for Psychotherapy Research, Department of Psychiatry, University of Pennsylvania, Philadelphia

Robert J. DeRubeis, University of Pennsylvania, Philadelphia

Louis Diguer, Laval University, Quebec, Canada

Paul Dudek, Community Mental Health Center for Gloucester County, Woodbury, NJ

Irene Elkin, School of Social Service Administration, University of Chicago

Marvin R. Goldfried, State University of New York at Stony Brook

William P. Henry, University of Utah, Salt Lake City

Leonard M. Horowitz, Stanford University, Stanford, CA

Mardi J. Horowitz, Department of Psychiatry, School of Medicine, University of California, San Francisco

Kenneth I. Howard, Northwestern University, Evanston, IL

Gregory G. Kolden, Department of Psychiatry and Behavioral Sciences, University of Wisconsin–Madison

Steven R. Krebaum, Department of Psychiatry, University of Texas Southwestern Medical Center at Dallas

Michael J. Lambert, Brigham Young University, Provo, UT
Lester Luborsky, Center for Psychotherapy Research, Department of Psychiatry, University of Pennsylvania, Philadelphia
Robert J. Lueger, Marquette University, Milwaukee, WI
Constance Milbrath, Department of Psychiatry, School of Medicine, University of California, San Francisco
Karla Moras, Center for Psychotherapy Research, Department of Psychiatry, University of Pennsylvania, Philadelphia
Kristin L. Nelson, Stanford University, Stanford, CA
Michelle G. Newman, Pennsylvania State University, University Park
Eric A. Person, Pennsylvania State University, University Park
Paul A. Pilkonis, Western Psychiatric Institute and Clinic, School of Medicine, University of Pittsburgh
A. John Rush, Department of Psychiatry, University of Texas Southwestern Medical Center at Dallas
Kelly A. Schmidt, George Washington University, Washington, DC
Dietmar Schulte, Ruhr-Universität, Bochum, Germany
Zindel V. Segal, Clarke Institute of Psychiatry/ Mt. Sinai Hospital, Department of Psychiatry, University of Toronto, Canada
M. Tracie Shea, Department of Psychiatry and Human Behavior, Brown University, Providence, RI
Charles H. Stinson, Department of Psychiatry, School of Medicine, University of California, San Francisco
Hans H. Strupp, Distinguished Professor of Psychology, Emeritus, Vanderbilt University, Nashville, TN
Ralph M. Turner, Department of Clinical and Health Psychology, Allegheny University of the Health Sciences, Philadelphia
Logan Zemp, Brigham Young University, Provo, UT

Preface

M easuring changes in personality and behavior as a result of psycho-therapeutic and pharmacological interventions has been a perennial problem facing practicing clinicians and researchers. The problem has been compounded as the number of studies dealing with therapy outcomes has increased over the years and the need for precision in comparing the results of diverse studies has become a major concern. In addition to a sizable number of methodological difficulties, researchers have noted the lack of agreement on outcome measures, which have differed from study to study. Even when identical measures have been used, they frequently have been applied in less than directly comparable ways. In short, the need for a standard set of measures—a core battery—has been apparent for about 25 years. An earlier effort along these lines by Irene Elkin (then Waskow) and Morris Parloff, as detailed in chapter 2, led to some progress, but the need for further steps has become increasingly apparent.

From our respective research perspectives, we have been interested for some years in grappling with the foregoing problem. As we pondered and discussed possible steps in developing a consensus, usually in the context of annual meetings of the Society for Psychotherapy Research, it seemed sensible to bring together a diverse group of researchers with expertise in measuring treatment outcomes in an effort to develop the basis for multiple core batteries for both homogeneous and heterogeneous patient populations. Specifically, we considered it desirable to develop core batteries for research with nonpsychotic adults in three major diagnostic categories: mood, anxiety, and personality disorders. As part of such an effort, a 2- to 3-day conference seemed best suited to start building a consensus. Accordingly, after extensive planning, such a conference was held on the campus of Vanderbilt University on March 12–14, 1994. We are grateful to Edward

Bein and Louis Castonguay for their content analysis of a questionnaire that helped us prepare for the conference.

In writing this book, we were greatly aided by a grant from the American Psychological Association (APA), which was matched by contributions from Vanderbilt University. In particular, we are grateful to Clifford S. Russell, Director of the Vanderbilt Institute for Public Policy Studies, who, in addition to providing financial support, aided our work in a variety of ways.

Thanks are also due to Russell G. Hamilton, Dean of Vanderbilt University's Graduate School, and George H. Sweeney, Associate Dean of the College of Arts and Science at Vanderbilt University.

Kay Houston and Meredith Dyer deserve special recognition for invaluable secretarial assistance.

We are indebted to Andrea Phillippi, Development Editor for APA Books, for a valuable critique of our manuscript and suggestions for improvement.

PART ONE

Overview of Assessing Psychotherapy Outcomes and the Development of Core Measures of Patient Change

1

Introduction

Michael J. Lambert, Hans H. Strupp, and Leonard M. Horowitz

The measurement of change in patients after psychological and pharmacological interventions has a long history dating back to the 1920s
(Lambert, Christensen, & DeJulio, 1983). Despite this long history, there
is no consensus about appropriate methods and measures for evaluating
patient improvement after treatment. This lack of consensus concerning
the choice of instruments for measuring outcomes has come to a head in
recent years with changes in mental health delivery systems characterized
by managed mental health care (Trabin, 1995). In the 1990s, more than
ever, there is an emphasis on accountability for services rendered—and
thus an era is under way in which professional practices rely on the measured effects of treatments. There is a need to develop a consensus about
which measures most accurately reflect patient improvement. This book is
an attempt to address such a need. We hope it will lead to the development
of several brief test batteries (core batteries) that can be used routinely to
assess treatment effects. Ultimately, our desire is to facilitate the highest
quality of patient care.

This book brings together a diverse group of experts in the field to
address the core battery idea in relation to three broad diagnostic areas:
mood, anxiety, and personality disorders. We believe that this book will

have important implications for clinical practice, providing routine methods for tracking patient progress in treatment. It also will be of interest to researchers, administrators, insurance providers, and policymakers. Although the material is geared to a sophisticated professional audience, advanced graduate students in professional psychology and postdoctoral fellows preparing for clinical research careers will also find the material relevant.

CHAPTERS IN THIS BOOK

This book is divided into six parts. Chapter 2 extends this introduction and seeks to provide a historical background to the development of the core battery idea. Chapter 2 introduces the reader to the issues to be discussed in subsequent chapters. It also summarizes the discussions at the American Psychological Association-sponsored core battery conference at Vanderbilt University.

The remaining chapters present the contributions of individual participants. Part Two consists of three chapters that focus on conceptual and methodological issues as well as problems surrounding the core battery concept. In chapter 3, Dietmar Schulte explores a paradigm from which to view therapeutic success. The paradigm is medical and examines outcome from the point of view of causes, symptoms, and final consequences, particularly as they are expressed in problems pertaining to role behavior. Furthermore, Schulte discusses the design of data collection methods and the clinical relevance of changes.

In chapter 4, Zindel Segal addresses the paradox of the need for measures to be sensitive to patient change and the vulnerability of patients to further episodes of illness. Thus, he emphasizes the importance of taking both a short view of outcome that involves symptomatic recovery while attending to factors that place patients at risk for future illness. His discussion of patient vulnerability and its assessment raises important questions about the contents of a core battery and the need to take a long view of outcome.

Marvin Goldfried (chap. 5) examines four major points that need to be addressed in the development of core batteries: (a) the development of a set of criteria for judging the value of specific measures; (b) issues related to battery development, such as the relative importance of generalized versus individualized outcome measurement; (c) content areas in need of assessment; and (d) a set of procedures for developing the batteries themselves. These points are all placed in the context of the evolutionary trends found in the psychotherapy outcome research enterprise.

Part Three consists of two chapters that focus on the development of a core battery for measuring change in patients who are diagnosed with an anxiety disorder. In chapter 6, Thomas Borkovec, Louis Castonguay, and Michelle Newman review the most frequently used outcome measures for posttraumatic stress disorder and social phobia. They provide a foundation for the selection of measures dealing with these two disorders without attempting to draw final conclusions about specific measures. They address major instruments of psychiatric diagnosis as well as target problems in these two disorders and discuss strengths and weaknesses of a number of scales. They also provide recommendations for data collection procedures, such as the need for 1-year follow-ups.

Paul Crits-Christoph and Mary Beth Connolly (chap. 7) examine measures used in studying the outcome of patients diagnosed with generalized anxiety disorder, obsessive–compulsive disorder, and specific phobia. They present a general core battery consisting of measures of general anxiety symptoms, depression, quality of life, and interpersonal problems, followed by recommendations for measures specific to each disorder. They also provide recommendations for defining such terms as remission, recovery, relapse, and reoccurrence.

In chapter 8, Monica Basco, Steven Krebaum, and John Rush discuss issues relevant to measuring outcome in depression and then survey the existing outcome measures of depression. Their survey includes measures of "caseness," clinician-administered rating scales, and self-report measures. In so doing, they apply four criteria in evaluating six diagnostic measures, 27 clinician rating scales, and 90 self-report measures that exist in the literature.

Part Four consists of six chapters that address the measurement of outcome across patients with mood disorders. In chapter 9, Larry Beutler considers issues that need to be addressed before developing a battery rather than focusing on specific instruments. He recommends criteria for selecting outcome instruments and outlines parameters within which certain dimensions should be measured. He presents examples of instruments that meet minimal standards.

Kenneth Howard, Robert Lueger, and Gregory Kolden (chap. 10) describe their phase model of psychotherapy as it applies to the measurement of progress and outcome of depression. They identify three treatment targets—distress, pathological signs, and disability in life functioning—as a way of organizing outcome assessment. After offering some sobering information about the problems of diagnosing depression, they review several relevant measures and offer general caveats about their limitations.

In chapter 11, Lester Luborsky, Louis Diguer, Robert DeRubeis, and Kelly Schmidt offer a two-stage approach to selecting outcome measures for a core battery. They list 10 principles for selecting outcome measures and provide illustrative measures that are suitable across many of the dimensions. They compare several measures across studies showing concordance in outcome evaluation.

Karla Moras (chap. 12) discusses issues and criteria that must be considered in battery developments and then proposes a core battery. She presents a useful table of content areas that should be covered by such a battery. She offers valuable suggestions for the widespread implementation of the battery and makes suggestions for developing a final consensus about its components and characteristics.

Leonard Horowitz, Kristin Nelson, and Eric Person (chap. 13) identify performance tasks that discriminate between depressed and nondepressed people and consider a battery of such tasks that might be used to assess the severity of depression. They thus propose a behavioral battery that would have several advantages over self-reported and clinician-assessed depressive distress. These proposals are embedded within a theory of depressive syndromes. The behavioral tasks are itemized and described in detail, with the goal of increasing their use in research.

Part Five focuses on a core battery for measuring outcome in the personality disorders. Whereas measuring change in patients diagnosed as suffering from anxiety and mood disorders has a long history in clinical research, measuring change in patients with personality disorder diagnoses is just beginning. In fact, if one surveys past research, there are literally hundreds of studies on patients with depression and anxiety disorders and dozens of meta-analytic reviews of this literature (Lambert & Bergin, 1994). By contrast, there are no more than six outcome studies on the personality disorders (with the exception of antisocial personality disorder). Many edited books have summarized measures recommended for assessing anxiety and depressive disorders (e.g., Barlow, Hayes, & Nelson, 1984; Bellack & Hersen, 1988; Corcoran & Fisher, 1995; Lambert et al., 1983; Wetzler, 1989). None of these books (again with the exception of antisocial personality disorder) has addressed outcome in the assessment of personality disorders. The lack of history for measuring change in most personality disorders makes the development of a core battery difficult, but a battery of measures is much needed at this time.

Part Five consists of five chapters that discuss relevant issues and recommendations. Although there is some overlap of ideas, for the most part the respective authors raise concerns and offer insights from their own research programs as well as their theoretical and conceptual orientations.

In chapter 14, Paul Pilkonis discusses the important place of diagnostic accuracy and the possibility of using "caseness" as an outcome. He suggests the use of a dimensional approach to resolve problems associated with the overlap of diagnostic categories. The dimensional aproach allows clinicians to identify poor prognostic profiles, a matter of considerable concern in outcome studies, because such patients tend to overuse medical as well as psychological services in addition to passing problems on to their offspring.

Tracie Shea (chap. 15) considers issues of general importance in developing a core battery in this area. She emphasizes the need for measures that are relatively free of theoretical bias. Such a battery would be brief and allow researchers to add measures that are not a part of the core. She emphasizes the importance of follow-up assessments and proposes a strategy for collecting pretreatment estimates of patient disturbance that minimize the confounding effects of Axis I psychopathology. Her position on the problems of dealing with the stability of disturbance in the personality disorders is worthy of careful consideration in research on personality disorders.

In chapter 16, Mardi Horowitz, Constance Milbrath, and Charles Stinson present a position that is grounded in their own theoretical model, but they make suggestions that appear to be appropriate for a variety of theoretical orientations. Horowitz and colleagues conceptualize people as having recurring states of mind rather than invariable traits. Their assessment strategies are based on the assumption that "existing official diagnostic criteria are transient compromises in an unsettled field." They draw attention to research and theory on states of mind while illustrating the ways in which these inner states can be identified and used to quantify patient personality change. They deal in depth with the assessment of personal schemas while conceptualizing "personality disorder" as the result of a person's vulnerability to enter states of mind in which certain views of self and others are used irrationally. Several measures are reviewed and critically evaluated, followed by creative suggestions for measuring modifications in these states of mind.

Ralph Turner and Paul Dudek (chap. 17) review obstacles in developing a core battery and propose a comprehensive model of outcome assessment with a minimum set of instruments. They raise questions about the validity and utility of the classification system of the fourth edition of the *Diagnostic and Statistical Manual of Mental Disorders* (American Psychiatric Association, 1994) and the implications for research on personality disorders. Obstacles include high comorbidity, variance of symptoms across different personality disorders, heterogeneity of symptoms within personality disorder categories, the structural and functional organization of personality, effects of differing theoretical perspectives on change, and the longitudinal nature of personality disorder. Despite these obstacles, the authors develop a model that deals effectively with many of the complexities in this area of assessment. Finally, they recommend measures that target specific individualized behaviors as well as standardized scales for measuring change in life functioning and substance abuse problems.

William Henry (chap. 18) explores conceptual issues in Axis II change measurement by attempting to distinguish between variables that can be quantified and hypothetical constructs that cannot be reduced to measurable entities. He also discusses the problem of comorbidity with both Axis I and Axis II disorders, pointing out the implications of different kinds of comorbidity for assessing change and for theory development. He completes his contribution by shifting from conceptual issues to a discussion of what should be measured and how it should be measured. He focuses on the value of the interpersonal model for conceptualizing and measuring change.

Finally, in Part Six (chap. 19), we provide the conclusions we have drawn from the authors and the conference. We also present a strategy for selecting measures for a core battery by describing an ongoing study in which existing measures of personality functioning are identified. We provide a list of criteria for judging these measures. A panel of expert judges is used to weigh each criterion and judge the extent to which each measure meets each criterion. The proposed study examines the five personality measures originally proposed at the conference plus an additional 15, identified from the literature. This procedure is proposed as a model for future research across the widest variety of patient disorders, providing a method for rank ordering measures in an unbiased fashion, thereby exposing whatever consensus does exist about a final core battery.

We hope the information and suggestions in this book provide a foundation and stimulus for future outcome research. The reader is provided with alternative conceptual schemes for organizing the assessment enterprise, criteria for selecting measures, and a tentative list of measures that could make up a core battery for outcome assessment. We hope this work will take the field a step closer to consensus on the value of a limited set of measures allowing greater integration of the outcome research that will be conducted in the coming decades.

REFERENCES

American Psychiatric Association. (1994). *Diagnostic and statistical manual of mental disorders* (4th ed.). Washington, DC: Author.

Barlow, D. H., Hayes, S. C., & Nelson, R. O. (1984). *The scientist practitioner: Research and accountability in clinical and educational settings.* Elmsford, NY: Pergamon Press.

Bellack, A. S., & Hersen, M. (1988). *Behavioral assessment: A practical handbook* (3rd ed.). Elmsford, NY: Pergamon Press.

Corcoran, K., & Fisher, J. (1995). *Measures for clinical practice* (Vols. 1 and 2). New York: Free Press.

Lambert, M. J., & Bergin, A. E. (1994). The effectiveness of psychotherapy. In A. E.

Bergin & S. L. Garfield (Eds.), *Handbook of psychotherapy and behavior change* (pp. 143–189). New York: Wiley.

Lambert, M. J., Christensen, E. R., & DeJulio, S. S. (Eds.). (1983). *The assessment of psychotherapy outcome.* New York: Wiley.

Trabin, T. (1995). Making quality and accountability happen in behavioral healthcare. *Behavioral Healthcare Tomorrow, 4*(3), 5–6.

Wetzler, S. (Ed.). (1989). *Measuring mental illness: Psychometric assessment for clinicians.* Washington, DC: American Psychiatric Association.

2

Overview and Summary of the Core Battery Conference

Leonard M. Horowitz, Hans H. Strupp,
Michael J. Lambert, and Irene Elkin

THE 1975 CORE BATTERY PROJECT

Several developments led to the March 1994 conference held at Vanderbilt University.[1] In many respects, the 1994 conference was a direct descendant of the Outcome Measures Project (OMP), which was sponsored by the Clinical Research Branch (then headed by Martin Katz) of the National Institute of Mental Health (NIMH). The OMP was designed to identify a battery of instruments that could be used across a variety of studies to evaluate the outcome of different forms of psychotherapy. The major impetus for the project was the difficulty experienced by investigators in the field of psychotherapy research (and others interested in the results of their research) in comparing and integrating the findings from different studies. One problem was the diversity of outcome measures used by different researchers. The OMP therefore focused on the selection of a core battery of outcome measures in the hope that "if researchers working in different settings with different treatment orientations were to use the same standard set of instruments, it would become possible to compare and integrate the results of different studies" (Waskow & Parloff, 1975, p. 3).

---

[1] This section was written by Irene Elkin (then Waskow), who initiated the project, working with Hussain Tuma and later with Morris Parloff.

11

The ultimate goal was to convene a small group of expert consultants to select a core battery on the basis of reviews of different areas of outcome assessment that could provide background material for their deliberations. For this purpose, several researchers in the fields of psychotherapy, personality assessment, and methodology were enlisted. They were asked to review a particular area of outcome evaluation and to recommend two or three of the best instruments then available.

The organization of these reviews and the guidelines for the reviewers revealed some of the underlying assumptions about outcome assessment and about the final nature of the battery. The reviews were organized in terms of perspective: of the patient, the therapist, a person relevant in the patient's life, and an independent clinical evaluator. Within the area of patient measures, they were broken down further into direct self-reports, tests and inventories, behavioral measures, physiological measures, and measures based on interviews and other verbal material. Reviewers were asked to focus on instruments appropriate for adult outpatient populations and to consider the following characteristics of the recommended measures: conventional psychometric information, populations for which the instrument is relevant, feasibility, nonoffensiveness, sensitivity to change, and relevance to more than one theoretical orientation.

The battery conference was held on November 30 and December 1, 1970. The invitation to the participants read as follows: "It is hoped that the battery will include both subjective and behavioral measures, taken from different vantage points in the therapy situation, and including constructs which are relevant to different theories of therapeutic change." The core battery that was recommended included the following instruments: The Psychiatric Status Schedule; the Hopkins Symptom Checklist (HSCL); Target Complaints, both patient and therapist forms; the Minnesota Multiphasic Personality Inventory; and either the Katz Adjustment Scales or the Personal Adjustment and Role Skills Scales.

In some ways, the process of selecting the battery and the ultimate choices made fulfilled the original expectations; in other ways they did not. An attempt was made to represent different rater perspectives, and this was accomplished. In terms of the request that "both subjective and behavioral measures" be included, one cannot consider any of the measures to be truly behavioral. Perhaps the greatest disappointment was the lack of an overall conceptual framework for the battery. As noted in *Psychotherapy Change Measures* (Waskow, 1975b),

> We had originally hoped ... that it would be possible for the conference to select a number of constructs or dimensions of change that should be tapped (for example, symptoms, self-awareness, interpersonal behavior and values) and to find measures for each of these. But since such a specification of constructs would, itself, have taken on a theoretical cast, the conferees chose a different and more "atheoretical" course. (p. 268)

That is, they selected

> a small group of instruments that made "empirical sense" to them— that, in aggregate, could provide basic information about the patient's status at the beginning and end of therapy and that would not be offensive to researchers and clinicians of diverse theoretical orientations. (Waskow, 1975b, p. 247)

A small book was published, entitled *Psychotherapy Change Measures* (Waskow & Parloff, 1975). Because many of the reviews that had been prepared as background material contained valuable overviews of conceptual and methodological issues and useful discussions of individual instruments (some of which were not included in the battery), they also were included in that volume. The chapter that presented the proposed core battery also included a summary of the proceedings of the battery conference, so that readers could profit from the expert consultants' discussion of many important issues related not only to the selection and use of the recommended instruments, but also to method development needs in this area. A final chapter, "Fantasied Dialogue with a Researcher" (Waskow, 1975a), provided a framework for the choice of instruments (in addition to those in the battery) relevant to the individual researcher's hypotheses and questions.

The OMP was the one major predecessor of the current effort to recommend a core battery (or batteries) for use in the assessment of psychotherapy outcome. After summarizing the history and products of this project, one may ask, What was its impact and what might we learn from it? Although chapters in *Psychotherapy Change Measures* are frequently cited in the literature and although there was probably an increased use of some of the individual instruments (e.g., the HSCL and its successor, the SCL-90) in psychotherapy outcome studies, the battery as a whole did not "catch on."

There were two major limitations of the OMP and the proposed battery, both of which can be (and to some extent already are) addressed in the current effort: (a) the failure to develop batteries specific to particular patient disorders and problems and (b) the lack of an overall conceptualization about domains of functioning to be included in a battery.

In recommending instruments for the proposed battery, the target population was seen as "adult outpatients." Although writings by Kiesler (1966) and Paul (1967), among others, had begun to focus the field on the importance of specificity issues, including the evaluation of outcome for specific patient populations, this was not reflected in either the instructions to the reviewers and conferees or in the final battery. At the time that the work on the OMP began, many psychotherapy researchers were still focusing on heterogeneous groups of patients. Although Waskow's (1975a) "Dialogue" chapter in *Psychotherapy Change Measures* did address the importance of focusing on constructs relevant to a particular patient population, this was not reflected in the OMP as a whole.

In the years since 1975, outcome research in psychotherapy has focused increasingly on specific patient populations. The impetus for this development has come from many quarters, including the continued growth of behavior therapy and the development of other brief psychotherapies targeting particular disorders, the wish—especially in the area of depression—to compare psychotherapies with targeted drug treatments, and the general lack of differential treatment effects when studying heterogeneous patient populations. With this increased focus on specific patient disorders and problems, an "all-purpose" outcome battery probably no longer seemed relevant to many researchers. This lesson greatly influenced the planning of the present conference, and the organizers decided to have the discussions focus separately on three specific patient populations: patients with anxiety disorders, mood disorders, and personality disorders. It also may be useful to consider batteries targeted for subgroups defined in ways other than by using the standard psychiatric nomenclature.

An even greater limitation of the OMP may have been the lack of a conceptual framework, of a consideration of the constructs or the domains of functioning that should be tapped by a proposed battery. The Dialogue chapter in *Psychotherapy Change Measures* attempted to compensate for this, at least in terms of demonstrating a process through which individual researchers could move from their respective conceptualizations about therapeutic change to specific constructs and then to the choice of instruments. However, the selection of the instruments in the battery itself was not based on such a process.

The participants in the battery conference felt that it would not be possible to specify constructs or dimensions of change without leaning toward one or another theoretical orientation. The care with which they considered whether particular instruments would be palatable to those with different theoretical orientations may have indeed been necessary in the early 1970s. However, the climate among researchers with different theoretical orientations has become somewhat warmer in recent years, especially with the integration movement in psychotherapy. Although many researchers will, of course, want to include measures particularly relevant to a specific therapeutic approach, we might well find agreement on a number of key constructs of therapeutic change. This lesson also influenced the planning of the present conference, and the organizers decided to have the participants identify domains that they agreed to be essential in any outcome study.

Finally, some general issues related to the wisdom of recommending a core battery or batteries need to be addressed. A reasonable concern is that the recommendation and use of a common battery may "freeze the field" (i.e., it may delay the development of new and better instruments). This danger can be illustrated by what has happened recently, at least in the field of depression, because of the informal acceptance of a "minibattery" of outcome instruments. Most major outcome studies of outpatient depression, especially those comparing drugs and psychotherapy, assess the extent of depressive symptomatology by using the Beck Depression Inventory (BDI; Beck, Rush, Shaw, & Emery, 1979) and the Hamilton Rating Scale for Depression (HRSD; Hamilton, 1967). This had the valuable effect of allowing researchers to compare results across studies, but there also may be some negative side effects.

Although the BDI and the HRSD have proved to be relatively sensitive measures of change in depressive symptomatology, they are not without their shortcomings, including psychometric problems and problems in the differential weighting of different areas of functioning. Perhaps most problematic, it is virtually impossible to compare scores as assessed from the two different perspectives used, those of the patient and the clinician, because of the different content in the two measures. There were at least two attempts, one by John Rush and the other by Eugene Paykel, to develop parallel instruments to measure depressive symptomatology from different rater perspectives. These might prove to be fruitful in allowing researchers not only to assess the severity of depression but also the discrepancy in how this is seen by the patient and by others. Yet, to be able to compare findings with those in other studies, investigators tend to keep using the BDI and the HRSD.

Another potential problem may be illustrated by the use of the HRSD. Because the same instrument is being used, investigators feel confident in comparing results across studies. Yet, the instrument may be used differently in different settings (e.g., with raters having different subjective anchors for specific points on a scale), perhaps partly because of the patient populations with which they have experience. The potential problem here is revealed by the fact that the relative magnitude of clinician HRSD scores and patient BDI scores are sometimes different in different settings. In addition, a recent survey of the HRSD literature revealed a number of alternate versions, alternate scoring procedures, and ad hoc revisions; apparently, more than 20 different versions of the HRSD exist (Grundy, Lunnen, Lambert, Ashton, & Tovey, 1994).

It is important, then, not to assume that use of the same instrument automatically allows one to compare numerical scores across studies. Researchers must address the issue, particularly in the use of clinician measures, of the standardization of instruments and scoring instructions, and the need for the development of "calibration samples" for the purpose of attaining cross-study reliability. The consequence of not attending to these issues may lead to an illusion of comparability where it does not exist.

THE TRIPARTITE MODEL

In the mid-1970s a group of researchers at Vanderbilt University studied negative effects in psychotherapy (Strupp, Hadley, & Gomes-Schwartz,

1977).[2] There had been little work done on this topic despite some notable exceptions (e.g., Lambert & Bergin, 1977). Renewed interest in the problem was sparked by a small contract that Morris Parloff, of NIMH, had awarded the Vanderbilt group. As work on the project started, it was noted that all forms of psychotherapy are designed to move a patient to a particular standard or norm, and the researchers soon discovered that any psychotherapeutic intervention that may have a good outcome also must be capable of having a poor outcome.

The Vanderbilt researchers also considered that one would have to look at psychotherapy outcomes from multiple perspectives and that a single rating was not adequate. For example, a therapy that results in a divorce might be judged as a good outcome, but it also might be regarded as a poor outcome. Or, to cite another example, if as a result of therapy a patient becomes more placid and less driven, is this a good outcome or a poor outcome? They concluded that clinical judgments of psychotherapeutic outcomes depend importantly on the values of the raters who are making the judgment. The researchers also had to consider the purpose for which patients enter psychotherapy, to remove or ameliorate a symptom, to find meaning in life, to actualize themselves, and so on.

The Vanderbilt researchers asked the following question: How can one determine whether a therapy has led to improvement, to deterioration, or to no change? It seems inevitable that people make certain assumptions that they use to develop a set of criteria for defining mental health (cf. Jahoda, 1958). Researchers also must consider the social and cultural ramifications of therapy-induced changes, the patient's place in society, his or her stage in life, and the general context in which the patient functions (Strupp & Hadley, 1977).

As already noted, one must take into account the vantage point of the judge, including the values to which the judge subscribes. As the exploration proceeded, the Vanderbilt researchers found it useful to differentiate three major parties who are interested in therapy outcomes: (a) society, including the significant figures in the patient's life; (b) the individual patient himself or herself; and (c) the mental health professionals who may have their clinical values.

---

[2] This section was written by Hans H. Strupp.

Society is concerned primarily with the maintenance of social relations, behavioral stability, predictability of behavior, and conformity to a social code. On the downside, psychotherapy can be used as an instrument of social control. Like it or not, however, society has become increasingly involved in the outcomes of psychotherapy. As far back as the 1970s, the problem of national health insurance came to the fore. The following passage by a psychiatrist, Knight Aldrich, succinctly stated the issue (Strupp & Hadley, 1977):

> As long as Jones paid me for his psychotherapy or friendship or however he wanted to use the time I sold him, it was none of Smith's business, but when Smith's taxes or insurance premiums began to contribute to my fee, Smith's interest in what I was doing with Jones increased. In other words, Smith now expects me to be accountable and in terms that he can understand. (p. 188).

Since that time, the issue of insurance claims and national health insurance has gained enormous prominence. Indeed, it is more important today than ever before.

The second party who is interested in psychotherapy outcomes is the individual client. What does the typical patient want? The patient wants to feel happy, content, satisfied, and enjoy feelings of well-being. Such an outcome may or may not coincide with the values of the society in which he or she lives. For example, the patient may define himself or herself as mentally sound, independent of society's or the mental health professionals' opinions.

Third, there are the interests of the mental health professional. Most mental health professionals see a patient's functioning within the framework of a theory of personality structure that defines mental health. The mental health professional's judgment often parallels the judgment of society or the patient, but there are times when it does not. Psychoanalysis, for example, may provide the most comprehensive and the most ambitious model of mental health and psychological functioning; it has been influential, but it has largely lost its prominence.

Consider further the implications of discrepant vantage points. As Table 1 shows, each person's mental health may be judged differently de-

Table 1

Primary Perspectives on Mental Health

Source	Standards and values	Measures
Society	Orderly world in which individuals assume responsiblity for their assigned social roles	Observations of behavior, extent to which individual fulfills society's expectations and measures up to prevailing standards
Individual	Happiness, gratification of needs	Subjective perceptions of self-esteem, acceptance, and well-being
Mental health professional	Sound personality structure characterized by growth, development, environmental mastery	Clinical judgment, aided by behavioral observations, psychological tests, and so on

NOTE: Adapted from "A Tripartite Model of Mental Health and Therapeutic Outcomes," by H. H. Strupp and S. W. Hadley, 1977, *American Psychologist, 32,* p. 190. Copyright 1977 by the American Psychological Association.

pending on whether society, the individual, or the mental health professional makes the judgment.

There is no conflict as long as each dimension is considered in isolation; however, if one is interested in a comprehensive picture of a patient's functioning, evaluations from single vantage points are inadequate. For example, preoccupation with intrapsychic forces and mechanisms may lead to a caricature of therapy as a way of life rather than as vehicle of change.

The Vanderbilt researchers then explored the implications of judgments of mental health from the foregoing major perspectives and concluded that these perspectives must be considered simultaneously in evaluating mental health or changes from psychotherapy. It seemed inevitable that in the final analysis, therapeutic outcomes are essentially value judgments and that one must make explicit the values that are brought to bear on such judgments.

WORK PRELIMINARY TO THE 1994 CONFERENCE

At the 1992 meeting of the Society for Psychotherapy Research (SPR), the idea of the core battery was brought up again. The discussants then formed a network of volunteers who would further study the issue of a core battery. The volunteers consisted of 40 psychologists and psychiatrists representing all of the major theories of therapy and all of the major treatment modalities.[3] Some participants specialized in anxiety disorders, some in mood disorders, and some in personality disorders.

The group simplified the task by focusing on outcome research with nonpsychotic adults. As a first step, it tried to generate a list of domains (or content areas) that generally are considered essential in outcome research. A *domain* was defined as any aspect of a person's functioning that ought to be considered when a psychotherapy researcher evaluates the effectiveness of a treatment. Each participant listed essential outcome domains, and the group's responses were collated. Three participants (Louis Castonguay, Edward Bein, and Leonard Horowitz) then performed a content analysis. The resulting categories are shown in the Appendix.

At a session of the 1993 SPR meeting, the group focused on broad questions about a core battery enterprise. Four questions guided the discussion: (a) What should a core battery look like? Different people have different images of a core battery, and needed to decide whether the term *core battery* should refer, at one extreme, to a small number of instruments that are recommended for every outcome study or, at the other extreme, to a flow diagram in book form that allows a researcher to identify instruments that can be used to assess domains that are considered essential for a given diagnostic category. (b) What needs to be measured? We needed to decide, for example, whether to include domains that are specific to particular theories (e.g., a measure of defense). (c) What criteria should be adopted in selecting measures? The criteria that one investigator emphasizes may differ from those that another investigator emphasizes, and we needed to determine whether a consensus can be reached. (d) Finally, what specific instruments should be included in the core battery?

---

[3] The group consisted of David M. Allen, Edward Bein, Lorna S. Benjamin, Ilse Burbiel, Franz Caspar, Louis Castonguay, Olivier Chambon, John F. Clarkin, Dolores Gallagher-Thompson, Klaus Grawe, William Henry, Clara E. Hill, Per Hoglend, Leonard M. Horowitz, Mardi J. Horowitz, Kelly Koerner, Janice L. Krupnick, Michael J. Lambert, Marsha M. Linehan, Steinar Lorentzen, Peter E. Maxim, Lovick C. Miller, Nancy E. Miller, J. Christopher Muran, Lisa M. Najavits, Frederick Newman, Ben Ogles, Linda J. Page, Paul A. Pilkonis, Robert Rosenbaum, Seth Isaiah Rubin, Dietmar Schulte, David A. Shapiro, Tracie Shea, M. Katherine Shear, Varda Shoham, Stephen Soldz, Hans H. Strupp, P. Forrest Talley, and Douglas Vakoch.

Hans Strupp, Michael Lambert, and Leonard Horowitz wanted to organize a conference that would be supported by the American Psychological Association (APA) and Vanderbilt University and that would bring together approximately 15 people with expertise in measurement to discuss these issues. APA and Vanderbilt University granted the funds, and the meeting took place at Vanderbilt University in March 1994.

To help the participants organize their thinking, each member of the invited core group was asked to draft a manuscript on some issue that he or she considered important in developing consensus in the evaluation of outcome. Expanded versions of these manuscripts form the body of the current book. At the conference proper, the participants were divided into three small working groups, each focusing on a separate diagnostic category: anxiety disorders, mood disorders, and personality disorders. Each group discussed each question with reference to its own particular diagnostic category. After the groups discussed a given question, they came together for a plenary session to compare their responses to that question and discuss differences among them.

In the following sections of this chapter, we summarize each group's discussion of the four questions. We present each group's summary and then examine the themes that were common to all groups and the notable differences among them.

SUMMARY OF ANXIETY DISORDERS
SMALL-GROUP DISCUSSION

What Should an Anxiety Disorder Core Battery Look Like?

The core battery that we envisioned would parallel the diagnostic categories of the fourth edition of the *Diagnostic and Statistical Manual of Mental Disorder (DSM–IV)*.[4] After a lively debate, we concluded that a core battery should enable us to classify each patient with anxiety disorder into one

---

[4] This section was compiled by Leonard M. Horowitz from the participants' reports. The discussion leader was Leonard M. Horowitz. The panelists were Thomas Borkovec, Paul Crits-Christoph, Marvin Goldfried, and Katherine Shear. The recorders were Louis G. Castonguay and Benjamin Johnson. The group members were Tracy D. Eells, Jorma Hannula, Mary P. Koss, Carlos Mirapeix, Barbara Saul-Krasse, and Dietmar Schulte.

of the following *DSM–IV* diagnostic categories: panic disorder (with or without agoraphobia), agoraphobia without panic disorder, specific phobia, social phobia, obsessive–compulsive disorder, posttraumatic stress disorder, acute stress disorder, generalized anxiety disorder, anxiety disorder due to a general medical condition, and anxiety disorder not otherwise specified. We also felt that a core battery should provide a *dimensional* assessment of each core feature of anxiety and avoidance behavior described by the various diagnostic categories. Furthermore, the measures themselves should include self-reports by the patient as well as judgments by clinicians, family members, and other independent assessors.

We envisioned two different types of core batteries: a *general* core battery of instruments that would be administered to every person suspected of having an anxiety disorder and a *specific* core battery that would describe patients with a specific anxiety disorder. Both general and specific core batteries should be short, efficient, and user-friendly. Ideally, the advantages of a battery would be so evident to investigators that they would want to use it and could compile data that eventually would influence future revisions of the *DSM*. We hoped that the battery also would be useful to practicing clinicians and compatible with other diagnostic systems (such as the *International Classification of Disease*) that are used in cross-cultural comparisons (e.g., by the World Health Organization).

In our view, a core battery should include specific domains (or content areas) that need to be assessed and instruments that are available for assessing those domains. It would expose domains that lack adequate measures and thereby help promote the development of new instruments. Important domains would probably include (a) the presenting problem (e.g., obsessive–compulsive disorder); (b) other related symptoms (e.g., symptoms of depression); (c) the person's degree of impairment in social and occupational functioning; and (d) other relevant characteristics (e.g., personality variables, self-evaluation, interpersonal difficulties). The measures that we envisioned would be theory-free; they would not be tied to a particular theory of psychopathology or treatment. As a result, the same core battery could be used to evaluate pharmacological and psychological treatments, individual and group treatments, private practice, and managed care treatments.

We envisioned core batteries to appear in a manual that also would contain three additional kinds of supplementary information. First, the manual would provide, for each relevant domain, a description of the available instruments, information needed for using them, references to the primary literature, relevant psychometric properties of the instruments, and a balanced evaluation of each instrument with respect to preestablished criteria. Second, the manual would provide information about other psychometrically sound measures that are not appropriate for a core battery (e.g., because they are tied to a specific theory of psychopathology or treatment). Such measures are indispensable in basic research concerning the mechanisms of psychopathology and treatment. For example, the manual might describe instruments that assess the "therapeutic alliance" (thought by psychodynamic theorists, among others, to mediate outcome) as well as instruments that assess "dysfunctional attitudes" (thought by cognitive–behavioral theorists to explain relapse).

Third, the manual would help systematize a variety of procedures that are not, strictly speaking, standardized tests (and therefore not appropriate for a core battery of psychometrically sound measures). For example, daily diaries are important procedures that are widely used to monitor and evaluate change in the treatment of panic disorder. Indeed, a recent NIMH conference on the assessment of panic disorder regarded the daily diary as an essential tool for assessing outcome. However, the procedure itself has not been standardized, norms do not exist, and psychometric properties are not known. Still, diaries are used to estimate the number and content of disturbing thoughts that the patient reports and the probability of a patient's entering or avoiding anxiety-arousing situations.

What Should an Anxiety Disorder Core Battery Measure?

We concluded that a core battery should include *both* a categorical and a dimensional measure of each symptom cited among the *DSM–IV* diagnoses. These measures would assess physiological arousal, phobic avoidance, worry, panic, obsessions and compulsions, social evaluation anxiety, and intrusive thoughts related to trauma. In addition, the comorbidity between anxiety and depression is so great that a general measure of both anxiety and depression should be included in the general core battery.

We also discussed whether nonsymptomatic measures should be part of a core battery (e.g., a measure of interpersonal difficulties or a measure of self-evaluation). We concluded that there frequently are treatment goals beyond those of symptom reduction, so that these other forms of change need to be assessed. For example, an increase in the patient's assertiveness may be highly relevant for treating anxiety disorders, so that changes in the patient's capacity for behaving assertively ought to be assessed.

In general, two domains must be represented in any general core battery for an anxiety disorder: (a) a description of salient symptoms (symptoms of anxiety disorders as well as other salient symptoms) and (b) a measure of the degree of impairment in work, social relationships, and family functioning. In addition, we probably need to assess the patient's self-evaluation, interpersonal patterns, subjective distress (or well-being), and utilization of services (e.g., number of visits to settings that provide mental health services or social services).

What Criteria Should Be Adopted in Selecting Measures for an Anxiety Disorder Core Battery?

The following criteria were recommended in selecting measures for a core battery: (a) Norms should be available that characterize patient and non-patient populations for any instrument that is to appear in a core battery. (b) The instrument should have demonstrated reliability and validity, and there should be psychometric information on various forms of reliability and validity. We recognize that high reliability is sometimes achieved at the expense of validity, but instruments should be identified that jointly optimize the two. (c) The instrument should be efficient, simple to use, and inexpensive; ideally, it should be in the public domain. (d) There should be data to show the instrument's sensitivity to change—the effect size expected from treatment compared with effect size of a no-treatment control group. (e) Ideally, the instrument would be adopted easily by practicing clinicians and relevant to their needs. (f) If an instrument is to be administered by a trained clinician, a systematic training procedure should be available. For example, master tapes might be available for calibrating clinicians' responses at different treatment sites. (g) Along with self-reports, the instruments should include measures that rely on the judgments of independent assessors. Most instruments in use today are self-reports, and we would like to broaden that scope.

What Measures Should Be Used in an
Anxiety Disorder Core Battery?

We did not feel able at that time to recommend specific measures for each of the recommended domains. Recommendations of specific instruments would require another meeting in which we would have to compile all existing measures of a given domain and evaluate each measure against the objective criteria described earlier. However, we did feel able to recommend *domains* and provide examples of instruments that are available for assessing those domains.

Our discussion focused on domains that we believed should be part of a *general* core battery for assessing anxiety disorders, and we recommended the following domains: (a) a diagnostic measure; (b) a general measure of anxiety; (c) a general measure of depression; (d) a measure of the person's degree of functional impairment in work, social relationships, and family functioning; (e) a measure of self-evaluation; (f) a measure of interpersonal functioning; and (g) a measure of service utilization. Each of these domains is described, with examples provided.

Diagnostic Measure

The diagnosis would be assessed in two ways; ideally, both would come from the same instrument. The instrument would be a structured interview that provides a categorical classification of the patient as well as a dimensional rating of each component symptom. Existing structured interviews include the Structured Clinical Interview for DSM-III-R (Spitzer, Williams, Gibbon, & First, 1988); the Diagnostic Interview Schedule (Robins, Helzer, Croughan, & Ratcliff, 1981); the Anxiety Disorders Interview Schedule–Revised (DiNardo & Barlow, 1988); the Schedule for Affective Disorders–Lifetime, Anxiety (Manuzza et al., 1986); and the Composite International Diagnostic Interview (Robins et al., 1989).

General Measure of Anxiety

Ideally, this measure would tap each of the seven core features of anxiety: physiological arousal (somatization), phobic avoidance, worry, panic attacks, obsessions and compulsions, social evaluation anxiety, and intrusive thoughts related to trauma. At present, we know of no instrument that systematically assesses all seven forms of anxiety. Because separate measures do exist for each type of anxiety, we considered the possibility of generating an omnibus measure by combining these instruments. However, different instruments probably yield score distributions that differ in skewness, and differences in the form of the distributions would affect the maximum possible degree of correlation between instruments. For example, a measure of panic attacks may yield a highly skewed distribution of scores, whereas a measure of worry may yield a normal distribution; as a result, the degree of possible correlation between panic and worry would be highly constrained (Pearson correlations above .30 may be statistically impossible). Because these constraints could affect the psychometric properties of the omnibus measure, it would be better to construct a measure without such built-in limitations. Other measures of general anxiety, however, do exist (although they do not assess all core features of anxiety). These measures include the State-Trait Anxiety Inventory (Spielberger, Gorsuch, & Lushene, 1968), the S-R Inventory of Anxiousness (Endler, Hunt, & Rosenstein, 1962), the Beck Anxiety Inventory (Beck, Epstein, Brown, & Steer, 1988), and the Hamilton Anxiety Scale (Hamilton, 1959).

General Measure of Depression

Because of the frequent comorbidity between anxiety and depression, we recommended a general measure of depression for the core battery as well. In our discussion, we wondered whether the patient's degree of subjective distress due to anxiety and depression could be assessed separately. We concluded, however, that subjective distress *per se* is difficult to disentangle from the intensity of symptoms themselves.

Measure of Functional Impairment

We were not able to identify a satisfactory measure of functional impairment. Some measures that do exist are the Global Assessment Scale (Endicott, Spitzer, Fleiss, & Cohen, 1976) and the Social Adjustment Scales (Weissman & Bothwell, 1976).

Measure of Self-Evaluation

One possible measure of self-evaluation is the Rosenberg Self-Esteem Scale (Rosenberg, 1965); another is the Introject scale Intrex of the Structural Analysis of Social Behavior (SASB) (Benjamin, 1986). A measure of self-evaluation seems particularly important for the anxiety disorders because changes in self-evaluation may occur after psychotherapy but not after pharmacotherapy.

Measure of Interpersonal Difficulties

We also recommend a measure of interpersonal functioning and interpersonal difficulties. One possible measure is the Inventory of Interpersonal Problems (L. M. Horowitz, Rosenberg, Baer, Ureño, & Villaseñor, 1988; L. M. Horowitz, Rosenberg, & Bartholomew, 1993); another is the SASB (Benjamin, 1974, 1979).

Measure of Service Utilization

Finally, we recommended a measure that reviews the patient's use of services. No specific instruments were named.

We also discussed possible measures for specific core batteries (i.e., measures for assessing specific anxiety disorders). Each specific disorder could be assessed with a *DSM*-based interview or self-report measure. Standardized semistructured diagnostic interviews include the Yale-Brown Obsessive Compulsive Scale (Goodman et al., 1989), the Social Avoidance and Distress Scale (Watson & Friend, 1969), and the Clinician Rating Scale for Assessing Current and Lifetime PTSD (Blake et al., 1990). Instruments based on people's self-reports provide dimensional assessments of the core features of each disorder. Examples include the Maudsley Obsessive Compulsive-Inventory (Hodgson & Rachman, 1977) for obsessive–compulsive disorder; the Anxiety Sensitivity Index (Peterson & Reiss, 1992) for panic disorder; the Penn State Worry Scale (Meyer, Miller, Metzger, & Borkovec, 1990) for generalized anxiety disorder; the Fear of Negative Evaluation (Leary, 1983; Watson & Friend, 1969) for social phobia; the Mississippi Scale (Keane, Caddell, & Taylor, 1988) for Combat-Related Posttraumatic

Stress Disorder; and the Fear Questionnaire (Marks & Mathews, 1979) or the Fear Survey Schedule (Wolpe & Lang, 1964, 1969) for specific phobia.

SUMMARY OF MOOD DISORDERS SMALL-GROUP DISCUSSION

What Should a Mood Disorders Core Battery Look Like?

The core battery we envisioned would be intended primarily for researchers and clinicians.[5] It should be useful whether the researcher is evaluating psychopharmacological or psychotherapeutic treatment. Other potentially interested parties include sponsors of treatment, such as insurance companies and federal agencies, who often pay for the treatment. Even though they would not be the primary audience, it seemed prudent to include measures in a proposed battery that also would serve their needs.

The battery should be reasonably easy to administer in a variety of clinical settings. Some of the measures in the battery should assess the diagnostic categories and symptoms described in the *DSM–IV*, but the measures themselves should not be tied exclusively to the *DSM–IV* because too close a tie might contribute adversely to the "reification" of the *DSM–IV* categories. We decided to focus on "major depression," hoping that our conclusions about this prototypic mood disorder would simplify the task for the other mood disorders.

We envisioned ourselves identifying outcome *domains* that need to be measured as well as instruments that assess those domains. The domains primarily would be ones that would enable us to detect change. We differentiated among three groups of outcome domains: (a) those considered essential across all diagnostic categories; (b) those considered essential within a specific diagnostic category (e.g., major depression); and (c) those considered supplementary yet potentially relevant to one or more diagnostic categories.

---

[5] This section was compiled by Leonard M. Horowitz from the participants' reports. The discussion leader was Larry E. Beutler. The panelists were Irene Elkin, Kenneth Howard, Lester Luborsky, Karla Moras, and John Rush. The recorders were Russell Hilliard and Leslie Seggar. The group members were Michael Barkham, Monica Basco, Robin B. Jarrett, Sharon Kofman, Gregory Kolden, A. Kuhr, Jack R. Leggett, Howard A. Liddle, Wayne Neff, Samuel Pfeifer, Arnold L. Schuster, Zindel Segal, David C. Speer, Timothy J. Strauman, David Tulsky, Suzanne S. Wandersman, and Spencer A. Ward.

Thus, we envisioned the final product to be a document that would first identify the *essential* outcome domains and describe instruments that exist for assessing each domain. This section would include references to the primary literature, relevant psychometric properties, and a balanced evaluation of each instrument relative to preestablished criteria. In addition, the document would identify *supplementary* domains and describe instruments that exist for assessing those domains. This section, for example, might describe measures that assess the risk of relapse and measures that assess treatment side effects. It also might include domains and existing instruments that would be used to test particular theories of psychotherapy, such as instruments that assess the therapeutic alliance and instruments that assess dysfunctional attitudes. Finally, the document would also describe procedures that are often used in outcome research but are not, strictly speaking, standardized tests. For example, a visual analogue scale is sometimes used to monitor and evaluate changes in depression, but the method has not been fully standardized (i.e., norms do not exist and psychometric properties are not known).

What Should a Mood Disorders Core Battery Measure?

We concluded that a core battery for major depression should at least assess the following essential domains: (a) a description of the presence of salient symptoms and their frequency of occurrence; (b) a measure of the severity of the patient's subjective distress; and (c) a measure of the patient's degree of impairment in life functioning, such as in work, self-care, social relationships, and family functioning. Measures of self-esteem, interpersonal patterns, and other aspects of personality also were discussed, but we did not agree as a group to include them among the essential domains of the core battery.

If possible, measures should assess both positive and negative aspects of these domains. For example, the Positive and Negative Affect Scales (Watson, Clark, & Tellegen, 1988) assess both. The measures should also reflect multiple perspectives: Subjective distress is best evaluated by self-report, life functioning by an external observer, and symptomatology by both. Symptoms of depression, for example, can be evaluated by the patient, by a clinician, and by other people in the patient's life.

We felt that all of the criterion diagnostic symptoms for major depression should be evaluated: (a) depressed mood; (b) diminished interest or pleasure in most activities; (c) significant weight loss or gain or a decrease or increase in appetite; (d) insomnia or hypersomnia; (e) psychomotor agitation or retardation; (f) fatigue or loss of energy; (g) feelings of worthlessness or excessive or inappropriate guilt; (h) diminished ability to think or concentrate; and (i) recurrent thoughts of death, suicidal ideation, or a suicide attempt.

Three other kinds of measures were also discussed. First, the comorbidity between anxiety and depression is so great that general measures of both depression and anxiety should be included in a core battery of essential measures; other comorbid symptoms (e.g., psychosis, drug and alcohol abuse) might also be assessed. Second, supplementary measures could also include measures that typically are used in studies of pharmacological treatment for anxiety and depression. One example is the Clinician Global Index (Othmer, 1989); another is a checklist of side effects of medication. Third, we considered individualized procedures such as goal attainment scaling but decided as a group not to include them in the core battery.

Ideally, a measure also would be included to show how cost-effective a treatment had been. Without this kind of information, psychotherapy research cannot have much of an impact on health care policy. Because psychotherapy researchers generally believe that psychotherapy is effective, we must convince the "managed care culture" of its effectiveness in their own terms. For that reason, there ought to be a way of expressing the cost of the treatment relative to the improvement in subjective well-being, functioning, and symptom removal. However, we realized the complexity of assessing the cost-effectiveness of psychosocial interventions, so that a measure of cost-effectiveness may be best viewed as a supplementary option at this time.

What Criteria Should Be Adopted in Selecting Measures for a Mood Disorders Core Battery?

The following criteria were recommended for selecting essential measures for a core battery: (a) Procedures for administering and scoring the instrument should be clear and standardized. (b) Norms should be available that characterize patient and nonpatient populations. (c) The instrument should have demonstrated reliability, and the measure of reliability should be appropriate for the domain for which it is intended. For example, internal consistency should be measured to demonstrate the stability of a "state" (e.g., depression), whereas test–retest reliability should be measured to demonstrate the reliability of a "trait." (d) The instrument should have demonstrated validity. It should discriminate patients from nonpatients, and its scores should correlate with other measures of the same construct. The instrument should be sensitive to the characteristic in question, but it also should discriminate that characteristic from other similar characteristics. (e) There should be data to show the instrument's sensitivity to change (i.e., the effect size expected from treatment compared with the effect size of a no-treatment control group). (f) The instrument should be efficient, easy to use, and feasible in clinical settings. It should be brief, and its use should require minimal training. It also should be inexpensive. If possible, it should be available in several languages. (g) Ideally, the instrument should be easy to use by clinicians (e.g., therapists, independent assessors). It should seem obviously relevant to clinical needs. (h) If an instrument is to be administered by a trained clinician, a systematic training procedure should be available. Master tapes, for example, might be available for calibrating clinicians' responses across studies and treatment sites. (i) The measure should be theory-free (i.e., it should not be tied to a particular theory of psychopathology or treatment). Then it could be used broadly by researchers of different theoretical persuasions. Psychometrically sound instruments that are tied to a particular theory of psychopathology or treatment might be suggested as supplementary options, but they would not be considered essential. (j) Along with self-reports, some measures should draw on the judgments of independent assessors. Most instruments in use today are self-reports, and we would like to broaden that scope. (k) Ideally, an instrument would provide both categorical and dimensional assessments. A categorical assessment reflects the presence or absence of a condition and indicates whether a patient has become "normal" as a result of treatment; a dimensional assessment, on the other hand, allows an investigator to evaluate the amount of improvement in symptom removal, subjective well-being, and functioning. Ideally, an instrument also would indicate critical score values that reflect a need for treatment. (l) It should be possible to administer the instrument before, during, and after treatment. We felt that one or more midtreatment assessments should be included in an outcome study to allow an investigator to trace the complete course of the patient's depression from the original-episode response to subsequent relapse, remission, recovery, and recurrence.

What Measures Should Be Used in a Mood Disorders Core Battery?

We felt that we were not able to recommend specific measures for each of the essential and supplementary domains. Before specific instruments can be recommended, an impartial panel of experts would have to compile all existing measures of a given domain and evaluate each measure against the objective criteria described earlier. However, we did feel able to identify essential domains and provide examples of instruments that are available for assessing those domains.

Our discussion focused on domains believed to be essential in a core battery that assesses major depression. The following domains were identified: (a) a measure of subjective distress; (b) a measure of general functioning that evaluates the person's disability in all areas of social role performance; and (c) a measure of the principal symptoms and associated symptoms. The last category would include an assessment of the *DSM–IV* diagnosis of major depression and an assessment of other comorbid *DSM–IV* diagnoses. Each of these domains is described and examples provided.

Measure of Subjective Distress

We discussed whether subjective distress is on the same continuum as subjective well-being and concluded that it is, but existing measures primarily assess negative rather than positive points along the continuum. Because subjective distress refers to the patient's experience, it is most directly assessed through the patient's self-report. One example is the Well-Being scale of the SF-36 Health Survey (Ware, 1991).

Measure of General Functioning

Several measures exist that assess a patient's functioning through clinician ratings. Examples of available instruments include the Global Assessment of Functioning (Americal Psychiatric Association, 1994) based on the Health-Sickness Rating Scale (Luborsky, 1962), the Progress Evaluation Scales (Ihilevich & Gleser, 1982), the Life Functioning Scales (Howard, Brill, Lueger, O'Mahoney, & Grissom, 1993), and the Social Adjustment Scales (Weissman & Bothwell, 1976).

Diagnostic Measure

The group recommended a structured diagnostic interview that would classify the patient on Axis I of the *DSM–IV*. Existing structured interviews include the Structured Clinical Interview for DSM–III–R (Spitzer et al., 1988) and the Diagnostic Interview Schedule (Robins, 1988).

Measure of Depressive Symptoms

A number of self-report measures of depression were named, including the BDI (Beck et al., 1979), the Self-Rating Depression Scale (Zung, 1965), and the Inventory of Depressive Symptoms (IDS; Rush et al., 1986; Rush, Hiser, & Giles, 1987). The IDS is available in parallel self-report (IDS-SR) and clinician-rated (IDS-C) forms. Another commonly used clinician-rated instrument is the HRSD (Hamilton, 1967).

SUMMARY OF PERSONALITY DISORDERS SMALL-GROUP DISCUSSION

Unlike anxiety and mood disorders, personality disorders have only a recent history in the official nomenclature.[6] This is true in terms of diagnosis, in which formal Axis II disorders are just more than a decade old. It is even more true when one considers that in controlled studies of treatment

---

[6] This section was compiled by Michael J. Lambert from the participants' reports. The discussion leader was Michael J. Lambert. The panelists were William Henry, Mardi Horowitz, Paul Pilkonis, and Tracie Shea. The recorders were Elana Newman and Marion Olmsted. The group members were Timothy Anderson, Carol Austad, Klaus Grawe, Raymond Headlee, David Ihilevich, Elaine Kersden, J. Christopher Muran, Cindy Notgrass, Andrew Phay, Cecilia Phillips, William Piper, Carol Jean Rogalski, Jeremy Safran, Shawn Taylor, and Ralph Turner.

effects, some disorders have not yet been studied (e.g., schizoid). These historical factors shaped, to a large degree, the task of developing a consensus about measuring outcome in patients with personality disorders.

What Should a Personality Disorders Core Battery Look Like?

Given the theoretical and nosological flux of Axis II diagnoses, a clear and quick consensus developed: The core battery should attempt to measure changes in individuals with personality disorders rather than changes in the personality disorder per se (along formal taxonomic lines). Recommending procedures for measuring the presence or absence of a categorical *DSM* diagnosis did not seem feasible. *DSM*-based approaches were seen as having little value in outcome assessment for a variety of reasons (e.g., some evidence of reliability but skepticism about validity, extensive comorbidity among disorders, poor fit between the psychological processes that define personality and a medically based categorical system). We felt that a dimensional approach would foster the interests of both basic and applied science. Thus, we moved away from the idea of specific batteries for specific personality disorders (or even major clusters) and toward recommending a brief atheoretical battery to which researchers could add measures most suitable for the purposes of their own research.

Research directed by theoretical interests would merely add measures directed at theoretical constructs. Research aimed at serving the needs of third-party payers and program evaluation would add client satisfaction and similar measures to the core battery.

The core battery would consist of measures aimed at assessing change in designated domains without requiring that a given instrument measure all domains of interest. The group tacitly agreed to pursue a single core battery for measuring change across settings, research purposes, and distinct personality disorders.

What Should a Personality Disorders Core Battery Measure?

The domains of interest included three areas: level of functioning, subjective state, and personality functioning. In addition to these three broad domains, we agreed that measures of level of functioning and subjective states should include both positive and negative indicators. That is, we felt that the battery should include measures not only of the absence of psychopathology but also some indication of positive mental health. Thus, a 2×2 matrix was proposed in which measures would be expected to address both positive and negative indicators.

Level of Functioning

The hallmark of all personality disorders is impairment of social and occupational functioning. Without impairment in these areas of life, personality problems fall short of the criterion that distinguishes normal from abnormal. Four categories of functioning were identified: interpersonal relations, social role functioning, self-care and physical health, and social costs.

Measures of functioning would assess interpersonal problems and strengths that manifest themselves in marriage and related intimate relationships, in the family, and in broader social interactions with friends and acquaintances. Measures of social role functioning would examine work, school, homemaking, and leisure life. Self-care and physical health measures would tap decreases and increases in self-damaging and health-promoting behaviors related to physical health and care, such as parasuicidal acts, exercise, nutrition, substance abuse, and the like. Social costs was a category about which we were more ambivalent. However, there was some consensus for including a separate measurement category for changes in behaviors relevant to societal costs. This category would include measures of use of social services, the criminal justice system, treatment utilization, including medical utilization and so on.

Subjective States

Although many patients with personality disorders may not directly complain about their subjective states (e.g., schizoid personality disorder), we felt that the majority would have recognizable and remediable subjective discomfort. Two categories were identified as most relevant: symptoms, such as anxiety and depression, and attitudes toward self, such as self-concept and self-esteem.

Personality Functioning

Although the first two categories were seen as important across the broad spectrum of psychological disorders, we viewed personality functioning as being especially relevant to the patient with a personality disorder. Furthermore, the personality functioning category was intended to facilitate assessment of both the underlying pathology and behavioral manifestations of personality disorder. This domain attempts to get at a more individual understanding of why people function and experience life as they do. This domain was most interesting to us because of its relevance to personality disorders, but it also was the most controversial because it is closely linked with specific theories that underlie treatments and many of the measures that have been developed for diagnostic purposes. Nonetheless, three subdomains were identified and agreed to with some reservations: maladaptive interpersonal styles or patterns, identity and role coherence, and habitual styles of affective control and expression.

Interpersonal patterns are maladaptive styles that have some links to personality theory such as the SASB (Benjamin, 1974) and more purely empirical strategies such as the Big Five personality factors (Costa & McCrae, 1992). Identity and role coherence is a dimension of measurement that attempts to assess a person's sense of self and feeling about self as captured by instruments that assess ego resiliency, integration, and coherence. Habitual styles of affective control and expression encompass expressive and temperamental tendencies (e.g., to be impulsive and unstable or to be overcontrolled). We recognized the potentially controversial nature of this domain because it clearly overlaps with the traditional psychodynamic idea of defense or coping styles. However, defensive patterns are included in an appendix to the *DSM–IV,* suggesting that the importance of this area of functioning has gained more widespread acceptance.

What Criteria Should Be Adopted in Selecting Measures for a Personality Disorders Core Battery?

Some formal attempts have been made to standardize criteria for evaluating outcome measures. Newman and Ciarlo (1994), for example, identified 11 criteria considered to be essential for outcome measures. The group was concerned with six criteria: psychometric adequacy, information source, length and comprehensiveness, breadth of use, ties to the *DSM,* and sensitivity to change. The need for validity data (e.g., discriminant validity) was considered to be essential because the emphasis in contemporary personality research has been on reliability. There was consensus on the importance of gathering outcome assessments from other sources besides the patient. Although this is the usual standard in the field, we noted that people with particular personality disorders make especially poor informants about their own functioning. At the same time, the clinician often is not in a position to observe the patient's daily functioning, making data gathered from significant others a high priority. Although noting the importance of brief assessments, we thought that the proper assessment of change in patients with personality disorders called for specific and broad assessments. This breadth was viewed as being essential to reflect changes in functioning that would result from effective treatments. The other form of breadth that was discussed emphasized measures that had been used by investigators other than the test developers. For inclusion in a core battery, we viewed this criterion as being essential.

Although personality disorder classification is in an unstable state and measures adhering solely to the *DSM* Axis II classification system would be of limited long-term value, we expected some advantage from characterizing patient samples in terms of Axis II disorders. Thus, structured interviews and self-report measures with links to the *DSM* were seen as important for theoretical and practical reasons and for comparability across studies, whereas their value as change measures was not highly regarded.

A final criterion was discussed without closure. It was suggested that data demonstrating sensitivity to change would be important but hard to find with measures aimed at personality functioning because so few outcome studies have been performed. Concern was expressed that some of the traits and criteria associated with personality functioning as reflected in the most widely used personality tests would be unlikely to change regardless of the type of intervention used. For example, items that ask about historical facts are not suitable for measuring change from pre- to posttesting or even follow-up testing. Including such measures in a core battery could result in negative (and misleading) findings in psychotherapy outcome studies. It was agreed that for measures of change, it is important to target traits that are expected to change while providing important baseline information for characterizing patient samples. Within the domain of personality functioning, this implies being prepared to undertake assessments that reflect pretherapy, posttherapy, and follow-up levels of personality functioning. The two separate purposes for assessing personality will require separate and distinct measures.

What Measures Should Be Used in a Personality Disorders Core Battery?

Specific measures were linked to the three dimensions of change (i.e., level of functioning, subjective state, and personality functioning), but the group acknowledged the need to develop a reference work listing measures for each. The reference work would include ratings of each measure with regard to the extent to which it meets the selection criteria.

Table 2 shows a summary of the consensus of conference participants. It is a matrix in which there are three major domains. The three domains are further divided to yield nine categories of measurement. The top two domains have both positive and negative valence that may need to be assessed using different instruments. The third domain (personality functioning) was not subdivided into positive and negative classifications. The measures listed in Table 2 are provided to give the reader the flavor and direction of activity by the working group, not for the purpose of providing the final recommendations of the conference because the choice of particular measures will require more effort than the conference time limits allowed.

As can be seen from Table 2, some domains had no specific measure and others had more than one. The process from here would be to select a minimal core battery that would recommend several measures that can be applied in future research.

In summary, the overall recommendations of individual group members were remarkably consistent with one another. Little time was spent discussing potentially divisive "big issues," and tangible progress was made. A general domain framework was agreed on, providing the outline for a core battery, and a handful of tentatively recommended specific instrument choices emerged. However, further work is needed to define more precisely some of the subdomains and to recommend specific measures

Table 2

Examples of Possible Measures for Outcome Assessment in Personality Disorders for Three Domains

Category	Positive valence	Negative valence	Valence
	Level of functioning		
Interpersonal relation	None listed	Inventory of Inter-personal Problem[a] SASB-Intrex Questionnaire[b]	
Social role functioning	Quality of Life Inventory[c] Progress Evaluation Scales[e]	Social Adjustment Scale[d] Global Level of Functioning[f]	
Self-care/physical health	None listed	None listed	
Social costs	None listed	None listed	
	Subjective states		
Traditional symptoms (anxiety, mood)	None listed	Brief Symptom Inventory[g]	
Attitudes toward self	Rosenberg Self-esteem[h] Self-efficacy[i] PANAS[j] Positive States of Mind[k]	None listed	
	Personality functioning		
Maladaptive interpersonal patterns			SNAP[l] SASB[b]
Themes of identity, role, and self-schema			Block Ego resiliency[m] Coherence Scale[n]
Styles of expression, defense, modes of control, temperament			Bond[o] Lerner & Lerner[n]

NOTE: SASB=Structural Analysis of Social Behavior; PANAS=Positive and Negative Affect Scales; SNAP=Schedule for Nonadaptive Personality.
[a] Horowitz, Rosenberg, et al. (1988). [b] Benjamin (1974). [c] Frisch, Cornell, Villanueva, & Retzlaff (1992). [d] Weissman & Bothwell (1976). [e] Ihilevich & Gleser (1982). [f] American Psychiatric Association (1994). [g] Derogatis & Melisaratos (1983). [h] Rosenberg (1965). [i] Bandura (1984). [j] Watson & Clark (1991). [k] Horowitz, Adler, & Kegeles (1988). [l] Clark (1993). [m] Block (1965). [n] Lerner & Lerner (1980). [o] Bond defensive styles; Bond et al. (1989).

that meet the criteria that were deemed essential for measuring change in patients with personality disorders.

SUMMARY: COMMON THEMES (AND DIFFERENCES) AMONG THE GROUPS

This section[7] describes the major themes that were common to all groups, as well as some of the differences.

What Should a Core Battery Look Like?

All three groups envisioned a core battery intended primarily for researchers and clinicians that could be used to evaluate any form of treatment. The anxiety and mood disorders groups felt that this battery should include at least one measure that assesses the diagnostic categories and symptoms described in the *DSM–IV,* although they also felt that measures of this kind should not be overemphasized because too close a tie to the *DSM–IV* might contribute adversely to the reification of the *DSM–IV* categories. The personality disorders group did not recommend assessing the diagnostic categories of the *DSM–IV.* In their view, the goal of a core battery would be to measure changes in people with personality disorders rather than recovery from a disorder per se. They also felt that the personality disorders described in *DSM–IV* have not been shown to have discriminant validity. Furthermore, they felt that the psychological processes that define personality are not clearly coordinated with the DSM categorical system.

All three groups agreed that the dimensional (rather than the categorical) assessment of core features of the disorders should be emphasized. They also agreed that the measures should include both self-reports by the patient and judgments by clinicians, family members, and other independent assessors. In addition, they differentiated between outcome domains that are essential to a core battery and outcome domains that should be considered supplementary or optional. Furthermore, measures that assess essential domains should not be tied to any particular theory of psycho-

---

[7] This section was written by Leonard M. Horowitz.

pathology or treatment, so that investigators of all theoretical orientations can use the same core battery regardless of whether they are evaluating pharmacological or psychological treatments, individual or group treatments, private practice, or managed care treatments.

The anxiety and mood disorders groups also differentiated among levels of core batteries. A specific core battery would contain instruments for assessing domains considered to be essential for a specific diagnostic category (e.g., obsessive–compulsive disorder); a general core battery would contain instruments considered to be essential for assessing a general diagnostic category (e.g., anxiety disorders); and a universal core battery would contain instruments for assessing domains considered to be essential for all diagnostic categories.

All groups envisioned a document consisting of several sections. The first section would identify essential outcome domains and describe instruments that are available for assessing those domains. This section would include references to the primary literature, relevant psychometric properties, and a balanced evaluation of each instrument with respect to preestablished criteria. Another section of the document would identify supplementary domains and describe instruments that assess those domains. This supplementary section, for example, might describe measures that assess the risk of relapse, measures that assess the side effects of treatment, and measures that assess patient satisfaction. This section also might identify outcome domains and instruments that exist for testing particular theories of psychotherapy (e.g., instruments that assess the therapeutic alliance and those that assess dysfunctional attitudes). A third section of the document would describe procedures that are often used in outcome research but are not, strictly speaking, standardized tests. For example, a visual analogue scale is sometimes used to evaluate changes in depression, and a daily diary is frequently recommended for assessing panic disorder. Neither procedure, however, has been standardized: Norms do not exist, and psychometric properties are not known.

What Needs to Be Measured?

All three groups concluded that the following domains need to be measured: (a) the severity of the patient's subjective distress; (b) the degree of impairment in the patient's life functioning (e.g., in work, self-care, interpersonal relationships, and family functioning); and (c) the salient symptoms and their frequency of occurrence. These domains and corresponding measures would therefore form a universal core battery.

The anxiety disorders and personality disorders groups considered two other domains essential to a general core battery: the patient's self-evaluation (e.g., self-esteem) and the patient's maladaptive interpersonal patterns. The anxiety disorders group also considered the patient's utilization of services an essential domain (e.g., the patient's number of visits to settings that provide mental health services or social services). The personality disorders group considered two other aspects of personality to be essential: the patient's identity and role coherence as well as his or her habitual styles of affective control and expression.

All three groups felt that the measures should, if possible, assess both positive and negative aspects of these domains. For example, the Positive and Negative Affect Scales (Watson & Clark, 1991; Watson et al., 1988) assess both.

What Criteria Should Be Adopted in Selecting Measures?

The three groups generally agreed that an instrument that is recommended for a core battery should meet the following criteria: (a) Procedures for administering and scoring the instrument should be clear and standardized. (b) Norms should be available that characterize patient and nonpatient populations. (c) The instrument should have demonstrated reliability, and the measure of reliability should be appropriate for the corresponding domain. For example, internal consistency is needed to demonstrate the stable one-time presence of a state, whereas test–retest reliability is needed to demonstrate the consistency over time of a trait. (d) The instrument should have demonstrated validity. It should discriminate patients from nonpatients, and its scores should correlate with other measures of the same construct. It should be sensitive to the characteristic in question, but it should also discriminate that characteristic from other similar characteristics. (e) The instrument should be efficient, easy to use, and feasible in clinical settings. It should be brief and inexpensive, and its use should require minimal training. If possible, it should be available in several languages. (f) Ideally, the instrument should be easy to use by clinicians (therapists, independent assessors) and obviously relevant to clinical needs. If it is to be administered by a trained clinician, a systematic training procedure should be available. Master tapes, for example, might be available for calibrating clinicians' responses across studies and treatment sites. (g) The measure should be theory-free (i.e., it should not be tied to a particular theory of psychopathology or treatment). Thus, it can be used broadly by researchers of different theoretical persuasions. Psychometrically sound instruments that are tied to a particular theory of psychopathology or treatment might be suggested as supplementary options, but they should not be considered essential. (h) It should be possible to administer the instrument before, during, and after treatment. One or more midtreatment assessments ought to be included in an outcome study to allow an investigator to trace the complete course of change from the original episode response to subsequent relapse, remission, recovery, and recurrence.

All three groups felt that data are needed to evaluate an instrument's sensitivity to change (i.e., the effect size expected from treatment compared with the effect size of a no-treatment control group). The personality disorders group expressed particular concern about this limitation among instruments used to assess personality; the sensitivity of those instruments to change especially needs to be evaluated. The anxiety and mood disorders groups also suggested that an instrument ideally should provide both categorical and dimensional assessments. A categorical assessment reflects the presence or absence of a condition and indicates whether a patient has become "normal" as a result of treatment. A dimensional assessment, on the other hand, allows an investigator to evaluate the amount of improvement in symptoms, subjective well-being, and functioning. Ideally, an instrument also would indicate critical score values that reflect a need for treatment.

Finally, the personality disorders group emphasized that a measure of change in personality calls for broad, rather than brief, assessments. Patients are not always ideal informants about their own functioning, nor is the clinician often in a position to observe the patient's daily functioning. Therefore, they emphasized the need for assessments by individuals other than the patient and the therapist.

What Measures Should Be Used?

All groups agreed that they could not recommend specific instruments for the essential outcome domains. Before specific instruments can be recommended, a panel of experts should compile all existing measures of that domain and evaluate each measure against the objective criteria described earlier. However, all groups did feel able to identify essential domains and provide examples of instruments that are currently available for assessing those domains.

The following domains were identified as being essential by all three groups and therefore belong in a universal core battery: (a) a measure of subjective distress; (b) a measure of general functioning that evaluates the person's disability in all areas of social role performance; and (c) a measure of the principal symptoms and associated symptoms. Each of these domains is described and examples provided.

Measure of the Severity of Subjective Distress

Subjective distress refers to the patient's experience and is most directly assessed through the patient's self-report. One example is the Well-Being scale of the SF-36 Health Survey (Ware, 1991); another is the brief Symptom Inventory (Derogatis & Melisaratos, 1983).

Measure of General Functioning

Several measures exist that assess a patient's functioning. Examples of available instruments include the Global Assessment of Functioning (American Psychiatric Association, 1994) based on the Health-Sickness Rating Scale (Luborsky, 1962), the Progress Evaluation Scales (Ihilevich & Gleser, 1982), the Life Functioning Scales (Howard et al., 1993), and the Social Adjustment Scales (Weissman & Bothwell, 1976).

Description of Salient Symptoms of Anxiety and Depression

Ideally, a general measure of anxiety would tap each of the seven core features of anxiety: physiological arousal (somatization), phobic avoidance, worry, panic attacks, obsessions and compulsions, social evaluation anxiety, and intrusive thoughts related to trauma. At present, we know of no instrument that systematically assesses all seven forms of anxiety. Measures of general anxiety, however, do exist, and they include the State-Trait

Anxiety Inventory (Spielberger, 1983), the S–R Inventory of Anxiousness (Endler et al., 1962), the Beck Anxiety Inventory (Beck et al., 1988), and the Hamilton Anxiety Scale (Hamilton, 1959).

Self-report measures of depression include the BDI (Beck et al., 1979), the Self-Rating Depression Scale (Zung, 1965), and the IDS (Rush et al., 1986, 1987). Two forms of the IDS are available: the IDS–SR and the IDS–C. The HRSD (Hamilton, 1967) is another commonly used clinician-rated instrument.

RECOMMENDATIONS

We thought the 2-day meeting was generally productive.[8] We felt, however, that further work is needed to achieve the original objective. In particular, we still need to examine all instruments that are available for assessing each essential domain, particularly (a) domains that belong in a universal core battery (essential for all diagnostic categories) and (b) those that belong in a general core battery (essential for anxiety disorders, for mood disorders, or for personality disorders).

Future work therefore should accomplish the following tasks. First, a panel of experts needs to scale the various criteria provided earlier for their relative importance in evaluating an instrument. That is, there is a need to apply conventional scaling procedures to determine what weight to attach to each criterion that was identified. Second, the panel needs to identify all instruments that exist for measuring each of the essential domains identified in response to the question of what measures should be used. To accomplish this task, the panel needs to compile a copy of each instrument plus the primary publications that provide data relevant to the various criteria. Third, the panel of experts needs to review the data on each instrument and rate that instrument with respect to each criterion. The experts' ratings then should be averaged across raters for each criterion, and a weighted sum across criteria then should be computed for each instrument. This weighted sum would constitute a measure of that instrument's quality. In this way, the different instruments that are available for a given

---

[8] This section was written by Leonard M. Horowitz.

essential domain could be ordered in terms of their respective quality. (This step is especially important because researchers seem to be developing premature allegiances to specific measures without having a well-articulated rationale for these allegiances.) Finally, the experts would write a narrative description of each instrument to provide a balanced evaluation of each instrument that would summarize its particular strengths and weaknesses. These descriptions then would enable users to determine which instrument would be particularly suitable for the user's own particular needs and purposes.

CONTENT AREAS THAT COULD POTENTIALLY BE ASSESSED (SPR PROJECT)

I. Contents that are normally assessed BEFORE AND AFTER treatment

1. Nature and degree of distress from target complaints _____

2. Symptomatic distress _____

   a. Measure of anxiety _____
   b. Measure of depression _____
   c. Degree of affective instability (lability) _____
   d. Substance abuse _____
   e. Sexual problems _____
   f. Evaluation of physical health _____

3. Distress from interpersonal functioning _____

   a. Interpersonal satisfaction _____
   b. Distress from specific types of interpersonal difficulties __
   c. Marital adjustment _____
   d. Family functioning _____

4. Self-evaluation, self-esteem, self-efficacy, self-acceptance _____

   a. Identity _____
   b. Self-destructive and self-defeating behaviors _____
   c. Adequacy in carrying out sociocultural and occupational roles _____

5. Personality Traits 1: Traits that describe orientation toward self and others _____

    a. Interpersonal styles _____
    b. Schemas of self and others; introject _____
    c. Dysfunctional attitudes _____
    d. Pathogenic beliefs regarding the self _____
    e. Maladaptive cognitive styles _____
    f. Attachment relationships and romantic relationships _____
    g. Autonomy–independence _____
    h. Separation–individuation _____
    i. Locus of control _____
    j. Developmental level _____

6. Personality Traits 2: Other personality traits relevant to treatment _____

    a. Ability to react emotionally _____
    b. Authenticity _____
    c. Creativity _____
    d. Problems of impulse control _____
    e. Cognitive functioning _____
    f. Neuropsychological assessments _____
    g. Insight and psychological mindedness _____
    h. Intrapsychic conflict _____
    i. Neuroticism _____
    j. Unresolved hostility and anger _____

7. Specific skills for coping flexibly with life demands _____

    a. Social and communication skills _____
    b. Assertiveness skills _____
    c. Problem-solving skills _____
    d. Parenting skills _____
    e. Other behavior deficits _____
    f. Use of social services _____

8. Resilence in coping flexibly with life demands _____

   a. Pattern of defenses _____
   b. Resourcefulness versus hopelessness _____
   c. Vulnerability to future episodes _____
   d. Ability to enter and leave states of mind _____

9. Life satisfaction and spiritual fulfillment _____

   a. Purpose and meaning in life _____
   b. Meaningful philosophy of life _____
   c. Construction of meaning _____
   d. Coming to terms with death and dying _____

10. *DSM-IV* diagnosis _____

   a. Evaluation of general psychological functioning _____

II. Contents that are normally assessed only BEFORE treatment

1. Stressful life events _____
2. Available social support _____
3. Readiness and motivation to change _____
4. Treatment expectations _____
5. Psychiatric history _____

III. Contents that are normally assessed only AFTER treatment

1. Satisfaction with treatment _____
2. Reasons for dropping out of treatment _____

REFERENCES

American Psychiatric Association. (1994). *Diagnostic and statistical manual of mental disorders* (4th ed.). Washington, DC: Author.

Bandura, A. (1984). Recycling misconceptions of perceived self efficacy. *Cognitive Therapy and Research, 8,* 231–255.

Beck, A. T., Epstein, N., Brown, G., & Steer, R. A. (1988). An inventory for measuring clinical anxiety: The Beck Anxiety Inventory. *Journal of Consulting and Clinical Psychology, 56,* 893–897.

Beck, A. T., Rush, A. J., Shaw, B. F., & Emery, G. (1979). *Cognitive therapy and depression.* New York: Guilford Press.

Benjamin, L. (1974). Structural Analysis of Social Behavior. *Psychological Review, 81,* 392–425.

Benjamin, L. (1986). Adding social and intrapsychic descriptors to Axis I of DSM–III. In T. Millon & G. Klerman (Ed.), *Contemporary issues in psychopathology* (pp. 599–638). New York: Guilford Press.

Benjamin, L. S. (1979). Use of Structural Analysis of Social Behavior (SASB) and Markov chains to study dyadic interactions. *Journal of Abnormal Psychology, 88,* 303–319.

Blake, D. D., Weathers, F. W., Nagy, L. M., Kaloupek, D. G., Klauminzer, G., Charney, D. S., & Keane, T. M. (1990). A clinician rating scale for assessing current and lifetime PTSD: The CAPS-1. *The Behavior Therapist, 13,* 187–188.

Block, J. (1965). *The challenge of response sets.* New York: Appleton-Century-Crofts.

Bond, M., Perry, C., Gautier, M., Goldberg, M., Oppenheim, J., & Simond, J. (1989). Validating self-report of defensive styles. *Journal of Personality Disorders, 3,* 101–112.

Clark, L. A. (1993). *Manual for the Schedule for Nonadaptive and Adaptive Personality (SNAP).* Minneapolis: University of Minnesota Press.

Costa, P. T., & McCrae, R. R. (1992). *NEO-PI-R professional manual.* Odessa, FL: Psychological Assessment Resources.

Derogatis, L. R., & Melisaratos, N. (1983). The Brief Symptom Inventory: An introductory report. *Psychological Medicine, 13,* 595–605.

DiNardo, P. A., & Barlow, D. H. (1988). *Anxiety Disorders Interview Schedule—Revised (ADIS-R).* New York: Graywinds Publications.

Endicott, J., Spitzer, R., Fleiss, J., & Cohen, J. (1976). The Global Assessment Scale. *Archives of General Psychiatry, 33,* 766–771.

Endler, N. S., Hunt, J. McV., & Rosenstein, A. J. (1962). An S-R inventory of anxiousness. *Psychological Monographs, 76* (17, Whole No. 536).

Frisch, M. B., Cornell, J., Villanueva, M. & Retzlaff, P. J. (1992). Clinical validation of the Quality of Life Inventory: A measure of life satisfaction for use in treatment planning and outcome assessment. *Psychological Assessment, 4,* 92–101.

Goodman, W. M., Price, L. H., Rasmussen, S. A., Mazure, C., Fleischmann, R. L., Hill, C. L., Heninger, G. R., & Charney, D. S. (1989). The Yale-Brown Obsessive-Compulsive Scale. *Archives of General Psychiatry, 46,* 1006–1011.

Grundy, C. T., Lunnen, K. M., Lambert, M. J., Ashton, J. E., & Tovey, D. R. (1994). The Hamilton Rating Scale for Depression: One scale or many? *Clinical Psychology: Science and Practice, 1,* 197–205.

Hamilton, M. (1959). The assessment of anxiety states by rating. *British Journal of Medical Psychology, 32,* 50–55.

Hamilton, M. (1967). Development of a rating scale for primary depressive illness. *British Journal of Social and Clinical Psychology, 6,* 278–296.

Hodgson, R. J., & Rachman, S. (1977). Obsession-compulsive complaints. *Behaviour Research and Therapy, 15,* 389–395.

Horowitz, L. M., Rosenberg, S. E., Baer, B. A., Ureño, G., & Villaseñor, V. S. (1988). Inventory of Interpersonal Problems: Psychometric properties and clinical applications. *Journal of Consulting and Clinical Psychology, 56,* 885–892.

Horowitz, L. M., Rosenberg, S. E., & Bartholomew, K. (1993). Interpersonal problems, attachment styles, and outcome in brief dynamic psychotherapy. *Journal of Consulting and Clinical Psychology, 61,* 549–560.

Horowitz, M. J., Adler, N., & Kegeles, S. (1988). A scale for measuring the occurrence of positive states of mind. *Psychosomatic Medicine, 50,* 477–483.

Howard, K. I., Brill, P. L., Lueger, R. J., O'Mahoney, M. T., & Grissom, G. (1993). *Integra outpatient tracking assessment: Psychometric properties.* Radnor, PA: Integra, Inc.

Ihilevich, D., & Gleser, G. D. (1982). *Evaluating mental-health programs: The Progress Evaluation Scales.* Lexington, MA: Lexington Books.

Jahoda, M. (1958). *Current concepts of positive mental health.* New York: Basic Books.

Keane, T. M., Caddell, J. M., & Taylor, K. L. (1988). Mississippi Scale for Combat-Related Posttraumatic Stress Disorder: Three studies in reliability and validity. *Journal of Consulting and Clinical Psychology, 56,* 85–90.

Kiesler, D. J. (1966). Some myths of psychotherapy research and the search for a paradigm. *Psychological Bulletin, 65,* 110–136.

Lambert, M. J., & Bergin, A. E. (1977). Therapist-induced deterioration in psychotherapy patients. In A. S. Gurman & A. M. Razin (Eds.), *Effective psychotherapy: A handbook of research* (pp. 452–481). Elmsford, NY: Pergamon Press.

Leary, M. R. (1983). A brief version of the Fear of Negative Evaluation Scale. *Personality and Social Psychology Bulletin, 9,* 371–375.

Lerner, P. M., & Lerner, H. D. (1980). Rorschach assessment of primitive defenses in borderline personality structure. In J. S. Kwawer, H. D. Lerner, P. M. Lerner, & A. Sugarman (Eds.), *Borderline phenomena and the Rorshach Test* (pp. 257–274). Madison, CT: International Universities Press.

Luborsky, L. (1962). Clinicians' judgments of mental health: A proposed scale. *Archives of General Psychiatry, 4,* 407–417.

Manuzza, S., Fyer, A., Klein, D., & Endicott, J. (1986). Schedule for Affective Disorders-Lifetime, Anxiety (SADS-LA): Rationale and conceptual development. *Journal of Psychiatric Research, 20,* 317–325.

Marks, I. M., & Mathews, A. M. (1979). Brief standard self-rating for phobic patients. *Behaviour Research and Therapy, 17,* 263–267.

Meyer, T. J., Miller, M. L., Metzger, R. L., & Borkovec, T. D. (1990). Development and validation of the Penn State Worry Questionnaire. *Behaviour Research and Therapy, 28,* 487–495.

Newman, F. L., & Ciarlo, J. A. (1994). Criteria for selecting psychological instruments for treatment outcome assessments. In M. E. Maruish (Ed.), *The use of psychological testing for treatment planning and outcome assessment* (pp. 98–110). Hillsdale, NJ: Erlbaum.

Othmer, E. (1989). *The clinical interview using DSM-III-R.* Washington, DC: American Psychiatric Press.

Paul, G. L. (1967). Strategy of outcome research in psychotherapy. *Journal of Consulting Psychology, 31,* 109–118.

Peterson, R. A., & Reiss, S. (1992). *Manual for the Anxiety Sensitivity Index* (2nd ed.). Worthington, OH: International Diagnostic Services.

Robins, L. N. (1988). *International classification in psychiatry: Unity and diversity.* New York: Cambridge University Press.

Robins, L., Helzer, J., Croughan, J., & Ratcliff, K. (1981). National Institute of Mental Health Diagnostic Interview Schedule. *Archives of General Psychiatry, 38,* 381–389.

Robins, L. N., Wing, J., Wittchen, H.-U., Helzer, J. E., Barbor, T. F., Burke, J., Farmer, A., Jablensky, R., Pickens, R., Regier, D. A., Sartorius, N., & Towle, L. H. (1989). The Composite International Diagnostic Interview: An epidemiological instrument suitable for use in conjunction with different diagnostic systems and in different cultures. *Archives of General Psychiatry, 45,* 1069–1077.

Rosenberg, M. (1965). *Society and the adolescent self-image.* Princeton, NJ: Princeton University Press.

Rush, A. J., Giles, D. E., Schlesser, M. A., Fulton, C. L., Weissenburger, J., & Burns, C. (1986). The Inventory for Depressive Symptomatology (IDS): Preliminary findings. *Psychiatry Research, 18,* 65–87.

Rush, A. J., Hiser, W., & Giles, D. E. (1987). A comparison of self-reported versus clinician-rated symptoms in depression. *Journal of Clinical Psychiatry, 48,* 246–248.

Spielberger, C. D. (1983). *Manual for the State-Trait Anxiety Inventory.* Palo Alto, CA: Consulting Psychologists Press.

Spielberger, C. D., Gorsuch, R. L., & Lushene, R. (1968). *Self-Evaluation Questionnaire.* Palo Alto, CA: Consulting Psychologists Press.

Spitzer, R. L., Williams, J. B., Gibbon, M., & First, M. B. (1988). *Structured Clinical Interview for DSM-III-R.* Washington, DC: American Psychiatric Press.

Strupp, H. H., & Hadley, S. W. (1977). A tripartite model of mental health and therapeutic outcomes. *American Psychologist, 32,* 187–196.

Strupp, H. H., Hadley, S. W., & Gomes-Schwartz, B. (1977). *Psychotherapy for better or worse: An analysis of the problem of negative effects.* Northwale, NJ: Jason Aronson.

Ware, J. E., Jr. (1991) *SF-36 Health Survey: Manual and interpretation guide.* Boston: Health Institute, New England Medical Center.

Waskow, I. E. (1975a). Fantasied dialogue with a researcher. In I. E. Waskow & M. B. Parloff (Eds.), *Psychotherapy change measures (DHEW Publication No. ADM 74–120,* pp. 274–327). Washington, DC: U.S. Government Printing Office.

Waskow, I. E. (1975b). Selection of a core battery. In I. E. Waskow & M. B. Parloff (Eds.), *Psychotherapy change measures (DHEW Publication No. ADM 74–120,* pp. 245–269). Washington, DC: U.S. Government Printing Office.

Waskow, I. E., & Parloff, M. B. (1975). *Psychotherapy change measures (DHEW Publication No. ADM 74–120).* Washington, DC: U.S. Government Printing Office.

Watson, D., & Clark, L. A. (1991). Self versus peer ratings of specific emotional traits: Evidence of convergent and discriminant validity. *Journal of Personality and Social Psychology, 60,* 927–940.

Watson, D., Clark, L. A., & Tellegen, A. (1988). Development and validation of brief measures of positive and negative affect: The PANAS scales. *Journal of Personality and Social Psychology, 54,* 1063–1070.

Watson, D., & Friend, R. (1969). Measurement of social-evaluation anxiety. *Journal of Consulting and Clinical Psychology, 33,* 448–457.

Weissman, M. M., & Bothwell, S. (1976). The assessment of social adjustment by patient self-report. *Archives of General Psychiatry, 33,* 1111–1115.

Wolpe, J., & Lang, P. J. (1964). A fear survey schedule for use in behaviour therapy. *Behaviour Research and Therapy, 2,* 27–30.

Wolpe, J., & Lang, P. J. (1969). *Fear Survey Schedule.* San Diego, CA: Educational and Industrial Testing Service.

Zung, W. W. (1965). A self-rating depression scale. *Archives of General Psychiatry, 12,* 63–70.

PART TWO

Conceptual and Methodological Issues

Dimensions of Outcome Measurement

Dietmar Schulte

ADVANTAGE AND NECESSITY OF A STANDARDIZED OUTCOME MEASUREMENT

The political requirement of quality assurance has been extended to psychotherapy, making it necessary to define appropriate criteria of therapeutic success. Without a theoretical foundation, previous classifications of various dimensions of success measurement will remain nonobligatory. If "healing" or "improvement of illness" is chosen as a common therapeutic goal, success has to be measured along several dimensions according to the general conception of disease in medicine. On the "causes and disease" dimension, there is no alternative to school-specific measures. On the "illness or symptoms" dimension, general symptom and disorder-specific measures are adequate. On the "consequences or sickness" dimension, measures across the different schools and disorders based on the sick role and the impairment of normal role behavior are possible. The method of measuring success includes the operationalization of the several success

From "How Treatment Success Could Be Assessed," by D. Schulte, 1995, *Psychotherapy Research, 5,* 281–296. Copyright 1995 by Guilford Press. Adapted with permission.

variables, the design of data collection, and the definition of success criteria.

In this chapter, detailed proposals about these criteria are presented, both for assessing the amount and significance of the change obtained as well as for the degree of goal attainment (clinical relevance). Against this background, conclusions for an appropriate measurement of success are drawn.

An adequate method of assessing the effect of psychotherapy is highly important to research, clinical practice, and health care and medical politics (Baumann, 1986; Strupp & Hadley, 1977). This last area in particular has gained in importance in the past few years. In 1984, the World Health Organization (WHO) introduced the program "Health 2000," calling on all member countries to introduce effective ways of quality assurance until 1990. In some countries (e.g., Germany), quality assurance is now a legal obligation. The definition of criteria for assessing the quality of outcome is the fundamental question for quality assurance in general.

In meta-analyses of outcome studies, the question of what is measured (i.e., the content of success and outcome measures) also is disregarded. The effect size criterion is defined only as the degree of change, regardless of the dimension on which the change is measured (Brown, 1987; Fiske, 1983; Grawe, Bernauer, & Donati, 1990; Kazdin, 1985; Shapiro, 1985; Smith & Glass, 1977; Wittmann & Matt, 1986).

Nonetheless, some studies have shown that the question of which variable should be used for assessing success is relevant: Changes are represented with different degrees of distinctness on different variables (Grawe, 1987; Smith & Glass, 1977; Wittmann & Matt, 1986). Standardized use of at least some measures would considerably increase the value of comparative treatment research.

A definition and decision about the content of success measures would be helpful in achieving some degree of standardization of outcome measures in psychological and pharmacological treatment studies and in evaluating clinical practice. The only way to reach this goal is through consensus. The international diagnostic system of the WHO (the *International Classification of Diseases [ICD]*) and the American Psychiatric Association (the *Diagnostic and Statistical Manual of Mental Disorders [DSM]*) were also developed by consensus, and they have led to substantial innovations in research and practice.

CLASSIFICATION OF SUCCESS MEASURES

In spite of the diverse attempts to systematize the different aspects of success, various authors agree (except Agras, 1989) that treatment outcome has to be assessed by multiple criteria (Lambert, Shapiro, & Bergin, 1986) on multiple dimensions (Lambert, Ogles, & Masters, 1992), by many methods ("multimethodically"; Seidenstücker & Baumann, 1978), and on many levels ("multimodally"; Fahrenberg, 1987). The proposed classification systems, however, are different.

Seidenstücker and Baumann (1978) suggested three dimensions: data source, measurement, and psychological functioning. *Source* pertains to the person who or institution that delivers the information: patient, therapist, relevant others, or independent observers. Lambert et al. (1986) added "institutional sources." The sources dimension can be found in all proposals.

On the measurement (or data) dimension, Seidenstücker and Baumann (1978) differentiated between experience (cognition and emotion), behavior, and performance, each of which is related to the present or past, and three biosomatic data categories (psychophysiological, neuropsychological, and biochemical). All these categories pertain to the patient. However, the target of treatment also can be a social relationship or a group (family) or social organization, which should be considered by an appropriate data category (Elliott, 1992). In addition to these extensions to social measures, further differentiations of the biological-biochemical categories also have been recommended (Baumann, Fähndrich, Stieglitz, & Woggon, 1990).

The third dimension, called "psychological functioning" by Seidenstücker and Baumann (1978), pertains to the content or constructs to be assessed. On this dimension Strupp (1978) differentiated between the feeling state (well-being), social functioning (performance), and personality organization (structure). However, Lambert et al. (1986) introduced a similar dimension, content, that is difficult to distinguish from the measurement dimension. They differentiated between intrapersonal (i.e., affect, behavior, and cognition), interpersonal, and social role performance. Elliott (1992) discriminated between the content (i.e., cognition, emotion, behavior, and physiology) and the realm (i.e., intrapersonal, interpersonal, and social role) dimensions.

Lambert, Ogles, et al. (1992; Lambert et al., 1986; see also Rosen & Proctor, 1981) introduced another dimension, technology, to differentiate between different diagnostic methods (e.g., observation) and different strategies to develop criteria (e.g., global posttreatment evaluation vs. descriptive pre–postcomparison). Elliott (1992) used several dimensions to describe the methodology of outcome measurement: evaluative directness (i.e., direct or indirect assessment of the treatment goal); baseline assessment (i.e., pretest or retrospective assessment of the amount of change); temporal unit (i.e., change in one session or the whole treatment); and timing or delay (time between treatment and assessment, such as during treatment, posttreatment, and follow-up; see also Rosen & Proctor, 1981). Parloff (1980) listed different criteria to judge success: effectiveness, relevance, breadth and stability of change, percentage of improved patients, efficiency, patient satisfaction, and ethics.

This diversity and variability of the classification systems reflects its nonbinding nature. A theoretical foundation has not been made; it has even been rejected on the grounds that a nontheoretical classification is necessary for studies from different therapeutic schools (Lambert, Masters, & Ogles, 1992).

PROPOSAL OF A CLASSIFICATION SYSTEM OF OUTCOME MEASUREMENT

The assessment of treatment success is not fundamentally different from the assessment of any other psychological construct in psychological research. The first step is a theoretical definition of the indexes or variables by which the construct should be represented. The second step determines how these variables can be operationalized and measured. A distinction between the content and the method of defining treatment success or treatment outcome is therefore necessary. These are not independent of each other; the method must correspond to the variables selected. Content and method are the main dimensions of a classification system of outcome measurement that are discussed in this chapter (see Figure 2).

CONTENT OF OUTCOME MEASURES

Treatment Goals

Treatment success basically means that intended goals are achieved. Standardization of treatment measures therefore implies common treatment goals. Is that possible?

Parloff (1967) differentiated between ultimate goals and mediating goals. Rosen and Proctor (1981) divided the mediating goals into instrumental goals representing stages on the way to the ultimate goals and intermediate goals required by the treatment methods. Treatment success is related to the ultimate goals, and reaching these is the criterion for terminating treatment.

It is doubtful, however, that a generally applicable definition of such ultimate goals is possible or that they should be determined individually for every single case (Mintz, 1980; Schulte-Bahrenberg, 1990). An appropriate method for evaluating individual treatments is the scaling of the attainment of individual goals (Cytrynbaum, Ginath, Birdwell, & Brandt, 1979; Mintz, 1980; Kiresuk & Sherman, 1968; Weinstein & Ricks, 1977). However, because researchers strive for generalizable statements, individualized goal criteria are less useful. (Averaging the goal attainment scaling over several patients—or even averaging the different goals of one patient—changes the criterion of success: It is no longer the specific goal but more generally the possibility of attaining individual goals.)

Lambert (1983) suggested developing specific test batteries for different disorders. In this case, the overcoming, healing, or improvement of the corresponding disorder or disease is chosen as the goal. This suggestion contradicts the assumption that the results of psychotherapy are not specific to certain disorders but consist, for instance, of overcoming demoralization (J. D. Frank, 1973) or maturation and self-development (Braaten, 1989).

Furthermore, the various psychotherapeutic schools define various ultimate goals in accordance with their theories. It often has been demanded that the assessment of the treatment outcome has to consider these specific goals to do justice to the treatment concerned (Elkin, Pilkonis, Docherty, & Sotsky, 1988; Gottman & Markman, 1978). On the other hand, it can be argued that common measures are necessary to compare different treatments. Accordingly, Lambert, Masters, et al. (1992) demanded atheoretical as well as theoretically founded measures.

However, *theory neutral* does not necessarily mean *atheoretical.* The various schools have some common aspects, bridging their differences. One common treatment goal is imposed on the various therapeutic schools from the outside, from society, or from medical policy: healing or improvement of physical or mental states that are termed *illness* in a legal sense. This goal of treatment has to be distinguished from other legitimate goals (e.g., improvement of quality of life, personality development, or self-development). Braaten (1989), for example, developed the Self-Development Project Check List-90, which is supposed to assess success in the sense of self-maturation or self-realization.

Treatment Success as Healing or Improvement of Disease

In the following discussion, treatment success will be defined as attainment of the goal of healing or improvement of (mental) diseases or as improvement of (psycho)pathological states. However, what various therapeutic schools understand as mental diseases or mental disorders—not in a legal but in a scientific sense—varies. This difference will become clearer as I take a more precise look at the general conception of disease in medicine (Schulte, 1990).

The term *disease* characterizes a common model serving to explain changes in a person that otherwise would be inexplicable by attributing this change to a disorder or a defect in the body or more generally in the individual. Thus, a distinction is made between the conspicuous level of symptoms and complaints, called the *illness,* and the level of the "defect in the person," the disease (see Figure 1). In turn, the disease is caused by one or several biological, psychological, or sociological factors. The "ill-being" (illness) can be perceived as a social fact to which the environment

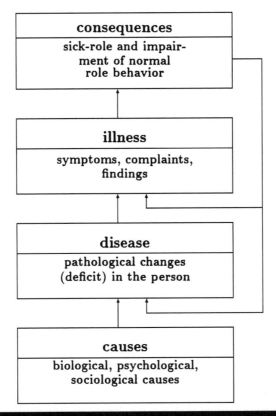

Figure 1

Levels of the general concept of disease.

and the person himself or herself relates with changed expectancies: The person is seen and treated as though he or she were sick. Parsons (1967) termed these changed expectancies the "sick role." The individual does not comply or complies only within limits to the normal role expectancy so that the specific role of the sick is ascribed to him or her.

This general concept of disease presumes the causal chain: causes → defect (disease) → manifestation (illness) → consequences (sick role). It is not a testable theory, but it can be seen as the fundamental paradigm (in Kuhn's, 1972, sense) of medicine. It is the basis for the development of specific theories for particular diseases. It serves as a guide to develop step-by-step hypotheses in medical research (i.e., that some complaints can be seen as symptoms of a specific, perhaps new disease, such as AIDS, that the central "defect" of this disease may be a viral infection, etc.; Häfner, 1981). Kuhn (1972) postulated that a paradigm cannot be falsified if it will die out among its proponents when a new and better paradigm is established. Against this background, treatment success can be described on four levels: no sick role or no restrictions of normal role behavior, no symptoms and complaints, no defect or disease, and perhaps no causes of disease.

The differences between the various psychiatric and psychotherapeutic schools relate primarily to the level of defect. In the medical tradition, psychiatry also assumes such a defect for psychological disorders, either as a somatic deviation or—in the tradition of Jaspers' (1965) psychopathology—as a defect of experience or a defect of the psyche. Psychoanalytic and psychodynamic theories also postulate an inner psychic defect, a central conflict. On the other hand, behavior therapy, humanism, social psychiatry, and systemic family therapy do not assume such a defect in the person, and to that extent they reject the medical model. The symtoms or complaints are directly attributed to specific causes. On the level of causes, however, there also are considerable differences between the various schools.

The disease paradigm makes it possible to point out fundamental differences as well as similarities, in the different psychiatric, psychological, and psychotherapeutic schools. This paradigm also gives the reasons for differences and common ground in measuring success.

Content Dimensions of Assessing Success

General standardization across schools is hard to achieve on the causes and disease levels. On these levels, only school-specific success criteria are currently appropriate.

For psychodynamic therapies, changes in ego functions, defense mechanisms, and interpersonal conflicts can be measured (Luborsky & Crits-Christoph, 1990; Schneider & Hoffman, 1992). In Rogerian counseling, the theoretically postulated discrepancy between the perceived and ideal self is measured by the Q-sort technique (Butler & Haigh, 1954). Behavior therapists have mainly used measures of target behaviors on the level of illness. Assessment of reinforcement (Cautela & Kastenbaum, 1967; Weiss, 1969) has not gained much acceptance, but there are instruments to assess cognitive variables (Bellack & Schwartz, 1976; Meichenbaum, 1976; Schwartz & Garamoni, 1986).

Psychiatric researchers look for markers of biochemical defects in mental disorders, such as spiperone binding sites in lymphocytis as a vulnerability marker in schizophrenia (Bondy & Ackenheil, 1987). The control of such markers consequently would be an additional success criterion in the view of biopsychiatry.

On the level of illness, treatment success means the reduction of the symptoms typical of the particular disease. Which symptoms are relevant for a certain disorder is defined in the operationalized diagnostic systems of the fourth edition of the *DSM* (*DSM–IV*) and the 10th edition of the *ICD* (*ICD–10*). On this level, disorder-specific measures of success are appropriate. There are already some proposals for such specific measures for some disorders, such as depression (E. Frank et al., 1991; Prien, Carpenter, & Kupfer, 1991), or for psychosomatic disorders (Blanchard & Schwarz, 1988). In addition to disorder-specific measures on the level of symptoms, a general decision across disorders and schools on a comprehensive rating of symptoms would be possible and useful, particularly to facilitate generalizations of treatment outcome or, conversely, symptom substitutions.

On the level of consequences, general measures across schools and disorders are possible. According to Parsons' (1967) theory of the sick role, a distinction can be made between the degree to which the sick role is assumed and the impairment of normal roles for which the person is socialized. Both can be assessed on the behavioral level and on the level of experience and subjective coping (see Exhibit 1).

The extent to which a person behaves according to the expectations of the sick role can be assessed in terms of the utilization of services of medical or mental care: frequency of rehospitalization, new treatments, notification of illness, and medication. The degree to which the sick role is assumed also can be subjectively assessed by the patient and significant others. Kassebaum and Baumann (1965), for example, developed a questionnaire that assesses the person's reaction to his or her illness: depen-

Exhibit 1

Consequences of Being Ill

Dimension	Sick role	Impairment of normal roles
Behavior	Utilization of health care services	Impairment with respect to work or professional efficiency, social activities, and social relations
Experience	Subjective experience of the sick role	Demoralization ■ No comprehension ■ No control ■ Reduced self-esteem

dency on others, being excused by others (reciprocity), claim to relief by reason of the sick role (role performance), and (lack of) self-responsibility for one's own illness (denial).

In accordance with the diversity of roles individuals are socialized for, impairments are possible in various role behaviors. In the *DSM* and the *ICD–10*, three areas are used to judge the severity of a disorder: impairment in professional efficiency, in social activities, and in social relations, including partnership and sexuality.

Impairment of normal roles is usually a considerable strain on the person. The experience of this impairment was termed "demoralization" by J. D. Frank (1973). The patients

> are conscious of having failed to meet their own expectations or those of others, or of being unable to cope with some pressing problem. . . . In other terms, to various degrees the demoralized person feels isolated, hopeless, and helpless, and is preoccupied with merely trying to survive. (J. D. Frank, 1973, p. 314)

Overcoming diseases also means overcoming the demoralization. Taylor (1983) presented a theory of cognitive adjustment to threatening events. People try in different ways to recover their former level of functioning. This adjustment process centers on three themes: (a) a search for meaning, (b) attempts to regain control over the event and over one's life more generally, and (c) trying to restore self-esteem. Questionnaires to assess demoralization in general (Dohrenwend, Levav, & Shrout, 1980) or some of its components could be used to operationalize this aspect of treatment success.

The differentiation between symptoms and consequences depends to some degree on the specific disorder. For depression, for instance, demoralization is a central symptom, not only a consequence. For a single patient, it can be difficult to decide whether a strange behavior is a symptom of the disorder or a consequence (e.g., the result of hospitalization).

Defining the disorder-specific measures on the level of symptoms (and on the level of disease and causes), these differences have to be taken into account. An overlap with some general measures of consequences are of minor relevance. Hence, treatment outcome should be assessed on three content dimensions according to the levels of the general concept of disease: (a) possibly on the (combined) levels of disease and causes by theory-specific measures on which the different schools could agree; (b) on the level of symptoms by disorder-specific measures and the use of an extensive instrument to assess general symptoms; and (c) on the level of consequences by means of some comprehensive measures across schools and disorders.

If the central deficit or the causes of a particular mental disorder will be detected unequivocally, measures on this level will be central. However, measures on the other levels will not be needless because the severity of the symptoms and the extent of the consequences also depends on personal and interpersonal variables, independent of the disease.

METHOD DIMENSIONS OF ASSESSING SUCCESS

In accordance with the success variable chosen, a specific methodological approach may have to be planned. The question of the appropriate method can be divided into three parts, reflecting three methodological dimensions of the classification system: operationalization of the success variables, defining the criteria, and design of data collection.

Operationalization

Operationalization involves deciding which method or instruments to use to measure the corresponding variables. This includes the decision about the data source: Should the data be gathered from the patient, from the therapist, from other members of the staff, from significant others, from or by neutral observers, by instruments, or by institutions? For measurement on the content dimension of illness, assessments by different people are necessary, and in the case of certain symptoms additional somatic measures must be taken.

Which diagnostic method is most appropriate has to be decided separately for each variable: questionnaires; self-rating; observation; content analysis; ratings; tests; projective tests; psychophysiological, neuropsychological, or biochemical methods; social analysis; and so on. Source and diagnostic methods are not independent.

Defining Criteria of Success

The value observed by means of the chosen instruments at the end of treatment is the basis for judging success. In addition, a comparison with a norm or a reference value is necessary. The result of this comparison constitutes the success criteria.

In principle, it is possible to distinguish between two kinds of comparisons: comparison with the pretreatment measure as the reference point (the result of this comparison characterizes the degree of change) and comparison with a goal or a norm (the result of this comparison is the degree of goal attainment). Although the pretreatment measure is an empirical value, the goal or norm value is based on a value judgment (which in turn can be suggested by empirical values, such as by the statistical average of a population).

The comparison can be done in three ways (see Exhibit 2): (a) a subjective rating, for which one measurement point at the end of treatment is in principle sufficient; (b) a computed difference between (at least) two

Exhibit 2		
Criteria to Characterize the Effectivity of Psychological and Pharmacological Treatment		
	Relation of postmeasures to	
Way of comparison	*State before treatment (change)*	*Goal or norm (goal attainment)*
Subjective rating (1-point measurement)	Change measurement	Contentment Social validation
Empirical difference (2-point measurement)	Computed difference	Individual goal attainment Normative comparison
Statistical definition	Reliable change Effect size	Clinical relevance

values, the measure at the end of treatment and either the pretreatment measure (to compute the degree of change), or a defined goal measure (to compute goal attainment); and (c) by statistical comparison, such as determining a patient's state at the end of treatment and comparing it with the range of values of a reference population. These criteria will now be briefly discussed.

Criteria of the Level of Change

Change measurement. The simplest form of this success criterion is a global, retrospective rating of the degree of change attained at the end of treatment. A more differentiated measure can be obtained using special methods of change measurements (Bereiter, 1963; Herold & Thomas, 1981; Stieglitz, 1986). It is not the performance or the state of the person at a given time that has to be assessed on an item of those questionnaires, but the degree of change since the beginning of treatment.

Computed difference. The most frequently used criterion to assess the degree of an obtained change is the difference between the pretreatment and posttreatment measure. The reliability of such difference values often has been criticized (Cronbach & Furby, 1970), but it seems to be less problematic and more useful than other conceivable measures such as residual values (Willett, Ayoub, & Robinson, 1991; Wittmann, 1988).

Reliable change and effect size. To test whether a patient's observed change from pre- to posttreatment is significant or reliable, Jacobson, Follette, and Revenstorf (1984; Christensen & Mendoza, 1986; Jacobson & Truax, 1991; Speer, 1992) proposed a reliable change index. The pre–post difference of one patient will be related to the standard error of measurement. The success criterion is the number of patients in this sample whose improvement is "of a sufficient magnitude to rule out chance as a plausible competing explanation" (Jacobson et al., 1984, p. 344).

The reliable change index characterizes the significance or probability level, but not the magnitude of change. The magnitude of change (or the degree to which the relation studied differs from zero) can be computed as the effect size, considering the standard deviation of the scores (Rosnow & Rosenthal, 1988). Effect sizes are computed mainly in meta-analyses, but they also can be used in original studies.

Criteria on the Level of Goal Attainment

Contentment. Measures of the patient's or the therapist's satisfaction, assessed as a global rating at the end of treatment, make it possible to draw inferences about the extent to which implicit goals are attained by the end of treatment. The acceptability of treatment and the relevance of the outcome also can be judged using social validation measures (Kazdin, 1977), that is, by an evaluation of significant others (e.g., the Treatment Evaluation Inventory of Kazdin, 1980; Kelley, Heffer, Gresham, & Elliott, 1989).

Goal attainment. The explicit comparison of a postscore with a norm or goal requires that it be defined. Goal or norm values can be set as a nominal value on an individually chosen scale, valid only for the patient concerned (a functional norm in Hofstätter's, 1957, sense). An elaborate way to assess the attainment of individual goals is the goal attainment scaling, already mentioned. The magnitude of the approximation to or the deviation from the goals defined for the individual case will be rated on one scale for each goal by the patient, by the therapist, or by others. Researchers, however, aim at generalizable statements and hence need universally valid goal criteria. It is sometimes proposed that therapists or researchers should define such common goals (Hollon & Flick, 1988; Kordy & Senf, 1985). Kendall and Grove (1988) suggested a "normative comparison" of the behavior of treated participants with that of nondisturbed participants. This implies standards of nondisturbed or normal behavior. The question remains whether these standards should be defined in the sense of ideal norms as a "state of perfection" (Hofstätter, 1957) or as the statistical average of a population (statistical norm).

Clinical relevance. In addition to the reliable change index, Jacobson et al. (1984; Jacobson, 1988; Jacobson & Revenstorf, 1988; Jacobson & Truax, 1991) also have proposed some methods to assess the clinical relevance of changes (see also Blanchard & Schwarz, 1988; Hayes & Haas, 1988; Nietzel & Trull, 1988). The basis of these indexes is the principle that the patient's postscore has to fall within the range of a normal population or outside the range of the dysfunctional population in order for him or her to be regarded as healthy or cured. The norm is defined as a statistical norm. The standard deviation of patients' pretreatment scores and, as much as possible, the standard deviation of a normal population will be used to compute limits that allow an assignment of each participant to the successfully or nonsuccessfully treated group of patients.

The criteria discussed so far characterize the effectiveness of a treatment. More complex statistical values can be formed by taking additional variables into consideration. If effectiveness is related to the necessary expenditure or cost, the efficiency of the treatment can be assessed (Yates, 1985). Taking the time factor into consideration by repeated measurement, it is possible to compute indexes of change over time using time-series analysis (Diekmann & Mitter, 1984; Morley & Adams, 1989, 1991; Revenstorf, 1979) or growth modeling (Francis, Fletcher, Stuebing, Davidson, & Thompson, 1991; Lehmacher & Lienert, 1980; Willett et al., 1991).

Design of Data Collection

Other aspects of success mentioned in some of the classifications discussed earlier, such as the time between treatment and measurement (Elliott, 1992) or the breadth and stability of change (Parloff, 1980), can be seen as various classes of generalization of treatment outcome. Four dimensions of generalization can be differentiated (Allen, Tarnowski, Simonian, Elliott, & Drabman, 1991; Drabman, Hammer, & Rosenbaum, 1979): generalization across time, settings, behaviors, and participants.

Generalization across time relates to the stability of the change obtained. It can be assessed by repeated follow-up measurement. It is mainly behavior therapists who would expect modifications to be limited to the situation (and to the behavior) that was focused on during treatment (e.g., changing of working behavior in school). To test the generalization to other settings, such as at home, measurements within the various settings are necessary.

To check the generalization across behaviors, such as from work to play, measurements of the different behaviors are necessary. However, that is not only a question of methodology but also of content. This also holds true for the question of generalization to other participants, such as other family members, which requires measurements of different individuals. When planning which measurements should be done in which settings, the generalization of results across time, settings, behaviors, and participants has to be considered.

CONCLUSIONS

To the extent the goal of treatment is seen as healing or improvement of diseases or mental disorders, there is no integrated measure to evaluate psychological and pharmacological treatment. *Disease* or *disorder* is a multilayer construct that needs operationalization on different dimensions (see Figure 2).

Also, the demand for obligatory and standardized measures can be met only in part. On the disease and causes dimension, if measurement on this dimension is considered necessary at all, theory-specific measures are unavoidable as long as one has to rely mainly on theoretical conjectures

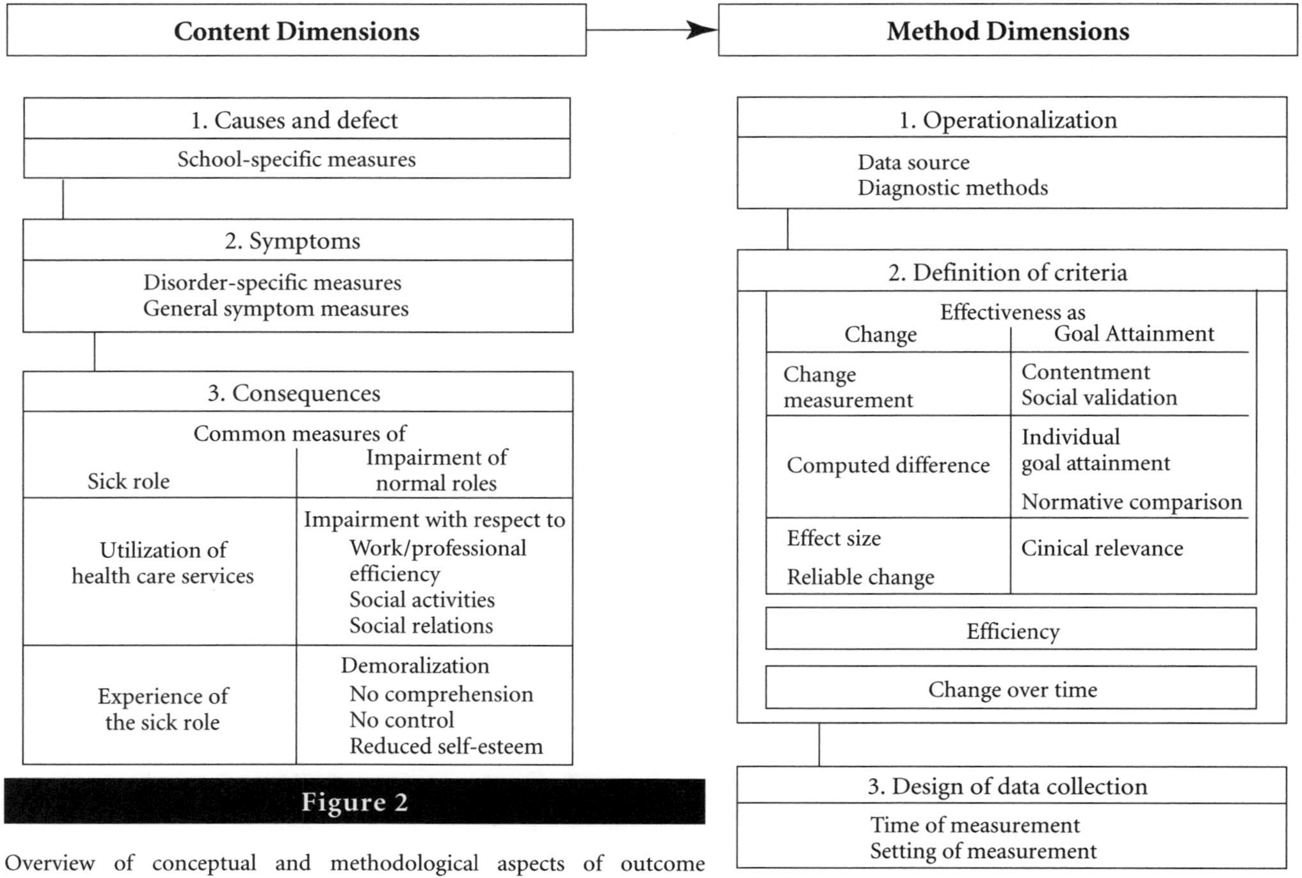

Content Dimensions

1. Causes and defect

School-specific measures

2. Symptoms

Disorder-specific measures
General symptom measures

3. Consequences

Common measures of	Impairment with respect to	Impairment of normal roles
Sick role	Work/professional efficiency Social activities Social relations	
Utilization of health care services		
Experience of the sick role	Demoralization No comprehension No control Reduced self-esteem	

Method Dimensions

1. Operationalization

Data source
Diagnostic methods

2. Definition of criteria

	Effectiveness as	Goal Attainment
Change		
Change measurement		Contentment Social validation
Computed difference	Individual goal attainment Normative comparison	
Effect size Reliable change	Clinical relevance	
Efficiency		
Change over time		

3. Design of data collection

Time of measurement
Setting of measurement

Figure 2

Overview of conceptual and methodological aspects of outcome measurement.

and as long as there is a dearth of adequate tested data about the causes of mental disorders.

On the dimension of illness, however, standardization is possible. A generally usable instrument for a complete measurement of symptoms and complaints would be desirable. In many studies, the SCL-90 (Derogatis, 1986) is being used. There are technological reasons (Baumann et al., 1990) for recommending this questionnaire: because of its frequent application, but not necessarily because of its content. In addition, it is necessary to compile specific instruments for each disorder by consensus.

Views on the possible consequences of illness, the impairment, and its personal implications are relatively uniform. On this dimension, there are no fundamental differences, only quantitative differences between the different disorders. The therapeutic schools have not dealt extensively with these questions, so a consensus about adequate operationalization of the consequences of being ill should be possible. This almost certainly holds for measures of the utilization of medical and social services. Because of the criteria chosen by the *DSM* and the *ICD–10,* it can be assumed that there is a consensus on the classification of impairments in terms of efficiency, social activities, and social relationships. It should be possible to reach an agreement about adequate instruments.

Regarding the design of data collection and the definition of criteria, there is increased standardization of procedure, at least in research. Follow-up measurements are seen as indispensable. As a result of methodological developments of criteria to assess the degree of success in the past few years, it would seem possible to reach general agreement on the three indices of effect size, reliable change, and clinical relevance.

Three fundamental decisions constitute the basis of the suggested system of success measurement: (a) the prescriptive decision for the treatment goal of healing or improvement of states that are seen as illness in a legal sense; (b) on the basis of this decision, the option for the paradigm of disease as the common basis for all therapeutic schools for distinguishing different content dimensions of success; and (c) the fundamental distinction between the determination of the content of the variables or indices of success on the one hand and the consequent decision for an appropriate methodology on the other.

These considerations are the reason for demanding multimodality and multimethodology and for measuring success on various dimensions. Measurement of treatment success is multifarious but not arbitrary.

REFERENCES

Agras, W. S. (1989). Treatment outcome evaluation methodology: An overview. *Advances in Behaviour Research and Therapy, 11,* 215–220.

Allen, J. S., Jr., Tarnowski, K. J., Simonian, S. J., Elliott, D., & Drabman, R. S. (1991). The generalization map revisited: Assessment of generalized treatment effects in child and adolescent behavior therapy. *Behavior Therapy, 22,* 393–405.

Baumann, U. (1986). Evaluation von Psychotherapie: Zugrundeliegende Forschungsbilder. *Zeitschrift für Klinische Psychologie, Psychopathologie und Psychotherapie, 34,* 169–178.

Baumann, U., Fähndrich, E., Stieglitz, R.-D., & Woggon, B. (1990). Probleme der Veränderungsmessung in Psychiatrie und Klinischer Psychologie. In U. Baumann, E. Fähndrich, R.-D. Stieglitz, & B. Woggon (Eds.), *Veränderungsmessung in Psychiatrie und Klinischer Psychologie* (pp. 15–43). Munich, Germany: Profil.

Bellack, A. S., & Schwartz, J. S. (1976). Assessment for self-control programs. In M. Hersen & A. S. Bellack (Eds.), *Behavioral assessment: A practical handbook* (pp. 111–142). Elmsford, NY: Pergamon Press.

Bereiter, C. (1963). Some persisting dilemmas in the measurement of change. In C. W. Harris (Ed.), *Problems in measuring change* (pp. 3–20). Madison: University of Wisconsin Press.

Blanchard, E. B., & Schwarz, S. P. (1988). Clinically significant changes in behavioral medicine. *Behavioral Assessment, 10,* 171–188.

Bondy, B., & Ackenheil, M. (1987). ^{3}H-spiperone binding sites in lymphocytes as possible vulnerability marker in schizophrenia. *Journal of Psychiatric Research, 21,* 521–529.

Braaten, L. J. (1989). The Self-Development Project List-90: A new instrument to measure positive goal attainment. *Small Group Behavior, 20,* 3–23.

Brown, J. (1987). A review of meta-analyses conducted on psychotherapy outcome research. *Clinical Psychology Review, 7,* 1–23.

Butler, J. M., & Haigh, G. V. (1954). Changes in the relation between selfconcepts and idealconcepts consequent upon the client-centered counseling. In C. R. Rogers & R. F. Dymond (Eds.), *Psychotherapy and personality change* (pp. 125–148). Chicago.

Cautela, J. R., & Kastenbaum, R. (1967). A reinforcement survey schedule for use in therapy. *Psychological Report, 20,* 1115–1130.

Christensen, L., & Mendoza, J. L. (1986). A method of assessing change in a single subject: An alteration of the RC index. *Behavior Therapy, 17,* 305–308.

Cronbach, L. J., & Furby, L. (1970). How should we measure "change"—Or should we? *Psychological Bulletin, 74,* 68–80.

Cytrynbaum, S., Ginath, Y., Birdwell, J., & Brandt, L. (1979). Goal attainment scaling: A critical review. *Evaluation Quarterly, 3,* 5–40.

Derogatis, L. R. (1986). Symptom-Check-Liste (SCL-90-R). In Collegium Internationale Psychiatriae Scalarunm (Ed.), *Internationale Skalen für die Psychiatrie.* Weinheim, Germany: Beltz.

Diekmann, A., & Mitter, P. (1984). *Methoden zur Analyse von Zeitverläufen.* Stuttgart, Germany: Teubner.

Dohrenwend, B. P., Levav, I., & Shrout, P. E. (1980). *Screening scales from the Psychiatric Epidemiology Research Interview (PERI).* Unpublished manuscript.

Drabman, R. S., Hammer, D., & Rosenbaum, M. S. (1979). Assessing the generalization in behavior modification with children: The generalization map. *Behavioral Assessment, 1,* 203–219.

Elkin, I., Pilkonis, P. A., Docherty, J. P., & Sotsky, S. M. (1988). Conceptual and methodological issues in comparative studies of psychotherapy and pharmacotherapy: II. Nature and timing of treatment effects. *American Journal of Psychiatry, 145,* 1070–1076.

Elliott, R. (1992). A conceptual analysis of Lambert, Ogles, and Master's conceptual scheme for outcome assessment. *Journal of Counseling and Development, 70,* 535–537.

Fahrenberg, J. (1987). Multimodale Diagnostik: eine Einleitung. *Diagnostica, 33,* 185–187.

Fiske, D. W. (1983). The meta-analytic revolution in outcome research. *Journal of Consulting and Clinical Psychology, 51,* 65–70.

Francis, D. J., Fletcher, J. M., Stuebing, K. K., Davidson, K. C., & Thompson, N. M. (1991). Analysis of change: Modeling individual growth. *Journal of Consulting and Clinical Psychology, 59,* 27–37.

Frank, E., Prien, R. F., Jarrett, R. B., Keller, M. B., Kupfer, D. J., Lavori, P., Rush, A. J., & Weissman, M. M. (1991). Conceptualization and rationale for consensus definitions of response, remission, recovery, relapse and recurrence in major depressive disorder. *Archives of General Psychiatry, 48,* 800–804.

Frank, J. D. (1973). *Persuasion and healing: Comparative study of psychotherapy* (2nd ed.). Baltimore: Johns Hopkins University Press.

Gottman, J., & Markman, H. J. (1978). Experimental design in psychotherapy research. In S. L. Garfield & A. E. Bergin (Eds.), *Handbook of psychotherapy and behavior change* (2nd ed., pp. 23–62). New York: Wiley.

Grawe, K. (1987). Die Effekte der Psychotherapie. In M. Amelang (Ed.), *Bericht über den 35: Kongreß der Deutschen Gesellschaft für Psychologie in Heidelberg 1986* (Vol. 2, pp. 515–534). Göttingen, Germany: Hogrefe.

Grawe, K., Bernauer, F., & Donati, R. (1990). Psychotherapien im Vergleich: Haben wirklich alle einen Preis verdient? Psychotherapie–Psychosomatik. *Medizinische Psychologie, 40,* 102–114.

Häfner, H. (1981). Der Krankheitsbegriff in der Psychiatrie. In R. Degkwitz & H. Siedow (Eds.), *Standorte der Psychiatrie: Vol. 2. Zum umstrittenen psychiatrischen Krankheitsbegriff* (pp. 16–54). Munich, Germany: Urban & Schwarzenberg.

Hayes, S. C., & Haas, J. R. (1988). A reevaluation of the concept of clinical significance: Goals, methods, and methodology. *Behavioral Assessment, 10,* 189–196.

Herold, E. S., & Thomas, R. E. (1981). Perceiving versus computed change: Can perceived measures tell us something that computed measures cannot? *Educational and Psychological Measurement, 41,* 701–707.

Hofstätter, P. R. (1957). Normalitätsbegriff. In P. R. Hofstätter (Ed.), *Das Fischer Lexikon: Psychologie* (pp. 217–221). Frankfurt am Main, Germany: Fischer.

Hollon, S. D., & Flick, S. N. (1988). On the meaning and methods of clinical significance. *Behavioral Assessment, 10,* 197–206.

Jacobson, N. S. (1988). Defining clinically significant change: An introduction. *Behavioral Assessment, 10,* 131–132.

Jacobson, N. S., Follette, W. C., & Revenstorf, D. (1984). Psychotherapy outcome research: Methods for reporting variability and evaluating clinical significance. *Behavior Therapy, 15,* 336–352.

Jacobson, N. S., & Revenstorf, D. (1988). Statistics for assessing the clinical significance of psychotherapy techniques: Issues, problems, and new developments. *Behavioral Assessment, 10,* 133–145.

Jacobson, N. S., & Truax, P. (1991). Clinical significance: A statistical approach to defining meaningful change in psychotherapy research. *Journal of Consulting and Clinical Psychology, 59,* 12–19.

Jaspers, K. (1965). *Allgemeine psychopathologie* (8th ed.). Berlin: Springer.

Kassebaum, G. G., & Baumann, B. O. (1965). Dimensions of the sick role in chronic illness. *Journal of Health and Human Behavior, 6,* 16–27.

Kazdin, A. E. (1977). Assessing the clinical or applied importance of behavior change through social validation. *Behavior Modification, 1,* 427–452.

Kazdin, A. E. (1980). Acceptability of alternative treatments for deviant child behavior. *Journal of Applied Behavior Analysis, 13,* 259–273.

Kazdin, A. E. (1985). The role of meta-analysis in the evaluation of psychotherapy. *Clinical Psychology Review, 5,* 49–62.

Kelley, M. L., Heffer, R. W., Gresham, F. M., & Elliott, S. N. (1989). Development of a modified treatment evaluation inventory. *Journal of Psychopathology and Behavioral Assessment, 11,* 235–247.

Kendall, P. C., & Grove, W. M. (1988). Normative comparisons in therapy outcome. *Behavioral Assessment, 10,* 147–158.

Kiresuk, T. J., & Sherman, R. E. (1968). Goal attainment scaling: A general method for evaluating comprehensive community mental health programs. *Community Mental Health Journal, 4,* 443–453.

Kordy, H., & Senf, W. (1985). Überlegungen zur Evaluation psychotherapeutischer Behandlungen. *Psychotherapie und medizinische Psychologie, 35,* 207–212.

Kuhn, T. S. (1972). *Die Struktur wissenschaftlicher Revolutionen.* Frankfurt, Germany: Suhrkamp.

Lambert, M. J. (1983). Introduction to assessment of psychotherapy outcome: Historical perspective and current issues. In M. J. Lambert, E. R. Christensen, & S. S. DeJulio (Eds.), *The assessment of psychotherapy outcome* (pp. 3–22). New York: Wiley.

Lambert, M. J., Masters, K. S., & Ogles, B. M. (1992). Measuring counseling outcome: A rejoinder. *Journal of Counseling and Development, 70,* 538–539.

Lambert, M. J., Ogles, B. M., & Masters, K. S. (1992). Choosing outcome assessment devices: An organizational and conceptual scheme. *Journal of Counseling and Development, 70,* 527–532.

Lambert, M. J., Shapiro, D. A., & Bergin, A. E. (1986). The effectiveness of psychotherapy. In S. L. Garfield & A. E. Bergin (Eds.), *Handbook of psychotherapy and behavior change* (3rd ed., 157–212). New York: Wiley.

Lehmacher, W., & Lienert, G. A. (1980). Nichtparametrischer Vergleich von Testprofilen und Verlaufskurven vor und nach einer Behandlung. *Psychologische Beiträge, 22,* 432–448.

Luborsky, L., & Crits-Christoph, P. (1990). *Understanding transference the Core Conflictual Relationship Theme method.* New York: Basic Books.

Meichenbaum, D. (1976). A cognitive-behavior modification approach to assessment. In M. Hersen & A. S. Bellack (Eds.), *Behavioral assessment: A practical handbook* (pp. 143–171). Elmsford, NY: Pergamon Press.

Mintz, J. (1980). *Tailoring psychotherapy outcome measures to fit the individual case.* Los Angeles: Brentwood Veterans Administration Hospital.

Morley, S., & Adams, M. (1989). Some simple statistical tests for exploring single-case time-series data. *British Journal of Clinical Psychology, 28,* 1–18.

Morley, S., & Adams, M. (1991). Graphical analysis of single-case time series data. *British Journal of Clinical Psychology, 30,* 97–115.

Nietzel, M. T., & Trull, T. J. (1988). Meta-analytic approaches to social comparisons: A method for measuring clinical significance. *Behavioral Assessment, 10,* 159–169.

Parloff, M. B. (1967). Goals in psychotherapy: Mediating and ultimate. In A. R. Mahrer (Ed.), *The goals of psychotherapy* (pp. 5–19). New York: Appleton-Century-Crofts.

Parloff, M. B. (1980). Psychotherapy and research: An analytic depression. *Psychiatry, 43,* 279–293.

Parsons, T. (1967). Definition von Gesundheit und Krankheit im Lichte der Wertbegriffe und der sozialen Struktur Amerikas. In A. Mitscherlich, T. Brocher, O. V. Mering, & K. Horn (Eds.), *Der Kranke in der modernen Gesellschaft* (pp. 57–87). Cologne, Germany: Kiepenheuer & Witsch.

Prien, R. F., Carpenter, L. L., & Kupfer, D. J. (1991). The definition and operational criteria for treatment outcome of major depressive disorder: A review of the current research literature. *Archives of General Psychiatry, 48,* 796–800.

Revenstorf, D. (1979). *Zeitreihenanalyse für klinische Daten: Methodik und Anwendungen.* Weinheim, Germany: Beltz.

Rosen, A., & Proctor, E. K. (1981). Distinctions between treatment outcomes and their implications for treatment evaluation. *Journal of Consulting and Clinical Psychology, 49,* 418–425.

Rosnow, R. L., & Rosenthal, R. (1988). Focused tests of significance and effect size estimation in counseling psychology. *Journal of Counseling Psychology, 35,* 203–208.

Schneider, W., & Hoffmann, S. O. (1992). Diagnostik und Klassifikation neurotischer und psychosomatischer Störungen. *Fundamenta Psychiatrica, 6,* 137–142.

Schulte, D. (1990). Psychische Gesundheit, psychische Krankheit, psychische Störung. In U. Baumann & M. Perrez (Eds.), *Lehrbuch Klinische Psychologie: Vol. 1. Grundlagen, Diagnostik, Ätiologie* (pp. 28–37). Bern, Switzerland: Huber.

Schulte-Bahrenberg, T. (1990). *Therapieziele, Therapieprozess und Therapieerfolg.* Bochum: Centaurus.

Schwartz, R. M., & Garamoni, G. L. (1986). Cognitive assessment: A multibehavior-multimethod-multiperspective approach. *Journal of Psychopathology and Behavioral Assessment, 8,* 185–197.

Seidenstücker, G., & Baumann, U. (1978). Multimethodale Diagnostik. In U. Baumann, H. Berbalk, & G. Seidenstücker (Eds.), *Klinische Psychologie: Trends in Forschung und Praxis* (Vol. 1, pp. 134–182). Bern, Switzerland: Huber.

Shapiro, D. A. (1985). Recent applications of meta-analysis in clinical research. *Clinical Psychology Review, 5,* 13–34.

Smith, M. L., & Glass, G. V. (1977). Meta-analysis of psychotherapy outcome studies. *American Psychologist, 32,* 752–760.

Speer, D. C. (1992). Clinically significant change: Jacobson and Truax (1991) revisited. *Journal of Consulting and Clinical Psychology, 60,* 402–408.

Stieglitz, R.-D. (1986). *Erfassung von Veränderungen: Theoretische und empirische Beiträge.* Berlin: Peter Oberhofer.

Strupp, H. H. (1978). Psychotherapy research and practice: An overview. In S. L. Garfield & A. E. Bergin (Eds.), *Handbook of psychotherapy and behavior change* (2nd ed., pp. 3–22). New York: Wiley.

Strupp, H. H., & Hadley, S. W. (1977). A tripartite model of mental health and therapeutic outcomes: With special reference to negative effects in psychotherapy. *American Psychologist, 32,* 187–196.

Taylor, S. E. (1983). Adjustment to threatening events: A theory of cognitive adaptation. *American Psychologist, 38,* 1161–1173.

Weinstein, M. S., & Ricks, F. A. (1977). Goal attainment scaling: Planning and outcome. *Canadian Journal of Behavioral Science, 9,* 1–11.

Weiss, R. L. (1969). Operant conditioning techniques in psychological assessment. In P. W. Reynolds (Ed.), *Advances in psychological assessment* (pp. 169–190). Palo Alto, CA.

Willett, J. B., Ayoub, C. C., & Robinson, D. (1991). Using growth modeling to examine systematic differences in growth: An example of change in the functioning of families at risk of maladaptive parenting, child abuse, or neglect. *Journal of Consulting and Clinical Psychology, 59,* 38–47.

Wittmann, W. W. (1988). Multivariate reliability theory: Principles of symmetry and successful validation strategies. In I. R. Nesselrode & R. B. Cattell (Eds.), *Handbook of multivariate experimental psychology* (pp. 505–560). New York: Plenum.

Wittman, W. W., & Matt, G. E. (1986). Meta-Analysen als Integration von Forschungsergebnissen am Beispiel deutschsprachiger Arbeiten zur Effektivität von Psychotherapie. *Psychologische Rundschau, 37,* 20–40.

Yates, B. T. (1985). Cost-effectiveness analysis and cost-benefit analysis: An introduction. *Behavioral Assessment, 7,* 207–234.

4

Implications of Priming for Measures of Change Following Psychological and Pharmacological Treatments

Zindel V. Segal

The desire for a modicum of unanimity in the development of a battery of assessment instruments to measure treatment outcome is nearly 20 years old (Waskow & Parloff, 1975) and remains largely unsatisfied (Lambert, 1992). A core battery of assessment devices is considered by some as being increasingly necessary for the field, not only for the momentum it could provide to those studying the process of behavior change after treatment but also as a corrective to the sometimes uninformed assessments of outcome currently used in the managed health care and national health insurance systems. A unified stance on this question would be an important first step in making the case for the benefits of psychological treatment and their need for continued support in an environment in which resources and accountability are becoming increasingly linked (VandenBos, 1993).

Although recognizing that the case for efficacy of psychological interventions will be put most forcefully if the psychotherapy community

I would like to acknowledge Mark Williams, John Teasdale, Rick Ingram, and Len Horowitz for valuable discussions of many of the ideas expressed in this chapter.

can speak with one voice on this issue, this unanimity has yet to be achieved. One of the explicit goals of convening the American Psychological Association's conference on measuring changes in patients following psychological and pharmacological treatments in 1994 was to enable psychotherapy to "put its own assessment house in order" in anticipation of the need for greater public education and professional documentation of the benefits of psychotherapy in the years to come.

The purpose of this chapter is to reflect on an apparent paradox that I believe surrounds the development of measures for gauging patient change after treatment. I describe how this may impede clinicians' ability to accurately assess the formal outcomes associated with psychotherapy compared with pharmacotherapy or at least to underestimate its impact. In addition, by drawing on recent studies of cognitive vulnerability to depression, I suggest one way of approaching this problem.

The paradox I refer to is the need for the measures to be both sensitive to recovery from disorder and vulnerability to future dysfunction. The context for these needs is created by the growing realization that many of the major mental disorders are recurrent in nature and bestow limitations in functioning on patients that often outlast the acute episode of the disorder (Keller, Lavori, Lewis, & Klerman, 1983; Weissman, 1988). For example, the fact that episodes of major depression respond well to short-term treatment has been used to bolster traditional views of this disorder as a condition that is self-limited in nature and associated with a favorable prognostic outcome. In this case, measures of treatment outcome that discriminated patients from nonpatients were adequate to the task because they could signal the presence of an episode (patient scores were not equal to nonpatient scores) and its resolution (patient scores were equal to nonpatient scores).

Yet, such measures may be judged to be less well suited when one considers that single episodes of depression are extremely rare, and if the time of observation is extended beyond 15 years they are practically never observed (Angst et al., 1973, p. 500). Furthermore, at least 50% of patients who recover from an initial episode of depression will have at least one subsequent depressive episode (Angst, 1988; Zis & Goodwin, 1979), and those patients with a history of two or more past episodes will have a 70–80% likelihood of recurrence in their lifetimes (Consensus Development Panel, 1985). In this case, recovered depressed patients' scores on a treatment outcome measure may equal nonpatients' scores, but this would be less than fully informative because an exclusive focus on changes in the initial symptom state may fail to adequately capture patients' predispositions to experience a return of the disorder. Put another way, a core assessment battery should reflect changes in symptom levels and changes in risk status attributable to treatment.

Whether outcome measures can satisfy these Januslike demands in the near future remains to be seen. It nevertheless seems important to work toward this capability. Most commonly, attempts to determine enduring risk have relied on follow-up assessments, with the rationale being that risk can be gauged in terms of the maintenance of posttreatment functioning over time. The problem with this view stems from its endorsement of a "traitlike" model of risk and can be seen in the enormous variance associated with predictions of follow-up status from posttreatment indexes. For example, patients may score in the improved range on measures of treatment outcome but still be at risk for symptom return in the not too distant future (as evidenced by the high rates of relapse after acute treatment with antidepressant medication [Consensus Development Panel, 1985] or in the case of patients receiving cognitive–behavioral therapy [CBT] Dysfunctional Attitudes Scale [DAS] scores decrease significantly with treatment but who go on to relapse [Thase et al., 1992; J. M. G. Williams, Healy, Teasdale, White, & Paykel, 1990]).

The approach described in this chapter is more situation specific. It requires specification of both the cognitive structures or representations that place patients at risk, as well as a paradigm for activating them temporarily during an assessment conducted once treatment has ended. In this way, one can evaluate the effects of treatment on the patient's ability to process information differently in the face of circumstances similar to those implicated in symptom onset. This then permits generalizations about the patient's ability to deal with such challenges on an ongoing basis.

In what follows, I describe a strategy that recently has been used in the cognitive–behavioral literature to study patients' reactivity after recovery from depression (Segal, Williams, Teasdale, & Gemar, 1996). Implications for designing measures of patient change after psychological or pharma-cological treatment are then outlined. Although situated in the affective disorders, there are little reason to believe that these principles would not apply to other conditions as well.

RELATION BETWEEN DEPRESSIVE SYMPTOMS AND MOOD-DEPENDENT ACCESSIBILITY OF COGNITIVE CONSTRUCTS

Measures of treatment outcome in depression should be calibrated to what is generally known about the effects of depressed mood on information processing because retrieval, recall, and attention partly determine the nature of patients' responses on these scales (J. M. G. Williams, Watts, MacLeod, & Matthews, 1988). Viewed from the perspective of semantic network theory (Bower, 1981; Ingram, 1984), an important aspect of de-pression is that negative concepts and negative events are rehearsed, lead-ing to extensive elaboration of related mnemonic structures that are highly interconnected with depression. Activation of part of such mnemonic structures will serve to activate other parts, making negative memories salient, for example. Consequently, future negative mood will bring to mind a wide range of related negative concepts and memories. Individuals who have, through early adverse life experiences or other means, strongly associated sadness with the activation of intensely negative constructs re-lated to profound loss, lack of self-worth, or global hopelessness will have formed a relatively durable and stable elaborative structure around the emotion of sadness (L. M. Horowitz & Malle, 1993).

Because of this dense interconnection among individual elements within this cognitive structure about depression (or depression schema), a patient's vulnerability to persistent states of depression can be defined in terms of the patterns of information processing that become activated in states of mild dysphoria (Segal et al., 1996). This hypothesis predicts mood-dependent changes in the accessibility of cognitive content (Teas-dale & Barnard, 1993) and has clear implications for the design of mea-sures of treatment outcome. It suggests that a patient's risk status can be determined primarily by differences in the patterns of information processing that become accessible once a person has initially become depressed or a mild depressed state has been induced.

According to this view, the thinking of vulnerable individuals may be normal when not in a negative mood state. However, as their mood becomes more depressed, these dormant dysfunctional sets of cognitive biases become active. This approach contrasts with views that emphasize constantly present and enduring differences in basic assumptions and attitudes as the primary vulnerability factors (Kovacs & Beck, 1978). The mood-dependent accessibility hypothesis does not deny the possible importance of enduring differences of the latter form. However, the dynamic emphasis of this newer approach means that differences between these groups will more likely be obtained if measures are taken when individuals are in a mildly depressed mood. As Persons and Miranda (1992) pointed out,

> patients treated with antidepressant medication "appear" to show changes in dysfunctional thinking during treatment. However, the mood-state hypothesis proposes that these patients still retain their dysfunctional attitudes; the attitudes are simply not reported because patients are in a positive mood at the time their attitudes are assessed. . . . The dysfunctional attitudes are present, but they are . . . inactive, and unavailable for report. . . . The mood induction (or other activation procedure) "turns on the light" that allows the investigator to observe real differences between groups that are hidden from view. (p. 497)

COMMENT ON THE NATURE OF PRIMING

Measures of mood-dependent accessibility typically require that the processes one is interested in assessing are already activated and "on-line" before testing can occur. This is usually accomplished by including a priming or induction task of some sort as part of the assessment procedure. Responses under two conditions (before and after the induction) then can be compared. The value of this approach is that it enables the study of vulnerability during the time when the patient is asymptomatic and, in this way, is compatible with posttreatment assessment.

In its most general usage, the term *priming* refers to a collection of procedures or techniques for the indirect activation of a hypothetical mental structure, often without the individual's conscious recollection that such activation has occurred (Hasher & Zacks, 1979; Segal & Ingram, 1994). This is frequently accomplished in two stages involving (a) the presentation of contextual features relevant to the targeted structure and (b) measuring the effects of this presentation at a later point in time. Changes in the chosen measures of the targeted structure as a function of exposure or nonexposure to the display provide an index of the magnitude of the priming effect (Graf & Schacter, 1985; Tulving & Schacter, 1990).

Activation of a cognitive structure can occur in two possible ways, either directly or indirectly. *Direct activation* usually follows exposure to an event whose content matches the type of information contained or represented in the structure (Teasdale, 1988; Warren, 1972). For example, an adolescent who gave up playing sports because she was frequently teased and picked last on teams may, as an adult, quit her company's softball team in response to jocular humor or good-natured taunting from coworkers; her past tendencies of responding to evaluation or ridicule by withdrawing may be reactivated by similar appraisals or performance demands in the present. *Indirect activation* of a cognitive structure occurs after exposure to an event whose content matches one of the elements constituting the structure and, through its interconnection with other elements, contributes to the reinstantiation of the entire organization (Bower, 1981; L. M. Horowitz & Prytulak, 1969). This process is frequently referred to as "spreading activation"; through associative linkages activation spreads through various elements until the entire structure can be considered activated. For instance, an employee's manager fails to acknowledge his greeting in the morning, leaving him feeling snubbed and puzzled. These affects may reflect a normative response to the situation, and, if they have not been frequently associated with self-deprecating thoughts, will probably pass after the employee has found a suitable explanation for the manager's behavior. If, however, these feelings are subelements of a larger cognitive–affective self-esteem structure, their activation will make it more likely that other affects, such as inadequacy and rejection, will come to mind, eventuating in at least a transient reinstantiation of the entire cognitive structure.

EMPIRICAL FINDINGS USING PRIMED AND UNPRIMED MEASURES OF VULNERABILITY

Segal and Ingram (1994) surveyed 29 studies examining the stability of cognitive variables by comparing scores taken during a depressive episode with those taken during remission, none of which used priming as part of their assessment strategy. The findings consistently pointed to the state-dependent nature of most of the measures of depressive cognition, including scales typically used in treatment outcome studies of depression (e.g., the DAS or the Attributional Style Questionnaire). Typical of this work is a study conducted by Bowers (1990) in which 30 depressed inpatients received one of three treatments: medication alone, relaxation therapy plus medication, or cognitive therapy plus medication. Posttreatment scores on the DAS were significantly lower than pretreatment scores for each group.

By contrast, there are relatively few studies that have included priming methods in their approach to assessment (Segal & Ingram, 1994, reviewed nine published studies). This is probably because of the recent focus on construct activation strategies in the literature, along with an allegiance to assessment paradigms based on shorter term outcomes in nonrecurrent conditions. Although not completely uniform, results from available priming studies do support the notion that priming before cognitive assessment allows for the detection of depressotypic cognitive variables in individuals who are theoretically at risk but not currently depressed. For example, in Teasdale and Dent (1987), formerly depressed patients and nondepressed control participants were tested on two occasions, once in a normal mood state and once after a depressed mood induction. Teasdale and Dent reported that recovered depressed patients did not differ from never-depressed participants in a normal mood state on measures of adjective recall. When a negative mood was induced, however, recovered depressed patients recalled more negative adjectives that had been endorsed as self-descriptive than did never-depressed individuals.

Perhaps the most direct indication of the importance of priming comes from considering the findings of two studies using similar methods with and without a priming manipulation. McCabe and Gotlib (1993) and Ingram, Bernet, and McLaughlin (1994) examined attentional biases in formerly depressed patients (patients at Time 2 in McCabe and Gotlib, 1993, and recovered depressed patients in Ingram et al., 1994), with the key difference being that the former study did not prime patients before testing them but the latter did. Consistent with the viewpoint being advocated, only the primed group of remitted depressed patients showed a performance decrement in the presence of negative content stimuli, whereas unprimed patients continued to perform in a manner no different from normal control participants.

Interestingly, construct activation effects have been obtained across several different levels of cognitive analysis (Ingram, 1990), offering some concurrent validity for the nature of the basic finding. For instance, in the presence of negative mood, dysfunctional cognition for those at risk appears evident in cognitive content (i.e., DAS scores; Miranda & Persons, 1988; Miranda, Persons, & Byers, 1990), information encoding and retrieval (adjective recall; Dent & Teasdale, 1988; Teasdale & Dent, 1987), and attention (tracking errors in a dichotic listening task; Ingram et al., 1994). Moreover, the lack of differences between vulnerable and non-vulnerable individuals in the various control (normal mood) conditions of these studies closely parallels previous research that has failed to find evidence of depressive cognitive processing after the depression abates (e.g., Lewinsohn, Steinmetz, Larson, & Franklin, 1981), that is, under ordinary conditions depressive cognitive processes cannot be detected after individuals are no longer depressed.

This last point illustrates the potential advantage of incorporating priming strategies in the design of treatment outcome measures. One could examine whether those psychological processes thought to underlie or drive the disorder were still contributing to the construction of the patient's experience, even in the presence of symptom or outcome scores that indicated that the patient was in the normal range of the distribution on the particular measure. One of the possible benefits to the field of considering this approach is that it would help to broaden the definition of effective treatment in a way that is consistent with the various change processes instigated through psychotherapy (Rice & Greenberg, 1984). An important task for all psychological therapies is to somehow reduce the probability that maladaptive patterns of responding, be they affective, cognitive, or behavioral, will be reactivated in the face of environmental challenges. Following from this view, one could speculate that at some future point in time a treatment's efficacy would be judged partly by how well it achieves this goal. I now consider how this framework can be adapted to the more traditional therapy assessment formats.

A ROLE FOR PRIMING IN THE DESIGN OF TREATMENT OUTCOME MEASURES?

The use of priming strategies in the realm of assessment is not unique to cognitive studies of depression or to psychology in general. As is the case with most hypothesized markers of risk (e.g., high levels of expressed emotion in families [Hooley, 1985]; cortisol suppression after a dexamethasone suppression test [Carroll et al., 1981]), priming bears on latent variables whose effects are discernible only under certain stressful or evocative conditions that are challenging to the individual. The need to understand how a system responds once it has been "challenged" is the premise under which many tests for biological markers of depression are conducted. As Hollon (1992) noted in this vein, there is a striking similarity between cognitive priming studies and dysregulation models that currently dominate in biological psychiatry. For instance, research in this domain has established that, after a psychological or pharmacological challenge, people vulnerable to depression will show evidence of dysregulation in key biological systems. Such dysregulation is not apparent under ordinary circumstances. Hollon (1992) further noted that the formulation of cognitive diathesis-stress models, which emphasize the importance of priming latent processes, predated the biological challenge paradigm by nearly two decades.

Going back to the use of these strategies for the assessment of treatment outcomes, priming methods used to ensure construct activation can be customized to better assess patients' psychological vulnerabilities after treatment. In the priming studies previously reviewed, sad mood served as an analogue to the potent environmental triggers that can reactivate cognitive structures that have been only minimally involved in on-line information processing. It may be possible to use interpersonal interactions that feature themes to which patients may be sensitive and that were the focus of work in therapy. Scenarios of loss, abandonment, rejection, shame, criticism, perfectionism, or other themes might be presented to patients on videotape. These could be derived from existing films or constructed anew. Patients would complete posttreatment measures before and after the viewing. This could be done by using the split-halfs of some of the more common outcome scales or by readministering the same measure.

If merely viewing the tape is not sufficiently evocative, patients may be asked to respond to probes about their perceptions of the nature of the interaction in emotionally relevant terms (e.g., How do you feel watching this? Does it bring anything to mind? How would you feel if you were in this situation? What could you do if you were in this situation? Are there any options you see for yourself in this situation as a result of the work you did in therapy?; Elliot, 1986; Genest & Turk, 1981). Of course, these paradigms would need to be validated through comparisons with the responses of nondepressed individuals, along with measures of changes in patients' moods elicited by the scenarios. Patients whose scores increased after their viewing of the scenario would be considered as showing a less positive response to treatment than patients with similar posttreatment scores, but no change in their scores as a result of viewing the interpersonal scenario. The extent to which the psychological tendencies reflected by these scores are changed through treatment and, if changed, how they contribute or protect the patient from future dysfunction are important benchmarks for any meaningful measure of benefit from such interventions.

In some ways, these procedures do not differ from the types of work that characterize the final stages of treatment in which a focus on how the patient sees himself or herself coping with future or anticipated stressors or challenges is discussed (e.g., Beck, Rush, Shaw, & Emery, 1979; M. J.

Horowitz, 1988; Linehan, 1993; Wachtel, 1993). The difference here is that, based on the empirical findings in depression vulnerability, it is being suggested as a formal addition to the larger assessment enterprise. I now consider the implications of this approach for studies in which the relative effects of psychosocial and somatic interventions are being gauged.

THE ROLE OF PRIMING IN ASSESSING THE EFFECTS OF PSYCHOTHERAPY AND PHARMACOTHERAPY

A central tenet of this chapter is that the paradox, by which the same outcome measure can signal two different posttreatment patient states, can be addressed by considering the implications of priming studies for the construction of treatment outcome measures. If one examines a commonly used outcome indicator such as the DAS, one finds that it shows a pattern of change in which pretreatment scores are usually elevated and in the dysfunctional range, whereas posttreatment scores are significantly lower and approach the mean of normal control samples. This is just what one would hope for, yet according to the priming or construct activation view, the lower DAS scores are less than an ideal reflection of the patient's posttreatment status. This is because they are not entirely informative about the patient's risk for future depression, a critical metric for judging the efficacy and effectiveness of psychotherapy for a recurrent and disabling disorder.

Imagine three possible outcomes after cognitive therapy for depression. In the first instance, the patient failed to respond to the intervention and so his or her scores at posttreatment are still in the elevated range on the Beck Depression Inventory, Hamilton Rating Scale for Depression, and DAS. The second and third patients are both treatment responders and evidence scores in the normal range on all three measures at the end of therapy. However, the second patient is at a higher risk for relapse after treatment and, although scoring in the normal range on the DAS, would be difficult to distinguish from the lower risk third patient on the basis of their posttreatment scores alone. The conclusions drawn about treatment efficacy would be that both patients responded to the intervention, and, although this is true at one level, the additional information about the treatment's effect on vulnerability to relapse or recurrence would be ignored. That priming and construct activation procedures can be used to assess this underlying level of risk is suggested by the work of Miranda and Persons (1988; Miranda et al., 1990) using the DAS to study vulnerability to depressive thinking styles. Their results indicate that mood predicts the occurrence of dysfunctional attitudes only in people who have a history of depression; as negative mood increases, people with a history of depression are more likely to endorse dysfunctional attitudes. In people without such a history, there is little evidence of a relationship between mood and dysfunctional attitude endorsement. Thus, people who are vulnerable to depression, as operationalized by having a previous episode, do seem to have distinctly negative attitudes, but these attitudes do not appear to be accessible until they experience a mild depressed mood.

Apart from having a method for identifying patients who continue to be at risk after psychological treatment, a second reason for adding a priming condition to posttreatment assessments is that it could help to demonstrate the effects of psychological interventions as being distinct from those attributable to pharmacological treatment. Hollon, Shelton, and Loosen (1991) described these differences in terms of the "symptom-suppressive" effects of antidepressant medication (pharmacotherapy) and the possible "prophylactic" effects of psychological treatments such as CBT. DeRubeis et al. (1990) suggested that a key difference between these two treatments may be that the former reduces the intensity of depressive symptomatology, whereas the latter teaches patients coping strategies or compensatory skills to use in the face of these symptoms. Both approaches work well for the acute episode of depression, but once patients are no longer depressed and they encounter new periods of sad mood or dysphoria, the patients receiving pharmacotherapy are at a disadvantage because they did not learn skills for handling these mood states. The patients receiving CBT presumably have learned a way to cope with their low moods and should be less likely to experience a relapse or recurrence in response to new episodes of low mood (Teasdale, Segal, & Williams, 1995).

If the data bear this out, then one would predict different reactions to a prime-based posttreatment assessment of patients who had responded to either CBT or pharmacotherapy. Consider, for example, how interesting it would be to compare patients who have recovered after either antidepressants or psychotherapy on a relevant outcome measure (e.g., in depression it might be negative thinking styles, negatively biased information processing, or narratives about the self) that tested patients under two conditions: euthymic mood and mild dysphoria. Perhaps both groups would respond similarly after the challenge, or perhaps the type of treatment received would make a difference and psychotherapy patients would score in the normal range on this measure under both conditions, whereas patients who had received antidepressants would have elevated scores after the induction. Studies of this kind could easily be added to existing or planned comparative outcome protocols at a negligible cost to their budgets and would allow these predictions to be put to the test. Finally, the data from one such study support the predictions outlined above (Segal, Gemar, & Williams, 1997).

SUMMARY

The addition of priming or construct activation procedures to measures of patient change after psychological or pharmacological treatment may provide the means to help identify measures most sensitive to the mechanisms underlying relapse or recurrence in depression or other disorders. A treatment's efficacy then could be judged not only by the magnitude of symptom reduction achieved but also on the basis of how well these mechanisms were altered so that, along with a measure of improvement in symptoms, one could also gauge patients' level of risk.

Advocates of psychotherapy often argue that this form of intervention allows patients to develop skills or new meanings for dealing with their symptoms and that this is an advantage over approaches that merely suppress symptoms and, with it, the opportunity to learn how to handle them differently. The use of outcome measures that assess such processes directly, often in the presence of a mild challenge, would augment a core assessment battery and contribute to the understanding of the ways in which differential therapeutics achieve their effects.

Some Qualifications

The ideas discussed in this chapter are consistent with the recent recommendations from a National Institute of Mental Health-sponsored conference (February 1995) on new research priorities for psychosocial treatment. At this meeting, there also was a call for the development of new assessment paradigms, along with the recognition of a need for an increased integration of basic science work with research on change mechanisms and processes (Pilkonis, 1995). The priming or construct activation approach to assessment might strike some as being premature given that little is known about how cognitive structures change as a result of successful treatment and the types of measures that can reflect this more or less directly (Barber & DeRubeis, 1989; Luborsky & Crits-Christoph, 1990). More specifically, demonstrating increased construct reactivity in recovered patients who are exposed to a prime does not indicate how much more at risk these individuals actually are than patients who do not show this effect. To say something meaningful about this, recovered patients would need to be tested, identified as being at risk, and then followed until they develop a new episode of dysfunction, and this work has yet to be done. What one is left with is a proposal, a rationale for why it might be worth considering and some early empirical data that suggest that it may be valid in a related context of inquiry. What is certain, however, is that until the field becomes serious about ensuring that assessments occur under conditions of adequate construct activation, psychologists will never know. Until then, the outcome measures will continue to hold the promise of prediction spiced with paradox.

REFERENCES

Angst, J. (1988). Clinical course of affective disorders. In T. Helgason & R. J. Daly (Eds.), *Depressive illness: Prediction of clinical course and outcome* (pp. 1–48). Berlin: Springer-Verlag.

Angst, J., Baastrup, P. C., Grof, P., Hippius, H., Poldinger, W., & Weis, P. (1973). The course of monopolar depression and bipolar psychoses. *Psychiatry, Neurology and Neurosurgery, 76,* 489–500.

Barber, J. P., & DeRubeis, R. J. (1989). On second thought: Where the action is in cognitive therapy for depression. *Cognitive Therapy and Research, 13,* 441–458.

Beck, A. T., Rush, A. J., Shaw, B. F., & Emery, G. (1979). *Cognitive therapy of depression.* New York: Guilford Press.

Bower, G. H. (1981). Mood and memory. *American Psychologist, 36,* 129–148.

Bowers, W. A. (1990). Treatment of depressed inpatients: Cognitive therapy plus medication, relaxation plus medication, and medication alone. *British Journal of Psychiatry, 156,* 73–78.

Carroll, B. J., Feinberg, M., Greden, J. F., Tarika, J., Albala, A. A., Haskett, R. F., James, N. M., Kronfol, Z., Lohr, N., Steiner, M., deVigne, J. P., & Young, E. (1981). A specific laboratory test for the diagnosis of melancholia. *Archives of General Psychiatry, 38,* 15–22.

Consensus Development Panel. (1985). NIMH/NIH consensus development conference statement on mood disorders: Pharmacological prevention of recurrences. *American Journal of Psychiatry, 142,* 469–476.

Dent, J., & Teasdale, J. D. (1988). Negative cognition and the persistence of depression. *Journal of Abnormal Psychology, 97,* 29–34.

DeRubeis, R. J., Evans, M. D., Hollon, S. D., Garvey, M. J., Grove, W. M., & Tuason, V. B. (1990). How does cognitive therapy work? Cognitive change and symptom changes in cognitive therapy and pharmacotherapy for depression. *Journal of Consulting and Clinical Psychology, 58,* 862–869.

Elliot, R. (1986). Interpersonal process recall (IPR) as a psychotherapy process research method. In L. S. Greenberg & W. Pinsof (Eds.), *The psychotherapeutic process: A research handbook* (pp. 503–527). New York: Guilford Press.

Genest, M., & Turk, D. C. (1981). Think-aloud approaches to cognitive assessment. In T. V. Merluzzi, C. R. Glass, & Y. M. Genest (Eds.), *Cognitive assessment* (pp. 233–269). New York: Guilford Press.

Graf, P., & Schacter, D. L. (1985). Implicit and explicit memory for new associations in normal and amnesic subjects. *Journal of Experimental Psychology: Learning, Memory, and Cognition, 11,* 501–518.

Hasher, L., & Zacks, R. T. (1979). Automatic and effortful processes in memory. *Journal of Experimental Psychology: General, 108,* 356–388.

Hollon, S. D. (1992). Cognitive models of depression from a psychobiological perspective. *Psychological Inquiry, 3,* 250–253.

Hollon, S. D., Shelton, R. C., & Loosen, P. T. (1991). Cognitive and pharmacotherapy for depression. *Journal of Consulting and Clinical Psychology, 59,* 88–99.

Hooley, J. M. (1985). Expressed emotion: A review of the critical literature. *Clinical Psychology Review, 5,* 119–139.

Horowitz, L. M., & Malle, B. F. (1993). Fuzzy concepts in psychotherapy research. *Psychotherapy Research, 3,* 131–148.

Horowitz, L. M., & Prytulak, L. S. (1969). Reintegrative memory. *Psychological Review, 76,* 519–531.

Horowitz, M. J. (1988). *Introduction to psychodynamics.* New York: Basic Books.

Ingram, R. E. (1984). Toward an information-processing analysis of depression. *Cognitive Therapy and Research, 8,* 443–478.

Ingram, R. E. (1990). Self-focused attention in clinical disorders: Review and a conceptual model. *Psychological Bulletin, 107,* 156–176.

Ingram, R. E., Bernet, C. Z., & McLaughlin, S. C. (1994). Attention allocation processes in depressed individuals. *Cognitive Therapy and Research, 18,* 317–332.

Keller, M. B., Lavori, P. W., Lewis, C. E., & Klerman, G. L. (1983). Predictors of relapse in major depressive disorder. *Journal of the American Medical Association, 250,* 3299–3304.

Kovacs, M., & Beck, A. T. (1978). Maladaptive cognitive structures in depression. *American Journal of Psychiatry, 135,* 525–533.

Lambert, M. J. (1992). Psychotherapy outcome research: Implications for integrative and eclectic therapists. In J. C. Norcross & M. R. Goldfried (Eds.), *Psychotherapy integration* (pp. 94–129). New York: Basic Books.

Lewinsohn, P. M., Steinmetz, J. L., Larson, D. W., & Franklin, J. (1981). Depression-related cognitions: Antecedent or consequence? *Journal of Abnormal Psychology, 90,* 213–219.

Linehan, M. M. (1993). *Cognitive behavioral treatment of borderline personality disorder.* New York: Guilford Press.

Luborsky, L., & Crits-Christoph, P. (1990). *Understanding transference.* New York: Basic Books.

McCabe, S. B., & Gotlib, I. H. (1993). Attentional processing in clinically depressed subjects: A longitudinal investigation. *Cognitive Therapy and Research, 17,* 359–377.

Miranda, J., & Persons, J. B. (1988). Dysfunctional attitudes are mood-state dependent. *Journal of Abnormal Psychology, 97,* 76–79.

Miranda, J., Persons, J. B., & Byers, C. (1990). Endorsement of dysfunctional beliefs depends on current mood state. *Journal of Abnormal Psychology, 99,* 237–241.

Persons, J. B., & Miranda, J. (1992). Cognitive theories of depression: Reconciling negative evidence. *Cognitive Therapy and Research, 16,* 485–502.

Pilkonis, P. A. (1995, June). *Future initiatives for psychotherapy research: Concerns from inside and outside NIMH.* Paper presented at the Society for Psychotherapy Research, Vancouver, British Columbia, Canada.

Rice, L. N., Greenberg, L. (Eds.). (1984). *Patterns of change: Intensive analysis of psychotherapy process.* New York: Guilford Press.

Segal, Z. V., Gemar, M., & Williams, S. (1997). *Differential cognitive effects to a mood challenge following response to either cognitive therapy or pharmacotherapy for unipolar depression.* Manuscript submitted for publication.

Segal, Z. V., & Ingram, R. E. (1994). Mood priming and construct activation in tests of cognitive vulnerability to unipolar depression. *Clinical Psychology Review, 14,* 663–695.

Segal, Z. V., Williams, J. M., Teasdale, J. D., & Gemar, M. C. (1996). A cognitive science perspective on the stress/neurobiology relationship in recurrent affective disorder. *Psychological Medicine, 26,* 371–380.

Teasdale, J. D. (1988). Cognitive vulnerability to persistent depression. *Cognition and Emotion, 2,* 247–274.

Teasdale, J. D., & Barnard, P. (1993). *Affect, cognition, and change.* Hillsdale, NJ: Erlbaum.

Teasdale, J. D., & Dent, J. (1987). Cognitive vulnerability to depression: An investigation of two hypotheses. *British Journal of Clinical Psychology, 26,* 113–126.

Teasdale, J. D., Segal, Z. V., & Williams, J. M. G. (1995). How does cognitive therapy prevent depressive relapse and why should attentional control (mindfulness) training help? *Behaviour Research Therapy, 33,* 25–39.

Thase, M. E., Simons, A. D., McGeary, J., Cahalane, J. G., Hughes, C., Harden, T., & Friedman, E. (1992). Relapse after cognitive behavior therapy of depression: Potential implications for longer courses of treatment. *American Journal of Psychiatry, 149,* 1046–1052.

Tulving, E., & Schacter, D. L. (1990). Priming in human memory systems. *Science, 247,* 301–306.

VandenBos, G. R. (1993). U.S. mental health policy: Proactive evolution in the midst of health care reform. *American Psychologist, 48,* 283–290.

Wachtel, P. (1993). *Therapeutic communication.* New York: Guilford Press.

Warren, R. E. (1972). Stimulus encoding and memory. *Journal of Experimental Psychology, 94,* 90–100.

Waskow, I. E., & Parloff, M. B. (1975). *Psychotherapy change measures.* Washington, DC: Department of Health, Education and Welfare.

Weissman, M. M. (1988). The epidemiology of panic disorder and agoraphobia. *Annual Review of Psychiatry, 7,* 54–66.

Williams, J. M. G., Healy, D., Teasdale, J. D., White, W., & Paykel, E. S. (1990). Dysfunctional attitudes and vulnerability to depression. *Psychological Medicine, 20,* 375–381.

Williams, J. M. G., Watts, F. N., MacLeod, C., & Matthews, A. (1988). *Cognitive psychology and emotional disorders.* New York: Wiley.

Zis, A. P., & Goodwin, F. K. (1979). Major affective disorders as a recurrent illness: A critical review. *Archives of General Psychiatry, 36,* 835–839.

5

Considerations in Developing a Core Assessment Battery

Marvin R. Goldfried

Before considering some of the issues involved in the development of a core outcome assessment battery, it is useful to conceptualize psychotherapy outcome research as having passed through three generations of development, beginning in the 1950s and ending in the 1990s (Goldfried & Wolfe, 1996).

From the early 1950s through the late 1960s, research was directed toward answering the question of whether psychotherapy is effective in bringing about personality change. Thus, the question was framed as if there were a presumably homogeneous intervention to deal with a general outcome (Strupp & Howard, 1992). The therapeutic interventions were primarily client-centered or psychodynamic in nature, and the measure of outcome tended to be global in nature (e.g., "improvement").

In the late 1960s, as different therapy procedures were developed for dealing with different clinical problems, the focus started to sharpen somewhat. Instead of addressing whether psychotherapy is effective, researchers conducted comparative outcome studies to determine which specific procedures were more effective in dealing with a particular clinical problem. In this second generation, participants in outcome research were selected according to more specific target problems (e.g., public speaking anxiety, unassertiveness), and different interventions based on written guidelines were compared with each other (e.g., desensitization, behavior rehearsal). The treatment procedures varied, but by and large they were behavioral and cognitive–behavioral in nature. Although this represented a methodological advance over the first generation, numerous criticisms came to the fore with this approach to outcome research, such as the tendency to use graduate students as therapists and volunteer participants rather than "real" patients or clients.

From the early 1980s to the present, a new and more highly refined methodological approach to studying therapy outcome evolved. Taking the lead from the NIMH (National Institute of Mental Health) Treatment of Depression Collaborative Research Program, the third generation of outcome research involved "clinical trials"; this was a clear reflection of the movement toward the medical model. In the clinical trial paradigm, different manual-based therapy interventions are compared to determine their effectiveness in treating patients or clients with various *Diagnostic and Statistical Manual of Mental Disorders* (DSM) Axis I disorders. The array of therapy approaches studied spans different theoretical orientations, with the goal being to determine which "pure form" therapeutic orientation is more effective in bringing about symptom reduction.

With the methodological refinements associated with our most recent generation of outcome research, there has been a renewed interest in addressing the dilemma of having outcome measures vary from study to study. This current interest in establishing a consensus on a core assessment battery for specific disorders represents a clear advancement over the earlier attempt by Waskow and Parloff (1975) to establish a single, generic outcome battery. Even so, a number of conceptual and methodological issues need to be considered. Four major points are discussed: (a) a set of criteria for judging the value of specific measures; (b) some of the issues associated with developing core batteries; (c) content areas in need of assessment; and (d) procedures for developing the batteries themselves.

CRITERIA FOR JUDGING THE VALUE OF SPECIFIC MEASURES

An important consideration in judging the value of measures to be included in a core outcome battery is that of *method variance* (i.e., variation resulting from the nature of the measurement procedure rather than what is being measured). To some extent, this issue has been acknowledged in previous discussions on psychotherapy outcome measures (e.g., Strupp & Hadley, 1977; Waskow & Parloff, 1975). In the psychometric literature, the classic article by Campbell and Fiske (1959) made a convincing case for assessing a given personality characteristic using multiple methods because the methods themselves may contribute to the obtained scores.

A variety of different methods are relevant for assessing therapy outcome, although each may not be conceptually appropriate or practical for evaluating all clinical problems. Still, it is useful to categorize different methods on the basis of whether they consist of naturalistic observations, situational tests, role playing, self-report, or physiological assessment.

Naturalistic Observations

Often serving as a criterion for the validation of other measures, direct observations in naturalistic settings may be relevant for measuring therapeutic outcome. These observations typically are implemented using some sort of coding scheme involving reliable judgments by trained coders. In addition to its utility as a measure of outcome in the more naturalistic setting, observations also may be used for categorizing certain aspects of a client's functioning within the session itself, often to determine an immediate, in-session impact or outcome (i.e., "little o").

From a practical point of view, it may not always be feasible to have trained observers rate aspects of a client's functioning. As a useful compromise, observations may be obtained by individuals in the client's naturalistic environment, such as relatives, friends, peers, or other significant individuals who have had the opportunity to observe the client. Although their reports may not be as detailed, precise, or objective as those of more highly trained observers, there is a definite advantage to obtaining information from individuals who can view the client over longer periods of time, in a wider variety of situations, and with minimal likelihood of reactivity resulting from the knowledge of being observed.

Situational Tests

In the case of naturalistic observation, there is often little control one has over the circumstances in which the patient's functioning is being assessed.

Because an individual's behavior may vary as a function of the situational circumstances, it may be appropriate to construct an observation within the context of a situational test, where the patient is confronted with events that are likely to elicit the type of behavior toward which the assessment is specifically directed. Thus, if an individual is anxious when speaking in front of groups of individuals, a situational test may be constructed involving public speaking, which may be used readily as an indication of therapeutic success. Other typical uses involve the evaluation of outcome in the treatment of specific phobias, such as the Behavioral Avoidance Test, wherein individuals approach specific objects or situations about which they are phobic (e.g., injections). In the case of situational tests, not only is there the option of observing the client's behavior, but it also is possible to obtain relevant subjective and physiological measures associated with anxiety.

Role-Playing Assessment

Although assessment within the context of role playing is somewhat similar to situational tests, it differs in that a role-playing assessment is much more clearly simulated, such that clients are asked to react as if the event were happening in real life. Thus, an example of a role play assessment might be one in which a socially anxious client is asked to interact with another person in the kind of social situation in which they have difficulties (e.g., asking a person for a date). As in the case of situational tests, assessment can be made not only of overt behavior but also of subjective and physiological indicators of anxiety.

Self-Report Assessment

Self-report assessment procedures can focus on a client's behavior, emotion, or thoughts. For self-reports of behavior, it is possible to determine the extent to which this form of assessment relates to more external observations of the same behavior. For subjective reports of anxiety or thoughts, the self-report method may be the only way to obtain information on the variable of interest.

Regardless of the content of the self-report, it may be obtained via paper-and-pencil measures or within the context of a structured interview.

Moreover, self-report of emotion and thoughts may be specific to particular situational circumstances (i.e., states), such as feelings and thoughts in the context of a situational test, or it may deal with more general patterns of functioning (i.e., traits), such as general symptomatology or belief systems.

Physiological Assessment

Particularly relevant to measuring outcome in the treatment of anxiety disorders is the need for physiological assessment. Although this may sometimes raise issues of feasibility, it nonetheless is crucial in the evaluation of changes in the overall level of activation (i.e., trait anxiety) or within the context of specific anxiety-provoking situations (i.e., state anxiety).

Apart from the issue of method variance, another factor that needs to be taken into account is the sensitivity of the measure to change. In considering whether a particular measure of outcome will be sensitive to change, it is important to consider the "difficulty level" of the assessment task and how it interacts with the power of the intervention. The difficulty level of the assessment procedure is the ease with which the assessment task can be handled in an anxiety-free fashion. For example, in the use of a situational test for assessing public speaking anxiety, one may vary the nature and length of the talk, as well as characteristics of the audience, all of which may make the task easy or difficult. If the task is too easy or too difficult, it may fail to provide a sensitive instrument for evaluating differences between treatment conditions. Moreover, therapeutic interventions provided in a less powerful fashion (i.e., an insufficient number of sessions) may fail to show any change whatsoever if the assessment situation is too difficult. To deal with this issue, I recommend having one's assessment procedure sample a range of difficulty levels to increase the likelihood of detecting change.

A final caution to keep in mind in judging the value of specific measures for an outcome battery is the extent to which the outcome measure closely parallels the nature of the intervention. For example, in some early research Linehan, Goldfried, and Goldfried (1979) conducted on the facilitation of assertiveness, one of the outcome measures used entailed a role-playing assessment of assertion. During the posttest assessment, however, some patients were noted "preparing" for this posttest by reviewing handouts that they received during one of the intervention conditions, which made use of role playing for training in assertiveness (e.g., "State what you want without being apologetic"). Participants in this condition no doubt had more of an advantage in doing well in these posttest assessments than did those who were observed in intervention conditions not entailing any role playing. The same comment can be made about the use of the self-report of cognitions as an outcome measure for cognitive interventions, as one may simply be obtaining a check on the manipulation and not a true measure of outcome.

ISSUES ASSOCIATED WITH DEVELOPING A CORE ASSESSMENT BATTERY

An issue that has been discussed over the years in assessing therapeutic outcome is the extent to which one can reasonably determine therapeutic success by developing generic measures or whether the measure of success should be individually tailored to the particular client (e.g., goal attainment scaling). To some extent, this issue may have been minimized as psychotherapy outcome research has moved away from studying personality change in general to change within the context of specific target populations. Thus, rather than asking the question "Is psychotherapy effective in producing change," more specific questions have been addressed for specific kinds of clinical issues, such as "Is cognitive–behavior effective in treating panic disorder?" However, whether this move toward greater diagnostic specificity successfully deals with this issue depends on whether one assumes the centrality of the *DSM* as a criterion for both selecting cases and evaluating change. The fact that core outcome batteries were organized according to diagnostic categories within the 1994 Consensus Conference on Measuring Change in Patients Following Psychological and Pharmacological Interventions reflects an assumption that *DSM* is the optimal way of "carving nature at its joints." Indeed, this is a basic assumption associated with current methodological state of the art; without the use of *DSM* diagnoses and therapy manuals, it is difficult if not impossible to obtain funding for outcome research.

During the conference itself, I found myself, a cognitive–behavior therapist, arguing with psychodynamic researchers about the place of measures other than those assessing *DSM* symptoms within a core battery. I took the position that variables such as interpersonal skills and self-concept were important to include as indexes of change, whereas my psychodynamic colleagues were of the opinion that symptom reduction should be the primary index. The irony of this was that I can recall similar discussions between psychodynamic and behavior therapists in the 1970s, except their positions were reversed. Psychotherapy researchers clearly have been socialized to think and behave differently over time.

A serious problem associated with the development of a core battery for evaluating whether psychotherapy successfully treats various "disorders" rather than intra- and interpersonal problems in living is that we as clinical researchers may fail to evaluate some of the key determinants or dynamics that are central to change. This danger can be illustrated by referring to a recent NIMH conference dealing with the attempt to develop standardized assessment measures for psychotherapy research on panic disorder (Shear & Maser, in press). During the conference, the importance of assessing mediator variables throughout the course of treatment was noted, such as evaluations of self-reports of panic frequency, anxiety-related thoughts, and other relevant variables. However, the conferees concluded that the evaluation of personality variables were *not* "essential" for measuring outcome. This conclusion was reached because the conferees noted the difficulty in measuring personality disorders and also because of the lack of clarity in "comorbidity" between Axes I and II. It is unfortunate that the saliency of the disorder conceptualization of outcome may have led the conferees to overlook the need to measure certain personality characteristics that often may be determinants or dynamics targeted within certain interventions (e.g., unassertiveness, unrealistically high standards for oneself).

Arkowitz (1989) has argued that insufficient attention has been paid to knowledge of psychopathology in the design and evaluation of therapeutic interventions, as demographic information and basic research on particular clinical problems can provide invaluable information on "what" needs to be changed. Thus, research findings that panic attacks temporally precede the development of agoraphobic avoidance have contributed to increased emphasis on working therapeutically with the panic attacks. Researchers and clinicians who specialize in a given clinical problem typically share a common pool of knowledge, and it is this shared experience that can help to shed light on key variables associated with a given problem, including those that would be important to include in an outcome battery.

CONTENT AREAS TO BE INCLUDED
IN A CORE ASSESSMENT BATTERY

Although it is certainly important to have symptom reduction as a central aspect of the core battery, it would be short-sighted if the battery did not go well beyond this. In the earlier attempt to develop a core assessment battery for psychotherapy outcome research, Waskow and Parloff (1975) had similarly hoped that conference participants would be able to agree on measures that could provide a wide array of information. As they envisioned it,

> by using a battery relevant for but not specific to any particular orientation of therapy, we would be able to evaluate the effects of different treatment approaches, not only in terms of the constructs relevant to the theoretical orientation of the particular therapists studied but also in terms of constructs relevant to other approaches and to more general concepts of therapeutic change and healthy functioning. By employing both across-the-board and more individualized measures, it should moreover be possible to test ideas about the specificity or more generalized nature of changes brought about by different treatment approaches. (Waskow & Parloff, 1975, p. 6)

The difficulty in developing a multifaceted core battery, however, involves the need to obtain a consensus about which variables to include. Indeed, this was the problem reported by Waskow and Parloff (1975):

> The conferees did not find it possible to orient their selection process around the coverage of particular constructs or dimensions of change, as we had originally hoped they could. The view prevalent at the conference was that the very specification of such dimensions is inevitably tied to one's particular theoretical orientation. Thus, it

would be extremely difficult to define such constructs in a way that
would be palatable to researchers of different orientations. (p. 247)

Despite the difficulties encountered some 20 years ago, I nonetheless
maintain that it is essential to arrive at a listing of potentially important
outcome variables that may cut across different orientations (e.g., patterns
of interpersonal relations, self-esteem). Knowledge of psychopathology
and personality can help move us beyond the *DSM* classification system
and theories of therapy to take into account the possible determinants or
dynamics that are associated with different clinical problems. As suggested
by Waskow and Parloff (1975), even if those of a given therapeutic orientation do not necessarily believe certain variables to be central to the
change process and ultimate outcome, it nonetheless is important to determine whether these variables do in fact change when therapy is implemented from within that particular orientation.

As any practicing clinician knows, a *DSM* diagnosis does not provide
sufficient information on how to proceed therapeutically. Despite the fact
that we can now obtain acceptable reliability in classifying individuals into
diagnostic categories, it is clear that a fair amount of heterogeneity exists
within a category, including variability that can have important therapeutic implications. This is known not only to practicing clinicians,
but also to psychotherapy researchers who also are practicing therapists
(Wolfe, 1994). Indeed, I once had occasion to ask two of the four authors
of a well-known manual on cognitive therapy of depression whether they
would use cognitive therapy with a patient who was depressed because of
a complicated grief reaction. Without hesitation, both independently responded with something like "Of course not! I would do grief therapy."

The theoretically based therapies outlined in the manuals used for
clinical trials tend to favor different classes of process variables as part
of their intervention (e.g., changing of thoughts, interpersonal patterns),
which are believed to result in symptom reduction. According to our
current research paradigm, patients sharing the same diagnostic label are
randomly assigned to a particular pure form intervention. The typical failure to find consistent differences across therapy orientations with this
research model certainly may be interpreted as reflecting the existence of
common therapeutic factors among the different therapies (Goldfried,

1980, 1995; Norcross & Goldfried, 1992). However, it also may be due to the failure to match specific interventions according to the particular determinants or dynamics likely to be maintaining the symptomatology.

For example, patients participating in clinical trials comparing the effectiveness of different forms of therapy for the treatment of depression, although sharing the same diagnosis, may vary according to psychosocial determinants. They may be depressed because of the unrealistically high standards they set for themselves, their sensitivity to rejection, an unfortunate work situation, interpersonal patterns that elicit a negative reaction from others, the failure to mourn a loss, an unassertive interpersonal pattern that makes it difficult for them to cope with various life situations, or an intolerable marriage. Although the practicing clinician would never think of randomly assigning a patient to a given form of therapy without carefully taking into account these essential determinants or dynamics, random assignment is a key component of our research paradigm. However, when following a cognitive model, a woman who is depressed because she interprets her husband's withdrawal in a negative way (e.g., "He doesn't care about me") would be helped to reevaluate the significance of his actions so that the depression-producing thoughts were reduced. If one were to take an interpersonal, or even cognitive–behavioral approach, the case formulation and consequent intervention would be different (Coyne, 1976; Goldsamt, Goldfried, Hayes, & Kerr, 1992). An exploration of the potential behavioral impact that the patient was having on her husband, as well as the intent or motivation for her behavior, would probably contribute to the formulation and the specific nature of the intervention. For example, the therapist might seek to determine whether, in her desire to receive nurturance and caring from her husband, she was acting in a way (e.g., being overly demanding) that was having a negative impact on her husband (e.g., withdrawal). Whereas cognitive therapy may be the intervention of choice in treating depressed individuals who are unduly sensitive to rejection, interpersonal therapy may be more appropriate in reducing symptomatology in those in whom the determinants or dynamics are more interpersonal.

Practicing therapists who are interested in benefiting from what the research literature has to offer have lamented the serious limitations of our outcome research paradigms (e.g., Fishman, 1981; Persons, 1991; Raw, 1993). Referring to the work being done in the 1970s, during the second generation of outcome research, Fishman (1981) observed that a methodological constraint that limited the generalizability of research findings to clinical practice was the fact that

> in their quest for "topographical equivalence," researchers tend to lump together all subjects with the same manifest problem, regardless of the etiological, mediational, contextual, and maintenance factors that underlie and act to perpetuate the maladaptive pattern. I think that we are sufficiently advanced in our thinking to accept the fact that underlying factors have to be taken into consideration in formulating any treatment program, yet rarely do researchers conduct fine-grain assessments to differentiate subjects according to these factors. (p. 244)

The need for outcome researchers to incorporate individualized case formulations into third-generation research protocols has more recently been underscored by Persons (1991), another practicing clinician.

There have been a few efforts to match the specific form of therapy with relevant patient characteristics. For example, Nelson-Gray (1991) reported some preliminary research findings suggesting that cognitive–behavior therapy interventions that were matched to specific formulations of the determinants of the depression (e.g., irrational beliefs, deficiencies in interpersonal behavior, or the lack of gratifying activities) were more likely to be effective than those that were not matched. Similarly, Jacobson, Holtzworth-Monroe, and Schmaling (1989) found that cognitive–behavioral marital interventions that were tailor-made to the needs of the particular couple were more effective than a standardized cognitive–behavioral intervention. Moreover, matching interventions according to stylistic characteristics of patients that are not necessarily determinants of the clinical problem has revealed that individuals who need to be in control of their lives responded better to interventions that were nondirective or paradoxical than those that were more directive in nature (Beutler & Consoli, 1992; Shoham-Salomon, Avner, & Neeman, 1989).

Until our current research methodology is changed, it is essential that all potential determinants or dynamics be evaluated as part of a standard assessment battery, which hopefully can shed light on the mechanisms associated with given interventions. Moreover, when a key mediator of change is targeted within a given intervention, this variable should also be part of the outcome battery because it is likely to determine the maintenance of symptom reduction over time. For example, if ability to use relaxation as a coping skill is part of a given intervention, the assessment of this coping skill at posttest may be a better predictor of maintenance than would posttest anxiety level.

Because any assessment of outcome needs to determine the maintenance of change over time, not solely outcome at the end of treatment, it is important that relevant measures of self-schema be included in an assessment battery (Goldfried & Robins, 1983). Research findings have shown that measures of self-efficacy—individuals' reports that they can successfully cope with certain situations—are more likely to predict future behavior than are individuals' past behavior. Individuals' efficacy expectations are associated with the types of situations they will place themselves in, the amount of effort they will expend in these situations, and how long they will persist in the face of obstacles. For example, a socially anxious man who does not perceive himself as being competent in heterosocial interactions may avoid going to parties; if he happens to be at one, he may make few if any attempts to interact with women; and if he does make the attempt to interact with a woman at the party, he may end the conversation if he does not receive a clear indication of interest.

Goldfried and Robins (1983) have argued that patients' views of themselves as being competent in handling certain types of life circumstances are important in determining the likelihood of therapeutic change being maintained over time because these subjective predictions "provide us with a useful index of the extent to which certain learning experiences have been cognitively processed and are being used by the individual to predict his or her future behavior" (Goldfried & Robins, 1983, p. 41).

Individuals' perceptions of their ability to cope with stressful situations has been found to be particularly linked to the degree of stress they experience when confronted with such situations (Lazarus & Launier,

1978). Wolfe (1992) has similarly placed the concept of self-experiencing at the core of anxiety disorders, arguing that

> such phenomena as spontaneous panic attacks, fear of fear, fear of losing control, fear of being trapped, catastrophic misinterpretations of somatic stimuli, and chronic worrying are all responses to tacitly governed experiences of self-endangerment. (p. 30)

Like Lazarus and Launier, Wolfe went on to suggest that a patient's subjective experience of self is essential to the very concept of anxiety, stating that

> when anxiety and the anxiety disorders are viewed from such a perspective, it becomes evident that these difficulties have most to do with painful and dangerous self-experience. The unifying phenomena in the various anxiety disorders, I suggest, are the chronic experiences of self-endangerment and the cognitive/emotional processes that emerge to deal with the sense of danger and the consequent loss of safety. (p. 34)

In light of the above, a measure of self-confidence is essential in an outcome battery for measuring change in anxiety disorders.

PROCEDURES FOR DEVELOPING CORE BATTERIES

The selection of any given core battery involves two steps: (a) determine the variables that are essential for inclusion and (b) determine how these may be best assessed. In the recent conference on assessing outcome in panic disorder research (Shear & Maser, in press), decisions were made only on the variables to be assessed rather than on the specific measures themselves.

In selecting specific assessment procedures based on the state of the art, there is certainly the advantage of making use of what is currently available and easily implemented. The obvious danger here is that the psychometric properties can often take second place in the consideration of what is "frequently used." A major dilemma to be confronted is how to decide on different measures of the same outcome variable when there is no clear-cut empirical superiority of one over the other. What is obviously needed are some careful comparative studies to determine the relative validity and sensitivity of varying measures of the same variable.

Consistent with the recommendation made by Waskow and Parloff (1975) in the earlier conference on the core battery, any decision made regarding assessment procedures must be updated periodically. To the extent that a consensus of specific measures can be achieved, these should be the methods of choice used in NIMH-funded research and in editorial decisions regarding publication of findings. At the same time, every effort must be made to prevent the maintenance of the status quo, and research should be supported to develop procedures that prove to be more efficacious or sensitive as indicators of successful therapeutic outcome.

SUMMARY

To understand the context in which the attempt is being made to develop a core assessment battery, I noted that we are currently in our third generation of psychotherapy outcome research. During the first generation (early 1950s to late 1960s), research was directed at determining if therapy was successful in producing personality change. In the second generation (late 1960s to late 1970s), different interventions were compared with regard to their effectiveness in treating specific target problems. From the early 1980s to the present, our outcome paradigm has been modeled after "clinical trials," in which the efficacy of theoretically based, manual-driven therapies are compared for their ability to deal with *DSM* Axis I disorders.

After providing an overview of different types of methodologies for assessing outcome (e.g., naturalistic observations, situational tests, role playing, self-report, and physiological assessment), I discussed some general issues in developing a core assessment battery. The shift from studying methods of changing intra- and interpersonal problems in living to that of treating disorders influences how we think about the intervention process and what constitutes appropriate measures of outcome. I argue that until the field moves to a new generation of outcome research that matches the particular intervention to account for the specific determinants or dynamics associated with a patient's symptomatology, our assessment batteries should include measures of relevant patient variables (e.g., self-schema) as well as symptomatology.

REFERENCES

Arkowitz, H. (1989). The role of theory in psychotherapy integration. *Journal of Integrative and Eclectic Psychotherapy, 8,* 8–16.

Beutler, L. E., & Consoli, A. J. (1992). Systematic eclectic psychotherapy. In J. C. Norcross & M. R. Goldfried (Eds.), *Handbook of psychotherapy integration* (pp. 264–299). New York: Basic Books.

Campbell, D. T., & Fiske, D. W. (1959). Convergent and discriminant validation by the multitrait-multimethod matrix. *Psychological Bulletin, 56,* 81–105.

Coyne, J. C. (1976). Depression and the response of others. *Journal of Abnormal Psychology, 85,* 186–193.

Fishman, S. T. (1981). Narrowing the generalization gap in clinical research. *Behavioral Assessment, 3,* 243–248.

Goldfried, M. R. (1980). Toward the delineation of therapeutic change principles. *American Psychologist, 35,* 991–999.

Goldfried, M. R. (1995). *From cognitive-behavior therapy to psychotherapy integration: An evolving view.* New York: Springer.

Goldfried, M. R., & Robins, C. (1983). Self-schema, cognitive bias, and the processing of therapeutic experiences. In P. C. Kendall (Ed.), *Advances in cognitive-behavioral research and therapy* (Vol. 2, pp. 35–80). New York: Academic Press.

Goldfried, M. R., & Wolfe, B. E. (1996). Psychotherapy and research: Repairing a strained alliance. *American Psychologist, 51,* 1007–1016.

Goldsamt, L. A., Goldfried, M. R., Hayes, A. M., & Kerr, S. (1992). Beck, Meichenbaum, and Strupp: A comparison of three therapies on the dimension of therapist feedback. *Psychotherapy, 29,* 167–176.

Jacobson, N. S., Holtzworth-Monroe, A., & Schmaling, K. B. (1989). Marital therapy and spouse involvement in the treatment of depression, agoraphobia, and alcoholism. *Journal of Consulting and Clinical Psychology, 57,* 5–10.

Lazarus, R. S., & Launier, R. (1978). Stress-related transactions between person and environment. In L. A. Pervin & M. Lewis (Eds.), *Perspectives in interactional psychology.* New York: Plenum.

Linehan, M. M., Goldfried, M. R., & Goldfried, A. P. (1979). Assertion training: Skill acquisition or cognitive restructuring. *Behavior Therapy, 10,* 372–388.

Nelson-Grey, R. O. (1991, November). Treatment matching for unipolar depression. In M. E. Addis (Chair), *Matching clients to treatment: Clinical and research considerations*. Symposium conducted at the meeting of the Association for the Advancement of Behavior Therapy, New York.

Norcross, J. C., & Goldfried, M. R. (Eds.). (1992). *Handbook of psychotherapy integration*. New York: Basic Books.

Persons, J. B. (1991). Psychotherapy outcome studies do not accurately represent current models of psychotherapy: A proposed remedy. *American Psychologist, 46,* 99–106.

Raw, S. D. (1993). Does psychotherapy research teach us anything about psychotherapy? *The Behavior Therapist, 16,* 75–76.

Shear, M. K., & Maser, J. D. (in press). Standardized assessment for panic disorder research. *Archives of General Psychiatry.*

Shoham-Salomon, V., Avner, R., & Neeman, R. (1989). You're changed if you do and changed if you don't: Mechanisms underlying paradoxical interventions. *Journal of Consulting and Clinical Psychology, 57,* 590–598.

Strupp, H. H., & Hadley, S. W. (1977). A tripartite of mental health and therapeutic outcomes: With special reference to negative effects in psychotherapy. *American Psychologist, 32,* 187–196.

Strupp, H. H., & Howard, K. I. (1992). A brief history of psychotherapy research. In D. K. Freedheim (Ed.), *History of psychotherapy: A century of change* (pp. 309–334). Washington, DC: American Psychological Association.

Wolfe, B. E. (1992). Self-experiencing and the integrative treatment of the anxiety disorders. *Journal of Psychotherapy Integration, 2,* 29–43.

Wolfe, B. E. (1994). Adapting psychotherapy outcome research to clinical reality. *Journal of Psychotherapy Research, 4,* 160–166.

Waskow, I. E., & Parloff, M. B. (1975). *Psychotherapy change measures*. Washington, DC: Department of Health, Education, and Welfare.

PART THREE

Core Batteries
for Assessment
of Anxiety Disorders

6

Measuring Treatment Outcome for Posttraumatic Stress Disorder and Social Phobia: A Review of Current Instruments and Recommendations for Future Research

Thomas D. Borkovec, Louis G. Castonguay,
and Michelle G. Newman

Over the past 40 years, the measurement of treatment outcome for psychological disorders has been a major source of disagreement among mental health researchers. The lack of clear and agreed on guidelines regarding what, how, and when to measure therapeutic change has prevented the accumulation of knowledge about the effectiveness of different interventions for particular disorders. As demonstrated in this book, however, some consensus currently seems to be emerging among researchers from diverse theoretical persuasions and professional backgrounds. There now seems to be a fair level of agreement on the main characteristics of core outcome batteries, the domains of human functioning that they should assess, and the psychometric qualities of the specific measures to be included. What is less clear, however, is whether it is possible at this point to achieve a consensus on a list of specific instruments to be commonly used in outcome studies of particular disorders. The main goal of this chapter is an attempt to lay the groundwork for future consensus by reviewing the most frequently used outcome measures for two specific dis-

We thank Charles Hines III and Frank Weathers for their assistance and are especially grateful to Liz Roemer for helping us to complete this chapter. Preparation of the chapter was supported in part by National Institute of Mental Health Grant MH-39172 to Thomas D. Borkovec.

orders: posttraumatic stress disorder (PTSD) and social phobia. Our intent is not to recommend a specific list of outcome measures to be used in all future treatment studies for these two disorders. Rather, we want to exemplify the type of review (although by no means exhaustive) that would provide the foundational step for ultimately selecting specific measures for use in core outcome batteries.

This chapter is a companion to chapter 7 in this book, which covers outcome assessment devices for generalized anxiety disorder, obsessive–compulsive disorder, and specific phobias. When combined, these two chapters provide a review of five of the six categories of anxiety disorders. Outcome measures for panic disorder (with or without agoraphobia) are not specifically addressed in either of these chapters because a core assessment battery related to this disorder has been recommended recently by the members of a National Institute of Health-sponsored workshop (Shear & Maser, 1994; see also chap. 15 in this book). Moreover, reviews of assessment scales for panic disorder also have recently been conducted by other experts in the field (J. G. Beck & Zebb, 1994; Rapee & Barlow, 1990).

In this chapter, we review the major instruments aimed at the assessment of psychiatric diagnoses and the measurement of the target problems. For the assessment of both diagnoses and target problem, we first discuss general issues and recommendations and then describe specific assessment devices for PTSD and social phobia. Instruments providing global assessment of anxiety and depression are also reviewed. Finally, recommendations regarding possible core batteries and general issues related to the measurement of treatment effectiveness are offered.

DIAGNOSTIC ASSESSMENT

With the introduction of third edition of the *Diagnostic and Statistical Manual of Mental Disorders* (*DSM–III;* American Psychiatric Association, 1980), a commitment was made by the American Psychiatric Association to increasingly base its nosological system on descriptive psychopathology and on periodic revisions of definitions in response to empirical results regarding the characteristics and nature of each of its disorders. The system, of course, continues to view psychological problems from the perspective of the medical model of disease and thus to categorize individuals on the basis of similar symptomatology into similar types of disorder. Such a view is in contrast to a psychological perspective, which sees human problems in terms of continuous dimensions of maladaptive psychological processes. Certainly an important preliminary decision regarding the possible development of a core battery of assessment methods rests on whether to work within the nosological approach or to recommend departure from its context. In this chapter, we have adopted the former approach, although much contained in the review of existing measures and issues relevant to a core battery can be applied easily to considerations of measurement from the point of view of continuous, dimensional assessment. We chose this approach for three reasons. First, although a nosological system implies philosophical and theoretical positions contrary to what many psychologists hold to be an accurate metaphor of human psychological problems, it does provide a widely prevalent way of identifying groups of anxious individuals who are homogeneous with respect to certain crucial descriptive features of specific psychological difficulties. As such, research conducted on *DSM* groups can provide additional, valid information about the dimensions of psychological processes underlying the features represented. Second, there is a practical issue about the funding of clinical research. The National Institute of Mental Health, the principal resource for grants, has a strong preference for proposals focused on diagnostic groups. Third, to choose the alternative approach, it would be necessary to agree on the specific dimensions on which to select participants for research and to provide evidence that adopting these definitions would yield results that are equally or more valid and reliable. Clinical psychologists have not yet reached a consensus on what those dimensions should be, nor have they examined the implications of this approach for the degree of homogeneity of participant samples so selected, a characteristic of research methodology that is important for the internal validity of empirical results obtained.

If clinicians are to work within the *DSM* system, selection of clients for outcome research requires reliable identification of clients who meet the diagnostic criteria for a particular disorder. We would therefore recommend the use of established interview methods for identifying appropriately diagnosed clients for inclusion in outcome investigations. Several semistructured interviews have been developed for the purpose of diagnosing all or most *DSM* categories: Structured Clinical Interview for DSM–III–R (SCID), Diagnostic Interview Schedule (DIS), Anxiety Disorder Interview Schedule (ADIS), and Schedule for Affective Disorders and Schizophrenia (SADS). Some of these interview methods have been more frequently used in studies of some disorders, as we describe in each disorder section. Certain general recommendations can be made, however, for the use of these as selection devices in outcome research.

Widely varying degrees of interrater reliability have been reported for each interview method and for several of the anxiety disorders. Reliable identification of homogeneous samples to reduce error in research conclusions is crucial. Consequently, a few recommendations relevant to this issue can be made.

First, the ideal method for selecting participants for research would require independent diagnostic interviews by separate assessors, both of whom agree on the client's principal diagnosis. The importance of doing so is greater for those disorders found in the past to have the poorer interrater reliabilities. Although such a procedure does not eliminate the possibility either of the inclusion of false-positive cases in the study or of the exclusion of true-positive cases, the likelihood of inclusion of clients who do not have the crucial diagnosis-relevant characteristics would be lessened markedly. Thus, error variance attributable to the presence of inappropriate clients would be reduced. Generalized anxiety disorder (GAD) provides a good example of the importance of this issue. Its kappas are routinely among the lowest in studies of diagnostic reliability of the anxiety disorders, even by interview methods that specialize in anxiety problems (e.g., $\kappa = .57$ via the revised ADIS [ADIS-R], Brown & Barlow, 1992). In our GAD project, which for several years has used dual diagnostic interviews, our second interviewer has ruled out 20–30% of the cases initially accepted by our first interviewer. This percentage thus reflects our best local estimate of the likelihood of false-positive cases that otherwise would have been admitted into a GAD investigation and would have decreased the signal-to-noise ratio in detecting treatment effects. The use of dual interviewers is, of course, an investment that is costly in terms of both finances and time commitment for clients and project personnel. The generation of more valid and reliable results is, however, worth that investment. Existing ambiguity in conclusions from both basic research and therapy outcome investigations may well be due simply to inclusion of clients who do not truly meet selection criteria and who thus create heterogeneity on the most crucial features of the problem being investigated. Less costly alternatives have been used in an effort either to exclude false-positive cases (e.g., review of interview materials by a second clinician) or to obtain local information for estimating likely reliability of the diagnostic decisions (e.g., diagnosis by a second interviewer who either conducts a separate interview on a subset of clients or who listens to audiotapes of a subset of interviews). None of these approaches is ideal from the viewpoint of exclusion of inappropriate clients and of increasing the internal validity of the investigation.

Second, the diagnostic interviews should be conducted by trained professionals who are knowledgeable about descriptive psychopathology and the *DSM* system and who are specifically trained in the type of interview used. Although some diagnostic interview schedules (the DIS and some of the specialized PTSD interviews described later) have been developed for use by trained paraprofessionals, we suggest that every effort should be made to maximize the reliability of diagnosis, for the reasons described earlier. Use of professional interviewers is likely to facilitate that goal unless considerable data from future research persuasively indicate otherwise.

Two further recommendations are made. First, the diagnostic interview should be repeated at the posttherapy assessments. The presence or absence of a diagnosable condition after therapy provides a clinically significant, dichotomous outcome measure, one that also facilitates communication of results to clinicians and researchers in psychiatry. Second, both current and lifetime diagnoses and their duration of occurrence should be determined to provide important information for characterizing the sample and for identifying individual differences in the history of problems that may be associated with treatment responsiveness or with differential response to types of treatments.

PTSD

Two types of structured diagnostic interview methods have been used in research on PTSD. The first type involves broad-based interviews that cover most or all *DSM* diagnostic categories and thus provide information on principal and comorbid disorders.

Full Diagnostic Assessment

The SCID (Spitzer, Williams, Gibbon, & First, 1990) has been the most commonly used diagnostic method in PTSD research (Keane, Weathers, & Kaloupek, 1992). It provides both current and lifetime diagnostic assessment, and its PTSD module evaluates all core *DSM* symptoms on 3-point scales (absent, subthreshold, and present). C. G. Watson's (1990) review of three studies (Davidson, Smith, & Kudler, 1989; Kulka et al., 1988; McFall, Smith, Mackay, & Tarver, 1990) with clinical samples indicated high kappas (.79–.82), sensitivity (.81–.89), and specificity (.92–.98), although Keane, Kolb, and Thomas (1988) reported a lower kappa (.68) in their sample of veterans. Highly trained professionals are required to administer the SCID.

The DIS (Robins & Helzer, 1985) has the advantage that paraprofessionals can learn its administration, and in clinical samples it has acceptable reliability and validity. Schlenger and Kulka (1987) reported a sensitivity of .87, a specificity of .73, and a kappa of .64 against SCID or clinical chart diagnoses, whereas C. G. Watson, Juba, Manifold, Kucala, and Anderson (1991) found higher levels for the DIS against their own diagnostic interview schedule (.92, .91, and .84, respectively). Breslau and Davis (1987) found adequate agreement between lay interviewers and psychiatrists among veterans with and without PTSD (sensitivity = .86, specificity = .82, and κ = .67). Its sensitivity (.23) and interrater reliability (κ = .28) suffered when used in epidemiological study of community samples, although its specificity remained high (.995; Kulka et al., 1991). Kulka et al. (1991) suggested that the DIS is at times worded in a confusing way and that the questions problematically assume that the client sees a connection between the traumatic event and the symptoms that are being experienced.

The ADIS (DiNardo & Barlow, 1988) is used commonly in anxiety disorder research, although few PTSD studies have used it for selection purposes. The interview can be administered by trained paraprofessionals. Early study of 43 veterans with its *DSM–III* version showed a kappa of .86 between an ADIS diagnosis and that of an experienced clinician (Blanchard, Gerardi, Kolb, & Barlow, 1986), although a more recent report on its interrater reliability for each anxiety disorder indicated low agreement for principal and additional diagnosis of PTSD on a small sample ($\kappa = .55$, $N = 8$; DiNardo, Moras, Barlow, Rapee, & Brown, 1993).

PTSD-Specific Diagnostic Assessment

The second approach has used relatively brief structured interviews that are limited specifically to the diagnosis of PTSD. These have been developed fairly recently, although useful psychometric information is already available for most of them.

The PTSD-Interview (PTSD-I) items cover all *DSM* symptom criteria for current and lifetime diagnosis, and the interview has been administered by paraprofessionals. The interview has shown strong sensitivity (.89), specificity (.94), and diagnostic agreement ($\kappa = .84$) against the DIS, with strong internal consistency (.92) and test–retest reliability (.95) among combat veterans (C. G. Watson et al., 1991).

The Structured Interview for PTSD (SI-PTSD; Davidson et al., 1989) also contains items relevant to PTSD core symptom criteria and has displayed good internal consistency (.94), sensitivity (.96), and specificity (.80) with a sample of veterans. However, the interview may suffer from poor stability, with a 2-week test–retest reliability of .71 on a subset of 14 participants who were selected for failing to show change over that interval on the Hamilton Rating Scale for Depression (HRSD). The total severity score correlated moderately with the Impact of Event subscales (described later) and the Hamilton anxiety and depression scales. Interrater agreement between nurse and psychiatrist raters on total severity scores was high (.97–.99), and diagnostic agreement between them was 100%. Against the SCID, the diagnostic decisions via the SI-PTSD had a kappa of .79, a sensitivity of .96, and a specificity of .80. Using a severity cutoff score of 16, sensitivity was .93 and specificity was 1.00. The interview has been administered by paraprofessionals.

The most recent interview schedule was developed in the context of research with female sexual assault survivors and nonsexual assault victims. The PTSD Symptom Scale-Interview (Foa, Riggs, Dancu, & Rothbaum, 1993) includes 17 rating scales assessing current core revised *DSM–III* (*DSM–III–R;* American Psychiatric Association, 1987) symptoms and has been administered by trained paraprofessionals. Curiously, the interview asks the client for symptom information "during the past two weeks," although the authors indicate that for diagnostic purposes, assessors also are to assess whether the duration of disturbance has lasted for at least 1 month. In its initial validation study, assault survivors were assessed 2 weeks after the assault and then at 5–6, 9–10, 12–14, and 24 weeks' postassault. Internal consistency was .85 for the total-scale severity (.65–.71 for the three symptom clusters) at the second assessment, 1-month test–retest reliability for the total score from the third to the fourth assessment was .80 (.66–.77 for clusters), and the kappa from independent administrations of the interview was .91 (the intraclass correlation for total severity was .97 and .93–.95 for clusters). Against the SCID given at 3 months' postassault, the sensitivity was .88, the specificity was .96, and the kappa was .94. The scale also correlated significantly with other measures of PTSD symptoms and with anxiety and depression measures given at the second assessment.

The Clinician Administered PTSD Scale (CAPS; Blake et al., 1995) appears to have a great deal of promise in that it was developed to circumvent previously identified problems with many PTSD interview methods. The CAPS covers all *DSM* PTSD symptoms with behaviorally anchored rating scales that contain separate frequency and intensity measures for each symptom. Unique among PTSD assessment methods, the CAPS also includes additional items that allow the interviewer to rate the impact of PTSD symptoms on social and occupational functioning, overall global severity, global change in symptoms since the last interview, assessor ratings of the likely validity of the client's responses, and an explicit time frame of 1 month for each item to ensure coexistence of all symptoms. Preliminary psychometric data have shown that the reliability and validity of the instrument are promising (Weathers et al., 1992). Test–retest reliability (.77–.96) and internal consistency (.85–.87) of the three PTSD symptom clusters are high, total severity scores correlate well with other measures of PTSD symptoms, and its cutoff score had a sensitivity of .84, specificity of .95, and kappa of .78 against the SCID. Its dichotomous decision rules for diagnosis had a kappa of .72. There are both lifetime and current diagnostic versions, and they can be administered by paraprofessionals if rigorously trained. In an effort to increase cost effectiveness, a computerized version of the CAPS was recently developed (Neal, Busuttil, Herapath, & Strike, 1994). Although it was tested on a small sample ($N = 40$), the computer version revealed good psychometric qualities, showing strong agreement with the clinician-administered version ($\kappa = .90$), sensitivity (.95), and specificity (.95). Moreover, a weekly symptom rating version (CAPS-2) for use in outcome investigations is being evaluated in current research.

Because of the promising data on the specialized PTSD interviews and the less than outstanding reliabilities of PTSD diagnoses by the full diagnostic schedules, we recommend that one of these specialized interviews be substituted for the PTSD module in the full interviews. This combination will yield thorough diagnostic assessment of all principal and additional diagnoses while providing more reliable diagnosis of PTSD itself.

Social Phobia

Full Diagnostic Assessment

In their review of diagnostic interviews for social phobia, Cox and Swinson (1995) noted that little interrater reliability information is available on the SCID. In a reliability study involving a wide range of clients and a large number of interviewers, Williams et al. (1992) determined a kappa of .47 for current social phobia and .57 for lifetime occurrence, although Skre, Onstad, Torgersen, and Kringlen (1991) found that diagnostic agreement on audiotaped interviews was higher ($\kappa = .72$) for the 12 clients with social phobia participating in their study. In an early study of the *DSM-III* ADIS, DiNardo et al. (1983) also reported fairly good agreement between independent interviews ($\kappa = .77$), although, again, the sample size of social phobic clients was small ($N = 8$). More reassuringly, Brown and Barlow (1992) found ADIS-R kappas of .77 among 45 clients with a principal diagnosis of social phobia and .66 among 84 clients with an additional diagnosis of social phobia. Finally, the SADS-LA has been found to yield good agreement between independent interviewers for principal or additional social phobia (.75 when the first interview was by a field rater and .69 when the first interviewer was an expert rater; Mannuzza et al., 1989), although conducting this interview requires considerably more time than the alternative schedules.

Social phobia subtypes, although referred to in the fourth edition of the DSM (DSM–IV; American Psychiatric Association, 1994) and frequently diagnosed in social phobia research (e.g., Heimberg, Hope, Dodge, & Becker, 1990; Herbert, Hope, & Bellack, 1992), are not specifically assessed with any available structured interview. The DSM–IV indicates that if a person fears "most social situations," he or she is classified within the "generalized social phobia subtype." Two other subtypes, not mentioned in the DSM–IV but reported in the literature, are "nongeneralized" (i.e., those who fear several social situations, but there are some areas of social functioning in which they are not anxious) and "circumscribed" (fear of one or two highly specific social situations). Despite no structured measure of these subtypes, researchers have reported interrater reliability ranging from .70 to 1.0 (e.g., Herbert et al., 1992; Hofmann, Newman, Ehlers, & Roth, 1995; Holt, Heimberg, & Hope, 1992; Turner, Beidel, & Townsley, 1992).

MEASUREMENT OF TARGET PROBLEMS

Dimensional assessment of target problems is important for providing measures of initial severity of the problems and for evaluating the degree of improvement generated by treatment. As for the diagnostic measures reviewed earlier, we offer general recommendations before describing specific measures of target problems.

The first general recommendation is that selected measures cover all relevant target problems and important aspects of those problems. What specific measures are chosen will vary depending on the disorder involved, but any significant problem commonly and directly associated with the target should be included, with assessment of its frequency, intensity, or duration as applicable.

The second general recommendation is that the set of instruments should include measures based on multiple perspectives. This most commonly has involved client self-report instruments and ratings by an independent clinical assessor. Such multimethod assessment ensures that at least two different perspectives form the basis of outcome evaluation. The independent assessor must necessarily be unaware of the treatment condition status of the client at any assessment period, and posttherapy ratings should be conducted by the same assessor who performed the ratings at the pretherapy assessment to prevent between-raters variance from influencing change scores.

Third, some form of daily diary is recommended. Ideally, such a client self-report measure should be obtained for a 2- to 4-week period before and after therapy to ensure some degree of stability, and its content should dimensionally assess relevant aspects of crucial target problems. This measurement approach is widely used in outcome studies for several anxiety disorders, and daily ratings provide a clinically meaningful mode of assessment of client experience that potentially provides important data of a different kind relative to pre–post questionnaires. Despite sufficient intuitive appeal of the daily diary as an important, additional method of assessment to warrant recommendation of its use, surprisingly little psychometric information in general is available on daily diaries. We next describe specific measures of target problems based on assessor ratings and client self-report for PTSD and social phobia, along with recommendations relevant to core battery development.

PTSD

Several options exist for the dimensional rating of PTSD problem areas, some of which are based explicitly on core *DSM* criteria.

DSM-Based Ratings by an Assessor

Global severity of diagnosed symptoms. Both the SCID (via GAF) and the ADIS interviews obtain the assessor's rating of the overall severity of any diagnosed disorder. That rating is a composite judgment that is typically based on the intensity, frequency, and degree of interference caused by the problems in daily functioning, and it can be used as a global outcome measure based on clinician judgment of disorder severity. Specific information on the psychometric properties of the such global severity scores could not be found.

PTSD-specific symptom ratings. Although none of the full diagnostic interviews include dimensional ratings by the assessor of the core PTSD symptoms, all of the recently developed, specialized PTSD diagnostic interviews do so. Each of these interviews allows for both dichotomous decisions about the presence or absence of each symptom or criterion (thus allowing use in diagnosis) and continuous scale assessment of each symptom (thus providing continuous measures of severity of individual symptoms, cluster severity, and total symptom severity for use as an outcome assessment). Research on some of the psychometric properties of these measures was reviewed earlier.

DSM-Based Ratings by the Client

The Mississippi Scale (Keane, Caddell, & Taylor, 1988) is a 35-item measure of PTSD symptoms, rationally constructed by experts and largely covering *DSM* criterion symptoms. It has both combat and civilian forms. In its original development, the former was found to have excellent sensitivity (.93), specificity (.89), test–retest reliability (.97), and internal consistency (α = .94; Keane et al., 1988) and has been found to be useful in both clinical settings (McFall, Smith, Roszell, Tarver, & Malas, 1990; Schlenger & Kulka, 1987) and community research (Kulka et al., 1991). A recent report (Lyons, Caddell, Pittman, Rawls, & Perrin, 1994), however, indicated that the Mississippi Scale for Combat-Related PTSD is vulnerable to faking. Lyons et al. (1994) found that a higher cutoff score than the one originally recommended (121 instead of 107) allowed a better differentiation of veterans with and without PTSD. Although the sensitivity of the scale remains good (.95) with the higher cutoff, its specificity is relatively low (.45). In terms of the presence or absence of PTSD, the combat-related form also shows strong convergent validity with the PTSD-I, DIS, and Minnesota Multiphasic Personality Inventory (MMPI) PTSD scale (C. G. Watson et al., 1994). With regard to severity level, the Mississippi Scale and the PTSD-I show stronger convergent validity than the two other measures (C. G. Watson et al., 1994). A short version (11 items) of the combat-related form has been tested recently (Fontana & Rosenheck, 1994); it showed good internal consistency, a strong correlation with the full scale, high sensitivity and specificity, and sensitivity to symptomatic change. In addition, significant relationships were found between the change in the short scale and clinicians' rating of improvement, number of treatment sessions received by clients, and duration of treatment.

As for the civilian form of the Mississippi Scale, a recent report indicated a relatively high internal consistency ($\alpha = .86$) but weaker measurement precision than the military version (Vreven, Gudanowski, King, & King, 1995). Although the scale is related to stressful life events, it was more strongly associated with an index of demoralization (Dohrenwend, 1982) than with the PTSD section of the DIS, suggesting that it may be more of an indicator of general distress than PTSD per se. These findings were consistent with a study by Lauterbach and Vrana (1996), who found that the Civilian Mississippi Scale correlated less with the Purdue Post-Traumatic Stress Scale (PPTSS) and the Impact of Event Scale than with general measure of depression and anxiety. As argued by Vreven et al. (1995), more studies addressing the psychometric qualities of the civilian version of the Mississippi Scale should be conducted, and further refinements of this version of the scale may be indicated.

A short self-report scale (15 items) was constructed by Figley (1989) to measure the *DSM–III* criteria of PTSD: the PPTSS. A recent study with Vietnam veterans showed that this scale has high internal consistency ($\alpha = .94$), a strong correlation with the Impact of Event Scale, and significant correlations with scales measuring exposure to combat and abusive violence (Hendrix, Anelli, Gibbs, & Fournier, 1994). Although the PPTSS discriminated between respondents who reported having received a diagnosis of PTSD sometime in their life and others who did not, we could find no measure of sensitivity or specificity against clinician assessor ratings.

Hammarberg (1992) developed the Penn Inventory for Posttraumatic Stress Disorders covering *DSM–III–R* criteria in its 26 items, and he provided preliminary psychometric data using both combat veterans and civilians who had been exposed to an oil rig explosion, along with non-PTSD veteran psychiatric and nonpsychiatric groups and nonveteran control groups. The item format is modeled after the Beck Depression Inventory (BDI); respondents select one of four choices for each symptom reflecting absence versus presence, degree, frequency, or intensity. Using a cutoff score for diagnosis, Hammarberg found that sensitivity (.90 and .94) and specificity (1.00 and 1.00) were good in both combat and civilian PTSD studies (and replicable in a cross-validation sample of veterans) and that there was strong internal consistency (α = .94) and test–retest reliability (.96) in the combat group.

Designed to be used with both veterans and nonveterans, the Los Angeles Symptom Checklist (LASC; King, King, Leskin, & Foy, 1995) is composed of 43 items. Of these, 17 measure the *DSM–III–R* criteria for PTSD, whereas the remaining 26 address general psychological distress. Using a large sample (N = 874) of heterogeneous participants (Vietnam veterans, battered women, adult survivors of child abuse, psychiatric outpatients, and high-risk adolescents), King et al. (1995) found that both the 17 items targeting the PTSD criteria and the scale as a whole had strong internal consistency (αs = .94 and .95, respectively). Test–retest reliability calculated on a subgroup of the same sample also was high (.90 and .94). The LASC has been predictive of trauma exposure, correlating significantly with the Combat Exposure Scale (Foy, Sipprelle, Rueger, & Carroll, 1984) and duration of a violent relationship (Houskamp & Foy, 1991). It also correlates moderately with the Impact of Event Scale. Rates of sensitivity and specificity against the SCID have varied from .70 to .78 and from .80 to .82, respectively (Houskamp & Foy, 1991; King et al., 1995).

The PTSD Symptom Scale interview (reviewed earlier) also has a parallel self-report version (PSS-SR; Foa et al., 1993) covering the 17 core *DSM–III–R* symptoms. Some items were rewritten from the interview form to increase their clarity, and several have examples provided to further aid clients in making their ratings. The same 2-week time frame present in the PSS-I is used, raising questions regarding its usefulness in diagnosis but not detracting from its use as a continuous outcome measure. In the validation study described earlier for the PSS-I, PSS-SR total scores were found to be internally consistent (αs = .91 and .78–.82 for the three symptom clusters), had a test–retest reliability of .74 (.56–.71 for clusters), and had significant correlations with other PTSD and anxiety measures that were somewhat higher than those obtained with the interview version. Against the SCID, sensitivity was .62, specificity was 1.00, and it correctly identified diagnostic status in 86% of the cases. The kappa coefficient of agreement between the interview and self-report versions was .73, and the correlation coefficient between total severity scores of the two versions was .80.

Non-DSM Questionnaires That Distinguish PTSD Clients From Control Groups

Clients with PTSD have been found to differ significantly from (mainly) nondisordered control groups on three instruments in common usage in clinical research. Cutoff scores on the first two measures also have been evaluated for their ability to classify correctly clients and nonclients.

From the MMPI, a 49-item PTSD Scale (PK) can be derived that significantly distinguishes veterans with and without PTSD (Keane, Malloy, & Fairbank, 1984). Several investigations reviewed by C. G. Watson (1990) have indicated sensitivities for cutoff scores ranging from .57 to .90 and specificities ranging from .53 to .95. A more recent study indicated a high level of correspondence between the 49 items of the PTSD scale administered separately or as part of the full MMPI (Lyons & Scotti, 1994). A 46-item scale based on the MMPI-2 appears to retain favorable properties (Lyons & Keane, 1992; Munley, Bains, Bloem, & Busky, 1995; Wetzel & Yutzy, 1994).

The SCL-90 contains a 28-item subscale that distinguishes PTSD caused by crime-related trauma in women from control participants (Saunders, Arata, & Kilpatrick, 1990) and has fair sensitivity (.75) and strong specificity (.90) against the DIS. Saunders et al. noted that the SCL-90 is a commonly used clinical assessment device and thus provides the opportunity for considerable archival research.

The most commonly used inventory in trauma research has been the Impact of Event Scale (Horowitz, Wilner, & Alvarez, 1979), which provides measures of two of the crucial PTSD symptoms (intrusions and avoidance/numbing). Internal consistency is high for both subscales (.78 and .82, respectively), as is test–retest reliability (.89 and .79, respectively), and the scale relates significantly to other measures of PTSD. It does not assess all PTSD symptoms, however.

A recent study with traumatized individuals in the United Kingdom (Neal, Busutti, Rollins, et al., 1994) investigated the convergent validity of the MMPI PTSD scale (PK), the SCL-90 (total scale), and the Impact of Event Scale. Significant correlations were found between the three scales in terms of the severity of the PTSD symptoms. Using the CAPS as a criterion, however, the Impact of Event Scale was found to be the most useful measure of the presence or absence of the disorder, with the highest positive predictive value and lowest misclassification error rate.

Social Phobia

DSM-Based Ratings by an Assessor

Global severity of diagnosed symptoms. As mentioned earlier, both the SCID (GAF) and the ADIS provide assessor ratings of the overall severity of any diagnosed disorder, including social phobia, of potential usefulness as an outcome measure.

Social phobia-specific symptom ratings. None of the existing diagnostic interview schedules provide assessor ratings of all individual diagnostic symptoms or criteria. They all are designed to yield only dichotomous (present or absent) information for the purpose of making diagnostic decisions. The ADIS, however, does obtain assessor ratings of both fear and avoidance of several social situations typical of the phobic stimuli for socially anxious individuals, thus providing clinician measures that are both somewhat related to diagnostic characteristics and are certainly useful for dimensional outcome assessment.

DSM Ratings by the Client

As with assessor ratings, no existing questionnaires or self-report inventories currently available include client ratings of all explicit *DSM* criteria. Several questionnaires have been developed, however, that provide either (a) general measures of fear and avoidance of situations involving evaluation by others or potential embarrassment and (b) measures of the severity of fear and avoidance in specific social situations that are commonly disturbing to socially anxious clients. These are described next.

Non-DSM Questionnaires by the Client

Developed more than two decades ago by D. Watson and Friend (1969), the Social Avoidance and Distress Scale (SAD), a 28-item true–false inventory of discomfort in and avoidance of interpersonal interaction situations, and the Fear of Negative Evaluation Scale (FNE), a 30-item true–false measure of fear and of other people's judgments have been used frequently in studies of social anxiety in student populations. Brief reviews (Heimberg, Hope, Rapee, & Bruch, 1988; Heimberg, Mueller, Holt, Hope, & Liebowitz, 1992) indicate good test–retest reliability, internal consistency, and construct validity in such groups. Only recently have these measures been evaluated in clinical samples, however. Turner, McCanna, and Beidel (1987) found that simple phobic clients alone scored significantly lower on both scales than other clients with *DSM–III* anxiety disorders on each questionnaire; groups with social phobia, panic disorder with or without agoraphobia, agoraphobia, generalized anxiety disorder, and obsessive–compulsive disorder did not differ. Oei, Kenna, and Evans (1991) found basically similar results. A lively debate about the use of the SAD and FNE in clinical social phobia research has resulted. Heimberg et al. (1988) argued that social anxiety is prevalent across all of the anxiety disorders and that the measures therefore are useful for assessing social anxiety. Turner and Beidel (1988), on the other hand, emphasized that neither questionnaire can be used as distinct measures of diagnosed social phobia. Moreover, their review of therapy outcome research employing these measures suggested restricted degrees of absolute change in the scores from pre- to posttest assessments. However, others have suggested that the decrease of fear of negative evaluation is the greatest predictor of treatment outcome in social phobia (Mattick & Peters, 1988; Mattick, Peters, & Clarke, 1989; Newman, Hofmann, Roth, & Taylor, 1994).

The Social Phobia subscale of the Fear Questionnaire (FQ; Marks & Mathews, 1979) is one of the most frequently used self-report assessment devices in the social anxiety and social phobia literature. Using 9-point rating scales of the degree of avoidance, the full questionnaire includes one item for the main target phobia, five items for each of three phobic areas (agoraphobia, social phobia, and blood phobia), and one item for any other phobia. Five associated (anxiety and depression) symptoms also are rated for degree of troublesomeness, and the global severity of all phobic symptoms is rated on a final 9-point scale. These items were selected originally on the basis of factor analyses by various collaborators of the responses to a larger pool of phobic situations provided by phobia client samples. In the original study, 7-day test–retest reliabilities were high for the main phobia (.93), the three phobia subscales (.82–.96), the total phobia score (.82), global phobic rating (.79), and the associated symptoms (.82). In a small sample of clients with agoraphobia, social phobia, and mixed phobia, significant improvement was seen on nearly all FQ scales; clients with agoraphobia improved more on the Agoraphobia scale than did the other groups with anxiety, the clients with social phobia tended to improve more on the Social Phobia subscale. Cox, Swinson, and Shaw (1991) and Cox and Swinson (1995) have reviewed psychometric information and concluded that the FQ has considerable reliability and validity among clinical samples. Oei, Gross, and Evans (1989) found that the FQ Social Phobia and Agoraphobia subscales accurately classified 90% of social phobic and panic with agoraphobia (PDA) clients in a discriminant function analysis. The FQ Agoraphobia subscale also has been found to be specifically sensitive to treatment effects among clients with agoraphobia (Mavissakalian, 1986), although it was not sensitive to improvement in specific avoidance during a behavioral test (Kinney & Williams, 1988). Cox et al. (1991) found in their own study that the FQ subscales and total score had good internal consistency (.69–.86) among SCID-diagnosed PDA and social phobic clients, the two clinic groups differed in predicted ways on the Agoraphobia and Social Phobia subscales, and discriminant function analysis indicated that 70% of the clients (77% of PDA and 60% of social phobic clients) could be identified correctly by the FQ Social Phobia subscale and 66% (72% of PDA and 58% of social phobic clients) by the FQ Agoraphobia subscale. With combined use of the two subscales, 76% of social phobic clients and 86% of PDA clients were classified accurately.

The Social Phobia and Anxiety Inventory (SPAI; Turner, Beidel, Dancu, & Stanley, 1989) was developed as a self-report measure that would be specific to diagnosable social phobia and would assess severity and critical features of the disorder (including its cognitive, behavioral, and somatic dimensions) in a variety of situations. From an initial pool of scales derived from available inventories and *DSM–III* criteria, items were selected that were endorsed by mental health professionals to be relevant to social phobia and that were found to empirically distinguish diagnosed socially anxious individuals (a mixed group of students and nonstudents) and nonanxious control individuals. The resulting SPAI includes 32 items that assess anxiety experiences in specific social situations (some items are rated separately for the presence of strangers, authority figures, opposite sex members, and people in general) as well as avoidance behavior, cognitions before and during social encounters, and common somatic reactions (e.g., sweating, heart palpitations, blushing, shaking, and need to urinate). To create a measure of social phobia independent of the social anxiety often experienced by agoraphobic clients, a 13-item Agoraphobia subscale based on *DSM–III* criteria and reflecting anxiety experienced in commonly avoided agoraphobic situations also was included; the total SPAI score is calculated by subtracting the Agoraphobia subscale from the Social Phobia subscale. A series of studies variously using diagnosed student and clinical social phobic clients, panic disorder clients with and without agoraphobia, obsessive–compulsive clients, and nonanxious control individuals has been conducted to evaluate the SPAI's psychometric properties (Beidel, Borden, Turner, & Jacob, 1989; Beidel, Turner, Stanley, & Dancu, 1989; Turner, Beidel, et al., 1989; Turner, Stanley, Beidel, & Bond, 1989). Test–retest reliability (.86) and alpha (.96 for the Social Anxiety subscale and .85 for the Agoraphobia subscale) have been high. Social phobic clients have scored significantly higher than all comparison groups on the SPAI, and discriminant function analyses have yielded classification accuracies of 67.9–74.4% With student samples, measures derived from the SPAI have been found to correlate significantly with significant-other ratings of the respondent on the SPAI (.63) and with daily monitoring of general distress in social situations (.47), distress from disturbing thoughts (.30), and entry into anxiety-provoking situations (.31). The SAD and FNE were found to correlate only with the general distress monitoring variable. With a clinic sample, significant relationships were found between SPAI-derived measures and daily diary scores on general distress (.43), frequency of disturbing thoughts (.36), and distress from the thoughts (.52); somatic and behavioral items also predicted pulse rate and length of speech, respectively, in a laboratory public speaking task. Using socially anxious and nonanxious individuals, two factor analysis studies of the SPAI have largely confirmed the existence of two factors reflecting the two a priori subscales, although factor analyses of the Social Phobia subscale by itself produced varying results, from basically a single factor to a five-factor identification (e.g., Osman, Barrios, Aukes, & Osman, 1995). A separate Q-factor analysis study on all SPAI items (both subscales) with predominantly clinical groups found homogeneity of diagnosed social phobic clients (all classified into the first factor, along with a majority of obsessive–compulsive clients), whereas agoraphobic clients were distributed over Factors 1–3, reflecting mild agoraphobia with high social anxiety, mild social anxiety with high agoraphobia, and significant symptoms in both domains.

Heimberg et al. (1992) felt that the numerous situations related to social phobia could be separated into two general categories (social interactions with others and situations in which the person is being observed), and they evaluated Mattick and Clarke's (1989) unpublished measures designed to assess these two domains: the Social Interaction Anxiety Scale (SIAS) and the Social Phobia Scale (SPS). The SIAS is a 20-item self-rating scale of the person's typical cognitive, affective, and behavioral reactions to various social interaction situations and seems to tap areas of anxiety characteristic of the generalized subtype of social phobia in the *DSM–III–R*. The SPS has 20 items rating a variety of situations involving observation by others and thus assesses anxiety more closely related to the *DSM* circumscribed subtype. Both Cox and Swinson (1995) and Heimberg et al. (1992) provided brief reviews of Mattick and Clarke's (1989) unpublished paper. The scales were developed with large samples of *DSM–III* social phobic clients, college students, and community volunteers and small samples of agoraphobic and simple phobic clients. Internal consistencies were found to be high (.88–.94), test–retest correlation on a small sub-sample of social phobic clients was in the .90s for both scales, social phobic clients scored significantly higher on both measures than nonanxious control individuals and agoraphobia clients, and neither measure correlated with social desirability. Within the social phobia sample, the two scales showed a correlation of .72. In their own study, Heimberg et al. (1992) found that *DSM–III–R* diagnosed social phobic clients scored significantly higher than matched community control individuals on both scales, and internal consistencies were high for both (.86–.93). Using a cutoff of 1 *SD* above the community mean, 82% of the clients via the SIAS and 73% via the SPS were identified correctly. Only a moderate degree of relationship between the two scales was found among this sample of social phobia clients ($r = .41$). As predicted, among social phobic clients the SIAS correlated more highly with other social interaction anxiety measures (both questionnaire and clinician ratings) than with performance (i.e., being observed) measures, whereas the SPS showed the converse. The generalized subtype of social phobia was associated with significantly higher scores on the SIAS but not on the SPS. Test–retest reliabilities, obtained only on a college subsample over a 1- to 2-week period, were .86 for SIAS and .66 for SPS.

In a recent study (Ries et al., 1996), three *DSM–III–R* social phobia groups (circumscribed, generalized, and generalized with avoidant personality disorder) were contrasted on behavioral performance tasks (public speaking and interacting with a confederate) as well as on the SPAI, SIAS, and SPS. The SPAI difference score and its Social Anxiety subscale both significantly discriminated the three groups from each other (generalized social phobia with avoidant personality scored the highest, and circumscribed social phobia scored the lowest), whereas only the circumscribed group scored lower than the two generalized groups on the SIAS and only the avoidant personality group scored higher than the circumscribed group on the SPS. The SIAS showed the highest correlations with measures of negative thinking as assessed by the Social Interaction Self-Statement Test (Glass, Merluzzi, Biever, & Larsen, 1982) during performance tasks, and only the SPS was significantly negatively related to the amount of time spent in the speech task.

DIMENSIONAL ASSESSMENT
OF GENERAL ANXIETY AND DEPRESSION

Because anxiety and depression are highly interrelated and prevalent among both anxiety and depression disorders and to facilitate comparability of results across outcome studies of both anxiety and depression, we recommend that pretherapy and posttherapy assessments of both general anxiety and depression levels be obtained in all therapy studies involving either type of problem. Again, both client and clinician ratings would be highly desirable to provide multiple methods of measurement.

Although it was developed with nonclinical respondents, the most commonly used general self-report measure of anxiety has been the State-Trait Anxiety Inventory (STAI; Spielberger, Gorsuch, & Lushene, 1970), especially its Trait version. More recently, the Beck Anxiety Inventory (BAI) is becoming popular because it was originally developed with clinical samples and because it has shown favorable psychometric characteristics. This 21-item questionnaire was initially found to have high internal consistency ($\alpha = .92$) and fair 1-week test–retest reliability ($r = .75$) in a large sample of clients with mood and anxiety disorders (A. T. Beck, Epstein, Brown, & Steer, 1988). Factor analysis revealed two components (somatic symptoms and subjective anxiety or panic symptoms), and the anxiety groups scored significantly higher than the depressed or control groups. The BAI total score correlated only .48 with the BDI, and it was more highly related to the Hamilton Anxiety Rating Scale (HARS; $r = .51$) than to the HRSD ($r = .25$). In a subsequent study with 367 clients with mixed anxiety disorders, A. T. Beck and Steer (1991) found that the BAI correlated .56 with the HARS, and factor analysis yielded four factors: Subjective Anxiety, Neurological Aspects of Anxiety, Autonomic Features, and Symptoms Characteristic of Panic Attacks. Alpha coefficients for these factors were .87, .86, .74, and .72, respectively. Clients with panic disorder both with and without agoraphobia scored significantly higher than clients with GAD on the Subjective Anxiety, Neurological Aspects of Anxiety, and Panic scales; neither the Autonomic Features subscale nor two factor analytically derived HARS subscales (Psychic and Somatic Symptoms) differed among the groups. A replication of the factor analysis was conducted by Steer, Ranieri, Beck, and Clark (1993), this time with a mixed group of 470 clients who had been diagnosed with mood disorder, anxiety disorder (panic disorder being most frequent), or other disorders (adjustment disorder representing the majority). Basically, the same four factors emerged. Internal consistency for the inventory was again high ($\alpha = .92$). Correlation with the BDI was higher than previously found ($r = .61$), but the BAI correlated more strongly with the SCL-90-R Anxiety subscale ($r = .81$) than did the BDI ($r = .62$), whereas the BDI related more to the SCL-90-R Depression subscale ($r = .82$) and the SCL-90 Global Severity Index ($r = .80$) than did the BAI ($rs = .62$ and $.75$, respectively). The groups with mood disorder and anxiety disorder had equivalent mean scores on the BAI and significantly higher scores than the third client group, although reanalysis comparing only clients with panic disorder and mood disorders indicated significantly higher scores for the former group. Finally, Fydrich, Dowdall, and Chambless (1992) found high alpha (.94) in a mixed (predominantly panic disorder) group of 71 clients and a fair 11-day test–retest reliability of .67. Clients with panic disorder with and without agoraphobia scored significantly higher than the group with residual other anxiety disorder. The BAI correlated moderately with the STAI Trait scale ($r = .58$) and the BDI ($r = .50$), and it was related more highly with daily diary assessments of anxiety ($r = .54$) than of depression ($r = .38$). The STAI Trait scale had a test–retest coefficient of .73, correlated poorly with daily diary measures of both anxiety ($r = .34$) and depression ($r = .36$), but was highly associated with the BDI ($r = .73$). As the authors noted, however, the BAI items relate more closely to the types of symptoms experienced by clients with panic disorder, and clinical studies investigating its psychometric properties have involved overrepresentation of those with panic disorder. Consequently, its usefulness as a general measure of anxiety with other clinical groups may be limited.

A relatively new instrument, the Endler Multidimensional Anxiety Scales (EMAS; Endler, Parker, Bagby, & Cox, 1991), holds promise for the self-report assessment of state and trait anxiety because preliminary information indicates that it can differentiate between depression and anxiety to a greater degree than other instruments such as the STAI. The EMAS State questionnaire has 20 items, half tapping cognitive-worry aspects of anxiety, half measuring autonomic-emotional aspects, and both having a solid factor-analytic foundation. The EMAS Trait questionnaire contains 60 items covering four factor analytically established situational domains (i.e., social evaluation, physical danger, ambiguous situations, and daily routines). Endler, Cox, Parker, and Bagby (1992) found that the BDI correlated at moderately high levels with STAI state and trait and EMAS state measures but at low levels with the four EMAS trait factors. STAI trait and state scores correlated in the high .60s, whereas correlations between EMAS state and trait total and subscale scores were considerably lower, ranging from .04 to .43. Both state and trait anxiety and depression could be significantly distinguished when the multidimensional scales of the EMAS were used. Internal consistencies were high for all EMAS scales (above .83). The primary problem for the EMAS is that it has not yet been evaluated systematically on clinical samples.

For client self-reports of depression, the BDI (A. T. Beck, Ward, Mendelson, Mock, & Erbaugh, 1961) is the most widely accepted and researched questionnaire. The most common clinician ratings for both anxiety and depression are the HARS (Hamilton, 1959) and the HRSD (Hamilton, 1960). Among depressed clients with or without additional panic disorder or agoraphobia, Maier, Buller, Philipp, and Heuser (1988) found intraclass correlations between two raters to be .74 for the total HARS, .73 for its Psychic Anxiety subscale, and .70 for its Somatic Anxiety subscale. The correlations between these three scores and assessor-rated global severity of anxiety were .63, .69, and .60, respectively, among clients with a principal anxiety disorder and .75, .80, and .85 among clients with principal depression disorders. Significant differences were apparent between clients with principal panic disorder without depression or agoraphobia and panic disorder with either major depression or agoraphobia, although the scores did not discriminate depression between those with and without additional anxiety disorders. In brief uncontrolled pharmacological trials, all scores declined significantly, except for the Somatic subscale among depresse clients; among anxious clients, changes in Total ($r = .73$), Psychic ($r = .76$), and Somatic ($r = .65$) scale scores correlated significantly with changes in the assessor's global severity ratings. More recently, Moras, DiNardo, and Barlow (1992) attempted to replicate the results of Riskind, Beck, Brown, and Steer's (1987) study, which explored the validity of a revised scoring method for the HARS and the HRSD. The latter investigation indicated that the revised system yielded a lower correlation between the Anxiety and Depression scales ($r = .15$) and better discrimination between clients with anxiety disorder and those with depression. The original scoring method had in the past produced correlations ranging from .53 to .89 between the two scales (Clark, 1989). Moras et al. (1992) compared the psychometric properties of the original and the revised scoring methods among a large group of clients with mixed anxiety disorders who had been diagnosed via dual ADIS-R interviews and administered the HARS and the HRSD during the interview. The revised scoring method produced interrater reliabilities of .65 and .78 for the Anxiety and Depression scales, respectively, similar to values of .65 and .82 for the original scoring method. Internal consistencies also were comparable across methods and between their study and the Riskind et al. (1987) investigation (alphas in the middle .70s to low .80s). They also found a considerably larger relationship between the two scales by revised scoring ($r = .61$) than did Riskind et al., although it was somewhat lower than that found using the original scoring method ($r = .78$). Discriminant function analyses accurately classified clients with anxiety disorder with and without additional mood disorders at comparable rates (77.7% for revised scores, and 76.5% for original scores).

CONCLUSION AND RECOMMENDATIONS

Clearly, several studies have been conducted to determine the psychometric properties of numerous measures of PTSD and social phobia. Further studies are expected in the near future since numerous instruments have been adapted for the *DSM–IV* (e.g., the ADIS, DIS, CAPS, PSS-SR), but virtually no data on their validity and reliability have been published. In addition, other instruments not covered in the previous section recently have emerged in the literature and are likely to receive researchers' attention (e.g., Briere, Elliott, Harris, & Cotman, 1995; Fournier, 1994; Glover et al., 1994; Hovens et al., 1994; Schneier et al., 1994). Based on the instruments that have received the most empirical attention, however, the time seems to be ripe for researchers to consider reaching a consensus on a list of measures to be adopted in all new treatment studies for PTSD and social phobia. As a preliminary step toward the delineation of core batteries, we hope that this and other chapters in this book will set the stage for a joint effort from leaders in the field to achieve such a crucial consensus on outcome measures.

By prioritizing various selection criteria (e.g., reliability, specificity, sensitivity), leaders in anxiety disorders research would be able to select from this chapter various instruments that measure PTSD and social phobia from different perspectives (i.e., client, clinician, observer). In addition, we would like to encourage researchers to adopt other instruments not discussed here, either because they have been associated with a particular theoretical orientation or because they have tapped a specific aspect of anxiety. For example, social skills tasks developed by cognitive–behavioral therapists have shown good psychometric qualities as measures of treatment outcome for social phobia (e.g., Mersch, Emmelkamp, Bogels, & Van Der Sleen, 1989; Turner, Beidel, Cooley, Woody, & Messer, 1994). Cognitive–behavior researchers also have developed a number of cognitive scales measuring, for example, the client's self-statements about heterosocial interactions (e.g., Social Interaction Self-Statement Test; Glass et al., 1982). Although this type of cognition is a specific target for cognitive–behavioral interventions, they are recognized as a defining feature of socially anxious individuals and therefore deserve the interest of researchers from other orientations. The psychometric qualities of these cognitive measures have been reviewed recently (Glass & Arnkoff, 1994), as has their relationship to treatment outcome (Feske & Chambless, 1995; Heimberg, 1994).

Psychophysiological measures also should be considered seriously by researchers of all theoretical persuasions when launching a major outcome study. Although such measures have been shown to be sensitive to the treatment of social phobia (e.g., Hofmann et al., 1995), they may be especially relevant to outcome studies for PTSD. Several investigations have shown that PTSD clients react with significantly greater physiological activity than do control groups in response to trauma-relevant material irrespective of the mode (e.g., slides, sounds, or narration) of presentation (cf. Litz & Weathers, 1994), and diagnostic accuracy can be incremented by the use of such measures (Gerardi, Keane, & Penk, 1989). A large-scale investigation further examining the usefulness of physiological assessment in the diagnosis of PTSD is currently under way (Keane, Kolb, & Thomas, 1992). It is unlikely, however, that psychophysiological assessment would become readily incorporated into core battery recommendations given problems with cost, availability, and specialized expertise necessary for obtaining, analyzing, and interpreting the data. However, if simple measures (e.g., heart rate) could be obtained during systematic presentations of individually determined trauma stimuli both before and after therapy, such measures would have the advantage of providing outcome assessments independent of client report or assessor ratings.

Not mentioned previously but nevertheless worthy of consideration for eventual specific core batteries are numerous instruments developed for subgroups of PTSD and social phobia. Examples of these instruments include Paul's (1966) Report of Confidence as a Speaker, validated on a public speaking anxious sample (Trexler, 1971), and the Trauma Symptom Checklist, validated with victims of sexual abuse (Elliott & Briere, 1992).

Finally, we offer a few general recommendations for consideration. These general recommendations address the important issues of associated clinical problems, global impairment, follow-up assessment, and improvement status.

Assessment of Associated Problems

We recommend that all additional Axis I diagnoses be recorded from diagnostic interviews given at all assessments. Since the elimination of most hierarchical exclusion decisions in earlier *DSM* versions, it is now possible to assign other diagnoses wherein diagnostic criteria are met but at a severity level lower than the principal diagnosis. Greater specification of client characteristics within the sample is thus provided. This has three useful implications: (a) Identification of additional diagnoses expands the possibility for dimensional assessment of other client characteristics; (b) the relationship of the presence or absence of additional diagnoses or types of diagnoses to responsiveness to treatment or types of treatment method becomes possible; and (c) the efficacy of treatment in reducing "comorbid" conditions not specifically targeted by the intervention can be determined (cf. Borkovec, Abel, & Newman, 1995). Overall severity ratings by the diagnostic assessor are recommended to provide outcome measures of each diagnosed condition. In conjunction with later suggestions about a hierarchical approach to core batteries, it also is worth considering the inclusion of other, agreed-on dimensional assessment devices by both assessor and client for each diagnosed disorder.

Global Impairment

We recommend that assessment of the degree of interference with daily living in occupational or school, social, marital, and family functioning be assessed at all assessment periods. Pretherapy evaluation of these areas provides information on the amount of impairment attributable to the disorder and provides an individual-differences variable for evaluating its influence on responsiveness to treatment or type of treatment. Posttherapy evaluation provides a clinically significant outcome measure. Such assessment is virtually absent from the outcome literature on PTSD and social phobia. Among the diagnostic interview methods, the ADIS contains a single assessor rating scale for each anxiety disorder (except for panic disorders), which varies among the disorders in terms of basing the rating on degree of impairment or a combination of impairment, intensity, or both. Instruments such as the Social Adjustment Scale (Weissman, 1993) specifically designed to measure client general functioning should be included in any core battery for anxiety disorders.

Follow-Up Assessment

It is essential to assess the long-term efficacy of therapy interventions. Three recommendations can be made. First, a minimum interval of 1 year should be used before reassessment. Second, measurement should be as complete as that contained in the original pretherapy assessment. Third, information on the type and frequency of interval treatments (both psychosocial and pharmacological) since postassessment, both for the original problem and other problems potentially related to it, should be obtained. Interpretation of follow-up results is confounded if clients have received additional treatments during the intervening period. Analyses with and without such clients will allow more valid inferences on maintenance of therapy gains and differential long-term efficacy between comparison conditions.

Defining Improvement Status

We also recommend that researchers not only determine whether treatment of PTSD and social phobia leads to statistically significant change but also to clinically significant change. Jacobson and Truax (1991) have provided guidelines that should be adopted in all major treatment outcome studies for PTSD and social phobia to define clinically significant change. A complementary strategy to measure client change is the construction of composite outcome measures. Turner and his colleagues have recently developed two composite measures for the treatment of social phobia: the Social Phobia Endstate Functioning Index (SPEFI; Turner, Beidel, Long, Turner, & Townsley, 1993), which compares the level of functioning after treatment with normal control group, and the Index of Social Phobia Improvement (ISPI; Turner, Beidel, & Wolff, 1994), which assess the degree of improvement from pre- to posttreatment. Tapping various domains of social phobia, the SPEFI and ISPI are based on the same five outcome measures representing multiple methods of assessment (self-reports, behavioral performance, and clinical ratings). We recommend that more composite indexes be developed and tested for the treatment of social phobia and PTSD. To facilitate the construction of the most useful composite indexes of outcome, we also recommend that more attention be given in the literature to the sensitivity of different measures to treatment response.

REFERENCES

American Psychiatric Association. (1980). *Diagnostic and statistical manual of mental disorders* (3rd ed.). Washington, DC: Author.

American Psychiatric Association. (1987). *Diagnostic and statistical manual of mental disorders* (3rd ed., rev.). Washington, DC: Author.

American Psychiatric Association. (1994). *Diagnostic and statistical manual of mental disorders* (4th ed.). Washington, DC: Author.

Beck, A. T., Epstein, N., Brown, G., & Steer, R. A. (1988). An inventory for measuring clinical anxiety: Psychometric properties. *Journal of Consulting and Clinical Psychology, 56,* 893–897.

Beck, A. T., & Steer, R. A. (1991). Relationship between the Beck Anxiety Inventory and the Hamilton Anxiety Rating Scale with anxious outpatients. *Journal of Anxiety Disorders, 5,* 213–223.

Beck, A. T., Ward, C. H., Mendelson, M., Mock, J., & Erbaugh, J. (1961). An inventory of measuring depression. *Archives of General Psychiatry, 41,* 561–571.

Beck, J. G., & Zebb, B. J. (1994). Behavioral assessment and treatment of panic disorder: Current status, future directions. *Behavior Therapy, 25,* 581–611.

Beidel, D. C., Borden, J. W., Turner, S. M., & Jacob, R. G. (1989). The Social Phobia and Anxiety Inventory: Concurrent validity with a clinic sample. *Behaviour Research and Therapy, 27,* 573–576.

Beidel, D. C., Turner, S. M., Stanley, M. A., & Dancu, C. V. (1989). The Social Phobia and Anxiety Inventory: Concurrent and external validity. *Behavior Therapy, 20,* 417–427.

Blake, D. D., Weathers, F. W., Nagy, L. M., Kaloupek, D. G., Gusman, F. D., Charney, D. S., & Keane, T. M. (1995). The development of a clinician administered PTSD Scale. *Journal of Traumatic Stress, 8,* 75–90.

Blanchard, E. B., Gerardi, R. J., Kolb, L. C., & Barlow, D. H. (1986). The utility of the Anxiety Disorders Interview Schedule (ADIS) in the diagnosis of the post-traumatic stress disorder (PTSD) in Vietnam veterans. *Behaviour Research and Therapy, 24,* 577–580.

Borkovec, T. D., Abel, J. L., & Newman, H. (1995). The effects of therapy on co-morbid conditions in generalized anxiety disorder. *Journal of Consulting and Clinical Psychology, 63,* 479–483.

Breslau, N., & Davis, G. C. (1987). Posttraumatic stress disorder: The etiologic specificity of wartime stressors. *American Journal of Psychiatry, 144,* 578–583.

Briere, J., Elliott, D. M., Harris, K., & Cotman, A. (1995). Trauma Symptom Inventory: Psychometrics and association with childhood and adult victimization in clinical samples. *Journal of Interpersonal Violence, 10,* 387–401.

Brown, T. A., & Barlow, D. H. (1992). Comorbidity among anxiety disorders: Implications for treatment and *DSM-IV. Journal of Consulting and Clinical Psychology, 60,* 835–844.

Clark, L. A. (1989). The anxiety and depressive disorders: Descriptive psychopathology and differential diagnosis. In P. C. Kendall & D. Watson (Eds.), *Anxiety and depression: Distinctive and overlapping features* (pp. 83–129). New York: Academic Press.

Cox, B. J., & Swinson, R. P. (1995). Assessment and measurement. In M. B. Stein (Ed.), *Social phobia: Clinical and research perspectives* (pp. 261–291). Washington, DC: American Psychological Association.

Cox, B. J., Swinson, R. P., & Shaw, B. F. (1991). Value of the Fear Questionnaire in differentiating agoraphobia and social phobia. *British Journal of Psychiatry, 159,* 842–845.

Davidson, J., Smith, R., & Kudler, H. (1989). Validity and reliability of the DSM-III criteria for posttraumatic stress disorder: Experience with a structured interview. *Journal of Nervous and Mental Disease, 177,* 336–341.

DiNardo, P. A., & Barlow, D. H. (1988). *Anxiety Disorders Interview Schedule–Revised (ADIS-R).* Albany, NY: Center for Stress and Anxiety Disorders.

DiNardo, P. A., Moras, K., Barlow, D. H., Rapee, R. M., & Brown, T. A. (1993). Reliability of DSM-III-R anxiety disorder categories: Using the Anxiety Disorders Interview Schedule–Revised (ADIS-R). *Archives of General Psychiatry, 50,* 251–256.

Dohrenwend, B. P. (1982). *Psychiatric Epidemiology Research Interview (PERI).* New York: Columbia University, Social Psychiatry Research Unit.

Elliott, D. M., & Briere, J. (1992). Sexual abuse trauma among professional women: Validating the Trauma Symptom Checklist-40 (TSC-40). *Child Abuse & Neglect, 16,* 391–398.

Endler, N. S., Cox, B. J., Parker, J. D., & Bagby, R. M. (1992). Self-reports of depression and state-trait anxiety: Evidence for differential assessment. *Journal of Personality and Social Psychology, 63,* 832–838.

Endler, N. S., Parker, J. D., Bagby, R. M., & Cox, B. J. (1991). Multidimensionality of state and trait anxiety: Factor structure of the Endler Multidimensional Anxiety Scales. *Journal of Personality and Social Psychology, 60,* 919–926.

Feske, U., & Chambless, D. L. (1995). Cognitive behavioral versus exposure only treatment for social phobia: A meta-analysis. *Behavior Therapy, 26,* 695–720.

Figley, C. R. (1989). *Helping traumatized families.* San Francisco: Jossey-Bass.

Foa, E. B., Riggs, D. S., Dancu, C. V., & Rothbaum, B. O. (1993). Reliability and validity of a brief instrument for assessing post-traumatic stress disorder. *Journal of Traumatic Stress, 6,* 459–473.

Fontana, A., & Rosenheck, R. (1994). A short form of the Mississippi Scale for Measuring Change in combat-related PTSD. *Journal of Traumatic Stress, 7,* 407–414.

Fournier, D. G. (1994). Validation of the Purdue Post-traumatic Stress Scale on a sample of Vietnam veterans. *Journal of Traumatic Stress, 7,* 311–318.

Foy, D. W., Sipprelle, R. C., Rueger, D. B., & Carroll, E. M. (1984). Etiology of post-traumatic stress disorder in Vietnam veterans: Analysis of premilitary, military, and combat exposure influences. *Journal of Consulting and Clinical Psychology, 52,* 79–87.

Fydrich, T., Dowdall, D., & Chambless, D. L. (1992). Reliability and validity of the Beck Anxiety Inventory. *Journal of Anxiety Disorders, 6,* 55–61.

Gerardi, R., Keane, T. M., & Penk, W. E. (1989). Utility: Sensitivity and specificity in developing diagnostic tests of combat-related post-traumatic stress disorder (PTSD). *Journal of Clinical Psychology, 45,* 691–703.

Glass, C. R., & Arnkoff, D. B. (1994). Validity issues in self-statement measures of social phobia and social anxiety. *Behaviour Research and Therapy, 32,* 255–267.

Glass, C. R., Merluzzi, T. V., Biever, J. L., & Larsen, K. H. (1982). Cognitive assessment of social anxiety: Development and validation of a self-statement questionnaire. *Cognitive Therapy and Research, 6,* 37–55.

Glover, H., Silver, S., Goodnick, P., Ohlde, C., Packard, P., & Hamlin, C. L. (1994). Vulnerability Scale: A preliminary report of psychometric properties. *Psychological Reports, 75,* 1651–1668.

Hamilton, M. (1959). The measurement of anxiety states by rating. *British Journal of Medical Psychology, 32,* 50–55.

Hamilton, M. (1960). A rating scale for depression. *Journal of Neurology, Neurosurgery, and Psychiatry, 23,* 56–62.

Hammarberg, M. (1992). Penn Inventory for Posttraumatic Stress Disorder: Psychometric properties. *Psychological Assessment, 4,* 67–76.

Heimberg, R. G. (1994). Cognitive assessment strategies and the measurement of outcome of treatment for social phobia. *Behaviour Research and Therapy, 32,* 269–280.

Heimberg, R. G., Hope, D. A., Dodge, C. S., & Becker, R. E. (1990). DSM-III-R subtypes of social phobia: Comparison of generalized social phobics and public speaking phobics. *Journal of Nervous and Mental Disease, 178,* 172–179.

Heimberg, R. G., Hope, D. A., Rapee, R. M., & Bruch, M. A. (1988). The validity of the Social Avoidance and Distress Scale and the Fear of Negative Evaluation Scale with social phobic patients. *Behaviour Research and Therapy, 26,* 407–410.

Heimberg, R. G., Mueller, G. P., Holt, C. S., Hope, D. A., & Liebowitz, M. R. (1992).

Assessment of anxiety in social interaction and being observed by others: The Social Interaction Anxiety Scale and the Social Phobia Scale. *Behavior Therapy, 23,* 53–73.

Hendrix, C. C., Anelli, L. M., Gibbs, J. P., & Fournier, D. G. (1994). Validation of the Purdue Post-Traumatic Stress Scale on a sample of Vietnam veterans. *Journal of Traumatic Stress, 7,* 311–318.

Herbert, J. D., Hope, D. A., & Bellack, A. S. (1992). Validity of the distinction between generalized social phobia and avoidant personality disorder. *Journal of Abnormal Psychology, 101,* 332–339.

Hofmann, S. G., Newman, M. G., Ehlers, A., & Roth, W. T. (1995). Psychophysiological differences between subgroups of social phobia. *Journal of Abnormal Psychology, 104,* 224–231.

Holt, C. S., Heimberg, R. G., & Hope, D. A. (1992). Avoidant personality disorder and the generalized subtype of social phobia. *Journal of Abnormal Psychology, 101,* 318–325.

Hovens, J. E., van der Ploeg, H. M., Bramsen, I., Klaarenbeek, M. T. A., Schreuder, J. N., & Rivero, V. V. (1994). The development of the Self-Rating Inventory for Posttraumatic Stress Disorder. *Acta Psychiatrica Scandinavica, 90,* 172–183.

Horowitz, M. J., Wilner, N., & Alvarez, W. (1979). Impact of Event Scale: A measure of subjective stress. *Psychosomatic Medicine, 41,* 207–218.

Houskamp, B. M., & Foy, D. W. (1991). The assessment of posttraumatic stress disorder in battered women. *Journal of Interpersonal Violence, 6,* 368–376.

Jacobson, N. S., & Truax, P. (1991). Clinical significance: A statistical approach to defining meaningful change in psychotherapy research. *Journal of Consulting and Clinical Psychology, 59,* 12–19.

Keane, T. M., Caddell, J. M., & Taylor, K. L. (1988). Mississippi Scale for Combat-Related Post-Traumatic Stress Disorder: Three studies in reliability and validity. *Journal of Consulting and Clinical Psychology, 56,* 85–90.

Keane, T. M., Kolb, L. C., & Thomas, R. T. (1988). *A psychophysiological study of chronic PTSD* (Department of Veterans Affairs Cooperative Study No. 334). Boston: V.A. Medical Center.

Keane, T. M., Malloy, P. F., & Fairbank, J. A. (1984). Empirical development of an MMPI subscale for the assessment of combat-related posttraumatic stress disorder. *Journal of Consulting and Clinical Psychology, 52,* 888–891.

Keane, T. M., Weathers, F. W., & Kaloupek, D. G. (1992). Psychological assessment of post-traumatic stress disorder. *PTSD Quarterly 3,* 1–3.

King, L. A., King, D. W., Leskin, G., & Foy, D. W. (1995). The Los Angeles Symptom

Checklist: A self-report measure of posttraumatic stress disorder. *Psychological Assessment, 2,* 1–17.

Kinney, P. J., & Williams, S. L. (1988). Accuracy and fear inventories and self-efficacy scales in predicting agoraphobic behavior. *Behaviour Research and Therapy, 26,* 513–518.

Kulka, R. A., Schlenger, W. E., Fairbank, J. A., Hough, R. L., Jordan, B. K., Marmar, C. R., & Weiss, D. S. (1988). *National Vietnam Veterans Readjustment Study (NVVRS): Description, current status, and initial PTSD prevalence estimates.* Research Triangle Park, NC: Research Triangle Park Institute.

Kulka, R. A., Schlenger, W. E., Fairbank, J. A., Jordan, B. K., Hough, R. L., Marmar, C. R., & Weiss, D. S. (1988). Assessment of posttraumatic stress disorder in the community: Prospects and pitfalls from recent studies of Vietnam veterans. *Psychological Assessment, 3,* 547–560.

Lauterback, D., & Vrana, S. (1996). Three studies on the reliability and validity of a self-report measure of post-traumatic stress disorder. *Assessment, 3,* 17–25.

Litz, B. T., & Weathers, F. W. (1994). The diagnosis and assessment of post-traumatic stress disorder in adults. In M. B. Williams & J. F. Sommer (Eds.), *Handbook of post-traumatic therapy* (pp. 20–37). Westport, CT: Greenwood Press.

Lyons, J. A., Caddell, J. M., Pittman, R. L., Rawls, R., & Perrin, S. (1994). The potential for faking on the Mississippi Scale for Combat-related PTSD. *Journal of Traumatic Stress, 7,* 441–445.

Lyons, J. A., & Keane, T. M. (1992). Keane PTSD Scale: MMPI and MMPI-2 update. *Journal of Traumatic Stress, 5,* 111–117.

Lyons, J. A., & Scotti, J. R. (1994). Comparability of two administration formats of the Keane Posttraumatic Stress Disorder Scale. *Psychological Assessment, 6,* 209–211.

Maier, W., Buller, R., Philipp, M., & Heuser, I. (1988). The Hamilton Anxiety Scale: Reliability, validity and sensitivity to change in anxiety and depressive disorders. *Journal of Affective Disorders, 14,* 61–68.

Mannuzza, S., Fyer, A. J., Martin, M. S., Gallops, M. S., Endicott, J., Gorman, J., Liebowitz, M. R., & Klein, D. F. (1989). Reliability of anxiety assessment: I. Diagnostic agreement. *Archives of General Psychiatry, 46,* 1093–1101.

Marks, I. M., & Mathews, A. M. (1979). Brief standard self-rating for phobic patients. *Behaviour Research and Therapy, 17,* 263–267.

Mattick, R. P., & Clarke, J. C. (1989). *Development and validation of measures of social phobia scrutiny fear and social interaction anxiety.* Unpublished manuscript.

Mattick, R. P., & Peters, L. (1988). Treatment of severe social phobia: Effects of guided exposure with and without cognitive restructuring. *Journal of Consulting and Clinical Psychology, 56,* 251–260.

Mattick, R. P., Peters, L., & Clarke, J. C. (1989). Exposure and cognitive restructuring for social phobia. *Behavior Therapy, 20,* 3–23.

Mavissakalian, M. (1986). The Fear Questionnaire: A validity study. *Behaviour Research and Therapy, 24,* 83–85.

McFall, M. E., Smith, D. E., Mackay, P. W., & Tarver, D. J. (1990). Reliability and validity of Mississippi Scale for Combat-Related Posttraumatic Stress Disorder. *Psychological Assessment, 2,* 114–121.

McFall, M. E., Smith, D. E., Roszell, D. K., Tarver, D. J., & Malas, K. (1990). Convergent validity of measures of PTSD in Vietnam combat veterans. *American Journal of Psychiatry, 147,* 645–648.

Mersch, P. P. A., Emmelkamp, P. M. G., Bogels, S. M., & Van Der Sleen, J. (1989). Social phobia: Individual response patterns and the effects of behavioural and cognitive interventions. *Behaviour Research and Therapy, 27,* 421–434.

Moras, K., DiNardo, P. A., & Barlow, D. H. (1992). Distinguishing anxiety and depression: Reexamination of the reconstructed Hamilton scales. *Psychological Assessment, 4,* 224–227.

Munley, P. H., Bains, D. S., Bloem, W. D., & Busky, R. M. (1995). Post-traumatic stress disorder and the MMPI-2. *Journal of Traumatic Stress, 8,* 171–178.

Neal, L. A., Busuttil, W., Herapath, R., & Strike, P. W. (1994). Development and validation of the Computerized Clinician Administered Post-traumatic Stress Disorder Scale-1-Revised. *Psychological Medicine, 24,* 701–706.

Neal, L. A., Busuttil, W., Rollins, J., Herapath, R., Strike, P. W., & Tunbull, G. (1994). Convergent validity of measures of post-traumatic stress disorder in a mixed and civilian population. *Journal of Traumatic Stress, 7,* 447–455.

Newman, M. G., Hofmann, S. G., Roth, W. T., & Taylor, C. B. (1994). Does behavioural treatment of social phobia lead to cognitive changes? *Behavior Therapy, 25,* 503–517.

Oei, T. P., Gross, P. R., & Evans, L. (1989). Phobic disorders and anxiety states: How do they differ? *Australian and New Zealand Journal of Psychiatry, 23,* 81–88.

Oei, T. P., Kenna, D., & Evans, L. (1991). The reliability, validity and utility of the SAD and FNE scales for anxiety disorder patients. *Personality and Individual Differences, 12,* 111–116.

Osman, A., Barrios, F. X., Aukes, D., & Osman, J. R. (1995). Psychometric evaluation of the Social Phobia and Anxiety Inventory in college students. *Journal of Clinical Psychology, 51,* 235–243.

Paul, G. L. (1966). *Insight vs. desensitization in psychotherapy: An experiment in anxiety reduction.* Stanford, CA: Stanford University Press.

Rapee, R. M., & Barlow, D. H. (1990). The assessment of panic disorder. In P. McReynolds, J. C. Rosen, & G. J. Chelune (Eds.), *Advances in psychological assessment* (pp. 203–227). New York: Plenum.

Ries, B. J., McNeil, D. W., Boone, M. L., Turk, C. L., Carter, L. E., & Heimberg, R. G. (1996). *Assessment of contemporary social phobia instruments with patient samples.* Manuscript in preparation, Oklahoma State University.

Riskind, J. H., Beck, A. T., Brown, G., & Steer, R. A. (1987). Taking the measure of anxiety and depression: Validity of the reconstructed Hamilton scales. *Journal of Nervous and Mental Disease, 175,* 817–820.

Robins, L. N., & Helzer, J. E. (1985). *Diagnostic Interview Schedule (DIS) Version III-A.* St. Louis, MO: Washington University.

Saunders, B. E., Arata, C. M., & Kilpatrick, D. G. (1990). Development of a crime-related post-traumatic stress scale for women within the Symptom Checklist-90-Revised. *Journal of Traumatic Stress, 3,* 439–448.

Schlenger, W. E., & Kulka, R. A. (1987, August). *Performance of the Fairbank-Keane MMPI scale and other self-report measures in identifying post-traumatic stress disorder.* Paper presented at the 95th Annual Convention of the American Psychological Association, New York.

Schneier, F. R., Heckelman, L. R., Garfinkel, R., Campeas, R., Fallon, B. A., Gitow, A., Street, L., Del Bene, D., & Liebowitz, M. R. (1994). Functional impairment in social phobia. *Journal of Clinical Psychiatry, 55,* 322–331.

Shear, M. K., & Maser, J. D. (1994). Standardized assessment for panic disorder research. *Archives of General Psychiatry, 51,* 346–354.

Skre, I., Onstad, S., Torgersen, S., & Kringlen, E. (1991). High interrater reliability for the Structured Clinical Interview for DSM-III-R Axis I (SCID-I). *Acta Psychiatrica Scandinavica, 84,* 167–173.

Spielberger, C. D., Gorsuch, R. L., & Lushene, R. E. (1970). *The State-Trait Anxiety Inventory: Test manual for Form X.* Palo Alto, CA: Consulting Psychologists Press.

Spitzer, R. L., Williams, J. B. W., Gibbon, M., & First, M. B. (1990). *User's guide for the structured clinical interview for DSM-III-R: SCID.* Washington, DC: American Psychiatric Press.

Steer, R. A., Ranieri, W. F., Beck, A. T., & Clark, D. A. (1993). Further evidence for the validity of the Beck Anxiety Inventory with psychiatric outpatients. *Journal of Anxiety Disorders, 7,* 195–205.

Trexler, L. (1971). *Rational-emotive therapy, placebo, and no-treatment effects on public speaking anxiety.* Unpublished doctoral dissertation, Temple University, Philadelphia (University Microfilms No. 71-31, 063).

Turner, S. M., & Beidel, D. C. (1988). Some further comments on the measurement of social phobia. *Behaviour Research and Therapy, 26,* 411–413.

Turner, S. M., Beidel, D. C., Cooley, M. R., Woody, S. R., & Messer, S. B. (1994). A multicomponent behavioural treatment for social phobia: Social effectiveness therapy. *Behaviour Research and Therapy, 32,* 381–390.

Turner, S. M., Beidel, D. C., Dancu, C. V., & Stanley, M. A. (1989). An empirically derived inventory to measure social fears and anxiety: The Social Phobia and Anxiety Inventory. *Psychological Assessment, 1,* 35–40.

Turner, S. M., Beidel, D. C., Long, P. J., Turner, M. W., & Townsley, R. M. (1993). A composite measure to determine the functional status of treated social phobics: The Social Phobia Endstate Functioning Index. *Behavior Therapy, 24,* 265–275.

Turner, S. M., Beidel, D. C., & Wolff, P. L. (1994). A composite measure to determine improvement following treatment for social phobia: The Index of Social Phobia Improvement. *Behaviour Research and Therapy, 32,* 471–476.

Turner, S. M., McCanna, M., & Beidel, D. C. (1987). Validity of the Social Avoidance and Distress and Fear of Negative Evaluation Scales. *Behaviour Research and Therapy, 25,* 113–115.

Turner, S. M., Stanley, M. A., Beidel, D. C., & Bond, L. (1989). The Social Phobia and Anxiety Inventory: Construct validity. *Journal of Psychopathology and Behavioral Assessment, 11,* 221–234.

Turner, S. M., Beidel, D. C., & Townsley, R. M. (1992). Social phobia: A comparison of specific and generalized subtypes and avoidant personality disorder. *Journal of Abnormal Psychology, 101,* 326–331.

Vreven, D. L., Gudanowski, D. M., King, L. A., & King, D. W. (1995). The civilian version of the Mississippi PTSD Scale: A psychometric evaluation. *Journal of Traumatic Stress, 8,* 91–109.

Watson, C. G. (1990). Psychometric posttraumatic stress disorder measurement techniques: A review. *Psychological Assessment, 2,* 460–469.

Watson, C. G., Juba, M., Manifold, V., Kucala, T., & Anderson, P. E. D. (1991). The PTSD Interview: Description, reliability, and concurrent validity of a DSM-III based technique. *Journal of Clinical Psychology, 47,* 179–188.

Watson, C. G., Plemel, D., DeMotts, J., Howard, M. T., Tuorila, J., Moog, R., Thomas, D., & Anderson, D. (1994). A comparison of four PTSD measures' convergent validities in Vietnam veterans. *Journal of Traumatic Stress, 7,* 75–82.

Watson, D., & Friend, R. (1969). Measurement of social-evaluative anxiety. *Journal of Consulting and Clinical Psychology, 33,* 448–457.

Weathers, F. W., Blake, D. D., Krinsley, K. E., Haddad, W., Huska, J. A., & Keane, T. M. (1992, October). *The Clinician Administered PTSD Scale—Diagnostic Version (CAPS-1): Description, use and psychometric properties.* Paper presented at the annual meeting of the International Society for Traumatic Stress Studies, Los Angeles.

Weissman, M. M. (1993). *Social Adjustment Scale.* New York: New York Psychiatric Institute.

Wetzel, R. D., & Yutzy, S. (1994). Effect of reducing cut-off scores on Keane's Post-traumatic Stress Disorder Scale. *Psychological Reports, 75,* 1296–1298.

Williams, J. B. W., Gibbon, M., First, M. B., Spitzer, R. L., Davies, M., Borus, J., Howes, M. J., Kane, J., Pope, H. G., Rounsaville, B., & Wittchen, H. (1992). The structured clinical interview for DSM-III-R (SCID): II. Multisite test-retest reliability. *Archives of General Psychiatry, 49,* 630–636.

7

Measuring Change in Patients Following Psychological and Pharmacological Interventions: Anxiety Disorders

Paul Crits-Christoph and Mary Beth Connolly

The purpose of this chapter is to make recommendations about measures that should be included in treatment outcome research on anxiety disorders. This chapter is a companion to the chapter by Borkovec and colleagues in this book (see chap. 6). Our chapter covers generalized anxiety disorder (GAD), obsessive–compulsive disorder (OCD), and specific phobias. Chapter 6 covers posttraumatic stress disorder, agoraphobia and panic disorder, and social phobia.

Before describing our recommended instruments, we make some preliminary comments about the philosophy that guided our recommendations. The first issue that is important to consider in developing a core battery of instruments is the purpose of the core battery. A common reason given for core batteries in treatment research, articulated in the chapter by Horowitz et al. in this book (see chap. 2), is the desire to make comparisons across studies, including meta-analyses. Meta-analytic reviews of the literature, however, can have different purposes. For example, a meta-analysis may be aimed at examining whether psychotherapy works at all (e.g., Smith & Glass, 1977) and consequently will include a broad range of studies of varying treatments and patient problems. More recent meta-analyses have focused on the question of what works for what kind of patient problem. For example, Dobson (1989) used the Beck Depression Inventory (BDI) as the sole outcome measure used for comparisons of the effects of cognitive therapy (CT; vs. other treatments) for depression. Another example is the review by the Agency for Health Care Policy and Research (1993). This latter review used the proportion of patients who met criteria for recovery from a depressive episode as their main outcome measure for cross-study comparisons. For these types of meta-analyses, a measure of the specific patient problem (e.g., depression) is crucial for making cross-study comparisons, assuming one does not rely on the questionable technique of combining effect sizes derived from much different types of outcome measures. Another type of review might focus on the effects of psychotherapy on some specific area of patient functioning, such as the one by Mintz, Mintz, Arruda, and Hwang (1992) on the effects of treatments of depression on work functioning. Rather than focusing solely on a specific patient symptom or problem, other meta-analyses might address the issue of generalizability of treatments to "real-world" populations. With questions about generalizability, other kinds of outcome measures, such as measures of comorbidity and general functioning, take on greater importance.

Paralleling the various questions that can be asked in meta-analyses are the variety of purposes of individual studies. Such purposes range from a highly controlled efficacy study under ideal conditions to "effectiveness" or services research. The latter typically is characterized by inclusion of a broader range of patients and therapists. Moreover, whereas controlled efficacy research often includes an assessment battery that involves many hours of patient time, with patients being compensated for their time, services research is usually conducted without major intrusions into the normal clinical operation. Thus, a core battery for broad application including both services research as well as clinical application (e.g., outcomes assessment for managed care) would need to be brief and efficient. A recommendation to include full structured diagnostic assessment instruments for Axis I and Axis II of the fourth edition of the *Diagnostic and Statistical Manual of Mental Disorders* (*DSM–IV;* American Psychiatric Association, 1994) would not be a practical recommendation for services research or outcome evaluation in managed care settings because of the large patient burden and because of the need for trained evaluators. However, these instruments are essential for controlled efficacy research. Our approach to these varying purposes is to recommend a full range of instruments. Investigators then can choose a subset of the full battery based on their specific purpose.

Another issue to consider is whether the instruments should be "atheoretical." As described in the chapter by Horowitz et al. (see chap. 2 in this book), the earlier attempt at a core battery by Waskow and colleagues specifically stayed away from instruments that they thought were too closely associated with a particular psychotherapy theoretical orientation. We think that implicit theoretical assumptions or values are part of any instrument, that it is not possible to be truly atheoretical. For example, the phenomenological approach that guides the *DSM–IV* system, which is seen as being central to most current treatment research, contains its own assumptions about what is important (i.e., disorders). Furthermore, the particular way the *DSM* carves up nature into pieces (disorders) may not be the only meaningful way to classify patients into disorders. Having said this, we think that the *DSM* disorders approach is an important component to a core battery at this point in time. Despite any problems that might exist with the *DSM–IV*, the system is widely used in mental health treatment, far more widely than any potential alternative system. In addition, the *DSM* can be seen as still in development and responsive (in future versions) to emerging findings about the reliability and validity of specific classifications. Thus, the *DSM–IV* is a reasonable starting point for recommendations about a core battery of assessment instruments. Assessment of *DSM–IV* categories is important to both inclusion and exclusion criteria for a study as well as for the measurement of outcome (e.g., is the disorder still present?). This is not to say that other variables are unimportant. To the contrary, in most studies the primary outcome measures will be continuous measures of patient symptoms and functioning. Furthermore, we also do not want to exclude studies of specific problematic behaviors that might not be captured in the current *DSM* system.

Like with the *DSM*, the decision to measure specific other outcome domains is not an atheoretical decision. The choice of domains such as social, interpersonal, and occupational functioning involve a theoretical choice or value decision about what is important in life. As the field develops, research on the extent to which certain types of functioning (e.g., interpersonal) predict symptom formation, relapse, or course of treatment can lend justification to the importance of assessing such an area of functioning. Such justification can even be expressed in terms of the financial costs to society due to impairments in certain areas of functioning. As Strupp and Hadley (1977) argued, however, patients, therapists, and society have different values and different preferences in terms of what kind of outcome is important. Our approach on this issue is to recommend instruments from a variety of perspectives while recognizing that, ultimately, such recommendations are guided by values. Information on the validity of measures, despite the fact that such tests of validity also are influenced by values, should guide recommendations and revisions to such recommendations over time.

A truly comprehensive approach to the selection of instruments to be included in a core battery would involve comparing the psychometric characteristics (e.g., reliability, validity, sensitivity to change) of the entire pool of relevant instruments. In the area of anxiety disorders, this pool is large. To make our task more manageable, we focus our attention on instruments that are recommended by experts in the area of anxiety disorder research, have been used widely in treatment research, or, in the case of a less widely known instrument, are relatively new and fill a void that no other instrument appears to fill. The opinions of experts were solicited as described in the chapter by Borkovec and colleagues (see chap. 6 in this book). Therefore, our final set of recommendations is determined partly by consensus opinion and partly by our own preferences. We do attempt, however, to provide detailed psychometric justification of our recommendations.

We adopt the perspective here that developed out of the APA (American Psychological Association) conference on measuring changes in patients following psychological and pharmacological interventions. We separate our recommendations into general (across all anxiety disorder) and specific core batteries (specific to each anxiety disorder). The recommendations for the general core battery are presented first.

GENERAL CORE BATTERY

Although general measures that would cut across anxiety disorder (or perhaps across all disorders) have appeal, particularly for broad reviews of the literature, we begin with a caution: Such general measures have greater or lesser relevance to different disorders. So, for example, a measure of general anxiety is highly relevant to measuring the outcome of patients with GAD, but it probably has little relevance to the outcome of treatment for many patients with specific phobias, who may have little general anxiety but intense anxiety when confronted with the particular stimulus to which they are phobic. General anxiety measures, however, may have another useful purpose: as an intake assessment to characterize the level of symptomatology in a given sample. As long as such measures are relatively brief, at the current time we would recommend several measures to be obtained at pretreatment, posttreatment, and follow-up assessments until evidence accumulates that for particular disorders they have little if any relevance. These instruments are reviewed next.

Hamilton Anxiety Rating Scale

The Hamilton Anxiety Rating Scale (HARS; Hamilton, 1959) is a clinician-administered measure. This scale was developed to measure symptom severity in patients with anxiety neurosis. It has been used extensively in efficacy studies of anxiolytic medications. The original scale had 13 items, although a 14-item version was later introduced (Guy, 1976; Hamilton, 1969) and became the version commonly used. The scale items cover anxious mood; tension; fears; and muscular, sensory, cardiovascular, respiratory, gastrointestinal, and autonomic symptoms of anxiety. An additional item assesses the patient's behavior during the interview. Each item is rated on a 0–4 scale, and the final scale score is the sum of the 14 items, ranging from 0 to 56.

Recently, a revision of the HARS and the Hamilton Rating Scale for

Depression (HRSD) has been proposed (Riskind, Beck, Brown, & Steer, 1987) that attempts to reduce the overlap between the scales. The revised HARS (HARS-R) consists of 16 items: 10 from the 14-item HARS and 6 from the HRSD, including insomnia (early awakening), agitation, psychic anxiety, somatic anxiety, hypochondriasis, and depersonalization. Another recent advance is the development of a structured interview for administering the HARS: the Hamilton Anxiety Rating Scale Interview Guide (HARS-IG; Bruss, Gruenberg, Goldstein, & Barber, 1994). The purpose of the HARS-IG is to provide the clinician with criteria to judge and rate symptom severity.

Several studies have examined the internal consistency of the HARS. Moras, DiNardo, and Barlow (1992) reported a Cronbach's alpha of .77. Using the HARS-IG, Bruss et al. (1994) reported a Cronbach's alpha of .79 for the 14-item HARS.

With regard to interrater reliability, Maier, Buller, Philipp, and Heuser (1988) reported an intraclass correlation coefficient (*ICC*) of .74 for the 14-item HARS. However, Bruss et al. (1994), using the HARS-IG, reported an *ICC* of .99 for the total of the 14 items when a second judge observed the interview and made ratings and an *ICC* of .96 when a second interview was conducted 1 day after the first interview.

One problem with the HARS is that it generally has been found to correlate highly with the HRSD. Clark (1989) reported correlations between these two scales ranging from .53 to .89. These correlations are partly a function of overlap in item content between the two scales (one HARS item concerns depressed mood and one HRSD item concerns psychic anxiety). This overlap prompted the development of the HARS-R (Riskind et al., 1987). The HARS-R was reported by Riskind et al. to have minimal overlap with the revised HRSD (2% shared variance). Moras et al. (1992), however, reported a higher amount of shared overlap (about 37%). In comparing their results with those of Riskind et al. (1987), Moras et al. pointed out that Riskind et al. used a "past week" inquiry about symptoms, whereas Moras et al. used a "past month" inquiry. Thus, although the revised scales appear to be an advantage over the original scales, the problem of overlap in the assessment of anxiety and depressive symptoms remains. Reducing the time interval of symptom inquiry to 1 week, however, may limit this overlap.

Space does not permit a thorough evaluation of the validity of the HARS. However, we report some selected studies to support the inclusion of the HARS in our core battery. Beck and Steer (1991) reported on the relation between the HARS and the Beck Anxiety Inventory (BAI; also included within our core battery). The total score of the 14-item HARS and the BAI was found to be .56 in a sample of 367 outpatients. Beck, Epstein, Brown, and Steer (1988) reported a similar coefficient (.51) for the relation between the HARS and the BAI in another sample.

An especially important characteristic of a scale recommended for a core battery for treatment research is whether the measure has demonstrated sensitivity to change. Table 1 shows a sampling of psychosocial and pharmacological treatment outcome studies of the HARS. Both within-conditions and across-conditions effect sizes are presented. Within-conditions effect sizes are calculated as the postmean minus the

Table 1

Hamilton Anxiety Rating Scale: Sensitivity to Change

Study	Treatment condition	Effect size	
		Within condition	Between condition
Power et al. (1990)	CT, DZ,	CT: 4.3	CT-PL: 1.2
	CT+DZ,	DZ: 2.2	DZ-PL: 0.39
	PL	CT+DZ: 2.9	CT+DZ-PL: 1.4
Barlow et al. (1992)	CT, REL,	CT: 1.4	CT-WL: 1.9
	combined	REL: 2.7	REL-WL: 1.9
	CT+REL, WL	Combined: 1.0	Combined-WL: 1.6
Borkovec and Costello (1993)	CBT, REL, ND	CBT: 2.3	CBT-ND: 0.90
		REL: 3.2	REL-ND: 0.71
Crits-Christoph et al. (1996)	Brief dynamic	1.41	

NOTE: CT = cognitive therapy; DZ = diazepam; PL = placebo; REL = relaxation; WL = waiting-list control; CBT = cognitive–behavioral therapy; ND = nondirective therapy.

premean, divided by the prestandard deviation; across-conditions effect sizes are calculated as the postmean of active treatment versus the postmean of control treatment, divided by the standard deviation of control condition. The data illustrate that the HARS is sensitive to change.

The BAI

The BAI (Beck, Epstein, et al., 1988) is our selection for a self-report measure of anxiety symptoms. The BAI is a 21-item measure developed to assess the severity of anxiety symptoms in clinical populations. The authors of the BAI stated that this scale was developed specifically to address the need for an instrument that would reliably discriminate anxiety from depression while also displaying convergent validity (Beck, Epstein, et al., 1988). Other self-report instruments for measuring anxiety (e.g., the State-Trait Anxiety Inventory; Spielberger, Gorsuch, & Lushene, 1970) have not been shown to adequately differentiate anxiety from depression (Dobson, 1985; Tanaka-Matsumi & Kameoka, 1986).

The BAI asks respondents to rate how much they have been bothered by each of the 21 anxiety symptoms over the past week on a 4-point scale from 0 (*not at all*) to 3 (*severely—I could barely stand it*). The final score is the sum of the 21 items, ranging from 0 to 63. Normative values on the BAI have been reported recently (Gillis, Haaga, & Ford, 1995). Beck et al. (1988) reported the internal consistency of the BAI to be .92 (Cronbach's alpha) and the short-term (1 week) test–retest reliability to be .75. Fydrich, Dowdall, and Chambless (1992) also reported good internal consistency ($\alpha = .94$) and a test–retest reliability of .67 for the BAI in a sample of 40 outpatients.

Regarding convergent validity, Beck, Epstein, et al. (1988) reported that the BAI correlated higher with the HARS (.51) than with the HRSD (.25). The BAI also correlated with a subscale assessing the hypothesized cognitive content of anxiety disorders (Cognition Checklist; Beck, Brown, Steer, Eidelson, & Riskind, 1987) more than it did with a subscale assessing the cognitive content of depressive disorders (.51 vs. .22). Moreover, the BAI differentiated patients with an anxiety disorder from those with a depressive disorder, as based on the criteria from the third edition of the

DSM (*DSM–III*). This differentiation held up regardless of whether the group of patients with anxiety disorders were "pure" (no secondary depressive disorder), had a primary diagnosis of anxiety disorder (whether a secondary depressive disorder existed), or had an anxiety disorder whether there was a primary or secondary depressive disorder. In another validity study of the BAI, Steer, Ranieri, Beck, and Clark (1993) reported that the BAI correlated higher with the SCL-90-R Anxiety subscale (.81) than it did with the SCL-90-R Depression subscale (.62). Fydrich et al. (1992) further found that the BAI correlated significantly higher with diary anxiety ratings (.54) than with diary depression ratings (.38).

Few treatment studies have yet used the BAI. In our own pilot study of the efficacy of brief dynamic therapy with GAD (Crits-Christoph, Connolly, Azarian, Crits-Christoph, & Shappell, 1996), we found a within-conditions effect size (pre–post) of 1.99 for the BAI, indicating that the measure was highly sensitive to change. Pre–post effect sizes for patients with GAD treated with CT can be calculated from the data presented by Sanderson, Beck, and Keswani (1994). For patients with GAD who were diagnosed with a personality disorder, the effect size was 1.00; for those without a personality disorder diagnosis, the effect size was 1.63. For patients with GAD who were treated with high-frequency CT (16–20 sessions over 6 months), Durham et al. (1994) found a pre–post effect size of 0.90; for low-frequency CT (8–10 sessions over 6 months), the effect size was 0.97. Pre–post effect sizes for CT in the treatment of GAD were found by Butler, Fennell, Robson, and Gelder (1991) to be 1.3; CT versus a waiting-list effect size in this study was 0.85. Thus, the BAI appears to be highly sensitive to change, at least in the treatment of GAD.

Other Domains of Functioning

In any treatment study of anxiety disorders, it is of interest to assess the impact of treatment on the broader context of the patient's life beyond the specific anxiety disorder. It is difficult to make definitive recommendations about such measures because the specific domains are likely to be a function of the investigator's hypotheses or the theoretical basis of the treatment approach (i.e., psychodynamic therapy views change in interpersonal patterns or views of self as of central importance but behavior therapy does not). However, we concur with the summary report of the conference on measuring changes in patients following psychological and pharmacological interventions that important areas for a core battery would include, at the least, other related symptoms and impairment in social and occupational functioning.

The most common related symptoms of interest are depressive symptomatology. To assess these symptoms, we recommend the BDI (see Beck, Steer, & Garbin, 1988, for a summary of the psychometric properties of this widely used instrument) and the HRSD (Hamilton, 1960) as parallel instruments to our recommendations for the BAI and HARS.

To assess more general domains of life functioning, we recommend the Quality of Life Inventory (QOLI; Frisch, Cornell, Villanueva, & Retzlaff, 1992). The QOLI consists of 17 items relevant to overall life satisfaction, including items related to work, love relationship, friendships, self-regard, standard of living, recreation, community, home, and so on. Respondents rate each item in terms of its importance to overall happiness and satisfaction and in terms of their satisfaction with the area. The product of the satisfaction and importance ratings for each area of life are computed and then an overall score is calculated by averaging all weighted satisfaction ratings that have nonzero importance ratings. Test–retest reliability coefficients for the QOLI range from .80 to .91, and internal consistency coefficients range from .77 to .89, across three clinical and three nonclinical samples. In terms of validity, the QOLI has demonstrated significant positive correlations with seven related measures of well-being and significant negative correlations with measures of general psychopathology, but in all cases the QOLI was not redundant with these other measures. Further research is needed to evaluate the sensitivity of the QOLI to therapeutic change.

We also recommend the Inventory of Interpersonal Problems (IIP; Horowitz, Rosenberg, Baer, Ureño, & Villaseñor, 1988) to measure problems occurring in relationships. The IIP is a 127-item self-report measure that contains six subscales. Internal consistency (Cronbach's alpha) and test–retest reliabilities, respectively, of the subscales are as follows: Assertive (.93 and .80), Sociable (.93 and .80). Intimate (.88 and .87), Submissive (.85 and .86), Responsible (.86 and .84), and Controlling (.82 and .81). The total score of the IIP also has a high test–retest reliability (.98; Horowitz et al., 1988). Change in IIP scores for patients in brief dynamic therapy was found to correlate highly (.80) with a composite measure of outcome (Horowitz et al., 1988).

Two short forms of the IIP have been developed. Alden, Wiggins, and Pincus (1990) developed a set of circumplex scales for the IIP consisting of eight 8-item scales. The 8-item subscales revealed good internal consistency, with Cronbach's alpha coefficients ranging from .72 to .85. Soldz, Budman, Demby, and Merry (1995) developed a 32-item short circumplex form designed for use in settings in which brevity is important. The eight subscales of this version as well as the total score revealed good internal consistency, with alpha coefficients ranging from .69 to .89. The test–retest correlations for a generic outpatient sample across an 8-week interval ranged from .61 to .83 for the eight subscales and the total score. This version of the IIP also revealed treatment responsiveness comparable to the long form, with effect sizes of -0.57 for the total score and effect sizes ranging from -0.34 to -0.58 for the subscale scores for a sample of 71 patients treated in short-term group therapy.

RECOMMENDATIONS FOR GAD

Diagnostic Instrument

The most commonly used instruments for obtaining *DSM* Axis I diagnoses in anxiety disorder treatment studies are the Structured Clinical Interview for DSM-IV (SCID; First, Spitzer, Gibbon, & Williams, 1994) and the Anxiety Disorders Interview Schedule–Revised (ADIS-R; DiNardo & Barlow, 1988). Using *DSM–III* criteria, Riskind, Beck, Berchick, Brown, and Steer (1987) reported a .79 kappa coefficient between diagnosticians using an SCID and raters using the SCID from videotape on the diagnosis of GAD. Skre, Onstad, Torgersen, and Kringlen (1991) reported a generalized kappa coefficient of .95 for *DSM–III–R* GAD using diagnoses made by a diagnostician and two raters who listened to audiotaped SCID interviews. A kappa of .57 (test–retest) was found for a GAD diagnosis by

DiNardo, Moras, Barlow, Rapee, and Brown (1993) using the ADIS-R for the *DSM–III–R*.

The diagnostic criteria for GAD were changed somewhat in the *DSM–IV*. These changes included reducing somatic symptom criteria from 6 out of 18 to 3 out of 6. In addition, worry must be experienced as being difficult to control. At the time of this writing, to our knowledge, no reliability studies have yet been performed using a structured interview for *DSM–IV*. Therefore, recommendations for choice of diagnostic instrument will need to be responsive to the emerging data on the *DSM–IV*.

Central Feature of GAD: Worry

The Penn State Worry Questionnaire (PSWQ; Meyer, Miller, Metzger, & Borkovec, 1990) is our recommendation for the assessment of the central feature of GAD. The PSWQ is a 16-item self-report measure, with each item rated on a 1–5 scale, yielding a total score ranging from 16 to 80. Gillis et al. (1995) recently reported on normative values of the PSWQ. The psychometric characteristics of the PSWQ have been reviewed recently by Molina and Borkovec (1994). Those authors reported that the PSWQ has shown high internal consistency reliability (ranging from .86 to .95) and high test–retest reliability (ranging from .74 to .93) across a variety of studies. In terms of validity, within an unselected student sample, the PSWQ was found to be highly correlated (.64) with a question about the percentage of the day spent worrying (Meyer et al., 1990), although no relation between these measures was found in a clinical GAD sample (Brown, Antony, & Barlow, 1992). Davey (1993) reported that the PSWQ correlated highly (.59 to .67) with two content-based measures of normal (nonclinical) worry. The PSWQ was found to be highly related to trait anxiety (.64), state anxiety (.49), and emotionality (.58; Meyer et al., 1990).

The PSWQ also has been found to differentiate GAD patients from patients with other anxiety disorders (Brown et al., 1992; Molina & Borkovec, 1994). Meyer et al. (1990) also found that a student sample diagnosed as GAD using a questionnaire had significantly higher PSWQ scores than did a sample that met some, but not all, criteria for GAD, with the latter group having higher scores than a sample that met no criteria for GAD.

The PSWQ also has been shown to be sensitive to change over treatment for GAD in two studies. Borkovec and Costello (1993) found PSWQ within-conditions pre–post effect sizes of 1.86 and 2.75 for cognitive–behavioral therapy (CBT) and applied relaxation therapy, respectively. Comparing CBT with nondirective therapy yielded a 0.85 effect size, whereas applied relaxation versus nondirective therapy showed a 0.60 effect size on the PSWQ. Crits-Christoph et al. (1996) found a 0.95 pre–post effect size on the PSWQ for brief dynamic therapy of GAD.

Response, Remission, Recovery, Relapse, and Recurrence

Investigators need to present their results of treatment outcome studies not only in terms of change on specific measures but also in terms of percentages of patients who have achieved an adequate response. If the treatment or follow-up period extends over a period of time, it also is important to classify patients in terms of whether their symptoms have remitted, whether they are fully recovered, or whether they have experienced a relapse or recurrence of the disorder. To date, researchers have failed to establish consensus definitions for the constructs of response, remission, recovery, relapse, and recurrence for anxiety disorders. The conceptualization of these constructs discussed by Frank et al. (1991) with regard to depression can be used as a starting point for defining these terms in the case of anxiety disorders. In describing the course of major depression, Frank et al. (1991) defined remission as a period in which the patient improves to the point that he or she is asymptomatic. A remission that lasts for a defined period of time is defined as a recovery. A relapse is defined as a return of symptoms during the remission, whereas a recurrence is defined as a return of symptoms during the recovery. The authors did not define a response because they limited their discussion to constructs that represented the course of a disorder, regardless of a treatment intervention. We suggest defining response as a remission that occurs after a treatment intervention.

Frank et al. (1991) suggested the operationalization of specific criteria for these constructs based on acceptable measures of symptoms. Using these criteria applied to the diagnosis of GAD, we suggest the use of *DSM–IV* diagnostic criteria as outlined in the SCID to define these terms. Thus, a patient would be seen as fully symptomatic if he or she met Criteria A through F for this disorder more days than not over a 6-month period as defined in the *DSM–IV.*

Remission and recovery then can be defined by choosing time cut-offs. We suggest defining a remission as a period of 3–6 months in which the patient is asymptomatic and a recovery as a period of greater than 6 months in which the patient is symptom-free. Although these time periods are arbitrary, they can serve as a starting point for arriving at consensus definitions of these important constructs across research studies. It is important that a consensus be reached if researchers are to draw conclusions about treatment efficacy based on reviews of the research literature.

RECOMMENDATIONS FOR OCD

Diagnostic Instrument

We recommend the inclusion of the ADIS-R (DiNardo & Barlow, 1988), which demonstrates good test–retest reliability for the diagnosis of OCD ($\kappa = .80$; DiNardo et al., 1993). In addition, Brown, Moras, Zinbarg, and Barlow (1993) found that the ADIS-R adequately distinguished between the diagnosis of OCD and GAD in a sample of 41 patients.

The SCID also is recommended in treatment studies of OCD because it has the advantage over the ADIS-R of a more thorough assessment of non-anxiety-disorder diagnoses. Segal, Hersen, and Van Hasselt (1994) reviewed the literature on the reliability of the SCID. Although most of the investigations reviewed by them suggest that the SCID is a reliable diagnostic instrument, only one investigation specifically evaluated the reliability of the diagnosis of OCD (Skre et al., 1991). That investigation revealed marginal interjudge agreement for the diagnosis of OCD ($\kappa = .40$). In light of these findings, we suggest the inclusion of the SCID with multiple independent interviews to ensure interrater reliability. In addition, the *DSM–IV* criteria for OCD have been reorganized, such that the criteria that the symptoms are unrelated to another Axis I disorder and that the individual recognizes that the symptoms that are unreasonable are no longer subsumed under Criterion A but form individual criteria for the disorder. Therefore, recommendations for choice of diagnostic instrument will need to be responsive to the emerging data on the *DSM–IV.*

Assessment of Target Rituals and Obsessions

Target Ratings

Many treatment studies on OCD have included global ratings of the severity of obsessions, compulsions, fears, avoidance, and urges. A complete review of all studies using such ratings is beyond the scope of this chapter. Instead, we review a few treatment studies for the methods used to rate targets. Foa, Steketee, Turner, and Fischer (1980) had an independent assessor rate the severity of compulsions, obsessions, main fears, urges to perform rituals, and degree of avoidance on a scale from 0 to 8. In later investigations (Foa, Steketee, & Grayson, 1985; Foa, Steketee, Grayson, Turner, & Latimer, 1984), each of these scales was completed by both an assessor and the patient. Boersma, Den Hengst, Dekker, and Emmelkamp (1976) had an independent observer, the therapist, and the patient rate the patient's severity of anxiety and avoidance on a 5-point scale. Both Rachman et al. (1979) and Marks, Stern, Mawson, Cobb, and McDonald (1980) first asked patients to identify four main rituals for which he or she sought treatment. Both an assessor and the patient then rated the patient's discomfort with the ritual and the time spent on the ritual on an 8-point scale.

Although target ratings as described earlier are widely used in treatment studies of OCD, some limitations suggest the need for further research. First, many of these ratings consist of single-item ratings for which there is no reliability information. Although independent assessors are often used, little information is provided about the interrater reliability of such measures. Efforts also are needed to review the validity of single item ratings of targets. Finally, the methods for rating targets need to be standardized to make results across studies comparable. Once such standardization occurs, target ratings would be an important part of a core battery for treatment studies of OCD.

Behavioral Observations

Behavioral observations of patient rituals also are important with OCD. Marks et al. (1980) and Rachman et al. (1979) used a behavioral avoidance test in which the patient is asked to engage in five tasks that lead to the ritual behavior. The assessor rated the patient's degree of avoidance and discomfort on a 0–8 scale. Using a slightly different methodology, Foa et al. (1984) had patients confront their feared stimuli. An independent assessor then rated the patient's subjective anxiety on a scale from 0 to 1,000. As with ratings of targets, efforts are needed to evaluate the reliability and validity of these behavioral ratings, as well as to establish standard methods for implementing behavioral assessments across studies.

Assessment of OCD Symptoms

Three measures are recommended for the assessment of obsessive–compulsive symptoms. The Yale-Brown Obsessive-Compulsive Scale (Y-BOCS; Goodman, Price, Rasmussen, Mazure, Delgado, et al., 1989; Goodman, Price, Rasmussen, Mazure, Fleischmann, et al., 1989) and the Compulsive Activity Checklist (CAC; Philpott, 1975) are reliable and valid measures that can be used to assess symptoms from the perspective of an independent assessor or a clinician. The CAC also has a self-report version that can be used along with the Maudsley Obsessional-Compulsive Inventory (MOCI; Hodgson & Rachman 1977) to assess symptoms from the patient's perspective. The following provides a brief review of the reliability and validity of these measures for use with patients with OCD. A comprehensive review of measures used to assess obsessions and compulsions was provided by Taylor (1995).

The Y-BOCS

The Y-BOCS is a 10-item, clinician-rated scale designed to assess the severity of OCD symptoms regardless of the type or number of obsessions or compulsions present. Ten items representing the patient's time spent on obsessions, interference with functioning, subjective distress, the patient's active resistance, and the patient's control over symptoms are each rated on a 0–4 scale on the basis of a semistructured interview. The scale provides a total score and Severity of Obsessions and Severity of Compulsions subscale scores.

In the first study of the reliability of the Y-BOCS, Goodman, Price, Rasmussen, Mazure, Delgado, et al. (1989) pilot tested the Y-BOCS on a sample of 6 patients with OCD. Six judges were asked to rate the Y-BOCS for each patient from the videotaped interview. The results indicated good interrater reliability ($ICC = .80$, $p < .05$). In the second investigation, Goodman et al. evaluated 40 patients meeting the *DSM–III* criteria for OCD. Four raters independently rated the videotaped Y-BOCS interviews. The results indicated excellent interrater reliability, with *ICC*s ranging from .86 to .98. In addition, the total score internal consistency was good, with alpha coefficients ranging from .88 to .91 across the raters.

Goodman, Price, Rasmussen, Mazure, Fleischmann, et al. (1989) also have investigated the validity of the Y-BOCS. A total of 80 patients with OCD, drawn from various medication trials for OCD, were evaluated using the Y-BOCS. The Y-BOCS revealed good convergent validity with two measures of OCD symptoms, the Clinical Global Impression Scale–OCD adaptation (Guy, 1976) and the NIMH Global Obsessive Compulsive Scale (Insel et al., 1983; Murphy, Pickar, & Alterman, 1982), with correlations of .74 and .67, respectively. The Y-BOCS demonstrated only moderate convergent validity with the MOCI. The investigators explained this moderate relationship as being a result of the MOCI being biased toward fear of contamination symptoms. The results indicated that patients identified as contamination focused had significantly higher scores on the MOCI ($p < .001$), but not the Y-BOCS, when compared with non-contamination-focused patients with OCD. Thus, the Y-BOCS seems better suited for the assessment of OCD symptoms across a wide range of obsessions and compulsions.

The discriminant validity of the Y-BOCS is more questionable (Goodman, Price, Rasmussen, Mazure, Fleischmann, et al., 1989). Across the patients sampled, the Y-BOCS correlated moderately with the HRSD and the HARS, with correlations of .60 and .47, respectively. The authors concluded that the Y-BOCS is a valid measure of the severity of OCD symptoms but that it should not be used as a diagnostic measure, especially with patients experiencing concurrent depression. Finally, the Y-BOCS demonstrated good sensitivity to change in 42 patients treated with 6–8 weeks of fluvoxamine or placebo. The authors reported that the Y-BOCS decreased 20–25% in patients on active medication, yet revealed no change in patients given placebo.

A comprehensive review of studies evaluating the Y-BOCS was provided by Taylor (1995). As evident in the investigations reviewed earlier, Taylor concluded that the Y-BOCS has good interrater reliability, internal consistency, and adequate convergent validity but poor discriminant validity. Taylor further reviewed studies indicating that the Y-BOCS has good test–retest reliability and is successful at discriminating patients with OCD from control participants. The Y-BOCS has not been used widely to assess change in symptoms over the course of treatment. Further research is needed to evaluate the sensitivity of this measure to therapeutic change.

The CAC

The CAC was developed originally as a 62-item assessor-rated scale (Philpott, 1975). The items for the CAC are designed to assess the degree to which obsessive–compulsive symptoms interfere with daily activities. The instrument has since been modified to include fewer items that can be completed directly by the patient. Marks, Hallam, Connolly, and Philpott (1977) published a 39-item version that can be completed by either the patient or an independent assessor.

In an evaluation of the psychometric properties of the CAC, Freund, Steketee, and Foa (1987) evaluated 77 patients using a modified 38-item version of the CAC. All patients met the *DSM–III* criteria for OCD. For a subset of 55 patients, two independent assessors rated the CAC in separate interviews. The results indicated adequate interrater reliability ($r = .62$, $p < .001$). The CAC further demonstrated stability over a 5- to 60-day test–retest period ($r = .68$, $p = .001$; $N = 33$). A factor analysis revealed two predominant factors representing washing behavior and checking behavior. Both the subscale scores and the total score for the CAC demonstrated good internal consistency, with alpha coefficients ranging from .89 to .93.

Freund et al. (1987) also reported good convergent and discriminant validity for the subscale scores using the 38-item assessor-rated version of the CAC. Patients identified as predominantly washers by an independent therapist scored significantly higher on the Washing subscale, $t(53) = 5.43$, $p < .001$, whereas patients identified as checkers scored significantly higher on the Checking subscale, $t(49) = 4.79$, $p < .001$. The CAC total score also demonstrated significant but moderate correlations with assessor-rated global measures of obsessive–compulsive symptoms and functioning. Furthermore, the CAC Washing and Checking subscales correlated .44 and .55 with the corresponding subscale scores of the MOCI, and the CAC total score correlated moderately with the Fear Survey Schedule III (FSS-III). Finally, the CAC was not correlated with measures of anxious mood, depression, or neurotic symptomatology.

Cottraux, Bouvard, Defayolle, and Messy (1988) examined the validity and structure of the French version of the CAC. One hundred eighty participants, who had a *DSM–III* diagnosis of OCD, agoraphobia with panic, or social phobia, each completed a revised 37-item self-report version of the CAC; there were 55 control participants. Across the sample, the scale demonstrated good internal consistency ($\alpha = .94$), and across the control participants the scale revealed moderate test–retest reliability after 1 month, $r(52) = .62$).

The CAC also demonstrated adequate validity in this investigation. The total score for the scale significantly differentiated patients with OCD from the other diagnostic and control groups. The total score also demonstrated good convergent validity, correlating significantly with a scale evaluating the total time spent per day in rituals.

Steketee and Freund (1993) evaluated further the psychometric properties of the 38-item self-report version of the CAC using a sample of patients with *DSM–III–R*-diagnosed OCD, other patients with anxiety disorder, and nonpsychiatric participants. In the first study, 150 participants completed the 38-item self-report version of the CAC and the Marlowe-Crown Social Desirability Scale (Crowne & Marlowe, 1964). The CAC total score revealed good internal consistency ($\alpha = .95$) across the entire sample. The results also indicated that patients with OCD scored significantly higher on the total score than patients with anxiety disorder, and nonpsychiatric participants. Finally, a small correlation was found between the CAC total score and the measure of social desirability ($r = .19$, $p = .06$).

The CAC has demonstrated good sensitivity to change across various active treatment conditions. Rachman et al. (1979) reported within-treatments effect sizes ranging from 0.83 to 1.75 for 40 patients with OCD who were treated with either clomiprimine plus exposure or clomiprimine plus relaxation. In a follow-up investigation, Mawson, Marks, and Ramm (1982) reported large effect sizes (7.7 for self-report and 18.6 for assessor-rated CAC) for these same patients over a 2-year follow-up period. Foa et al. (1984) reported effect sizes ranging from 1.75 to 2.40 across 15 sessions of either exposure, response prevention, or a combination of exposure plus response prevention for 32 patients diagnosed with *DSM–III* OCD. Two smaller studies by Insel et al. (1983) and Perse, Greist, Jefferson, Rosenfeld, and Dar (1987) showed modest within-groups effect sizes. Insel et al. (1983) reported effect sizes of 0.14–0.38 for 13 patients treated with either clogyline or clormiprimine, whereas Perse et al. (1987) reported an effect size of 0.38 for 16 patients treated with fluvoxamine. Overall, these investigations suggest that the CAC is sensitive to treatment change.

In two investigations, the CAC has also differentiated the treatment gains of patients in active treatments and those assigned to a control condition. Rachman et al. (1979) reported between-groups effect sizes ranging from 0.44 (self-report) to 0.55 (assessor rated) for patients treated with clomiprimine plus exposure compared with patients treated with placebo plus exposure. Perse et al. (1987) reported a between-groups effect size of 0.38 for patients treated with fluvoxamine versus placebo. Although these effect sizes are modest, they suggest that the CAC is sensitive to differences between active treatments and control conditions.

The CAC appears to demonstrate adequate to good internal consistency, interrater reliability, and test–retest reliability. The CAC also demonstrates acceptable convergent validity, with moderate correlations between the CAC and other measures of obsessive–compulsive symptoms emerging across studies. Taylor (1995) suggested that the CAC demonstrates weak discriminant validity because it appears to correlate moderately with measures of non-OCD symptoms. However, both Freund et al. (1987) and Sternberger and Burns (1990a) found significant correlations between the CAC and other measures of OCD symptoms but no relationship between the CAC and measures of non-OCD symptomatology. Finally, the CAC appears to adequately discriminate patients with OCD from patients with other anxiety disorders and control groups, as well as differentiating patients with OCD who are primarily washers from those who are primarily checkers. This review of the literature includes many different versions of the CAC. As suggested by Taylor (1995), we suggest the inclusion of both the self-report and assessor-rated 38-item versions of the CAC because this version has been implemented most often and thus demonstrates the most evidence regarding reliability and validity.

The MOCI

The MOCI is a 30-item self-report measure designed to assess the presence or absence of obsessive–compulsive symptoms. Hodgson and Rachman (1977) designed the instrument by defining 30 items from a pool of 65 items that differentiated 50 obsessional patients from 50 nonobsessional neurotic patients. A principal-components analysis of 100 obsessional adults revealed four factors representing checking, cleaning, slowness, and doubting. All subscales revealed adequate internal consistency, with alpha coefficients ranging from .7 to .8.

Hodgson and Rachman (1977) also provided information about the validity of the Cleaning and Checking subscales. Namely, therapists' retrospective ratings of 42 patients' cleaning and checking behavior was associated with patients' subscale scores ($\gamma = .70$). In addition, the change in questionnaire total scores across behavioral treatment was moderately correlated with therapists' and patients' global ratings of improvement. A test–retest of the MOCI using 50 adult night-school students revealed a moderate association after a 1-month interval ($\tau = .80$). The authors concluded that the total obsessional score and the Cleaning and Checking subscale scores are reliable and valid measures of obsessional behavior. They suggested further research on the Slowness and Doubting subscales.

Sternberger and Burns (1990a) reported good internal consistency for the MOCI total score ($\alpha = .75$) and modest internal consistency for the Washing and Checking subscales (αs $= .54$ and .58, respectively) in a sample of 579 college students. The results also indicated adequate test–retest reliability ($r = .69$) over a 6- to 7-month interval for the MOCI. As with the CAC, the authors reported a valid pattern of correlations between the MOCI total score and the SCL-90-R subscale scores, with the highest correlation emerging between the MOCI total score and the SCL-90-R Obsessive-Compulsive subscale.

In a follow-up study, Sternberger and Burns (1990b) evaluated 11 participants with MOCI scores in the top 2% and 11 participants with scores in the 50th percentile 6–7 months after the original investigation. All participants were asked to complete an ADIS-R interview (DiNardo, O'Brien, Barlow, Waddell, & Blanchard, 1983) to evaluate the validity of the MOCI scores. The results indicated that those with OCD reported significantly more obsessions, $t(20) = 5.60$, $p < .001$, and compulsions, $t(20) = 2.17$, $p = .04$, than the comparison group in the ADIS interviews.

The MOCI has not been used widely as a measure of obsessive–compulsive symptoms in studies of treatment efficacy. However, two investigations suggest that the MOCI might be sensitive to therapeutic change and differences between active treatments and control groups. Perse et al. (1987) reported a within-treatments effect size of 0.44 for 20 patients treated with fluvoxamine. Foa et al. (1984) reported more impressive effect sizes that ranged from 1.96 to 2.78 for 32 patients treated with either exposure, response prevention, or exposure plus response prevention. Regarding active treatments versus control groups, Perse et al. reported a between-groups effect size of 0.5 for fluvoxamine versus placebo. Although further research is needed to evaluate the sensitivity of the MOCI, these results indicate that the MOCI is a sensitive measure.

In summary, the MOCI demonstrated moderate internal consistency for the total score and for the Checking and Cleaning subscale scores. These scales also demonstrated adequate test–retest reliability. However, as suggested consistently in this literature, the Slowness and Doubting subscales reveal poor psychometric properties and should be modified before inclusion in an outcome battery. The MOCI also demonstrated adequate convergent validity and seems to be best suited for assessing common types of obsessive–compulsive behavior, such as washing and checking.

Response, Remission, Recovery, Relapse, and Recurrence

As with our recommendation for GAD, we suggest the use of *DSM–IV* diagnostic criteria as outlined in the SCID to define these terms. Thus, a patient would be seen as fully symptomatic if he or she met Criteria A through E for OCD over a 4-week period as defined in the *DSM–IV*. A patient would be seen as clinically asymptomatic if he or she did not meet one of the five criteria or had not been symptomatic for at least 4 weeks. For OCD, we suggest defining a remission as a period of 4–8 weeks in which the patient is asymptomatic and a recovery as a period of greater than 8 weeks in which the patient is symptom-free.

RECOMMENDATIONS FOR SPECIFIC PHOBIA

Diagnostic Instrument

As reviewed by Segal, Hersen, and Van Hasselt (1994), few investigators have specifically evaluated the reliability of the Structured Clinical Interview for DSM-III-R (SCID-P) for the diagnosis of specific phobia (formerly known as simple phobia). One investigation by Skre et al. (1991), in which independent judges completed the SCID simultaneously from a single interview, indicated that the SCID yielded good reliability for the presence of specific phobia ($\kappa = .70$). Further research is needed to evaluate the reliability of the SCID-P in diagnosing specific phobia as defined in the *DSM–IV*.

DiNardo et al. (1993) presented evidence that the ADIS-R also has good reliability for the presence of specific phobia. In a test–retest evaluation of the ADIS-R, the investigators reported an interrater reliability (kappa) for the ADIS-R in the diagnosis of specific phobia of .82. On the basis of the current literature, we recommend the inclusion of either the SCID-P or the ADIS-R for all studies of specific phobia.

Assessment of Phobic Symptoms

Target Ratings

A review of the treatment studies for specific phobia indicate that many studies use target ratings of fear and avoidance in the assessment of treatment outcome. For example, Beckman, Vrana, May, Gustafson, and Smith (1990) rated patients on a scale ranging from 0 to 100 representing the patient's degree of fear, and Chambless (1990) used the 0–100 scale to rate the patient's degree of anxiety. Ost, Salkovskis, and Hellstrom (1991) had patients complete two 0–8 scales representing the degree of fear experienced and the degree of avoidance of the feared stimuli. In this latter investigation, independent assessors also rated the patient's severity of phobia on a scale ranging from 0 to 8. As in treatment studies of OCD, ratings of patients' fears and avoidance have the potential to be an important part of outcome batteries for studies of specific phobia, yet efforts are needed to develop reliable and valid standard methods for implementing target ratings.

Behavioral Assessments

A survey of the treatment literature on specific phobia indicates that many researchers used ratings made during behavioral tests. A few studies are described here to illustrate the types of behavioral tests used. Merluzzi, Taylor, Boltwood, and Gotestam (1991) implemented an exposure test in which patients were asked to perform 17 tasks. The time taken to perform each task was measured as an indication of the patient's level of avoidance. In a similar design, Ost et al. (1991) rated patients on a scale ranging from 0 to 12 representing the patient's success in approaching a feared stimuli. Chambless (1990) and Chambless and Woody (1990) used the behavioral avoidance test in which patients are rated on a scale ranging from 0 to 2 representing the degree of avoidance for each of three individually tailored situations. As with the target ratings described earlier, these behavioral assessments have potential for representing specific change in phobic symptoms. However, it is necessary that standard procedures be adopted across investigations to make study comparisons possible.

The FSS-III

The FSS-III was developed by Wolpe and Lang (1964) as a self-report measure for use with clinical populations. The items include anxiety stimuli that were encountered the most frequently in the clinical practice of behavior therapy. The items were originally defined across six broad domains, including animal stimuli, tissue damage or illness, death, classical phobic stimuli, social stimuli, noises, and miscellaneous. Patients are asked to complete a 5-point Likert scale for each item indicating the degree to which they are bothered by the item.

Arrindell (1980) evaluated the factor structure of the FSS-III based on a sample of 703 individuals with phobias. The author reported a five-factor solution representing social fears, agoraphobic fears, fears of injury, death, and illness, fears of sexual and aggressive scenes, and fears of harmless animals. Arrindell reported good internal consistency for the five subscale scores (αs = .79–.91) and for the FSS-III total score (α = .95). Two of the subscales of the FSS-III also demonstrated good convergent validity. The Agoraphobic Fears subscale demonstrated a high association with the agoraphobic dimension of the SCL-90 (r = .80, p < .0001), and the Social Fears subscale correlated highly with the Social Inadequacy Scale of the SCL-90 (r = .65, p < .0001).

Arrindell and Van Der Ende (1986) reevaluated the factor structure of the FSS-III using a sample of 191 heterogeneous psychiatric inpatients. The authors reported that the five-factor solution reported by Arrindell (1980) also represented the data from their sample. The reliability of the FSS-III also was consistent with the previous analyses by Arrindell, with alpha coefficients ranging from .81 to .92 for the subscales and an alpha of .96 for the total score.

The FSS-III has demonstrated good reliability in multiple investigations. There also is evidence of convergent validity with other fear measures. Further research is needed to fully evaluate the validity of the measure as well as the sensitivity of the FSS-III to change across treatment. The FSS-III is currently recommended for assessment of anxiety symptoms in studies of specific phobia.

Response, Remission, Recovery, Relapse, and Recurrence

In the case of specific phobia, the constructs of response, remission, recovery, relapse, and recurrence can be defined using the guidelines outlined by Frank et al. (1991), discussed earlier. An episode of a specific phobia can be said to occur when a patient experiences the criteria of the disorder as outlined in the *DSM–IV* for a period of at least 4 weeks. A remission then would be defined as a period in which the patient is asymptomatic for 4–8 weeks, whereas a recovery can be defined as an asymptomatic period lasting greater than 8 weeks. As described earlier, a relapse can be defined as a return to symptoms during the remission period, whereas a recurrence would be a return of symptoms during a recovery period.

CONCLUDING COMMENTS

One issue we have not discussed is the nature of follow-up outcome assessments. In terms of instruments, we recommend using the same instruments described earlier for follow-up assessments. Because a follow-up period is typically uncontrolled, we also suggest an assessment of the type and frequency of psychosocial and pharmacological treatments during the follow-up period, as well as an assessment of the medical conditions experienced during this period. These variables then can be used to understand the changes seen from posttherapy to follow-up. To standardize the timing of follow-up evaluations across research protocols, we suggest at a minimum that follow-up assessment be conducted at 1 and 2 years after intake. The reason that follow-up should be timed to intake, rather than termination of treatment, is that the influence of naturally occurring change over time is controlled. This is particularly important for the assessment of treatment dropouts and protocol violators (who should be evaluated at all follow-up assessment points), as well as to control the inevitable variations in time to completion of the protocol that occurs when treatment consists of a certain number of sessions.

As discussed earlier, the battery suggested here is broad and time-consuming because it is intended to be a comprehensive battery for use with anxiety disorders. It is assumed that researchers will choose from this battery assessments that meet the their own needs and values. In studies in which time allows, we recommend adding the Structured Clinical Interview for Axis II DSM-IV (SCID-II; First, Spitzer, Gibbon, Williams, & Benjamin, 1994) at intake evaluations. Although the addition of the SCID-II may expand the assessment time needed, we think that it is important to evaluate the presence of personality disorders as possible predictors of treatment outcome.

Although our recommended instruments are a reasonable starting point for a core battery for anxiety disorders, we reiterate the inherent problems in designing a core battery. This includes the issue of varying purposes of research projects described in the introduction. Another important issue briefly mentioned previously is the changing nature of the *DSM*. To the extent that the definition of some specific disorders has changed, instruments for assessing the new disorders have to be created, and old instruments need to be reevaluated, particularly in terms of their ability to discriminate certain anxiety disorders from other disorders. Because many instruments are relatively new, data on sensitivity to change from psychosocial and pharmacotherapy treatments need to be further evaluated. All of these limitations of the core battery concept suggest that any core battery should be reassessed on a regular basis. On the one hand, such a process is necessary so that new developments (new *DSM* definitions, new instruments) can be properly taken into account. On the other hand, frequent revision of a core battery would, to some extent, defeat one of the purposes of such a battery: to compare results across accumulating studies in the literature. This dilemma, however, is inherent to the early stage of research on psychiatric disorders and treatments for such disorders.

REFERENCES

Agency for Health Care Policy and Research, U.S. Public Health Service. (1993). *Clinical practice guideline number 5—Depression in primary care: Vol. 2. Treatment of major depression.* Rockville, MD: U.S. Public Health Service.

Alden, L. E., Wiggins, J. S., & Pincus, A. L. (1990). Construction of circumplex scales for the Inventory of Interpersonal Problems. *Journal of Personality Assessment, 55*, 521–536.

American Psychiatric Association. (1994). *Diagnostic and statistical manual of mental disorders* (4th ed.). Washington, DC: Author.

Arrindell, W. A. (1980). Dimensional structure and psychopathology correlates of the Fear Survey Schedule (FSS-III) in phobic population: A factorial definition of agoraphobia. *Behavior Research and Therapy, 18*, 229–242.

Arrindell, W. A., & Van Der Ende, J. (1986). Further evidence for cross-sample invariance of phobic factors: Psychiatric inpatient ratings of the Fear Survey Schedule—III. *Behavior Research and Therapy, 24*, 289–297.

Barlow, D. H., Rapee, R. M., & Brown, T. A. (1992). Behavioral treatment of generalized anxiety disorder. *Behavior Therapy, 23*, 551–570.

Beck, A. T., Brown, G., Steer, R. A., Eidelson, J. I., & Riskind, J. H. (1987). Differentiating anxiety from depression: A test of the cognitive content-specificity hypothesis. *Journal of Abnormal Psychology, 96*, 179–183.

Beck, A. T., Epstein, N., Brown, G., & Steer, R. A. (1988). An inventory for measuring clinical anxiety: Psychometric properties. *Journal of Consulting and Clinical Psychology, 56*, 893–897.

Beck, A. T., & Steer, R. A. (1991). Relationship between the Beck Anxiety Inventory and the Hamilton Anxiety Rating Scale with anxious outpatients. *Journal of Anxiety Disorders, 5*, 213–223.

Beck, A. T., Steer, R. A., & Garbin, M. G. (1988). Psychometric properties of the Beck Depression Inventory: Twenty-five years of evaluation. *Clinical Psychology Review, 8*, 77–100.

Beckman, J. C., Vrana, S. R., May, J. G., Gustafson, D. J., & Smith, G. R. (1990). Emotional processing and fear measurement synchrony indicators of treatment outcome in fear of flying. *Journal of Behavior Therapy and Experimental Psychiatry, 21*, 153–162.

Boersma, K., Den Hengst, S., Dekker, J., & Emmelkamp, P. M. G. (1976). Exposure and response prevention in the natural environment: A comparison with obsessive-compulsive patients. *Behavior Research and Therapy, 14*, 19–24.

Borkovec, T. D., & Costello, E. (1993). Efficacy of applied relaxation and cognitive–behavior therapy in the treatment of generalized anxiety disorder. *Journal of Consulting and Clinical Psychology, 61*, 611–619.

Brown, T. A., Antony, M. M., & Barlow, D. H. (1992). Psychometric properties of the Penn State Worry Questionnaire in a clinical anxiety disorders sample. *Behaviour Research and Therapy, 30*, 33–37.

Brown, T. A., Moras, K., Zinbarg, R. E., & Barlow, D. H. (1993). Diagnostic and symptom distinguishability of generalized anxiety disorder and obsessive-compulsive disorder. *Behavior Therapy, 24,* 227–240.

Bruss, G. S., Gruenberg, A. M., Goldstein, R. D., & Barber, J. (1994). The Hamilton Anxiety Rating Scale Interview Guide: Joint interview and test-retest methods for inter-rater reliability. *Psychiatry Research, 53,* 191–202.

Butler, G., Fennell, M., Robson, P., & Gelder, M. (1991). Comparison of behavior therapy and cognitive–behavior therapy in the treatment of generalized anxiety disorder. *Journal of Consulting and Clinical Psychology, 59,* 167–175.

Chambless, D. L. (1990). Spacing of exposure sessions in treatment of agoraphobia and simple phobia. *Behavior Therapy, 21,* 217–229.

Chambless, D. L., & Woody, S. R., (1990). Is agoraphobia harder to treat? A comparison of agoraphobics' and simple phobics' response to treatment. *Behavior Research and Therapy, 28,* 305–312.

Clark, L. A. (1989). The anxiety and depressive disorders: Descriptive psychopathology and differential diagnosis. In P. C. Kendall & D. Watson (Eds.), *Anxiety and depression: Distinctive and overlapping features* (pp. 83–129). New York: Academic Press.

Cottraux, J., Bouvard, M., Defayolle, M., & Messy, P. (1988). Validity and factorial structure study of the Compulsive Activity Checklist. *Behavior Therapy, 19,* 45–53.

Crits-Christoph, P., Connolly, M. B., Azarian, K., Crits-Christoph, K., & Shappell, S. (1996). An open trial of brief supportive-expressive psychotherapy in the treatment of generalized anxiety disorder. *Psychotherapy, 33,* 418–430.

Crowne, D., & Marlowe, D. (1964). *The approval motive.* New York: Wiley.

Davey, G. C. L. (1993). A comparison of three worry questionnaires. *Behaviour Research and Therapy, 31,* 51–56.

DiNardo, P. A., & Barlow, D. H. (1988). *Anxiety Disorders Interview Schedule—Revised (ADIS-R).* Albany: Phobia and Anxiety Disorders Clinic, State University of New York.

DiNardo, P. A., Moras, K., Barlow, D. H., Rapee, R. M., & Brown, T. A. (1993). Reliability of DSM-III-R anxiety disorder categories using the Anxiety Disorders Interview Schedule-Revised (ADIS-R). *Archives of General Psychiatry, 50,* 251–256.

DiNardo, P. A., O'Brien, G. T., Barlow, D. H., Waddell, M. T., & Blanchard, E. B. (1983). Reliability of DSM-III anxiety disorder categories using a new structured interview. *Archives of General Psychiatry, 40,* 1070–1074.

Dobson, K. S. (1985). The relationship between anxiety and depression. *Clinical Psychology Review, 5,* 307–324.

Dobson, K. S. (1989). A meta-analysis of the efficacy of cognitive therapy for depression. *Journal of Consulting and Clinical Psychology, 57,* 414–419.

Durham, R. C., Murphy, T., Allan, T., Richard, K., Treliving, L. R., & Fenton, G. W. (1994). Cognitive therapy, analytic psychotherapy, and anxiety management training for generalized anxiety disorder. *British Journal of Psychiatry, 165,* 315–323.

First, M. D., Spitzer, R. L., Gibbon, M., & Williams, J. B. W. (1994). *Structured Clinical Interview for Axis I DSM-IV disorders: Patient Edition (SCID-I/P, Version 2.0).* Biometrics Research Department, New York State Psychiatric Institute.

First, M. D., Spitzer, R. L., Gibbon, M., Williams, J. B. W., & Benjamin, L. (1994). *Structured Clinical Interview for DSM-IV Axis II personality disorders (SCID-II, Version 2.0).* Biometrics Research Department, New York State Psychiatric Institute.

Foa, E., Steketee, G., & Grayson, J. B. (1985). Imaginal and in vivo exposure: A comparison with obsessional-compulsive checkers. *Behavior Therapy, 16,* 292–302.

Foa, E., Steketee, G., Grayson, J. B., Turner, R. M., & Latimer, P. R. (1984). Deliberate exposure and blocking of obsessive-compulsive rituals: Immediate and long term effects. *Behavior Therapy, 15,* 450–472.

Foa, E. B., Steketee, G., Turner, R. M., & Fischer, S. C. (1980). Effects of imaginal exposure to feared disasters in obsessive-compulsive checkers. *Behavior Research and Therapy, 18,* 449–455.

Frank, E., Prien, R. F., Jarrett, R. B., Keller, M. B., Kupfer, D. J., Lavori, P. W., Rush, A. J., & Weissman, M. M. (1991). Conceptualization and rationale for consensus definitions of terms in major depressive disorder. *Archives of General Psychiatry, 48,* 851–855.

Freund, B., Steketee, G. S., & Foa, E. B. (1987). Compulsive Activity Checklist (CAC): Psychometric analysis with obsessive-compulsive disorder. *Behavioral Assessment, 9,* 67–79.

Frisch, M. B., Cornell, J., Villanueva, M., & Retzlaff, P. J. (1992). Clinical validation of the Quality of Life Inventory: A measure of life satisfaction for use in treatment planning and outcome assessment. *Psychological Assessment, 4,* 92–101.

Fydrich, T., Dowdall, D., & Chambless, D. L. (1992). Reliability and validity of the Beck Anxiety Inventory. *Journal of Anxiety Disorders, 6,* 55–61.

Gillis, M., Haaga, D. A. F., & Ford, G. T. (1995). Normative values for the Beck Anxiety Inventory, Fear Questionnaire, Penn State Worry Questionnaire, and Social Phobia and Anxiety Inventory. *Psychological Assessment, 7,* 450–455.

Goodman, W. K., Price, L. H., Rasmussen, S. A., Mazure, C., Delgado, P., Heninger, G. R., & Charney, D. S. (1989). The Yale-Brown Obsessive Compulsive Scale II: Validity. *Archives of General Psychiatry, 46,* 1012–1016.

Goodman, W. K., Price, L. H., Rasmussen, S. A., Mazure, C., Fleischmann, R. L., Hill, C. L., Heninger, G. R., & Charney, D. S. (1989). The Yale-Brown Obsessive Compulsive Scale I: Development, use, and reliability. *Archives of General Psychiatry, 46,* 1006–1011.

Guy, W. (1976). *ECDEU assessment manual for psychopharmacology* (DHEW Publication No. 76-338). Washington, DC: U.S. Department of Health, Education, and Welfare.

Hamilton, M. (1959). The assessment of anxiety states by rating. *British Journal of Medical Psychology, 32,* 50–55.

Hamilton, M. (1960). A rating scale for depression. *Journal of Neurological and Neurosurgical Psychiatry, 23,* 56–62.

Hamilton, M. (1969). Diagnosis and rating of anxiety. *British Journal of Psychiatry Special Publication No. 3,* 76–79.

Hodgson, R. J., & Rachman, S. (1977). Obsessional-compulsive complaints. *Behaviour Research and Therapy, 15,* 389–395.

Horowitz, L. M., Rosenberg, S. E., Baer, B. A., Ureño, G., & Villaseñor, V. S. (1988). Inventory of Interpersonal Problems: Psychometric properties and clinical applications. *Journal of Consulting and Clinical Psychology, 56,* 885–892.

Insel, T. R., Murphy, D. L., Cohen, R. M., Alterman, I., Kilts, C., & Linnoila, M. (1983). Obsessive–compulsive disorder: A double-blind trial of clomiprimine and clorgyline. *Archives of General Psychiatry, 40,* 605–612.

Maier, W., Buller, R., Philipp, M., & Heuser, I. (1988). The Hamilton Anxiety Scale: Reliability, validity and sensitivity to change in anxiety and depressive disorders. *Journal of Affective Disorders, 14,* 61–68.

Marks, I. M., Hallam, R. S., Connolly, J., & Philpott, R. (1977). *Nursing in behavioral psychotherapy.* London: Royal College of Nursing.

Marks, I. M., Stern, R. S., Mawson, D., Cobb, J., & McDonald, R. (1980). Clomiprimine and exposure for obsessive-compulsive rituals. *British Journal of Psychiatry, 136,* 1–25.

Mawson, D., Marks, I. M., & Ramm, L. (1982). Clomiprimine and exposure for chronic obsessive-compulsive rituals: Two year follow-up and further findings. *British Journal of Psychiatry, 140,* 11–18.

Merluzzi, T. V., Taylor, C. B., Boltwood, M., & Gotestam, K. G. (1991). Opioid antagonist impedes exposure. *Journal of Consulting and Clinical Psychology, 59,* 425–430.

Meyer, T. J., Miller, M. L., Metzger, R. L., & Borkovec, T. D. (1990). Development and validation of the Penn State Worry Questionnaire. *Behaviour Research and Therapy, 28,* 487–495.

Mintz, J., Mintz, L. I., Arruda, M. J., & Hwang, S. S. (1992). Treatments of depression and the functional capacity to work. *Archives of General Psychiatry, 49,* 761–768.

Molina, S., & Borkovec, T. D. (1994). The Penn State Worry Questionnaire: Psychometric properties and associated characteristics. In G. C. L. Davey & F. Tallis (Eds.), *Worrying: Perspectives on theory, assessment, and treatment* (pp. 249–290). New York: Wiley.

Moras, K., DiNardo, P. A., & Barlow, D. H. (1992). Distinguishing anxiety and depression: Reexamination of the reconstructed Hamilton scales. *Psychological Assessment, 4,* 224–227.

Murphy, D. L., Pickar, D., & Alterman, I. S. (1982). Methods for the quantitative assessment of depressive and manic behavior. In E. I. Burdock, A. Sudilovsky, & E. Gershon (Eds.), *The behavior of psychiatric patients* (pp. 355–392). New York: Marcel Dekker.

Ost, L. G., Salkovskis, P. M., & Hellstrom, K. (1991). One-session therapist-directed exposure vs. self-exposure in the treatment of spider phobia. *Behavior Therapy, 22,* 407–422.

Perse, T. L., Greist, J. H., Jefferson, J. W., Rosenfeld, R., & Dar, R. (1987). Fluvoxamine treatment of obsessive-compulsive disorder. *American Journal of Psychiatry, 144,* 1543–1548.

Philpott, R. (1975). Recent advances in the behavioral assessment of obsessional illness: Difficulties common to these and other measures. *Scottish Medical Journal, 20,* 33–40.

Power, K. G., Simpson, R. J., Swanson, B. A., & Wallace, L. A. (1990). A controlled comparison of cognitive-behavior therapy, diazepam, and placebo, alone and in combination, for the treatment of generalized anxiety disorder. *Journal of Anxiety Disorders, 4,* 267–292.

Rachman, S., Cobb, J., Grey, S., MacDonald, G. B., Mawson, D., Sartory, G., & Stern, R. (1979). The behavioural treatment of obsessional-compulsive disorders, with and without clomiprimine. *Behaviour Research and Therapy, 17,* 467–478.

Riskind, J. H., Beck, A. T., Berchick, R. J., Brown, G., & Steer, R. A. (1987). Reliability of DSM-III diagnoses for major depression and generalized anxiety disorder using the structured clinical interview for DSM-III. *Archives of General Psychiatry, 44,* 817–820.

Riskind, J. H., Beck, A. T., Brown, G., & Steer, R. A. (1987). Taking the measure of anxiety and depression validity of the reconstructed Hamilton Scales. *Journal of Nervous and Mental Disease, 175,* 474–479.

Sanderson, W. C., Beck, A. T., & Keswani, L. (1994). Cognitive therapy for generalized anxiety disorder: Significance of comorbid personality disorders. *Journal of Cognitive Psychotherapy, 8,* 13–18.

Segal, D. L., Hersen, M., & Van Hasselt, V. (1994). Reliability of the Structured Clinical Interview for DSM-III-R: An evaluation review. *Comprehensive Psychiatry, 35,* 316–327.

Skre, I., Onstad, S., Torgersen, S., & Kringlen, E. (1991). High interrater reliability for the Structured Clinical Interview for DSM-III-R Axis I (SCID-I). *Acta Psychiatrica Scandinavica, 84,* 167–173.

Smith, M. L., & Glass, G. V. (1977). Meta-analysis of psychotherapy outcome studies. *American Psychologist, 32,* 752–760.

Soldz, S., Budman, S., Demby, A., & Merry, J. (1995). A short form of the Inventory of Interpersonal Problems circumplex scales. *Assessment, 2,* 53–63.

Spielberger, C., Gorsuch, A., & Lushene, R. (1970). *The State-Trait Anxiety Inventory.* Palo Alto, CA: Consulting Psychologists Press.

Steer, R. A., Ranieri, W. F., Beck, A. T., & Clark, D. A. (1993). Further evidence for the validity of the Beck Anxiety Inventory with psychiatric outpatients. *Journal of Anxiety Disorders, 7,* 195–205.

Steketee, G., & Freund, B. (1993). Compulsive Activity Checklist (CAC): Further psychometric analyses and revision. *Behavioral Psychotherapy, 21,* 13–25.

Sternberger, L. G., & Burns, G. L. (1990a). Compulsive Activity Checklist and the Maudsley Obsessional-Compulsive Inventory: Psychometric properties of two measures of obsessive-compulsive disorder. *Behavior Therapy, 21,* 117–127.

Sternberger, L. G., & Burns, G. L. (1990b). Maudsley Obsessional-Compulsive Inventory: Obsessions and compulsions in a nonclinical sample. *Behavioural Research and Therapy, 28,* 337–340.

Strupp, H. H., & Hadley, S. W. (1977). A tripartite model of mental health and therapeutic outcomes. *American Psychologist, 32,* 187–196.

CRITS-CHRISTOPH AND CONNOLLY

Tanaka-Matsumi, J., & Kameoka, V. A. (1986). Reliabilities and concurrent validities of popular self-report measures of depression, anxiety, and social desirability. *Journal of Consulting and Clinical Psychology, 54,* 328–333.

Taylor, S. (1995). Assessment of obsessions and compulsions: Reliability, validity, and sensitivity to treatment effects. *Clinical Psychology Review, 15,* 261–296.

Wolpe, J., & Lang, P. J. (1964). A fear survey schedule for use in behaviour therapy. *Behavioural Research and Therapy, 2,* 27–30.

PART FOUR

Core Batteries for Assessment of Mood Disorders

8

Outcome Measures of Depression

Monica Ramirez Basco, Steven R. Krebaum,
and A. John Rush

S everal major objectives are addressed by measurement of the clinical
features of depression. The most common objective is assessment of
the somatic, affective, cognitive, and behavioral features of the disorder.
These features are assessed before and during the acute, continuation, and
maintenance phases of treatment to evaluate treatment efficacy. Evaluation
of other noncriterion symptoms that accompany depressive symptomatology (e.g., anxiety, psychosis) also may be relevant to assessing the
outcome of treatment. In addition, the evaluation of the quality of life
of individuals with depression, including their social, interpersonal, and
occupational functioning, provides an essential perspective in evaluating
treatment outcome. The personal and economic costs (e.g., side effects,
time away from work, family problems) and benefits (e.g., symptom relief,
enhanced psychosocial functioning, relapse prevention) provide for cost–
benefit evaluation of treatment.

This chapter was supported in part by a Mental Health Clinical Research Center grant from the National
Institute of Mental Health (MH-41115) to the Department of Psychiatry, University of Texas Southwestern
Medical Center, Dallas, Texas.

The major treatment objectives for depression are outlined in the Depression Guideline Panel's report (1993). In acute phase treatment, remission of symptoms and restoration of psychosocial function are the primary goals. In the continuation phase, prevention of relapse is the key objective. These two phases of treatment often are followed by a maintenance phase aimed at prevention of a recurrence (a new episode) of depression. Patient evaluation, whether structured or unstructured, is necessary for the practitioner to determine whether the treatment has accomplished these goals. That is, measurement provides clinically relevant information that may affect both strategic and tactical decisions in treatment planning and implementation. Symptom and psychosocial functioning measurements can establish the efficacy of treatment in both clinical practice and outcome research.

Another objective of measurement in research is to identify prescriptive and prognostic predictors. Prescriptive predictors inform clinicians about which treatment among many is preferred for a particular patient. For example, should the patient receive an antidepressant medication or psychotherapy or, in another instance, one type of medication as opposed to another? Prognostic predictors provide a gauge of the likelihood that a given individual will respond to a particular treatment. Assessment of prescriptive and prognostic predictors is particularly useful if conducted before the initiation of treatment for depression. For example, assessment also may establish clinical subtypes of depression (e.g., endogenous, melancholic, atypical) or overall severity or chronicity that may affect treatment selection.

The processes involved in treatment also can become the foci of measurement (e.g., the degree to which patients follow treatment recommendations, attend appointments, bond with the therapist, change attitudes, develop new relationships, etc.). The processes measured depend on the clinical or research objectives being addressed.

Finally, administrators, third-party payers, and policymakers may wish to know the economic and personal costs of depressive illness and their treatments (e.g., side effects, inconvenience) as well as the benefits of treatment. These measurements include both direct and indirect costs and benefits realized by the treatment (e.g., cost offsets). For example, health care utilization may be reduced and individuals may be able to return to work after remediation of their illness.

WHAT TO MEASURE

Although the rationale for evaluation of treatment outcome is straightforward, when and how to measure these elements is less obvious. How often should the benefits and costs associated with treatment outcome be assessed? Which outcome measures are most informative? Clinical research historically has had the luxury of a multiplicity of measures and perspectives to gauge the efficacy of a treatment. These include self-report measures, clinician rating scales, reports by significant others, and ratings by independent evaluators who do not know the type of treatment received by patients. These complex measurement strategies are used because there is evidence that outcome results can differ depending on the perspective of the assessor (see Elkin, Pilkonis, Docherty, & Sotsky, 1988).

In clinical practice, one can use patient self-report measures, clinician rating scales, or both to simplify the process. In psychopharmacological trials, clinician ratings have been found to be slightly more sensitive to change in patient status than self-report measures (Depression Guideline Panel, 1993). These measurement scales often include both criterion signs and symptoms and associated signs and symptoms of depression. For example, in an attempt to be inclusive of associated and criterion symptoms, the Hamilton Rating Scale for Depression (HRSD; M. Hamilton, 1960, 1967) has grown over the years from 17 items (in the original) to 28–32 items in various modifications. A simpler approach is to identify the criterion symptoms of the syndrome (e.g., major depression) and evaluate only these (e.g., nine for major depression) to establish whether individuals do or do not meet criteria for caseness at various points in time in the course of treatment. The disadvantage is that documenting merely the presence or absence of meeting all criteria for a disorder, such as major depression, may lead clinicians to overlook subsyndromal symptom levels that are associated with a poorer long-term prognosis (Depression Guideline Panel, 1993).

The measurement of psychosocial functioning is more complex. The expected level of functioning may depend on the age, general medical fitness, and lifestyles of each individual (e.g., adolescent, adult, or geriatric patients; unemployed people; students; homemakers; or those fully employed outside the home). Psychosocial functioning can be gauged with simple questions about interpersonal, social, occupational, familial, and child-rearing functions, or it can be assessed more completely using a variety of psychosocial measures. Psychosocial improvement appears to follow symptom improvement in most cases of major depression (Mintz, Mintz, Arruda, & Hwang, 1992).

The economic and personal costs of treatment such as stress, pain, suffering, and inconvenience are important factors in program and policy planning. One way to assess indirect treatment costs is through a variety of rating scales that detail various treatment side effects. In this case, the overall inconvenience or impact of the side effects, rather than the specific types, are of primary interest. In addition, the economic cost of treatment both in its delivery and in terms of cost offsets must be measured in some way. For example, a comparison of previous and subsequent health care service utilization may suggest an improvement in health status if fewer services are needed after successful treatment of the depression.

In addition, the longer term complications associated with an illness and the associated treatment can be assessed. For example, there is evidence that when depression is present along with a general medical condition, the prognosis of both the general medical and psychiatric disorder is worse than when the depression is uncomplicated. We know of no well-established methods for measuring such costs. An assessment of both the costs and benefits of an intervention can contribute to the overall strategic decision of whether to embark on the treatment.

REQUIREMENTS OF MEASURES

As suggested earlier, the range of possible assessment measures and strategies for depression is broad. In this chapter we focus on three groups: measures of "caseness" (i.e., meeting or no longer meeting criteria for major depression), clinician-administered rating scales of depressive symptoms, and self-report measures of depressive symptoms. A literature search on the measurement of depression produced references for 6 diagnostic measures, 27 clinician rating scales, and 90 self-report measures.

Several criteria were applied to select a subset of measures in the three categories that we review. The first criterion was that the measure specifically assess symptoms of depression. This eliminated measures of anxiety, psychosis, mania, and other symptoms often associated with depression. Although clinical trials often include a broader range of measures, in clinical practice the outcome of treatment of depression generally would focus on the primary symptoms of that disorder.

The second criterion was that psychometric data suggest adequate reliability and validity. We discuss the appropriateness of the subject types sampled in the development and evaluation studies of each measure as well as the appropriateness of the validity and reliability assessments used.

The third criterion was that the measure be tested in populations with mood disorders. This eliminated measures used exclusively with dysphoric college students or other nonpatient populations. Measures were not excluded if psychometric development included use in nonpatient populations and with depressed individuals. Our goal was to identify measures that would be appropriate for assessment of individuals with depressive symptoms.

The fourth criterion was that the measure be sensitive to change in symptomatology after treatment for depression. A measure whose score did not change when there were other indicators that symptoms had improved would not be useful for clinical purposes. This would include trait-like measures such as the Attributional Style Questionnaire (Peterson et al., 1982) that demonstrate patterns common in individuals with depression that may not change when remission of symptoms occurs.

TARGET POPULATIONS

Clinician ratings and self-report measures of depressive symptoms generally are developed for use with individuals of varying ages, socioeconomic backgrounds, diagnostic subtypes, and both genders. That is, they are considered multiuse measures. Some caution is warranted, however, when using depression rating scales with individuals on whom normative or psychometric data were not collected. For example, a measure developed and normed on inpatients may not be appropriate for outpatients. Similarly, measures developed and normed on one ethnic or demographic group may not be appropriate for others. In addition, the method of administration intended for a measure should not be altered. For example, it may not be appropriate to administer a clinician rating scale by simply reading the response options to a patient and asking him or her to select the one that best describes his or her symptoms. Likewise, measures intended for in-person clinical interviews may not be appropriate for administration by phone.

SURVEY OF MEASURES

The following overview of measures for depression provides brief descriptions of each measure and summarizes the available psychometric data. The measures fall into the following categories: structured diagnostic interviews, clinician rating scales, global illness ratings, and self-report instruments.

STRUCTURED DIAGNOSTIC INTERVIEWS

The Structured Clinical Interview for DSM-IV – Clinician Version

The original research version of the Structured Clinical Interview for DSM–IV (SCID-IV) is a structured clinical interview that assesses symptoms of major psychiatric disorders as defined by the fourth edition of the *Diagnostic and Statistical Manual of Mental Disorders* (*DSM–IV*; American Psychiatric Association, 1994). Each module (e.g., mood disorders, anxiety disorders, psychotic disorders, substance abuse) of the SCID-IV assesses essential symptoms of each disorder. If the patient interviewed reports the essential symptoms, the remainder of symptoms are assessed. If essential or primary symptoms are not present, the evaluator skips the remainder of the questions and goes to the next disorder or module. Instructions are provided that guide the evaluator through the interview. *DSM–IV* criteria are included next to the prompting questions to assess that symptoms, and a place for indicating the presence or absence of the symptom is provided. Decision cues are provided to help clinicians summarize the information obtained before proceeding to the next disorder. The SCID-IV allows for assessment of both current and past psychiatric episodes or disorders.

The Structured Clinical Interview for DSM–IV–Clinician Version (SCID-CV; First, Spitzer, Gibbon, & Williams, 1995) is a modified version of the parent research SCID that was designed for ease in administration in clinical settings. The SCID-CV consists of a reusable administration booklet that contains the diagnostic criteria and prompting questions and a separate scoring sheet to record patient responses and to summarize diagnostic data. Full assessment of less commonly diagnosed disorders has been replaced with screening questions for these disorders (e.g., fear of going out alone in agoraphobia). A positive response prompts clinicians to use the *DSM–IV* to more fully assess symptoms of these disorders. The SCID-CV reduces administration time and complexity of the research version of the SCID and still allows for a thorough evaluation of psychiatric disorders.

The Schedule for Affective Disorders and Schizophrenia–Change Version

The Schedule for Affective Disorders and Schizophrenia (SADS; J. Endicott & Spitzer, 1978) was constructed to provide a structured format to assess the current and lifetime presence of Research Diagnostic Criteria (RDC; Spitzer, Endicott, & Robins, 1978) diagnoses. The Change Version of the SADS (SADS-C) is used to assess an individual's symptoms during the past week. The SADS-C consists of 45 items, of which 20 describe various aspects of depression. Most items are rated on 1- to 6-point scales with brief descriptions at anchor points. Higher scores indicate greater symptom severity. The authors reported that it is possible to derive an HRSD score from the SADS-C scores. The SADS-C is appropriate for use by experienced clinicians who complete extensive training. The authors recommended that the raters be psychiatrists, clinical psychologists, or psychiatric social workers. Interrater reliability assessment in a sample of 150 inpatients ranged from .82 to .99 for summary scales, and more than 90% of individual scale items correlated .60 or higher (J. Endicott & Spitzer, 1978). The intraclass correlations of scale measures of depression ranged from .95 to .97. Test–retest reliabilities of the depression scales ranged from .78 to .88 (J. Endicott & Spitzer, 1978). The concurrent validity of the SADS-C is seen in the correlation of .92 between extracted HRSD and regular HRSD scores (J. Endicott, Cohen, Nee, Fleiss, & Sarantakos, 1981). The SADS-C frequently has been used as an outcome measure and has been found to be sensitive to change in treatment studies, even among outpatients.

The Diagnostic Interview Schedule

The Diagnostic Interview Schedule (DIS; Robins, Helzer, Croughan, & Ratcliff, 1981) is a structured diagnostic interview that can be used by lay interviewers or clinicians to make diagnoses by the third edition of the *DSM* (*DSM–III;* American Psychiatric Association, 1980), the Feighner criteria (Feighner et al., 1972), and RDC. Diagnoses are made on a lifetime basis, and the status of symptoms is specified as either current or in remission based on the date that the most recent symptoms were experienced. The interview contains 263 items. All symptom questions and follow-up probes are specified. Each symptom is rated on a 5-point scale (1 = *not present,* 5 = *present*). Training to administer the measure is required, with recommendation that lay interviewers receive at least 1 week of intensive training followed by an additional week of supervised practice. The DIS is appropriate for use in the general population, clinical, and research settings, where the goal is to make specific psychiatric diagnoses. Unlike the SCID-IV (First et al., 1995), it does not include optional skipouts or omissions. Each question is read verbatim to the respondent, who responds either yes or no. The authors reported that it requires approximately 45– 75 min to administer. Computer programs are available to generate diagnoses, and it includes all Feighner, all RDC (but only primary and secondary subtyping of major depressive disorder), and 32 of 150 *DSM–III* disorder groupings. The programs can provide all diagnoses regardless of hierarchical rules, total symptom counts, the number of criteria met for each diagnostic group, and whether the diagnosis is positive. When lay interviewers' ratings were compared with psychiatrists' ratings using the DIS (and psychiatrists could ask further questions they deemed necessary), the agreement on the diagnosis of depression was approximately 80% for all three sets of diagnostic criteria (Robins et al., 1981). The authors reported that sensitivity (i.e., the percentage of psychiatrists' diagnoses confirmed by a lay interviewer) ranged from 41% to 100%, whereas specificity (i.e., the percentage of persons not found to have a diagnosis confirmed by a lay interviewer) ranged from 84% to 100%. The mean kappa was .69, the mean sensitivity was 75%, and the mean specificity was 94% (Robins, Helzer, Ratcliff, & Seyfried, 1982). Criterion validity also was seen in comparing DIS interviews with medical charts in 167 patients. Sixty-three percent of all chart diagnoses were identified by the psychiatrists' DIS, and the lay interviewers identified an average of 55% of these diagnoses (Robins et al., 1982). The authors commented that current disorders and severe disorders are diagnosed more accurately than disorders in remission or borderline conditions.

CLINICIAN RATING SCALES

There are many clinician rating scales that assess the severity of depressive symptomatology. Ratings generally are based on observations made by the clinician and by reports from the patient, family members, and hospital-based staff if the patient is hospitalized. The following is a summary of clinician rating scales for depression. Although they all attempt to assess the most common symptoms of depression, such as changes in mood, cognition, behavior, and physical symptoms, they vary greatly in structure, format, and item coverage. Table 1 provides a summary of these measures, including the number of items and criterion symptoms covered, usefulness in demonstrating clinical change, and psychometric strength.

Table 1

Summary of Clinician Rating Scales of the Severity of Depressive Symptoms

Measure	No. of items	No. of DSM–IV criteria for MDD (out of 9)	Shows change in treatment	Training required?	Good psycho-metrics?	Comments
Association for Methodology and Documentation in Psychiatry III	140	7	Yes	Yes	++	Usually used for diagnosing, especially in Europe
Brief Psychiatric Rating Scale	18	1	Yes	Yes	++	Broad psychopathology scale; not specific to depression used in antipsychotic trials.
Clinical Global Impression Scale	1	N/A	Yes	No	±	Standard in medication trials
Clinical Interview for Depression	36	8	Yes	Yes	+	Not often an outcome measure
Comprehensive Psychopathological Rating Scale	67	7	Unknown	Yes	±	Not often an outcome measure
Cronholm–Ottosson Depression Scale	8	4	Yes	Yes	+	Occasionally used in medical trials
Diagnostic Interview Schedule	263	9	Yes	Yes	+	An epidemiologic tool sometimes used in trials
Hamilton Rating Scale for Depression	17–28	7	Yes	Yes	+	Gold standard in United States; has 15 versions; 17 items missing some criterion symptoms; some items are confounded

Measure						Comments
Inventory of Depressive Symptomatology for Clinicians	28	9	Yes	Yes	+	Includes all criterion symptoms as well as melancholic and atypical features; self-report and clinician versions match
Montgomery-Asberg Depression Rating Scale	10	6	Yes	Yes	+	Often an outcome measure in medication trials
Newcastle Scales	35	5	Yes	Yes	+	Divides respondents into endogenous and neurotic subtypes
Raskin Three-Area Depression Scale	3	N/A	Yes	No	±	Often used in medication trials
Schedule for Affective Disorders and Schizophrenia–Change Version	45	9	Yes	Yes	+	Similar to Lifetime diagnostic version
Depression Status Inventory	20	8	Unknown	No	+	Some items same as Self-Report Version

NOTE: *DSM–IV* = fourth edition of the *Diagnostic and Statistical Manual of Mental Disorders*; MDD = major depressive disorder; N/A = not applicable; ± = fair; + = good; ++ = very good.

Association for Methodology and Documentation
in Psychiatry III

The Association for Methodology and Documentation in Psychiatry III (AMDP-III; Angst & Woggon, 1983) was developed to document psychopathological and somatic symptoms in Germany, Switzerland, and Austria. This clinician rating consists of five parts, each of which is printed on a separate piece of paper, and covers demographic data, life events, historical data, psychopathological symptoms, and somatic signs. The AMDP-III is appropriate for assessing a broad range of symptoms, including the assessment of depression, mania, schizophrenia, psychosis, and side effects of medications. One hundred psychopathological symptoms and 40 somatic signs are rated. Each sign and symptom is assessed during an unstructured interview across four dimensions: (a) accessibility (i.e., is the necessary information available); (b) certainty (i.e., the reliability of the information); (c) presence of symptoms and signs; and (d) severity of symptoms and signs (i.e., mild, moderate, or severe). Symptoms that cannot be ascertained or are not certain are rated as "not ascertained." Each sign and symptom is rated over a defined period (e.g., 24 hr), and ratings combine both subjective (reported by patient) and objective (noted by doctor, family member, etc.) information. Training is required to administer the measure, and the use of a manual is vital in documenting symptoms on the AMDP-III sheets. Scoring rules are not available. Nine primary factors have been found: paranoid hallucinating, depressive, psychoorganic, manic, hostile, autonomic, apathetic, obsessive–compulsive, and neurological (Baumann, Pietzcker, & Woggon, 1983). These were identified through factor analysis, with the exception of neurological, which was based on clinical considerations. Interrater reliability coefficients were higher for the syndromes than for individual symptoms, but 43 symptoms showed good interrater reliability ($\kappa \geq .60$, $\geq 80\%$ agreement), whereas 25 showed moderate interrater reliability (κs $= .40–.59$, $70–78\%$ agreement; Kuny et al., 1983). The authors reported that the content validity of the measure was good given the broad range of symptoms covered. The measure is sensitive to changes in symptoms and shows results similar to the HRSD concerning changes in depressive symptoms (Angst, Dittrich, &

Woggon, 1979). The AMDP-III has been used primarily in Europe and assesses only seven of the *DSM–IV* criterion symptoms of depression.

The Clinical Interview for Depression

The Clinical Interview for Depression (Paykel, 1985) is a 36-item rating scale for use by a trained rater in conjunction with a semistructured interview. Items are rated on a 7-point scale, and each anchor point includes descriptions of one or all of the following: severity, frequency, and quality. The 7-point scale ranges from 1 *(absent)* to 7 *(extremely severe)*. An exception, depressive delusions, is rated on a 4-point scale. Higher scores indicate greater symptom severity. No cutoff scores or other interpretative guidelines are provided. Specified prompting questions are provided for each item, but they may be modified. Further probing at the interviewer's discretion is required to make specified ratings. Most items are rated on the patient's retrospective account of the past week, but a few items, such as suicidal ideation, are rated as the maximum severity shown in the past week. Some items are rated based on observations of certain behavior in the interview. Administration time is 30–45 min. A short form is available for repeated administrations. Interrater reliability of simultaneous independent ratings of psychiatrists and nonpsychiatrists revealed mean correlations of .81 and .82, respectively (Chipman & Paykel, 1974; Paykel & Griffith, 1983). The scale has impressive levels of reliability. For example, agreement within 1 point on each 7-point scale was found in 95% of psychiatrist ratings and 97% of nonpsychiatrist ratings. The measure has two subscales, Anxiety and Depression, that were developed on an a priori basis. The validity of the Clinical Interview for Depression is supported by its sensitivity to change in patients with antidepressant treatment (Haskell, DiMascio, & Prusoff, 1975). Concurrent validity can be seen in the correlation of Depression total scores with other measures of depression such as the HRSD (rs = .53–.70), Raskin Three-Area Depression Scale (rs = .54–.73), the Brief Psychiatric Rating Scale (BPRS; rs = .34–.59), and Clinical Global Impression (rs = .62–.71; Paykel, Parker, Penrose, & Rassaby, 1979; Rowan, Paykel, & Parker, 1982). The Clinical Interview for Depression has been used in treatment studies in the United States and Britain.

The Comprehensive Psychopathological Rating Scale

The Comprehensive Psychopathological Rating Scale (CPRS; Asberg, Montgomery, Perris, Schalling, & Sedvall, 1978) is a 67-item rating scale that assesses a broad range of psychiatric symptomatology from a semi-structured clinical interview. Symptoms include mood changes, anxiety, physical symptoms, cognitive functioning, psychotic symptoms, and ob-servable behavior. Clinicians rate each symptom on a 0–3 scale, with higher numbers suggesting greater severity of symptoms. Ratings are based on both patient interview and observation. Interrater reliability assessment in a sample of 49 patients ranged from .33 to .99 (Asberg et al., 1978). The concurrent validity of the CPRS was evaluated by comparing the total score and two items tapping sad mood with the Cronholm-Ottosson De-pression Rating Scale in 20 depressed inpatients. Correlation with total CPRS score was .77, with the two items for sad mood correlating .63 and .74. This suggested that the CPRS has some degree of concurrent validity. However, the psychometric strength of the full measure remains some-what questionable. It includes only seven criterion symptoms of depres-sion. There is no information available about its sensitivity to clinical change.

The Cronholm-Ottosson Depression Scale

The Cronholm-Ottosson Depression Scale (Cronholm & Ottosson, 1960) is a clinician rating scale of depressive symptoms that was originally de-signed to be sensitive to changes with antidepressant medication or elec-troconvulsive therapy (ECT). The eight items are each rated on a Likert scale from 0 to 6, with higher scores indicating greater symptom severity. Item content includes depressed mood, anxiety, depressive thoughts, sui-cidal tendencies, sleep disturbance, intellectual retardation, emotional in-difference, and motor retardation. Scores range from 0 to 48. The authors did not report suggested cutoff scores for interpretation. However, a re-duction in pretreatment scores of 50% or more equaled global clinical scores of moderate-to-excellent improvement (Bech, 1991). The measure had interrater reliability correlations of .86 to .97 (Bech, 1991). Cronholm, Schalling, and Asberg (1974) found that total scores correlated .63 with the

Beck Depression Inventory (BDI) and .87 with scores on a nurse rating scale, suggesting it has a reasonable level of concurrent validity. Factor analysis revealed one general dimension of severity of depressive states. The authors asserted that this scale is a purer measure of depression than the HRSD for use in antidepressant treatment studies because the HRSD includes items that might be side effects of antidepressants. However, this scale does not include all of the criterion items for the diagnosis of a major depressive episode.

The HRSD

The HRSD (M. Hamilton, 1960, 1967) is a clinician rating scale designed to assess the severity of depression in individuals who have been diagnosed already. It is likely the most commonly cited outcome measure in depression literature. The HRSD has been used in 17-, 21-, 24-, and 28-item versions, but the 17-item is the most commonly used. Each of the 17 items is rated by a clinician on either a 3- or a 5-point scale, with equal weighting of intensity and frequency of each symptom. The total score is derived by summing the item scores. Scores greater than 24 indicate severe depression (inpatients), whereas scores less than 17 suggest mild symptoms (outpatients) and scores less than 7 indicate an absence of depression. The HRSD has an interrater reliability correlation of $r = .90$ (M. Hamilton, 1960). Knesevich, Biggs, Clayton, and Ziegler (1977) found HRSD change scores to be correlated .68 with global change scores. There are little data on the internal consistency of the measure, but Schwab, Bialow, and Holzer (1967) found that individual items correlated with whole scores .45 to .78. Numerous studies have shown significant differences in the HRSD scores of normal controls and depressed persons, thus supporting its discriminant validity. The measure has a reasonable level of concurrent validity as it has been found to correlate approximately .60 with self-report measures (Rehm, 1981) and .98 or better with global clinical ratings (e.g., Knesevich et al., 1977). The 17-item HRSD does not include all of the criterion symptoms for the diagnosis of a major depressive episode (e.g., weight gain, over eating, over sleeping) it has some items confounded (e.g., pain complaints with fatigue or irritability and anxiety) and it differentially weights some items over others (e.g., 0–3 vs. 0–5 scored items). Despite these weaknesses, the HRSD remains the gold standard in the field for the assessment of depression.

The Inventory of Depressive Symptomatology for Clinicians

The Inventory of Depressive Symptomatology for Clinicians (IDS-C; Rush et al., 1986) was designed to measure specific signs and symptoms of depression in both inpatients and outpatients. This 28-item questionnaire was developed as both a self-report measure (IDS-SR) and a clinician rating scale (IDS-C). Each item is rated on a 0–3 scale, with higher scores representing greater severity of symptoms. Twenty-six of the 28 items contribute to a final score. The total score ranges from 0 to 78. The IDS-C includes all criterion items for a major depressive episode, as well as endogenous symptoms and most atypical symptoms. (A 30-item revised version contains all atypical symptoms.)

Interrater reliability for the IDS-C was .96 for the 30-item version (Rush, Gullion, Basco, Jarrett, & Trivedi, 1996). These values differ significantly and support the construct validity of the measure. The internal consistency of the IDS-C was high, with a Cronbach's alpha rating of .88 in the original test sample (Rush et al., 1986). In a larger sample of depressed patients ($N = 434$), Cronbach alphas were .67 for both the 28-item and 30-item IDS-C (Rush et al., 1996). When adding remitted depressed and normal control participants to create a larger sample ($N = 552$), the Cronbach alpha was .92 for the 28-item version of the IDS-C and .94 for the 30-item version of the IDS-C (Rush et al., 1996). The IDS-C correlated .61 with the BDI and .92 with the HRSD. A factor analysis on a sample of 353 patients completing the IDS-C showed three factors: Cognitive/Mood Symptoms, Anxiety/Arousal Symptoms, and Vegetative Symptoms (Rush et al., 1996). The IDS was designed to improve on the sensitivity of the HRSD.

The Montgomery-Asberg Depression Rating Scale

The Montgomery-Asberg Depression Rating Scale (MADRS; Montgomery & Asberg, 1979) is a clinician rating of depression that was designed to be sensitive to treatment effects. The 10-items, which were empirically selected from patient samples, are rated on a 0- to 6-point scale. Anchors are provided for every other point (0 indicates an absence of the symptom, and 6 represents its most extreme form). Scores range from 0 to 60, with higher scores suggesting greater symptom severity. The authors did not report suggested cutoff scores or other interpretation of scores.

The MADRS had interrater reliability correlations of .87–.97 for independent ratings of conjoint interviews. The MADRS has been shown to be highly correlated with the HRSD (rs = .89 to .98) and with global clinical ratings of severity (r = .89). It also has been shown to be highly sensitive in its evaluation of response to treatment. The authors reported a point–biserial correlation between response category and change scores of .70, which was superior to that of the HRSD. Only six of the nine criterion symptoms of depression are included in the MADRS.

The Newcastle Scales

The Newcastle scales (Carney, Roth, & Garside, 1965) were developed from factor analysis of 35 items that the authors felt would discriminate depressive subtypes. The Newcastle Diagnostic Scale (N-1) is a clinician rating scale that is made up of 10 items that were most highly correlated with diagnosis. On the diagnostic scale, 8 items are positively weighted and 2 items are negatively weighted, with scores ranging from −2 to 12. Different items have different weights, and only items that are present are scored; others are ignored. The scale is intended to provide a dichotomous classification of patients, with scores of 6 or higher indicating endogenous depression and less than 6 neurotic. The 10 items best predicting ECT response were selected to constitute the Newcastle ECT Prediction Scale. This scale is constructed similarly to the N-1, with 5 items having positive weights and 5 items having negative weights. Thus, scores range from −12 to 11. A total score of 1 or higher would be considered to predict good ECT outcome, whereas a score of less than 1 would suggest poor outcome. The authors reported that interrater reliability obtained on 11 patients resulted in concordance on diagnosis or good or bad outcome in every case. However, they did not report values of the correspondence between scores. Concurrent validity was reported between clinician diagnosis and scale diagnosis, with 89 or 97 patients being accurately classified. However, the same clinician made both ratings, which might have artificially inflated this value. Discriminant validity was supported in terms of ECT response, in which individuals classified as endogenous did significantly better than those classified as neurotic ($p < .001$) after 3 months of ECT (Carney & Sheffield, 1972). However, this finding was not replicated by Abou-Saleh and Coppen (1983), who found that patients with Newcastle scores in the middle range responded better to either ECT or medication than did those in the higher and lower ranges. This suggests that the utility of using the Newcastle scales to predict outcome is questionable. Carney and Sheffield (1972) found that there was no correlation between HRSD scores and endogenous or neurotic classification by the Newcastle ECT Prediction Scale.

The Depression Status Inventory

The Depression Status Inventory (DSI; Zung, 1972) is a clinician rating scale that was developed as an adjunct to the Self-Rating Depression Scale (SRDS; Zung, 1965). It consists of 20 items that cover the same content as the SRDS. Ratings are made on a 4-point Likert scale ranging from 1 (*none*) to 4 (*severe*). Scores range from 25 to 100, with higher scores indicating greater severity of symptoms. Scoring involves summing the raw scores and converting them to DSI z scores. Although no clear cutoff scores were recommended, a mean DSI z score of 61 was found in depressed samples. This was significantly higher than z scores obtained for other diagnostic groups, thus supporting its discriminant validity. Internal consistency estimates using an odd–even split-half reliability were reported to be .81. The DSI had an interrater reliability correlation of .91 using simultaneous raters (Zung, 1985). The DSI has been shown to be correlated .87 with the SRDS. It includes eight of the criterion symptoms of depression. Its sensitivity to clinical change has not been established.

SELF-REPORT MEASURES

Table 2 provides a summary of the depression self-report measures described next. There are many similarities among these measures, including symptom coverage. However, they appear to vary in acceptability to the clinical and research communities as well as in convention of usage. The more popular measures (e.g., the BDI, the SRDS, the SCL-90) tend to correlate highly with one another and with clinician rating scales. This finding often is cited by their developers as evidence of content validity.

The BDI

Perhaps the most widely used measure of depressive symptoms is the BDI (Beck, Ward, Mendelson, Mock, & Erbaugh, 1961). This 21-item self-report measure was designed to assess the intensity of depression in psychiatric patients and to detect depression in normal populations. Items are rated on a 0- to 3-point scale, with higher numbers indicating greater symptom severity. The total score ranges from 0 to 63. Cutoff scores vary with the population used: general depression screening greater than 13, medical screening greater than 10, and research uses greater than 21. Depression scores less than 4 are considered mild or low, 14–20 is considered moderate, and 21 or higher is considered severe. Beck, Steer, and Garbin (1988) summarized 25 years of research on the BDI. They found that across studies of various subject populations, the average internal consistency rating of the BDI was .87 (range = .48–.86). There is considerable evidence for the content, concurrent, discriminant, and construct validity of the BDI. Correlations between clinical ratings and the BDI range from .55 to .96 across studies, and the mean correlation for a psychiatric population is .72. It has been found to correlate .61 –.87 with the HRSD across studies and is highly correlated with self-report measures of depressive symptoms (Beck et al., 1988).

The BDI contains more items tapping depressive cognitions than are found in most depression measures. This has made it an ideal outcome measure for studies of cognitive therapy. It is used commonly in both clinical and research settings because it is easy to administer and score. Patients can complete the measure at home or in the waiting room, add up the score, and report the value to their therapist or psychiatrist. Because of its bias toward changes in depressive cognitions, it may not indicate clinical change for interventions that target other symptomatology.

Table 2

Summary of Self-Report Measures of Depressive Symptoms

Measure	No. of items	No. of DSM–IV criteria for MDD (out of 9)	Shows change in treatment	Good Psycho-metrics?	Comments
Beck Depression Inventory	21	8	Yes	+++	Widely used; cognitive symptoms prominent
Carroll Rating Scale for Depression	52	7	Yes	++	Self-report version of 17-item DRS; HRSD w/similar limitations (does not cover overeating, oversleeping, or weight gain)
Center for Epidemiological Studies Depression Scale	20	7	Yes	+	Usually used in population surveys
Depression Adjective Checklist	32–34	1	Unknown	±	Adjectives checked; very state dependent
Depression Self-Rating Scale	16	7	Unknown	+	Not commonly used in medication efficacy trials
General Health Questionnaire	28	6	Unknown	+	Screen used in general medical patients; "fake good" is noted
Hopkins Symptom Checklist	90 (or 35)	7	Yes	+	Includes 9 symptom clusters
Inventory to Diagnose Depression	22	9	Yes	+	Includes all endogenous and melancholic symptoms; often used to screen

Scale					
Inventory of Depressive Symptomatology	28	Yes	9	+	Includes all criterion symptoms as well as melancholic and atypical features; self-report and clinician versions match
Irritability-Depression-Anxiety Scale	18	Yes	6	+	Not often used as an outcome measure
Leeds Scales for the Self-Assessment of Anxiety and Depression	22	Unknown	6	±	Screens for depressive and anxiety disorders
Levine-Pilowsky Depression Questionnaire	57	Yes	6	±	Some predictive validity of ECT response
Minnesota Multiphasic Personality Inventory Depression Scale	60	Yes	6	±	Norms available; no distinct time frame used
Plutchik-van Pragg Self-Report Depression Scale	34	Unknown	9	+	Screen designed to tap *DSM–III* criteria
Profile of Mood States	65	Yes	5	+	Adjective list; state dependent; rarely used as an outcome measure
Symptom Rating Test	30–56	Yes	8	±	Anxiety and depressive symptoms
Vietnamese Depression Scale	15	Unknown	4	±	Good sensitivity and specificity for screening depressed Vietnamese
Visual Analogue Mood Scale	1	No	0	–	Simple; correlates 0.7 with HRSD
Wakefield Self-Assessment Depression Inventory	12	Unknown	8	±	Screen replaced by Leeds
Self-Rating Depression Scale	20	Unknown	8	±	Matches clinician rating scale version

NOTE: *DSM–IV* = fourth edition of the *Diagnostic and Statistical Manual of Mental Disorders*; *DSM–III* = third edition of the *DSM*; DRS = Depression Self-Rating Scale; HRSD = Hamilton Rating Scale for Depression; w/ = with; ECT = electroconvulsive therapy; – = weak; ± = fair; + = good; ++ = very good; +++ = excellent.

The Carroll Rating Scale for Depression

The Carroll Rating Scale for Depression (CRSD; Feinberg & Carroll, 1985) is a 52-item self-report measure of symptom severity. Each item is rated as being absent or present, with 1 point contributing toward a total score for each symptom present. A cutoff score of 10 is recommended when using the CRSD as a screening instrument for depression. Split-half reliabilities on 3,725 CRSD ratings were .87 (odd- vs. even-numbered items) and .97 (first vs. second half). The concurrent validity of the CRSD is supported by its correlation with the HRSD (rs = .66–.85; Carroll, Fielding, & Blashki, 1973; Feinberg, Carroll, Smouse, & Rawson, 1981; Nasr, Altman, Rodin, Jobe, & Burg, 1984).

The advantage of the CRSD is its similarity in item coverage to the HRSD. This would allow for better comparability of clinician ratings using the HRSD and the CRSD. Unfortunately, the CRSD has the same item limitations as the HRSD, overlooking reverse vegetative symptoms.

The Center for Epidemiological Studies Depression Scale

The Center for Epidemiological Studies Depression Scale (CES-D; Markush & Favero, 1973; Radloff, 1977) is a 20-item self-report measure that surveys depressive symptomatology. Each item is rated on a 0 *(rarely)* to 3 *(most or all of the time)* scale for severity of symptoms over the previous week. It is not intended to be a symptom severity or diagnostic measure but a survey or screen of depressive symptoms in psychiatric, general medical, and community populations. Total scores range from 0 to 60. A cutoff score of 16 or higher has been proposed, which results in a false-positive rate of 6.1% and a false-negative rate of 36.4% (Myers & Weissman, 1980). The test–retest reliability is moderate for up to 8 weeks posttest (r = .57) and lower at longer retest intervals (r = .32 at 1 year; Radloff, 1977). Concurrent validity was demonstrated in correlations with other measures of depression such as the SRDS (r = .90) and the BDI (r = .81) in a sample of recovered depressed patients (Weissman, Prusoff, & Newberry, 1975). Content validity is supported in that the CES-D items were selected from depression scales that tap the major components of depressive symptomatology. Depressed patients scored higher than other psychiatric groups on the CES-D, acutely depressed patients scored higher than remitted depressed individuals, and it differentiated between psychiatric patients and community control individuals, providing other evidence of its validity (Weissman, Sholomskas, Pottenger, Prusoff, & Locke, 1977).

Because this measure was intended for use in surveys, it may not be as useful as a treatment outcome measure as other scales developed for this purpose. For future surveys, the CES-D will require updating to match the changes in the *DSM–IV*.

The Depression Adjective Checklist

The Depression Adjective Checklist (DACL; Lubin, 1965) is a 32- to 34-item self-report checklist that assesses transient depressive mood and feelings. The DACL consists of 22 positive and either 10 (Versions A–D) or 12 (Versions E–G) negative adjectives that are checked by respondents if they apply to how the person is feeling today or in general. A score is derived by deducting the total number of negative adjectives endorsed by the individual from the number of positive adjectives endorsed. Seven versions of the DACL have been developed and may be used interchangeably. Normative data are available for students, senior citizens, adolescent delinquents, depressed and nondepressed psychiatric patients, and a community sample of 3,000 adults (Levitt & Lubin, 1975). Split-half reliability correlations ranged from .82 to .93 in normal control individuals and from .86 to .93 in psychiatric patients. One-week test–retest reliability correlations ranged from .19 to .24, suggesting that the DACL taps transient symptomatology. The internal consistency reliability indexes for male respondents were .79–.88 and .85–.90 for female respondents (Lubin, 1965). Although all correlations were significant at the .05 level, the correlations between the DACL and other depression symptom severity measures were meager (rs = .39–.47 with the MMPI Depression scale and .4–.66 with BDI). This suggests minimal concurrent validity.

The DACL may be too state dependent to be used as a measure of treatment outcome. Although it is not uncommon for symptoms of depression to vary from day to day, the test–retest correlations reported for the DACL suggest too much instability in measurement to accurately reflect changes depressive symptomatology with treatment. For research on transient mood states in nonpatient populations, the DACL may be more sensitive to variations in mood than depression self-report measures that assess criterion symptoms.

The Depression Self-Rating Scale

The Depression Self-Rating Scale (D-S; von Zerssen, Strian, & Schwarz, 1974) is a self-rating scale for the evaluation of depressive mood. The measure was initially developed in German but has been translated into English, French, Italian, Japanese, Russian, and Spanish. This 16-item Likert scale was developed for use in medical settings and has two parallel forms, the D-S and D-S'. Items are rated on a 0- to 3-point scale ranging from *not true* to *completely true*. A scoring key is required because *not true* may be assigned either 0 or 3 points depending on the direction of the scoring. The total scores range from 0 to 48, with higher scores indicating greater symptom severity. The mean scores for the D-S were 24.1 for depressed inpatients, 19.2 for other psychiatric inpatients, and 6.3 for the general population. These differences are significant, supporting the construct and discriminant validity of the measure. Scores from 0 to 10 are considered "normal." There was a high correlation between the two forms, with correlations ranging from .76 to .91 across populations (von Zerssen, 1985). Split-half reliability estimates of the measure, upgraded by Spearman-Brown, ranged from .80 to .91. Among medical patients, total scores on the D-S correlated .91 with the HRSD before treatment and .89 after treatment (von Zerssen et al., 1974). This supports the concurrent validity of the measure.

The D-S has not been fully tested as a treatment outcome measure in clinical trials. Therefore, information about its utility as a measure of change after treatment of depression is unavailable.

The General Health Questionnaire

The General Health Questionnaire (GHQ; Goldberg, 1978) is a 28-item self-report measure of current somatic symptoms, anxiety, insomnia, social dysfunction, and severe depression. Each item is rated on a 3-point Likert-type scale, with higher scores suggesting greater symptomatology. A 30- and a 60-item version of the GHQ are available. The GHQ was intended to detect psychiatric illness in primary care or general medical out-patients. Cutoff scores are 11 of 12 for the 60-item version, 4 of 5 for the 30-item version, and 5 for the 28-item version (Vieweg & Hedlund, 1983). Factor analysis on the 60-item GHQ resulted in the following factors: De-pression, Sleep Disturbance, Somatic/General Illness, Social Dysfunction, and Anxiety. The split-half reliabilities in a sample of 853 psychiatric out-patients were .78–.95, with higher correlations for the 60-item scale. Test–retest reliabilities for 26 neurology patients over a 5- to 7-day period were .85 using the 30-item GHQ and .51–.90 in a 6-month retest interval with varying groups of psychiatric outpatients. The concurrent validity of the GHQ is supported by its concurrence with standard psychiatric interviews (rs = .70–.83), Profile of Mood States (POMS; r = .90), BDI (r = .72), and Beck Hopelessness Scale (r = .69; Vieweg & Hedlund, 1985). The criterion-related validity of the GHQ when compared with diagnoses made by the SADS and the Present State Examination showed sensitivity of up to 88% and specificity up to 93% across studies (see the review by Vieweg & Hedlund, 1983).

The GHQ makes a unique contribution to the assessment of depres-sion in medical populations. Although it does not assess all criterion symp-toms of depression, it does appear to assess symptoms that may be more indicative of depression concurrent with a general medical condition.

The Hopkins Symptom Checklist

The Hopkins Symptom Checklist-90 (HSCL-90; Derogatis, Lipman, & Covi, 1973) is a 90-item self-report symptom scale that covers a broad range of symptoms, including depressive and anxiety symptoms. Re-spondents read a list of complaints or problems and rate the extent they were bothered or distressed by them in the past week. Each item is rated on a 5-point Likert scale (1 = *not at all,* and 5 = *extremely*). Factor analy-sis of the HSCL-90 on 300 nonpsychotic outpatients with symptoms of depression and anxiety revealed eight significant factors: Somatization, Phobic-Anxiety, Retarded Depression, Agitated Depression, Obsessive-Compulsive, Interpersonal Sensitivity, Anger-Hostility, and Psychoticism (Derogatis, Lipman, Rickels, Uhlenhuth, & Covi, 1974). This is an im-provement over the five primary symptom dimensions of the 58-item

HSCL: Somatization, Obsessive-Compulsive, Interpersonal Sensitivity, Depression, and Anxiety. Internal consistency of these five dimensions revealed alpha coefficients ranging from .84 to .87. Test–retest reliability over 1 week for the five dimensions ranged from .75 to .85 (Derogatis et al., 1974). When clinician pairs rated individuals using the HSCL, with one questioning and one observing, intraclass correlations ranged from .64 to .80 over the five factors. The depression cluster and depression factors of the HSCL-90 have demonstrated good internal consistency and test–retest reliability ($rs = .82-.90$). Concurrent validity of the depression dimension can be seen in significant correlations with the MMPI Content Depression scale ($r = .75$) and Cluster Depression scale ($r = .68$; Derogatis, Rickels, & Rock, 1976).

The HSCL or the more current SCL-90 is particularly useful in a population with varying types of psychiatric symptomatology. It can be used to screen psychiatric symptoms when a specific disorder is unknown. The total score summarizing all factors can be used as a measure of general psychological distress. Because of its broad symptom coverage, it is not the most economical measure of depressive symptomatology.

Inventory to Diagnose Depression

The Inventory to Diagnose Depression (IDD; Zimmerman, 1983) is a 22-item self-report inventory designed specifically for the assessment of depression. It was designed originally to make diagnoses by the *DSM–III*, but it has been modified to reflect *DSM–III–R* (American Psychiatric Association, 1987) scoring criteria. The IDD is not intended solely as a diagnostic instrument; it also quantifies the severity of depressive illness. Items are rated on 5-point scales, with 0 indicating no disturbance and 2 or higher indicating clinical levels. Item scores are combined to give an overall estimate of depressive severity. The IDD covers the entire range of symptoms used to diagnose major depressive disorder. The test–retest reliability over 1 day is .98, and split-half reliability is .93 (Zimmerman, Coryell, Corenthal, & Wilson, 1986). The internal consistency of the measure also is strong ($\alpha = .92$; Zimmerman et al., 1986). Concurrent validity of the measure is evidenced by high correlations with other self-report measures such as the BDI ($r = .87$) and clinician ratings such as the HRSD ($r = .80$) and the CSRS ($r = .81$; Zimmerman et al., 1986). The IDD diagnosis also was found to agree with clinical diagnosis ($\kappa = .66$; Zimmerman et al., 1986) and structured diagnostic interview (97.2% agreement overall with DIS classification, and chance corrected agreement was .51; Zimmerman & Coryell, 1987).

The IDD appears to be a useful, multipurpose measure. It includes symptoms of endogenous (RDC) and melancholic (*DSM–III* criteria) depression and covers all nine criterion symptoms of depression.

The Inventory of Depressive Symptomatology–Self-Report Version

The Inventory of Depressive Symptomatology–Self-Report Version (IDS-SR; Rush et al., 1986) parallels the clinician rating scale version in both content and wording of items. Twenty-eight items assess criterion symptoms of major depression as well as endogenous and atypical symptoms on a 0 to 3 scale. A 30-item version adds the remainder of atypical depression symptoms. The mean scores for the 28-item version of the IDS-SR were 36.5 for depressed outpatients, 21.8 for other diagnostic groups, and 2.1 for normal control participants (Rush et al., 1996). These values differ significantly, supporting the construct validity of the measure. The Cronbach's alpha of .85 suggests high internal consistency. In a sample of 434 depressed patients, the Cronbach's alpha of the IDS-SR was .77 (Rush et al., 1996). Adding normal control participants to create a larger sample ($N = 552$), the Cronbach's alpha level increased to .93. The IDS-SR was highly correlated with the BDI ($r = .78$) and the HRSD ($r = .67$), providing support for its concurrent validity. Factor analysis results matched findings from the IDS-C by showing three factors: Cognitive/Mood symptoms, Anxiety/Arousal symptoms; and Vegetative symptoms (Rush et al., 1996). The IDS-SR has the advantage of thorough symptom coverage. The availability of parallel clinician and self-report versions allows for easy and direct comparison of symptom status from both subjective self-report and more objective clinician perspectives.

Irritability-Depression-Anxiety Scale

The Irritability-Depression-Anxiety Scale (IDA; Snaith, Constantopoulos, Jardine, & McGuffin, 1978) is an 18-item self-report questionnaire that assesses depression, anxiety, and inwardly and outwardly directed irritability. Each item is rated on a scale of 0–3, but the direction of the scoring varies with each item. The IDA is scored by adding the total item scores. Questions are asked of the present state or proceeding day or two. The IDA has four subscales: Depression (5 items), Anxiety (5 items), Inward Irritability (4 items), and Outward Irritability (4 items). The Depression subscale is made up of questions about sadness of mood, guilt, suicidal ideation, retardation, late insomnia, loss of energy, loss of appetite, and loss of weight. The maximum scores for the Anxiety and Depression subscales are 15, and the Irritability scales are 12. Snaith et al. reported a suggested cutoff of 4 or 5 for the Depression subscale, 7 or 8 for the Anxiety subscale, and 5 or 6 for either of the Irritability subscales. For the Depression subscale, use of this cutoff resulted in 8% of controls being misclassified and 14% of patients misclassified. The internal consistency of the subscales were calculated using the Spearman-Brown method, in which subscales were halved in various ways, and resulting coefficients ranged from .70 to .93 (Snaith et al., 1978). Interrater reliability is supported by significant correlations ranging from .80 to .90 for paired ratings, and concurrent validity of the measure is supported by significant correlations between the Depression scale scores and psychiatric ratings of depression ($r = .75$; Snaith et al., 1978).

The IDA, although not often used as a treatment outcome measure, makes a contribution to the depression assessment literature by providing a measure of irritability. This may be particularly useful for patients who suffer from irritable depressions or bipolar II disorder with irritable hypomanic episodes. Item coverage includes only six of the nine criterion symptoms of depression.

Leeds Scales for the Self-Assessment of Anxiety and Depression

The Leeds Scales (Snaith, Bridge, & Hamilton, 1976) are a revision of the Wakefield Self-Assessment Depression (SAD) Inventory that was then subjected to item analysis. Ten items were added that cover somatic symptoms, self-blame, tension, fear, and suicidal thoughts. The resulting 22-item self-report scale is rated on a 4-point Likert scale ranging from *not at all* to *definitely*. The content of the scale contains items reflecting symptoms of both anxiety and depression. The measure has two 6-item subscales that measure general depression and anxiety, and a cutoff score of 6 or 7 is recommended to distinguish between "healthy" and "sick." The psychometric properties of the measure have not been well established. Reliability estimates have not been reported. However, the concurrent validity of the measure is supported through correlations with global clinician ratings of anxiety and depression, which ranged from .72 to .87 for the specific scales and from .83 to .85 for the general scales (Snaith et al., 1976).

The Leeds Scales of Anxiety and Depression fall short in documentation of their psychometric properties. Item coverage is not complete for criterion symptoms, and no information is currently available regarding its sensitivity to changes in depressive symptoms with treatment.

The Levine-Pilowsky Depression Questionnaire

The Levine-Pilowsky Depression Questionnaire (LPD; Pilowsky, Levine, & Boulton, 1969) is a 57-item self-report measure of depression. Items were selected from standard psychiatric texts and are responded to as yes or no. Wallace and Boulton's (1968) method was used to group respondents into three groups on the basis of their responses to the questionnaire and other respondent characteristics, including age, marital status, sex, and length of illness. Class A was considered to represent a mixed group of depressive reactions, Class B corresponded well with endogenous depression, and Class C was composed of individuals with nondepressive syndromes. Phi coefficients were calculated between each item and each class to identify which items significantly differentiated between classes. Class B patients were more likely to be treated with ECT and to show a better response to this treatment than were Class A patients (Pilowsky & Boulton, 1970). In addition, items corresponding to a high B score were more likely to change after ECT (Pilowsky & McGrath, 1970). Concurrent validity of the LPD depression score can be seen in its correlation with the SRDS ($r = .88$). Although the association between clinical diagnosis and LPD diagnostic classification was significant, $\chi^2 (4, N = 367) = 53.5, p < .001$, the LPD identified only 33.3% of respondents who had been diagnosed by clinicians with nonendogenous depression, 58.6% with endogenous depression, and 59.1% with no depressive syndrome (Pilowsky, 1979). Thus, it appears the LPD may have limited diagnostic utility. This may be partly because this 57-item scale assesses only six of the nine criterion symptoms of depression.

The MMPI Depression Scale

The MMPI Depression scale (Hathaway & McKinley, 1942) is commonly used in the United States as a screening measure for the presence of depression. The MMPI Depression scale consists of 60 empirically derived true–false items, 49 of which were selected because they discriminated between a group of manic-depressive and normal individuals and 11 which discriminated between depressed and other psychiatric patients (Hathaway & McKinley, 1942). The full test takes 45 min to 2 hr to complete, but the MMPI Depression scale alone can be completed in 5–10 min. Item content covers somatic, cognitive, affective, social interpersonal, and behavior symptoms as well as five items not easily classified. Numerous researchers have examined the reliability of the MMPI scales. Split-half reliabilities of the MMPI Depression scale ranged from .35 to .84, with the median being in the low .70s (Dahlstrom & Welsh, 1960). Test–retest reliabilities over 1 week were .82 (Derogatis et al., 1976). However, estimates of test–retest reliability are problematic because the MMPI lacks a specific time frame, which may limit its usefulness in outcome research. Raw scores are converted to t scores, and a score of 70 or more has been traditionally considered clinically significant. Interpretative guidelines suggest that a t score of 67.19 indicates mild, 74.45 indicates moderate, and 87.90 indicates marked depression (N. Endicott & Jortner, 1975; Greene, 1980). The concurrent validity of the MMPI Depression scale can be seen in correlations with other depressive measures such as the BDI ($r = .60$) and the HSCL-90 ($r = .69$). Although the discriminant validity of the measure has been criticized because of intercorrelations among the MMPI scales, particularly its correlation with anxiety, group differences between depressed and nondepressed samples were found. Using Wilcoxon's test of equality of distributions, depressed samples ($M = 84.15, SD = 13.28$) were significantly different from nondepressed groups ($M = 68.52$,

$SD = 15.32, p < .0001$). The hit rates of the measure when compared with depression diagnosis based on diagnostic interview and BDI score revealed test sensitivity (true-positives) of 78% and test specificity (true-negatives) of 75% (Nelson & Cicchetti, 1991). The positive predictive power (i.e., the ratio of true-positives to all positive results) was .93, whereas the negative predictive power (i.e., the ratio of true-negatives to all negative results) was .43 (Nelson & Cicchetti, 1991). Because item content changes in the Depression scale were slight from the revision of the MMPI to the MMPI-2 (3 items were deleted and 2 were reworded), these results are also expected to apply to the MMPI-2.

The Plutchik-van Praag Self-Report Depression Scale

The Plutchik-van Praag Self-Report Depression Scale (PVP; Plutchik & van Praag, 1987) is a 34-item self-report measure tapping *DSM–III* symptoms of major depression on a 5-point Likert-type scale ranging from *a lot less* to *a lot more*. Scores range from 0 to 68. Scores of 20–25 suggest probable depression. A cutoff score of 16 maximizes sensitivity while controlling specificity. The measure assesses symptoms occurring in the 2 weeks before administration of the measure. Plutchik and van Praag (1987) reported a coefficient alpha of .93 and provided evidence for its discriminant validity by demonstrating significant differences in the scores of depressed patients and normal control students, $t(76) = 3.37, p < .001$, as well as patients with schizophrenia, $t(57) = 2.66, p < .001$. The concurrent validity of the PVP is supported by significant correlations with the SRDS ($r = .82$), the BDI ($r = .83$), and the CES-D Scale ($r = .91$; Plutchik & van Praag, 1987).

Although the PVP assess all nine criterion symptoms of depression, little is known about its sensitivity to changes in symptoms after treatment. It was intended to be a screening instrument for depression rather than a symptom severity measure.

The POMS

The POMS (McNair, Lorr, & Droppleman, 1981) is a self-report measure that consists of 65 adjectives that describe mood states. Each item is rated on a 5-point scale, on which individuals are asked to rate how they feel "right now." The POMS was factor analyzed, and six factors were found: Tension-Anxiety, Depression-Dejection, Anger-Hostility, Vigor-Activity, Fatigue-Inertia, and Confusion-Bewilderment. Overlay sheets are used to score the scales. Fifteen items make up the Depression scale, with content consisting primarily of affect items and a few verbal-cognitive items. Scores on the Depression scale range from 0 to 60. Norms are available for the measure, and college-age norms for the Depression scale were 13.1 for men and 14.8 for women (McNair et al., 1981). Subsequent factor-analytic studies have supported the factor structure found by the authors and support its reliability (Boyle, 1987). Concurrent validity of the POMS can be seen in its correlation with other measures of depression such as the SRDS ($rs = .65-.93$; Frazier, 1987). Discriminant validity is found in its ability to distinguish between university and Veterans Administration samples (Little & Penman, 1989). The POMS also has been shown to be sensitive to change in depression with treatment (Little & Penman, 1989). However, items have high face validity, and the instrument may be criticized because of the potential influence of social desirability effects in responses. It has been used little because of its limited item content.

The Symptom Rating Test

The Symptom Rating Test (SRT; Kellner & Sheffield, 1973) is a 56-item self-report measure of psychological distress. Subscales include Anxiety, Depression, Somatic Symptoms, and Inadequacy. A 30-item short-form is also available. Each item is rated on a 0–3 scale ranging from *not at all* to *extremely, could not have been worse,* respectively. Items are summed to provide a total score. The SRT has a 24-hr test–retest reliability of .94 for outpatients and .92 for inpatients. The authors reported that conventional split-half reliability was not performed because items were not psychometrically equivalent. However, the split-half reliability of changes in outpatient SRT scores after 1 month was .89. The discriminant validity was demonstrated by showing significant differences ($p < .001$) in scores between neurotic patients and normal control individuals. In addition, SRT scores decreased significantly ($p < .001$) after 3 weeks of treatment with antidepressant medications. Evidence for the SRT's concurrent validity can be found in its correlations with the SRDS ($r = .66$), the HRSD ($rs = .65–.72$), and with psychiatrist ratings ($rs = .55–.95$). The SRT includes eight criterion symptoms of depression. However, its correlations with more widely accepted measures of depression are weaker than other self-report measures of depression, perhaps because of its broader item coverage.

Vietnamese Depression Scale

The Vietnamese Depression Scale (Kinzie et al., 1982) is included as an example of outcome measures designed for use with diverse ethnic or cultural groups. The Vietnamese Depression Scale is a self-report instrument developed in the Vietnamese language. It describes the thoughts, feelings, and behaviors common among depressed Vietnamese individuals. The original scale consisted of 43 items that were field tested using a psychiatric clinical group and a matched community sample. Fifteen items were found to account for 96% of the variance of the sum of scores for the original 45 items. The items cover symptoms such as "down-hearted and low-spirited," "shameful and dishonored," and "sad and bothered." The 15 items are rated on a 3-point continuum, with item scores summed to get the total score. Higher scores indicate greater symptom severity. The mean score for the depressed group was 17.5, and for the matched community sample is was 4.9. Scores range from 0 to 34. A cutoff score of 13 is recommended, which correctly classified 91% of the patient group and 96% of the community sample. Although the authors did not report data on reliability, the measure appears to have good discriminant validity. Discriminant function analysis of summary scores predicted group membership (100% of the respondents were correctly classified). Thus, the measure has both good sensitivity and specificity.

The Visual Analogue Mood Scale

The Visual Analogue Mood Scale (VAMS; Aitken, 1969) is a rectangular card 100 × 35 mm on which the following instruction is printed, "How is your mood right now? A mark on the line toward the left represents your worst mood, toward the right, your best." The VAMS score is determined by measuring in millimeters the distance from the left of the card to the respondent's mark. Scores range from 0 to 100, with higher scores representing more positive mood. No cutoff scores or ranges were suggested by the authors. Test–retest reliability over 24 hr between two samples of psychiatric inpatients revealed mean correlations of .61 and .73 (Folstein & Luria, 1973). Mean correlation coefficients within individuals of .32 and .48 were found. Folstein and Luria (1973) examined the concurrent validity of the measure and found correlations of −.64 and −.67 with the SRDS. Significant correlations also were found with some scales of the Clyde Mood Scale, such as Friendliness (rs = .39 and .45), Clear Thinking (rs = .33 and .60), and Unhappy (rs = −.46 and −.56). Other evidence of the validity of the VAMS can be seen in that it discriminates between groups, in which orthopedic patients scored higher than schizophrenic patients, and schizophrenic or manic patients scored higher than depressed patients. This provides evidence of the discriminant validity of the measure.

The VAMS may be more useful in research environments testing the effects of mood states on other psychological and biological measures. It is favored by many for its simplicity in administration. It does not measure any specific symptoms of depression and does not show change with treatment.

The Wakefield SAD Inventory

The Wakefield SAD Inventory (Snaith, Ahmed, Hehta, & Hamilton, 1971) was developed by selecting 10 items from the SRSD and adding 2 items on anxiety. The resulting 12-item self-report inventory contains items rated from 0 (*no, not at all*) to 3 (*yes, definitely*). Scores range from 0 to 36, with higher scores indicating greater symptom severity. A cutoff score of 14 or 15 is recommended for classification as depressed, and using this results in only 3% of depressed and 7.5% of normal control participants being misclassified. Test–retest reliabilities of individuals before and after administration of ECT were .68. Validity of the measure is supported by correlations with the HRSD across various stages of treatment (r = .87). Snaith et al. also correlated scores after deleting the somatic items from the HRSD and obtained a correlation of .89. They concluded that little is lost by excluding somatic symptoms from the inventory. However, the authors reported that the Wakefield SAD Inventory has been superseded by the Leeds Scales, which they reported are superior.

The SRDS

The SRDS (Zung, 1965) is a 20-item self-report scale designed for use in patients with a primary diagnosis of depression or as a screening measure for depression in the general population. The items are intended to represent three domains: mood (2 items), somatic concomitants (8 items), and psychological concomitants (10 items). Each of the 20 items is rated on a 4-point Likert scale in terms of frequency from 1 (*a little of the time*) to 4 (*most of the time*). The total score is obtained by dividing the sum of the item raw scores by the maximum possible score of 80 and then multiplying by 100. The range of scores is 25–100. Zung (1965) provided cutoff scores as follows: below 50 is in the normal range, 50–59 indicates minimal-to-mild depression, 60–69 indicates moderate depression, and 70+ indicates severe depression. Zung (1974) found that a cutoff score of 50 or more correctly classified 88% of the depressed patients and also correctly classified 88% of normal individuals. Thus, sensitivity and specificity were .88. A split-half correlation of even and odd SRDS items was .73 (Zung, 1974). Internal consistency is further supported by the alpha coefficient calculation for reliability ($\alpha = .92$). Although the SRDS discriminates between depressed and nondepressed samples (Carroll et al., 1973), it appears to have limited usefulness for discriminating between depressed individuals. The measure was not able to discriminate between severely ill inpatients, moderately ill day hospital patients, and mildly ill outpatients, whereas the HRSD was able to make these discriminations. Evidence of the concurrent validity of the measure can be seen in correlations with other depression measures such as the HRSD ($rs = .37-.60$) and the MMPI Depression scale ($r = .70$; Carroll et al., 1973). The SRDS may serve as a useful brief assessment of depression, but it may not be the instrument of choice for estimating depressive severity despite its popularity. Because it is one of the oldest and most studied measures of depressive symptomatology, it has held its position as a standard in the field despite its weaknesses. Several measures developed after the SRDS assessed their psychometric strength by comparison with this original scale.

GLOBAL ILLNESS RATING SCALES

The Clinical Global Impression Scale

The Clinical Global Impression Scale (Guy, 1976) is a 7-point Likert-type scale assessing overall clinical status of the patient in terms of improvement. It ranges from 1 (*normal*) to 7 (*among the most extremely ill*). The psychometric properties of this measure have not been established, but it has been found to be sensitive to change in patients treated for depression.

Raskin Three-Area Depression Scale

The Raskin Three-Area Depression Scale (Raskin, Schulterbrandt, Reatig, & McKeon, 1970) is a clinical rating scale completed by the clinician. It represents three separate depressive clusters on 5-point Likert scales. Ratings are made on verbal report, behavior, and somatic or secondary signs. Total scores range from 0 to 12. The psychometric properties of this measure have not been reported, but it has been used in studies of treatment outcome (e.g., Klerman, DiMascio, Weissman, Prusoff, & Paykel, 1974).

The Global Assessment of Functioning

The Global Assessment of Functioning (GAF; American Psychiatric Association, 1994) has undergone several modifications over the years since its initial development by Luborsky (1962) as the Health-Sickness Rating Scale. In the most recent version published as part of the *DSM–IV* (American Psychiatric Association, 1994), the GAF is a clinician rating scale in which the degree of impairment in functioning caused by psychiatric illnesses and their psychosocial sequelae are rated on a 1–100 scale. Severity of symptomatology, degree of impairment in various aspects of daily functioning (e.g., personal hygiene, work, and social relations), personal safety (e.g., suicidality or risk to others), behavioral changes (e.g., influenced by psychotic symptoms), and causation of symptomatology (e.g., expectable given stressors) are integrated into a singular rating that reflects how well the patient is currently functioning. Clinicians can rate the highest level of functioning achieved in the past year as a marker of either the chronicity of the psychiatric illness or of the level of functioning likely to be achieved following treatment for an acute episode. There are no current psychometric data available on the newest version of the GAF. Despite this, the GAF is one of the most widely used symptom severity and psychosocial functioning scales available.

RELATED DOMAINS

Cognitive Symptoms of Depression

Beck, Rush, Shaw, and Emery (1979) provided a psychological model for the conceptualization and treatment of depression. The basic premise is that negative emotions are stimulated, maintained, and escalated by depressogenic cognitions, such as distorted schemas about the world that set the stage for the generation of negative automatic thoughts after either an internal or external stimulus event. Although it is difficult if not impossible to determine whether negative thinking precipitates negative emotional shifts or vice versa, there is considerable evidence that cognitive therapy (Beck et al., 1979), which remediates and reduces negative thinking, improves depressive symptoms (e.g., Rush, Beck, Kovacs, & Hollon, 1977). The following is a summary of the psychometric properties of three measures of negative cognitions that are commonly used in treatment outcome studies of cognitive therapy for major depression.

The Hopelessness Scale

The Hopelessness Scale (HS; Beck, Weissman, Lester, & Trexler, 1974) is a 20-item self-report scale that assesses pessimistic expectations. Hopelessness is a predictor of suicidal risk (Beck et al., 1974) and therefore is important in the assessment of the severity of depression. Each of 20 statements are rated true or false by the respondent. Items are scored as 0 or 1 and are summed to provide a total score. The internal consistency of the HS is high, with coefficient alphas (Kuder–Richardson formula) ranging from .91 for a sample of 78 psychiatric patients (Mendonca, Holden, Mazmanian, & Dolan, 1983) to .93 for a sample of 294 hospitalized patients (Beck et al., 1974). HS total scores correlated significantly with clinical ratings of hopelessness in a general practice sample ($r = .74, p < .001$) and in a suicide attempter sample ($r = .62, p < .001$).

The Dysfunctional Attitudes Scale

The Dysfunctional Attitudes Scale (DAS; Weissman, 1979) is a 40-item self-report measure of attitudes or beliefs such as perfectionism, concern about approval from others, beliefs about being happy, or feelings of inadequacy. These dysfunctional attitudes are proposed to be common among individuals suffering from depression. Each item is rated on a 7-point scale ranging from *agree very much* to *disagree very much*. Some items are reversed in scaling to avoid response bias. The average score for students reporting depressive symptoms was 130.26 ($SD = 29.60$) and 114.46 ($SD = 25.10$) for nondepressed students. Weissman (1979) reported a test–retest reliability correlation of .84 over an 8-week period. Internal consistency is high, with coefficient alphas ranging from .89 to .92 (Weissman, 1979). There was modest support for the concurrent validity of the DAS in its correlations of .36 and .47 ($p < .001$) with two depression measures among college students (Weissman, 1979). More supportive evidence of its validity is reported by E. W. Hamilton and Abramson (1983), who found significant differences between depressed and nondepressed psychiatric patients and nondepressed volunteers on this measure.

Automatic Thoughts Questionnaire

The Automatic Thoughts Questionnaire (ATQ; Hollon & Kendall, 1980) is a questionnaire designed to assess the degree of belief in 30 negative thoughts similar to those hypothesized to occur only during the symptomatic depressed state (Beck, 1976). The ATQ discriminates depressed and nondepressed individuals. Split-half reliability was .97 ($p < .001$). All ATQ item–total correlations were significant at the .001 level. In 348 college students, the ATQ correlated significantly with the BDI and MMPI Depression scale ($p < .001$). In a patient sample, the ATQ was significantly associated with depressive symptoms (Eaves & Rush, 1984).

Manic and Psychotic Symptomatology

Individuals suffering from severe episodes of major depression may experience psychotic symptomatology such as delusions or hallucinations. These symptoms remit as the depression remits. Those with persistent psychotic symptoms (despite remission of depression) and recurrent episodes of major depression may have schizoaffective disorder, depressed type. The Brief Psychiatric Rating Scale (BPRS) is a commonly used clinician rating scale of psychotic symptomatology. For those who suffer from bipolar I or bipolar II disorders, hypomanic or manic symptomatology may be present either in combination with episodes of major depression (i.e., mixed states) or alone. There are several mania rating scales available. The Bech-Rafaelsen Mania Scale (BRMS) and the Young Mania Rating Scale (YMRS) have the most thorough symptom coverage and are commonly used in treatment outcome studies.

The BRMS

The BRMS (Bech, Bolwig, Kramp, & Rafaelsen, 1979) is a clinician-rated scale designed to quantitatively assess the severity of the manic state in diagnosed patients. It consists of 11 items rated on a 5-point scale, with the total score comprising a summation of all items. The BRMS had an interrater reliability correlation (the Kendall coefficient of concordance) of .95, and the interobserver reliability correlation ranged from .97 to .99 (Bech et al., 1979). Homogeneity of the BRMS ranged from .72 to .94 on 10 of the items excluding sleep, which was .48 when correlated to the total scale score (Bech et al., 1979).

The BRMS items load more heavily on aggressive symptomatology, hypersexuality, impaired judgment, appearance, and behavior and less heavily on impulsivity, mood, sleep, and speech (Goodwin & Jamison, 1990).

The YMRS

The YMRS (Young, Biggs, Ziegler, & Meyer, 1978) allows for both ratings of individual symptoms and a global measure allowing clinicians to provide an overall rating of manic symptomatology. There is considerable overlap in symptom coverage with the BRMS.

The YMRS differs from the BRMS in its item coverage. The YMRS places more emphasis than the BRMS on hypersexuality, appearance, cognition, sleep, psychomotor activity, and speech and relatively less emphasis on aggression, judgment, impulsivity, and behavior (Goodwin & Jamison, 1990).

The Global Mania Rating Scale (GMRS) is a 3-item addendum to the YMRS, which includes a global 0- to 4-point rating scale (1 = *not at all*, 4 = *very much*) of verbal report, behavior, and secondary symptoms (e.g., loud, hypersexual, unkempt) of mania. The global measure is included to allow the clinician to summarize general clinical impressions of the severity of the patient's symptoms.

The BPRS

The BPRS (Overall & Gorham, 1962) is an 18-item clinical rating scale of symptom severity including five symptom clusters: thinking disturbance, anxious depression, withdrawal/retardation, hostile/suspiciousness, and agitation/excitement. Ratings are made for each item on a 7-point scale ranging from *not present* to *extremely severe* after interviewing a patient. Training is required to administer the measure reliably. A summation of the ratings for the 18 items provides a total global score. A 50% reduction in the total score represents a response to short-term treatment (Overall & Hollister, 1985). Interrater reliability derived for independent ratings by pairs of clinicians of joint patient interviews was .75 for the total score and .85 for factor scores (Overall & Hollister, 1985). Overall and Gorham (1962) reported a kappa reliability estimate of .80 for depressive disorders using the BPRS. The BPRS has good criterion-related validity when compared with final clinical diagnosis by the RDC ($N = 150$, 95% agreement; Overall & Hollister, 1985). Eighty-four percent of patients receiving a final diagnosis of depression were identified by the BPRS (Overall & Hollister, 1985).

Psychosocial Functioning Scales

The Social Adjustment Scale–Self-Report

Perhaps the most widely used measure of psychosocial functioning in the depression literature is the Social Adjustment Scale–Self-Report (SAS-SR;

Weissman & Bothwell, 1976). The SAS-SR is a 40-item self-report measure of instrumental and expressive role performance. Items are rated on a 5-point scale, with higher scores indicating impairment. The measure has a high level of internal consistency; it had a mean alpha coefficient of .74, and the mean test–retest reliability was .80 across two time periods (Weissman, Prusoff, Thompson, Harding, & Myers, 1978). The concurrent validity of the SAS-SR has been demonstrated by Weissman et al. (1978) through differentiation between psychiatric patients and community control participants as well as by showing significant differences between acute and recovered depressed patients.

The Quality of Life Scale

The Quality of Life Scale (QOLS; Lehman, 1983) is a structured interview designed to assess four components of quality of life across eight life domains. The life domains are living situation, family, social relations, leisure activities, work, finances, personal safety, and health. The four components of quality of life are (a) personal characteristics (demographics and clinical characteristics); (b) objective indicators; (c) subjective indicators (i.e., patient self-report); and (d) global well-being measures. Lehman reported the construct validity of the objective indicators in each life domain to be adequate. The respondent also rates the quality of his or her life for the eight life domains by selecting a rating on a visual 7-point scale with descriptors such as "delighted" for a rating of 7 and "terrible" for a rating of 1. The internal consistency for these items ranged from .67 to .87. The QOLS also includes three global measures of well-being. First, patients are asked twice during the interview "How do you feel about your life in general?" The 1–7 scale is used for these two ratings. Scale 2 consists of items that assess positive well-being. Scale 3 requires the respondent to choose from two dichotomous response alternatives to complete the phrase "I think my life is . . ." (e.g., miserable-enjoyable). The test–retest reliability of the three global well-being scales ranged from .74 to .87.

This measure, which allows for both patients' subjective rating of the quality of their lives as well as more objective ratings by clinicians, has been used primarily in populations of severely and persistently mentally ill individuals. It has not yet been tested in samples of depressed outpatients.

However, the domains of interest are relevant to the daily functioning of individuals with depressive disorders.

Ways of Coping Questionnaire

The Ways of Coping Questionnaire (WOC; Folkman & Lazarus, 1988) is a 63-item questionnaire designed to measure coping processes by identifying the thoughts and actions used by an individual to cope with a specific stressful encounter. It yields scores on eight coping scales: Confrontive Coping, Distancing, Self-Controlling, Seeking Social Support, Accepting Responsibility, Escape-Avoidance, Planful Problem Solving, and Positive Reappraisal. Individuals respond to each item on a 4-point Likert scale indicating the frequency with which each strategy is used. Cronbach's coefficient alphas for the eight scales (.66–.79; Folkman & Lazarus, 1988) are higher than the alpha coefficients reported for most other coping measures. Construct validity is supported by findings consistent with theoretical predictions that (a) coping consists of both problem-focused and emotion-focused strategies and (b) coping is a process.

The Psychosocial Adjustment to Illness Scale–Self-Report

The Psychosocial Adjustment to Illness Scale–Self-Report (PAIS-SR; Derogatis, 1977) is a 46-item self-report inventory designed to assess the quality of a patient's psychosocial adjustment to a current medical illness or its residual effects in the following areas: health care orientation, vocational environments, domestic environment, sexual relationships, extended family relationships, social environment, and psychological distress. Each item is rated on a 4-point (0–3) scale. On the basis of a sample of cardiac patients, the internal consistency of the subscales ranged from .47 to .85, with six of seven domains having reliability coefficients of .62 or higher. The PAIS-SR appears to have an acceptable level of construct validity. Previous studies have shown that the PAIS-SR correlated .81 with global clinical ratings and .60 (Derogatis & Derogatis, 1990) with self-report measures of psychosocial adjustment, thus supporting its convergent validity. The PAIS-SR scores of dialysis patients also have been found to be consistent with physicians' ratings of patients' adjustment. Although this measure has not been tested on depressed patients, its construction and content are a notable improvement over existing social adjustment measures used in the psychiatric literature. The item ratings rely more on patients' subjective experience in coping with several key psychosocial spheres that can be affected by depression rather than relying on the identification of discrete behaviors (e.g., number of days missed from work) as indicators of adjustment.

Interpersonal Functioning

There are consistent data to show that individuals who suffer from depression are likely to have problematic interpersonal relationships (e.g., Barnet & Gotlib, 1988; Basco, Prager, Pita, Tamir, & Stephens, 1992; Bothwell & Weissman, 1977). Marital discord is common among those who suffer from depression, and likewise depression is common among those who suffer from severe marital discord. Remediation of the depression without additional treatment for interpersonal problems appears to place people at greater risk for early relapse of depression after treatment (Krantz & Moos, 1987; Rounsaville, Weissman, Prusoff, & Herceg-Baron, 1979).

The following is a sample of more commonly used measures of interpersonal functioning. They can be used to assess the concurrence of depression and relationship problems and can be administered after treatment to assess improvement.

The Dyadic Adjustment Scale

The Dyadic Adjustment Scale (DAS; Spanier, 1976) is a 32-item self-report measure assessing the quality of marriages or similar dyads. Higher scores indicate greater satisfaction. Spanier (1976) reported an alpha reliability of .96 and supported its content, criterion-related, and construct validity via correlations with the Marital Adjustment Test (Locke & Wallace, 1959), factor analysis of the scale, and a significant contrast between normal and divorced couple groups. Basco et al. (1992) found significant differences in the DAS scores of depressed patients and their spouses as compared with normal control couples before treatment.

The Clinician Rating of Adult Communication

The Clinician Rating of Adult Communication (CRAC; Basco, Birchler, Kalal, Talbott, & Slater, 1991) is a 20-item marital communication assessment instrument that was designed to organize the casual observations of clinicians by focusing their attention on behaviors that have been found to empirically distinguish maritally distressed from nondistressed couples. Examples of behaviors assessed include problem solving, attribution of blame, involvement, aggression, and listening skills. Each CRAC item is scored on a 1–3 scale, with higher scores indicating poorer skills. Basco et al. (1991) found the CRAC to be internally consistent with part–whole correlations on the five subscales ranging from 75.3% to 83.3%, whereas intraclass correlations among four raters ranged from .91 to .95. Support for the validity of the CRAC was found in its correspondence with a state-of-the-art observational coding system, its relationship to ratings of marital satisfaction, and its concordance with couple's perceptions of their conflict management behavior. Basco et al. (1992) scored videotaped communication samples of depressed patients and their spouses as well as control couples. CRAC scores for the depressed couples were significantly higher than for the control couples, suggesting greater impairment in basic interpersonal communication skills.

The Interpersonal Competence Questionnaire

The Interpersonal Competence Questionnaire (ICQ; Buhrmester, Furman, Wittenberg, & Reis, 1988) is a 40-item self-report measure of self-perceptions of competence and comfort in social situations. It was designed to measure five domains of interpersonal competence: initiating relationships, disclosing personal information, asserting displeasure with others, providing emotional support and advice, and managing interpersonal conflict. Scores for each of the five dimensions are derived by averaging the eight items representing each factor. Four-week test–retest reliability for the five subscales were adequate, with reliabilities ranging from .69 (Conflict Management) to .89 (Initiation). Internal consistency reliabilities for the five scales ranged from .77 to .87. Concurrent and discriminant validity for the five scales was established via correlations with various measures of dating skills, assertion, social reticence, and emotional sensitivity, among others. Total scores correlated negatively with loneliness and positively with well-being, energy, and social self-esteem.

WHEN TO MEASURE

The choice of when to administer symptom severity or diagnostic measures depends on the intended purpose of the assessment. In clinical practice, diagnostic measures are used initially to guide treatment planning. In conjunction with a diagnostic assessment, clinician rating scales and patient self-report measures can be used to assess the initial severity of depressive symptoms. When readministered after initiation of treatment or after a treatment-free observation period, these measures can assess clinical change. Measures can be administered as often as is clinically useful, such as at each treatment visit, at fixed intervals (e.g., monthly), or only at the end of treatment. In the latter case, clinical judgment is the primary indicator of change, and the symptom severity or diagnostic measures are used to document or validate clinical impressions.

In research protocols, diagnostic and symptom severity measures are used more systematically to determine whether patients meet inclusion and exclusion criteria for participation in studies. For example, do patients meet the criteria for the psychiatric disorder under study? Are their symptoms severe enough to require treatment, to detect change if the intervention is successful, or to be certain that they unequivocally have the disorder under study?

Both diagnostic and symptom severity measures can be used at the end of treatment to determine treatment outcome. A threshold score often is established below which a positive response to treatment is declared. For example, a score of less than 10 on the HRSD (M. Hamilton, 1960, 1967) could be considered evidence of a positive response to treatment for depression. Caseness is a second indicator of treatment response. Does a given individual still meet diagnostic criteria for the disorder for which he or she has received treatment (e.g., does he or she still meet *DSM–IV* criteria for major depression?). If the goal of treatment was relapse prevention, response may be indicated by a failure to meet diagnostic criteria for the disorder under study.

Symptom rating scales can be used to determine the efficacy of an intervention by measuring the amount of change in symptom severity that occurred within an individual from baseline (pretreatment) levels to end-of-treatment levels. Depending on the instrument used, an absolute number or percentage of change with individuals can be used as a measure of the degree of response to treatment. This prevents the problem of defining a priori an arbitrary cutoff score (e.g., HRSD scores < 10) that indicates treatment response.

If two or more treatment groups are being compared and individuals are randomly assigned to these groups, the end-of-treatment symptom severity scores can be compared to determine the relative efficacy of the interventions. Similarly, the mean percentage of change within individuals or the frequency of diagnostic caseness can be compared across groups at the end of treatment to examine the advantages of each.

More commonly, several (e.g., weekly, each visit) ratings of symptom severity are conducted during an individual's participation in a treatment study. Frequently repeated measures have the added advantage of guiding the treatment process for interventions that are symptom focused. They also allow for examination of the stability of the treatment response when several ratings during the final phases of the intervention are available. Single end-point assessments in patients with mood disorders may be misleading given that symptomatology naturally fluctuates over time. It is possible that the final rating may suggest treatment response, but those conducted before and after the final treatment visit may indicate greater symptomatology.

In summary, there are many choices of measures and strategies available in the assessment of depressive symptoms. To select the best strategy, it is important to first clearly identify the intended purpose of the assessment. Examples include initial diagnostic evaluation for treatment planning and assessment of treatment outcome. Second, measures should be selected to assess the symptoms of interest. This might include a rating of specific mood and physical symptoms of depression or simply a global rating of clinical improvement. Each measure taps a slightly different grouping of symptoms. Likewise, treatment interventions might target some specific symptoms more than others. Assessment measures can be selected that will be sensitive to changes in the symptoms of interest. Third, a plan for the timing of assessments should be developed that provides the clinician or researcher with the information that is most useful in evaluating the patient, the intervention, or both.

REFERENCES

Abou-Saleh, M. T., & Coppen, A. (1983). Classification of depression and response to antidepressive therapies. *British Journal of Psychiatry, 143,* 601–603.

Aitken, R. (1969). Measurement of feelings using visual analogue scales. *Proceedings of the Royal Society of Medicine, 62,* 989–996.

American Psychiatric Association. (1980). *Diagnostic and statistical manual of mental disorders* (3rd ed.). Washington, DC: Author.

American Psychiatric Association. (1987). *Diagnostic and statistical manual of mental disorders* (3rd ed., rev.). Washington, DC: Author.

American Psychiatric Association. (1994). *Diagnostic and statistical manual of mental disorders* (4th ed). Washington, DC: Author.

Angst, J., Dittrich, A., & Woggon, B. (1979). Reproduzierbarkeit der Faktoren-strukltur des AMP-Systems. *International Pharmacopsychiatry, 14,* 319–324.

Angst, J., & Woggon, B. (1983). The validity of the AMP system for its use in clinical psychopharmacology. In J. Angst, U. Baumann, D. Bobon, H. Helmchen, & H. Hippius (Eds.), *Modern problems of pharmacopsychiatry: Vol. 20. AMDP-system in pharmacopsychiatry* (pp. 174–184). Basel, Switzerland: Karger.

Asberg, M., Montgomery, S. A., Perris, C., Schalling, D., & Sedvall, G. (1978). A comprehensive psychopathological rating scale. *Acta Psychiatrica Scandinavica,* (Suppl. 271), 5–28.

Barnet, P. A., & Gotlib, I. H. (1988). Psychosocial functioning in depression: Distinguishing among the antecedents, concomitants, and consequences. *Psychological Bulletin, 104,* 97–126.

Basco, M. R., Birchler, G. R., Kalal, B., Talbott, R., & Slater, M. A. (1991). The Clinician Rating of Adult Communication (CRAC): A clinician's guide to the assessment of interpersonal communication skill. *Journal of Clinical Psychology, 47,* 368–380.

Basco, M. R., Prager, K. J., Pita, J. M., Tamir, L. M., & Stephens, J. J. (1992). Communication and intimacy in the marriages of depressed patients. *Journal of Family Psychology, 6,* 1–11.

Baumann, U., Pietzcker, A., & Woggon, B. (1983). Syndromes and scales in the AMP-system. In J. Angst, U. Baumann, D. Bobon, H. Helmchen, & H. Hippius

(Eds.), *Modern problems of pharmacopsychiatry: Vol. 20. AMDP-system in phar-macopsychiatry* (pp. 74–87). Basel, Switzerland: Karger.

Bech, P. (1991). The Cronholm-Ottosson Depression Scale: The first depression scale designed to rate changes during treatment. *Acta Psychiatrica Scandinavica, 84,* 439–445.

Bech, P., Bolwig, T. G., Kramp, P., & Rafaelsen, O. J. (1979). The Bech-Rafaelson Mania Scale and the Hamilton Depression Scale: Evaluation of homogeneity and inter-observer agreement. *Acta Psychiatrica Scandinavica, 59,* 420–430.

Beck, A. T. (1976). *Cognitive therapy and emotional disorders.* Madison, CT: International Universities Press.

Beck, A. T., Rush, A. J., Shaw, B. F., & Emery, B. (1979). *Cognitive therapy of depression.* New York: Guilford Press.

Beck, A. T., Steer, R. A., & Garbin, M. G. (1988). Psychometric properties of the Beck Depression Inventory: Twenty-five years of evaluation. *Clinical Psychology Review, 8,* 77–100.

Beck, A. T., Ward, C. H., Mendelson, M., Mock, J. E., & Erbaugh, J. K. (1961). An inventory for measuring depression. *Archives of General Psychiatry, 4,* 561–571.

Beck, A. T., Weissman, A. N., Lester, D., & Trexler, L. (1974). The measurement of pessimism: The Hopelessness Scale. *Journal of Consulting and Clinical Psychology, 42,* 861–865.

Bothwell, S., & Weissman, M. M. (1977). Social impairments four years after an acute depressive episode. *American Journal of Orthopsychiatry, 47,* 231–237.

Boyle, G. J. (1987). A cross-validation of the factor structure of the profile of mood states: Were the factors correctly identified in the first instance? *Psychological Reports, 60,* 343–354.

Buhrmester, D., Furman, W., Wittenberg, M. T., & Reis, H. T. (1988). Five domains of interpersonal competence in peer relationships. *Journal of Personality and Social Psychology, 55,* 991–1008.

Carney, M. W. P., Roth, M., & Garside, R. F. (1965). The diagnosis of depressive syndromes and the prediction of E.C.T. response. *British Journal of Psychiatry, 111,* 659–674.

Carney, M. W. P., & Sheffield, B. J. (1972). Depression and the Newcastle scales: Their relationship to Hamilton's scale. *British Journal of Psychiatry, 121,* 35–40.

Carroll, B. J., Fielding, J., & Blashki, T. (1973). Depression rating scales: A critical review. *Archives of General Psychiatry, 28,* 361–366.

Chipman, A., & Paykel, E. S. (1974). How ill is the patient at this time? Cues determining clinician's global judgments. *Journal of Consulting and Clinical Psychology, 42,* 669–674.

Cronholm, B., & Ottosson, J. O. (1960). Experimental studies of the therapeutic action of electroconvulsive therapy in endogenous depression: The role of the electrical stimulation and of the seizure studies by variation of stimulus and modification by lidocaine of seizure discharge. *Acta Psychiatrica Neurologica Scandinavica, 35* (Suppl. 145), 69–97.

Cronholm, B., Schalling, D., & Asberg, M. (1974). Development of a rating scale for depressive illness. In P. Pichot (Ed.), *Modern problems of pharmacopsychiatry: Vol. 7. Psychological measurements in psychopharmacology* (pp. 139–150). Paris: Karger/Basel.

Dahlstrom, W. G., & Welsh, G. S. (1960). *An MMPI handbook: A guide to use in clinical practice and research.* Minneapolis: University of Minnesota Press.

Depression Guideline Panel. (1993). *Depression in primary care: Vol. 2. Treatment of major depression: Clinical practice guideline, number 5* (AHCPR Publication No. 93-0551). Rockville, MD: U.S. Department of Health and Human Services.

Derogatis, L. R. (1977). *Psychosocial Adjustment to Illness Scale—Self Report Version.* Towson, MD: Clinical Psychometric Research.

Derogatis, L. R., & Derogatis, M. F. (1990). *PAIS & PAIS-SR administration, scoring & procedures manual-II.* Towson, MD: Clinical Psychometric Research.

Derogatis, L. R., Lipman, R. S., & Covi, L. (1973). The SCL-90: An outpatient psychiatric rating scale. *Psychopharmacology Bulletin, 9,* 13–28.

Derogatis, L. R., Lipman, R. S., Rickels, K., Uhlenhuth, E. H., & Covi, L. (1974). The Hopkins Symptom Checklist (HSCL). In P. Pichot (Ed.), *Modern problems of pharmacopsychiatry: Vol. 7. Psychological measurements in psychopharmacology* (pp. 79–110). Basel, Switzerland: Karger.

Derogatis, L. R., Rickels, K., & Rock, A. F. (1976). The SCL-90 and the MMPI: A step in the validation of a new self-report scale. *British Journal of Psychiatry, 128,* 280–289.

Eaves, G., & Rush, A. J. (1984). Cognitive patterns in symptomatic and remitted unipolar major depression. *Journal of Abnormal Psychology, 93,* 31–40.

Elkin, I., Pilkonis, P. A., Docherty, J. P., & Sotsky, S. M. (1988). Conceptual and methodological issues in comparative studies of psychotherapy and pharmacotherapy: II. Nature and timing of treatment effects. *American Journal of Psychiatry, 145,* 1070–1076.

Endicott, J., Cohen, J., Nee, J., Fleiss, J., & Sarantakos, S. (1981). Hamilton Depression Rating Scale. *Archives of General Psychiatry, 38,* 98–103.

Endicott, J., & Spitzer, R. L. (1978). A diagnostic interview: The Schedule for Affective Disorders and Schizophrenia. *Archives of General Psychiatry, 35,* 837–844.

Endicott, N., & Jortner, S. (1975). Objective measures of depression. In W. Dahlstrom, G. Welsh, & L. Dahlstrom (Eds.), *An MMPI handbook: Research applications* (pp. 145–146). Minneapolis: University of Minnesota Press.

Feighner, J. P., Robins, E., Guze, S. B., Woodruff, R. W., Winokur, G., & Munoz, R. (1972). Diagnostic criteria for use in psychiatric research. *Archives of General Psychiatry, 26,* 57–63.

Feinberg, M., & Carroll, B. J. (1985). The Carroll Rating Scale for Depression. In N. Sartorius & T. A. Ban (Eds.), *Assessment of depression* (pp. 188–200). New York: Springer-Verlag.

Feinberg, M., Carroll, B. J., Smouse, P., & Rawson, S. G. (1981). The Carroll Rating Scale for Depression III: Comparison with other rating instruments. *British Journal of Psychiatry, 138,* 205–209.

First, M. B., Spitzer, R. L., Gibbon, M., & Williams, J. B. W. (1995). *Structured Clinical Interview for DSM-IV Axis I Disorders—Clinician Version.* New York: New York State Psychiatric Institute, Biometrics Research Department.

Folkman, S., & Lazarus, R. S. (1988). Coping as a mediator of emotion. *Journal of Personality and Social Psychology, 54,* 466–475.

Folstein, M. F., & Luria, R. (1973). Reliability, validity and clinical application of the Visual Analogue Mood Scale. *Journal of Psychological Medicine, 3,* 479–486.

Frazier, S. E. (1987). Comparison of two depression inventories: An examination of construct validity. *Psychological Reports, 60,* 1219–1222.

Goldberg, D. P. (1978). *Manual of the General Health Questionnaire.* London: NFER-Nelson Publishing.

Goodwin, F. K., & Jamison, K. R. (1990). *Manic-depressive illness.* New York: Oxford University Press.

Greene, R. (1980). *The MMPI: An interpretive manual.* New York: Grune & Stratton.

Guy, W. (1976). *ECDEU assessment manual for psychopharmacology, revised* (DHEW Publication No. ADM 76-338). Washington, DC: U.S. Government Printing Office.

Hamilton, E. W., & Abramson, L. Y. (1983). Cognitive patterns and major depressive disorder: A longitudinal study in a hospital setting. *Journal of Abnormal Psychology, 92,* 173–184.

Hamilton, M. (1960). A rating scale for depression. *Journal of Neurology, Neurosurgery and Psychiatry, 23,* 56–62.

Hamilton, M. (1967). Development of a rating scale for primary depressive illness. *British Journal of Social and Clinical Psychology, 6,* 278–296.

Haskell, D. S., DiMascio, A., & Prusoff, B. (1975). Rapidity of symptom reduction in depressions treated with amitriptyline. *Journal of Nervous and Mental Disease, 160,* 24–33.

Hathaway, S. R., & McKinley, J. C. (1942). A multiphasic personality schedule (Minnesota): III. The measurement of symptomatic depression. *Journal of Psychology, 14,* 73–84.

Hollon, S. D., & Kendall, P. C. (1980). Cognitive self-statements in depression: Development of an automatic thoughts questionnaire. *Cognitive Therapy and Research, 4,* 383–395.

Kellner, R., & Sheffield, B. F. (1973). A self-rating scale of distress. *Psychological Medicine, 3,* 88–100.

Kinzie, J. D., Manson, S. M., Vinh, D. T., Tolan, N. T., Anh, B., & Pho, T. N. (1982). Development and validation of a Vietnamese-language depression rating scale. *American Journal of Psychiatry, 139,* 1276–1281.

Klerman, G., DiMascio, A., Weissman, M., Prusoff, B., & Paykel, E. (1974). Treatment of depression by drugs and psychotherapy. *American Journal of Psychiatry, 131,* 186–191.

Knesevich, J. W., Biggs, J. T., Clayton, P. J., & Ziegler, V. E. (1977). Validity of the Hamilton Rating Scale for Depression. *British Journal of Psychiatry, 131,* 49–52.

Krantz, S. E., & Moos, R. H. (1987). Functioning in life context among spouses of remitted and nonremitted depressed patients. *Journal of Consulting and Clinical Psychology, 55,* 353–360.

Kuny, S., von Luckner, N., Banninger, R., Baur, P., Eichenberger, G., & Woggon, B. (1983). Interrater reliability of AMDP and AMP symptoms. In D. Bobon, U. Baumann, J. Angst, H. Helmchen, & H. Hippius (Eds.), *Modern problems of pharmacopsychiatry: Vol. 20. AMDP-system in pharmacopsychiatry.* Basel, Switzerland: Karger.

Lehman, A. F. (1983). The well-being of chronic mental patients: Assessing their quality of life. *Archives of General Psychiatry, 40,* 369–373.

Levitt, E. E., & Lubin, B. (1975). *Depression: Concepts, controversies and some new facts.* New York: Springer.

Little, K., & Penman, E. (1989). Measuring subacute mood changes using the Profile of Mood States and visual analogue scales. *Psychopathology, 22,* 42–49.

Locke, H. J., & Wallace, K. M. (1959). Short marital adjustment and prediction tests: Their reliability and validity. *Marriage and Family Living, 21,* 251–255.

Lubin, B. (1965). Adjective checklists for the measurement of depression. *Archives of General Psychiatry, 12,* 57–62.

Luborsky, L. (1962). Clinicians' judgments of mental health. *Archives of General Psychiatry, 7,* 407–417.

Markush, R. E., & Favero, R. V. (1973). Epidemiologic assessment of stressful life events, depressed mood, and psychophysiological symptoms: A preliminary report. In B. S. Dohrenwend & B. P. Dohrenwend (Eds.), *Stressful life events: Their nature and effects* (pp. 171–190). New York: Wiley.

McNair, D. M., Lorr, M., & Droppleman, L. F. (1981). *EDITS manual for the Profile of Mood States.* San Diego, CA: Educational and Industrial Testing Service.

Mendonca, J. D., Holden, R. R., Mazmanian, D. S., & Dolan, J. (1983). The influence of response style on the Beck Hopelessness Scale. *Canadian Journal of Behavioural Science, 15,* 237–247.

Mintz, J., Mintz, L. I., Arruda, M. J., & Hwang, S. S. (1992). Treatments of depression and the functional capacity to work. *Archives of General Psychiatry, 49,* 761–768.

Montgomery, S. A., & Asberg, M. (1979). Montgomery-Asberg Depression Rating Scale: A new depression scale designed to be sensitive to change. *British Journal of Psychiatry, 134,* 382–389.

Myers, J., & Weissman, M. (1980). Use of a self-report symptom scale to detect depression in a community sample. *American Journal of Psychiatry, 137,* 1081–1084.

Nasr, S., Altman, A., Rodin, M., Jobe, T., & Burg, B. (1984). Correlation of the Hamilton and Carroll Depression Rating Scales: A replication study among psychiatric outpatients. *Journal of Clinical Psychiatry, 45,* 167–168.

Nelson, L. D., & Cicchetti, D. (1991). Validity of the MMPI Depression scale for outpatients. *Psychological Assessment: A Journal of Consulting and Clinical Psychology, 3,* 55–59.

Overall, J. E., & Gorham, D. R. (1962). The Brief Psychiatric Rating Scale. *Psychological Reports, 10,* 799–812.

Overall, J. E., & Hollister, L. E. (1985). Assessment of depression using the Brief Psychiatric Rating Scale. In N. Sartorius & T. A. Ban (Eds.), *Assessment of depression* (pp. 159–178). New York: Springer-Verlag.

Paykel, E. S. (1985). The clinical interview for depression. In N. Sartorius & T. A. Ban (Eds.), *Assessment of depression* (pp. 304–315). New York: Springer-Verlag.

Paykel, E. S., & Griffith, J. H. (1983). *Community psychiatric nursing for neurotic patients: The Springfield Controlled Trial.* Unpublished manuscript, Royal College of Nursing, London.

Paykel, E. S., Parker, R. R., Penrose, R. J., & Rassaby, E. (1979). Depressive classification and prediction of response to phenelzine. *British Journal of Psychiatry, 134,* 572–581.

Peterson, C., Semmel, A., von Baeyer, C., Abramson, L. Y., Metalsky, G. I., & Seligman, M. E. P. (1982). The Attributional Style Questionnaire. *Cognitive Therapy and Research, 6,* 287–299.

Pilowsky, I. (1979). Further validation of a questionnaire method for classifying depressive illness. *Journal of Affective Disorders, 1,* 179–185.

Pilowsky, I., & Boulton, D. M. (1970). Development of a questionnaire-based decision rule for classifying depressed patients. *British Journal of Psychiatry, 16,* 647–650.

Pilowsky, I., Levine, S., & Boulton, D. M. (1969). The classification of depression by numerical taxonomy. *British Journal of Psychiatry, 115,* 937–945.

Pilowsky, I., & McGrath, M. D. (1970). The effect of electro-convulsive therapy on responses to a depression questionnaire: Implications for taxonomy. *British Journal of Psychiatry, 117,* 685–688.

Plutchik, R., & van Praag, H. M. (1987). Interconvertability of five self-report measures of depression. *Psychiatry Research, 22,* 243–256.

Radloff, L. S. (1977). The CES-D Scale: A self-report depression scale for research in the general population. *Applied Psychological Measurement, 3,* 385–401.

Raskin, A., Schulterbrandt, J. G., Reatig, N., & McKeon, J. J. (1970). Differential response to chlorpromazine, imipramine, and placebo: A study of subgroups of hospitalized depressed patients. *Archives of General Psychiatry, 23,* 164–173.

Rehm, L. P. (1981). Assessment of depression. In M. Hersen & A. S. Bellack (Eds.), *Behavioral assessment: A practical handbook* (2nd ed., pp. 246–295). New York: Pergamon Press.

Robins, L. N., Helzer, J. E., Croughan, J., & Ratcliff, K. S. (1981). National Institute of Mental Health Diagnostic Interview Schedule. *Archives of General Psychiatry, 38,* 381–389.

Robins, L. N., Helzer, J. E., Ratcliff, K. S., & Seyfried, W. (1982). Validity of the Diagnostic Interview Schedule, Version II: DSM-III diagnoses. *Psychological Medicine, 12,* 855–870.

Rounsaville, B. J., Weissman, M. M., Prusoff, B. A., & Herceg-Baron, R. L. (1979). Marital disputes and outcome in depressed women. *Comprehensive Psychiatry, 20,* 483–490.

Rowan, P. R., Paykel, E. S., & Parker, R. R. (1982). Phenelzine and amitriptyline:

Effects on symptoms of neurotic depression. *British Journal of Psychiatry, 140,* 475–483.

Rush, A. J., Beck, A. T., Kovacs, M., & Hollon, S. D. (1977). Comparative efficacy of cognitive therapy and pharmacotherapy in the treatment of depressed outpatients. *Cognitive Therapy and Research, 1,* 17–37.

Rush, A. J., Giles, D. E., Schlesser, M. A., Fulton, C. L., Weissenburger, J., & Burns, C. (1986). The Inventory of Depressive Symptomatology (IDS): Preliminary findings. *Psychopharmacology Bulletin, 22,* 985–990.

Rush, A. J., Gullion, C. M., Basco, M. R., Jarrett, R. B., & Trivedi, M. H. (1996). The inventory of depressive symptomatology (IDS): Psychometric properties. *Psychological Medicine, 26,* 477–486.

Schwab, J. J., Bialow, M. R., & Holzer, C. E. (1967). A comparison of two rating scales for depression. *Journal of Clinical Psychology, 23,* 94–96.

Snaith, R. P., Ahmed, S. N., Hehta, S., & Hamilton, M. (1971). The assessment of the severity of primary depressive illness: The Wakefield Self-Assessment Depression Inventory. *Psychological Medicine, 1,* 143–149.

Snaith, R. P., Bridge, G., & Hamilton, M. (1976). The Leeds Scales for the Self Assessment of Anxiety and Depression. *British Journal of Psychiatry, 128,* 156–165.

Snaith, R. P., Constantopoulos, A. A., Jardine, M. Y., & McGuffin, P. (1978). A clinical scale for the self-assessment of irritability. *British Journal of Psychiatry, 132,* 164–171.

Spanier, G. B. (1976). Measuring dyadic adjustment: New scales for assessing the quality of marriage and similar dyads. *Journal of Marriage and the Family, 38,* 15–28.

Spitzer, R. L., Endicott, J., & Robins, E. (1978). Research Diagnostic Criteria: Rationale and reliability. *Archives of General Psychiatry, 36,* 773–782.

Vieweg, B. W., & Hedlund, J. L. (1983). The General Health Questionnaire (GHQ): A comprehensive review. *Journal of Operational Psychiatry, 14,* 74–81.

von Zerssen, D. (1985). Clinical Self-Rating Scales (CSRS) of the Munich psychiatric information system (PSYCHIS Munchen). In N. Sartorius & T. A. Ban (Eds.), *Assessment of depression* (pp. 270–303). New York: Springer-Verlag.

von Zerssen, D., Strian, F., & Schwarz, D. (1974). Evaluation of depressive states, especially in longitudinal studies. In P. Pichot (Ed.), *Psychological measurements in psychopharmacology* (Vol. 7, pp. 189–202). Basel, Switzerland: Karger.

Wallace, C. S., & Boulton, D. M. (1968). An information measure for classification. *Computer Journal, 11,* 185–194.

Weissman, M. M. (1979). The Dysfunctional Attitudes Scale: A validation study. *Dissertation Abstracts International, 40*(b), 1389–1390.

Weissman, M. M., & Bothwell, S. (1976). Assessment of social adjustment by patient self-report. *Archives of General Psychiatry, 33,* 1111–1115.

Weissman, M. M., Prusoff, B., & Newberry, P. B. (1975). *Comparison of the CES-D, Zung, Beck Self Report Depression Scales.* (Tech. Rep. No. ADM 42-74-83). Rockville, MD: National Institute of Mental Health.

Weissman, M. M., Prusoff, B. A., Thompson, W. D., Harding, P. S., & Myers, J. K. (1978). Social adjustment by self-report in a community sample and in psychiatric outpatients. *Journal of Nervous and Mental Disease, 166,* 317–326.

Weissman, M. M., Sholomskas, D., Pottenger, M., Prusoff, B. A., & Locke, B. Z. (1977). Assessing depressive symptoms in five psychiatric populations: A validation study. *American Journal of Epidemiology, 106,* 203–214.

Young, R. C., Biggs, J. T., Ziegler, V. E., & Meyer, D. A. (1978). A rating scale for mania: Reliability, validity and sensitivity. *British Journal of Psychiatry, 133,* 429–435.

Zimmerman, M. (1983). *The Inventory to Diagnose Depression.* Unpublished manuscript, University of Iowa, Iowa City.

Zimmerman, M., & Coryell, W. (1987). The Inventory to Diagnose Depression (IDD): A self-report scale to diagnose major depressive disorder. *Journal of Consulting and Clinical Psychology, 55,* 55–59.

Zimmerman, M., Coryell, W., Corenthal, C., & Wilson, S. (1986). A self-report scale to diagnose major depressive disorder. *Archives of General Psychiatry, 43,* 1076–1081.

Zung, W. W. K. (1965). A self-rating depression scale. *Archives of General Psychiatry, 12,* 63–70.

Zung, W. W. K. (1972). The Depression Status Inventory: An adjunct to the Self-Rating Depression Scale. *Journal of Clinical Psychology, 28,* 539–543.

Zung, W. W. K. (1974). The measurement of affects: Depression and anxiety. In P. Pichot (Ed.), *Psychological measurements in psychopharmacology* (Vol. 7, pp. 170–188). Basel, Switzerland: Karger.

Zung, W. W. K. (1985). Zung Self-Rating Depression Scale and Depression Status Inventory. In N. Sartorius & T. A. Ban (Eds.), *Assessment of depression* (pp. 221–231). New York: Springer-Verlag.

9

Measuring Changes in Patients Following Psychological and Pharmacological Interventions: Depression

Larry E. Beutler

The advancement of any science depends on the development of reliable and valid measures of relevant phenomena. The need for a standard method of measurement is clearly apparent in mental health treatment outcome research, in which the modal methodology includes the development of one or more instruments to measure phenomena that are of specific interest to the objectives of each study (Beutler & Crago, 1983; Lambert, 1994). Unfortunately, these special-purpose instruments are seldom developed on independent samples, and many lack rudimentary evidence of reliability and validity. This practice presents a major obstacle to translating research findings into practice, not only because these instruments violate accepted procedures for test development, but also because the diverse array of instruments used have an inexact and inconsistent relationship both to one another and to the construct under investigation. Yet, there are some decided advantages to developing instruments whose function, purpose, and scores are specific to the objectives of a particular study. They potentially provide a clearer test of theory-specific hypotheses than more general-purpose instruments, and the process of developing such instruments is one avenue toward improving the measures currently in existence. Balancing the advantages and the disadvantages of general versus study-specific measures is one of the most pressing and difficult problems facing clinical researchers.

On its face, the need for a set of commonly accepted measures that can be used in all treatment outcome research has intuitive appeal as a means of improving generalization across studies, samples, and methods. This procedure also parallels many areas of physical and biomedical science, in which such standardization of measurement across laboratories is routine. However, when the constructs that are being measured are abstract ideas rather than physical entities and arise from widely diverse theories, the development of a restrictive standard invariably excludes parameters that are considered central by some investigators while including concepts that are irrelevant to others. Thus, two previous efforts (Lambert, Christensen, & DeJulio, 1983; Waskow & Parloff, 1975) to develop a consensus recommendation for a battery of measures to assess outcome in treatment research have failed to generate either enthusiastic endorsement or investigator compliance. The failure of these two efforts may be attributed to two factors: (a) The diverse theoretical leanings that characterize the field result in the need for a theoretical hegemony of measurement devices and (b) reluctance among investigators to adopt a standard list of procedures when doing so is likely to discourage the development and use of new instruments that are sensitive to specific populations and treatments.

In this chapter I consider what a core assessment battery should, and conceivably could, look like. I suggest methods to resolve the question of what constructs should be assessed, how one might assess these constructs, and the criteria for the selection of measurement devices.

WHAT TO MEASURE?

Faced with the dilemma created by the desirability of introducing standardization in the field on one hand and the failure of previous efforts to achieve acceptance on the other, one must seek an alternative to the strategy of proposing a list of specific instruments. A promising possibility is to identify domains of assessment and standards for developing and using assessment instruments that would apply across studies. Three domains in which standardization may be possible come readily to mind: (a) identification of a core set of dimensions that should be assessed representing the patient, treatment, and outcome; (b) specification of the parameters within which these dimensions should be measured; and (c) delineation of the criteria with which the measurement instruments should comply.

Dimensions

The first concern in identifying a standard assessment procedure is to define the minimal number and type of dimensions that are to be measured. Rather than identifying an unordered list of specific areas, there are advantages to prioritizing several basic dimensions that range in specificity and importance. Some dimensions are of sufficiently broad interest to warrant incorporation into treatment research generally, whereas others have their greatest benefit to research only with particular populations or problems, such as major depression, anxiety disorders, or schizophrenia. Still other dimensions will be relevant for measurement only in research on particular theoretical viewpoints.

For example, the value of obtaining information on demographic and environmental variables, symptoms of depression and anxiety, and diagnostic data is generally accepted as valuable for all treatment research to ensure generalizability of findings. However, some variables, such as aspects of the treatment process, will be of much more specific and limited interest to various investigators. There are at least four levels of generality that can define the domains in which measurement might be developed.

Level 1: General Patient and Treatment Parameters

The first domain of common assessment applies to concepts and principles that apply broadly to treatment research in the mental health arena. This domain defines a baseline set of characteristics or variables that can be applied to all treatment studies, regardless of the particular symptoms or diagnoses that characterize the population under study. These dimensions are relevant either because of tradition and use in clinical practice, or because they are necessary to understand the nature of the research sample of patients, therapists, and treatments used in a particular study.

Some of these variables reflect characteristics of the patient sample as they enter treatment, such as social-familial history, psychiatric history, diagnoses, target symptoms, level of functional impairment, distress level, and the method of entering study. Symptom severity measures of depression and anxiety also are of general interest and probably should be included in all outcome studies. Assessment of these dimensions will complement symptom-specific outcome variables in assessing change.

Although the nature of these general variables is self-explanatory, in most respects some bear further explanation. For example, a measure of patient diagnosis would serve several functions that would make it of value in all treatment outcome studies. In mixed samples, diagnosis would allow comparisons to other settings and would permit an evaluation of the moderating effects of Axis I and Axis II characteristics. In diagnostically homogeneous studies, reliable assessment of diagnoses will ensure sample representativeness and define the limits of generalization that are warranted. Similarly, measures both of functional impairment, emotional well-being, chronicity, and subjective distress would allow an assessment of general change in psychiatric severity, including comparisons across studies of effectiveness and efficacy, regardless of the specific population to which the study is addressed. Strupp and Hadley's (1977) suggestion of an external rating of severity of functional impairment also is particularly noteworthy.

Level 2: Assessment of Depression

Although symptom measures of depression and anxiety severity ideally would be included in a core battery for treatment research, generally a more specific assessment of characteristic and particular symptom constellations will be important in research devoted to the study of populations that are characterized by major or minor depression, anxiety disorders, or any other specific set of diagnoses. The types of measures to be used at this level of specificity should include assessment of specific, diagnosis-related symptoms that would include a reliable and standard diagnostic classification and identification of the specific qualifiers that contributed to the patient's diagnosis. Related dimensions, such as those indicating severity and chronicity, also should be included. Reliable diagnosis would ensure the presence of a reasonably homogeneous sample on relevant symptom presentations and would permit future replication and generalization. Compliance with diagnostic criteria also would serve as a measure of change with treatment as these dimensions are assessed across time.

In addition, both self-reported and clinician ratings of subjective distress and symptom severity, respectively, would allow an assessment of treatment effectiveness and efficacy. Such measurement will allow a determination of the social significance and need for treatment, as well as the broad impact of treatment-related response on clinical presentations. These measures would provide continuous measures, to complement the categorical one provided by diagnosis, in the assessment of outcomes.

Level 3: Measures of Treatment Integrity and Composition

Given the importance of determining what qualities moderate treatment outcome, it would be advantageous for researchers to include a measure of treatment integrity, both to identify the components of the treatment provided and to ensure that the designated treatment is actually being provided. Measures of clinician skill at providing this treatment, indexes indicating intensity and frequency of treatment, and measures of clinician and patient backgrounds also should be routinely noted.

Other general variables to assess as part of process measurement include aspects of treatment, such as the mode of treatment delivery, the nature and integrity of the treatment delivered, and the quality of treatment relationship. As many of these dimensions connote, a temporal dimension is an important aspect of treatment process and should be a part of all treatment research. Temporal measurement should include the measures defined in the second-level assessment procedure described earlier, as applied during and at the end of treatment and at some follow-up point.

Level 4: Theory-Specific Measures

At the most study-specific level of assessment, procedures should be incorporated in all research that will help develop understanding both of the particular patients most affected by the treatment and of the mechanisms or variables that accomplish and accompany change. Of the first type, those that contribute understanding of the patients who are most affected by treatment, initial characteristic traits and response styles that might be thought to predispose particularly strong or weak responses to the treatments under study should be assessed initially. Aspects of coping style, Axis II pathology, hostility and resistance patterns, availability of social support, and the problem-solving phase are examples that have been studied in prior literature (Beutler & Clarkin, 1990).

Of the second type, those characteristics that accompany and contribute to change, aspects of in-treatment states, and transitory reactions should be identified to allow an assessment of how treatment exerts both positive and negative effects. The specific dimensions selected by a given investigator should reflect either empirically or theoretically derived constructs that are of interest to the investigators or of relevance to the theoretical models underlying the treatments.

Parameters of Measurement

Every construct that appears initially to be a reflection of treatment effectiveness of treatment outcome proves to be more complex than originally thought. A seemingly simple measure of symptom severity, for example, not only varies as a function of who observes it—patient, therapist, significant other, independent clinician—but it also varies in many other parameters. Depression, for example, is at once a symptom of dysphoria, a syndrome composed of related but discrete signs, and a theoretical construct. As a symptom, it varies in level or intensity; as a syndrome, it varies in pattern and chronicity; and as a theoretical construct it varies in etiology and function. Reflecting this variation, different investigators incorporate, to different degrees, those aspects of the symptom that are of particular concern from their own perspectives.

The diversity of concepts relating to improvement, both within constructs and across studies, makes the acceptance of a discrete battery of tests to assess outcome in the treatment of any disorder, such as depression, highly unlikely. Identifying the principles of assessment that should guide the selection of instruments is more likely to be helpful and acceptable to researchers. Construct diversity and face validity are key requirements for the development of standard measures of treatment outcomes. Whatever dimensions are selected as standard fare for outcome research, the value of their measurement across studies is likely to be directly proportional to the degree that the recommended measures reflect face validity and theoretical interest. To serve these diverse roles, researchers should attempt to include measures that balance the assessment of narrow and commonly accepted aspects of change: theory-specific aspects of the change process. That is, it must reflect both the diversity of the construct under consideration and allow latitude for investigators to explore aspects of the condition and its treatment of their own interest.

Efforts should be made to distinguish between the overt signs and symptoms of the syndrome, the severity of impairment, and the theoretical understructures that guide assessment and treatment. This requires that investigators apply multiple measures of key constructs whenever possible, deriving from different theoretical aspects and rating sources. Because not all possible permutations of sources and theoretical distinctions can be assessed for all variables, investigators would be well advised to sample key combinations of sources and theoretical frames and to describe the dimensions selected in a careful and thoughtful manner. Following the logic of latent construct analysis, measuring key constructs from at least two rating sources ensures some stability and generalizability to the dimension.

The role of investigator judgment is more pronounced in a proposal such as this than in one that recommends a specific battery of instruments. The investigator is and should remain the final judge of how the measures are used and what aspects, facets, or subdimensions are included in the assessment. For example, among the standard list of dimensions proposed in the foregoing section, some are included to facilitate the disclosure of potential treatment moderators (e.g., background, therapist characteristics, expectancies, etc.). Others are reflective of the treatment outcome itself (e.g., diagnosis, symptom severity, target symptoms, etc.). The class of variable of greatest interest to the research project will partially determine the degree to which one focuses most on ensuring a broad multitheoretical perspective, a specific theoretical principle, and the common, rather than unique, sources of assessment variance. When addressing process and moderator dimensions, for example, concern should be with ensuring that a broad range of theoretically or empirically derived aspects of the variable are represented among the outcome measures. For this purpose, several theoretically diverse instruments may be used to capture the processes of change. Alternatively, when attention is directed at effectiveness and efficacy, it will be advantageous to use instruments that concentrate on the common variances among several rating sources (patient, therapist, observer, etc.) and instruments. In this latter case, the source of the ratings would be more important than the breadth of theories represented and would be emphasized to ensure adequate representation of the perspectives that represent those who have a vested interest in the patient's condition. Thus, for these latter dimensions, the tripartite model originally proposed by Strupp and Hadley (1977) is of greatest importance.

Of course, concentration on face validity, diversity, and common variance among measures still will have limited value for addressing the lack of standardization across studies. The scientific value of a standardized procedure requires that the constructs measured in one study are similar to those measured in others. Hence, other criteria are required for selecting measurement devices, beyond the concepts of face validity, construct diversity, and theoretical integrity. Thus, criteria must include principles of selection that ensure psychometric integrity in the selection of instruments.

Psychometric Criteria

Measures vary widely in their construction, method of administration, reliability, and validity. Although standards could be defined specifically to apply to each and all of these variations, a simple principle may suffice. It should be the responsibility of the investigator to address the psychometric integrity of the instruments used and particularly to demonstrate the construct validity of the instruments selected. Sound procedures should be used and described for demonstrating construct validity. Investigators should be required to justify the need for a new instrument before electing to replace established instruments with specifically developed ones in a given study. In those instances in which new instruments are justified, investigators should demonstrate that they understand the importance of using independently derived samples and methods and that they used appropriate test development procedures. Specifically, investigators should demonstrate that the instruments selected or developed have normative data by which scores can be interpreted, that reliability estimates are available that are appropriate to the particular use of the instrument, that the instruments have construct validity, and that other forms of validity (e.g., predictive validity, sensitivity, specificity, etc.) have been established as appropriate to the objectives of the study.

Placing emphasis jointly on the parsimonious use of instruments that have demonstrated both construct validity and have normative information will ensure that a common construct was being investigated across studies. It also will ensure that if investigators have developed new instruments, a relationship exists between the common constructive elements in the new ones and the established ones. Because this chapter was initiated with a view to measuring depression in treatment outcome studies, this construct can serve to illustrate my proposals.

MEASURING DEPRESSION

I have recommended that subjective distress, diagnosis, symptoms of depression and anxiety, and other targeted symptoms be among the dimensions measured consistently across treatment outcome studies. Treatment studies of depression can be used to illustrate the use of tests that capture these constructs. Diagnoses along the depressive spectrum can be reliably measured, and these can be used in studies of homogeneous populations to determine whether a participant meets the entry criteria. In studies of heterogeneous populations, assessing the diagnosis of a depressed individual may provide information to evaluate the role of moderator variables as well as providing an index of the degree of functional impairment.

Depression also is measured along a continuum of severity. Because it is closely correlated with measures of distress and overall symptom intensity (Dobson, 1985; Feldman, 1993), it is a useful index of subjective distress for studies of mixed and various populations. In studies of depressed populations, it serves as a target symptom for evaluating the efficacy of treatment.

Depressive syndromes as well as symptoms are implicated in many different psychiatric conditions; depression is a frequent secondary symp-

tom of other disorders, and measures of depressive severity mark improvement in level of dysfunction and distress across a variety of treatments.
Moreover, there are a number of well-established and easily administered
instruments that can be used for assessing depression, representing different perspectives and different facets of the depressive spectrum. Rather
than recommending the use of one or more of these for all purposes, I
present several acceptable methods, as examples, in the following paragraphs. The measures illustrated have been selected with the objectives of
ensuring that the instruments have sufficient breadth to assess syndromes,
intensity, and related symptoms. The instruments have demonstrated at
least minimal construct validity.

Syndrome Measures

In the previous paragraphs of this chapter I have emphasized the importance of including measures representing different sources of ratings in
treatment research. Here, I provide information on instruments that represent the perspectives both of clinicians and of the patient and that result
in a diagnostic classification of patients that include disorders within the
depressive spectrum.

The Schedule for Affective Disorders and Schizophrenia was developed by Spitzer and Endicott (1975) and was one of the earliest efforts to
reliably assess major affective disorders and schizophrenia using a structured interview. This procedure predates both the third edition of the *Diagnostic and Statistical Manual of Mental Disorders (DSM–III;* American
Psychiatric Association, 1980) and the other structured diagnostic interviews to be presented here. Some versions (Endicott et al., 1982) of this
method allow for the assessment of change in the patient's clinical presentation over as short a time as 1 week. This flexibility makes the procedure
useful for assessing outcomes among targeted groups as well as allows the
assessment to serve as a measure for establishing the entry criteria of participants. The construct validity and reliability of the instrument have been
established.

The Diagnostic Interview Schedule (DIS; Robins, Helzer, Croughan,
& Ratcliff, 1981) is a structured diagnostic interview based on the *DSM–
III.* It has been used extensively to ensure the presence of diagnostically

homogenous patient or participant subgroups and can be administered effectively through interactive computer. The DIS can be used to establish a primary diagnosis of major depression and to rule out comorbid psychiatric conditions.

The Structured Clinical Interview for DSM – III – R (SCID; Spitzer, Williams, & Gibbon, 1986) has modules for assessing both Axis I and Axis II disorders and is being updated to be consistent with the nosology of the fourth edition of the *DSM (DSM–IV;* American Psychiatric Association, 1994). The interview format is determined strictly by revised *DSM–III (DSM– III–R;* American Psychiatric Association, 1987) criteria, and preliminary studies reveal acceptable reliability scores. For research purposes, raters are trained extensively on criteria-based videotape samples to ensure comparability. To ensure reliability and construct validity, the training must be both intensive initially and frequently repeated to prevent rater drift.

The Millon Clinical Multiaxial Inventory – II (MCMI – II; Millon, 1987) is a revision of the original 175-item MCMI (Millon, 1983). It is a multidimensional self-report instrument. The self-report format allows a patient's perspective to be added to the diagnostic classification process in studies that are focused on a specific depressive syndrome.

The MCMI yields scales that are designed to reflect syndromes that parallel *DSM–III–R* diagnostic criteria. Several clusters of scores are obtained; the most relevant ones for our purposes are a cluster that reflects basic personality styles that are designed to correspond with the Axis II disorders, one that assesses more severe personality patterns and that corresponds with schizotypal, borderline, and paranoid personality disorders, and one that corresponds with Axis I disorders and syndromes. This latter cluster includes the spectrum of anxiety syndromes, somatoform disorder, bipolar I disorders, dysthymic disorder, alcohol and drug dependence disorders, major depression, delusional disorder, and psychotic processes (Millon & Davis, 1995).

Symptom and Severity Measures

Although most symptom measures are based on patient self-report, there also are interview measures available that allow an assessment of depression from different perspectives. In either case, these methods are distinguished from the syndrome measures by the provision of a continuous measure of intensity of depressive symptoms, independent of whether the signs and criteria of a syndrome of depression are met.

For example, the Hamilton Rating Scale for Depression (Hamilton, 1967) provides one of the most used independent ratings of patient dysphoria. The scale taps areas such as sleep disturbances, libido and sexual functioning disturbances, somatic complaints associated with depression, suicide ideation, guilt, and anergia. The clinical utility and reliability of this instrument have been well documented (Endicott, Cohen, Nee, Fleiss, & Sarantakos, 1981), and it has been used in a wide variety of studies to reflect clinician judgments of symptom severity.

The Beck Depression Inventory (Beck, 1978) is an easily administered and frequently used self-report device for assessing changes in depressive symptoms. It is readily applied in a repeated measures design and reliably assesses depression level (Beutler & Crago, 1983). Scores on this test also correspond closely with self-report measures of anxiety and general distress, making it a useful tool for evaluating subjective discomfort in studies of general and nondepressive populations.

Facets of Functioning Related to Depression

Depression is a complex phenomenon, as a syndrome, as a set of symptoms, and as the basis for theories of psychopathology and its treatment. Thus, at least when it is used as a target symptom in research, it is important to obtain observations of its impact from those outside of the patient and the clinician and to include measures that reflect on various theoretical vantage points. Partly because of their theoretical as well as practical importance, when at-risk populations are studied, it is important to obtain information regarding the interpersonal, social, and self-destructive behaviors that may be associated with depressive thoughts and feelings.

The Social Adjustment Scale (Weissman & Bothwell, 1976) is made up of 42 questions relating to everyday adjustment and performance, the content of which partially reflects an interpersonal theory of depression. Forms are available for obtaining information both from the patient and from significant others. The questions cover areas such as impairment and adequacy in social role performance at work and home, leisure activities, relationships with significant others, integrity of the family unit, and economic self-support, all of which are thought to be relevant to the development and treatment of depression from an interpersonal framework. Available norms allow comparisons to be made both to nonpatient and various patient samples.

The Scale for Suicidal Ideation (Beck, Kovacs, & Weissman, 1979) is an interview-based instrument that is designed to quantify clinical indicators of suicide potential. From a theoretical model of crisis adaptation and management, this scale attempts to assess the intensity of current suicidal intent by tapping self-destructive thoughts and wishes, suicidal threats, overt suicide plans, and depressive cognition. It uses a flexible format that allows the clinician to elicit as much information as possible in each area to accurately determine the presence of suicidal behaviors and to estimate the probability of future suicidal acts.

The Hopelessness Scale (Beck, Weissman, Lester, & Trexler, 1974) is a 20-item, self-report, true–false questionnaire that can complement clinician judgments of suicide potential from the theoretical vantage point of cognitive therapy. The Hopelessness Scale, in particular, assesses that aspect of clinical depression that most closely relates to suicidal behavior. The scale has good internal consistency and concurrent validity and is sensitive to relatively small changes in depression and suicidal thoughts over time.

CONCLUDING COMMENTS

Depression is not only one of the most prevalent psychiatric disorders in developed countries, but depressive symptoms are the most frequently observed psychiatric symptoms both among patients with other psychiatric conditions and among those with transitory life stress and medical conditions. Accordingly, I have proposed some guidelines that may guide the selection of instruments by which to assess and measure outcome of treatment. These guidelines specify the dimensions, parameters, and criteria by which measurements should be selected, and some of these guidelines are illustrated in the description of various measurement devices that are frequently used in the study of depression.

The guidelines presented here suggest that if depression is the primary problem or symptom of interest to investigators, it should be measured from several perspectives, at both symptomatic, syndromal, and theoretical levels and across several related domains of experience. It should be assessed both as a syndrome and as a set of symptoms, thus emphasizing both its qualitative and quantitative properties, and assessment should include related symptoms and domains of experience (e.g., interpersonal, cognitive, and self-destructive).

This chapter has presented examples of instruments that have at least content and construct validity and good reliability and that measure depression from different perspectives. These instruments illustrate the presence of tests that can evaluate symptom intensity and subjective distress, provide self-reports of depression, and reflect the observations of both experts and significant others. These various perspectives and measurement domains are advantageously included in all treatment research on patients who have various syndromes. In addition, a measure that identifies patients and participants' diagnostic status is warranted for defining treatable groups and for providing the diagnostic information that may be valuable for an assessment of treatment moderating variables.

REFERENCES

American Psychiatric Association. (1980). *Diagnostic and statistical manual of mental disorders* (3rd ed.). Washington, DC: Author.

American Psychiatric Association. (1987). *Diagnostic and statistical manual of mental disorders* (3rd ed., rev.). Washington, DC: Author.

American Psychiatric Association. (1994). *Diagnostic and statistical manual of mental disorders* (4th ed.). Washington, DC: Author.

Beck, A. T. (1978). *Depression inventory.* Philadelphia: Center for Cognitive Therapy.

Beck, A. T., Kovacs, M., & Weissman, A. (1979). Assessment of suicidal intention: The Scale of Suicide Ideation. *Journal of Consulting and Clinical Psychology, 47,* 343–352.

Beck, A. T., Weissman, A., Lester, D., & Trexler, L. (1974). The measurement of pessimism: The Hopelessness Scale. *Journal of Consulting and Clinical Psychology, 42,* 861–865.

Beutler, L. E., & Clarkin, E. (1990). *Systematic treatment selection: Toward targeted therapeutic interventions.* New York: Brunner/Mazel.

Beutler, L. E., & Crago, M. (1983). Self report instruments. In M. J. Lambert, E. R. Christensen, & S. DeJulio (Eds.), *The assessment of psychotherapy outcome.* New York: Brunner/Mazel.

Dobson, K. S. (1985). The relationship between anxiety and depression. *Clinical Psychology Review, 5,* 307–324.

Endicott, J., Cohen, J., Nee, J., Fleiss, J., & Sarantakos, S. (1981). Hamilton Depression Rating Scale. *Archives of General Psychiatry, 38,* 98–103.

Endicott, J., Nee, J., Fleiss, J. L., Cohen, J., Williams, J. B. W., & Simon, R. (1982). Diagnostic criteria for schizophrenia: Reliabilities and agreement between systems. *Archives of General Psychiatry, 39,* 884–889.

Feldman, L. A. (1993). Distinguishing depression and anxiety in self-report: Evidence from confirmatory factor analysis on nonclinical and clinical samples. *Journal of Consulting and Clinical Psychology, 61,* 631–638.

Hamilton, M. (1967). Development of a rating scale for primary depressive illness. *British Journal of Social and Clinical Psychology, 6,* 278–296.

Lambert, M. J. (1994). Use of psychological tests for outcome assessment. In M. E. Maruish (Ed.), *The use of psychological testing for treatment planning and outcome assessment* (pp. 75–97). Hillsdale, NJ: Erlbaum.

Lambert, M. J., Christensen, E. R., & DeJulio, S. S. (Eds.). (1983). *The assessment of psychotherapy outcome.* New York: Wiley.

Millon, T. (1983). *Millon Clinical Multiaxial Inventory manual* (3rd ed.). Minneapolis, MN: National Computer Systems.

Millon, T. (1987). *Manual for the Millon Clinical Multiaxial Inventory–II (MCMI–II).* Minneapolis, MN: National Computer Systems.

Millon, T., & Davis, R. (1995). Putting humpty-dumpty back together again: Using the Millon Clinical Multiaxial Inventory in psychological assessment. In L. E. Beutler & M. Berren (Eds.), *Integrative assessment of adult personality* (pp. 240–279). New York: Guilford Press.

Robins, L. N., Helzer, J. E., Croughan, J., & Ratcliff, K. S. (1981). National Institute of Mental Health Diagnostic Interview Schedule: Its history, characteristics, and validity. *Archives of General Psychiatry, 38,* 381–389.

Spitzer, R. L., & Endicott, J. (1975). *The Schedule for Affective Disorders and Schizophrenia (SADS).* New York: Biometrics Research Division, New York State Psychiatric Institute.

Spitzer, R. L., Williams, J. B. W., & Gibbon, M. (1986). *The Structured Clinical Interview for DSM III–R–Patient Version.* New York: Biometrics Research Department, New York State Psychiatric Institute.

Strupp, H. H., & Hadley, S. W. (1977). A tripartite model of mental health and therapeutic outcomes. *American Psychologist, 32,* 187–196.

Weissman, M. M., & Bothwell, S. (1976). Assessment of social adjustment by patient self-report. *Archives of General Psychiatry, 33,* 111–115.

Waskow, I. E., & Parloff, M. B. (Eds.). (1975). *Psychotherapy change measures* (NIMH Publication No. 74-120). Rockville, MD: National Institute of Mental Health.

10

Measuring Progress and Outcome in the Treatment of Affective Disorders

Kenneth I. Howard, Robert J. Lueger, and
Gregory G. Kolden

It is generally recognized that the process of change in psychotherapy is multidimensional. Moreover, progress and outcome in each of these dimensions have a cumulative temporal course so that both shape and amount of change are relevant to judging outcomes. How can one understand this multidimensional change with different amounts and types of treatments for affective disorders? In this chapter, we show that the operationalization and assessment of the course of improvement is tied closely to conceptions of illness, the nature of diagnosis, and evaluative perspective (e.g., patient, therapist, nonparticipant observers). We discuss how the psychometric characteristics of operational definitions of affective disorders define the sensitivity of change in marking treatment progress. Finally, we offer a phase model as a prototype for the evaluation of progress and outcome in the treatment of affective disorders and argue that a multidimensional phase model is the most comprehensive approach yet to incorporating these varied issues.

This work was partially supported by Grants RO1 MH42901 and KO5 MH00924 from the National Institute of Mental Health. We are grateful for the statistical work of Bruce Briscoe and the helpful comments of the Northwestern/Chicago psychotherapy research group.

THE CONCEPT OF ILLNESS

According to the dictionary (*American Heritage Electronic Dictionary*, 1993), *illness* is a "disease of body or mind; poor health; sickness." *Disease*, in turn, is defined as "a pathological condition of a part, an organ, or a system of an organism resulting from various causes, such as infection, genetic defect, or environmental stress, and characterized by an identifiable group of signs or symptoms." Where, full circle, a *pathological condition* is "the anatomic or functional manifestations of a disease."

Three aspects of a pathological condition are distinguished in our phase model of psychotherapy (Howard, Lueger, Maling, & Martinovich, 1993): subjective upset or distress (feeling sick), presence of pathological signs or symptoms, and disability in life functioning (interference with the person's role performances). These aspects are relevant to any conception of illness.

A (cause) pathogen is another important aspect of a pathological condition. Causes, however, are generally specific to a particular theoretical explanation. Insofar as pathogens can be identified, they constitute another domain for the assessment of treatment.

THE NATURE OF DIAGNOSIS

The dictionary defines *diagnosis* as "the art of identifying a disease [cause] from its signs and symptoms." Diagnosis is an essential element of all professions. The practitioner is given a set of observations (e.g., a leaky faucet, a car that will not start, a headache, a cough, depressed mood, fearful anxiety) and is expected to determine a causal diagnosis that accounts for these observations (e.g., a worn-out washer, a dead battery, dysfunctional thinking, childhood trauma) and that defines the corrective action to be taken. However, many diagnoses deviate from this ideal model and merely involve renaming the symptoms (e.g., glaucoma is defined by excess pressure in the eye) without implicating any specific causal agent. These descriptive diagnoses are, however, based on diagnostic procedures and can guide symptomatic treatment.

Psychiatric diagnoses are essentially descriptive and syndrome based; they do not impart causal information. If a patient manifests a certain constellation of symptoms (i.e., a syndrome), he or she is assigned a diagnosis. This diagnosis is used to explain why the patient is having these symptoms (e.g., the patient is having sleep difficulties because he or she is depressed—we know he or she is depressed, in part, because of the presence of sleep difficulties). There is a tendency to infer that a pathogen has been isolated and treatment will focus on its eradication. In fact, however, we have just renamed the symptoms and are faced with the dilemma that there are many causes (theoretical explanations) of depression. Moreover, some of these potential causes (e.g., dysfunctional thinking, object loss, neurotransmitter imbalance) also are potential causes for other syndromes. Consequently, these causes become the focus of interventions rather than the diagnosed disorder. This state of affairs is reflected in the many clinical trials that do not use diagnosis as a major outcome criterion (i.e., that do not report the number of patients who no longer qualify for the inclusion-criterion diagnosis).

Few pathogen-based diagnoses exist in the psychiatric nomenclature. Pathogen-based diagnoses have an identifed necessary or sufficient cause that, when the pathogen is treated, will lead to an alleviation of the pathological condition. Thus, treatments for pathogen-based diagnoses tend to be specific.

By contrast, syndome-based diagnoses tend to be common in psychiatric nosology. Diagnoses are derived from multiple symptom criteria, many of which share characteristics with several disorders (e.g., poor concentration is a symptom of both mood and anxiety disorders). Thus, symptom criteria are seldom completely sensitive or specific to the diagnostic category. As a result, heterogeneous symptom scales are commonly used to measure treatment outcomes.

Depression, in general, is a syndrome-based diagnosis rather than a pathogen-based diagnosis. Moreover, it is a heterogeneous disorder and a psychiatric condition that is commonly comorbid with a variety of other Axis I as well as Axis II disorders. Research on the treatment of depression has been characterized by the use of a wide variety of self-report symptom measures (see Moran & Lambert, 1983). Factor analyses of the symptoms of depression as measured by one of the most common of these self-report measures, the Beck Depression Inventory (BDI; Beck, Ward, Mendelson,

Mock, & Erbaugh, 1961; Beck, Shaw, & Emery, 1979), have shown that three clusters of symptoms can be identified: mood motivation, self-denigration, and vegetative disturbances (Startup, Rees, & Barkham, 1992; Steer, Beck, Riskind, & Brown, 1987). Each of these three clusters can be evident to a varying degree in patients with depression. Furthermore, several treatments, each perhaps focusing on a different combination of symptoms, may effectively reduce symptoms.

Syndrome-based diagnoses for heterogeneous disorders such as depression require multidimensional measurement for comprehensive progress and outcome assessment. Broad content domains should be sampled. At least three important aspects of pathological conditions have been identified in the phase model of psychotherapy: subjective distress, signs and symptoms, and impaired role functioning. Progress and outcome of treatments for mood disorders should be assessed in at least these three domains. Other theory-driven domains specific to hypothesized pathogens also might be included in such assessments (e.g., expectations of hopelessness, dysfunctional attitudes, level of object relations).

RELIABILITY AND TREATMENT
IMPLICATIONS OF DIAGNOSES

There has been a persistent dilemma throughout the history of science: The more training it takes to observe a phenomenon, the less generalizable is that phenomenon to the common language used to describe that observation. In psychology, this dilemma is manifested in the training of raters. For example, if it takes 10 hr of training to obtain acceptable interrater reliability for the rating of "friendliness," no one outside of the study could know what was meant by the term *friendliness* unless he or she could receive the same training. In this instance, the investigator (in fairness) should call the variable "what I mean by friendliness" or "friendliness as defined uniquely in my study."

What does this have to do with mood disorders? In clinical trials (whether pharmacological or psychosocial), specially trained clinicians are used commonly to conduct structured diagnostic interviews to select their patient samples. Thus, the results of such studies can be generalizable to practice only if the therapist has the necessary training (or inclination) to conduct such interviews (e.g., the Structured Clinical Interview for DSM-III-R [SCID]; Spitzer, Williams, Gibbon, & First, 1988) or if there is a high enough correspondence between a diagnosis based on such structured interviews and ordinary clinical diagnosis (in which case one would not need the structured interview in the first place). Because practicing clinicians seem to be reluctant to get the necessary training or to spend valuable clinical time in administering structured diagnostic procedures, one is left to depend on the latter "if."

What is the relationship between structured (e.g., the SCID) diagnoses and clinical diagnoses? In the clinic that is the site of our study of psychotherapy utilization (Howard et al., 1991), each patient was given a 1- to 2-hr clinical screening interview before being assigned to treatment. At the conclusion of that interview, the clinician assigned diagnoses from the revised third edition of the *Diagnostic and Statistical Manual of Mental Disorders (DSM–III–R;* American Psychiatric Association, 1987). As part of our research program, 204 participating patients also were given an SCID interview by a research clinician. In this sample, 95 patients (47%) were diagnosed (on the basis of the SCID) as having a major depression, dysthymia, or a depressive syndrome. Of these, 48% also qualified for at least one other (nondepressive) Axis I diagnosis. Table 1 shows the primary Axis I diagnoses that were assigned by clinical screening interviewers for

Table 1

Axis I Clinic Diagnoses for Patients With an Axis I (SCID) Diagnosis of Depression, Dysthymia, or Depressive Syndrome (*N* = 90)

Diagnosis	*n*	%
Major depression	48	53
Adjustment disorders	16	18
No Axis I diagnosis	16	18
Anxiety disorders	7	9
Other	3	3

NOTE: SCID = Structured Clinical Interview for DSM-III-R.

90 of these patients. As can be seen, only 53% of these patients also received an (either primary or secondary) Axis I diagnosis of depression, dysthymia, or depressive syndrome from the clinical screener.

Based solely on clinical interviewer diagnoses, 42% of the 204 patients received an intake diagnosis of clinical depression. Of these, 38% also were given at least one other (nondepressive) Axis I diagnosis, and 47% were given an Axis II diagnosis. As Table 2 shows, the majority of these patients (68%) also received an SCID diagnosis of major depression, dysthymia, or depressive syndrome. It appears that Axis I diagnoses (at least of depression) based on structured interviews or on clinical interviews do not show enough correspondence to be interchangeable and that there is considerable comorbidity of these conditions. This lack of correspondence is not surprising, of course, because it was the putative unreliability (and invalidity) of clinical diagnoses that led to the development of structured systems such as the SCID in the first place.

The implication of these findings is that clinicians cannot use their own diagnoses of affective disorders as a basis for using procedures that have been shown to be effective in clinical trials that used structured diagnostic interviews to select appropriate patients. First, they will misdiagnose a significant number of patients (if the SCID is the standard for validity). In our sample, clinicians identified only 53% of the SCID-diagnosed depressions. Second, a significant number (32%) of clinically

Table 2

SCID Diagnoses for Patients With a Clinical Axis I Diagnosis of Major Depression, Dysthymia, or Depressive Syndrome ($N = 81$)

Diagnosis	n	%
Depression	48	59
No Axis I diagnosis	19	23
Adjustment disorders	7	9
Other	5	6
Anxiety disorders	2	2

NOTE: SCID = Structured Clinical Interview for DSM-III-R.

diagnosed depressions will not qualify for this diagnosis on the basis of the SCID. The only remedy would be for clinicians to obtain a formal diagnostic workup for all patients, either by learning the procedures themselves or by referring patients to trained diagnosticians.

Why are clinicians reluctant to learn how to conduct structured diagnostic interviews? Why has a new diagnostic speciality service not developed? It must be the case that clinicians have no constructive use for diagnoses because therapists offer only a single service (their own brand of psychotherapy) to a general class of patients (people who feel the need for or are coerced into going for psychotherapy). Because therapists tend to have only one "treatment package" to offer, the diagnosis of the patient becomes irrelevant and thus not worth the time and money to obtain. All a practitioner needs to determine is that the patient needs treatment and is likely to benefit from what the therapist has to offer.

In addition, the syndrome-based diagnostic system does not seem precise enough to determine treatment decisions. In our sample of SCID-diagnosed patients with depression, 48% of them qualified for an additional SCID Axis I diagnosis. In the sample of clinical diagnoses, 38% received an additional clinical Axis I diagnosis and 47% received a clinical Axis II diagnosis. It is clear from these findings that many patients cannot be categorized neatly within the current diagnostic system.

SELF-REPORT ASSESSMENTS OF DEPRESSION

Self-report measures of depression promise a more cost-efficient alternative to the structured clinical interviews that clinicians are reluctant to use in making diagnoses of their patients. How do self-report diagnoses compare with clinician diagnoses or with structured clinical interview diagnoses?

The BDI (Beck et al., 1979, 1961) is the most widely used self-report measure of the symptoms of depression in clinical trials (Beck, Steer, & Garbin, 1988) and of the severity of depression in diagnosed patients (Piotrowski, Sherry, & Keller, 1985). The BDI typically asks the individual to "describe thoughts and feelings you may have had in the past month," although different time intervals such as a week or the past 3 weeks have been used. The BDI fully covers six of the nine symptoms for the diagnosis of major depression from the fourth edition of the *DSM* (*DSM–IV*; American Psychiatric Association, 1994) and partially covers two others (sleep difficulty but not increased sleep; losses in appetite, but not increases), and it does not address psychomotor activity and agitation. Beck et al. (1988) explained the absence of these two *DSM–IV* symptoms from the BDI: Including sleep and appetite increases would increase false-positives for a depressive diagnosis, and changes in psychomotor activity must be observed rather than self-reported to be a reliable index.

Although the BDI is a sensitive measure of depression, it is not a sufficiently specific measure of the syndrome of depression. Community and student samples have shown that individuals can score high on the BDI without having diagnosable conditions. The second Sheffield Psychotherapy Project, which examined the comparative effectiveness of two individual psychotherapies for depression, found that of 293 potential patients who exceeded a BDI cutoff score of 16, 139 (47%) met *DSM–III* criteria for a diagnosis of major depression (Startup et al., 1992). Of the group with a diagnosis of major depression (mean BDI = 24.5, *SD* = 6.73), 55% (*n* = 76) also met criteria for a diagnosis of either generalized anxiety disorder or panic disorder. Basing diagnoses on structured clinical interviews yields heterogeneous diagnostic groups, and diagnoses from self-report measures of depression do not correspond with diagnoses from structured clinical interviews.

For purposes of our large, systematic naturalistic study, we developed a symptom checklist (Current Symptoms [CS]; Howard, Brill, Lueger, O'Mahoney, & Grissom, 1993) based on the menus of the *DSM–III–R*. One of the subscales of the CS is Major Depression. This CS scale asks fully about six of the nine *DSM–IV* symptoms for major depression, partially about one other symptom (lethargy but not restlessness), and does not ask about appetite or weight changes or about fatigue or loss of energy. On the basis of this subscale, it can be determined whether, by self-report, the patient qualifies for this diagnosis of major depression. Using this criterion, 66% of patients would be diagnosed as exhibiting a major depression at intake. Table 3 shows the SCID diagnoses for these patients. As can be seen, 58% of these self-report-based patients with major depression also

Table 3

SCID Diagnoses for Patients With a Self-Report Symptom-Based Axis I Diagnosis of Major Depression ($N = 19$)

Diagnosis	n	%
Depression	11	58
No Axis I diagnosis	5	26
Bipolar disorders	2	11
Panic disorder	1	5

NOTE: SCID = Structured Clinical Interview for DSM-III-R.

qualified for an SCID diagnosis of major depression, dysthymia, or depressive disorder. Table 4 shows the clinical diagnoses for a sample of self-report-based patients with major depression. Here, 53% were assigned a depressive diagnosis at intake. It seems clear that diagnoses based on our self-report algorithm also do not correspond with diagnoses from standard or structured clinical interviews.

EVALUATIVE PERSPECTIVE

Outcome is clearly in the eyes of the beholder. In an earlier article, Krause and Howard (1976) described six perspectives (sets of beholders) regarding the outcome of psychotherapy: patients, therapists, clients, managers,

Table 4

Clinic Diagnoses for Patients With a Self-Report Symptom-Based Axis I Diagnosis of Major Depression ($N = 19$)

Diagnosis	n	%
Major depression	10	52
Bipolar disorder	3	15
No Axis I diagnosis	2	11
Adjustment disorders	2	11
Other Axis I	2	11

Table 5

Outcome Perspectives and Criteria

Perspective	Criteria				
	Well-being	Symptoms	Functioning	Pathogen	Cost
Patients	×				
Therapists		×		×	
Clients			×		
Managers					×
Sponsors			×	×	×
Researcher		×	×	×	

sponsors, and researchers (see Table 5). It seems reasonable that these perspectives would place differential value on the four aspects of illness.

Patients are the ones who (often initiate and) directly receive treatment. It is likely that their major concern will be with feeling better (subjective well-being). Therapists are the ones who deliver the treatment. It is likely that their major concern will be the elimination of symptoms (and identified pathogens). Clients are people or institutions whose interests are intended to be served by the treatment. Although patients also are usually the clients, there are many situations in which the client is a parent, supervisor, or institution (e.g., school, court). The major concern of the client is likely to be the actual functioning (behavior) of the patient. Managers are the ones who make decisions about the allocation of treatment resources. Their concern will be with treatment efficiency in attaining the goals that have been set for them by sponsors. Sponsors are the institutions that pay for the treatment. Their concern will be with patient functioning and treatment cost—some trade-off between what the treatment costs and what gains there will be in such things as enhanced job performance or medical utilization (cost offset). Finally, researchers are the ones who are concerned with the application of proper methodology for establishing and measuring the efficacy of the treatment.

Not only do these parties bring different emphases to the evaluation of the treatment, they also bring different standards of evidence. For example, the patient is probably the only stakeholder who directly knows and is most concerned with feeling well or at least better. From another point of view (e.g., the therapist, the researcher), patient well-being may appear entirely illusory. In the same vein, the researcher may hold statistically (or clinically) significant change on an established instrument (e.g., the BDI) as the criterion for progress or outcome.

We contend that whatever criteria are used to justify the initiation of treatment (e.g., a "medical necessity" criterion) also should be used to evaluate the progress and outcome of that treatment. In most cases the patient initiates the treatment, and this is usually motivated by subjective criteria (e.g., feeling badly enough to seek professional help). Treatment then is terminated by patients because they no longer deem professional help necessary, or they have concluded that the treatment they are getting is not making them feel sufficiently better.

When (nonpatient) clients initiate treatment, it is because the patient's behavior is problematic. However, clients seldom are party to the decision to terminate treatment. For example, for a substance-dependent person (e.g., alcoholic, drug addict) to receive supplemental security income disability payments from the Social Security Administration (SSA), that person must be in treatment. In this case the SSA becomes the client. Although the status of the patient is reviewed periodically by the SSA to assess improvement, the decision to terminate usually remains the patient's decision.

Therapists seldom tell patients that they (patients) do not need to enter treatment. Like most professionals, therapists will find something that needs fixing. In the main, therapists, managers, sponsors, and researchers do not initiate treatment, but each could determine the need for treatment and evaluate progress and outcome using criteria that are most relevant to their perspectives. Again, the most important consideration is that the criteria used to assess the need for treatment also be used to assess the progress and outcome for that treatment.

ASSESSING DEPRESSION FROM THE PATIENT'S PERSPECTIVE

In addition to being an economical mode of assessment, self-report measurement of depression represents the patient's perspective (at least in part). Furthermore, it is the patient's concerns that most frequently serve as the basis for engagement in therapy.

Self-report measures of depression vary in their coverage of *DSM*-specified symptoms of depression, in scale intent or purpose (i.e., criterion validity), and in the probes used to elicit self-descriptions. Three self-report measures of depression—the BDI, the Minnesota Multiphasic Personality Inventory (MMPI) Depression scale (Hathaway & McKinley, 1989), and the Self-Rating Depression Scale (Zung, 1965)—were reviewed thoroughly by Moran and Lambert (1983) as potential measures of psychotherapy outcome for the treatment of patients with depression. Since Moran and Lambert's (1983) review, the BDI has been the subject of a meta-analytic review, the MMPI has been revised, and the concept of clinical significance has become a popular approach to assessing therapeutic outcomes. In addition, three other measures of depression—the Center for Epidemiological Studies-Depression scale (Radloff, 1977), the SCL-90-R Depression subscale (Derogatis, 1974; Derogatis & Cleary, 1977), and the CS (Howard, Brill, et al., 1993) Depression subscale—have gained prominence in research assessing therapeutic gain in the treatment of depression.

The concept of the clinical significance approach (cf. Jacobson & Truax, 1991) also has gained prominence in the past decade. This approach to assessing therapeutic progress and outcome requires normative data from patient and nonpatient samples and stability estimates from nonpatient samples for specific time intervals. Thus, the psychometric properties of self-report instruments are important considerations in this methodology. The greater the internal consistency and stability in a nonpatient sample, the more sensitive is the measure to therapeutic changes. In Table 6, we present some psychometric characteristics of the six self-report measures of depression mentioned earlier.

The internal consistency estimates (coefficient alpha) of the measures are generally moderately high (.80s and lower .90s). The test–retest stability estimates vary greatly, in part because of the wide range of time intervals assessed. The standard error of measurement, which can be computed from either internal consistency or stability estimates, is useful for determining whether two measures (e.g., intake and Session 10) on the same individual are different, whether an observed score is different from a cutoff score, and whether patient and nonpatient groups differ on the

Table 6

Reliability of Six Self-Report Measures of Depression

Measure and group	Internal consistency	SEM as a % of *SD*	Stability	SEM as a % of *SD*
BDI				
Patients	.86	37.5	.65	59.2
Nonpatients	.81	43.6	.78	46.9
CES-D				
Patients	.90	31.6	.53	68.6
Nonpatients	.85	38.7	.54	67.8
CS				
Patients	.88	34.6	.77	48.0
Nonpatients	NA	NA	NA	NA
MMPI-2-D				
Patients	NA	NA	NA	NA
Nonpatients	.64	51.0	.77	48.0
SCL-90-R-D				
Patients	.82	NA	.90	NA
Nonpatients	.86	NA	.81	NA
SRDS				
Patients	.88	NA	NA	NA
Nonpatients	.93	NA	NA	NA

NOTE: SEM = standard error of measurement; BDI = Beck Depression Inventory; CES-D = Center for Epidemiological Studies-Depression scale; CS = Current Symptoms; MMPI-2-D = Minnesota Multiphasic Personality Inventory-2 Depression scale; SCL-90-R-D = SCL-90-R Depression scale; SRDS = Self-Rating Depression Scale; NA = not available.

measure. The lower the ratio of the standard error of measurement to the standard deviation, the more sensitive the measure is to assessing therapeutic change. Using the internal consistency estimates to calculate standard errors of measurement, we see in Table 6 that the standard errors of measurement are about 0.3–0.5 *SD*. A one-tailed (predicted improvement or no improvement) test at the 90% confidence level would require approximately 0.5 *SD* to show significant improvement using internal consistency estimates and approximately 0.75 *SD* using stability estimates.

Limited data are available on head-to-head comparisons of these self-report measures of depression in therapy contexts. The overall mean effect sizes of BDI and Self-Rating Depression Scale measures on the same patients were not significantly different as reported in one meta-analytic review (Lambert, Hatch, Kingston, & Edwards, 1986). The BDI and SCL-90 were compared for the measurement of reliable improvement in the NIMH Treatment of Depression Collaborative Study Project Report Data (TDCS) by Ogles, Lambert, and Sawyer (1995). Using a two-tailed 95% probability level to assess reliable change, patients in the TDCS who completed at least 12 sessions were classified as improved, not improved, or deteriorated on the basis of BDI and SCL-90 scores. Of the patients receiving psychotherapy for depression, 43.9% were reliably improved on both measures. Moreover, the same proportion was judged reliably improved using the clinician report on the Hamilton Rating Scale for Depression (HRSD).

Compared with clinicians' ratings, self-report measures of depression may underestimate initial levels of depression, especially when patients are defensive. Comparisons of self-report and clinician ratings later in therapy generally yield higher correlations (Lambert et al., 1986; Radloff, 1977; Sayer et al., 1993). In addition, the BDI has been shown in several reviews to produce significantly smaller effect sizes than the HRSD (Edwards et al., 1984; Lambert et al., 1986). A meta-analysis (Tan & Lueger, 1995) of 12 studies of the treatment of depression, mostly with some form of cognitive therapy, showed that effect sizes were consistently larger for clinician ratings on the HRSD than for self-reported depression on the BDI. Reliable improvement also tended to be higher for the HRSD than the BDI; also, the HRSD reached dosage by Session 6, whereas the BDI reached dosage by Session 8. Nevertheless, the probability of being better off when assessed by the HRSD (.91) at Session 8 was not much higher than the probability assessed by the BDI (.87).

THE PHASE MODEL OF THERAPEUTIC OUTCOMES:
A PROTOTYPE FOR TREATMENT EVALUATION

We propose the phase model of psychotherapy as a prototype for the assessment of treatment progress and outcome in mood disorders. Three domains of therapeutic change (corresponding to aspects of pathological conditions) have been identified: subjective well-being, symptomatic distress, and life functioning. Moreover, Howard, Lueger, et al. (1993) demonstrated that improvement in subjective well-being potentiates and precedes symptomatic improvement and that symptomatic improvement potentiates and precedes improvement in life functioning. Furthermore, these domains show successive lags in the point at which change is most pronounced (Martinovich, 1995). Subjective well-being improves early in treatment and shows a dose effect (50% improvement) of approximately 4 sessions. Symptoms improve more slowly, reaching dosage in approximately 12 sessions for the majority of depressive symptoms (Kopta, Howard, Lowry, & Beutler, 1994). Life functioning improves last of the three outcome categories and requires in excess of 20 sessions to achieve 50% dosage (Lueger & Howard, 1994; Mintz, Mintz, Arruda, & Hwang, 1992).

Elsewhere, Lueger, Howard, and Smart (1994) demonstrated that psychotherapy patients diagnosed with structured clinical interviews as having depressive disorders improved more slowly than patients diagnosed with anxiety disorders, with adjustment disorders, or with no disorders. Patients with both anxiety and depressive disorders improved at the slowest rate; these comorbid patients began nearly 0.50 *SD* worse than the average patient and typically did not achieve dosage in 20 sessions. All three components of the phase model showed different rates of improvement depending on the diagnosis. Life functioning particularly showed the adverse effects of comorbid diagnosis of anxiety and depression.

CONCLUDING COMMENTS

The selection of treatment evaluation assessment instruments is strongly influenced by evaluative perspectives and the sometimes-unique priorities of the stakeholders involved. The phase model explicitly recognizes that change in psychotherapy is multifaceted. As such, it offers an empirically valid prototype for measuring change in mood disorders that also is conceptually relevant to the interests of the stakeholders involved in this enterprise.

We reiterate an elegantly simple rule: The criteria used to justify the initiation of treatment also should be the criteria used to evaluate the progress and outcome of that treatment. Patients tend to be most concerned with subjective well-being. Some patients also will share with clients and sponsors (purchasers) concern for their functioning. These patients likely will be motivated to continue in treatment for longer treatment durations. Yet, we have seen that functioning improves slowly for patients with affective disorders, particularly those who are comorbid for anxiety and depressive disorders.

Therapists, although attentive to patient distress, are likely to mark change by focusing on the symptoms of patients or in analogues for the pathogens believed to produce the symptoms. As it is, therapists are likely to offer a single service that differs only in nuances and not in active ingredients across patient presentations of affective disorders. At present, use of the pathogen domain by therapists is more a treatment rationale than a measure of progress and outcome in psychotherapy. On the other hand, if the therapist persuades the patient to change or convert the initial justification for treatment to a pathogen rationale, the patient may join the therapist in recognizing success or failure by changes in symptoms or pathogen.

If the diagnosis of affective disorders is not the reason patients come to psychotherapy, then diagnosis is only a marker variable for therapists or researchers. However, we have argued that therapists may not make valid diagnoses, at least compared with structured clinical interviews. Thus, use of diagnoses as an outcome variable in the treatment of affective disorders is mainly the province of researchers.

Outcome research is now largely responsive to the increased influence of care managers, whose objective is the efficiency and effectiveness of treatment. Managers are likely to look at the rates of response (sessions to dosage) for patient (subjective well-being), therapist (symptomatic remission), and client or sponsor (life functioning) perspectives. The degree of influence of each of these parties on the manager will determine the focus of the manager's need for outcome assessment information.

REFERENCES

American Heritage Electronic Dictionary. (1993). Boston: Houghton Mifflin.

American Psychiatric Association. (1987). *Diagnostic and statistical manual of mental disorders* (3rd ed., rev.). Washington, DC: Author.

American Psychiatric Association. (1994). *Diagnostic and statistical manual of mental disorders* (4th ed.). Washington, DC: Author.

Beck, A. T., Shaw, B. F., & Emery, G. (1979). *Cognitive therapy of depression.* New York: Guilford Press.

Beck, A. T., Steer, R. A., & Garbin, M. G. (1988). Psychometric properties of the Beck Depression Inventory: Twenty-five years of evaluation. *Clinical Psychology Review, 8,* 77–100.

Beck, A. T., Ward, C. H., Mendelson, M., Mock, J., & Erbaugh, J. (1961). An inventory for measuring depression. *Archives of General Psychiatry, 4,* 561–571.

Derogatis, L. R. (1974). The Hopkins Symptom Checklist (HSCL): A self-report symptom inventory. *Behavioral Science, 19,* 1–15.

Derogatis, L. R., & Cleary, H. (1977). *SCL-90R administration, scoring, and procedures manual.* Baltimore: Clinical Psychometric Research.

Edwards, B. C., Lambert, M. J., Moran, P. W., McCully, T., Smith, K. C., & Ellingson, A. G. (1984). A meta-analysis comparison of the Beck Depression Inventory and the Hamilton Rating Scale for Depression as measures of treatment outcome. *British Journal of Clinical Psychology, 23,* 93–99.

Hathaway, S. R., & McKinley, J. C. (1989). *MMPI-2: Manual for administration and scoring.* Minneapolis: University of Minnesota Press.

Howard, K. I., Brill, P., Lueger, R. J., O'Mahoney, M. T., & Grissom, G. (1993). *Integra Outpatient Tracking Assessment: Psychometric properties.* Radnor, PA: Integra.

Howard, K. I., Lueger, R. J., Maling, M. S., & Martinovich, Z. (1993). A phase model of psychotherapy: Causal mediation of outcome. *Journal of Consulting and Clinical Psychology, 61,* 678–685.

Howard, K. I., Orlinsky, D. E., Saunders, S. M., Bankoff, E. A., Davidson, C. V., & O'Mahoney, M. T. (1991). Northwestern University–University of Chicago Psychotherapy Research Program. In L. E. Beutler & M. Crago (Eds.), *Psychotherapy research: An international review of programmatic studies* (pp. 65–73). Washington, DC: American Psychological Association.

Jacobson, N. S., & Truax, P. (1991). Clinical significance: A statistical approach to defining meaningful change in psychotherapy research. *Journal of Consulting and Clinical Psychology, 59,* 12–19.

Kopta, S. M., Howard, K. I., Lowry, J. L., & Beutler, L. E. (1994). Patterns of symptomatic recovery in psychotherapy. *Journal of Consulting and Clinical Psychology, 62,* 1009–1016.

Krause, M. S., & Howard, K. I. (1976). Program evaluation in the public interest:

A new research methodology. *Community Mental Health Journal, 12,* 291–300.

Lambert, M. J., Hatch, D. R., Kingston, M. D., & Edwards, B. C. (1986). Zung, Beck, and Hamilton rating scales as measures of treatment outcome: A meta-analytic comparison. *Journal of Consulting and Clinical Psychology, 54,* 54–59.

Lueger, R. J., Howard, K. I., & Smart, B. (1994, February). *The effectiveness of psychotherapy with anxiety and mood disorders: Contributions of the dose-effect and phase models.* Paper presented at the NIMH Conference on Research Methodology, Bethesda, MD.

Lueger, R. J., & Howard, K. I. (1994, June). *Assessing life change of psychotherapy patients.* Paper presented at the international meeting of the Society for Psychotherapy Research, York, England.

Martinovich, Z. (1995). *A growth curve analysis of the phase model components.* Unpublished doctoral dissertation, Northwestern University, Evanston, IL.

Mintz, J., Mintz, L., Arruda, M., & Hwang, S. (1992). Treatments of depression and the functional capacity to work. *Archives of General Psychiatry, 49,* 761–768.

Moran, P. W., & Lambert, M. J. (1983). A review of current assessment tools for monitoring changes in depression. In M. S. Lambert, E. R. Christensen, & S. S. DeJulio (Eds.), *The assessment of psychotherapy outcome* (pp. 263–303). New York: Wiley.

Ogles, B. M., Lambert, M. J., & Sawyer, J. D. (1995). Clinical significance of the National Institute of Mental Health Treatment of Depression Collaborative Research Program Data. *Journal of Consulting and Clinical Psychology, 63,* 321–326.

Piotrowski, C., Sherry, D., & Keller, J. W. (1985). Psychodiagnostic test usage: A survey of the Society for Personality Assessment. *Journal of Personality Assessment, 49,* 15–29.

Radloff, L. S. (1977). The CES-D Scale: A self-report depression scale for research in the general population. *Applied Psychological Measurement, 1,* 358–401.

Sayer, N. A., Sackeim, H. A., Moeller, J. R., Prudic, J., Devanand, D. P., Coleman, E. A., & Kiersky, J. E. (1993). The relations between observer-rating and self-report of depressive symptomatology. *Psychological Assessment, 5,* 350–360.

Spitzer, R. L., Williams, J. B. W., Gibbon, M., & First, M. B. (1988). *Structured Clinical Interview for DSM-III-R.* Washington, DC: American Psychiatric Press.

Startup, M., Rees, A., & Barkham, M. (1992). Components of major depression examined via the Beck Depression Inventory. *Journal of Affective Disorders, 26,* 251–260.

Steer, R. A., Beck, A. T., Riskind, J. H., & Brown, G. (1987). Relationships between the Beck Depression Inventory and the Hamilton Rating Scale for Depression in depressed outpatients. *Journal of Psychopathology and Behavioral Assessment, 9,* 327–339.

Tan, L., & Lueger, R. J. (1995, June). *Dose-effect models of improvement for the treatment of depression: 50% symptom reduction vs. reliable improvement criteria.* Paper presented at the international meeting of the Society for Psychotherapy Research, Vancouver, British Columbia, Canada.

Zung, W. W. K. (1965). A self-rating depression scale. *Archives of General Psychiatry, 12,* 63–70.

11

A Core Battery of Measures of Depression and Principles for Their Selection

Lester Luborsky, Louis Diguer, Robert J. DeRubeis, and Kelly A. Schmidt

W hen—not *if*—the next set of researchers set about to restudy the outcomes of psychotherapies for depression, they will need guidance about how to choose from among the many possible measures. There have been many such studies of outcomes, there will be many more, and the choices of measures are still difficult.

Assembling core batteries that suit major diagnoses is a currently popular goal that is shared by the planners of the American Psychological Association's conference on the selection of core batteries. In accord with this goal, our contribution to the conference is accomplished here through (a) a description of a proposed core battery for patients diagnosed with major depression, chronic depression, or both and (b) a set of principles, along with some supporting data, that offer reasons for the selection of these measures for evaluating change in depression.

This chapter was supported in part by Research Scientist Awards from the National Institute on Drug Abuse (DA00168-23A) and the National Institute of Mental Health (NIMH; MH40710-22) to Lester Luborsky; partially supported by supplement to MH-39673 from the NIMH's Affective and Anxiety Disorders Branch to Lester Luborsky for a study of major depression; and by a Center for Psychotherapy Research grant (P50MH45178) to Paul Crits-Christoph.

SOURCES OF SUPPORTING DATA
FOR A PROPOSED BATTERY

Our supporting data comes from a study involving initial, termination, and follow-up assessments of 49 patients diagnosed with either major depression or chronic depression (Luborsky, Diguer, et al., 1996). All patients were treated using short-term, manual-guided supportive–expressive dynamic psychotherapy, which has a usual limit of 16 sessions (Luborsky, et al, 1995). Other comparison data came from the major clinical trial studies of depression, particularly the National Institute of Mental Health (NIMH) Collaborative Study of Depression (Elkin, Parloff, Hadley, & Autry, 1985; Elkin et al., 1989).

A revered ancestor of the present effort to assemble a core battery was Waskow and Parloff's (1975) guide, which was sponsored by the NIMH. An updated review in the same useful genre was presented by McCullough (1993). These previously suggested batteries were mostly not specific for each psychiatric diagnosis. Our aim, by contrast, was to make a representative selection of measures that would provide a more diagnosis-specific core battery for an important psychiatric diagnosis: depression. Athough there is no evidence for the benefits of distinctive core batteries for different psychiatric diagnostic groups, it is a good working assumption that such batteries are valuable. We also assume that some researchers will make use of this proposed core battery, although previous core batteries have not been relied on much in the studies so far, as we know from the experience with Waskow and Parloff's (1975) core battery as surveyed by McCullough (1993).

A PROPOSED CORE BATTERY OF MEASURES
FOR PATIENTS WITH DEPRESSION

In this chapter, we discuss the measures in our proposed battery (also see the Appendix, with references about each one). These measures were selected to reflect the application of a set of principles and domains for the selection of the measures. Our final list of measures actually is a reduced core battery that combines the measures that are common to two larger batteries: one for major depression and one for chronic depression. It is much shorter than either in that it consists only of the measures that are common to both batteries.

PRINCIPLES FOR THE SELECTION OF MEASURES IN THE CORE BATTERY

The specific principles used for selecting each measure are listed in the Appendix, and the rationale for each is explained briefly in the sections that follow. For more detail, see Luborsky and Fiske (1995).

This question must occur to all readers though: Would other experts in psychotherapy research agree about the importance of each principle and each measure? To anticipate this question, we made the Appendix into a questionnaire and administered it to six experts who each had at least 8 years of experience with psychotherapy outcome studies. Their ratings were made on a 1–4 scale, defined as follows: 4 = a principle that is very important to include in choosing measures; 3 = a principle that is moderately important to include; 2 = a principle that is marginal; and 1 = a principle that is not important to include. The experts were mostly in close agreement with us, with mean ratings close to 4, except for Principles 7–10, which were close to 3.

Principle 1: The Battery of Measures Should Include Measures of General Functioning

It is essential to include measures of general functioning (Principle 1) along with measures of specific symptoms (Principle 2). The inclusion of both types of measures will enable comparisons of the amount of benefit on each type of outcome measure. The measures that are specific to the patient's symptoms should show more improvement than the general outcome measures. That finding appeared in the Penn Psychotherapy Study (Luborsky, Crits-Christoph, Mintz, & Auerbach, 1988) and should be examined in other samples.

Another reason for inclusion of both general functioning measures and specific symptom-related measures is to be able to examine the relative predictive capacity of each type of measure. There is evidence that measures of the severity of impairment of general functioning typically predict outcome better than the severity of the target symptom. In a sample ($N = 49$) of depressed patients diagnosed according to criteria from the revised third edition of the *Diagnostic and Statistical Manual of Mental Disorders* (*DSM–III–R*; Luborsky, Diguer, et al., 1996), the measures of general functioning were stronger predictors than the measures of symptom severity. The same finding emerged before from a study of opiate-addicted patients in psychotherapy (Woody et al., 1983). We suggest several useful measures of general functioning.

Psychological Health

Both the Health-Sickness Rating Scale (HSRS; Luborsky, 1962, 1975b; Luborsky, Diguer, Luborsky, McLellan, et al., 1993) or the Global Assessment of Functioning (GAF) version of the HSRS (Endicott, Spitzer, Fleiss, & Cohen, 1976) are included in this listing because they are essentially alternate forms of the same clinical observer measure. These two scales correlate highly with one another because the scale points of the GAF and even its wording are derived from the HSRS. In four studies they correlated at .9 or above with each other (Luborsky, Diguer, Luborsky, McLellan, et al., 1993). The HSRS and the GAF are recommended because of their high reliability, contribution to the prediction of outcomes of psychotherapy (Luborsky et al., 1993), and their low cost of application. In our article on chronic versus nonchronic depression (Luborsky, Diguer, et al., 1996), for example, we found psychological health as measured by the HSRS and GAF to be the best predictor of outcome. Furthermore, initial GAF correlated .64 with a linear model that combined initial Hamilton Rating Scale for Depression (HRSD), comorbid Axis I diagnosis, the length of the current episode of depression, and the number of previous episodes of depression. Psychological health measures appear to be able to summarize the condition of patients suffering from depression.

Global Improvement

A judgment of improvement requires that the judge know the initial state of the patient. However, global improvement is recommended on the bases of both economy (it takes little time to assess) and common usage (Luborsky, 1975a). However, there is an additional reason: In contrast to the HSRS and GAF measures of change, ratings of improvement do not require the operation of residualizing the gain. As Mintz, Mintz, Arruda, and Hwang (1992) found, and as is reported in Luborsky et al. (1988), a clinical judgment of global improvement appears to involve a mental operation that corrects for initial level; we deducted this because the residualized gain score correlated highly with the clinical judge's improvement ratings.

Social Assets

This topic includes job functioning, marital functioning, and other assets as assessed by the Social Assets Scale (Luborsky, Todd, & Katcher, 1973). The importance of Principle 1 is most dramatically illustrated by the comparative assessment of depressive symptoms relative to functional capacity to work as reviewed by Mintz et al. (1992). They found only 10 studies among 4,000 outcome studies in which the impact of treatment of depression on the functional capacity to work was reported. In the 10 studies, with 827 patients, a return to the capacity for work functioning took longer to achieve than improvement in depression. Also improvements in work satisfaction and interest came before improvements in depressive disorders in 50% of the patients.

Maturity of Relationships (Observer) and Self-Report

Because the Core Conflictual Relationship Theme (CCRT) evaluates only the pattern of relationships, an important additional dimension also needs to be evaluated: the maturity of the relationships in the pattern (as illustrated in Kasabakalian-McKay, 1995). The scales by Weston, Barends, Leigh, Mendel, and Silbert (1988), which measure maturity of object relations, can be applied to the same relationship narratives used for estimating the CCRT. The quality of the relationships, including the capacity to form an alliance, can be estimated by a questionnaire, such as the Helping Alliance (Luborsky, Barber, et al., 1996).

Capacity to Internalize the Gains (Self-Report)

The capacity to internalize the gains of the psychotherapy is essential for all patients, and for a few patients it can be a critical deficit (Luborsky, 1984, pp. 26–28). Until Orlinsky and Geller (1993) developed one, there were no self-report measures of this capacity. These measures include specific capacities that correlate with outcome, such as the arousal of positive feeling associated with representations of the therapist and the recall of the problem-solving methods worked out in therapy.

Principle 2: The Battery Should Include Severity of the Symptoms of Depression and Major Characteristics of the Depression and Associated Disorders

Severity of the Depression

Such a variable might make a difference predictively, but there is only slight evidence to support it. With depressed patients, for example, Luborsky, Diguer, et al. (1996) found that the measure was not a good predictor in a sample of depressed patients whose depression ranged from mild to moderately severe (very severe and psychotic depression were not included).

For the severity of depressive symptoms the measures should include self-rated measures, such as the Beck Depression Inventory (BDI), and observer-rated measures, such as the HRSD. Luborsky, Diguer, et al., 1996 found that an observer-rated scale of depression (the HRSD) was a better predictor of psychological health outcome than was a self-report scale (the BDI). For goals of treatment, the measures should include the target symptom measure (Battle et al., 1966).

The degree to which the depression interferes with the person's capacity to function should be measured as it is in the measures of general functioning. This dimension varies considerably from patient to patient; some patients are able to keep up the level of their work and relationships despite moderately severe depression, and some are not.

Nonchronic Major Versus Chronic Major Depression

The diagnosis of depression is best guided by the *DSM–III–R* or the fourth edition of the *DSM* (*DSM–IV*). This chronic versus nonchronic distinction is worth making as an aid to research, but the evidence is mixed that the distinction makes a difference in the prediction of outcome of the psychotherapy. It did not for Luborsky, Diguer, et al. (1996), and it did for

Thase et al. (in press): Chronic depression was not treated as effectively as nonchronic depression.

Specific chronicity measures need to be specified. These include length of current illness, number of previous episodes, years since the first episode, and age. Measures of chronicity combined with other measures of severity add a slight increment to the predictability of outcomes (Luborsky, Diguer, et al., 1996).

Personality Disorder

The addition of a measure of personality disorder (e.g., the Structured Clinical Interview for DSM-II) to a measure of general functioning should make a difference predictively, but it has operated inconsistently; it did for Diguer, Barber, and Luborsky (1993) and Shea, Pilkonis, Beckham, and Collins (1990), but it did not for Luborsky, Diguer, et al. (1996).

Principle 3: The Measures Should Represent Dimensions From the Major Psychotherapeutic Orientations, Especially the Dynamic and the Behavioral

It sometimes is noted that assessment batteries are deficient in theory-relevant measures. Persons (1991) pointed to this deficiency in measures that are relevant to cognitive–behavioral psychotherapy. The coverage of assessment measures in most studies is even more deficient in measures that are relevant to the theory of dynamic change. We provide examples of theory-relevant measures of dynamic dimensions that should be used:

Self-Understanding

There have been many attempts to make such measures (Connolly, Crits-Christoph, Schweizer, & Shappell, 1966; Crits-Christoph & Luborsky, 1990b; Luborsky, 1953; Morgan, Luborsky, Crits-Christoph, Curtis, & Solomon, 1982), but there are no established measures.

Central Relationship Pattern

The assessment of the central relationship pattern by the CCRT provides a well-established measure that shows similarities to the concept of the transference pattern (Luborsky, 1990, in press). The CCRT is distinctive for each person, and it shows changes that are associated with the benefits of psychotherapy. For example, the degree of positivity of relationship interactions increases for improved patients (Crits-Christoph & Luborsky, 1990a. Luborsky, in press).

Mastery of Conflictual Patterns

A reliable and valid measure of mastery has been constructed (Grenyer, 1994). The measure is theoretically important in dynamic psychotherapy, and it correlates with the benefits of psychotherapy (Grenyer, 1994; Grenyer & Luborsky, 1996).

Maturity of Defenses

This appears to make a difference in outcomes (Perry, 1993).

Examples of theory-relevant measures of cognitive–behavioral therapy include the following:

The Attributional Style Questionnaire (Seligman, Abramson, Semmel, & von Baeyer, 1979) and the Dysfunctional Attitudes Scale (Weissman, 1979) are now widely used measures. A third one, the Ways of Responding Questionnaire, is becoming used more and more as a measure of cognitive skill (Barber & DeRubeis, 1989, 1992).

Principle 4: The Measures Should Include the Major Assessment-Relevant Spheres

These spheres include (a) intrapsychic, such as the CCRT, (b) interpersonal such as the Inventory of Interpersonal Problems, and (c) external stress, such as the Psychiatric Epidemiology Research Interview (PERI).

Principle 5: The Measures Should Include the Three Major Vantage Points

The two main ones are the patient self-report and observer judgments. A third vantage point is objective measures, such as biochemical ones, which have been lacking in consistent validity.

Principle 6: The Measures Should Include Those That Are Predictors of Outcome in Psychotherapy

It is important for valid comparative treatment studies that the groups should be equalized at the intial point in terms of the predictive measures.

Equalization is not always achieved by random assignment. Two measures that are especially central in this equalization are psychological health (Luborsky et al., 1993) and antisocial personality (Woody, McLellan, Luborsky, & O'Brien, 1985).

Although comparisons of outcomes of different forms of psychotherapy typically yield nonsignificant differences (Luborsky, Singer, & Luborsky, 1975; Luborsky, Diguer, Luborsky, Singer, & Dickter, 1993; Smith, Glass, & Miller, 1980), it happens occasionally that significant differences appear. On those occasions, initial group differences in the level of the predictive measures may be responsible. In fact, it is a good hypothesis that when significant differences in outcomes appear between treatments, extrinsic factors (e.g., differences in initial levels of the patient's psychiatric severity, the therapists' level of skill) are more likely to be implicated than intrinsic factors (e.g., the relative merits of the treatments themselves).

Principle 7: Each Patient's Achievement of Specific Goals Should be Assessed

The way to measure a patient's achievement of specific goals is through an initial measure of each patient's goals and a termination measure of the achievement of those goals. The usefulness of using methods of this type, such as the target complaints measure (Battle et al., 1966), was illustrated in the Penn Psychotherapy Study (Luborsky et al., 1988), in which the gain in the target complaints was slightly larger than the gain in the general functioning measures. This finding should be compared with findings of other studies because it seems logical that change in the area of the patient's specific goals will continue to be found to be more prominent than changes in more general dimensions.

Principle 8: The Measures Should Include a Representative Sample of the Most Widely Used Ones

This criterion provides for continuity with past studies and simplifies comparisons among studies. An example of a conventionally used simple outcome measure is the Improvement Scale (Luborsky, 1975a). Others are the HSRS, the GAF, and the BDI.

Principle 9: The Cost of Assessment Needs to Be Considered and Weighed Relative to Usefulness of the Results

Questionnaires tend to be most economical to use despite their well-known limits. A *DSM–IV* based assessment, however, may still be useful despite its costliness. By contrast, the Rorschach may not be cost-effective for many studies.

Principle 10: Psychometric Properties

The most basic of psychometric properties that need careful research are the reliability and validity of the measures.

SUMMARY

To deal with the task of selecting the measures for a core battery, we have relied on a two-stage approach: (a) assembling the most useful principles for the selection of measures and (b) choosing the best measures that fit each principle. The decisionmaking about the selection of principles was aided by a study of 49 depressed patients in time-limited dynamic psychotherapy (Luborsky, Diguer, et al., 1996) compared with major studies of depression, especially the NIMH collaborative study of the treatment of depression (Elkin et al., 1985, 1989). Ten such principles were listed, and each measure in the proposed battery was identified in terms of the principles that informed its selection. The 10 principles that led to the measures were:

1. inclusion of measures of general functioning
2. inclusion of measures of the major characteristics of the symptoms of depression
3. measures representing major dimensions from the major psychotherapeutic orientations
4. measures selected from the major assessment-related spheres such as intrapsychic, interpersonal, and external
5. from the major vantage points such as self-report and observer
6. the predictors of outcomes
7. special measures of achievement of goals

8. the most widely used measures
9. the cost of assessment
10. the essential psychometric properties

In future studies, it would be a relief to be able to compare results obtained from studies that used the same core battery. We were able to do only a bit of this comparison across samples with the Penn sample versus the collaborative study of depression sample (e.g., with the HSRS, GAF, and the BDI) and were able to show considerable similarity in results on these two measures (Luborsky, Diguer, et al., 1996).

Having come to the end of this task for now, we may ask a more general question: "Are these principles and proposed measures likely to be different for depression than for other diagnoses such as anxiety?" Our answer is that most of the time, the principles and measures will be the same across different diagnoses. But, a major area of difference will likely be in the specific measures of the main symptom chosen for each study.

PRINCIPLES AND RELATED MEASURES FOR
A DEPRESSION CORE BATTERY

___1. *General Functioning*
  ___Psychological health GAF/HSRS (or HSRS Global with the 7 criteria, mean; observer)
  ___Global Improvement Rating Scale (observer; Luborsky, 1975a)
  ___Social Assets Scale (Luborsky, Todd, & Katcher, 1973; self-report)
    ___Marital status
    ___Education
    ___Employment
    ___Occupation
  ___Maturity of relationships (Weston, Barends, Leigh, Mendel, & Silbert, 1988; observer)
  ___Capacity to internalize gains (Orlinsky & Geller, 1993)
___2. *Main specific symptoms and related symptoms*
  ___Main diagnosis (and related diagnoses)
    ___*DSM–IV* (Axis I; observer)
  ___Severity
    ___Beck Depression Inventory (Beck, Steer, Garbin, 1988; self-report)
    ___Hamilton Rating Scale for Depression (Hamilton, 1960; observer)
  ___Interference of depression with capacity to function
  ___Chronicity
    ___Length of current illness
    ___Number of prior episodes
    ___Years since first episode
  ___Personality disorder (Axis II)

___3. *Representing different types of treatments*
  ___Dynamic
    ___Self understanding (Crits-Christoph & Luborsky, 1990;
      (Morgan, Luborsky, Crits-Christoph, Curtis, & Solomon,
      1982).
    ___Core Conflictual Relationship Theme (CCRT or related
      measures; Luborsky, in press; observer)
    ___Mastery of conflictual pattern (Grenyer, 1994; observer)
    ___Defenses (observer; Perry, 1993)
  ___Cognitive
    ___Attributional style (ASQ; Seligman, Abramson, Semmel, &
      von Baeyer, 1979; self-report)
    ___Dysfunctional Attitudes Scale (Weissman, 1979; self-report)
    ___Cognitive skills (Ways of Responding questionnaire; Barber &
      De Rubeis, 1992)
___4. *Major spheres*
  ___Intrapsychic (e.g., SASB [Benjamin, 1974], CCRT)
  ___Interpersonal (e.g., SASB, CCRT, IIP [Horowitz, Rosenberg,
    Baer, Ureño, & Villaseñor, 1988])
  ___External stress (e.g., PERI)
___5. *Assessment vantage points*
  ___Self-report
  ___Observer rating (therapist; diagnostician-evaluator)
  ___Objective test (e.g., biological measures)
___6. *Special predictors of outcome*
  ___GAF (Endicott, Spitzer, Fleiss, & Cohen, 1976); HSRS (Lubor-
    sky, 1975a)
  ___Antisocial personality (Woody, McLellan, Luborsky, & O'Brien,
    1985)
___7. *Achievement of patient's goals*
  ___Target complaints (Battle et al., 1966)
  ___Goal attainment
___8. *Common usage*
___9. *Cost of measure*
___10. *Psychometric properties*

NOTE. GAR = Global Assessment of Functioning; HSRS = Health-Sickness Rating Scale; *DSM–IV* = fourth edition of the *Diagnostic and Statistical Manual of Mental Disorders,* ASQ = Attributional Style Questionnaire; SASB = Structural Analysis of Social Behavior; IIP = Inventory of Interpersonal Problems; PERI = Psychiatric Epidemiology Research Interview.

REFERENCES

Barber, J. P., & DeRubeis, R. J. (1989). On second thought: Where the action is in cognitive therapy for depression. *Cognitive Therapy and Research, 13,* 441–457.

Barber, J. P., & DeRubeis, R. J. (1992). The Ways of Responding: Development and initial validation of a scale to assess compensatory skills. *Behavioral Assessment, 14,* 93–115.

Battle, C., Imber, S., Hoehn-Saric, R., Stone, A. R., Nash, C., & Frank, J. D. (1966). Target complaints as criteria of improvement. *American Journal of Psychotherapy, 20,* 184–192.

Beck, A. T., Steer, R. A., & Garbin, M. G. (1988). Psychometric properties of the Beck Depression Inventory: Twenty-five years of evaluation. *Clinical Psychology Review, 8,* 77–100.

Benjamin, L. S. (1974). Structural analysis of social behavior. *Psychological Review, 81,* 392–425.

Connolly, M. B., Crits-Christoph, P., Schweizer, E., & Shappell, S. (1966, June). *Change in self-understanding of interpersonal patterns across supportive expressive psychodynamic psychotherapy.* Paper presented at the annual meeting of the Society for Psychotherapy Research, Amelia Island, FL.

Crits-Christoph, P., & Luborsky, L. (1990a). Changes in CCRT pervasiveness during psychotherapy. In L. Luborsky & P. Crits-Christoph (Eds.), *Understanding transference—The CCRT method* (pp. 133–146). New York: Basic Books.

Crits-Christoph, P., & Luborsky, L. (1990b). The measurement of self-understanding. In L. Luborsky & P. Crits-Christoph (Eds.), *Understanding transference: The CCRT method* (pp. 189–196). New York: Basic Books.

Diguer, L., Barber, J., & Luborsky, L. (1993). Three concomitants: Personality disorder, psychiatric severity and outcome of dynamic psychotherapy of major depression. *American Journal of Psychiatry, 150,* 1246–1248.

Elkin, I., Parloff, M., Hadley, S., & Autry, J. (1985). NIMH treatment of depression collaborative research program: Background and research plan. *Archives of General Psychiatry, 42,* 305–316.

Elkin, I., Shea, T., Watkins, J., Imber, S., Sotsky, S., Colins, J., Glass, D., Pilkonis, P., Leber, W., Docherty, J., Fiester, S., & Parloff, M. (1989). National Institute of Mental Health Treatment of Depression Collaborative Research Program: General effectiveness of treatments. *Archives of General Psychiatry, 46,* 971–982.

Endicott, J., Spitzer, R., Fleiss, J., & Cohen, J. (1976). The Global Assessment Scale: A procedure for measuring overall severity of psychiatric disturbance. *Archives of General Psychiatry, 33,* 766–771.

Grenyer, B. (1994). *Mastery Index I: A research and scoring manual.* University of Wollongong, Australia.

Grenyer, B., & Luborsky, L. (1996). Dynamic change in psychotherapy: Mastery of interpersonal conflict. *Journal of Consulting and Clinical Psychology, 64,* 411–416.

Hamilton, M. (1960). A rating scale for depression. *Journal of Neurology, Neurosurgery, and Psychiatry, 23,* 56–62.

Horowitz, L. M., Rosenberg, S. E., Baer, B. A., Ureño, G., & Villaseñor, V. S. (1988). Inventory of Interpersonal Problems: Psychometric properties and clinical applications. *Journal of Consulting and Clinical Psychology, 56,* 885–892.

Kasabakalian-McKay, R. (1995). *Referential Activity, object relation, and affiliative trust-mistrust as predictors of treatment outcome in short-term supportive-expressive psychotherapy for major depression.* Unpublished doctoral dissertation, Adelphi University.

Luborsky, L. (1953). Self-interpretation of the TAT as a clinical technique. *Journal of Projective Techniques, 17,* 217–223.

Luborsky, L. (1962). Clinicians' judgments of mental health: A proposed scale. *Archives of General Psychiatry, 7,* 404–417.

Luborsky, L. (1975a). Assessment of outcome of psychotherapy by independent clinical evaluators: A review of the most highly recommended research measures. In I. E. Waskow & M. B. Parloff (Eds.), *Psychotherapy change measures* (DHEW Publication No. ADM 74-120, pp. 233–242). Washington, DC: U.S. Government Printing Office.

Luborsky, L. (1975b). Clinicians' judgments of mental health: Specimen case descriptions and forms for the Health-Sickness Rating Scale. *Bulletin of the Menninger Clinic, 35,* 448–480.

Luborsky, L. (1984). *Principles of psychoanalytic psychotherapy: A manual for supportive-expressive (SE) treatment.* New York: Basic Books.

Luborsky, L. (1990). The convergence of Freud's observations about transference with CCRT evidence. In L. Luborsky & P. Crits-Christoph (Eds.), *Understanding transference: The CCRT method* (pp. 251–266). New York: Basic Books.

Luborsky, L. (in press). Core Conflictual Relationship Themes (CCRT): A basic case formulation method. In T. Eells (Ed.), *Handbook of psychotherapy case formulation*. New York: Guilford Press.

Luborsky, L., Barber, J. P., Siqueland, L., Johnson, S., Najavits, L. M., Frank, A., & Daley, D. (1996). The Revised Helping Alliance questionnaire–II (HAq-II). Psychometric properties. *Journal of Psychotherapy Research and Practice, 6,* 260–271.

Luborsky, L., Crits-Christoph, P., Mintz, J., & Auerbach, A. (1988). *Who will benefit from psychotherapy? Predicting therapeutic outcomes.* New York: Basic Books.

Luborsky, L., Diguer, L., Barber, J. P., Cacciola, J., Moras, K., Schmidt, K., & De-Rubeis, R. (1996). Factors in outcomes of short-term dynamic psychotherapy for chronic versus non-chronic major depression. *Journal of Psychotherapy Research and Practice, 5,* 152–159.

Luborsky, L., Diguer, L., Luborsky, E., McLellan, A. T., Woody, G., & Alexander, L. (1993). Psychological health as a predictor of the outcomes of psychotherapy. *Journal of Consulting and Clinical Psychology, 61,* 542–548.

Luborsky, L., Diguer, L., Luborsky, E., Singer, B., & Dickter, D. (1993). The efficacy of dynamic psychotherapies. Is it true that everyone has won so all shall have prizes? In N. Miller, L. Luborsky, J. P. Barber, & J. Docherty (Eds.), *Psychodynamic treatment research: A handbook for clinical practice* (pp. 447–514). New York: Basic Books.

Luborsky, L., & Fiske, D. W. (1995). Principles for designing studies of the process and efficacy of psychotherapies. In P. E. Shrout & S. T. Fiske (Eds.), *Personality research, methods, and theory: A Festschrift honoring Donald W. Fiske* (pp. 295–312). Hillsdale, NJ: Erlbaum.

Luborsky, L., Mark, D., Hole, A. V., Popp, C., Goldsmith, B., & Cacciola, J. (1995). Manual for supportive-expressive (SE) dynamic therapy of depression: Adaptation of the general SE manual. In J. Barber & P. Crits-Christoph (Eds.), *Dynamic therapy manuals for Axis I diagnoses* (pp. 13–42). New York: Basic Books.

Luborsky, L., Singer, B., & Luborsky, E. (1975). Comparative studies of psychotherapies: Is it true that "everyone has won and all must have prizes?" *Archives of General Psychiatry, 32,* 995–1008.

Luborsky, L., Todd, T. C., & Katcher, A. H. (1973). A self-administered social assets scale for predicting physical and psychological illness and health. *Journal of Psychosomatic Research, 17,* 109–120.

McCullough, L. (1993). Standard and individualized psychotherapy outcome measures: A core battery. In N. Miller, L. Luborsky, J. P. Barber, & J. P. Docherty (Eds.), *Psychodynamic treatment research: A handbook for clinical practice* (pp. 469–496). New York: Basic Books.

Mintz, J., Mintz, I., Arruda, J., & Hwang, S. (1992). Treatment of depression and the functional capacity to work. *Archives of General Psychiatry, 49,* 761–768.

Morgan R., Luborsky, L., Crits-Christoph, P., Curtis, H., & Solomon, J. (1982). Predicting the outcomes of psychotherapy by the Penn Helping Alliance Rating Method. *Archives of General Psychiatry, 39,* 397–402.

Orlinsky, D., & Geller, J. (1993). Patients' representations of their therapists and therapy: New measures. In N. E. Miller, L. Luborsky, J. P. Barber, & J. P. Docherty (Eds.), *Psychodynamic treatment research: A handbook for clinical practice* (pp. 243–468). New York: Basic Books.

Perry, J. C. (1993). Defenses and their effects. In N. E. Miller, L. Luborsky, J. P. Barber, & J. P. Docherty (Eds.), *Psychodynamic treatment research: A handbook for clinical practice* (pp. 274–307). New York: Basic Books.

Persons, J. B. (1991). Psychotherapy outcome studies do not accurately represent current models of psychotherapy. *American Psychologist, 46,* 99–106.

Seligman, M. E. P., Abramson, L. Y., Semmel, A., & von Baeyer, C. (1979). Depressive attributional style. *Journal of Abnormal Psychology, 88,* 242–247.

Shea, M. T., Pilkonis, P. A., Beckham, E., & Collins, J. F. (1990). Personality disorders and treatment outcome in the NIMH Treatment of Depression Collaborative Research Program. *American Journal of Psychiatry, 147,* 711–718.

Smith, M., Glass, G., & Miller, T. I. (1980). *The benefits of psychotherapy.* Baltimore: The Johns Hopkins University.

Thase, M. Reynolds, C., Frank, E., Simons, A., Garamoni, G., McGeary, J., Harden, T., Fasiczka, A., & Cahalane, J. (in press). Response to cognitive behavior therapy in chronic depression. *Journal of Psychotherapy Practice and Research.*

Waskow, I., & Parloff, M. (1975). *Psychotherapy change measures* (DHEW Publication No. ADM 74-120). Washington, DC: U.S. Government Printing Office.

Weissman, A. N. (1979). *The Dysfunctional Attitudes Scale: A validation study.* Unpublished manuscript, University of Pennsylvania, Philadephia.

Weston, D., Barends, A., Leigh, J., Mendel, M., & Silbert, D. (1988). *Manual for coding object relations and social cognition from interview data.* Unpublished manuscript, University of Michigan, Ann Arbor.

Woody, G., Luborsky, L., McLellan, A. T., O'Brien, C., Beck, A. T., Blaine, J., Herman, I., & Hole, A. V. (1983). Psychotherapy for opiate addicts: Does it help? *Archives of General Psychiatry, 40,* 639–645.

Woody, G., McLellan, A. T., Luborsky, L., & O'Brien, C. (1985). Sociopathy and psychotherapy outcome. *Archives of General Psychiatry, 42,* 1081–1086.

12

Toward a Core Battery for Treatment Efficacy Research on Mood Disorders

Karla Moras

WHY A CORE BATTERY?

The idea of a standard core battery to assess the outcomes of mental health treatments elicits rare consensus and enthusiasm from researchers. A core battery would provide a common metric for studies of the same or related problems and thereby facilitate conclusions about the replicability and generalizability of outcome findings for available treatments. In other words, if widely adapted, a core battery would help create a cohesive and cumulative body of findings from treatment outcome studies. This benefit makes the development of such a battery one of the fastest and most cost-effective ways to obtain practice-relevant conclusions from the research of many different investigators and from the public funds that support much of their work.

GUIDING PRINCIPLES

How might a core battery be constructed? What principles should guide the effort? Consensus on these questions is predictably lower than consensus on the value of a core battery. This chapter illustrates using the decision-making goals of the consumers of mental health treatment out-come research to guide measure selection for a core battery. Other strate-gies for developing a core battery are described elsewhere in this book. Also, Lambert, Ogles, and Masters (1992) presented an excellent overview of the main dimensions that need to be considered when constructing a set of measures for psychotherapy outcome research.

One premise adopted here is that it is useful to link a core battery for treatment outcome research to the American Psychiatric Association's psy-chodiagnostic classification system, the fourth edition of the *Diagnostic and Statistical Manual of Mental Disorders* (*DSM–IV;* American Psychiat-ric Association, 1994). The same premise was adopted by the organizers of the 1994 American Psychological Association (APA)-sponsored confer-ence for which this chapter was prepared: The conference structure fol-lowed the *DSM* system. This chapter is focused on a core battery for stud-ies of what are labeled *mood disorders* in the two most recent editions of the *DSM* (American Psychiatric Association, 1987, 1994) but more com-monly known as depression or depressive disorders. To simplify the dis-cussion, a specific mood disorder, major depressive disorder, from the *DSM–IV* was selected as a focus.

The discussion here assumes that the core battery will be used for out-come studies of outpatient treatments for depression. Although overlap in core batteries for studies of inpatient and outpatient treatments can be expected, some differences are also likely. For example, a core battery for inpatient treatments probably would include a behavioral measure to be completed by nursing staff. It also is assumed that the battery will be used in treatment research with adults, young adulthood through middle age, but not necessarily through older adulthood. Finally, it is assumed that the battery will be suitable for use in outcome studies that are designed to evaluate the efficacy of treatments (i.e., study designs that use experimental methods, such as random assignment and the inclusion of a placebo con-trol condition, to determine whether a treatment is associated with bene-ficial effects). However, a core battery that is useful for efficacy studies also should be well suited for more naturalistic, effectiveness studies, which are conducted to evaluate the generalizability of a treatment's effects that are found in efficacy studies. In fact, it is highly desirable that any core battery adopted for treatment efficacy research on a problem or disorder also be suitable for effectiveness studies.

CHAPTER ORGANIZATION AND TOPICS

An audience-focused strategy for structuring a core battery is illustrated in this chapter, followed by the nomination of a few measures for a core battery for *DSM–IV* (American Psychiatric Association, 1994) major depressive disorder. Certain contents and features of measures are suggested as criteria to guide selection of measures for a core battery for outcome studies of depression. The chapter concludes with brief reviews of a few measures that meet some of the recommended content criteria and are currently widely used in treatment research on depression. The measures are highlighted mainly because their inclusion in a core battery would contribute to the comparison of at least some findings from treatment research on depression during the past 10 years with those obtained with a new core battery. Specific topics addressed are the pros and cons of a *DSM*-linked battery, the main audiences for mental health treatment outcome research, the type of information sought by each audience, the content and features of a core battery that could meet the aims of the various audiences, and measures to consider for a core battery for outcome research on depression.

STRATEGY FOR DEVELOPING A CORE BATTERY

Linking a Core Battery to the *DSM* Nomenclature: Pros and Cons

The last major effort to create a core battery for mental health treatment research (Waskow & Parloff, 1975) was not linked to the version of the *DSM* that existed at the time. Thus, one must ask the following question: What are the rationale and implications for linking a core battery to the *DSM*? Some central, current issues are discussed next.

Pros

A major shift in treatment outcome research in the United States occurred since Waskow and Parloff's (1975) National Institute of Mental Health

(NIMH)-sponsored conference on developing a core battery for psycho-therapy outcome research. The shift was spurred by the American Psychiatric Association's publication in 1980 of a much revised edition (third) of their *DSM* (*DSM–III;* American Psychiatric Association, 1980). One aim of the *DSM–III* was to improve the reliability of diagnoses that could be made with the system (Garfield, 1986). Psychiatric treatment researchers, in particular, had called attention to the poor reliability of diagnoses as they were defined in the second edition of the *DSM* (*DSM–II;* American Psychiatric Association, 1968) and to the serious handicaps posed by this problem for treatment and psychopathology research (Spitzer & Fleiss, 1974).

Because of various sociopolitical forces, the *DSM–III* had a profound impact on mental health treatment research in the United States. For example, it became essentially imperative to use *DSM* diagnostic criteria to select study samples for outcome research proposed in federal grant applications submitted to the NIMH. The situation in 1997 remains much the same. Thus, one important reason to link a core battery to the *DSM* is to increase the probability that the battery will be used in federally funded treatment outcome research because such research tends to be particularly influential on practice. Second, special effort was taken to make the newest edition of the *DSM*, the *DSM–IV* (American Psychiatric Association, 1994), compatible with the 10th edition of the *International Statistical Classification of Diseases and Related Health Problems* (World Health Organization, 1992). Thus, a core battery that is linked to the *DSM* could facilitate cross-cultural comparison of treatment outcome findings as well as cross-cultural psychopathology research. (Rothblum, Solomon, & Albee, 1986, presented a contrary view of the foregoing issues).

Cons

Many psychotherapeutically oriented treatment researchers and many more nonpsychiatrist mental health practitioners essentially reject the *DSM–III* (American Psychiatric Association, 1980) and subsequent editions of it (Rothblum, et al., 1986, presented a comprehensive critique of the *DSM–III.*) The main criticisms of both groups focus on the *DSM*'s clinical value. Two of the most common criticisms of this type are that the *DSM* is based on a medical model of psychopathology and that it does not classify individuals in the most treatment-relevant ways. The second criticism is closely tied to the first. What is viewed as problematic about the medical model?

Applying the medical model to mental health problems suggests that they are fundamentally similar to medical conditions, that is, their principal causes are organic anomalies of some type (e.g., biological, biochemical, neurobiological). This premise logically implies a second one about treatment strategies, namely that the most efficacious treatments are likely to be somatic (e.g., pharmacological agents) rather than psychological or behavioral. A third assumption that arises from the medical analogy is that sets of somatic and cognitive (e.g., concentration difficulties) symptoms provide a treatment-relevant nomenclature to classify mental health problems. Hence, for example, in the *DSM–IV* (American Psychiatric Association, 1994), several somatic and cognitive symptoms (e.g., appetite disturbance, fatigue, concentration problems, sleep disturbance) dominate the operational definition of major depressive disorder. Furthermore, most if not all of the pharmacological agents recommended to treat major depressive disorder affect one or more of the somatic and cognitive symptoms that define the disorder. (Millon, 1986, presented a less critical view of the medical model's influence on the *DSM*.)

In contrast to the foregoing, many psychotherapeutically oriented treatment researchers and practitioners believe that somatic and other symptoms of *DSM*-defined depression (and of anxiety as well) are often epiphenomena of other *nonorganic* problems that create and maintain the symptoms. The posited causes tend to be psychological or behavioral (or both) in nature (e.g., maladaptive patterns of interacting with one's significant others; basic beliefs about oneself, one's future, and how the world works; low self-esteem). Nonmedical models of depression also imply different treatment strategies than do medical models. In general, nonmedical perspectives (a) note that symptoms of depression and anxiety often prompt mental health contacts because the symptoms are distressing and sometimes debilitating but (b) caution against misconstruing the symptoms to be the primary problem or proper focus of treatment.

A second potential problem with linking a core battery to the *DSM* is that the *DSM* includes several categories of disorders (e.g., mood disorders, anxiety disorders, eating disorders). Somewhat different core batteries would need to be constructed for treatment research on each category of disorder. Furthermore, the battery for each category probably would need modification for research on the different disorders within the category (e.g., bipolar disorder vs. major depressive disorder in the mood disorders category).

A third problem with linking a core battery to the *DSM* is that such a link could help reify the nomenclature. From a scientific perspective, even the most recent edition is most appropriately regarded as a nomenclature in progress rather than a classification system that has notable evidence for its reliability and validity. As stated in the introduction of the *DSM–IV,* "these diagnostic criteria and the DSM-IV classification of mental disorders reflect a consensus of current formulations of evolving knowledge in our field" (American Psychiatric Association, 1994, p. xxvii).

The foregoing discussion suggests that linking a core battery to the *DSM* system has at least four notable disadvantages. First, the battery is likely to be rejected in principle by some treatment researchers and therefore will be used less widely. Second, the majority of nonpsychiatrist mental health practitioners are likely to reject or be disinterested in outcome findings based on the core battery, markedly limiting the impact on practice of findings. Third, adopting a core battery that is too closely or completely linked to the *DSM* could result in premature reification of the system rather than stimulating further examination of it and alternative nomenclatures. A fourth consideration is the complexity of developing a core battery that is linked closely to the *DSM* because of the number of categories of disorders and the number of disorders within each category.

Potential Audiences for a Core Battery for Major Depression

The strategy for constructing a core battery illustrated here starts by identifying the main consumers of mental health treatment outcome research. Next, the kind of information from outcome research that is of primary interest to each audience is identified. But first, what is the rationale for an audience-focused strategy to construct a core battery?

The ultimate aim of mental health treatment outcome research is to obtain applied (i.e., clinically informative) data. Such data are sought mainly to inform interested parties (e.g., patients, mental health professionals) about the probable benefits and costs of alternative treatments for various problems and how and with whom the benefits can be best achieved. Because of its applied aims, treatment research has tended to have a broader range of audiences than does more basic research. However, recent and profound changes in the United States regarding financing all forms of health care have both broadened the audiences of mental health outcome research and drawn researchers' attention to types of information wanted by different audiences (e.g., the length of time and probable costs to achieve a treatment's main effects). Thus, treatment outcome research can now have a more direct and quicker public health impact than it has in the past if it produces information wanted by various interested audiences.

The audiences of mental health research tend to seek somewhat different types of information, potentially leading to a core battery that has many measures. Identification of only the audiences who have the most vested interest in treatment outcome findings would help keep the number of measures in a battery small, a particularly desirable feature from the perspective of treatment researchers. Twenty years ago, Krause and Howard (1976) identified six groups of interested parties or "perspectives" on psychotherapy outcomes. Krause and Howard's list is surprisingly complete and current in terms of identifying the main audiences for treatment outcome findings that could be obtained with a core battery. The six groups are patients, therapists, clients, managers, sponsors, and researchers.

Patients are those who directly receive treatment, and therapists are those who conduct it. When considering treatments for adult outpatients, the client audience is composed either of individuals other than the patient (e.g., spouse) or of institutions (e.g., court system) whose interests are served by a person's treatment. Managers are individuals who make decisions about the allocation of treatment such as the utilization reviewers used by health maintenance organizations. Sponsors are a heterogeneous audience that includes various organizations and individuals who pay for mental health treatment for large numbers of people such as insurance companies, managed care companies, employers, and government agencies. Two groups of researchers potentially are most interested in a core battery for mental health treatment studies: treatment outcome and psychopathology researchers.

Goals and Needs of the Audiences

What are the primary information needs of each of the six audiences? Most want information to help with their decision-making priorities and responsibilities. Some of the priorities of each of the six audiences are described next, beginning with the two types of research audiences: treatment outcome and psychopathology.

Treatment Outcome Researchers

In general, treatment outcome researchers want to obtain data that will contribute to a cumulative body of findings from their and other investigators' studies. Data are sought that can be interpreted confidently as indicating which treatments are efficacious, in what ways (e.g., which symptoms, aspects of functioning, and phenomenological experience are affected), and for how long for various disorders and problems. Treatment researchers also want to ascertain the comparative efficacy of different treatments for the same problems. The preceding goals subsume others, such as identifying the variables that contribute to a treatment's efficacy (e.g., how long, at what frequency, and by whom and to whom must a treatment be administered to achieve which benefits)? Investigators also want to be able to evaluate the conventions and accepted "facts" that guide their research. Thus, current knowledge and assumptions play a major role in determining the kinds of measures that treatment outcome researchers want at any point in time.

For example, the results of some outcome studies of major depressive disorder suggest that severity of depression is related to differential efficacy of common alternative treatments for depression (e.g., Elkin et al., 1989). Thus, many investigators now want to include measures of the severity of depressive symptoms in their studies (e.g., Thase, Simons, Cahalane, McGeary, & Harden, 1991). Another important consideration now for treatment research on depression is the potential for recurrence of clinically significant depression. Also, a core battery for major depressive disorder should be consistent with one important recent attempt to standardize outcome assessment for treatment research on depression by creating operational definitions for some of its most commonly used terms: remission, recovery, recurrence, and relapse (Frank et al., 1991). This effort included specification of some measures in the operational definitions.

Psychopathology Researchers

Some psychopathology researchers strive to develop a classification system that "carves nature at the joints" (Kendell, 1975). Researchers of this orientation have cited the high comorbidity rates of many *DSM* disorders (i.e., the fact that many if not most individuals in clinical samples meet criteria for more than one disorder; Maser & Cloninger, 1990) as evidence against the validity of some of the disorders in the *DSM*. Two current psychopathology questions specific to *DSM–IV* major depressive disorder are as follows: (a) What is the relationship between dysthymic disorder and major depressive disorder (e.g., are they qualitatively different disorders, or is major depressive disorder the episodic occurrence of increased severity of symptoms of dysthymic disorder; Koscis, 1990)? (b) Do qualitatively different subtypes of major depressive disorder exist? (This question arises in part from findings that some depressed patients' symptoms respond completely to some pharmacological agents and others' symptoms do not.)

Patients

Patients' principal questions include the following: (a) What type of treatment will most quickly and completely alleviate the problems they are experiencing? (b) Is the treatment feasible for them (e.g., in terms of costs, medical contraindications, side effects, availability in their travel area? (c) What alternative treatments are feasible and how do their outcomes compare with those of the quickest and most fully efficacious treatment? (d) How can a competent provider of the most feasible treatment be identified?

Clients

Because this audience is heterogeneous (e.g., court system, spouses, and significant others), it can have a variety of goals. The court system as client often mandates individuals to receive treatment for substance abuse or physically abusive behavior within the family. Courts do not generally mandate treatment for depression. However, when suicide risk is present, the legal system is an interested party because of its role in commitment proceedings. When spouses or significant others are the audience of treatment outcome research on depression, they are interested in suicide risk if their loved one has revealed suicidal ideation, in other symptoms of depression such as ability to function in work and parenting roles, and in ability to meet other homelife responsibilities and participate in family and social activities.

Therapists

Therapists generally want to know the specific effects a treatment can have, about how long it takes to achieve those effects, how to identify patients for whom the treatment is most likely to have the desired effects, and how to perform the treatment. They also want to know how to modify it when individuals do not manifest the expected responses to the recommended interventions.

Managers

To facilitate their primary responsibility of making decisions about the allocation of treatment resources (e.g., how many treatment sessions should be allowed for a particular problem), managers seek two types of information from treatment research: (a) what effects alternative treatments can be expected to have and (b) what the expected rate of change is in the outcomes (e.g., symptom alleviation) associated with a treatment. Data on the expected rate of change help managers evaluate whether a particular patient is meeting normative expectations for progress in a form of treatment. Such information helps them decide whether the treatment plan or therapist (or both) should be changed.

Sponsors

The potential interests of institutions that pay for mental health services include the following: (a) which treatment will potentiate the changes that the institution is most interested in paying for (e.g., improved work productivity, fewer sick days, better functioning in social roles such as parenting, less illegal behavior); (b) how much it will cost to achieve the desired changes; (c) how cost-effective the alternative treatments are; and (d) what the likely trade-offs are (e.g., in terms of desired changes and costs to achieve them, providing vs. not providing the treatment).

Core Battery Measures That Could Meet Audience Goals

Measures have two primary dimensions that determine their utility for a core battery for treatment outcome research: content and features. The term *content* refers to the topics covered by a measure's items and the constructs that an instrument is designed to assess. Content is the fundamental determinant of the information that can be obtained with a measure (although the information obtained also is determined largely by the study design, such as how frequently a measure is administered). The term *features* refers to qualities of measures, such as psychometric adequacy and ease of administration. Table 1 shows contents of a core battery for major depressive disorder that would meet some of the goals of each of the six audiences. Table 2 lists features of measures that also are needed to meet some of each audience's goals.

Contents of a Core Battery
for *DSM–IV* Major Depressive Disorder

The content areas included in Table 1 were influenced greatly by the current research procedures and biases of investigators who are now conducting federally funded treatment outcome research on outpatient depression. The list is likely to differ somewhat from one constructed from a systematic poll of all six interested audiences. Despite this limitation, the list is useful because it contains content categories that probably would be endorsed by many investigators who now do treatment research on major depressive disorder and similar *DSM* mood disorders such as dysthymic disorder. I will briefly describe each content category listed in Table 1.

Symptoms

The diagnostic criteria that are used in the *DSM* to define disorders are commonly termed *symptoms.* When a *DSM*-defined disorder is the focus of a treatment, the most widely used measures of a treatment's efficacy are

Table 1

Suggested Content for Core Battery for Major Depressive Disorder by Audience

Measure content	Researchers		Clients				Sponsors			
	Treatment outcome	Psycho-pathology	Patients	Significant others	Public agencies	Thera-pists	Managers	Govern-ment agencies	Employer	Insurance companies and man-aged care
Symptoms	X	X	X				X	X	X	X
DSM–IV major depression criteria	X	X								
Anxiety	X	X	X							
Subjective distress	X		X	X		X			X	
Functioning	X	X	X	X	X	X	X	X	X	X
Global	X						X	X	X	

Work	X				X	
Interpersonal	X		X			
Social roles	X		X	X	X	X
Diagnostic status	X	X				X
Principal diagnosis	X	X		X		
Comorbid diagnosis	X	X				
Quality of life	X	X	X	X	X	
Costs of treatment	X	X	X	X	X	X
Savings of treatment	X	X	X	X	X	X
Side effects of treatment	X		X	X		

NOTE: X identifies contents that are of primary relevance for each audience's decision-making priorities with information from treatment outcome research. Blanks do not mean that an audience is not interested in a content: Either the content is not central to the audience's decision-making priorities or audience members diverge on the content. Blanks in a subcategory of a content that is marked X for an audience (e.g., Work under the Functioning heading) mean that the content is of interest to an audience, although the subcategories of interest vary within the audience. DSM–IV = fourth edition of the Diagnostic and Statistical Manual of Mental Disorders.

changes in some or all of the *DSM* diagnostic criteria or symptoms that define the disorder.

The symptom content in Table 1 includes both the *DSM–IV* (American Psychiatric Association, 1994) symptoms for major depressive disorder and anxiety symptoms. Both anxiety and depression symptoms are included because treatment and psychopathology research on samples selected on the basis of criteria from the *DSM–III* (American Psychiatric Association, 1980) and revised third edition of the *DSM* (*DSM–III–R;* American Psychiatric Association, 1987) consistently has shown that individuals who meet criteria for major depressive disorder also often have symptoms of various *DSM* anxiety disorders (e.g., Sanderson, Beck, & Beck, 1990) and vice versa (e.g., Barlow, DiNardo, Vermilyea, Vermilyea, & Blanchard, 1986; Brown & Barlow, 1992; Moras, DiNardo, Brown, & Barlow, 1994). For example, high rates of cooccurrence have been reported between major depressive disorder and obsessive–compulsive disorder (Barlow et al., 1986; Brown & Barlow, 1992; Moras et al., 1994). Furthermore, several studies of both patient and nonpatient samples have shown high correlations between widely used measures of depression and anxiety symptoms such as the Hamilton Rating Scale for Depression (HRSD; Hamilton, 1960) and the Hamilton Anxiety Rating Scale (HARS; Hamilton, 1959); for example, Pearson product–moment correlations range from .53 to .89 according to Clark (1989). Similarly high correlations have been found for both self-report and observer-rated measures (Clark, 1989; Gotlib & Cane, 1989).

The cooccurrence of anxiety and depression symptoms and disorders has prompted theories of the relationship between depression and anxiety, often with the aim of revising the *DSM* to make it more consistent with the high rates of cooccurrence of symptoms that now define disorders that are conceptualized as distinct (e.g., Clark & Watson, 1991). The findings on the relationship between anxiety and depression indicate that a core battery for treatment research on major depressive disorder should include measures of anxiety symptoms to advance both treatment and psychopathology research on depression. For example, one important treatment question is the impact of copresent anxiety symptoms on the efficacy of treatments for major depressive disorder (e.g., Hecht, von Zerssen, Krieg, Possl, & Wittchen, 1989).

Subjective Distress

The term *subjective distress* as used here means the severity of concern, psychological pain, or other distress that is associated from the patient's perspective with a problem for which he or she is being treated. Two reasons support including a measure of the subjective distress associated with the problems targeted by a treatment. Reduction in subjective distress indicates that a treatment is associated with a valued benefit: It means that a person at least experiences some relief. A second reason to include a measure of subjective distress is that the *DSM* requires that a set of symptoms must be associated with subjective distress or functional impairment to qualify as a "disorder," that is, a deviation from normalcy (American Psychiatric Association, 1994; Anthony et al., 1994). In fact, one change made in the *DSM–IV* (American Psychiatric Association, 1994) was the addition of subjective distress, functional impairment, or both to the diagnostic criteria for many disorders.

Functioning

Some type of impairment or deterioration in functioning frequently prompts a mental health treatment contact. For example, the inability to maintain the required rate of productivity at work and reduced sexual interest in one's partner often are associated with a major depressive disorder. Functional impairment, in turn, can create additional stressors for a person, such as potential job loss and heightened conflict in relationships that normally are sustaining to him or her.

Several domains of functioning help maintains one's sense of well-being, as well as the support received from and the well-being of others with whom an individual has frequent contact or to whom he or she has major responsibilities. Specific domains include work, and interpersonal (e.g., personal relationships including friends and family) and social roles (e.g., parenting, spouse).

Measures of functioning in a core battery for depression treatment research will provide an index of improvement in or restoration of function. Return to former levels of functioning commonly is viewed as an important criterion of the efficacy of any health-related treatment. A second reason to include a measure of functioning was mentioned in the previous section on subjective distress: The presence of functional impairment is one of the criteria used in the *DSM* to justify designating a condition a "disorder," as distinguished from being within normal limits.

Diagnostic Status

Diagnostic status denotes all the *DSM* diagnoses for which a person currently meets diagnostic criteria. A method to assess current *DSM* diagnoses is critically important to include in a core battery at this point in the history of treatment outcome research for reasons stated before on the pros of linking a core battery to the *DSM* system. Also, diagnoses need to be obtained for studies of treatments that target specific *DSM* disorders because the presence of the disorder must be a primary inclusion criterion. Also, if a treatment is being examined for its efficacy for a specific disorder, a primary index of efficacy is whether the treatment is associated with recovery from the disorder. Thus, diagnostic status needs to be assessed at least at termination as well as at intake.

The previously mentioned finding of high comorbidity rates between certain *DSM* mood and anxiety disorders also is relevant to core battery assessment of diagnostic status. Comorbidity findings of major depressive disorder with anxiety disorders (e.g., Barlow et al., 1986; Moras et al., 1994; Sanderson et al., 1990) and with *DSM* Axis II personality disorders (e.g., Shea et al., 1992) support the recommendation that comprehensive diagnostic assessments (i.e., *DSM* Axis I and Axis II disorders) be done at least at intake for treatment outcome research on major depressive disorder. One reason for this recommendation is that comorbidity findings indicate that considerable diagnostic heterogeneity can exist in study samples that are selected based only on the presence of major depressive disorder, for example. This source of heterogeneity cannot be detected without comprehensive diagnostic assessment at intake. Moreover, diagnostic heterogeneity data are crucial for evaluating the comparability of study samples when outcome findings for specific disorders are not replicated. Comprehensive diagnostic assessment also can help identify patient characteristics that are associated with a treatment's efficacy, a type of information that is of major interest to several audiences of treatment research. Finally, comprehensive diagnostic assessment will contribute to psychopathology research on the *DSM*.

Quality of Life

Quality of life is a construct that recently has gained more attention from treatment researchers (Endicott, Nee, Harrison, & Blumenthal, 1993), although its value as an outcome variable for mental health treatment research has long been recognized (e.g., Strupp & Hadley, 1977). In general, the construct refers to all nonpathological, positive aspects of mental and physical health, including a person's pleasure and satisfaction in the basic domains of life experience (e.g., family, work, social and leisure time activities). Specific definitions of quality of life have been developed, such as "an individual's subjective evaluation of the degree to which his or her most important needs, goals, and wishes have been fulfilled" (Frisch, cited in Frisch, Cornell, Villaneuva, & Retzlaff, 1992, p. 93).

One reason to include a measure of quality of life in a core battery is to tap the positive experiences associated with good adjustment and mental health. Most measures used in treatment outcome research assess the relative presence or absence of symptoms or problems (e.g., Frisch, et al., 1992). However, some evidence exists that the absence of negative states is not isomorphic with the presence of positive states (e.g., Diener & Emmons, 1984; Watson, Clark, & Cary, 1988). Furthermore, the inclusion of a quality-of-life measure is particularly important in studies of treatments for depression because a common aspect of depression is reduced enjoyment in many aspects of life (e.g., a key diagnostic criterion for *DSM–IV* major depressive disorder is "markedly diminished interest or pleasure in all, or almost all, activities most of the day" [American Psychiatric Association, 1994, p. 327]).

Cost of Treatment

Data on the basic cost of a treatment (e.g., the average fee per session for the level of mental health professional required to conduct a Treatment × Average Number of Sessions to Achieve Recovery) are a priority for several audiences of treatment outcome research. Cost is a fundamental determinant of a person's access to a particular treatment. Cost data also are a major variable used by managed care systems to determine which treatments they will provide.

Cost data are weighed against outcome data when sponsoring institutions make decisions about what treatments they will cover and to what extent (e.g., how many sessions). For some audiences, relevant cost data include both the tangible and intangible resources that are needed to procure psychotherapy. For example, tangible costs in addition to session fees include parking or baby sitter costs, travel expenses, and loss of revenue during the time needed to attend and travel to and from sessions. Even the most basic cost data rarely if ever have been collected in treatment outcome studies, perhaps partly because treatment typically is offered free or at substantially reduced rates in studies.

Savings of Treatment

During the past 5–10 years, various potential third-party payers for mental health services have closely and more publicly scrutinized available treatments. One effect has been that treatment outcome researchers have become more interested in asssessing the benefits of treatments other than the direct benefits that typically have been asssessed (e.g., symptom alleviation). Specific contents in the savings category include medical utilization (e.g., the number of visits to primary care practitioners) and sick days taken.

Comprehensive cost and savings data on treatments together constitute what often is referred to as "cost-effectiveness data." This type of information is a top priority for sponsors.

Side Effects of a Treatment

As used here, the term *side effects* refers to negative or unwanted effects associated with a treatment (e.g., dry mouth and nausea are side effects of many antidepressant medications). Historically, side effects have been assessed in psychopharmacology outcome research but ignored in psychotherapy outcome research. The difference is partly because the U.S. Food and Drug Administration (FDA) monitors testing and approval of psychotropic drugs, and side effect assessment is a required component of the testing because drugs can be associated with lethal and other medically serious reactions. Assessment of side effects has been incorporated by psychopharmacology researchers into their outcome studies of drugs that already have FDA approval. By contrast, potential negative side effects of psychotherapy (e.g., having despondent feelings after a session when one thinks about material that was discussed; expressing criticism and anger at one's spouse in unproductive ways) almost never are measured in outcome studies.

The decision-making goals of several of the audiences listed in Table 1 could be facilitated by (a) including in psychotherapy studies measures of common side effects of pharmacological agents used to treat depression and (b) developing side effect measures for psychotherapeutic interventions and using them in both psychotherapy and psychopharmacology studies. Parallel side effect data would allow more direct and complete cost–benefit comparisons of alternative treatments for the same problems.

Features of Measures for a Core Battery

Ten desirable features of measures for a core battery for major depression are presented in Table 2. Most of the features were listed by A. John Rush at the APA core battery conference in March 1994. Some features, such as psychometric adequacy, also were independently highlighted by other conference participants. The sections that follow describe how the features shown in Table 2 contribute to the aims of the six audiences of treatment outcome research.

Adequate Psychometrics

The scientific worth of data obtained with a measure is fundamentally determined and limited by its psychometric features (e.g., the reliability and validity of the scores that a measure can yield). Fleiss (1986), an expert on the design and analysis of treatment outcome studies, observed the following:

> The most elegant design of a clinical study will not overcome the damage caused by unreliable or imprecise measurement. The requirement that one's data be of high quality is at least as important a component of proper study design as the requirement for randomization, double blinding, controlling when necessary for prognostic factors, and so on. (p. 1)

The integral importance of the psychometric adequacy of measures to the validity of conclusions that can be drawn from outcome studies (Kraemer

Table 2

Features of Measures for a Core Battery for Major Depressive Disorder by Audience

Measure features	Researchers		Clients					Sponsors		
	Treatment outcome	Psycho-pathology	Patients	Significant others	Public agencies	Thera-pists	Managers	Govern-ment agencies	Employer	Insurance companies and man-aged care[a]
Adequate psychometrics[b]	X	X	X	X	X	X	X	X	X	X
Quick to complete	X	X	X			X				
Cheap	X	X	X							
Easy to administer	X	X								

Short training	X	X	X		X
Parallel versions	X	X		X	X	X
Multilingual versions	X	X	X		X
Clinically informative	X		X	X	X
Useful across treatments	X		X	X	X	X
Atheoretical	X	X			

NOTE: Most of the features were listed by A. John Rush in his presentation at the APA core battery conference. X identifies features of measures that are of primary relevance for the decision-making priorities of each audience.

[a]A battery of measures with all the features of interest to treatment researchers (Xs in first column) also might be used by managed care companies.

[b]Xs across this row are intended to underscore the fundamental importance of adequate psychometric properties for measures in a core battery.

& Telch, 1992) makes it a priority for all audiences. Standard and well-accepted procedures exist for evaluating a measure's psychometric features (e.g., Nunnally, 1978).

Obvious relevant psychometric features of measures include the reliability and validity of data that can be obtained with them. Other highly desirable psychometrically relevant features of measures are the availability of (a) standardized administration and training procedures and materials and (b) score norms for both the specific patient group with which a measure is to be used and for normal nonpatients who do not have the problems assessed by a measure.

Measures to be completed by independent clinical evaluators or by therapists require one psychometric feature that is virtually ignored in outcome research: evidence for the interrater reliability of ratings made by study personnel with a "gold standard" set of ratings made by raters external to the study. When clinical evaluators or therapists complete measures, interrater reliability figures computed for the study raters are necessary but not sufficient to determine whether the scores are likely to be comparable to these obtained with the same measure in other studies. The study evaluators and therapists also must be shown to have interrater reliability with some nonstudy standard reference set of ratings to ensure that the ratings made for a study are not idiosyncratic. That is, study raters need to be calibrated with an external standard.

The need to assess interrater reliability with an external standard requires that a measure have both master training videotapes or the like (with accompanying master score sheets) that can be administered to a study's raters to train them, and another set of master reliability tapes to evaluate the raters' interrater reliability. In this way, the comparability of the data obtained in a particular study with a common standard can be determined.

Quick to Complete

This feature is a top priority of treatment outcome researchers. They seek it because many measures typically are used in outcome studies, most of which require a patient's time, whether self-report or via an interview conducted by a clinical evaluator. Investigators worry about the "burden" associated with time-consuming batteries because they think that long assessments contribute to participant dropout or missing data. Both types of attrition create fundamental problems for interpreting outcome results from randomized clinical trials (e.g., Howard, Cox, & Saunders, 1990). Thus, investigators almost always will prefer a measure that can be completed more quickly to a measure with the same type of content that takes longer. Speed of completion is so important to researchers that it often tempts them to override psychometric adequacy, the critically important feature of a measure from a scientific standpoint.

Ease of Administration

Ease of administration refers to the procedures and instructions necessary to obtain data with a measure. This feature also is highly valued by researchers. The less complicated a measure is to administer (e.g., it requires only that a research assistant or receptionist hand a questionnaire and a pencil to a patient and includes simple, self-explanatory instructions), the more likely the measure will be administered correctly so that valid and complete data will be obtained with every administration.

Short Training Time

This feature refers to the amount of instruction and training that must be provided to those who administer or complete a measure. For example, many self-report measures of symptoms of depression used in treatment outcome research, such as the Beck Depression Inventory (BDI; Beck & Steer, 1992b), require essentially no training. Other commonly used measures such as the HRSD (Hamilton, 1960), which are designed to be administered by a clinically experienced interviewer, require training to attain adequate interrater reliability among a study's interviewers, at minimum (reliability with an external standard as previously discussed and validity are other important psychometric features of such measures that typically are ignored in current outcome research). Researchers tend to prefer measures that require little training because they reduce costs and use of other resources (e.g., the investigator's time to train individuals to administer measures).

Costs

Researchers also desire instruments that are inexpensive. The cost of a measure tends to be determined largely by the training time required, the prior skills and other qualifications required to administer it, and the time required to administer it during a study.

Parallel Versions

This features refers to versions of a measure to be completed by respondents who can provide different perspectives on a patient's status on the variables of interest. For example, when symptoms of depression are an outcome variable, researchers are interested in several perspectives on them: the patient's, a clinically trained independent evaluator's, the therapist's, and individuals who have ongoing contact with the patient such as family members and coworkers.

The desirability of parallel versions of a measure depends on the variable being assessed. Sometimes one perspective is viewed as being more valid than others. For example, a trained clinical evaluator's assessment of diagnostic status generally is viewed as the most valid perspective on *DSM* diagnosis, but several perspectives on a person's functioning are regarded as valid, such as the patient's, a clinical evaluator's, and a third party's (e.g., a spouse or employer).

Some audiences other than researchers seek information from more than one perspective on a treatment's efficacy. For example, practitioners generally are interested in outcome findings from the patient's perspective, but they also want to know the opinions of the study therapists who conducted the treatment. The court system often wants to know an independent evaluator's impression of a treatment's efficacy because the court system generally refers individuals for treatment when members of society view them as having a problem, but the individuals themselves do not necessarily agree.

Multilingual Versions

Both mental health treatment outcome and psychopathology research would benefit from the use of instruments that are available in several languages (e.g., English, Spanish, German, French). Multilingual instruments would facilitate cross-cultural studies and comparison of studies done in different countries on the same disorder. Multilingual versions also would help American investigators meet current federal guidelines for inclusion of ethnic minorities in studies.

Clinically Informative

As stated previously, the main aim of treatment outcome research is to provide clinically informative findings to the audiences who have vested interests in mental health treatment. For example, patients, therapists, and treatment researchers are interested in (a) the types of symptom and other changes associated with a treatment, (b) the rate at which the changes occur, and (c) the final status likely to be achieved (e.g., full recovery, functioning exceeding premorbid levels, reduced severity of the problem but rarely within the normal range). Therapists, managers, and some types of sponsors also want to know what clinical and other pretreat ment characteristics indicate that a person is likely to benefit from a particular treatment approach because such information facilitates patient–treatment matching. The same three audiences also would like criteria to help them assess when a treatment is not progressing at an expected rate and when unexpected deterioration is occurring. Such information helps with decisions about discontinuing or modifying a treatment.

Useful Across Treatments

Measures that can be applied to different treatments are particularly valuable because they allow comparison of potential alternative treatments for the same disorders. Applicability to both pharmacological and psychotherapeutic treatments is a high priority for research on depression because both modalities are typically offered for it.

Atheoretical

When used in the context of treatment research, the term *atheoretical* generally means not specific to a particular theory of psychotherapy. Being atheoretical also would qualify a measure for the preceding feature, useful across treatments. Atheoretical is distinguished here from useful across treatments because both are important to researchers. A measure could be useful across treatments, but not atheoretical in the sense of not linked to a specific theory of psychotherapy or psychopathology. Atheoretical measures in a core battery would be more likely to be used by many treatment researchers and thus would facilitate a fundamental goal for a core battery: widespread use.

POSSIBLE MEASURES

Overview

Now that content and feature criteria have been identified that could guide selection of measures for a core battery for outcome studies of *DSM–IV* (American Psychiatric Association, 1994) major depressive disorder, I suggest a few potential measures for evaluation for the battery. The measures are mentioned because they (a) are designed to assess one or more of the content areas listed in Table 1 and (b) currently are widely used in both pharmacotherapy and psychotherapy treatment outcome research on depression. The latter criterion was adopted for two reasons. First, both pharmacological and psychotherapeutic interventions are used commonly and recommended to treat depression now. Thus, for treatment research on depression, it is particularly important to identify measures that are acceptable to both pharmacologically oriented and psychotherapeutically oriented investigators so that they will be used in studies of both modes of treatment. Second, it is useful to begin selection of measures for a core battery by evaluating commonly used measures. If they meet agreed-on selection criteria, including them in a battery will contribute to the comparability of findings of existing and future studies.

The measures highlighted in the sections that follow were not systematically evaluated according to the features listed in Table 2. That would be a next step. Rather, a few features of each measure that are relevant to its full evaluation are described.

Content Areas Covered

Recently published treatment outcome studies of depression do not generally include measures of all the content areas listed in Table 1. Widely used measures cannot be identified for several of the content areas: subjective distress associated with depression, most aspects of functioning (i.e., work, interpersonal, social roles), quality of life, costs of treatment, savings of treatment, and side effects of treatment. The failure to find commonly used measures for some of the content areas (quality of life, costs of treatment, and savings of treatment) is due to the relative recency with which investigators have noted their importance to the audiences for treatment research. No commonly used measure can be identified for side effects for two reasons. First, as mentioned earlier, side effects are not typically assessed in treatment studies of psychotherapy. Second, it does not appear that a single side effect measure is commonly used in pharmacotherapy research on depression. Also, study reports often do not identify the side effect measure used.

Symptoms: *DSM–IV* Major Depressive Disorder Diagnostic Criteria

The *DSM–IV* (American Psychiatric Association, 1994) lists nine symptoms as part of the diagnostic criteria for a major depressive episode (MDE):[1] depressed mood, markedly diminished interest or pleasure in activities, weight change or appetite change or both, insomnia or hypersomnia, psychomotor agitation or retardation, fatigue or loss of energy, feelings of worthlessness or excessive or inappropriate guilt, diminished ability to think or concentrate or indecisiveness, and recurrent thoughts of death or suicidal ideation or a suicide plan or attempt. The 27-item HRSD (Hamilton, 1960) that is included in the Structured Interview Guide for the Hamilton Depression Rating Scale (SIGH-D; Williams, 1988) assesses all nine symptoms, including both extremes of the three *DSM–IV* diagnostic criteria that have both an excessive and inadequate pole (i.e., appetite and weight gain or loss, hyper- or hyposomnia, psychomotor disturbance). The 21-item self-report BDI (Beck & Steer, 1992b; Beck, Steer, & Garbin, 1988) recently was revised (BDI–II; Beck, Steer, & Brown, 1996) specifically to include the *DSM–IV* criteria for MDE. The only symptom that is not assessed is weight gain or loss. The 21-item format was retained in the BDI–II, but the time frame of the inquiry was changed from past week to past 2 weeks to be consistent with the *DSM–IV* criteria for MDE.

A measure of one of the nine *DSM–IV* diagnostic criteria, suicide ideation, also merits note even though the measure is not yet widely used in treatment outcome research on depression: the Scale for Suicide Idea-

---

[1] The relationship between the terms *major depressive disorder* and *major depressive episode* in the fourth edition of the *Diagnostic and Statistical Manual of Mental Disorders* (American Psychiatric Association, 1994) is as follows: The diagnosis of major depressive disorder is assigned based on the presence of the diagnostic criteria for major depressive episode.

tion (SSI; Beck, Kovacs, & Weissman, 1979). Both the BDI–II and the HSRD include an item about suicidal thoughts. However, the inclusion of a detailed measure of suicidality in a core battery for treatment research on depression merits consideration due to the critical clinical significance of the symptom for both treatment research and practice, the importance of the symptom for psychopathology research on depression, and its potential importance to knowledge about prediction of suicide. The latter could contribute in an important way to the welfare of patients, as well as to the court system's role in commitment proceedings.

The HRSD

The HRSD is probably the most frequently used observer-rated measure of symptoms of depression in clinical treatment research. The HRSD has a long history of use in treatment research on depression, particularly pharmacotherapy research. Several years ago, the SIGH-D (Williams, 1988) was developed to guide interviewers' administration of HRSD items. Despite the widespread use of the SIGH-D, no master reliability tapes are available for the SIGH-D for cross-study interrater reliability assessment and calibration of raters, a critical psychometric feature of observer-rated measures that was discussed earlier in this chapter. A limited number of training tapes are available.

The widespread use of the HRSD makes it potentially highly valuable as a measure that could be used to compare the outcomes of treatments for depression. Unfortunately, this potential has not been realized fully because several versions of the HRSD exist that are distinguished by the number of items (e.g., 17-item version, 21-item version, 24-item version, 27-item version), and investigators often do not specify the version used in their studies. (Each of the standard versions with more items includes all the items in the shorter versions.) Thus, if the HRSD is recommended for inclusion in the core battery, the version recommended must be specified.

As noted earlier, the 27-item version must be used to assess all nine of the *DSM–IV* (American Psychiatric Association, 1994) diagnostic criteria for MDE. It is not recommended that only those items from the 27-item version that correspond to the *DSM–IV* criteria for MDE be administered because this would reduce the comparability of HRSD findings with prior study findings and because doing so would reduce the value of the data for psychopathology research on depression. One psychometric consideration about the HRSD merits mentioning both because it is a basic psychometric issue for the HRSD and because it is relevant to version specification. The issue is low discriminant validity between HRSD scores and scores on a companion measure of a putatively different construct, the HARS (Hamilton, 1959).

Riskind, Beck, Brown, and Steer (1987) tried to remedy the foregoing problem by recombining both the HRSD and HARS items into two scales in a way that yielded a lower correlation between scores on them. Unfortunately, the Riskind et al. (1987) finding of excellent discriminant validity between their reconstructed HRSD and HARS ($r = .15$) was not replicated in the only published study that attempted to do so (Moras, DiNardo, & Barlow, 1992). However, Moras et al. (1992) did find that scores on the reconstructed HRSD and HARS were less highly correlated than were scores on the original scales ($rs = .61$ and $.78$, respectively). Based on the finding of improved discriminant validity, Moras et al. (1992) recommended that investigators use the 21-item version of the HRSD because the reconstructed HRSD requires some items that are on the 21-item version but not the 17-item version. However, use of the 27-item version of the HRSD would satisfy both this consideration and allow all nine *DSM–IV* symptoms of major depressive disorder to be assessed. (The Riskind et al., 1987, reconstructed HRSD also requires one item from the 14-item HARS; Guy, 1976; Hamilton, 1959.)

Another consideration for using the HRSD in a core battery to assess symptoms of depression is the time frame of the inquiry. The time frame used for the HRSD typically is the past week. A patient is asked to consider how he or she has been feeling during the past 7 days when responding to each item. However, the *DSM–IV* diagnosis of MDE requires that five of the nine symptoms be present daily or most every day for the past 2 weeks. If the core battery includes a structured diagnostic interview for making *DSM–IV* diagnoses, the time frame for the HRSD inquiry need not be set at 2 weeks if the diagnostic instrument is used in a way that will collect data on all nine symptoms for the past 2 weeks.

The BDI–II

The BDI (Beck & Steer 1992b; Beck, Steer, & Garbin, 1988) probably is the most widely used self-report measure of symptoms of depression in published research. The revised version, BDI–II (Beck et al., 1996), is likely to have the same or even wider use pattern, due to its compatibility with *DSM–IV* criteria. It is relatively quick to complete (5–10 min) and easy to administer (self-explanatory instructions). Parallel versions for completion from other perspectives, such as clinical evaluators and therapists, are not available. As noted previously, the time frame for inquiry of the BDI–II is the past 2 weeks.

The SSI

Both a self-report and a clinician-administered version have been developed for the SSI (Beck et al., 1979). A training manual for the clinician-administered version of the SSI exists, which includes three master videotapes with accompanying master score sheets that illustrate administration and rating of the SSI (Newman & Baranackie, 1992).

Symptoms: Anxiety

The HARS

The 14-item HARS (Hamilton, 1959) is not now widely used in treatment research on depression, although it is for treatment research on anxiety. The HARS is mentioned here because of the aforementioned cooccurrence of symptoms of depression and anxiety. Relatively recently, a structured interview guide for the 14-item version of the HARS (Guy, 1976; Hamilton, 1959) was developed by Bruss and colleagues (Bruss, Gruenberg, Goldstein, & Barber, 1994).

The Beck Anxiety Inventory

Beck Anxiety Inventory (BAI; Beck, Epstein, Brown, & Steer, 1988; Beck & Steer, 1992a) is not now widely used in treatment research on depression, although it is for studies of anxiety. It is a 21-item self-report instrument that is similar to the BDI–II. It is mentioned here for the same reason that the HARS is (i.e., the importance of including measures of anxiety symptoms in studies of treatments for depression).

Functioning

One measure of global functioning is widely used in treatment research on depression, but no measures of the specific domains of functioning listed in Table 2 are widely used. The commonly used measure of global functioning is the Global Assessment of Functioning (GAF), also known as Axis V in the *DSM–IV* (American Psychiatric Association, 1994) and *DSM–III-R* (American Psychiatric Association, 1987). The GAF is printed in the *DSM–IV* manual. It is a 0- to 100-point observer-rated scale that typically is completed in treatment research by clinical evaluators, therapists, or both.

The scale points all are multidimensional, requiring the rater to take into account severity of symptoms and functioning in several areas (e.g., work, social, interpersonal relationships). Thus, a GAF score can be interpreted as a global judgement of overall level of functioning across several domains.

The GAF can be rated for different time frames (e.g., current, highest level in the past year). Currently, no standard administration procedures (e.g., a standard set of questions to obtain information needed to assign a GAF score), training materials, or cross-site reliability materials exist for the GAF, and interrater reliability figures can be low when specific training and calibration procedures are not used (see Williams et al., 1992, for more on the reliability of the GAF). The GAF is included in the Structured Clinical Interview Guide for *DSM–IV.* The Interview is an excellent source of information for GAF ratings.

Diagnostic Status

The Structured Clinical Interview Guide for *DSM–IV* Axis I Disorders Patient Edition (SCID-P; First, Spitzer, Gibbon, & Williams, 1996) is a semistructured interview to facilitate the assessment of *DSM–IV* Axis I diagnoses (e.g., mood disorders, anxiety disorders, schizophrenia, and other psychotic disorders). The SCID-P is designed to be administered to a patient by an experienced clinical evaluator. It consists of several "modules," each of which is used to diagnose a category of *DSM–IV* disorders. Training materials were available for the previous, *DSM–III–R* version of the SCID-P (Spitzer, Williams, Gibbon, & First, 1990), that is, an administration manual and several master training videotapes with accompanying scored SCID forms. Similar materials eventually will be available for the current SCID-P.

Administration of the SCID-P modules for all *DSM–IV* Axis I disorders can be time-consuming (e.g., 3 hr or more) depending on the number of different disorders an individual has and his or her response style. No interrater reliability data are yet available for the SCID-P for the *DSM–IV*. However, interrater reliability figures were reported for the SCID-P for the *DSM–III–R* (Williams et al., 1992). In general, the values were disappointing, but they could have been due partly to methodological limitations of the reliability study (e.g., several different versions of the SCID-P were used over the course of the study).

A version of the SCID also exists for assessing the *DSM–IV* Axis II personality disorders (First, Spitzer, Gibbon, Williams, & Benjamin, 1994). However, other structured interviews also have been developed to assess *DSM* personality disorders (e.g., the Personality Disorder Examination; Loranger et al., 1994), and the SCID for Axis II to date has not been more widely used than the other available instruments in depression treatment research.

Principal Versus Secondary Diagnoses

DSM diagnoses are commonly obtained in treatment studies of depression. However, procedures rarely are used to systematically assess the relative severity of all the diagnoses for which an individual meets criteria. The aforementioned findings on the comorbidity of *DSM* Axis I and Axis II disorders indicate the value of distinguishing the various disorders for which an individual meets criteria by their relative severity on some dimension (e.g., the severity of the symptoms that are associated with each disorder in terms of functional impairment, subjective distress, or both). Such a procedure, for example, (a) allows only individuals to be selected for a study whose "principal" disorder (i.e., most severe) is the disorder of interest, thereby reducing somewhat the heterogeneity of a study sample; (b) facilitates clear and complete presentation of descriptive diagnostic data on study samples; and (c) facilitates psychopathology research.

One relatively simple 0- to 8-point scale has been developed to assign severity ratings to diagnoses. It is included in the Anxiety Disorders Interview Schedule for DSM-IV (Brown, DiNardo, & Barlow, 1994). The scale points range from *absent* (0) to *severe* (8), with severe anchored as "very severely disturbing/disabling." Basic instructions for rating the scale also are available,[2] but no master training and calibration tapes exist yet.

REMAINING WORK

The main purpose of this chapter has been to illustrate an audience-focused strategy to guide selection of measures for a core battery for treatment outcome research on depression. The goal of the strategy is to maximize the potential impact on public health and clinical practice of findings from treatment research by obtaining data that are useful for the decision-making priorities of the primary consumers of treatment outcome research. Other strategies for constructing a core battery exist, as illustrated in this book. The basic recommendation of this chapter is not that an audience-focused strategy should be adopted to guide the development of a core battery for treatment research on depression. Rather, (a) a systematic strategy of some type should guide its development and an audience-focused strategy merits consideration and (b) a core battery should be developed.

One point discussed in the chapter is critical for maximizing the scientific value of any observer-rated measures included in a core battery (e.g., measures rated by clinical evaluators or therapists). Standard master training tapes, interrater reliability tapes, and calibration materials need to be made available for such measures. Although training tapes are available for some measures (e.g., HRSD), tapes to evaluate the reliability of study raters' scores with those of raters external to the study are rarely available now, even for the most widely used instruments. The development of such materials would be a major contribution to the core battery effort, as well as to treatment research.

Finally, no mention has been made yet of a strategy to promote wide-

---

[2] Instructions for rating the 0- to 8-point Severity scale from the Anxiety Disorders Interview Schedule for DSM–IV (Brown et al., 1994) can be obtained from Karla Moras, Department of Psychiatry, University of Pennsylvania, 3600 Market Street, 7th Floor, Philadelphia, PA 19104-2648.

spread adoption of a core battery by all treatment outcome researchers, those who are pharmacologically oriented or psychotherapeutically oriented, and those who espouse diverse forms of psychotherapy within the psychotherapeutically oriented group. The history of the last similar attempt to create a core battery for treatment research (Waskow & Parloff, 1975) suggests that researchers are unlikely to spontaneously adopt a core battery. Thus, to successfully complete the work started by the March 1994 APA-sponsored core battery conference, three additional steps seem necessary: (a) evaluate potential measures by agreed-on criteria to select a final recommended battery, (b) develop a plan for disseminating the battery and effectively encouraging its widespread use, and (c) implement the dissemination plan. Successful achievement of the next steps is one of the most effective interventions that treatment outcome researchers can make to maximize the public health impact of their work at this crucial time for mental health treatment in the United States.

REFERENCES

American Psychiatric Association. (1968). *Diagnostic and statistical manual of mental disorders* (2nd ed.). Washington, DC: Author.

American Psychiatric Association. (1980). *Diagnostic and statistical manual of mental disorders* (3rd ed.). Washington, DC: Author.

American Psychiatric Association. (1987). *Diagnostic and statistical manual of mental disorders* (3rd ed., rev.). Washington, DC: Author.

American Psychiatric Association. (1994). *Diagnostic and statistical manual of mental disorders* (4th ed.). Washington, DC: Author.

Anthony, M. A., Moras, K., Meadows, E. A., DiNardo, P. A., Utech, J. E., & Barlow, D. H. (1994). The diagnostic significance of the functional impairment and subjective distress criterion: An illustration with the DSM-III-R anxiety disorders. *Journal of Psychopathology and Behavioral Assessment, 16,* 253–263.

Barlow, D. H., DiNardo, P. A., Vermilyea, B. B., Vermilyea, J., & Blanchard, E. (1986). Co-morbidity and depression among the anxiety disorders. *Journal of Nervous and Mental Disease, 174,* 63–72.

Beck, A. T., Epstein, N., Brown, G., & Steer, R. A. (1988). An inventory for measuring clinical anxiety: Psychometric properties. *Journal of Consulting and Clinical Psychology, 56,* 893–897.

Beck, A. T., Kovacs, M., & Weissman, A. (1979). Assessment of suicidal intention: The Scale for Suicide Ideation. *Journal of Consulting and Clinical Psychology, 47,* 343–352.

Beck, A. T., & Steer, R. A. (1992a). *Beck Anxiety Inventory manual.* San Antonio, TX: Psychological Corporation.

Beck, A. T., & Steer, R. A. (1992b). *Beck Depression Inventory manual.* San Antonio, TX: Psychological Corporation.

Beck, A. T., Steer, R. A., & Brown, G. K. (1996). *BDI–II manual* (2nd ed.). San Antonio, TX: Psychological Corporation.

Beck, A. T., Steer, R. A., & Garbin, M. G. (1988). Psychometric properties of the Beck Depression Inventory: Twenty-five years of evaluation. *Clinical Psychology Review, 8,* 77–100.

Brown, T. A., & Barlow, D. H. (1992). Comorbidity among anxiety disorders: Implications for treatment and *DSM–IV. Journal of Consulting and Clinical Psychology, 60,* 835–844.

Brown, T. A., DiNardo, P. A., & Barlow, D. H. (1994). *Anxiety Disorders Interview Schedule for DSM-IV.* Albany, NY: Graywind Publications.

Bruss, G. S., Gruenberg, A. M., Goldstein, R. D., & Barber, J. P. (1994). Hamilton Anxiety Rating Scale interview guide: Joint interview and test–retest methods for interrater reliability. *Psychiatry Research, 53,* 191–202.

Clark, L. A. (1989). The anxiety and depressive disorders: Descriptive psychopathology and differential diagnosis. In P. C. Kendall & D. Watson (Eds.), *Anxiety and depression: Distinctive and overlapping features* (pp. 83–129). New York: Academic Press.

Clark, L. A., & Watson, D. (1991). Tripartite model of anxiety and depression: Psychometric evidence and taxonomic implications. *Journal of Abnormal Psychology, 100,* 316–336.

Diener, E., & Emmons, R. A. (1984). The independence of positive and negative affect. *Journal of Personality and Social Psychology, 47,* 1105–1107.

Elkin, I., Shea, M. T., Watkins, J. T., Imber, S. D., Sotsky, S. M., Collins, J. F., Glass, D. R., Pilkonis, P. A., Lear, W. R., Docherty, J. P., Fiester, S. J., & Parloff, M. B. (1989). NIMH Treatment of Depression Collaborative Research Program: I. General effectiveness of treatments. *Archives of General Psychiatry, 46,* 971–982.

Endicott, J., Nee, J., Harrison, W., & Blumenthal, R. (1993). Quality of Life Enjoyment and Satisfaction Questionnaire: A new measure. *Psychopharmacology Bulletin, 29,* 321–326.

First, M. D., Spitzer, R. L., Gibbon, M., & Williams, J. B. W. (1996, January). *Struc-*

tured Clinical Interview for DSM–IV Axis I disorders: Patient Edition (SCID-I/P, Version 2.0). New York: Biometrics Research Department, New York State Psychiatric Institute.

First, M. D., Spitzer, R. L., Gibbon, M., Williams, J. B. W., & Benjamin, L. (1994). *Structured Clinical Interview for DSM–IV Axis II personality disorders* (SCID-II, Version 2.0). New York: Biometrics Research Department, New York State Psychiatric Institute.

Fleiss, J. L. (1986). *The design and analysis of clinical experiments.* New York: Wiley.

Frank, E., Prien, R. F., Jarrett, R. B., Keller, M. B., Kupfer, D. J., Lavori, P. W., Rush, A. J., & Weissman, M. M. (1991). Conceptualization and rationale for consensus definitions of terms in major depressive disorder: Remission, recovery, relapse, and recurrence. *Archives of General Psychiatry, 48,* 851–855.

Frisch, M. B., Cornell, J., Villaneuva, M., & Retzlaff, P. J. (1992). Clinical validation of the Quality of Life Inventory: A measure of life satisfaction for use in treatment planning and outcome assessment. *Psychological Assessment, 4,* 92–101.

Garfield, S. L. (1986). Problems in diagnostic classification. In T. Millon & G. Klerman (Eds.), *Contemporary directions in psychopathology: Toward the DSM-IV* (pp. 99–114). New York: Guilford Press.

Gotlib, I. H., & Cane, D. B. (1989). Self-report assessment of depression and anxiety. In P. D. Kendall & D. Watson (Eds.), *Anxiety and depression: Distinctive and overlapping features* (pp. 131–169). New York: Academic Press.

Guy, W. (1976). *NCDEU assessment manual for psychopharmacology* (DHHS Publication No. ADM 91-338). Washington, DC: U.S. Department of Health, Education, and Welfare.

Hamilton, M. (1959). The assessment of anxiety states by rating. *British Journal of Medical Psychology, 32,* 50–55.

Hamilton, M. (1960). A rating scale for depression. *Journal of Neurology, Neurosurgery, and Psychiatry, 23,* 56–62.

Hecht, H., von Zerssen, D., Krieg, C., Possl, J., & Wittchen, H.-U. (1989). Anxiety and depression: Comorbidity, psychopathology, and social functioning. *Comprehensive Psychiatry, 30,* 420–433.

Howard, K. I., Cox, W. M., & Saunders, S. M. (1990). Attrition in substance abuse comparative treatment research: The illusion of randomization. In L. S. Onken & J. D. Blaine (Eds.), *Psychotherapy and counseling in the treatment of drug abuse* (pp. 66–79, DHHS Publication No. ADM 90-1722). Washington DC: U.S. Government Printing Office.

Kendell, R. E. (1975). *The role of diagnosis in psychiatry.* Oxford, England: Blackwell Scientific.

Koscis, J. H. (1990). Chronic depression versus treatment refractory depression: Evaluation and treatment. In S. P. Roose & A. H. Glassman (Eds.), *Treatment strategies for refractory depression* (pp. 193–204). Washington, DC: American Psychiatric Press.

Kraemer, H. C., & Telch, C. F. (1992). Selection and utilization of outcome measures in psychiatric clinical trials: Report on the 1988 MacArthur Foundation Network I Methodology Institute. *Neuropsychopharmacology, 7,* 85–94.

Krause, M. S., & Howard, K. I. (1976). Program evaluation in the public interest: A new research methodology. *Community Mental Health Journal, 12,* 291–300.

Lambert, M. J., Ogles, B. M., & Masters, K. (1992). Choosing outcome assessment devices: An organizational and conceptual scheme. *Journal of Counseling and Development, 70,* 527–534.

Loranger, A. W., Sartorius, N., Andreoli, A., Berger, P., Vuchheim, P., Channabusavanna, S. M., et al. (1994). The International Personality Disorder Examination—The World Health Organization: Alcohol, Drug Abuse, and Mental Health Administration International Pilot Study of Personality Disorders. *Archives of General Psychiatry, 51,* 215–224.

Maser, J. D., & Cloninger, C. R. (Eds.). (1990). *Comorbidity of mood and anxiety disorders.* Washington, DC: American Psychiatric Press.

Millon, T. (1986). On the past and future of the DSM-III: Personal recollections and projections. In T. Millon & G. Klerman (Eds.), *Contemporary directions in psychopathology: Toward the DSM-IV* (pp. 29–70). New York: Guilford Press.

Moras, K., DiNardo, P. A., & Barlow, D. H. (1992). Distinguishing anxiety and depression: Reexamination of the reconstructed Hamilton scales. *Psychological Assessment, 4,* 224–227.

Moras, K., DiNardo, P. A., Brown, T., & Barlow, D. H. (1994). *Comorbidity, functional impairment, and depression among the DSM-III-R anxiety disorders.* Unpublished manuscript, Center for Stress and Anxiety Disorders, State University of New York at Albany.

Newman, C. E., & Baranackie, K. (1992). *Scale for Suicide Ideation (SSI): Interviewer instruction manual.* Unpublished manuscript, University of Pennsylvania, Philadelphia.

Nunnally, J. C. (1978). *Psychometric theory* (2nd ed.). New York: McGraw-Hill.

Riskind, J. H., Beck, A. T., Brown, G., & Steer, R. A. (1987). Taking the measure of anxiety and depression: Validity of the reconstructed Hamilton scales. *Journal of Nervous and Mental Disease, 175,* 474–479.

Rothblum, E. D., Solomon, L. J., & Albee, G. W. (1986). In T. Millon & G. Klerman

(Eds.), *Contemporary directions in psychopathology: Toward the DSM-IV* (pp. 176–189). New York: Guilford Press.

Sanderson, W. C., Beck, A. T., & Beck, J. (1990). Syndrome comorbidity in patients with major depression or dysthymia: Prevalence and temporal relationships. *American Journal of Psychiatry, 147,* 1025–1028.

Shea, M. T., Elkin, I., Imber, S. D., Sotsky, S. M., Watkins, J. T., Collins, J. F., Pilkonis, P. A., Beckham, E., Glass, D. R., Dolan, R. T., & Parloff, M. B. (1992). Course of depressive symptoms over follow-up: Findings from the National Institute of Mental Health Treatment of Depression Collaborative Research Program. *Archives of General Psychiatry, 49,* 782–787.

Spitzer, R. L., Williams J. B. W., Gibbon, M., & First, M. D. (1990). *Structured Clinical Interview for DSM-III-R Patient Edition (SCID-P), Version 1.0.* Washington, DC: American Psychiatric Press.

Spitzer, R. L., & Fleiss, J. L. (1974). A reanalysis of the reliability of psychiatric diagnosis. *British Journal of Psychiatry, 125,* 341–347.

Strupp, H. H., & Hadley, S. W. (1977). A tripartite model of mental health and therapeutic outcomes: With special reference to negative effects in psychotherapy. *American Psychologist, 32,* 187–196.

Thase, M. E., Simons, A. D., Cahalane, J. F., McGeary, J., & Harden, T. (1991). Severity of depression and response to cognitive behavior therapy. *American Journal of Psychiatry, 148,* 784–789.

Waskow, I. E., & Parloff, M. B. (1975). *Psychotherapy change measures* (DHEW Publication No. ADM-74-120). Washington, DC: U.S. Government Printing Office.

Watson, D., Clark, L. A., & Cary, G. (1988). Positive and negative affectivity and their relation to anxiety and depressive disorders. *Journal of Abnormal Psychology, 97,* 346–353.

Williams, J. B. W. (1988). A structured interview guide for the Hamilton Depression Rating Scale. *Archives of General Psychiatry, 45,* 742–747.

Williams, J. B. W., Gibbon, J., First, M. B., Spitzer, R. L., Davies, M., Borus, J., Howes, M. J., Kane, J., Pope, H. G., Rounsaville, B., & Wittchen, H.-U. (1992). The Structured Clinical Interview for DSM-III-R (SCID) II: Multisite test-retest reliability. *Archives of General Psychiatry, 49,* 630–636.

World Health Organization. (1992). *ICD classification of mental and behavioral disorders: Clinical descriptions and diagnostic guidelines.* Geneva, Switzerland: Author.

13

Using Empirical Research Findings to Develop a Behavioral Measure of Depression: A Proposed Direction for Future Research

Leonard M. Horowitz, Kristin L. Nelson,
and Eric A. Person

THE PROBLEM

Contemporary measures of subjective distress, such as those described in this book, rely almost exclusively on paper-and-pencil self-reports. Measurement based on self-reports, however, is rife with methodological difficulties (see, e.g., Froyd & Lambert, 1989). As noted earlier in this book, patients are not always accurate in reporting their distress (e.g., Weinberger, Schwartz, & Davidson, 1979), nor are they always willing to divulge distress; they sometimes underreport the level of their distress to please a therapist after treatment or to justify an early termination. By the same token, therapists are not always accurate judges of a patient's distress. The therapist's judgment usually is based on the patient's self-report, and therapists understandably are highly motivated to describe their own treatment as effective.

Self-report measures of depression, for example, are notoriously unstandardized. Approximately 200–300 studies are conducted each year examining the effectiveness of different interventions in treating psychologi-

The preparation of this article was supported by the John D. and Catherine T. MacArthur Foundation Program on Conscious and Unconscious Mental Processes. It was also supported by Kaiser Foundation Research Institute Grant 114-9724.

cal disorders. One review of studies published in 20 major journals over a 5-year period revealed nearly 1,500 distinct measures of outcome (Froyd & Lambert, 1989), 60% of which were used exactly once. The overwhelming majority of these measures were patient self-report measures, and a large subset concerned the treatment of depression. Even semistructured interviews, such as the Hamilton Rating Scale of Depression (Hamilton, 1960, 1967), depend on each patient's self-report, which then is translated into an "independent" evaluator's judgment. Anxiety is easier to operationalize behaviorally, but studies of anxiety have shown that many individuals who describe themselves as nonanxious are, physiologically and behaviorally, often as anxious as people who describe themselves as anxious (e.g., Weinberger, Schwartz, & Davidson, 1979).

THE PROPOSED SOLUTION

In this chapter we consider the possible future use of behavioral tasks to assess the severity of a syndrome such as depression. More than a dozen laboratory-derived performance measures have been identified in recent years that differentiate between depressed and nondepressed people (markers of depression). The approach described in this chapter is organized around our theory of a psychiatric syndrome, which helps coordinate empirical findings that provide these markers. These performance tasks then can be combined into a test battery to form a (multimethod) behavioral measure that is free of the kinds of response biases that plague self-report measures.

ADVANTAGES OF A BEHAVIORAL MEASURE

A behavioral measure of depression would have a number of advantages. For one thing, it would identify depression in individuals who are motivated to underreport their level of distress. Therefore, once the measure is developed and standardized, it could be used to identify individuals whose self-report of improvement at termination was inconsistent with their performance on the behavioral tasks. Such individuals would seem to be at particular risk for relapse. Second, the performance measure could be used to compare depressed patients who have received different forms of treatment: pharmacotherapy, individual psychotherapy, or a psychoeducational group treatment. According to the theory described later, a *psychological* variable that is operationalized by one of the laboratory tasks (e.g., the number of false alarms on a recognition task) should be particularly responsive to a *psychological* treatment. Therefore, patients receiving pharmacotherapy might not show the same degree of change on a performance-based measure as they show on a self-report measure, suggesting a greater vulnerability to relapse when the medication is removed. In general, then, a behavioral measure might be more sensitive to subtle changes that are not detected by self-report measures.

Third, self-report measures of depression differ in their respective emphases on particular symptoms of depression. For example, some self-report instruments contain more interpersonal items (e.g., "I feel guilty much of the time"), whereas others contain more impersonal items (e.g., "I have difficulty sleeping at night"). Therefore, people with an interpersonal depression (e.g., feeling abandoned, isolated, rejected) generally would obtain higher scores on measures that emphasize interpersonal content. The performance tasks, on the other hand, are content-free with respect to interpersonal versus intrapersonal forms of depression, so people with the two types of depression would get evaluated on a more nearly common denominator. For this reason, group differences observed on a paper-and-pencil test might disappear (or even reverse themselves) on a performance measure of depression.

The tasks that are to be part of our proposed battery can be organized around our theory of a psychiatric syndrome. We therefore present our theory first. We then describe implications of the theory and laboratory tests that have been used to support these implications for the syndrome *depression*. Finally, we show how the laboratory tasks might be combined into a behavioral battery for assessing depression that is independent of self-report.

A THEORY OF THE PSYCHIATRIC SYNDROME

The work of psychotherapy is designed to treat syndromes and other sources of subjective distress, but a unifying theory does not exist to guide thinking about syndromes, help systematize accumulating information, and clarify related phenomena such as comorbidity between syndromes.

To meet this need, we have proposed a theory that makes use of the theoretical construct of a schema. A *schema* is defined as a collection of internal representations that are interrelated and function together as a unit. This definition contains three important points. First, it claims that the elements of the schema are representations—of behaviors, thoughts, feelings, expectancies, bodily sensations, and the like. That is, a schema not only contains representations of cognitive states (e.g., beliefs, thoughts), but it also contains representations of sensory states (e.g., bodily sensations), affective states (e.g., feelings, moods), and behavioral states (e.g., actions). Second, the representations are interrelated. Any two elements that have co-occurred frequently in the past generally have a stronger associative link than two that have rarely co-occurred. For example, people who are frequently depressed would have experienced the co-occurrence of depressive thoughts and characteristic bodily sensations more often than people who are rarely depressed. As a result, their schema for depression should show stronger interelement associative links than that of nondepressed people. Third, the definition states that the elements function as a unit. That is, the interrelations among the elements are relatively stable over time.

A clinical syndrome itself is regarded as a complex aggregate of interrelated organismic events that vary to some extent from occasion to occasion within one person. If these organismic events are represented in a schema, the schema constitutes a blueprint that influences future occurrences of the syndrome as a whole. To be clear about the origin of the schema, we need to make the following distinctions.

Organismic Event

When a stimulus event produces a particular reaction (e.g., bad news instigates a depressive reaction), that reaction is a complex aggregate of interrelated events in the organism that induce and reinforce one another (e.g., bodily sensations, feelings, thoughts, perceptions, expectancies, etc.). The stimulus that produces the reaction would vary from occasion to occasion within a given person, so the reaction as a whole also would vary from occasion to occasion. On one occasion, a particular feeling might be especially salient; on other occasions, some perception, thought, or bodily sensation might be more salient. The organismic events that make up the complex reaction each become stored as a mental representation, and the mental representations that co-occur across many occasions become interrelated.

Schema

A schema is said to exist if the representations are interrelated and form a unit that is stable over time. The model assumes that mental representations with the strongest associative bonds become elements of the schema, a blueprint of the modal (or typical) reactions across occasions. The schema, as a modal summary of previous organismic events, should be relatively stable from one occasion to the next.

Prototype

To some extent, schemas differ from one person to the next. One person's schema of depression might emphasize cognitive elements, and another person's might emphasize affective elements or bodily sensations. By assessing the schemas of different people who are depressed, one could determine which elements are generally the most frequent in a population of depressed individuals. As a summary across many depressed individuals, it would correspond to a kind of average (modal) schema across people (Horowitz & Malle, 1993), forming the *prototype* of depression. A prototype of depression thus is viewed as the modal schema across depressed individuals. A textbook description of depression is an attempt to characterize the prototype of depression. The more elements a person's own schema shares with this prototype, the more the person's modal experience would approximate the average clinician's conception and the higher the probability that an outside observer would judge that person to be depressed (Horowitz, French, & Anderson, 1982; Horowitz, French, Lapid, & Weckler, 1982; Horowitz, Post, French, Wallis, & Siegelman, 1981; Horowitz, Weckler, & Doren, 1983; Horowitz, Wright, Lowenstein, & Parad, 1981).

IMPLICATIONS AND SUPPORTIVE EVIDENCE

This view of a syndrome has several implications that can help organize findings from the empirical literature. We describe seven implications, and the empirical procedures that follow provide the (performance-based) measures of depression.

Implication 1: Schematicity

When we say that a schema exists, we mean that existing elements (mental representations) are associatively interconnected. The term *schematicity* denotes the mean interelement associative strength. To study a schema empirically, one would need to operationalize the associative strength between pairs of elements. We have found, for example, that people with a history of depression (hence who are schematic for depression) more often report that mental states such as "sad," "depressed," "guilty," or "tired" go together than do people without a history of depression (Malle & Horowitz, 1995).

The schematicity of a syndrome explains why negative thoughts about the self are such powerful predictors of anxiety (Cacioppo, Glass, & Merluzzi, 1979; Galassi, Frierson, & Sharer, 1981), depression (Ross, Mueller, & de la Torre, 1986), and coping styles (Kendall et al., 1979). Negative thoughts about the self often are part of a tight schema, so they typically co-occur with other elements of dysfunctional syndromes. Showers (1992) found that people with such thoughts (i.e., low self-esteem), more than people with high self-esteem, cluster negative characteristics when describing themselves. According to our model, this clustering of negative self-descriptions occurs because negative self-descriptions cited by those with low self-esteem come from a highly schematic syndrome.

Implication 2: Redintegrative Phenomena

When a subset of elements of a schema is activated, the entire schema tends to get activated. We use the older term *redintegration* to indicate that a part of a unit reactivates the whole unit (Horowitz & Prytulak, 1969). Various writers (e.g., Bower, 1981; Collins & Loftus, 1975) have assumed that the activation of one element induces activation in an associated element that is proportional to the strength of association between the two elements. These writers have also assumed that activations arising from two different associated elements summate. For this reason, an element that is associated with two already-activated elements can become more intensely activated than either of the original elements. This principle explains why the activation induced in a schema with tightly interconnected elements can greatly exceed the activation induced by the initial stimulus: A relatively minor environmental event activates elements that are so highly interrelated with other elements that the entire schema gets activated and the activation persists for some time. According to this view, depressive reactions can be instigated by relatively minor stimuli and can be greatly out of proportion to the original environmental event.

Because the activation of a subset of elements tends to activate the entire schema, other elements of the schema also get activated even though these other elements may have nothing to do with the original stimulus situation. As one example, suppose we identified people who are vulnerable to depression but are not currently depressed, and suppose they completed the Dysfunctional Attitudes Scale (DAS; Weissman, 1979), a measure of negative thinking. Would we expect the two groups to differ in their negative thinking given that neither group was currently depressed? Miranda and Persons (1988) identified comparable groups of women, one known to be vulnerable to depression and the other known not to be vulnerable to depression. At the time that the women were first tested, neither group was depressed, so the vulnerable group's schema for depression was not activated. Under this condition, neither group showed evidence of negative thinking on the DAS. The investigators then induced a sad mood in each group using the Velten (1968) mood induction procedure. That procedure should activate the negative schema in the vulnerable women, but the nonvulnerable women had no schema to be activated. Therefore, sadness induction should activate a network of depression elements only in vulnerable individuals. That is exactly what happened. The vulnerable women now endorsed negative thoughts on the DAS, but the nonvulnerable group did not. Thus, the laboratory task induced negative thoughts only in women who had a depression schema. Miranda and Persons happened to use the Velten procedure to expose latent negative thinking in vulnerable people, but other procedures also might be used to activate a depression schema (e.g., playing sad music, showing a sad film).

We have observed another example of redintegration that occurs when a depressed person describes a mild experience of sadness. According to the theory, elements of the mild experience would, during the telling, tend to redintegrate elements of the schema, so a listener should have difficulty

345

determining whether the reported experience was mild or severe. On a laboratory task, we (1996) had respondents describe three different occasions on which they felt "sad, blue, or down," a time when they felt just a little bit sad, one when they felt moderately sad, and one when they felt very sad. Nondepressed people generated three clearly differentiable episodes, which naive raters could easily order from mild to severe. However, the episodes generated by a depressed person were harder to differentiate.

Implication 3: Comorbidity Between Syndromes

The term *comorbidity* usually refers to the co-occurrence of two different syndromes within the same individual. Many patients with panic disorder, for example, are also depressed (Brown & Barlow, 1992), so panic and depression are frequently comorbid. According to our model, at least three forms of comorbidity exist. In one form, a relatively circumscribed syndrome (e.g., low self-esteem) itself constitutes a subset of elements of a larger syndrome (e.g., depression), so activation of the first induces activation in the second. In a second form, the two syndromes said to be comorbid have overlapping elements, so the activation of those common elements concomitantly redintegrates both syndromes. For example, negative cognitions about the self (e.g., thoughts about one's own incompetence, expectancies of personal failure, pessimism about future obstacles, anticipation of future suffering) could be part of a person's schema for panic and part of the person's schema for depression. Therefore, whenever those cognitions get activated, the person would probably experience both panic and depression, possibly complicating the treatment.

In a third form of comorbidity, the individual has two distinct syndromes with nonoverlapping elements (e.g., one for panic and one for depression). For example, a person who experienced depression primarily in somatic form (e.g., feels tired, is unmotivated, overeats) might at other times experience panic (e.g., shortness of breath, palpitations, nausea). Even though the two syndromes occurred in the same person, they would not overlap in elements, so they probably would not occur at the same time. The term *comorbidity* therefore has at least two different meanings: One implies that the two syndromes typically co-occur (because of overlapping elements), whereas the other implies that they occur within the same person but on separate occasions.

If the prototypic features of depression and panic were empirically identified, then for each patient we could systematically determine whether each syndrome exists and, if so, whether the two syndromes possess overlapping elements. If overlapping elements exist, they would seem to be a particularly important target of treatment; if they were not treated, they would keep activating both syndromes. Although comorbidity is associated with a poor prognosis (Maser & Cloninger, 1990), the poor prognosis may apply only if the comorbid syndromes have overlapping elements. If elements do not overlap, the two syndromes could be treated separately.

Implication 4: Incompatible (Contrasting) Syndromes Within a Person

Sometimes two syndromes contain elements that are incompatible with one another. For example, a schema for paranoid rage and a schema for paranoid depression might contain incompatible elements: The former might include (a) a judgment that someone else is to blame for current frustrations; (b) feelings of anger and indignation; and (c) wishes for revenge, dominance, and control. On the other hand, the latter might include (a) a judgment that the *self* is to blame for current frustrations; (b) feelings of shame and pessimism; and (c) a resignation that the self is submissive, powerless, and helpless. Because of these contrasting components, a person may be unable to experience the two schemas simultaneously, although it would be possible to shift from one schema to the other. In this case, alternating states could occur within the same period but not at the same time. Some readers will argue that *any* two syndromes can co-occur, but we think not. We believe that a person with contrasting schemas can only *alternate* between rage and depression, just as a person with anorexia can alternate between self-starvation and bulimia, a person with manic–depression can alternate between a manic episode and a depressive episode, or a person with borderline personality disorder can alternate between love/idealization and hate/devaluation of the same individual. As one schema is activated, the other would have to be deactivated (suppressed) because corresponding elements of the two schemas are incompatible.

These implications—the principles of schematicity, redintegration, comorbidity, and incompatibility—describe aspects of syndromes that have not been described before, and they are easily applied to a broad range of syndromes, including depression. The remaining three implications are already familiar from the literature on depression.

Implication 5: Cognitive Facilitation

If an individual has a tight schema for a given syndrome, then that schema should be easily activated because the activation of any subset of elements would activate the entire schema. The person therefore could be efficient in processing information about that construct. For example, the person would gain ready access to component elements and exhibit a rich array of associations to those elements. The person therefore would exhibit faster perceptual recognition, faster processing in making complex decisions, and better recall of content organized around the syndrome.

Cognitive Facilitation: Reaction Times

As one simple example, recognition thresholds should be affected by schematicity. The model claims that a few elements, when activated, should redintegrate the full schema, thereby activating all the other elements of the schema. According to a well-established principle (Howes & Solomon, 1951; Solomon & Postman, 1952), a stimulus that occurs frequently in an individual's experience has a lower recognition threshold than a stimulus that occurs less frequently. Therefore, elements of the schema (as words flashed on a screen) should be recognized faster by schematic people than by nonschematic people.

Cognitive Facilitation: Memory

A similar effect is evident for memory. Dunbar and Lishman (1984) compared hospitalized depressed patients and nondepressed control individuals in recalling words with a positive, neutral, or negative connotation. Thirty-six words were presented individually on cards. The words then were intermingled with 36 other words, and the participants had to indicate which words were old and which were new. For each class of words, the investigators computed the hit rate, the number of false alarms, and the value of d', a measure of sensitivity that corrects for a participant's bias to say "old." An analysis of the d' data showed a significant interaction between the subject group (depressed vs. control) and the type of words (negative, neutral, or positive). Depressed individuals more sensitively recognized negative words correctly, whereas control individuals more sensitively recognized positive words correctly. The presence of a depressed person's depression schema apparently facilitates the recognition of words with a negative connotation.

Implication 6: Cognitive Bias (Misperceptions, Intrusions, and False Alarms)

Once a syndrome is activated by some stimulus, people who are schematic for the syndrome should produce more schema-related misperceptions of the stimulus than people who are not; they also should produce more intrusions and false alarms on a test of recognition or recall of the stimulus. The reason for the misperception, intrusion, or false alarm is that when one or two elements of the schema redintegrate the complete schema, other elements are activated incidentally. These other elements are activated every time the schema gets redintegrated, so they become relatively more accessible to the person. Therefore, schematic individuals whose elements have in fact been incidentally activated should more often "perceive" and "remember having perceived" these elements, even though the elements were not actually part of the presented stimulus. According to the theory, people who are schematic for a syndrome do in fact experience the activation of schematic elements, but many of the activated elements have been activated "internally" rather than by objective external stimuli; hence, the designation *misperception, intrusion,* or *false alarm.*

Zuroff, Colussy, and Wielgus (1983) compared depressed and nondepressed women in their memory for words. First, the women were shown a list of 20 positive and 20 negative adjectives, and they rated themselves on each; they also noted which 10 words from each set were the most self-descriptive. Then, after 1 hr, 2 days, and 7 days, the participants were asked to recall words from each set that they had selected as the most self-descriptive. The depressed individuals recalled more negative adjectives than the nondepressed individuals, but they also produced more negative intrusions. A recognition test also was administered after 7 days. On the recognition task, the depressed respondents recognized more negative adjectives than did the nondepressed individuals, but they also produced more negative false alarms. Beta, the signal detection measure that describes how lax or stringent a criterion the respondent has used to judge whether the stimulus had appeared before, was significantly lower for depressed individuals (they used a less stringent criterion in claiming to have seen words related to depression). Thus, the depressed respondents displayed a response bias for "recognizing" negative content, a bias that apparently led them to produce more intrusions in recall and more false alarms in recognition.

The response bias also helps explain other differences that have been observed in the depression literature. For example, depressed people underestimate the frequency with which they have been reinforced on laboratory tasks (Buchwald, 1977; DeMonbreun & Craighead, 1977; Nelson & Craighead, 1977; Wener & Rehm, 1975). If a failure (nonreinforcement) activates a depression schema, causing other negative elements to be activated, then the totality of negative consequences would in fact be greater for depressed individuals. Similarly, studies have shown that depressed people recall negative life events more quickly than nondepressed people (Lloyd & Lishman, 1975; Teasdale & Fogarty, 1979). One explanation is that the depression schema is activated so often in the depressed person that the set of events considered negative is in fact large.

Implication 7: Interference

If a stimulus activates a schema, it activates the many elements of that schema, and the activation of those elements could interfere with some other ongoing performance. For example, the Stroop Color-Word Test (Stroop, 1935) is often used to demonstrate this interference. The test contains words that are printed in different colors, and the respondent is asked to name the color of the ink as quickly as possible, ignoring the meaning of the words themselves. If the words happen to redintegrate a schema, the activation of that schema's many richly interconnected elements could not be ignored, thereby interfering with color naming. Therefore, color naming should take longer. Thus, words that activate a schema would interfere more with color naming than would control words that did not activate any particular schema. Words related to a syndrome therefore should take relatively longer to color-name than other words.

For example, stimulus words (e.g., *discouraged*) should activate a depression schema for depressed people but not for nondepressed people. Therefore, depressed people should take longer to name the color of words such as discouraged. Gotlib and McCann (1984) used the Stroop procedure to test this hypothesis. Depressed (schematic) and nondepressed respondents were presented with 50 words connoting depression, 50 words connoting mania, and 50 neutral words. Each word was presented in a different color, and the participants had to name the color. The results showed that depressed individuals took longer to name the color of words with depressive meaning. Similar results have been reported by Klieger and Cordner (1990) and by Gotlib and Cane (1987) for depressed psychiatric patients.

Gotlib and McCann (1984) also induced a sad mood in nondepressed individuals using the Velten mood induction procedure, but they found no increase in color naming latency after the sad mood was induced. Nondepressed individuals were apparently not vulnerable to depression and did not have a schema for depression that could be activated by inducing sadness. On the other hand, people who are vulnerable to depression (even if they are not actually depressed at the time of testing) do show the interference effect (Williams & Nulty, 1986).

BEHAVIORAL TASKS DESCRIBED IN THE LITERATURE: A POTENTIAL BATTERY

The findings just reviewed suggest behavioral tasks that could be used as a multimethod, performance-based approach for assessing the presence of (and recovery from) the syndrome *depression*. Assuming that the tasks are positively correlated on average, we could aggregate a person's performance across the various tasks to produce a behavioral measure of depression that had higher internal consistency (generalizability) than any of the individual tasks (Cronbach, Gleser, Nanda, & Rajaratnam, 1972). Each behavioral task is given a short title for ease of reference.

The first two tasks diagnose depression through the principle of schematicity (i.e., two elements are more strongly interassociated if they are part of a schema). In the *describe yourself: negative clustering task*, after a successful treatment, the syndrome should show less schematicity than it had shown before treatment. Therefore, the patient should be less likely to cluster negative characteristics when describing the self (Showers, 1992); the probability that one negative self-description follows another should decline after a successful treatment. In the *subjective conditional probability task*, the mean interitem associative strength between elements of the network should be lower than it had been before treatment (Malle & Horowitz, 1995). If a patient is asked to judge the likelihood that one element of the schema characteristically accompanies another element (e.g., "If you felt lonely, what is the probability that you would also feel tired?"), the mean rating should come to resemble values typically observed among nonschematic (i.e., nondepressed) people.

The following three tasks are diagnostic of depression through the principle of redintegration (i.e., one activated element tends to reinstate the entire schema). In the *sad music redintegration task*, after a successful treatment, the activation of one element should no longer activate the complete schema as readily as it had done before (Miranda & Persons, 1988). If, after a successful treatment, sad music were used to induce a sad mood, the sad feelings should no longer induce other elements of depression. In the *blurring of mild-to-severe experiences of sadness task*, people who have become less schematic for a syndrome should then be more apt to recount three experiences that differ in the degree of depression so that objective raters, hearing the episodes, could now readily rank order them as the patient had intended.

The following four tasks are diagnostic of depression through the cognitive facilitation that results from a schema. In the *"like me" reaction time task*, when a person who is schematic for a construct is asked to judge whether a trait is "like me," the person can retrieve the trait from memory and respond "yes" more rapidly to a word from that schema than to some other word (Markus, 1977). After a successful treatment, however, this difference should become attenuated as the schema has become less available. In the *tachistoscopic recognition task,* the difference also should be evident in tachistoscopic recognition thresholds. Before treatment, depressed people should perceive words more rapidly that connote depression than words that do not (Postman, Bruner, & McGinnies, 1948), but this difference should diminish after a successful treatment. In the *free-recall task,* cognitive facilitation also should be evident in the person's memory for words from a relevant schema (Dunbar & Lishman, 1984). Depressed respondents, for example, might be shown words with a positive, neutral, or negative connotation and asked to recall the words. Depressed people would recall relatively more words from the negative category. In the *recognition memory task,* the words that had been presented might then be intermingled with new words, and each respondent would be asked to indicate which words were old and which were new. Before treatment, a depressed person should recognize more depressed words correctly, but after a successful treatment that advantage should decline.

The following three tasks are diagnostic through the response bias that results from a schema (i.e., elements of an available schema are themselves highly available). In the *measure of beta in the recognition task,* depressed people should show a high value of beta (i.e., a response bias) on the recognition task described earlier for words connoting depression, indicating a lax criterion in judging that a negative word had appeared before. The value of beta should diminish after a successful treatment. In the *frequency estimate of positive reinforcements task,* when depressed respondents are asked, before treatment, to estimate the frequency with which they have been reinforced on a laboratory task, they underestimate the frequency of reinforcements (Buchwald, 1977; DeMonbreun & Craighead, 1977; Nelson & Craighead, 1977; Wener & Rehm, 1975). After a successful treatment, however, their estimates should become more accurate. In the *ease of recalling negative events task,* the person recalls negative life events. Depressed people recall negative events relatively more easily than do nondepressed people (Lloyd & Lishman, 1975; Teasdale & Fogarty, 1979), but after a successful treatment the difference between the two should diminish.

The final task is diagnostic of depression through the principle of interference (i.e., the activation of a schema initiates processes that can interfere with other ongoing activity). In the *Stroop effect task,* the Stroop procedure can be used with depressed people to examine interference in color naming that occurs for words connoting depression. Before treatment, stimulus words such as *discouraged* should take relatively longer to color-name than neutral words, but after a successful treatment that difference should diminish.

Each of these procedures would make up one task in a multimethod behavioral battery of tasks. To validate the battery, various criteria of improvement—including the patients' self-reports and judgments by both the therapist and an independent evaluator—would help identify the most discriminating behavioral tasks. Performance on each task would be converted into standard scores and combined into an overall measure of change. Once the measure was perfected, we could assess change in depression independently of the patient's self-report. We then would be able to study people whose self-reports and behavioral scores are discrepant and test the hypothesis that patients are particularly at risk for relapse if their self-reports indicate improvement when their behavioral performance does not.

PROCEDURAL DETAILS OF THE BEHAVIORAL TASKS

During an evaluation session, a staff therapist might first explore the patient's presenting complaint and background. The following five behavioral tasks then could be administered in the following order: ease of recalling negative events, blurring of mild-to-severe experiences of sadness, describe yourself: negative clustering, "like me" reaction time, and subjective conditional probability. A second visit might be scheduled a week later, and the patient could be tested on the remaining seven behavioral tasks in the following order: Stroop effect, tachistoscopic recognition, free recall, recognition memory, measure of beta in the recognition task, frequency estimate of positive reinforcements, and sad music redintegration. Procedural details are described next.

Ease of Recalling Negative Events

Patients are instructed to describe three different occasions on which they felt "sad, blue, or down": a time when they felt just a little bit sad, a time when they felt moderately sad, and a time when they felt very sad. Each patient's description of each experience is tape-recorded and transcribed verbatim. As the patient describes each incident, his or her response latency is recorded (in seconds) from the end of the interviewer's instruction to the beginning of the patient's reply (Horowitz, Weckler, Saxon, Livaudais, & Boutacoff, 1977). In addition, every tale is transcribed verbatim to include speech disruptions: false starts, stammers, pauses, extraneous sounds, and so on. A frequency count of the various speech disruptions that occur before the patient begins telling the actual tale reflects the person's difficulty retrieving the incident (and talking about it). At the end of each tale, the patient also rates the intensity of the experience, its vividness, and his or her ease of remembering details. The duration of the tale also is recorded. Depressed people recall tales more easily by all measures and spend more time in telling the tale.

Blurring of Mild-to-Severe Experiences of Sadness

The verbatim descriptions obtained are then presented in random order to three raters, who judge which episode was mild, which was moderate, and which was severe. If the correct order of the mild-to-severe episode is designated 1, 2, and 3, a rater's actual ordering (e.g., 3, 1, and 2) can be compared with the correct order: The difference of each judged position from the correct position is squared and summed (in the example, the sum is 6), and these values are summed across the three raters. (If all raters place all episodes in the correct positions, the sum is 0.) We have found the largest discrepancies for the episodes told by depressed people.

Describe Yourself: Negative Clustering

The patient then is asked to describe himself or herself. This task is modeled after the procedures used by Showers (1992), Cantor, Markus, Niedenthal, and Nurius (1986), and Markus and Wurf (1987). Patients are asked to generate a list of words or phrases that describe themselves in social situations outside the family. They are told that the descriptors could be personality characteristics, thoughts, feelings, or behaviors—"whatever represents the way you think about yourself in social situations." They list items in the order in which the items come to mind. The degree of clustering of negative characteristics in the person's portrayal is then assessed. Clustering methods measure the likelihood that one negative characteristic is followed by another negative characteristic. After a patient generates the list, he or she is asked to indicate whether each descriptor is mostly positive, mostly negative, or both positive and negative. On the average, people list approximately 10 descriptors. The typical percentage of negative terms in the list is 37%. An arcsine transformation is usually used to stabilize the variance of proportion data in analyses. The clustering index that is most commonly used is the adjusted ratio of clustering (ARC; Murphy, 1979; Roenker, Thompson, & Brown, 1971). The maximum ARC value is 1.0, corresponding to perfect clustering of descriptors, and an ARC of zero means that the extent of clustering is equal to that expected by chance given the relative proportion of positive and negative descriptors. Depressed people tend to have higher ARC scores (i.e., one negative descriptor tends to follow another), whereas nondepressed people are more likely to intermix positive and negative descriptors (Showers, 1992).

"Like Me" Reaction Time

The patient is then shown a list of personality traits and asked to judge, as quickly as possible, whether each trait is "like me." Fifty words from the Big Five personality traits (Goldberg, 1992) are presented, and the patient's reaction time is assessed for each. Words are included in the list that are elements of the depression prototype (e.g., unenergetic, unassertive, discontented), and other words (matched for social desirability, word length, and word frequency) also are included in the list (e.g., unadventurous, unkind, stingy). The list also contains a number of comparable positive (socially desirable) words. The words are presented by computer, and the patient's response latency is recorded. The latencies then are examined for words to which the person responded yes ("like me"). Words that are part of a schema produce a faster reaction time (Bruch, Kaflowitz, & Berger, 1988, Study 2; Markus, 1977; Markus, Crane, Bernstein, & Siladi, 1982, Study 2). According to the existing evidence, a depressed patient's reaction times for those words judged "like me" that are part of the depressive schema should be relatively faster.

Subjective Conditional Probability

The patient is then shown a list of traits selected from different measures of depression (e.g., tired, lonely, discouraged, and guilty). Each word is paired with every other word, and the patient is asked to judge whether they "go together." The exact procedure has been described by Malle and Horowitz (1995). For each pair, the patient is asked to judge the likelihood that one characteristic accompanies the other (e.g., "If you felt lonely, what is the probability that you would also feel tired?"). Depressed people report higher subjective probabilities than do nondepressed people.

Stroop Effect

Ten words connoting depression and 10 neutral words matched for word length, word frequency, and vividness of meaning are used in the Stroop procedure, replicating the procedures of Gotlib and McCann (1984), Klieger and Cordner (1990), Williams and Nulty (1986), and Segal, Hood, Shaw, and Higgins (1988). A practice card and two test cards are needed. On one test card, the 10 depressed words are each repeated five times in varying colors; on the other test card, the 10 neutral words are each repeated five times in varying colors. First, a practice task familiarizes the patient with the procedure. The patient then is tested on the card with neutral words, naming the color of the 50 words as quickly as possible. Then, after a short break, the patient is tested on the card with depressed words. The Stroop effect refers to the difference in the time needed for color-naming words on each of the two cards. As an interpolated activity, the patient then watches a 4-min selection from a library of film clips (Gross & Levenson, 1993) designed to produce a reliable feeling of well-being in most people. The patient also completes a brief questionnaire rating the film clip to eliminate any residual effects of the Stroop task.

Tachistoscopic Recognition

The procedure used by Postman et al. (1948) and Vanderplas and Blake (1949) is then used to assess the patient's recognition latency for depressed versus neutral words. Fifty words taken from depression inventories (e.g., sad, guilty, discouraged) are matched with 50 other words for word length, word frequency, and vividness of meaning. Following the standard procedure, the words are presented tachistoscopically in random order. Each word is exposed three times for 0.01 s. If the patient fails to recognize the word, three exposures each last 0.03 s, and so on. The duration at which the word is recognized is recorded as the perceptual threshold. Depressed patients should recognize words that connote depression more rapidly than words that do not, and the difference in recognition latency should exceed that for nondepressed individuals. Errors are also analyzed following the method used by Postman et al. (1949) and Vanderplas and Blake (1949).

Free Recall

This task is adapted from the procedure of Dunbar and Lishman (1984). The patients are shown a list of 36 words, one by one, on a computer, each word appears for 2 s. The list contains 12 positive words, 12 neutral words, and 12 negative words shown in random order. After the patients have seen the entire list, they are asked to write down whatever words they can remember in the order the words come to mind. The number of negative words and the proportion of recalled words that are negative are both recorded. Depressed patients are expected to recall more negative words by both measures.

Recognition Memory

Another list of words then is presented on the computer consisting of the same 36 words, together with 36 new words that are comparable in semantic and formal properties. As each of the 72 words is presented, the patient is asked to indicate which words are old and which are new. For each word, we can then determine the proportion of positive and negative words that the respondent correctly recognizes as old and new and the proportion of each that the respondent incorrectly labels old and new, thereby determining the patient's hit rate, the number of false alarms, and the value of d' (i.e., the measure of sensitivity that corrects for the person's bias to say "old"). An analysis of the d' data has shown that depressed and nondepressed patients differ in their sensitivity to each category of words.

Measure of Beta in the Recognition Task

The recognition data also are used to assess the depressed patients' bias to "recognize" (incorrectly) new words that have a depressive connotation. From each patient's recognition data, beta can be computed. Beta is a measure that describes how lax or stringent a criterion the patient has used to judge whether that stimulus word had appeared before. A measure of bias also can be determined from intrusions that occur in the free-recall data of the free-recall task. Three raters judge whether each intrusion belongs to the positive, negative, or neutral category. Depressed patients are expected to include more intrusions from the negative category.

Frequency Estimate of Positive Reinforcements

This task is based on the procedure of Wener and Rehm (1975). It consists of 40 trials presented by a computer. On each trial, a blurred consonant–vowel–consonant trigram stimulus appears on the computer screen for half a second, followed by a series of five choices (labeled *A* through *E*); the patient is asked to select the choice that best matches the original stimulus. No choice is actually correct, but a green or red light appears at the end of the trial to signify that the patient's choice had been correct (green) or not correct (red). A green light occurs on 28 of the 40 trials (70%), and a red light occurs on the remaining 12 trials (30%). After all trials have been completed, the patient is asked to judge the difficulty of the task and the number of times that he or she had been correct (i.e., to estimate the number of times the green light had occurred). Using the patient's standard error of measurement, we can determine whether each patient's judged frequency of reinforcement differed significantly from the correct answer (28). Wener and Rehm (1975) showed that nondepressed people, on the average, estimated 29.5 correct responses (not significantly different from 28) but that depressed people estimated 22.5 correct responses (significantly lower than 28).

Sad Music–Film Redintegration

The following procedure is adapted from that of Miranda and Persons (1988). To begin with, a happy mood is induced in each participant. The participant watches a short selection from a library of film clips (Gross &

Levenson, 1993) that reliably produces a feeling of well-being in most people; at the same time, "elation-inducing" music is played softly on a cassette tape recorder. The music that is usually used for this purpose is a passage from "Coppelia" by Delibes, recorded at normal speed. The patient then completes a short form of the Positive and Negative Adjective Schedule (PANAS; Watson, Clark, & Tellegen, 1988) to assess his or her degree of positive and negative affect. For each of 20 adjectives describing affect, the patients rate their affect on a 5-point scale ranging from 1 *(right now I feel very slightly or not at all like this)* to 5 *(right now I feel very much like this)*. The patient also completes an abbreviated version (Form 1) of the DAS (Weissman, 1979) to assess the dysfunctional thinking that is supposed to accompany the activation of the depression schema.

A sad mood is then induced. The patient watches a short selection from the library of film clips (Gross & Levenson, 1993) that reliably produces a feeling of sadness; at the same time, sad music is played softly. The music usually used for this purpose (see, e.g., Clark, 1983; Sutherland, Newman, & Rachman, 1982) is from Prokofiev's "Russia Under the Mongolian Yoke" from the soundtrack of the film *Alexander Nevsky,* recorded at half speed. The patient again completes the PANAS and another abbreviated version of the DAS (Form 2). Although both depressed and nondepressed patients are expected to show a change in affect after the film–music manipulation, only the depressed patients are expected to show a greater endorsement of dysfunctional attitudes after the sad mood is induced.

To reinstate a positive mood, another film is shown that reliably induces a happy mood. Each film presentation takes approximately 4 min, and the entire procedure should take no longer than 20 min.

POSSIBLE APPLICATIONS: STEPS IN ESTABLISHING NORMS AND TESTING HYPOTHESES

1. *Demonstrate that the behavioral tasks differentiate between depressed and nondepressed patients (as they do between dysphoric and nondysphoric students).* Every participant's performance before treatment could be examined on each of the 12 behavioral tasks. On the negative clustering task,

for example, the score would be the ARC score; on the Stroop task, it would be a difference between two color-naming latencies. For each task, a mean performance score would be computed for depressed and nondepressed patients. Then, for each of the 12 tasks, the effect size for depression would be computed. The final results would show the magnitude of the effect size for each task.

2. *Compare the patients' pretreatment performance on the behavioral tasks with their pretreatment paper-and-pencil measures of depression.* Each patient, before treatment, could complete self-report measures of depression (e.g., the Beck Depression Inventory, the Self-Rating Depression Scale, the Center for Epidemiological Studies Depression Scale, the Inventory of Depressive Symptomatology), and these self-report scores (individually or aggregated) could be correlated with each of the 12 performance measures to determine whether the different paper-and-pencil measures correlate differentially with the performance measures. Any performance measure that does not relate at all to the other measures of depression could then be eliminated from the battery of tasks.

3. *Determine whether a depressed patient's performance on each behavioral task "improves" after a successful treatment.* Using the paper-and-pencil measures, the patients then could be classified into three groups according to their level of improvement: those who improved the most (z scores above .44), those who improved the least (z scores below $-.44$), and those in between. Each posttreatment performance measure of each patient could be examined to determine whether that task is sensitive to change in depression. Statistical comparisons would be needed to show (a) that a change in performance on the behavioral tasks is sensitive only to changes in depression, not to changes in other types of symptoms, and (b) that a change in the patient's performance does not occur merely as a result of retesting. This analysis thus will evaluate the specificity and the sensitivity of each performance task.

4. *Compile norms and determine psychometric properties of the battery as a whole.* Means, standard deviations, and other descriptive statistics of the frequency distribution could be determined separately for each performance measure. Scores on the individual tasks could be correlated with one another, and, assuming that they are all positively correlated with one

another and significantly correlated with the paper-and-pencil criterion, they could be standardized and aggregated to yield a single behavioral measure of depression. Then the distribution of composite measures could be described, providing overall norms for a pretreatment patient population, as well as measures of reliability and internal consistency.

5. *Identify people whose paper-and-pencil self-reports of improvement at termination are at odds with their behavioral performance and examine their reports at follow-up.* We could then test the hypothesis that a depressed patient's performance at termination is a predictor of relapse at follow-up. First, for depressed patients, one could examine the correlation between the paper-and-pencil measure and the performance measure. Each measure of improvement could be standardized, and those patients could be identified whose composite paper-and-pencil measure (z) exceeds .44 (the top third of the distribution) but whose composite performance measure is below $-.44$ (the bottom third of the distribution). This group of patients could be compared with those patients whose scores on the two measures are congruent (z exceeds .44 on both measures). The two groups are expected to differ at follow-up in the level of their paper-and-pencil self-reported depression; the former group is expected to show a relapse at follow-up. One could also identify patients with a discrepancy in the opposite direction—patients who show substantially more progress on their performance tasks than they report on their paper-and-pencil measures—and examine their status at follow-up.

6. *Compare the improvement of patients in different types of treatment using the behavioral measure of improvement.* We could also compare patients who received pharmacotherapy with patients who received psychotherapy and with patients who participated in a psychoeducational group. Pharmacotherapy is thought to reduce the availability of the depression schema as a whole by preventing activation of somatic elements, but it is not thought to change the composition of the depression schema per se. If the schema itself is not modified by treatment, the performance measure should reflect the continued presence of the still-intact depression schema even though self-report measures would suggest genuine improvement. Therefore, the depressed patients in the different treatment conditions could be compared on the self-reported paper-and-pencil measures and on the performance measures.

7. *Compare patients with different subtypes of depression on the performance tasks.* In earlier studies, we differentiated between depressed patients who reported primarily *interpersonal* distress and those who reported primarily *impersonal (intrapersonal)* distress (e.g., Meresman, Horowitz, & Bein, 1995). The amount of distress that is reported by such groups depends partly on the content of the items on the instruments used to assess depression. If interpersonal items such as "I feel guilty much of the time" are less numerous across paper-and-pencil measures than impersonal items such as "I have difficulty sleeping at night," then people with interpersonal distress would obtain generally lower scores on measures of depression, not because their distress is genuinely lower but because the paper-and-pencil test items sensitive to their type of depression are less numerous. On the other hand, the performance tasks that are used to measure depression are content-free with respect to inter- versus intrapersonal forms of depression, so people with the two types of distress would get evaluated on a common scale. Therefore, the following analysis could be used to determine whether a difference on the paper-and-pencil measure disappears (or even reverses itself) on the performance measures.

Contrasting groups could be formed using the Depressive Experiences Questionnaire and the Inventory of Interpersonal Problems to differentiate between depressed patients whose suffering is interpersonal and those whose suffering is not. Three subgroups of depressed patients could be formed: patients with a clear preponderance of interpersonal distress, patients with an ambiguous mixture of the two, and patients with a clear preponderance of impersonal distress. The groups then could be compared on their pretreatment amount of depression, as measured by their self-reports on the paper-and-pencil measures and their scores on the performance measures. Even if the three groups differed in their mean self-report scores, we would expect the performance measure to show comparable severity of distress before and after treatment, comparable rates of improvement, and comparable degrees of relapse at follow-up.

SUMMARY

In this chapter we have suggested a future direction for measuring the severity of a syndrome before and after treatment. Twelve behavioral procedures were described that have successfully differentiated between depressed and nondepressed people. We organized these procedures around our neoassociationist theory of a syndrome. Similar procedures could be used to assess the severity of other syndromes. After the procedures have been refined and standardized, norms could be obtained and the resulting performance-based measure could assess outcome independently of the person's self-report. We hope that these procedures will help overcome the methodological problems inherent in self-report measures and also help clarify the nature of a syndrome.

REFERENCES

Bower, G. H. (1981). Mood and memory. *American Psychologist, 36,* 129–148.

Brown, T. A., & Barlow, D. H. (1992). Comorbidity among anxiety disorders: Implications for treatment and DSM-IV. *Journal of Consulting and Clinical Psychology, 60,* 835–844.

Bruch, M. A., Kaflowitz, N. G., & Berger, P. (1988). Self-schema for assertiveness: Extending the validity of the self-schema construct. *Journal of Research in Personality, 22,* 424–444.

Buchwald, A. M. (1977). Depressive mood and estimates of reinforcement frequency. *Journal of Abnormal Psychology, 86,* 443–446.

Cacioppo, J. T., Glass, C. R., & Merluzzi, T. V. (1979). Self-statements and self-evaluations: A cognitive-response analysis of heterosocial anxiety. *Cognitive Therapy and Research, 3,* 249–262.

Cantor, N., Markus, H., Niedenthal, P., & Nurius, P. (1986). On motivation and the self-concept. In R. M. Sorrentino & E. T. Higgins (Eds.), *Handbook of motivation and cognition: Foundations of social behavior* (pp. 96–121). New York: Guilford Press.

Clark, D. M. (1983). On the induction of depressed mood in the laboratory: Evaluation and comparison of the Velten and musical procedures. *Advances in Behavioural Research and Therapy, 5,* 27–49.

Collins, A. M., & Loftus, E. F. (1975). A spreading-activation theory of semantic processing. *Psychological Review, 82,* 407–428.

Cronbach, L. J., Gleser, G. C., Nanda, H., & Rajaratnam, N. (1972). *The dependability of behavioral measurements: Theory of generalizability for scores and profiles.* New York: Wiley.

DeMonbreun, B. G., & Craighead, W. E. (1977). Distortion of perception and recall of positive and neutral feedback in depression. *Cognitive Therapy and Research,* *1,* 311–329.

Dunbar, G. C., & Lishman, W. A. (1984). Depression, recognition-memory and hedonic tone: A signal detection analysis. *British Journal of Psychiatry, 144,* 376–382.

Froyd, J. E., & Lambert, M. J. (1989). *A review of measures used to assess psychotherapy outcome.* Unpublished manuscript, Brigham Young University, Provo, UT.

Galassi, J. P., Frierson, H. T., & Sharer, R. (1981). Behavior of high, moderate, and low test anxious students during an actual test situation. *Journal of Consulting and Clinical Psychology, 49,* 51–62.

Goldberg, L. R. (1992). The development of markers of the Big-Five factor structure. *Psychological Assessment, 4,* 26–42.

Gotlib, I. H., & Cane, D. B. (1987). Construct accessibility and clinical depression: A longitudinal investigation. *Journal of Abnormal Psychology, 96,* 199–204.

Gotlib, I. H., & McCann, C. D. (1984). Construct accessibility and depression: An examination of cognitive and affective factors. *Journal of Personality and Social Psychology, 47,* 427–439.

Gross, J. J., & Levenson, R. W. (1993). Emotional suppression: Physiology, self-report, and expressive behavior. *Journal of Personality and Social Psychology, 64,* 970–986.

Hamilton, M. (1960). A rating scale for depression. *Journal of Neurology, Neurosurgery, and Psychiatry, 23,* 56–62.

Hamilton, M. (1967). Development of a rating scale for primary depressive illness. *British Journal of Social and Clinical Psychology, 6,* 278–296.

Horowitz, L. M., French, R. deS., & Anderson, C. A. (1982). The prototype of a lonely person. In L. Peplau & D. Perlman (Eds.), *Loneliness: A sourcebook of current theory, research, and therapy* (pp. 183–205). New York: Wiley Interscience.

Horowitz, L. M., French, R. deS., Lapid, J. S., & Weckler, D. (1982). Symptoms and interpersonal problems: The prototype as an integrating concept. In J. Anchin & D. Kiesler (Eds.), *Handbook of interpersonal psychotherapy* (pp. 168–189). Elmsford, NY: Pergamon Press.

Horowitz, L. M., & Malle, B. F. (1993). Fuzzy concepts in psychotherapy research. *Psychotherapy Research, 3,* 131–148.

Horowitz, L. M., Post, D. L., French, R. deS., Wallis, K. D., & Siegelman, E. Y. (1981). The prototype as a construct in abnormal psychology: 2. Clarifying disagreement in psychiatric judgments. *Journal of Abnormal Psychology, 90,* 575–585.

Horowitz, L. M., & Prytulak, L. S. (1969). Redintegrative memory. *Psychological Review, 76,* 519–531.

Horowitz, L. M., Weckler, D. A., & Doren, R. (1983). Interpersonal problems and symptoms: A cognitive approach. In P. Kendall (Ed.), *Advances in cognitive-behavioral research and therapy* (pp. 81–125). London: Academic Press.

Horowitz, L. M., Weckler, D., Saxon, A., Livaudais, J., & Boutacoff, L. (1977). Discomforting talk and speech disruptions. *Journal of Consulting and Clinical Psychology, 45,* 1036–1042.

Horowitz, L. M., Wright, J. C., Lowenstein, E., & Parad, H. W. (1981). The prototype as a construct in abnormal psychology: 1. A method for deriving prototypes. *Journal of Abnormal Psychology, 90,* 568–574.

Howes, D. H., & Solomon, R. L. (1951). Visual duration threshold as a function of word-probability. *Journal of Experimental Psychology, 41,* 401–410.

Kendall, P. C., Williams, L., Pechacek, T. F., Graham, L. E., Shisslack, C., Herzoff, N. (1979). Cognitive-behavioral and patient education interventions in cardiac catherization procedures: The Palo Alto Medical Psychology Project. *Journal of Consulting and Clinical Psychology, 47,* 49–58.

Klieger, D. M., & Cordner, M. D. (1990). The Stroop task as measure of construct accessibility in depression. *Personality and Individual Differences, 11,* 19–27.

Lloyd, G. G., & Lishman, W. A. (1975). Effects of depression on the speed of recall of pleasant and unpleasant experiences. *Psychological Medicine, 5,* 173–180.

Malle, B. F., & Horowitz, L. M. (1995). The puzzle of negative self-views: An explanation using the schema concept. *Journal of Personality and Social Psychology, 68,* 470–484.

Markus, H. (1977). Self-schemata and processing information about the self. *Journal of Personality and Social Psychology, 35,* 63–78.

Markus, H., Crane, M., Bernstein, S., & Siladi, M. (1982). Self-schemas and gender. *Journal of Personality and Social Psychology, 42,* 38–50.

Markus, H., & Wurf, E. (1987). The dynamic self-concept: A social psychological perspective. *Annual Review of Psychology, 38,* 299–337.

Maser, J. D., & Cloninger, C. R. (Eds.). (1990). *Comorbidity of mood and anxiety disorders.* Washington, D.C.: American Psychiatric Press.

Meresman, J. F., Horowitz, L. M., & Bein, E. (1995). Treatment assignment, dropout, and outcome of depressed patients who somaticize. *Psychotherapy Research, 5,* 245–257.

Miranda, J., & Persons, J. B. (1988). Dysfunctional attitudes are mood-state dependent. *Journal of Abnormal Psychology, 97,* 76–79.

Murphy, M. D. (1979). Measurement of category clustering in free recall. In C. R. Puff (Ed.), *Memory organization and structure* (pp. 51–83). New York: Academic Press.

Nelson, R. E., & Craighead, W. E. (1977). Perception of reinforcement, self-reinforcement, and depression. *Journal of Abnormal Psychology, 86*, 379–388.

Postman, L., Bruner, J. S., & McGinnies, E. (1948). Personal values as selective factors in perception. *Journal of Abnormal and Social Psychology, 43*, 142–154.

Roenker, D., Thompson, C., & Brown, S. (1971). Comparisons of measures for the estimation of clustering in free recall. *Psychological Bulletin, 76*, 45–48.

Ross, M. J., Mueller, J. H., & Torre, M. de la (1986). Depression and trait distinctiveness in the self-schema. *Journal of Social and Clinical Psychology, 4*, 46–59.

Segal, Z. V., Hood, J. E., Shaw, B. F., & Higgins, E. T. (1988). A structural analysis of the self-schema construct in major depression. *Cognitive Therapy and Research, 12*, 471–485.

Showers, C. (1992). Evaluatively integrative thinking about characteristics of self. *Personality and Social Psychology Bulletin, 18*, 719–729.

Solomon, R. L., & Postman, L. (1952). Frequency of usage as a determinant of recognition threshold for words. *Journal of Experimental Psychology, 43*, 195–201.

Stroop, J. R. (1935). Studies of interference in serial verbal reactions. *Journal of Experimental Psychology, 18*, 643–662.

Sutherland, G., Newman, B., & Rachman, S. (1982). Experimental investigations of the relations between mood and intrusive, unwanted cognitions. *British Journal of Medical Psychology, 55*, 127–138.

Teasdale, J. D., & Fogarty, S. J. (1979). Differential effects of induced mood on retrieval of pleasant and unpleasant events from episodic memory. *Journal of Abnormal Psychology, 88*, 248–257.

Vanderplas, J. M., & Blake, R. R. (1949). Selective sensitization in auditory perception. *Journal of Personality, 18*, 252–266.

Velten, E. (1968). A laboratory task for induction of mood states. *Behaviour Research and Therapy, 6*, 473–482.

Watson, D., Clark, L. A., & Tellegen, A. (1988). Development and validation of brief measures of positive and negative affect: The PANAS scales. *Journal of Personality and Social Psychology, 54*, 1063–1070.

Weinberger, D. A., Schwartz, G. E., & Davidson, R. J. (1979). Low anxious, high-anxious, and repressive coping styles: Psychometric patterns and behavioral and physiological responses to stress. *Journal of Abnormal Psychology, 88*, 369–380.

Weissman, A. N. (1979). *The Dysfunctional Attitudes Scale: A validation study. Disser-*

tation Abstracts International, 40, 1389–1390. (University Microfilms No. 79-19, 533).

Wener, A. E., & Rehm, L. P. (1975). Depressive affect: A test of behavioral hypotheses. *Journal of Abnormal Psychology, 84,* 221–227.

Williams, J. M. G., & Nulty, D. D. (1986). Construct accessibility, depression and the emotional Stroop task: Transient mood or stable structure? *Personality and Individual Differences, 7,* 485–491.

Zuroff, D. C., Colussy, S. A., & Wielgus, M. S. (1983). Selective memory and depression: A cautionary note concerning response bias. *Cognitive Therapy and Research, 7,* 223–232.

PART FIVE

Core Batteries
for Assessment of
Personality Disorders

14

Measurement Issues Relevant to Personality Disorders

Paul A. Pilkonis

A major impediment to progress in the area of personality disorders has been the lack of consensus about issues of measurement, although thoughtful discussions are available about several of the most prominent concerns: the usefulness of categorical versus dimensional approaches to assessment (Dowson & Berrios, 1991; Livesley, Jackson, & Schroeder, 1992; Trull, Widiger, & Guthrie, 1990); the advantages and disadvantages of different sources of information (self-report vs. informants vs. clinical diagnosis vs. structured research diagnosis; Zimmerman, 1994); discrepancies between instruments, even when using the same kind of data (Perry, 1992); the relative lack of attention paid to alternative ways in which caseness can be operationalized (Kraemer, 1992; Zarin & Earls, 1993); and the absence of gold standards for validity (Faraone & Tsuang, 1994), which has resulted in a greater emphasis on reliability and fewer efforts to ensure external validity. The present chapter is not intended to be exhaustive, however, and I focus here on four issues: problems in case

Preparation of this chapter was supported in part by National Institute of Mental Health Grant MH44672. Bryan Neighbors, Elizabeth Corbitt, and Sally Popper made suggestions about the discussion of the social costs of personality disorders.

identification with personality disorders; the importance of assessing interpersonal functioning and performance in major social roles; intrapersonal variables to consider for inclusion in a common assessment battery; and the need to measure the social costs of personality disorders. I also suggest some instruments that may be promising across these domains.

PROBLEMS IN CASE IDENTIFICATION

If change in diagnostic status (ill vs. well) is regarded as an important outcome (as is often the case in studies of Axis I disorders), determination of diagnostic status on Axis II becomes a critical issue in measurement. In traditional epidemiological approaches, there are three methods used to define "caseness": clinical diagnosis (i.e., people seeking treatment are cases when the doctor says they deserve a diagnosis); research diagnosis (which usually relies on a structured assessment, often administered by a clinician); or self-reports on a screening measure (Goldberg, 1992).

Each of these methods has different advantages and disadvantages, and none can claim to be a "gold standard." The advent of structured interviews for diagnosing psychiatric disorders is usually hailed, however, as the most important recent advance for studies of classification, largely on the basis of the improved reliability that such interviews provide. Systematic inquiry about the symptoms and signs of Axis I disorders is now an accepted part of any clinical research endeavor. Similar approaches have been applied to the diagnosis of Axis II disorders, and this extrapolation has indeed led to improved reliability.

Three interviews have received the largest share of research attention: the Personality Disorder Examination (PDE; Loranger, 1988), the Structured Interview for DSM-III-R Personality (Pfohl, Blum, Zimmerman, & Stangl, 1989), and the Structured Clinical Interview for *DSM-III-R* Personality Disorders (SCID-II; Spitzer, Williams, Gibbon, & First, 1989). Interrater reliabilities (kappa coefficients) for assessing the presence versus absence of any PD with these structured approaches range from .41 to .89 (Arntz et al., 1992; Brent, Zelenak, Bukstein, & Brown, 1990; Loranger, Susman, Oldham, & Russakoff, 1987; O'Boyle & Self, 1990; Pilkonis et al.,

1995; Pilkonis, Heape, Ruddy, & Serrao, 1991; Standage & Ladha, 1988; Stangl, Pfohl, Zimmerman, Bowers, & Corenthal, 1985).

Validity, however, is more problematic. The definition of Axis II disorders describes an inferred or latent construct reflected in a longitudinal history of dysfunction, lack of flexibility, subjective distress, and impairment in major social roles, as well as a specific personality style. Ideally, the measurement of such a latent construct will incorporate manifest indicators in each of these areas. Nonetheless, the interviews developed for Axis II diagnosis tend to rely heavily on inquiry about the traits that characterize the personality style alone, with secondary inquiry about specific behavioral examples, personal estimates of impairment and distress, or both. One can endorse this approach as a necessary first step, but it is important to acknowledge that there is limited assessment of the functional severity of the disorder, only partial information about the social and developmental history that puts the clinical material in a longitudinal perspective, and no simple antidote for the distortions introduced by social desirability response biases. These limitations may constrain validity, and my and my colleagues' experience has been that structured interviews, by focusing on personality traits and styles, underdiagnose PDs in clinical samples in a specialty care setting (Pilkonis et al., 1995).

Given the assumptions about the longitudinal stability of PDs and the evidence for consistency of personality traits in adulthood (McCrae & Costa, 1990), it is unlikely that large changes in the shape of a patient's personality profile will be found after treatment. It is more reasonable to expect decreases in the elevation of such a profile, but even these changes are difficult to interpret because of state–trait issues. For example, the literature on relationships between neuroticism and depression illustrates that scores on personality tests decrease (often markedly) when patients are less symptomatic. For a start, there is a need for better models of how state versus trait elements influence such scores (e.g., Kendler, Neale, Kessler, Heath, & Eaves, 1993).

Another concern about validation is raised by the lack of evidence for the discriminant validity of individual PDs in the psychiatric nomenclature. Mixed (or "not otherwise specified") and multiple diagnoses are the rule rather than the exception in studies of Axis II assessment. Also, when patients meet criteria for multiple diagnoses (Oldham et al., 1992), the evidence is equivocal about whether such diagnoses aggregate within the a priori clusters (A, B, and C) proposed (Bell & Jackson, 1992; Dowson & Berrios, 1991; Kass, Skodol, Charles, Spitzer, & Williams, 1985; Livesley et al., 1992). These issues have generated a debate about the usefulness of categorical versus dimensional approaches to assessment (Dowson & Berrios, 1991; Livesley et al., 1992; Trull et al., 1990), and dimensional approaches are increasingly regarded as more promising. In general, what is needed are models of personality incorporating higher levels of generality, a smaller number of broad constructs (cf. Junker & Pilkonis, 1993), and an emphasis on dimensional approaches to assessment. Dimensional models may be especially useful if they can be used to define "core" areas of pathology requiring intervention or to generate profiles of patients with the poorest prognoses and a tendency to use the health care system in excessive or inappropriate ways.

A central issue that follows from a preference for dimensional approaches is the need to develop a consensus about the dimensions to be incorporated into comprehensive models of "normal" or "abnormal" personality (Strack & Lorr, 1994). There are several possible candidates available: the Big Five factor model (Widiger & Trull, 1992); the factor-analytic studies (and instruments) of L. A. Clark (1993; L. A. Clark, McEwen, Collard, & Hickok, 1993) and Livesley et al. (1992); the Structural Analysis of Social Behavior developed by Benjamin (1993); the dimensional model proposed by Siever and Davis (1991); and the psychobiological model of Cloninger, Svrakic, and Przybeck (1993). As a part of our own assessment work, my colleagues and I have done exploratory analyses of dimensional Axis II data. Dimensional scores for each PD were created by summing consensus ratings for the individual features (absent = 0, probable = 1, and definite = 2) of each disorder, and these dimensional "subscales" were then factor analyzed. These initial analyses suggested a four-factor structure: (a) an Aggression factor (including both covert and overt aggression, with high positive loadings [>.40] for paranoid, passive–aggressive, narcissistic, sadistic, and borderline features); (b) a Disinhibition, or lack of constraint, factor (with high positive loadings for antisocial and histrionic features and high negative loadings for obsessive–compulsive and avoidant traits); (c) an Anxious-Ambivalent Attachment factor (with high positive loadings for self-defeating, dependent, borderline, and avoidant features); and (d) a Schizotypal factor (with high positive loadings for schizotypal, schizoid, and avoidant features and a high negative loading for histrionic traits). These factors accounted for 64.3% of the variance in the dimensional scores of the revised third edition of the *Diagnostic and Statistical Manual of Mental Disorders (DSM–III–R)*.

If categorical distinctions are still desirable because of their clarity, such distinctions can be made either qualitatively or quantitatively from a core set of dimensions. Qualitatively, it would be possible to identify distinctive blends of core dimensions that have particular clinical significance. Profiles across core dimensions will not be random but will cluster with variable densities in multidimensional space. Quantitatively, thresholds on any dimension or set of dimensions could be determined by decision-theory and signal-detection analyses (Kraemer, 1992) accompanied by clear statements about their utilities in different populations and different settings and their ability to predict some validating criterion. In general, relatively little attention has been paid to strategies other than the *DSM* decision rules for case identification of PDs: "The prevalent use of structured psychiatric interviews has not been accompanied by adequate attention to the problem of determining a diagnosis once the information is obtained" (Zarin & Earls, 1993, p. 197).

There is another step that needs to be included (and that is implicit in the strategy of identifying critical dimensional profiles). To converge on a common set of dimensions is to ignore, for the individual person, the contextual or motivational meaning of these dimensions:

> Thus, for example, what is seen as social timidity, social phobia, or inhibition, and may contribute to a diagnosis of either a schizoid or an avoidant personality disorder, may in fact reflect the cautiousness of a deeply paranoid individual, or the fear of exposure of a narcissistically grandiose individual, or a reaction formation against exhibitionistic tendencies in a hysterical individual. (Kernberg & Clarkin, 1997, p. 2)

Therefore, one needs a superordinate model that links specific traits to organizing principles and structures of personality.

INTERPERSONAL PROBLEMS AND OUTCOMES

My work on PDs grows out of an interpersonal tradition (Benjamin, 1993) and relies heavily on attachment theory, with the assumption that attachment styles provide a "deep structure" that exerts an organizing influence on personality and its disorders throughout the life span: "Intimate attachments to other human beings are the hub around which a person's life revolves, not only when he is an infant or a toddler or a schoolchild but throughout his adolescence and his years of maturity as well" (Bowlby, 1980, p. 442). Given this commitment to theory, it has seemed most promising to focus on changes in interpersonal relatedness and functioning in major social roles when attempting to capture changes in outcome in patients with PDs. From a pragmatic perspective, it is also useful to identify decreases in functional impairment and improvements in role performance as "clinically significant" outcomes that are compelling for patients, therapists, and other audiences. Although personality profiles and traits may not change markedly, it does seem reasonable to expect to see benefits in interpersonal terms with effective treatments.

A consensus needs to be reached about the domains that should be assessed when doing a comprehensive review of social functioning. Given my interest in attachment theory, I begin with an examination of close ties and work outward toward other forms of social integration and engagement. Thus, relevant areas to measure (in adult patients) include marital and other intimate relationships, parenting, and extended family relationships. Moving beyond relationships with first-degree relatives requires attention to broader social ties (e.g., friends, acquaintances, coworkers, neighbors), the capacity for productive work, and generativity in social roles outside the family. Finally, because the person with the PD is not always the one who suffers the most, I attempt to assess distress imposed on others (both close and more distant ties).

In an ongoing assessment study of patients with PDs (Pilkonis et al., 1995), my colleagues and I have developed a measure for alternative aspects of personality disorder that includes 5-point ratings for occupational functioning, marital or intimate relationships, parenting, broader social ties, subjective distress, and distress imposed on significant others. At intake, correlations between these ratings and an overall rating of Axis II severity demonstrated the closest relationships with occupational functioning ($r = .68$), general social relationships (.62), and distress imposed on significant others (.53). When the variables were inspected as a group in an exploratory stepwise multiple regression equation, four predictors were included in the analysis: occupational functioning ($\beta = .71$), distress imposed on others ($\beta = .44$), subjective distress ($\beta = .21$), and functioning in marital or intimate relationships ($\beta = .20$). This regression equation produced a multiple correlation of .85 (adjusted $R^2 = .69$), suggesting that these variables account for a large proportion of the variance in judgments of Axis II severity.

Because current approaches to measurement are labor-intensive (both in the proper application of interview techniques and the formulation of consensus diagnoses), examining the utility and validity of self-reports as "Stage I" screening procedures (Dohrenwend, 1990) and as outcome measures has assumed greater importance. One goal is to identify instruments that are valid as well as brief, that are applicable in both clinical and nonclinical settings, and that have sufficient predictive power to guide the selection of samples for more intensive, "Stage II" assessment and treatment. Using the Inventory of Interpersonal Problems (IIP; Horowitz, Rosenberg, Baer, Ureño, & Villaseñor, 1988) and a sample of 145 psychiatric patients, my colleagues and I developed five new subscales reflecting interpersonal difficulties (Pilkonis, Kim, Proietti, & Barkham, 1996). Three subscales—Interpersonal Sensitivity (11 items), Interpersonal Ambivalence (10 items), and Aggression (7 items)—were based on items that distinguished between patients with any versus no PD. Two subscales—Need for Social Approval (9 items) and Lack of Sociability (10 items)—were based on items that distinguished between patients with a Cluster C (anxious, internalizing) PD and all others. These scales reflect the nature of interpersonal problems most characteristic of patients with PDs, and a continuing aim will be to investigate their use both as prospective screening tools and as outcome measures.

INTRAPERSONAL VARIABLES TO CONSIDER

Subjective distress, usually operationalized in the form of common psychological symptoms, is perhaps the least controversial area requiring assessment. If nothing else, clinicians hope to relieve their patients' symptoms with treatment, and there is evidence suggesting that patients with PDs report more symptomatic distress than patients without these disorders (Shea, Glass, Pilkonis, Watkins, & Docherty, 1987). Also, there have been some creative attempts to link changes in different symptoms to alternative personality constellations (Hull, Clarkin, & Kakuma, 1993).

Many approaches have been taken to assessing self-image; self-esteem; and mental representations of self, other, and self in relation to others. These approaches usually suggest some form of a cognitive diathesis (e.g., negative self-schema, role relationship models, core conflictual relationship themes, internalized object relations) indicating a chronic vulnerability to affective distress in the face of life circumstances perceived as threatening or painful. In some ways, such efforts harken back to Mischel's (1973) arguments on behalf of a social–cognitive approach to personality.

Unfortunately, there is little consensus about methods or measures in this area. At least one theme, however, deserves attention: that of the contrast between individuals whose positive sense of self depends on the availability of close relationships versus those whose self-esteem is more influenced by issues of autonomy, achievement, and self-definition. These two types of schemas have been discussed by several authors, often in the context of relationships between personality and depression (Pilkonis, 1988): Arieti and Bemporad (needs for a dominant other vs. a dominant goal), Beck (sociotropy vs. autonomy), Blatt (anaclitic/dependent vs. introjective/self-critical developmental lines), Bowlby (anxious attachment vs. compulsive self-reliance), and Main (preoccupied/enmeshed vs. dismissing adult attachment styles). These themes also have been linked empirically to the *DSM–III–R* PDs, with the promising conclusion that "the sociotropic/dependent and autonomous/self-critical personality styles are both significantly associated with Axis II psychopathology in outpatients" (Ouimette, Klein, Anderson, Riso, & Lizardi, 1994, p. 747). Given this convergence despite different theoretical starting points, it may be worthwhile to promote efforts to measure these schemas in more standard fashion.

SOCIAL COSTS OF PDs

In my own assessment work, I begin with an assumption about the social costs of PDs. I assume that a significant proportion of the morbidity in both the mental health care and physical health care systems can be understood most straightforwardly in Axis II terms. I do this to (a) encourage the use of chronic disease (rather than acute illness) models when conceptualizing psychiatric disorders and (b) desensitize clinicians to the use of Axis II diagnoses. PDs have pejorative connotations that tend to polarize clinicians, but PDs can be described in everyday terms and "behavioral" language as generalized failures of adaptation, persistent dysfunctional interpersonal relationships, and chronic impairments in the ability to love, to work, or both. In these terms, PDs carry large "burden of illness" costs: repeated treatment failures in the mental health care sector, inappropriate utilization of the primary care sector, treatment costs for family members, substance abuse, and so on. Researchers need to expand their assessment efforts to include an accounting of such costs, although, again, they are confronted with little or no consensus about relevant methodologies and variables. Initial attempts at cost-effectiveness analysis with mental health problems have tended to rely on self-report methodologies and to focus on treatment utilization, treatment costs associated with different disorders, and decreases in such costs after an adequate course of treatment (e.g., Kamlet et al., 1993). Accounting for broader costs and benefits and addressing quality-of-life issues are relatively undeveloped enterprises.

The literature on the social costs of PDs consists primarily of anecdotal reports and case studies about the burdens associated with these patients and discussions of the need for more comprehensive approaches to their care (e.g., Cohen, Shapiro, Manson, & Kondi, 1985; Holmes, 1988; Lewin & Sharfstein, 1990; McGlashan, 1993; Nehls & Diamond, 1993). These reports are consistent with the usual clinical wisdom (i.e., patients with PDs create significant interpersonal strains and generate substantial costs within the health care system).

Among the researchers who have reported on larger samples and included more systematic data collection, the literature can be divided into investigations of the costs and burdens generated within the physical health care system and the mental health care system. In the primary care system, Casey and Tyrer (1990) found a 28% 1-year prevalence of PDs in two general medical practices in England among 358 patients who had already been identified as having "conspicuous psychiatric morbidity." Patients with PDs had more social dysfunction than those without PDs, and "the robustness of this finding was independent of mental state" (Casey & Tyrer, 1990, p. 264). In the 3 years after diagnosis, psychologically impaired patients with PDs also displayed greater morbidity and had more frequent contact with psychiatric services (Tyrer & Sievewright, 1988). In a community survey with 249 respondents, Reich, Boerstler, Yates, and Nduaguba (1989) identified 26 individuals with *DSM–III* PDs and 167 individuals who had no features of PD and who served as a comparison group. Individuals with PDs were more likely to have been hospitalized for medical reasons during the prior year (38% vs. 17%). Reich et al. also emphasized the association in women ($r = .50$) between "flamboyant" PD scores and visits to a primary care physician for mental health reasons. In another investigation focusing specifically on somatization disorder, 61% of 94 patients with this disorder qualified for one or more Axis II diagnoses on the SCID-II (Rost, Akins, Brown, & Smith, 1992), and the authors emphasized the need for further research to "understand the relationship of personality disorders in SD [somatization disorder] patients to clinically important variables such as frequency of help seeking, functional impairment, health care expenditures, and readiness for psychiatric referral" (p. 325).

In the mental health care system, borderline PD has been associated with higher levels of service use in emergency room, day care, and inpatient settings (Perry, Lavori, & Hoke, 1987). In that study, patients with borderline personality disorder were compared with those with antisocial personality disorder and bipolar II disorder. In a survey of the worst recidivists in 196 state hospitals, patients with diagnoses of schizophrenia, bipolar disorder, and PD were overrepresented (Geller, 1992); the potential severity of the first two diagnoses is often acknowledged, but the major impact of PDs on functional impairment and repeated hospitalization is less frequently discussed.

In ongoing assessment studies of Axis II disorders (Pilkonis et al., 1995; Pilkonis et al., 1991), my colleagues and I collected follow-up data on treatment utilization for a 1-year period. In a sample of 86 patients, those with Cluster B PDs used more treatment sessions than did those with Cluster C PDs (23.5 vs. 9.1) and had the highest risk of hospitalization during the follow-up period. Nine patients (10.5%) were hospitalized during follow-up; all had Cluster B diagnoses, and 8 of the 9 were rated as "marked" at intake in terms of Axis II severity. As a way of proceeding further with this work, my colleagues and I are attempting to identify and validate a "high-risk" profile for patients with PDs. In addition to a Cluster B diagnosis and marked severity (i.e., a score of 70 or higher on a 100-point scale of Axis II severity developed as an analog to the Global Assessment Scale for Axis I), other current indicators include a lifetime history of substance abuse; a marital history other than a single, stable marriage; traits of aggression and impulsivity; and an anxious-ambivalent adult attachment style.

A comprehensive discussion of the potential social costs of PDs also should include some comments about their possible transgenerational effects. It is common for both clinicians and social observers to assert that there are consistencies across generations in the occurrence of sexual abuse, physical abuse, family violence, and substance abuse, all of which are frequent markers of PDs. PDs also may exert transgenerational effects in more subtle ways. For example, there is a large body of work examining the influence of maternal depression on early child development that has shown that depression is associated with diminished quality of mother–child interaction, decreased likelihood of secure attachment, impaired cognitive development, and less adaptive affect regulation (Gelfand & Teti, 1990). At the same time, a smaller number of studies have emphasized the heterogeneity of maternal and infant behavior in dyads in which the mothers are depressed (Cox, Puckering, Pound, & Mills, 1987). Little of this literature has examined the extent to which maternal personality might account for such heterogeneity. In their National Institute of Mental Health longitudinal sample, for example, Radke-Yarrow and Zahn-Waxler (1991) found that, using the PDE, 65% of mothers with affective disorders but only 19% of control mothers received a PD diagnosis. Thus, it is likely that when one compares groups of depressed and nondepressed individuals, one also is comparing groups in which levels of PD differ. In studies that do show differences, it is possible that a chronic condition such as a PD may be more of an influence on maternal interactive capability than an episode of depression.

INSTRUMENTS TO CONSIDER

Given the constraints of a less-than-ideal research world, it may be useful to try to provide practical suggestions about instruments valuable in current work. The best instruments, of course, are those that are both valid and efficient. Such instruments should probably reflect at least two measurement perspectives: the perspective of the patient (which is certainly efficient to assess via self-report questionnaires) and the perspective of the other (typically a therapist, independent clinician, or informant from the patient's social network; see Shedler, Mayman, & Manis, 1993, on the value of measures incorporating clinical judgments). With increased concerns about social and monetary costs, the "other" also may be a health care administrator, legislator, or other decision maker.

In the area of personality traits and features, four self-report measures are candidates for common assessment batteries: the Schedule for Non-adaptive and Adaptive Personality (SNAP; L. A. Clark, 1993), the Dimensional Assessment of Personality Pathology (Livesley et al., 1992), the Wisconsin Personality Disorders Inventory (Klein et al., 1993), and the Personality Assessment Inventory (Morey, 1991). The advantages of these measures include their development in the context of specific assessment traditions or models and their developers' attention to psychometric concerns and principles. From the perspective of the other, I prefer the PDE (Loranger, 1988) when used by a clinician who also has access to other pertinent clinical data and who does not simply administer the interview as if it were a verbal self-report. The advantages of the PDE include the availability of a manual with detailed instructions for scoring each item, a clinically attractive format organized around relevant themes (e.g., work, interpersonal relations, affect regulation), and the use of some open-ended questions to explore these themes.

In the area of interpersonal problems, the IIP (Horowitz et al., 1988) is a valuable self-report measure. I continue to look for interview and clinical measures of social functioning that may have particular relevance for PDs (cf. Goldman, Skodol, & Lave, 1992). I have examined various instruments assessing adult attachments, and a prominent candidate here is the Adult Attachment Interview (Main, Kaplan, & Cassidy, 1985). My colleagues and I have developed our own version of a comprehensive social and developmental history, the Interpersonal Relations Assessment (Heape, Pilkonis, Lambert, & Proietti, 1991), and prototypes of adult attachment styles that can be scored from it. Assessments of social role performance can be done using the Social Adjustment Scale (Schooler, Hogarty, & Weissman, 1979); an interview developed in the United Kingdom, the Adult Personality Functioning Assessment (Hill, Harrington, Fudge, & Rutter, 1990), also is available for this purpose.

Three instruments are candidates for use as self-report indicators of schemas about relatedness (social approval, dependency) versus self-definition (perfectionism, self-criticism): the Sociotropy-Autonomy Scale (D. A. Clark & Beck, 1991), the Depressive Experiences Questionnaire (Blatt, Quinlan, Chevron, McDonald, & Zuroff, 1982), and the Dysfunctional Attitudes Scale (see Imber et al., 1990, for the results of a factor analysis of this latter scale).

These suggestions are not intended to be definitive; rather, they are offered to try to promote continued work in this area. In general, it is an exciting time for work on measurement—in part, because of recent progress in the development of quantitative tools useful for psychometric purposes (e.g., Hambleton, Swaminathan, & Rogers [1991] on item response theory; Meehl [1995] on "taxometrics"). The goal is to encourage such work in the area of PDs where the need is great and the potential payoffs are large.

REFERENCES

Arntz, A., van Beijsterveldt, B., Hoekstra, R., Hofman, A., Eussen, M., & Sallaerts, S. (1992). The interrater reliability of a Dutch version of the Structured Clinical Interview for DSM–III–R Personality Disorders. *Acta Psychiatrica Scandinavica, 85,* 394–400.

Bell, R. C., & Jackson, H. J. (1992). The structure of personality disorders in *DSM–III. Acta Psychiatrica Scandinavica, 85,* 279–287.

Benjamin, L. S. (1993). *Interpersonal diagnosis and treatment of personality disorders.* New York: Guilford Press.

Blatt, S. J., Quinlan, D. M., Chevron, E., McDonald, C., & Zuroff, D. (1982). Dependency and self-criticism: Psychological dimensions of depression. *Journal of Consulting and Clinical Psychology, 50,* 113–124.

Bowlby, J. (1980). *Loss: Sadness and depression.* New York: Basic Books.

Brent, D. A., Zelenak, J. P., Bukstein, O., & Brown, R. V. (1990). Reliability and validity of the Structured Interview for Personality Disorders in adolescents. *Journal of the American Academy of Child and Adolescent Psychiatry, 29,* 349–354.

Casey, P. R., & Tyrer, P. (1990). Personality disorder and psychiatric illness in general practice. *British Journal of Psychiatry, 156,* 261–265.

Clark, D. A., & Beck, A. T. (1991). Personality factors in dysphoria: A psychometric refinement of Beck's Sociotropy-Autonomy Scale. *Journal of Psychopathology and Behavioral Assessment, 13,* 369–388.

Clark, L. A. (1993). *Manual for the Schedule for Nonadaptive and Adaptive Personality (SNAP).* Minneapolis: University of Minnesota Press.

Clark, L. A., McEwen, J. L., Collard, L. M., & Hickok, L. G. (1993). Symptoms and traits of personality disorder: Two new methods for their assessment. *Psychological Assessment, 5,* 81–91.

Cloninger, C. R., Svrakic, D. M., & Przybeck, T. R. (1993). A psychobiological model of temperament and character. *Archives of General Psychiatry, 50,* 975–990.

Cohen, L. M., Shapiro, E., Manson, J. E., & Kondi, E. S. (1985). The high cost of treating a psychiatric disorder as a medical/surgical illness. *Psychosomatics, 26,* 453–455.

Cox, A. D., Puckering, C., Pound, A., & Mills, M. (1987). The impact of maternal depression in young children. *Journal of Child Psychology and Psychiatry, 28,* 917–928.

Dohrenwend, B. P. (1990). The problem of validity in field studies of psychological disorders revisited. *Psychological Medicine, 20,* 195–208.

Dowson, J. H., & Berrios, G. E. (1991). Factor structure of *DSM–III–R* personality disorders shown by self-report questionnaire: Implications for classifying and assessing personality disorders. *Acta Psychiatrica Scandinavica, 84,* 555–560.

Faraone, S. V., & Tsuang, M. T. (1994). Measuring diagnostic accuracy in the absence of a "gold standard." *American Journal of Psychiatry, 151,* 650–657.

Gelfand, D. M., & Teti, D. M. (1990). The effects of maternal depression on children. *Clinical Psychology Review, 10,* 329–353.

Geller, J. L. (1992). A report on the "worst" state hospital recidivists in the U.S. *Hospital and Community Psychiatry, 43,* 904–908.

Goldberg, D. (1992). A classification of psychological distress for use in primary care settings. *Social Science and Medicine, 35,* 189–193.

Goldman, H. H., Skodol, A. E., & Lave, T. R. (1992). Revising Axis V for *DSM–IV:* A review of measures of social functioning. *American Journal of Psychiatry, 149,* 1148–1156.

Hambleton, R. K., Swaminathan, H., & Rogers, H. J. (1991). *Fundamentals of item response theory.* Thousand Oaks, CA: Sage.

Heape, C. L., Pilkonis, P. A., Lambert, J., & Proietti, J. M. (1991). *Interpersonal relations assessment.* Pittsburgh: University of Pittsburgh, Department of Psychiatry.

Hill, J., Harrington, R., Fudge, H., & Rutter, M. (1990). *Adult Personality Functioning Assessment (APFA).* Liverpool: University of Liverpool, Department of Psychiatry.

Holmes, J. (1988). Supportive analytical psychotherapy: An account of two cases. *British Journal of Psychiatry, 152,* 824–829.

Horowitz, L. M., Rosenberg, S. E., Baer, B. A., Ureño, G., & Villaseñor, V. S. (1988). Inventory of Interpersonal Problems: Psychometric properties and clinical applications. *Journal of Consulting and Clinical Psychology, 56,* 885–892.

Hull, J. W., Clarkin, J. F., & Kakuma, T. (1993). Treatment response of borderline inpatients: A growth curve analysis. *Journal of Nervous and Mental Disease, 181,* 503–508.

Imber, S. D., Pilkonis, P. A., Sotsky, S., Elkin, I., Watkins, J., Collins, J., Shea, T., Leber, W., & Glass, D. (1990). Mode-specific effects among three treatments for depression. *Journal of Consulting and Clinical Psychology, 58,* 352–359.

Junker, B. W., & Pilkonis, P. A. (1993). Personality and depression: Measurement and modeling issues. In M. Klein, M. T. Shea, & D. J. Kupfer (Eds.), *Personality and depression* (pp. 133–170). New York: Guilford Press.

Kamlet, M. S., Paul, N., Greenhouse, J., Kupfer, D. J., Frank, E., & Wade, M. (1993). *Cost-utility analysis of maintenance treatment for recurrent depression.* Pittsburgh: University of Pittsburgh, Department of Psychiatry.

Kass, F., Skodol, A. E., Charles, E., Spitzer, R. L., & Williams, J. B. W. (1985). Scaled ratings of *DSM–III* personality disorders. *American Journal of Psychiatry, 142,* 627–630.

Kendler, K. S., Neale, M. C., Kessler, R. C., Heath, A. C., & Eaves, L. J. (1993). A longitudinal twin study of personality and major depression in women. *Archives of General Psychiatry, 50,* 853–862.

Kernberg, O., & Clarkin, J. F. (1997). *The personality disorders: Empiricism in search of a theory.* Manuscript in preparation, Cornell Medical Center.

Klein, M. H., Benjamin, L. S., Rosenfeld, R., Treece, C., Husted, J., & Greist, J. H. (1993). The Wisconsin Personality Disorders Inventory: Development, reliability, and validity. *Journal of Personality Disorders, 7,* 285–303.

Kraemer, H. C. (1992). *Evaluating medical tests: Objective and quantitative guidelines.* Newbury Park, CA: Sage.

Lewin, R., & Sharfstein, S. S. (1990). Managed care and the discharge dilemma. *Psychiatry, 53,* 116–121.

Livesley, W. J., Jackson, D. N., & Schroeder, M. L. (1992). Factorial structure of traits delineating personality disorders in clinical and general population samples. *Journal of Abnormal Psychology, 101,* 432–440.

Loranger, A. W. (1988). *Personality Disorder Examination (PDE) manual.* Yonkers, NY: DV Communications.

Loranger, A. W., Susman, V. L., Oldham, J. M., & Russakoff, L. M. (1987). The Personality Disorder Examination: A preliminary report. *Journal of Personality Disorders, 1,* 1–13.

Main, M., Kaplan, N., & Cassidy, J. (1985). Security in infancy, childhood and adulthood: A move to the level of representation. *Monographs of the Society for Research in Child Development, 50*(1–2, Serial No. 209).

McCrae, R. R., & Costa, P. T., Jr. (1990). *Personality in adulthood.* New York: Guilford Press.

McGlashan, T. (1993). Sexual abuse and psychopathology: Commentary. *Psychiatry, 56,* 217–221.

Meehl, P. E. (1995). Bootstraps taxometrics: Solving the classification problem in psychopathology. *American Psychologist, 50,* 266–275.

Mischel, W. (1973). Toward a cognitive social learning reconceptualization of personality. *Psychological Review, 80,* 252–283.

Morey, L. C. (1991). *Personality Assessment Inventory (PAI) professional manual.* Odessa, FL: Psychological Assessment Resources.

Nehls, N., & Diamond, R. J. (1993). Developing a systems approach to caring for persons with borderline personality disorder. *Community Mental Health Journal, 29,* 161–172.

O'Boyle, M., & Self, D. (1990). A comparison of two interviews for DSM–III–R personality disorders. *Psychiatry Research, 32,* 85–92.

Oldham, J. M., Skodol, A. E., Kellman, H. D., Hyler, S. E., Rosnick, L., & Davies, M.

(1992). Diagnosis of DSM–III–R personality disorders by two structured interviews: Patterns of comorbidity. *American Journal of Psychiatry, 149,* 213–220.

Ouimette, P. C., Klein, D. N., Anderson, R., Riso, L. P., & Lizardi, H. (1994). Relationship of sociotropy/autonomy and dependency/self-criticism to *DSM–III–R* personality disorders. *Journal of Abnormal Psychology, 103,* 743–749.

Perry, J. C. (1992). Problems and considerations in the valid assessment of personality disorders. *American Journal of Psychiatry, 149,* 1645–1653.

Perry, J. C., Lavori, P. W., & Hoke, L. (1987). A Markov model for predicting levels of psychiatric service use in borderline and antisocial personality disorders and bipolar type II affective disorder. *Journal of Psychiatric Research, 21,* 215–232.

Pfohl, B., Blum, N., Zimmerman, M., & Stangl, D. (1989). *Structured Interview for DSM–III–R Personality (SIDP-R).* Iowa City: University of Iowa, Department of Psychiatry.

Pilkonis, P. A. (1988). Personality prototypes among depressives: Themes of dependence and autonomy. *Journal of Personality Disorders, 2,* 144–152.

Pilkonis, P. A., Heape, C. L., Proietti, J. M., Clark, S. W., McDavid, J., & Pitts, T. (1995). The reliability and validity of two structured diagnostic interviews for personality disorders. *Archives of General Psychiatry, 52,* 1025–1033.

Pilkonis, P. A., Heape, C. L., Ruddy, J., & Serrao, P. S. (1991). Validity in the diagnosis of personality disorders: The use of the LEAD standard. *Psychological Assessment: Journal of Consulting and Clinical Psychology, 3,* 46–54.

Pilkonis, P. A., Kim, Y., Proietti, J. M., & Barkham, M. (1996). Scales for personality disorders developed from the Inventory of Interpersonal Problems. *Journal of Personality Disorders, 10,* 355–369.

Radke-Yarrow, M., & Zahn-Waxler, C. (1991). Research on children of affectively ill parents: Some considerations for theory and research on normal development. *Development and Psychopathology, 2,* 349–366.

Reich, J., Boerstler, H., Yates, W., & Nduaguba, M. (1989). Utilization of medical resources in persons with DSM–III personality disorders in a community sample. *International Journal of Psychiatry in Medicine, 19,* 1–9.

Rost, K. M., Akins, R. N., Brown, F. W., & Smith, G. R. (1992). The comorbidity of DSM–III–R personality disorders in somatization disorder. *General Hospital Psychiatry, 14,* 322–326.

Schooler, N., Hogarty, G., & Weissman, M. M. (1979). Social Adjustment Scale II (SAS–II). In W. A. Hargreaves, C. C. Attkisson, & J. E. Sorenson (Eds.), *Resource materials for community health program evaluators* (DHEW Publication No.

ADM 79-328). Washington, DC: U.S. Department of Health, Education, and Welfare.

Shea, M. T., Glass, D., Pilkonis, P. A., Watkins, J., & Docherty, J. (1987). Frequency and implications of personality disorders in a sample of depressed outpatients. *Journal of Personality Disorders, 1,* 27–42.

Shedler, J., Mayman, M., & Manis, M. (1993). The *illusion* of mental health. *American Psychologist, 48,* 1117–1131.

Siever, L. J., & Davis, K. L. (1991). A psychobiological perspective on the personality disorders. *American Journal of Psychiatry, 148,* 1647–1658.

Spitzer, R. L., Williams, J. B. W., Gibbon, M., & First, M. B. (1989). *Structured Clinical Interview for DSM–III–R Personality Disorders (SCID–II, 9/1/89 version).* New York: New York State Psychiatric Institute, Biometrics Research Department.

Standage, K., & Ladha, N. (1988). An examination of the reliability of the Personality Disorder Examination and a comparison with other methods of identifying personality disorders in a clinical sample. *Journal of Personality Disorders, 2,* 267–271.

Stangl, D., Pfohl, B., Zimmerman, M., Bowers, W., & Corenthal, C. (1985). A structured interview for the *DSM–III* personality disorders: A preliminary report. *Archives of General Psychiatry, 42,* 591–596.

Strack, S., & Lorr, M. (Eds.). (1994). *Differentiating normal and abnormal personality.* New York: Springer.

Trull, T. J., Widiger, T. A., & Guthrie, P. (1990). Categorical versus dimensional status of borderline personality disorder. *Journal of Abnormal Psychology, 99,* 40–48.

Tyrer, P., & Sievewright, N. (1988). Studies of outcome. In P. Tyrer (Ed.), *Personality disorder: Diagnosis, management and course* (pp. 119–136). London: Wright.

Widiger, T. A., & Trull, T. J. (1992). Personality and psychopathology: An application of the five-factor model. *Journal of Personality, 60,* 363–393.

Zarin, D. A., & Earls, F. (1993). Diagnostic decision making in psychiatry. *American Journal of Psychiatry, 150,* 197–206.

Zimmerman, M. (1994). Diagnosing personality disorders: A review of issues and research methods. *Archives of General Psychiatry, 51,* 225–245.

15

Core Battery Conference: Assessment of Change in Personality Disorders

M. Tracie Shea

It goes without saying that the development of a core battery for use in outcome studies has the potential to improve the cumulative knowledge of the field. The issue of unknown comparability across studies is a nagging one that too often results in a frustrating difficulty in drawing conclusions about treatment effectiveness. There are at least two ways in which lack of knowledge about comparability across studies can be a problem. One is the nature of the sample (i.e., whether respondents in different studies that are focusing on the same problems or pathology are truly similar, at least in terms of the nature and severity of the targeted problems). The value of a core battery in this sense would be as a sort of metric, allowing more confidence in the comparability of the nature and severity of the targeted pathology in different studies.

The second advantage would be to increase comparability across studies in the assessment of the change associated with the treatments under study. How change is assessed naturally is critical to the conclusions of a treatment study, and measures vary considerably in terms of reliability and sensitivity to change. In addition, studies often differ in their definitions of a successful treatment outcome, such as definitions of "remission" or "recovery."

Despite the large amount of attention given in recent years to the diagnosis of personality disorders (PDs), little has been written about measuring change in these disorders. This is relatively uncharted territory and one that is in much need of development. There clearly are numerous issues that must be considered in the development of a core battery in this particular area. In this chapter, I consider some of these, including (a) suggestions for a general approach to developing a core battery; (b) some specific methodological issues related to assessment of change in PDs; and (c) suggestions for measures that might be included in a core battery.

GENERAL APPROACH TO A CORE BATTERY

A central obstacle to establishing a core battery, of course, is obtaining agreement among investigators concerning the best measure or measures to include. A perception by investigators that a proposed measure is less relevant than their own preferred measures naturally results in reluctance to spend the additional time and expense associated with a measure that they otherwise would not be using. In the area of PDs, this difficulty is perhaps intensified by the multiple theoretical conceptualizations and definitions of PDs. Theoretical formulations of PDs relevant to treatment have included psychodynamic approaches (Kernberg, Selzer, Koenigsberg, Carr, & Appelbaum, 1989), cognitive approaches (e.g., Beck & Freeman, 1990), behavioral approaches (e.g., Linehan, 1993), interpersonal approaches (Benjamin, 1993), and biological approaches (Siever & Davis, 1991). Particularly in terms of assessment of change, preferences for a core battery will be likely to differ among investigators with different treatment orientations. Agreement regarding measurement to provide characterization of the sample may seem to be less of a problem because the intent for this purpose is more descriptive, focusing more on "surface" behaviors and less on theoretical explanatory constructs for such behaviors. Even in terms of the characterization of the sample, however, there may be differences in opinions about the optimal measure or measures. For example, the Wisconsin Personality Disorders Inventory (Klein et al., 1993) assesses personality disorders as described in the revised third edition of the *Diag-*

nostic and Statistical Manual of Mental Disorders (*DSM–III–R*), but does so from an interpersonal perspective in an attempt to increase the validity of assessment. An investigator working from a cognitive perspective may have a different viewpoint about increasing validity of assessment even at this more descriptive level. Clearly, inclusion of measures relevant to all theoretical approaches in a "core" battery would not be feasible.

It might be useful to approach the development of a core battery for PDs in two phases (see Figure 1). The first phase would focus on more descriptive measures of both sample characterization and change. Important domains for coverage for such descriptive measures include assessment of functioning (e.g., overall, work, relationships), subjective distress, and the maladaptive patterns of interpersonal traits and behaviors. Of these domains, agreement about assessment of the personality traits and behaviors is likely to be the most difficult. In this regard, it is important to emphasize that the intent of this aspect of a core battery would be to provide a metric to allow comparability across studies rather than assessment

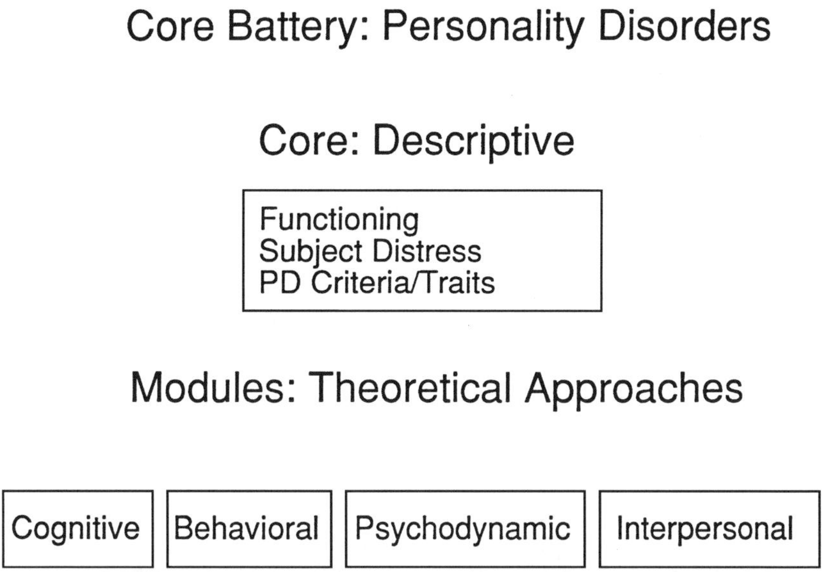

Core Battery: Personality Disorders

Core: Descriptive

> Functioning
> Subject Distress
> PD Criteria/Traits

Modules: Theoretical Approaches

| Cognitive | Behavioral | Psychodynamic | Interpersonal |

Figure 1

A suggested approach to developing a core battery for personality disorders.

of etiological or dynamic mechanisms underlying the surface traits and behaviors. Other measures would be included to best address questions related to mechanisms or targeted areas of change.

The measures recommended from this phase would be the "core" core battery, to be included in all treatment studies. Such measures, although devoid of theoretical assumptions about change, would be aimed at assessing outcome on variables that would be clinically relevant for any treatment approach. The emphasis on objective indexes of functioning also would be relevant to the needs of the managed care environment.

The second phase would focus on developing a consensus on measures to be included in subgroups or "modules" of core batteries associated with each relevant theoretical approach. Groups of investigators associated with each approach could be formed to make such recommendations. The focus of these groups would be assessment of change according to theoretically driven hypotheses about mechanisms or targets of change (e.g., use of defenses or core conflicts for studies of psychodynamic treatments). A goal could be to agree on at least one measure that would be recommended for use in all treatment studies of that theoretical approach. Investigators would also include other measures in their studies to capture aspects of change in which they are more specifically interested. Investigators interested in testing hypotheses about specific mechanisms of change also might include a measure from a module of the core battery associated with another treatment approach (e.g., psychodynamic vs. cognitive change).

Use of such an approach (i.e., core measures recommended for use in all studies, together with modules of recommended measures by theoretical approach) should allow reasonable comparability across studies while maintaining a battery of reasonable length.

METHODOLOGICAL ISSUES: ASSESSMENT OF CHANGE IN PDs

Two primary questions of treatment studies are whether change has occurred and, if it has, whether it is maintained. Typically, these questions are addressed by comparing the assessments at intake and termination of treatment and at some point after treatment (i.e., at follow-up). Because PDs are conceptualized as long-standing, enduring patterns of traits and behaviors, change must be measured in terms of such long-standing traits and behaviors. Thus, it is important that the initial pretreatment assessment be a valid measure of the patient's typical and long-term functioning. It is likely that, for the majority of patients with PDs, treatment will be sought when they are in crisis or experiencing increased levels of depression, anxiety, or general distress. Their current (pretreatment) level of functioning and symptomatic distress thus may not reflect their typical, more characteristic level. Not only symptoms, but also the maladaptive behavioral patterns, are likely to be intensified. Most diagnostic assessment measures of PDs require that the criteria be present for a minimal period of time (e.g., 5 years), to be rated as positive. Thus, a PD diagnosis in theory is based on longer term functioning. It remains possible, however, that if currently depressed or anxious, individuals' reports of their long-term functioning may be negatively distorted. This concern has been frequently cited, particularly with regard to the influence of depression on self-reports of personality (e.g., Hirschfeld et al., 1983). The possibility of distortion is particularly relevant to the PD criteria that overlap with Axis I disorders such as depression (e.g., low self-esteem, interpersonal sensitivity, anger, irritability). Positive change on such criteria after treatment could, then, be reflective of a decrease in depression or general distress and return to one's typical level of functioning rather than of a change in the PD.

Even if the PD criteria and diagnoses obtained at pretreatment are accurate reflections of long-term functioning, it is not clear that the posttreatment assessment of the criteria, and thus the assessment of change, would be valid. This is because the initial diagnosis covers a time span (e.g., 5 years) that is likely to be much longer than the course of treatment. Assessment of the presence of the criteria at posttreatment thus will be constricted, and it is possible that "improvement" may be due to the effects of differential sampling of behavior rather than to the treatment (Endicott & Shea, 1990). This is particularly true for those criteria that, although diagnostically important, are likely to be less frequently manifested (e.g., suicide gestures or attempts, devastated when relationships end, etc.).

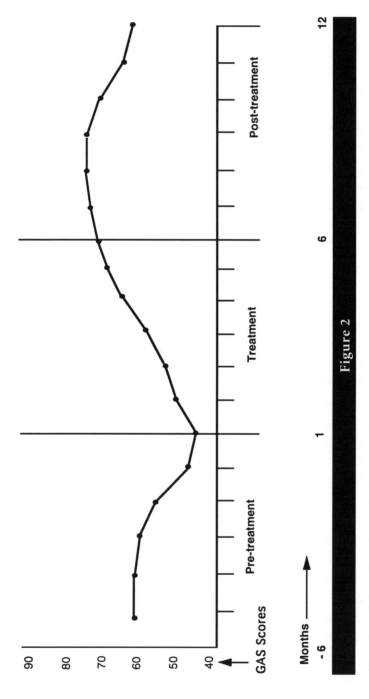

Figure 2

Illustration of a hypothetical example of change in functioning using a longitudinal approach to assessment.

Such complications argue for longitudinal assessment of the maladaptive behaviors and traits associated with the PDs under study and of the level of functioning, both at baseline and after the treatment intervention. At baseline, such assessment might include retrospective monthly ratings of global functioning over the past year or ratings of best and worst level of functioning over the past year or a longer period of time. Frequency and severity of the targeted behaviors and traits also could be assessed for the preceding year (vs. simply ascertaining the presence of the diagnosis). Although retrospective and thus subject to the limits of retrospective assessment, this approach should come closer to establishing the typical level of functioning, or true baseline for assessing change.

Similarly, outcome assessment should be longitudinal, covering a longer period of time than simply the past week or month. Pre- and posttreatment measures should cover similar intervals of time to avoid the "behavior sampling" bias.

Figure 2 shows a hypothetical example of change using the longitudinal approach. Monthly ratings on the Global Assessment Scale (GAS) are illustrated for three time intervals: (a) 6 months before treatment, (b) a 6-month treatment interval, and (c) 6 months after treatment. The comparison of interest would be functioning during the 6-month pretreatment interval versus the 6-month posttreatment interval rather than just status at intake and posttreatment. (Six months is illustrated for convenience, although a longer time period before and after treatment might be used). Again, because the objective of treatments of PDs is to effect changes in long-term patterns of maladaptive behavior, assessing change from pre- to posttreatment, as is typically done in studies of anxiety or depression, is likely to be misleading. Some of the change assessed may be associated with temporary stress-related fluctuations in functioning and distress. A longitudinal assessment should be more sensitive to meaningful changes.

POSSIBLE MEASURES FOR A CORE BATTERY

As noted, recommendations for measures of outcome that would be relevant for any treatment approach might be considered separately from recommendations for theoretically driven measures of the outcome of interest to specific treatment approaches. Here, I consider only the former. Measures relevant to three aspects of such change are considered: functioning, subjective distress, and the specific behaviors and traits associated with PDs.

Measures of Functioning

Two well-established and commonly used measures of functioning include the GAS (or the similar Global Assessment of Functioning Scale; Endicott, Spitzer, Fleiss, & Cohen, 1976) and the Social Adjustment Scale (Weissman & Paykel, 1974). The GAS assesses overall symptoms and impairment. The Social Adjustment Scale (including the self-report and the interview versions) covers five major areas of functioning: work (employed, housewife, student), social and leisure activities, relationships with extended family, marital (partner) role, and parental role.

Measures of Subjective Distress

Subjective distress is important to assess given that it is one of the criteria involved in the diagnosis of PDs; it is also an important aspect of outcome. Adhering to the *DSM* definition of PD would imply assessment of distress associated with the traits and behaviors that constitute PD. How to define such distress, however, is unclear, and determining its source would not be an easy task. Two aspects of subjective distress might be targeted. Measures of symptomatic distress, such as the Brief Symptom Inventory, may be relevant as an index of subjective distress. A broader perspective on subjective distress might be captured by measures of quality of life or satisfaction.

PD Behaviors and Traits

Assessment of PDs (for sample characterization as well as for change) is made more difficult by the lack of clarity in the conceptualization of these disorders, as defined by Axis II. Despite the value of Axis II in drawing attention to the PDs, the current diagnostic scheme is limited by the categorical nature of the system, the extensive overlap among diagnoses, the heterogeneity within disorders, and the lack of clarity concerning the constructs covered by the PDs (Livesley, 1995; Shea, 1992, 1995). Many would agree that these disorders should be considered "prototypes" rather than as real disorders (i.e., in the sense of "disease" or "syndromes"). A dimensional approach to assessment of these disorders has frequently been proposed. Some have proposed a dimensional (continuous) assessment of each of the Axis II disorders, using degree to which the criteria are present or actual number of criteria present, as the continuous measure. A more complex proposal is to assess dimensions that underlie and cross-cut all of the PDs, although there is no consensus regarding which of the many dimensional systems is to be preferred (Widiger & Sanderson, 1995).

In terms of sample characterization, measures assessing the Axis II disorders do have the advantage of adhering more closely to the current diagnostic nomenclature. Measures that adhere to the current diagnostic nomenclature, however, would not provide much insight into the nature of change. Measures derived from theoretical models, as discussed earlier, will provide a fuller and richer picture. Even on a descriptive level, however, assessment of dimensions that underlie the PDs would provide a fuller and more clinically relevant picture of change than assessments of change in diagnostic status or number of criteria. Livesley, Jackson, and Schroeder (1989) have attempted to delineate such dimensions through a series of factor analyses, using self-report scales that they developed to assess each of the traits associated with PDs. Using an oblique rotation, they identified 15 components accounting for 75.1% of the total variance: affective reactivity, rejection, social apprehensiveness, compulsive behaviors, stimulus seeking, insecure attachment, diffidence, intimacy problems, interpersonal disesteem, narcissism, conduct problems, restricted expression, identity disturbance, and obsessionality. Some of these components describe aspects of more than one PD; for example, restricted expression is relevant to schizoid, schizotypal, paranoid, and obsessive–compulsive PDs. Also, the components tend to be more specific than the *DSM* PDs, many of which would require combinations of components for a full description. Antisocial personality disorder, for example, would include conduct problems plus interpersonal disesteem (Livesley et al., 1989).

Through a somewhat different process, Clark (1993) also identified 15 dimensions believed to underlie the PDs. The 15 cross-cutting dimensions are assessed by scales included in the Schedule for Nonadaptive and Adaptive Personality (SNAP). The scales, which have been shown to be internally consistent and relatively independent of each other, include impulsivity, propriety, workaholism, manipulativeness, mistrust/cynicism, schizotypal thought, aggression, suicide potential, detachment, exhibitionism, entitlement, and dependency (Clark, 1993). An advantage of the SNAP is the inclusion of scales that assess the Axis II disorders as well as the cross-cutting dimensions.

Use of such dimensions in assessments of change in PDs would have the advantage of examining change in a more targeted fashion while remaining descriptive. It would be possible to examine change on behaviors and traits that are targeted by the treatment approach under investigation versus those that are not targeted and not expected to change. However, these measures would need to be modified to cover the relevant time intervals. The construction of each of the two self-report measures noted was based on solid psychometric procedures, and both would be good candidates for a core battery (although shorter versions might be necessary).

SUMMARY AND CONCLUSIONS

Development of a core battery to assess change in PDs would make an important contribution to the field and is also, I believe, feasible. The approach I have taken here is to suggest phases of development, starting with more descriptive and concrete, but also clinically relevant, aspects of change that should be of interest for any treatment approach. Recommendations for theoretically relevant measures could follow, based on in-depth consideration by investigators associated with each relevant theoretical approach (e.g., psychodynamic, interpersonal, cognitive, behavioral, biological). I have suggested that among possible descriptive measures of change, a focus solely on change in PD criteria and diagnoses would be limited and that assessment of functioning, subjective distress, and the trait dimensions underlying the PDs would be more informative. I also have emphasized the importance of a longitudinal perspective for assessment of change in PDs. Some specific measures of functioning, and of PD traits using a dimensional approach, have been considered.

There are several important issues that I have not addressed, among these the validity of the self-reported personality descriptions of patients with PDs; the desirability of including alternative sources and types of data in PD assessment; and reliability and general validity of PD assessments. The issues of perspective and sources of data are important directions for future work. I do not believe there are currently enough data to warrant recommendation of such measures in a core battery; hopefully, future work will be informative in this regard. As a general strategy, it would make sense to update a core battery periodically to incorporate advances in assessment.

With regard to reliability, establishment of adequate reliability among raters within a given research project or research group is, of course, a minimum requirement. What is usually unknown, however, is the extent to which raters in different research groups would agree. If interview measures are recommended as part of a core battery, another suggestion is to develop a series of "calibration" tapes, including "expert" ratings. Different research groups could use such tapes to calibrate their own ratings with a standard. Although not as ideal as test–retest reliability, such a mechanism would improve cross-site agreement and enhance the benefits of a core battery (i.e., comparability across studies).

REFERENCES

Beck, A. T., & Freeman, A. a. A. (1990). *Cognitive therapy of personality disorders.* New York: Guilford Press.

Benjamin, L. S. (1993). *Interpersonal diagnosis and treatment of personality disorders.* New York: Guilford Press.

Clark, L. A. (1993). *Manual for the Schedule for Nonadaptive and Adaptive Personality (SNAP).* Minneapolis: University of Minnesota Press.

Endicott, J., & Shea, M. T. (1990). Measurement of change in personality disorders. *Psychopharmacology Bulletin, 25,* 572–577.

Endicott, J., Spitzer, R. L., Fleiss, J. L., & Cohen, J. (1976). The Global Assessment Scale: A procedure for measuring overall severity of psychiatric disturbance. *Archives of General Psychiatry, 33,* 766–771.

Hirschfeld, R. M. A., Klerman, G. L., Clayton, P. J., Keller, M. B., McDonald-Scott, P., & Larkin, B. H. (1983). Assessing personality: Effects of depressive state on trait measurement. *American Journal of Psychiatry, 140,* 695–699.

Kernberg, O. F., Selzer, M., Koenigsberg, H., Carr, A., & Appelbaum, A. (1989). *Psychodynamic psychotherapy and borderline patients.* New York: Basic Books.

Klein, M. H., Benjamin, L. S., Rosenfeld, R., Treece, C., Husted, J., & Greist, J. (1993). The Wisconsin Personality Disorders Inventory: Development, reliability, and validity. *Journal of Personality Disorders, 7,* 285–303.

Linehan, M. M. (1993). *Cognitive-behavioral treatment of borderline personality disorder.* New York: Guilford Press.

Livesley, W. J. (Ed.) (1995). *The DSM-IV personality disorders.* New York: Guilford Press.

Livesley, W. J., Jackson, D. N., & Schroeder, M. L. (1989). A study of the factorial structure of personality pathology. *Journal of Personality Disorders, 3,* 292–306.

Shea, M. T. (1992). Some characteristics of the Axis II criteria sets and their implications for assessment of personality disorders. *Journal of Personality Disorders, 6,* 377–381.

Shea, M. T. (1995). Interrelationships among categories of personality disorder. In W. J. Livesley (Ed.), *The DSM-IV personality disorders* (pp. 397–406). New York: Guilford Press.

Siever, L. J., & Davis, K. L. (1991). A psychobiological perspective on personality disorders. *American Journal of Psychiatry, 148,* 1647–1658.

Weissman, M. M., & Paykel, E. S. (1974). *The depressed woman: A study of social relationships.* Chicago: University of Chicago Press.

Widiger, T. A., & Sanderson, C. J. (1995). Toward a dimensional model of personality disorders. In W. J. Livesley (Ed.), *The DSM-IV personality disorders* (pp. 423–458). New York: Guilford Press.

16

Assessing Personality Disorders

Mardi J. Horowitz, Constance Milbrath,
and Charles H. Stinson

People with personality disorders (PDs) are hard to assess. Many of the existing scales are time-consuming, based on self-report, and not yet well enough aligned to quantitative evidence of clinical validity. We see two possible tactics. One tactic is to assume the menu-based criteria from the third and fourth editions of the *Diagnostic and Statistical Manual of Mental Disorders* (*DSM–III* and *DSM–IV*, respectively; American Psychiatric Association, 1980, 1994) and the ninth and tenth editions of the *International Classification of Diseases* for making PD diagnoses are valid and to define self-report and observer-based ratings on the listed symptoms. A second tactic is to struggle with more complex theories, to develop better typologies and individualized approaches, while assuming that the existing official diagnostic criteria are transient compromises in an unsettled field. Both tactics are valuable. We follow the latter tactic and discuss complex approaches in this chapter. We consider four aspects of formulating pretherapy characteristics of patients and consider some self- and observer-based measures for each aspect. We also consider qualitative noncategorical formulations in a section on role relationship model configurations.

We draw attention to a systematic approach that includes problematic phenomena, varied states of mind, systematic beliefs about self and others (person schemas), and habitual defensive control processes. These four are components of a configurational approach to formulation of a patient with a PD (M. J. Horowitz, 1979/1997).

Phenomena description selects salient experiences to explain. For the PDs, this includes many types of aberrant social behaviors. The concept of *varied states of mind* implies that these maladaptive social patterns of an individual are not static. People do not have invariable personality traits; in different states they may even exhibit contradictory and polar-opposite behaviors. In one state the person may be excessively sadistic and in another state self-impairingly masochistic.

Attention to variation (e.g., being excessively submissive in one state and excessively domineering in another state) allows researchers to treat diversity in a person as signal rather than noise. That is why our term *person schemas* implies that an individual may have multiple self-concepts and relationship views as well as associated scripts for interpersonal transactions. The topic of *habitual defensive control processes* implies state-dependent ways of blunting emotion. The goal of defensive controls is to avoid entry into painful emotional states. The states of the individual thus vary in terms of access to knowledge. Some views of personal identity may be used to ward off other self-concepts. For example, in some states, views of self as submissive may be used defensively to avoid the dangers of being too domineering.

ASSESSMENT OF PHENOMENA

Impaired activities and functional incapacities at work, in caretaking, and in intimate relationships are important to assess. Self- and observer reports are ideal. Self-reports are covered in other chapters in this book. One observer-based approach we have found useful is called the Patterns of Individualized Change Scale (Kaltreider, DeWitt, Weiss, & Horowitz, 1981; Weiss, Horowitz, & Wilner, 1984). Data can be displayed in star plots from judgments made by evaluations before and after treatment. Results are illustrated in the book *Personality Styles and Brief Psychotherapy* (M. J. Horowitz, Marmar, Weiss, DeWitt, & Rosenbaum, 1984), and an example from page 106 is shown in Figure 1. Likert scales ranging from 1 to 7 are anchored by prose on each of the symptomatic, self-oriented, and

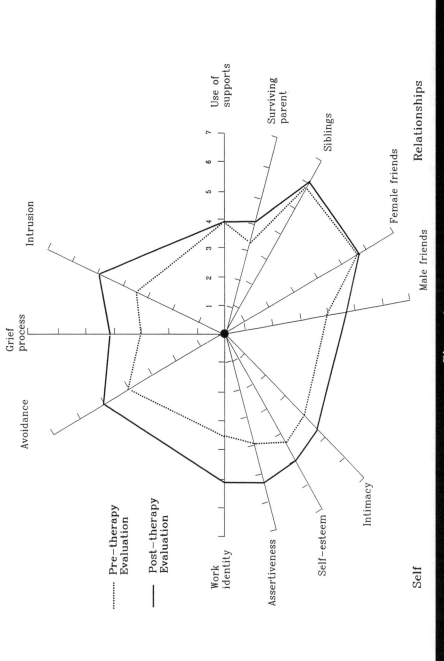

Figure 1

The pattern of change.

Table 1

Positive States of Mind

State	Unable to have it	Trouble having it	Limited in having it	Have it well	Not relevant to me
1. *Focused attention:* Feeling able to work on a task you want or need to do, without many distractions from within yourself.	0	1	2	3	4
2. *Productivity:* Feeling of flow and satisfaction without severe frustrations, perhaps while doing something new to solve problems or to express yourself creatively.	0	1	2	3	4
3. *Responsible caretaking:* Feeling that you are doing what you should do to take care of yourself or someone else in a way that helps meet life's necessities.	0	1	2	3	4
4. *Restful repose:* Feeling relaxed, without distractions or excessive tension, without difficulty in stopping it when you want to.	0	1	2	3	4
5. *Sensuous nonsexual pleasure:* Being able to enjoy bodily senses, enjoyable intellectual activity, doing things you ordinarily like, such as listening to music, enjoying the outdoors, lounging in a hot bath.	0	1	2	3	4
6. *Sensuous sexual pleasure:* Being able to feel erotic and enjoy sexual exchange, as in kissing, caressing, or intercourse.	0	1	2	3	4
7. *Sharing:* Being able to commune with others in an empathic, close way, perhaps with a feeling of joint purposes or values.	0	1	2	3	4

Directions: Circle 0 to 4 for each type of experience according to the *past 7 days:* 0 = unable to have it; 1 = trouble having it; 2 = limited in having it; 3 = have it well; and 4 = not relevant to me.

relationship-oriented scales as reported by Kaltreider, DeWitt, Weiss, and Horowitz (1981) and Kaltreider, DeWitt, Lieberman, and Horowitz (1981).

ASSESSMENT OF STATES OF MIND

By assessing recurrent states of mind before and after a treatment process, one may assess some types of change. We agree that states such as rage, despair, anxiety, and guilt should be assessed. We argue that ratings of impairments of positive states of mind also be considered as important in people with PDs.

We suggest the Positive States of Mind (PSOM) Scale, shown in Table 1. As can be seen, the PSOM Scale measures seven states that may be reduced in individuals with PDs. If impaired ability to have the kind of states shown in Table 1 is present before therapy, and if the ability to experience that state is increased as a consequence of treatment, that change is salient to outcome appraisals.

The PSOM Scale is a validated method for repeated assessment (M. J. Horowitz, Adler, & Kegeles, 1988). The PSOM Scale applies to experiences during the past week. Weekly repeated measures during treatment can be taken. A quantitative single measure of slope (for the trajectory of change during the treatment) can be used in statistical analyses. The pre- and posttherapy values can be compared between treatment groups in clinical trials.

Observer Ratings

We have used observer ratings to rate videotapes for states of mind. We record an interview and then assess the frequency of deflections from well-modulated states. These deflections may be into shimmering, undermodulated, and overmodulated states according to definitions shown in Table 2. Judges were able to reliably score each 30 s of recorded videos for predominant state. We found that shimmering and undermodulated states were useful indexes of the degree of unresolved conflict (M. J. Horowitz, Milbrath, Ewert, & Sonneborn, 1994; M. J. Horowitz, Milbrath, Jordan, et al., 1994; M. J. Horowitz, Stinson, Curtis, et al., 1993).

Individualized state descriptions also can be obtained; an example is shown in Table 3. These could be assessed by observers for intensity and

Table 2

Definitions of States of Mind in Terms of Apparent Control of Emotionality

State of mind	Definition
Undermodulated states	Undermodulated states appear to the observer as if the individual has dysregulation of emotional expression. This leads to appraisals of the individual as impulsive, uncontrolled, or experiencing intrusive concepts and emotions. Sharp increases in the intensity of expressions may suddenly appear as the individual experiences flares, surges, or pangs of emotion. The observer may experience surges of emotion as an empathic response or perhaps feel a wish to intervene in a way that will help the patient regain control.
Well-modulated states	Well-modulated states exemplify a relatively smooth flow of expressions. Affective displays appear genuine and, regardless of intensity, are expressed in a poised manner. The observer may feel subjective interest and empathy, with a sense of being connected to the individual and the material presented. The observer appraises the individual as being engaged in an organized process of communication without major discords between verbal and nonverbal modes of expression.
Overmodulated states	Overmodulated states are characterized by excessive control of expressive behavior. The individual seems stiff, enclosed, masked, or walled off. To the observer, the individual's emotional displays—if present—may seem feigned or false. The observer appraises the individual as being distant from genuine communication. Therefore, the observer may feel disconnected from the individual, even bored or inattentive.
Shimmering states	During shimmering states, the observer notes the individual shifting rapidly between undercontrolled emotions and overcontrolled emotion. The observer may recognize discordant signs of expression in verbal and nonverbal modes. The clashing signals may occur simultaneously or within a brief period of time.

Table 3

States of Mind of Mr. A. (Following the Format for Step 2 of Configurational Analysis)

State of mind	Description
Undermodulated	
Panic	Severely distraught, anxious at losing bodily control, intense fear, goes "yellow and rigid."
Pressured	Agony, lack of confidence ("in over my head"), hearing a whining self-voice in his mental auditory imagery, insecure, anxiously uncertain, obsessive doubting on self-evaluations in this state. He calls this "going crazy," but it has no psychotic features.
Distraught	Mixed emotions of hard-to-distinguish swift pangs of shame, rage, and fear.
Quick temper	Flaring up of anger that is expressed too readily or intensely to others.
Well-modulated	
Expansive excitement	Mobilized enjoyment, expansive
Earnest activity	Very sincere, face and voice intent, coherent, intelligent feelings, creative, productive.
Overmodulated	
Uninterested	Mask of social communication while "leaking" his lack of interest in the social situation.
As-if lighthearted	Collegial to boyish chitchat, engagingly communicated with animation but feels inwardly disengaged.

NOTE: From *Person Schemas and Maladaptive Interpersonal Patterns* (p. 109), by M. J. Horowitz, 1991, Chicago: University of Chicago Press. Copyright 1991 by University of Chicago Press. Adapted with permission.

frequency before and after therapy. In addition, new states might index change. Improvement can be assessed in terms of a reduction in frequency of dreaded and maladaptive states, as well as in movement of expression of a problematic affect such as anger from an undercontrolled rage state to a more well-modulated, irritated state.

PERSON SCHEMAS

A person is "personality disordered" because of his or her vulnerability to enter states in which he or she irrationally uses certain views of self and other. One advantage of defining idiographic states in evaluations of patients is that one can begin to define self- and other-views for each state. These beliefs may be characteristic of the state.

A variety of measures to tap beliefs or transactional patterns by self-report (the Inventory of Interpersonal Problems, Schedule for Nonadaptive and Adaptive Personality, Temperament and Character Inventory, Millon Multiaxial Inventory, and INTREX) are discussed in other chapters in this book, as are analogous observer ratings such as the Structural Analysis of Social Behavior (SASB) and the fixed categories of the Core Conflictual Relationship Theme (CCRT). Here, we discuss some other measures and their potential. The first is a quick but usefully repeatable self-report measure of self-regard.

Self-Report: The Self Regard Questionnaire

The Self Regard Questionnaire (see Exhibit 1) takes 1 min per respondent to administer, and it assesses one's current (the past week) sense of coherence. We have found this measure, taken 6 months after loss, to be associated with a difference between normal and pathological grief reaction assessed at 14 months; the measure had test–retest reliability and good internal consistency (M. J. Horowitz, Sonneborn, Sugahara, & Maercker, 1996).

Quantitative Observer Report: Organizational Level of Self- and Other-Schematization

We have used an observer measure of developmental level that yields scores ranging from normal to neurotic, to narcissistic, to psychotic loss of identity sense. This scale is presented in Table 4 (M. J. Horowitz, 1992).

Exhibit 1

The Self Regard Questionnaire (SRQ)

Instructions: Please circle one number for each question below indicating your average over the past 7 days, including today

Sense of my facial appearance

1	2	3	4	5	6	7	8	9	10

Least healthy I can really look

Most healthy I can really look

Sense of fatigue

1	2	3	4	5	6	7	8	9	10

Most tired I can really feel

Least tired I can really feel

Sense of healthy body

1	2	3	4	5	6	7	8	9	10

Least healthy my body can feel

Most healthy my body can feel

Sense of healthy mind

1	2	3	4	5	6	7	8	9	10

Least healthy my mind can feel

Most healthy my mind can feel

Sense of my identity as a whole person

1	2	3	4	5	6	7	8	9	10

Least clear sense of myself as a whole person

Most clear sense of myself as a whole person

Table 4

Organizational Level of Self and Other Schematization

Mode	Description
Mode 5 Normal	Such individuals have a well-developed supraordinate self (a schema of several self-schemas) and function from a relatively unitary position of self as agent and having values about long-standing issues. They have conflicts and negative moods and own these as "of the self." Conflicts are between various realistic pros and cons or limitations of real relationships. Conflicts tend to be consciously handled well through the use of well-modulated restraints, renunciations, sublimations, choices, wisdom, humor, or even resignation. The person is able to achieve intersubjectivity or "we-ness" and to empathically know that another is separate with equivalent characteristics to his or her own, also experiencing wishes, fears, emotional reactions, conflicts, memories, and fantasies.
Mode 4 Neurotic	Such individuals have self-schemas of a realistic nature. Yet, in some situations, these individuals experience contradictory aims of self as agent of action and self as critic that are not resolved in a reasonable time by rational choices. For example, they may see themselves continually as both intending to express some aim in behavior and opposing such expression on moral grounds, with indecisive repetitive rumination on the theme or repetitive doing and undoing actions. Enduring, unresolved enactments of conflicts about sexuality, love, attention, responsibility, and power indicate this mode.

Mode 3 Narcissistically vulnerable	These individuals are often able to maintain a cohesive and relatively realistic self-schema, but there are states of exception; in these situations, they are vulnerable to a sense of self-impoverishment, to a loss of a sense of self-cohesion, to grandiosity, or to externalization and internalization of characteristics of self and other at an unrealistic level. For example, a person with enduring grandiose delusions confined to a sphere of creativity or sexuality might be assigned this mode, as would a person who consistently disowned personal aggressive behavior, although it was flagrantly obvious to others. Some others are viewed irrationally as if extensions of self (self objects).
Mode 2 Borderline	These individuals are not able to stabilize self-cohesion that includes positive and negative self-schemas in a supraordinate schema of schemas. Rather, they have various self-schemas that are each only part of the actual self and various schemas of others that include only part of the actual behavior of others. Composites that are all good may be dissociated from composites that are all bad.
Mode 1 Fragmented	These individuals have a self and other differentiation that is only partial and transitory. At times they display or experience a significant level of confusion of self with other, or they regard self and other as merged or interchangeable. Parts of the bodily self may be disowned or dissociated.

NOTE: Modes derived and revised from Gedo and Goldberg (1973) and M. J. Horowitz (1979/1987). Midpoint scores such as 3.5 may be used.

411

We used this as a dispositional variable. It produced disposition, by process, by outcome associations in brief dynamic therapy for stress response syndromes (M. J. Horowitz et al., 1984). In long-term therapy, it could be used as a change measure to gauge improved integration.

Qualitative Observer Report: Role Relationship Model Configurations

We can go beyond self- and observer ratings to inference of particular dilemmas and dysfunctional beliefs about self and other using person schematic theories and methods. Various ways for formulating habitual but irrational views about self and others are detailed in the edited book *Person Schemas and Maladaptive Interpersonal Patterns* (M. J. Horowitz, 1991). These techniques condense salient information from narratives obtained in evaluation therapy sessions. Change can be assessed as before–after, early–late therapy differences in degree or irrationality, or internal, unintegrated contradictions.

Various methods, such as SASB codings (Hartley, 1991), the CCRT (Crits-Christoph & Luborsky, 1990; Luborsky & Crits-Christoph, 1990), and the Role Relationship Models Configuration (RRMC; M. J. Horowitz, Eels, Singer, & Salovey, 1995) were used to find repetitive and maladaptive views. The SASB can code aberrant social acts at a small unit of analysis. These SASB codes can fit into a somewhat larger measure, the CCRT. The RRMC contains these, and it is conceptually a more complex and larger unit of analysis (see chap. 13 of *Person Schemas* for a particular case example using each method). The RRMC adds a format for multiple self-concepts, multiple intentions, and multiple other-role possibilities, and it can put these multiplicities into motivational and defensive layers. It can usefully qualify personal dilemmas of how wish is linked to fear and can show characterological compromise formations when inhibitions of social possibilities are used as a way out of irrational beliefs in wish–fear linkages.

The RRMC is a systematic approach for recording inferred conflicts. The theme for an RRMC may be a specific person, a particular event, or alternative self-schemas (e.g., as strong or weak). An RRMC shows motivation and emotion. It contains role relationship models (RRMs) that are strongly desired and strongly feared (called *dreaded*). Desired RRMs may be associatively linked to dreaded RRMs. The wish–fear dilemma that results may be avoided by compromise RRMs. RRMs that serve as compromises avoid the threat of a belief that acting on an intention will inevitably lead into dreaded consequences. Defensive compromises are called either *quasi-adaptive* or *problematic* in an RRMC depending on whether they are relatively adaptive (nonsymptomatic) or maladaptive (symptomatic). Even the quasi-adaptive compromise may be a personality problem because it inhibits optimum development.

An illustration of one RRM is shown in Figure 2. The format for putting several RRMs into a configuration (RRMC) is shown in Figure 3. The instructions for how to form RRMs and RRMCs follow. For some patients, a three-person rather than two-person format may be preferable.

The desired RRM at the lower right quadrant of the RRMC contains wishes for good relationships and relief from distress (e.g., loneliness, despair, terror). The dreaded RRM at the lower left quadrant of the RRMC contains the worst fears of the theme. This does not mean that the dreaded RRM contains only unwanted elements. Wishes may occur early in the script schema of an RRM and fears later. It is the RRM as a whole, and as a whole in association with the other RRMs of the RRMC, that leads it to be placed in the dreaded position.

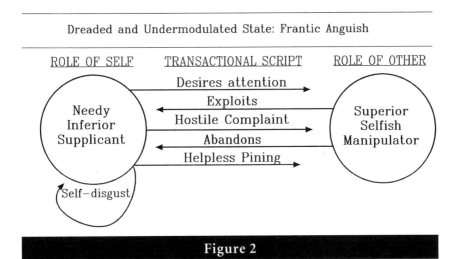

Dreaded and Undermodulated State: Frantic Anguish

ROLE OF SELF   TRANSACTIONAL SCRIPT   ROLE OF OTHER

Needy Inferior Supplicant

Desires attention
Exploits
Hostile Complaint
Abandons
Helpless Pining

Superior Selfish Manipulator

Self–disgust

Figure 2

A role relationship model.

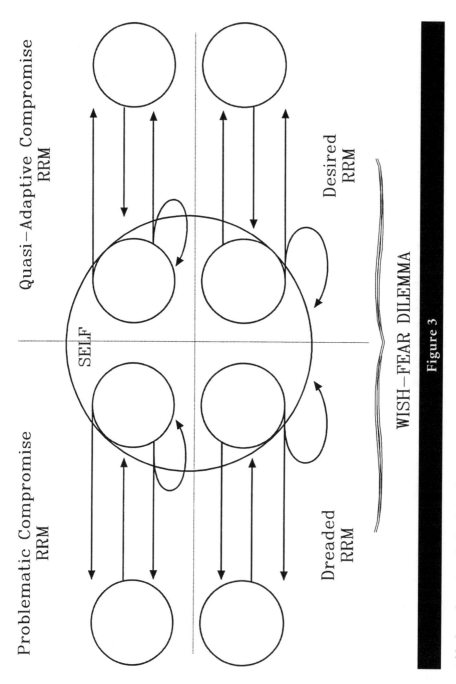

Quasi–Adaptive Compromise RRM

Problematic Compromise RRM

SELF

Desired RRM

Dreaded RRM

WISH–FEAR DILEMMA

Figure 3

A blank configuration of role relationship models (RRMs).

The quasi-adaptive compromise RRM in an RRMC is attempted by the person in association with the wishes and fears in the desired and dreaded RRMs. For example, a wish to rid oneself of the other might be the first action depicted in both the dreaded and desired RRMs. The desired RRM might be a schema for achieving that goal without guilt. The dreaded RRM might be that riddance equaled destruction of the other, leading to shame, guilt, remorse, or punishment. Any idea about riddance of the other might be too dangerous to contemplate because it could evoke a dreaded state organized by the beliefs of the dreaded RRM. A compromise might be to organize thought and action according to an RRM of staying with but remaining insulated from the other and to stifle desires. Change might be assessed as a revision of states and beliefs organized by dysfunctional and irrational RRMs.

As mentioned, the problematic compromise RRM also is a compromise with the conflict between wishes and fears in the desired and dreaded RRMs. It may occur when the more adaptive compromise RRM cannot be maintained. The problematic compromise RRM is better than the most dreaded consequences of acting on a theme, but it still evokes some problems such as anxious tension. Often, these are related to presenting symptoms. For example, staying with a person whom one wants to be rid of may lead to anxious tension or arguments, and the hostility "in the air" may be seen as problematic, but not as bad as the guilt depicted in a script schema for destructive elimination of the other in a dreaded RRMC.

RRMCs can be formed on the basis of few interviews. Studies of reliability using two different designs have been satisfactory (Eells, Horowitz, et al., 1995; M. J. Horowitz & Eells, 1993). In the first study, judges reliably rated ($r = .6$) the goodness of fit of four sets of psychotherapy onset videotapes to four different RRMCs. Judges matched the RRMCs to the correct respondents significantly more than to the incorrect respondents. In the second study, two independent teams, one at the University of California, San Francisco (UCSF), and one at Yale University, took five transcripts of discourse from the first five psychotherapy sessions of each of 2 respondents and followed two different systematic RRMC derivation procedures. The teams produced six to eight RRMCs for each case, one for each of the significant self–other relationships repeatedly described in the transcripts

(Horowitz et al., 1995). Raters then reliably agreed in rating contrasts and agreements between the RRMs and the RRMCs from the teams from Yale University and the UCSF (intraclass correlations of .89 for RRMs and .79 for RRMCs, respectively; Eells, Horowitz, et al., 1995).

The RRMC method is a qualitative formulation that therapists may use in treatment. It fits into a system called *configurational analysis* (M. J. Horowitz, 1997). One can assess a treatment process by seeing whether the focus selected by the therapist matches the contradictions, discrepancies, or conflicts contained within the RRMCs of the patient. One can also contrast a therapy that uses RRMCs as a case formulation method shared with the patient with one that does not add this ingredient. The RRMCs also could be used to assess change before and after treatment. Judges could assess, on a Likert scale, the degree of change.

Multidimensional Scaling Approaches

A variety of studies have been conducted to examine the convergent validity between person schemas assessed from discourse and the responses of participants in tasks in which they were asked to list descriptors for significant others and for different selves (e.g., past, future) and then were asked to rate each target object on all descriptors. The results then could be studied using multidimensional scaling. In several instances, the results of the multidimensional scaling have been similar to the RRMCs as formulated by clinicians (Eells, Fridhandler, & Horowitz, 1995; Hart, Stinson, Field, Ewert, & Horowitz, 1995; Merluzzi, 1991; Tunis, Fridhandler, & Horowitz, 1990). We make this point because this approach, in either of two forms—the Self and Object Matrix Approach (Hart et al., 1995) or the perspace approach (Kihlstrom & Cunningham, 1991)—gives a set of tasks that can lead to before–after outcome data. For example, the degree of discrepancy between the real and ideal self could be assessed before and after treatment.

There are a variety of other ways to assess views of self and other. Personality researchers increasingly recognize that there is neither a single internal working model of others nor a single model or core belief about the identity of the self (Bartholomew & Horowitz, 1991; Collins & Read, 1994; Markus & Nurius, 1986). We review some of the approaches that approach this complex issue from attachment theory. This domain of adult personality assessment is new and relatively unknown to many psycho-therapy researchers. We discuss it in some detail for this reason. Decisions on what to use from it in assessing person schemas may be premature at this time, but relevant issues are raised that can be resolved in a few years.

Assessing Attachment Status

When Bowlby's (1973) attachment theory was first debated in the Tavis-tock seminars (1959–1963), many clinicians and researchers viewed an individual's attachment style as a trait laid down early in a child's life that remained relatively stable into adulthood. Evidence from studies that re-peatedly assessed attachment disputed this position. For example, when familial circumstances altered the quality of caregiving, children shifted their attachment status (e.g., Egeland & Farber, 1984). Moreover, studies that assessed infants' attachment responses to mothers and fathers indi-cated that attachment patterns could be different with each parent (Bridges, Connell, & Belsky, 1988; Lamb, 1978; Main & Weston, 1981). As a result, attachment began to be viewed as a construct in interaction with cur-rent qualities of a relationship rather than as a stabilized trait (Sroufe & Fleeson, 1988).

Interview-Based Assessments

In the past decade, attachment research has extended its inquiry into peer relationships of young adults (Bartholomew & Horowitz, 1991), romantic relationships (Collins & Read, 1990; Hazan & Shaver, 1987), and marital relationships (Feeney, Noller, & Callan, 1994; Kobak & Hazan, 1991), and a variety of methods to assess adult attachment status have developed. One of the best approaches was developed by Main and Goldwyn (1991). It is based on an extended clinical interview about attachment history. Discrep-ancies and incoherences in the presented representations are used as in-dexes for classification.

Adult Attachment Interview and Scoring

The Adult Attachment Interview (AAI) is a semistructured clinical inter-view that attempts to elicit descriptions both at the level of general seman-tic summaries and at the level of specific episodic memories for individuals' relationships with their parents and with their children. Although content contributes significantly to the assessment, scoring of the interview relies heavily on the coherency and consistency of remembrances and on how well an individual has integrated and can reflect on the remembered experiences. In arriving at a score, 15 scales are scored on a 9-point Likert scale that have detailed anchor descriptions for each of the scale points. Five of the scales pertain to the individual's reported experiences, 9 relate to the person's state of mind to the presented material, and the final scale obtains a rating of overall coherency.

These lead to the determination of three typologies that correspond to infant categories derived for the Strange Situation (Ainsworth, Blehar, Waters, & Wall, 1978): secure, enmeshed, and detached. In one study (Main, Kaplan, & Cassidy, 1985), the correspondence between classifications of the infant based on the Strange Situation and the mother based on the AAI was strong ($r = .62$, $p < .001$). Secure mothers tended to have securely attached infants, whereas mothers who appeared overinvolved and preoccupied with their attachments had babies who were anxiously attached. Detached mothers who disclaimed their own attachment needs and appeared overly self-reliant had babies who were avoidant in the Strange Situation.

Attachment Q-Sort

Kobak (1989) developed a 100-item Q-set based on Main and Goldwyn's (1991) attachment classification system. The Q-items relate to aspects of information processing, emotion regulation, and working models of self and parents revealed in attachment interviews (Dozier & Kobak, 1992). Using a forced distribution sort based on the AAI, interrater reliabilities of composite (across all items) Q-sort ratings ranged from .60 to .91 across participants and had a mean of .73 (Kobak, Cole, Ferenz-Gillies, Fleming, & Gamble, 1993; secure/anxious and deactivating/hyperactivating).

The Relationship Questionnaire

Bartholomew (1990; Bartholomew & Horowitz, 1991) considered that there may be two types of avoidant individuals: those who are dismissing of the importance of relationships and report no experience of distress and those who report a great deal of distress and discomfort in close relationships. She argued further that if Bowlby's (1973) theory is studied, four typologies rather than three are logically derived. The typologies are based on whether a person has a positive or negative self-image and a positive or negative image of significant others. Three overlap with Main and Goldwyn's (1991) typologies. Secure and preoccupied were defined by Main and Goldwyn as autonomous and enmeshed. A third, dismissing, includes the overly self-reliant individuals who are dismissing of their need for close relationships. These types were captured by Main and Goldwyn's detached category. Bartholomew added a fourth type, fearful, to describe individuals who avoid close relationships because they are afraid of intimacy.

The measure consists of four short paragraphs describing the four attachment prototypes. These were empirically verified in several studies (see Griffin & Bartholomew, 1994). After reading or listening (or both) to an attachment interview, a respondent receives a rating of 1–7 based on his or her similarity to each of the four prototypes: secure, dismissing, preoccupied, and fearful. Raters also make a number of specific Likert judgments on six 9-point Likert scales that overlap with Main and Goldwyn's (1991) scales. These include the following: (a) parental acceptance remembered by the respondent; (b) parental rejection remembered by the respondent; (c) the degree of role reversal in the relationship with the parent; (d) parental idealization reported by the respondent; (e) the degree of parental involvement reported by the respondent; and (f) report of use of parent as a secure base when upset as a child.

The interview used by Bartholomew (1990; Bartholomew & Horowitz, 1991), although based on the AAI, was modified to gather information about current friendships, romantic relationships, feelings about close relationships, and perspectives about how others evaluate the self. Although an extensive discussion of the merits of this measure is not possible here, data presented by Griffin and Bartholomew (1994) and Bartholomew and Shaver (1995) suggest both convergent (comparisons with interviewed based measures including the AAI) and discriminant (comparisons with other personality measures) validity.

Pilkonis (1988) described five personality prototypes based on the quality of attachments. The prototypes were developed by extracting from the literature two lists of features associated with either socially dependent or autonomous depressives that were then grouped according to their association by 20 clinical experts. A subsequent cluster analysis of the groupings produced five clusters. Three appeared under the higher order cluster of autonomy as obsessive–compulsive features, defensive separation, and lack of interpersonal sensitivity, and two appeared under the higher order cluster of dependency as excessive dependency and borderline features. This intracluster similarity indexes between items in a cluster ranged from .47 for lack of interpersonal sensitivity to .56 for defensive separation. In subsequent research, Pilkonis, Heape, and Proietti (1992) related these prototypes to *DSM* Axis II diagnosis in a group of patients suffering from major depression. Examining the prevalence of PDs in relation to attachment, they found the greatest characterological impairment in the most purely dependent patients and the least in the most purely autonomous patients. Patients with mixed attachment classifications fell in the middle on diagnosis.

Pilkonis (Pilkonis, Heape, & Proietti, 1992) developed a semistructured interview called the Interpersonal Relations Assessment on which prototype judgments can be based. This interview is similar in many respects to the AAI, but it does not elicit specific examples of summary evaluations of relationships. Each prototype is rated for a person on a 6-point scale ranging from *not at all* to *an extreme degree*. The categories also are ranked for a person. If a person does not receive at least a 4 (characteristic) on one of the scales, he or she is not assigned a category. If at least one rating of 4 is obtained, the ranks are examined. The first two ranks determine the classification. If both are in the autonomous cluster, the person is classed as such; if in the dependent cluster, the person is classed as dependent; and if mixed between the two, the person receives a mixed classification. Although Pilkonis et al. found these useful and predictive for individuals with depression, it is unclear how useful these prototypes would be for other types of diagnoses.

Self-Report Assessments

Hazan and Shaver (1987) applied the Ainsworth et al. (1978) taxonomy to romantic love, using first a "love quiz" to prime individuals' love experiences. Respondents were asked to choose one of three alternative self-in-relationship descriptions. The love quiz was a 95-item questionnaire divided into three parts. In Part 1, respondents used a Likert scale to rate 56 items describing their most important relationships. Part 2 contained items related to the attachment history of their most important relationship. Part 3 pertained to mental models and a more general attachment history including the three alternative attachment prototypes. Respondents select the prototype that best describes them. Classification results from their first study paralleled those obtained in mother–infant studies, with 56% of the respondents identifying themselves as secure, 25% as avoidant, and 19% as anxious-ambivalent. More recently, Hazan and Shaver (1990) extended their inquiry into attachment relationships to include its relation to work. They argued that work is functionally equivalent to exploration, a key component in Bowlby's (1973) attachment theory. This era witnessed the development of several self-report measures (e.g., see Collins & Read, 1990; Levy & Davis, 1988).

The Reciprocal Attachment Questionnaire, developed by West and Sheldon-Keller (1994), is a 43-item questionnaire that has separate subscales to assess patterns of attachment described by Bowlby (1973) and criteria characteristics of adult attachment. Four subscales measure attachment patterns, and five subscales measure the characteristics. The four attachment pattern subscales are Angry Withdrawal, Compulsive Care Giving, Compulsive Self-Reliance, and Compulsive Care-Seeking. The five subscales measuring characteristics are Proximity-Seeking, Separation Protest, Feared Loss, Available Responsiveness, and Use of Attachment Figure.

West and Sheldon-Keller (1994) conducted considerable psychometric work on this measure with both nonpatient (n = 136) and patient (n = 110) samples. The internal consistency of the four attachment pattern scales ranged from .70 to .80, and test–retest reliabilities ranged from .54 to .79. The subscales for attachment characteristics had alpha coefficients ranging from .71 to .85 and test–retest reliabilities ranging from .68 to .82. When test–retest reliabilities were disattenuated for measurement error, they ranged from .60 to .97. Discriminant validity of the characteristic subscales was indicated by their ability to correctly classify 80% of a clinical patient population and nonpatient population as well as by other studies (see West & Sheldon-Keller, 1994). Besides having good psychometric properties, this instrument also has the advantage of studies that suggest normative values (West, Sheldon, & Reiffer, 1987; West & Sheldon-Keller, 1992) and that relate it to several personality types as well as to clinical samples (West, Keller, Links, & Patrick, 1993; West & Sheldon, 1988).

Measurement Issues

Studies of concurrent assessments of adult status with respect to past relationship patterns with parents in some cases show relatedness (i.e., Bartholomew & Horowitz, 1991), but in others they do not (see Parker, Barrett, & Hickie, 1992). In a recent meta-analysis by Baldwin and Fehr (1995) of a number of studies, some with multiple samples that used Hazan and Shaver's (1987) self-reported prototyping measure, repeated assessments yielded an instability of about 30%. That is, roughly one third of the respondents changed their self-reported classification on retest. The authors discounted measurement unreliability as a factor because when they compared concurrent self-reported categorical attachment with measures that provided a continuous score on each category, the agreement was 96.5%. When the same measures given at different times were compared, agreement fell to approximately 63%. These authors pointed out that the validity of the attachment construct was not in question because even the crudest measures of the construct produced meaningful discriminations. Instead, Baldwin and Fehr suggested that rather than being a measurement issue, the observed instability resulted from "psychologically meaningful variability," variability that is introduced by the current accessibility of one or another of the multiple relational schemas held by an individual.

Current accessibility may be determined by the state of the person's current relationships, the person's current state of mind, and by the most chronically accessible relational schema. Although the latter factor would bias toward stability, the other two factors could result in instability. The authors concluded that the meaning of these instabilities should be the subject of some future research attention. We propose that researchers should consider a strategy that uses multiple methods and multiple assessments of the construct as a way of defining a person's relationship style (Campbell & Fiske, 1959).

Another related measurement issue is the relative merits of operationalizing attachment as discrete typologies, one of which fits each individual, or as one or more underlying relationship dimensions along which individuals can vary (Feeney et al., 1994; Griffin & Bartholomew, 1994; Sharfe & Bartholomew, 1994). That is, with respect to specific relationships, individuals can vary along a single dimension or multiple underlying dimensions. In their review, Baldwin and Fehr (1995) reported that stability is somewhat better for continuous measures of attachment. Bartholomew and Horowitz (1991) also found a surprising consistency in attachments for parents and peers using a continuous measurement approach. Nevertheless, some researchers find that if the two types of measures are taken at the same time, they show high agreement (e.g., Baldwin & Fehr, 1995).

HABITUAL DEFENSIVE CONTROL PROCESSES

Issues of control and self-regulation about emotional themes constitute another level of assessment useful in the measurement of PDs. A list of classical psychoanalytic ego-defense mechanisms such as those proposed and defined by Vaillant (1992), Perry and Cooper (1989), and Bond et al. (1989) could be used. Unfortunately, lists of defense mechanisms, although found to be reliable in some studies (Perry & Cooper, 1989), are difficult to apply and were not accepted as a potential new axis in the *DSM–IV.* For that reason, a finer grading system of categories of defensive control processes may be more useful (M. J. Horowitz, et al., 1992). Horowitz, Markman, Stinson, Ghannam, and Fridhandler (1990) proposed a set of categories that adhere to the convergent states and person's schemas language of integrating psychodynamics and cognitive–behavioral points of view (L. M. Horowitz, Rosenberg, Baer, Ureño, & Villaseñor, 1988). These are shown in Table 5 (M. J. Horowitz & Stinson, 1995; M. J. Horowitz, Sonneborn, et al., 1996; M. J. Horowitz, Znoj, & Stinson, 1996). Horowitz and Stinson (1995) reported the operational definitions for episodes of consciousness; Horowitz, Znoj, Stinson (1996) reported the operational definitions for communicative manifestations; and M. J. Horowitz, Sonneborn, et al. (1996) presented a simplified format for nonresearch clinicians.

Table 5

Defensive Control Processes

Process	Description
	Content
Shifting attention	Avoids conscious thought, discourse, or action on important unresolved topics by shifting attention to another topic; the shifts may be deliberate (suppression) or may involve less conscious automatic choices (repression, dissociation, disavowal, or denial).
Juggling concepts about a topic	Shifts too often among ideas or emotional valences of ideas, thus preventing a potentially affect-related deepening train of thought; irrelevant details may be amplified. Vital links between ideas and feelings, and between cause and effect, may be obscured.
Sliding meanings and values	Adjusts conceptual weighting by minimizing or exaggerating intentions or emotional salience; the resulting appraisal errors and rationalizations may preserve self-esteem or reduce affect ("sweet lemons" or "sour grapes").
Premature disengaging from topics	Declares important topics or actions "finished" before reaching closure despite awareness of unresolved dilemmas and contradictions, effectively blocking potentially emotional review of important memories or anticipation of likely future events (e.g., interpersonal tensions).
	Form
Blocking apt modes of representation	Ineffectively represents ideas and feelings about a topic, engaging either in verbal intellectualizations or in preoccupying fantasies. Both can lead to failure to engage in effective action planning. Discourse may lack imagery, metaphors, and clarity or else may be excessively metaphoric with poor translation of visual images into clear, concrete, meaningful ideas. Both can reduce reactive emotions.

Shifting time span	Shifts from most pertinent to alternative less relevant temporal contexts (e.g., distant past, recent past, here and now, immediate future, distant future) in a manner that avoids or reduces emotionality (e.g., shifts to past memories apparently to avoid confrontation with current relationship difficulties or future jeopardy).
Using poor ideational linkage strategies	Uses intellectualized analysis of generalities when reflective contemplation or recollection of personalized issues and emotional memories is more appropriate; conversely, may use creatively wide-ranging associations when careful adaptive planning is more appropriate. The results may be isolated from identity and emotional responses.
Engaging inappropriate arousal levels	Shifts to an inappropriate level of arousal specifically when addressing a problematic topic; becomes dull, listless, or sleepy or else becomes too excited to do effective contemplation.

Person schemas

Shifting self–other roles	Abruptly shifts to alternate views of self and other or switches attributes of self and others (projection, role reversal, displacement, compensatory grandiosity, etc.), avoiding dreaded states of fear, shame, rage, and guilt.
Rigidly stabilizing compromise roles	Rigidly assumes compromise roles and views of self and other, apparently avoiding desired ones that may have associations with dreaded ones (e.g., wish–fear dilemmas); consequences include avoiding threatening situations and dysphoric emotion, as well as withdrawal, numbing, excessive self-preoccupations, and lack of satisfaction.
Altering valuation schemas	Shifts to an alternate set of values for appraising self or other with idealizing or devaluating consequences (e.g., unrealistically attributing blame to another, unrealistically criticizing oneself, etc.).

425

We define actual manifestations in observation of recorded discourse. Znoj, Horowitz, Field, Bonanno, and Maercker (1996) have found that observers can achieve reliability for the communicative versions of the specific categories of control processes, and we have already reliably and validly analyzed signs of some of them on raw data from psychotherapy transcripts (M. J. Horowitz, Milbrath, Reidbord, & Stinson, 1993) and from video recordings (M. J. Horowitz et al., 1994; M. J. Horowitz, Stinson, et al., 1993). Znoj, Horowitz, Bonanno, Stinson, and Maercker (1996) showed test–retest reliability of a control process report questionnaire, and judges reliably scored the categories.

Deployments of even habitual defensive control processes are state dependent. That is, in some states of mind, especially undermodulated states, a person may attempt to use more severe distortions and inhibitions or may fail to do so but still give signs of doing so. The individual might exhibit anxious and clinging attachment behavior. In well-modulated states, the individual may use less pathological forms of defensive control and exemplify more secure attachments or more confident independence. Judges will find this hard to assess, and self-reports will be incomplete. Thus, to assess habitual defensive control processes and person schemas, one probably will have to rely on a way of filtering out variations in the "crucible of clinical judgment." This type of research is too frequently demeaned as "too complex," but it may generate the new hypotheses needed to understand clinical issues of personality problems.

The reason we argue that intensive, even single-case, research is so important is that this issue of defensive control processes is a crucial area of distinction between psychodynamic and cognitive–behavioral therapies. Most therapists agree on the importance of enduring irrational beliefs about self and others as a source of maladaptive interpersonal patterns. The idea that there are some self-concepts that are used in defense against other self-concepts, that there are some roles in a relationship that actually are reversals of more feared roles, or that people have a variety of ways of distorting and inhibiting warded-off sets of information is still hotly debated. There is a need for empirical evidence of defensive control processes to produce a general and integrated theory of psychotherapy.

CONCLUSION

There is not yet a great battery for assessing PDs, and a great deal of new theory is under debate. Exciting advances in measurement need to occur before there is agreement on a core battery for general use. In this chapter we have explored some approaches that take a states-of-mind and multiple self-concepts approach, one that includes characterological defensiveness in the conceptualization of how patients with PDs may present themselves.

REFERENCES

Ainsworth, M., Blehar, M., Waters, E., & Wall, S. (1978). *Patterns of attachment: A psychological study of the Strange Situation.* Hillsdale, NJ: Erlbaum.

American Psychiatric Association. (1980). *Diagnostic and statistical manual of mental disorders* (3rd ed.). Washington, DC: Author.

American Psychiatric Association. (1994). *Diagnostic and statistical manual of mental disorders* (4th ed.). Washington, DC: Author.

Baldwin, M., & Fehr, B. (1995). On the instability of attachment style ratings. *Personal Relationships, 2,* 247–261.

Bartholomew, K. (1990). Avoiding of intimacy: An attachment perspective. *Journal of Social and Personal Relationships, 7,* 147–178.

Bartholomew, K., & Horowitz, L. (1991). Attachment styles among young adults: A test of a four-category model. *Journal of Personality and Social Psychology, 61,* 226–244.

Bartholomew, K., & Shaver, P. R. (1995). Methods of assessing adult attachment: Do they converge? In M. J. Horowitz (Ed.), *Person schemas: Self and interpersonal relationships, Part II.* Manuscript submitted for publication.

Bond, M., Perry, C., Gautier, M., Goldenberg, M., Oppenheim, J., & Simond, J. (1989). Validating self-report of defensive styles. *Journal of Personality Disorders, 3,* 101–112.

Bowlby, J. (1973). *Attachment and loss: Separation.* New York: Basic Books.

Bridges, L. J., Connell, J. P., & Belsky, J. (1988). Similarities and differences in infant-mother and infant-father interaction in the Strange Situation: A component process analysis. *Developmental Psychology, 24,* 92–100.

Campbell, D. T., & Fiske, D. W. (1959). Convergent and discriminant validation by the multitrait-multimethod matrix. *Psychological Bulletin, 56,* 81–105.

Collins, N., & Read, S. J. (1990). Adult attachment, working models, and relationship quality in dating couples. *Journal of Personality and Social Psychology, 58,* 644–663.

Collins, N., & Read, S. (1994). Cognitive representations of attachment: The structure and function of working models. In K. Bartholomew & D. Perlman (Eds.), *Attachment processes in adulthood: Vol. 5. Advance in personal relationships* (pp. 53–90). Bristol, PA: Kingsley.

Crits-Christoph, P., & Luborsky, L. (1990). The perspective of patients versus clinicians in the assessment of central relationship themes. In L. Luborsky & P. Crits-Cristoph (Eds.), *Understanding transference: The Core Conflictual Relationship Theme method* (pp. 197–208). New York: Basic Books.

Dozier, M., & Kobak, R. R. (1992). Psychophysiology and attachment interviews: Converging evidence for deactivating strategies. *Child Development, 63,* 1473–1480.

Eells, T., Fridhandler, B., & Horowitz, M. (1995). Self schemas and spousal bereavement: Comparing quantitative and clinical evidence. *Psychotherapy, 32,* 270–282.

Eells, T. D., Horowitz, M. J., Singer, J., Salovey, P., Daigle, D., & Turvey, C. (1995). The role relationship models method: A comparison of independently derived case formulations. *Psychotherapy Research, 5,* 161–175.

Egeland, B., & Farber, E. (1984). Infant-mother attachment: Factors related to its development and change over time. *Child Development, 55,* 753–771.

Feeney, J. A., Noller, P., & Callan, V. J. (1994). Attachment style, communication and satisfaction in the early years of marriage. In K. Bartholomew & D. Perlman (Eds.), *Attachment processes in adulthood: Vol. 5. Advance in personal relationships* (pp. 269–308). Bristol, PA: Kingsley.

Gedo, J., & Goldberg, A. (1973). *Models of the mind.* Chicago: University of Chicago Press.

Griffin, D. W., & Bartholomew, K. (1994). The metaphysics of measurement: The case of adult attachment. In K. Bartholomew & D. Perlman (Eds.), *Attachment processes in adulthood: Vol. 5. Advance in personal relationships* (pp. 17–52). Bristol, PA: Kingsley.

Hart, D., Stinson, C., Field, N., Ewert, M., & Horowitz, M. (1995). A semantic space approach to representations of self and other in pathological grief: A case study. *Psychological Science, 6*(2), 96–100.

Hartley, D. (1991). Assessing interpersonal behavior patterns using Structural Analysis of Social Behavior (SASB). In M. J. Horowitz (Ed.), *Person schemas and mal-*

adaptive interpersonal patterns (pp. 221–260). Chicago: University of Chicago Press.

Hazan, C., & Shaver, P. (1987). Romantic love conceptualized as an attachment process. *Journal of Personality and Social Psychology, 52,* 511–524.

Hazan, C., & Shaver, P. R. (1990). Love and work: An attachment-theoretical perspective. *Journal of Personality and Social Psychology, 59,* 270–280.

Horowitz, L. M., Rosenberg, S. E., Baer, B. A., Ureño, G., & Villaseñor, V. S. (1988). Inventory of Interpersonal Problems: Psychometric properties and clinical implications. *Journal of Consulting and Clinical Psychology, 56,* 885–892.

Horowitz, M. J. (1987). *States of mind.* New York: Plenum. (Original work published 1979).

Horowitz, M. J. (1988). *Introduction to psychodynamics.* New York: Basic Books.

Horowitz, M. J. (Ed.). (1991). *Person schemas and maladaptive interpersonal patterns.* Chicago: University of Chicago Press.

Horowitz, M. J. (1992). Formulation of states of mind in psychotherapy. In N. G. Hamilton (Ed.), *From inner resources: New directions in object relations psychotherapy* (pp. 75–83). Northvale, NJ: Jason Aronson.

Horowitz, M. J. (1994). Configurational analysis and the use of role-relationship models to understand transference. *Psychotherapy Research, 3,* 184–196.

Horowitz, M. J. (1997). *Formulation as a basis for planning psychotherapy.* Washington, DC: American Psychiatric Press.

Horowitz, M. J., Adler, N., & Kegeles, S. (1988). A scale for measuring the occurrence of positive states of mind. *Psychosomatic Medicine, 50,* 477–483.

Horowitz, M. J., Cooper, S., Fridhandler, B., Perry, J. D., Bond, M., & Vaillant, G. E. (1992). Control processes and defense mechanisms. *Journal of Psychotherapy Practice and Research, 1,* 324–336.

Horowitz, M. J., & Eells, T. D. (1993). Case formulations using role-relationship model configurations: A reliability study. *Psychotherapy Research 3,* 57–68.

Horowitz, M. J., Eells, T., Singer, J., & Salovey, P. (1995). Role relationship models for case formulation. *Archives of General Psychiatry, 53,* 627–632.

Horowitz, M. J., Markman, H. J., Stinson, C. H., Ghannam, J. H., & Fridhandler, B. (1990). A classification theory of defense. In J. Singer (Ed.), *Repression and dissociation: Implications for personality theory, psychopathology and health* (pp. 61–84). Chicago: University of Chicago Press.

Horowitz, M. J., Marmar, C., Weiss, D., DeWitt, K., & Rosenbaum, R. (1984). Brief psychotherapy of bereavement reactions: The relationship of process to outcome. *Archives of General Psychiatry, 41,* 438–448.

Horowitz, M. J., Milbrath, C., Ewert, M., & Sonneborn, D. (1994). Cyclical patterns of states of mind in psychotherapy. *American Journal of Psychiatry, 151*(2), 1767–1770.

Horowitz, M. J., Milbrath, C., Jordan, D. S., Stinson, C. H., Ewert, M., Redington, D. J., Fridhandler, B., Reidbord, S. P., & Hartley, D. (1994). Expressive and defensive behavior during discourse on unresolved topics: A single case study. *Journal of Personality, 62,* 527–563.

Horowitz, M. J., Milbrath, C., Reidbord, S., & Stinson, C. H. (1993). Elaboration and dyselaboration: Measures of expression and defense in discourse. *Psychotherapy Research, 3,* 278–293.

Horowitz, M. J., Sonneborn, D., Sugahara, C., & Maercker, A. (1996). Self regard: A new measure. *American Journal of Psychiatry, 153,* 382–385.

Horowitz, M. J., & Stinson, C. H. (1995). Consciousness and processes of control. *Journal of Psychotherapy and Practice and Research, 4,* 123–139.

Horowitz, M. J., Stinson, C., Curtis, D., Ewert, M., Redington, D., Singer, J., Bucci, W., Mergenthaler, E., & Milbrath, C. (1993). Topics and signs: Defensive control of emotional expression. *Journal of Consulting and Clinical Psychology, 61,* 421–430.

Horowitz, M. J., Znoj, H. J., & Stinson, C. H. (1996). Defensive control processes: Use of theory in research, formulation, and therapy of stress response syndromes. In M. Zeidner & N. Endler (Eds.), *Handbook of coping* (pp. 532–553). New York: Wiley.

Kaltreider, N., DeWitt, K., Lieberman, R., & Horowitz, M. J. (1981). Individualized approaches to outcome assessment: A strategy for psychotherapy research. *Journal of Psychiatric Treatment and Evaluation, 3,* 105–111.

Kaltreider, N., DeWitt, K., Weiss, D. S., & Horowitz, M. J. (1981). Patterns of Individual Change Scales. *Archives of General Psychiatry, 38,* 1263–1269.

Kihlstrom, J. F., & Cunningham, R. L. (1991). Mapping interpersonal space. In M. J. Horowitz (Ed.), *Person schemas and maladaptive interpersonal patterns* (pp. 311–336). Chicago: University of Chicago Press.

Kobak, R. R. (1989). *The Attachment Interview Q-Set.* Unpublished manuscript, University of Delaware, Newark.

Kobak, R. R., Cole, H. E., Ferenz-Gillies, R., Fleming, W. S., & Gamble, W. (1993). Attachment and emotion regulation during mother-teen problem solving: A control theory analysis. *Child Development, 64,* 231–245.

Kobak, R. R., & Hazan, C. (1991). Attachment in marriage: Effects of security and accuracy of working models. *Journal of Personality and Social Psychology, 60*, 861–869.

Lamb, M. (1978). Qualitative aspects of mother-infant and father-infant attachments. *Infant Behavior and Development, 1,* 265–275.

Levy, M. B., & Davis, K. E. (1988). Lovestyles and attachment styles compared: Their relations to each other and to various relationship characteristics. *Journal of Social and Personal Relationships, 5,* 439–471.

Luborsky, L., & Crits-Christoph, P. (1990). *Understanding transference: The CCRT method.* New York: Basic Books.

Main, M., & Goldwyn, R. (1991). *Adult attachment rating and classification system.* Unpublished manuscript, University of California, Berkeley.

Main, M., Kaplan, N., & Cassidy, J. (1985). Security in infancy, childhood and adulthood: A move to the level of representation. *Monographs for the Society of Research in Child Development, 50*(1–2), 66–104.

Main, M., & Weston, D. (1981). The quality of the toddler's relationship to mother and father: Related to conflict behavior and the readiness to establish new relationships. *Child Development, 52,* 932–940.

Markus, H., & Nurius, P. (1986). Possible selves. *American Psychologist, 41,* 954–969.

Merluzzi, T. V. (1991). Representation of information about self and other: A multidimensional scaling analysis. In M. J. Horowitz (Ed.), *Person schemas and maladaptive interpersonal patterns* (pp. 155–166). Chicago: University of Chicago Press.

Parker, G. B., Barrett, E. A., & Hickie, I. B. (1992). From nurture to network: Examining links between perceptions of parenting received in childhood and social bonds in adulthood. *American Journal of Psychiatry, 149,* 877–885.

Perry, J. C., & Cooper, S. H. (1989). An empirical study of defense mechanisms: I. Clinical interview and life vignette ratings. *Archives of General Psychiatry, 46,* 444–452.

Pilkonis, P. A. (1988). Personality prototypes among depressives: Themes of dependency and autonomy. *Journal of Personality Disorders, 2,* 144–152.

Pilkonis, A., Heape, C., & Proietti, J. (1992). *Adult attachment styles, personality disorder and treatment outcome in depression.* Unpublished manuscript, University of Pittsburgh.

Sharfe, E., & Bartholomew, K. (1994). Reliability and stability of adult attachment patterns. *Personal Relationships, 1,* 23–43.

Sroufe, A., & Fleeson, J. (1988). The coherence of family relationships. In R. A. Hinde & J. Stevenson-Hinde (Eds.), *Relationships within families: Mutual influences* (pp. 27–47). Oxford, England: Clarendon Press.

Tunis, S. L., Fridhandler, B., & Horowitz, M. J. (1990). Identifying schematized views of self with significant others: Convergence of qualitative and clinical methods. *Journal of Personality and Social Psychology, 59,* 1279–1286.

Vaillant, G. E. (1992). *Ego mechanisms of defense: In clinical practice and in empirical research.* Washington, DC: American Psychiatric Press.

Weiss, D. S., Horowitz, M. J., & Wilner, N. (1984). Stress Response Rating Scale: A clinician's measure. *British Journal of Clinical Psychology, 23,* 202–215.

West, M., Keller, A., Links, P., & Patrick, J. (1993). Borderline disorder and attachment pathology. *Canadian Journal of Psychiatry, 18,* 16–22.

West, M., & Sheldon, A. (1988). Classification of pathological attachment patterns in adults. *Journal of Personality Disorders, 2,* 153–159.

West, M., & Sheldon-Keller, A. (1992). The assessment of dimensions relevant to adult reciprocal attachment. *Canadian Journal of Psychiatry, 37,* 600–606.

West, M., & Sheldon-Keller, A. (1994). *Patterns of relating: An adult attachment perspective.* New York: Guilford Press.

West, M., Sheldon, A., & Reiffer, L. (1987). An approach to the delineation of adult attachment: Scale development and reliability. *Journal of Nervous and Mental Disease, 175,* 738–741.

Znoj, H., Horowitz, M., Bonanno, G., Stinson, C., & Maercker, A. (1996). *Control processes in bereaved subjects: A new measure for coping with severe emotional distress.* Manuscript submitted for publication.

Znoj, H., Horowitz, M., Field, N., Bonanno, G., & Maercker, A. (1996). *Emotional regulation: The Sense of Self-Control Questionnaire.* Manuscript submitted for publication.

17

Outcome Evaluation of Psychosocial Treatment for Personality Disorders: Functions, Obstacles, Goals, and Strategies

Ralph M. Turner and Paul Dudek

P atients with personality disorders (PDs) present with complex symptoms and intricate networks of problems that are among the most difficult and challenging psychosocial dysfunctions that clinicians encounter. This complexity is amplified because these and other PD characteristics are not simply a problem the person is suffering with but are in fact central to the identity of that person. Consequently, a PD is a major mental health problem. Bolstering this view, research indicates that 30–50% of outpatients have a PD (Koenigsberg, Kaplan, Gilmore, & Cooper, 1985) and that 15% of inpatients are hospitalized primarily for problems caused by a PD (Widiger & Weissman, 1991). Other data suggest that almost half of psychiatric inpatients have a comorbid PD that significantly affects their response to treatment (Loranger, 1990). It also has been estimated that PDs are relatively common in the general population, with a prevalence of 10–18% (Reich, 1989; Weissman, 1993; Zimmerman & Coryell, 1989).

The recognition of the severity of PDs as a major mental health problem has led to the development of manualized treatments and clinical outcome studies (Clarkin et al., 1992; Linehan, 1993; Munroe-Blum & Marziali, 1987; Stevenson & Meares, 1992; Turner, 1988, 1989). As this research accelerates, it is reasonable to begin to consider establishing a core outcome battery to systematize and guide future research to avoid the problems that plague the anxiety and depression treatment literature: an assortment of outcome measures that preclude accurate comparisons and interpretations of effectiveness across studies.

FUNCTIONS OF A CORE OUTCOME BATTERY

There are many obstacles to developing a core outcome battery for PD treatment research, to be sure, but by developing at least a minimal outcome model now, future research can be guided and directed to solve the existing problems. A fundamental benefit is that a core outcome battery might systematize psychosocial research on the PDs. Second, the specification of a routine, if limited, set of measures might aid in furthering the understanding the structural organization of personality. If successful, a thoroughgoing and structured core outcome battery might also provide new epidemiological and etiological data on the PDs. This would create complementary synergism between psychosocial treatment research and epidemiological and etiological research. In addition, specification of a comprehensive model of outcome assessment might enable researchers to focus on causal relations between treatment components and types, or degrees, of outcomes.

Consequently, despite the many obstacles described in the next section of this chapter, we believe that it is worthwhile to propose a structure for a core PDs outcome battery and to suggest a minimal set of instruments that should be used in future studies. Our recommendations for a core outcome battery for the PDs are made in the spirit of the original Waskow and Parloff (1975) effort, enlightened by the lessons of the history of that effort.

One of the most important lessons from that endeavor is that a core outcome battery must avoid specifying instruments aimed at measuring causal mechanisms of action. Because theoretical viewpoints differ significantly, investigators will not adhere to a core battery that incorporates theory-specific constructs. For a core battery to be used, the domains of assessment and instruments selected must focus on specific symptom outcomes and impact level, or community functioning, outcomes. In other words, a discrimination needs to be made between measures of the outcomes of treatment and the causal mechanisms of treatment. A second lesson learned from the Waskow and Parloff (1975) effort is that if the core battery is developed for a heterogeneous set of psychiatric problems, it will not be used. The core battery must focus on specific homogeneous groups of problems, or avoid stipulating measures for the problem level of analysis altogether.

The results of our attempt serve only as a first approximation to the problem. Further work will be required. For example, in the future researchers will need to focus on breaking the PDs into meaningful and manageable clusters of shared outcome phenomena so that more specificity can be obtained in defining multiple core outcome batteries. In addition, new instrument development is required to attend to sensitively measuring change in PD status.

OBSTACLES TO THE PDs CORE BATTERY

The feasibility of developing a core outcome battery for the PDs is controversial at best. Despite our enthusiasm for the task, our perspective about the viability of a core outcome battery for the PDs is similar to the conclusions Bergin and Lambert (1978) reached about the utility of a core outcome battery for clinical disorders in general 15 years ago: "A standard assessment does seem desirable though not yet feasible." The PDs, taken globally, present too many problem types and dimensions to yield easily to the core outcome battery concept. There is no specificity of problems when one speaks of the PDs globally. Also, there currently are practical restraints on the feasibility of administering a core outcome battery for the PDs. To adequately address all the relevant outcome phenomena would require an outcome battery that would be too time-consuming and difficult for patients to complete. In other words, the patient burden would be too high.

Questions About the Validity and Utility of the Diagnostic and Statistical Manual Classification System

One of the most significant issues centers on the validity of the fourth edition of the *Diagnostic and Statistical Manual of Mental Disorders DSM–*

IV; American Psychiatric Association, 1994) diagnostic system (Clark, 1995; Jackson & Livesley, 1995; Schwartz, Wiggins, & Norko, 1995). Different models of PD classification have been offered, and many investigators question whether the correct domain has been sampled (Clark, 1995; Davis & Millon, 1995; Jackson & Livesley, 1995; Schwartz et al., 1995). There is controversy about whether a formal system of PD diagnosis should be a categorical or continuous dimensional system (Blashfield & McElroy, 1995; Widiger & Sanderson, 1995). Throughout the next decade, researchers will have to continue to search for an acceptable common ground framework for diagnosis.

Comorbidity of the PD Diagnoses

The extensive degree of comorbidity among the PDs has caused some researchers to question the validity of the *DSM–IV* system (T. Shea, 1995). Even if one accepts the concept that comorbidity represents a valid scientific phenomenon, how does one manage the wide variety of patterns of comorbidity found in any PD diagnosis in an outcome study? It would be extremely difficult to find a truly homogeneous sample of patients with PDs for an outcome study, and if investigators were to do so, they would simultaneously reduce the external validity of their study.

Variance of Symptom Presentation Across the PDs

Perhaps one of the most salient pragmatic reasons that the core battery concept is not possible for the PDs is that people with PDs have a wide variety of symptoms, affective states, and cognitive problems. Patients with PDs enter treatment in a variety of ways. Some patients are seen for episodes of Axis I disorders that are comorbid with the PD. In this case, the measurement of Axis I problems perhaps becomes paramount. Even if Axis II problems are the most important measurement area of change, investigators must be sure that they are not confusing Axis I properties with Axis II properties. Some patients with PDs enter treatment because of a life-threatening behavior directly related to the PD (e.g., parasuicidal behavior related to borderline personality disorder [BPD] or histrionic PD). Others enter treatment because of pressure from family or coworkers (e.g., narcissistic PD) but do not believe they have a problem. Still, other patients enter treatment because of an adjustment disorder (short-lived depression due to rejection or job loss). This diversity of presenting problems is made more obvious by simply comparing just three of the *DSM–IV* PDs on prototypic descriptive behavioral, affective, and cognitive dimensions. For instance, as Millon (1990) has pointed out, in the behavioral domain, the schizotypal, borderline, and paranoid PDs show a wide array of protypical behavioral expression:

- Schizotypal: aberrant, peculiar, gauche, odd, and bizarre
- Borderline: precipitate, impulsive, and too desultory
- Paranoid: vigilant, tenacious, and resistant to external influence and control

In the affective domain, these same disorders again show a vast array of emotional patterns:

- Schizotypal: alert, agitated, and frantic
- Borderline: dramatic and unstable mood swings
- Paranoid: cold and churlish, edgy, envious, and jealous

Turning to the cognitive domain, these three PDs show large differences in their patterns of cognitive styles:

- Schizotypal: tangential and autistic
- Borderline: changeable, unstable, and unsettled
- Paranoid: distrustful, fearful, and guarded

Thoughtful consideration of the vast array of behavioral, emotional, and cognitive problems presented by the full set of PD classes leads to the conclusion that the PDs, taken globally, are too diverse to permit the use of a common outcome battery. Finally, when one remembers that this wide array of symptoms is only a prototype and that each individual human being is unique, the diversity of problems and symptoms presented by the PDs is genuinely overwhelming. Comorbidity with Axis I and Axis II disorders only serves to confound this problem further still. Adding to this complexity, it is becoming evident that there are subgroups, or clusters of patients, even among specific PDs.

Heterogeneity Within PD Categories

Subgroups, or subtypes of patients, within a diagnostic class is another factor that adds heterogeneity to samples of patients with PDs who would be enrolled in an outcome study. Recent research suggests that several distinct subgroups may make up the broader diagnostic groups. Hurt, Clarkin, Munroe-Blum, and Marziali (1992) identified three clusters of patients with BPD. Each cluster is defined by a specific constellation of BPD criteria. Hurt et al. argued that treatment strategies will be prescriptively different for the different clusters of patients with BPD. Turner, Mukhopadhyay, and Dudek (1994) cross-validated the findings of Hurt et al. (1992). Using hierarchical cluster analysis to cluster patients with BPD into homogeneous subgroups is multidimensional scaling to generate meaning interpretations for those subgroups, Turner et al. identified a four-group model for patients with BPD. Although differing slightly, these findings support the Hurt et al. (1992) view that patients with BPD can be classified into clusters on the basis of their prototypical clinical presentations. Following up on this work, Turner (1994a) also used hierarchical cluster analysis and multidimensional scaling to identify subgroups of people with histrionic and narcissistic PDs. In brief, the analyses suggested that multiple clusters of patients with histrionic and narcissistic PDs are embedded within each of these diagnostic classes.

Thus, it is not sufficient to speak of the patient with borderline, histrionic, or narcissistic PD. These subclusters have their own specific problem profile that differs among patients with borderline, histrionic, and narcissistic PDs. Consequently, one could expend considerable effort simply developing a comprehensive outcome battery for patients with BPD, narcissistic PD, or the dramatic-impulsive cluster at a higher level of inclusion.

The Structural and Functional Organization of Personality

The functional organization of personality presents yet another challenge to the application of a core outcome battery for treatment research. It is critical to recognize that personality is structured and organized. Human personality is organized, and personality organization forms an integral part of the therapeutic problem. Messer and Warren (1990) and Pervin

(1990) referred to this characteristic as the *structural criterion*. Personality is not merely a collection of individual traits, nor is it made up of atomistic bits of disconnected behavior. Personality is patterned.

Not only are there parts, there also is a piecing together of the parts in such a way that they make up an integrated structure (Pervin, 1990). Thus, a collection of individual variables (states or traits) does not constitute a needed perspective or outcome unless it is ordered hierarchically and interrelated holistically. This structural criterion also implies a degree of consistency in personality functioning, even if the behavioral manifestations of that structure differ in varying situations. Millon (1990) expanded this point by specifying both functional and structural domains for conceptualizing the PDs.

The central point we are attempting to make by focusing on the functional and structural aspects of personality functioning is that in developing a core outcome battery for the PDs, one must remember that the structure and organization of personality is the focal problem. Furthermore, different theoretical perspectives hypothesize differing functional and structural characteristics. We believe that concern about measurement in the context of the structural and functional components of personality change are, and will remain, one of the stumbling blocks to the development of a core outcome battery.

Differing Theoretical Perspectives of Change

Related to the structural concern, another significant impediment to the development of a PD core outcome battery is that different theoretical treatment approaches have different viewpoints about what should change during the course of treatment. Messer and Warren (1990) vigorously argued that it is unwise and impossible to create a core outcome battery for the psychosocial treatment of PDs, and they recommended that a core outcome battery for research on the PDs is to be avoided at all costs. Messer and Warren also argued that the terms of the differing personality theories and the goals of the related systems of psychotherapy are incommensurable. They pointed out that the theories and treatment models are embedded in a value structure that determines what is most important to know about and change in the individual. Accordingly, the terms of the theories dictate the methods and content of evaluation, and, consequently, the types of results obtained and their interpretations are embedded in the theories also. Thus, the specification of an outcome battery is a value-laden decision specific to each theoretical model. Such value-laden choices cannot be avoided. Rather, they reflect what each theoretical position believes is important in understanding and modifying human functioning.

The Pervasiveness, Severity, and Trait-Longitudinal Nature of PDs

Finally, consideration of the pervasiveness of dysfunction, the severity of dysfunction, and the trait-longitudinal nature of PDs presents other obstacles to a core outcome battery (M. T. Shea, 1992). By its structural nature, a PD affects every area of the person's life. Thus, no one discrete domain of life functioning can be targeted for change, as is typically the case with an anxiety disorder. This means that measurement must cover the patient's entire life, which is an extensive task.

Measuring the severity of a PD is made difficult by the pervasiveness of the symptoms and because the diagnostic classes within the *DSM–IV* system range from mild disturbance (e.g., avoidant) to severe disturbance (e.g., schizotypal and borderline). Yet, assessment of severity is necessary because a PD diagnosis is made only when sufficient criteria for a diagnosis are met and it is demonstrated that the person is significantly impaired in daily functioning. Unfortunately, little work had been done on PD severity measures.

More problematic still is that PDs are defined by evidence of long-term severity and pervasiveness of the symptoms. In other words, the criteria for the *DSM–IV* PDs are assumed to be traits. How does one measure the change in a trait and what time frames are to be used for comparative purposes?

A PD CORE OUTCOME BATTERY MODEL

Although the concerns and complications that we have raised are valid, and although the PDs present unique and difficult challenges for both the researcher and the clinician, we do need a standardized outcome battery now. Daily, clinicians are treating these patients in clinics and need a set of measures to aid treatment planning and assess patients' progress. Moreover, researchers are developing innovative treatments for the PDs and conducting clinical trials on these treatments; consequently, they need a comprehensive outcome battery to standardize communication and actualize progress.

So, despite the obstacles we have raised, we still believe that a minimal treatment outcome battery can be developed for PD research that will provide some order and comparability across studies. As we attempt to develop a core battery model, we try to attend to the issues raised. First, we consider some ideal goals and criteria for selecting measures to be used in a PDs core outcome battery. Next, we develop a strategy for conceptualizing the PDs core battery. Finally, we develop a structure based on these considerations.

Criteria for the PDs Outcome Battery

The criteria we recommend for the PDs core outcome battery are similar to those that are suggested by the other participants in this project. To begin with, the instruments should have at least adequate reliability and validity coefficients. In addition, they should be sensitive to measuring change during the core of psychotherapy. To these three base criteria we add that the measures should (a) be ecologically valid; (b) show good construct validity; (c) attend to the multiple perspectives of outcome; (d) attend to clinical significance with norms and cutoff scores for normal and abnormal functioning; (e) attend to both positive and negative outcomes; (f) limit the burden on participants in studies; and (g) be useful in both funded studies and in studies conducted in real-world clinical settings. Three of these criteria require further elaboration. By the term *ecological validity,* we mean that the measures should be clearly meaningful in terms of tapping functioning that the general public values. Construct validity dually implies that a measure shows good convergent and discriminant validity (i.e., the measure correlates well with measures of similar constructs and exhibits virtually no correlation with measures of purportedly dissimilar constructs). Finally, measures in the battery should be usable by individuals forming the multiple perspectives on psychotherapy outcome: the patient, the therapist, independent evaluators, and significant others in the patient's life. All that should be needed to use an instrument by these multiple perspectives is a simple rewording to reflect the differing frames of reference.

There is probably little disagreement about the criteria for evaluating potential instruments for a PDs core outcome battery. When conflict arises, it is usually about the structure of the battery (i.e., what is to be measured).

The Structure of Psychotherapy Outcome Assessment

A significant part of this conflict is caused by the lack of an adequate structure for conceptualizing the facets of psychotherapy outcome. The lack of a clear structure leads to confusion between variables measuring the impact of treatment and variables measuring the process, or mechanisms of change, of treatment.

Our starting point for developing a structural model for PD outcome research is derived from the models proposed by Kendall and Norton-Ford (1982) and Strupp and Hadley (1977). These models posit a number of ideals that lead to useful guidelines for outcome assessment. The first guideline specifies that therapy outcome research use a variety of measures of outcome that use multiple sources of input. The inventory of sources for psychotherapy outcome data include assessments of client self-report; client task performance; therapists' judgments and ratings; observations by trained, unbiased, observers who do not know the experimental conditions; ratings by significant people in the patient's life; and independent judgments by professionals. In addition to these multiple sources of data, multiple targets of assessment must be considered. For instance, the researcher should measure mood, cognitions, psychological and psychosocial adjustment, vocational status, the quality of interpersonal relationships, or dimensions of personality. Third, the evaluation model must focus on assessment of change over time. This places a high value on examining the durability of therapeutic outcomes. Finally, Kendall and Norton-Ford made a critically important distinction between the *specifying level* and *impact level* of outcome measurement. The term *specifying level of measurement* refers to the specific symptoms and problems targeted for change. This might be parasuicide or affective deregulation in the case of patients with BPD. Alternatively, it might be changing the tacit expectation of other's responses when an exploitive narcissistic patient enters into an interpersonal situation in which empathy is called for. The term *impact level of measurement* refers to the more global ramifications of treatment. This might involve improved work functioning after treatment. It might involve the patient pursuing an enhanced role in the community after treatment. It also might include improved global psychological health. This distinction, between the specifying and impact levels, helps to place overt symptoms and severity and issues of life-role functioning in balance. In addition, it guides us toward separating measures of the outcomes of treatment from the mechanisms of treatment.

In the following sections, we add three elements to this basic structural model of outcome research. These three elements attend to the special issues entailed in evaluating the treatment of people with PDs. The first component includes incorporating a uniform diagnostic system. Second, we suggest extending the specifying and impact levels of measurement to a more thoroughgoing system that preserves the functional relationships of the components of personality and aids in examining the mechanisms of change. The third facet involves including a more robust multiple indicator model for increasing the reliability and validity of measurement.

Uniform Diagnostic System

We start with the position that a uniform diagnostic procedure is required across studies. Of course, which diagnostic system to use is controversial, as is shown by the other chapters in this book. Yet, we are certain that diagnoses from the *DSM–IV*, the tenth edition of the *International Classification of Diseases (ICD–10)*, or both need to be conducted before treatment enrollment. Whichever system is adopted for the core outcome battery, diagnosis of both Axis I symptom disorders and complete diagnostic coverage of the PDs is the optimal strategy. The primary goal is to ensure that researchers know what type of patients are being treated in a study and the exact nature of their comorbidity. We do not recommend that this assessment be used as a change measure of PD because diagnosis is based on the trait-longitudinal view of PDs. However, we do believe that change in the specific diagnostic symptoms of the PDs be assessed separately at the specifying outcome level. This second type of diagnostic change assessment requires that the time line for symptom assessment be shortened to a more immediate time range to allow comparable pretreatment and posttreatment assessment.

Levels of Outcome Assessment

The definition of outcome often is confused with theoretical mechanisms of change. *Outcome* is defined by the *Random House Webster's Electronic Dictionary* (1992) as "a final product or end result." In psychotherapy research, this definition implies that outcome measurement per se needs to focus on assessing the extent and severity of the patients' problems, their functional capacity, and the presence or absence of a diagnosable disorder. Changes in working models of role relationships or in social skill reflect theoretically specified routes to reducing patients' problems, improving their work role functioning, or eliminating their mental health diagnoses. What we may observe empirically is that changes in the theoretical mechanisms do mediate changes in the outcome indicators. On the other hand, we also might discover empirically that the posited theoretical mechanisms do not mediate the reduction of symptoms or the elimination of diagnoses.

As we stated earlier, Kendall and Norton-Ford (1982) added important clarity to the categorization of types of outcome assessment in clinical trials. Their concept of the specifying level and impact level of outcome measurement helps to distinguish between measuring overt symptoms and diagnosis on the one hand and daily functioning in relationships, work, and social activities on the other. The specifying level of measurement refers to the specific symptoms and problems targeted for change. The impact level of measurement refers to the more global ramifications of treatment. To this model we add a third level that we call the *structural causal mechanisms of change level* of outcome analysis. This level of outcome includes measures of theoretically specific constructs such as working models of role relationships, social skill functioning, anxiety tolerance, or the results of a structured analysis of social behavior. These measures all reflect theoretically specified routes to the specifying and impact outcomes of reducing patients' problems, improving their work role functioning, or eliminating their mental health diagnoses. Outcomes assessed at this level of analysis often are treated as the final outcome of psychotherapy. This is a mistaken notion because such measures reflect theoretically important changes but not the remission of symptoms or a diagnosis.

Figure 1 illustrates our structural model of psychotherapy outcome assessment based on the considerations described earlier. In this model, the definition of treatment is considered to be a manifest variable that is under the control of the investigators. Treatment might involve only one intervention with a nonrandomized sample of patients, or it might involve two or more alternative intervention modalities with a fully randomized sample of patients. At this level, measurement assesses the integrity and completeness of the intervention administered. The second level of the model consists of the specification of moderator variables. These most often are manifest variables containing demographic information on patient and therapist characteristics or other important facets of the environment from which the sample is drawn. Moderator variables serve the function of enhancing or dampening down the outcomes of a treatment. For instance, one may find that certain diagnostic types do not respond to a particular intervention but that other diagnostic types react dramatically to it.

The third level of our model represents the structural causal mechanisms of change outcomes. Included here are measures of constructs that the therapy theory argues are vital for good outcome and that the treatment itself targets for change. In Figure 1, we have included only one causal mechanism construct to retain some simplicity in the diagram, but there may be as many causal mechanism constructs as the theoretical proposition purports there to be. Again, examples of structural causal mechanism outcomes might include (a) improved problem-solving capacity, (b) improved social skills, (c) improved cognitive hygiene, (d) movement from an interpersonal style of cold and harsh to warm and receptive

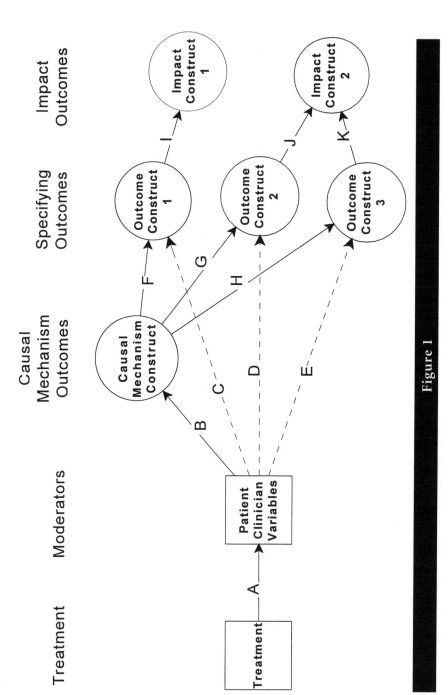

Figure 1

Personality disorders core outcome battery model.

on a structured assessment of social behavioral analysis, (e) a healthier set of role relationship models to guide behavior and emotion, (f) improved quality of the therapeutic alliance with the therapist, or (g) emotional resolve and closure regarding unfinished business. The critical concept to grasp is that all of these outcomes are mediators of the genuine treatment outcomes, not final end products, in and of themselves.

To be valid and important outcome constructs, treatment must substantially affect these mediating, or structural, causal mechanisms. In other words, the path labeled *B* must be large and significant. In addition, the definition of a genuine mediation process requires the paths labeled *C, D,* and *E* to be large when they are assessed in the absence of Path B, but small or near zero when they are assessed with Path B included in the model. Such a situation implies that the treatment influences the final outcome only by working through the causal mechanism construct. Empirically, treatment may or may not affect the measures at this level of analysis. If, for instance, Path B is a small nonsignificant value but Paths C, D, or E are large and statistically significant, the hypothesis that the purported causal mechanism mediates, or is involved at all, in determining treatment outcome is falsified. Furthermore, even if Path B is large, if Paths F, G, and H are large and significant, the mediating hypothesis is falsified. The psychotherapy research literature is filled with examples of investigators being able to demonstrate that a treatment can change measures at the structural causal mechanism level of analysis but that this change does not affect diagnosis or patients' problem severity. This is why many investigators continue to insist that theory-specific measurement be a component of outcome batteries. However, this insistence only reflects the continued confusion between outcome measures of structural mechanisms and the genuine final outcomes of treatment: the reduction of symptoms associated with a diagnosis and the problems in patients' lives.

The fourth level in our model is the specifying outcome level. It is already obvious that we consider this level to represent the existence or absence of a mental health diagnosis and the extent and severity of problems patients have relative to the diagnosis. With regard to PDs, from our perspective, this consists of either a *DSM–IV* or *ICD–10* diagnosis plus severity ratings to index the extent to which the diagnosed disorder reduces patients' daily role functioning.

The fifth level of assessment in the model is the impact level, and it corresponds to Kendall and Norton-Ford's (1982) original definition. The impact level of measurement refers to the global ramifications of treatment. This might involve improved work functioning, parenting functioning, and sexual functioning, or household functioning after treatment. It might involve the patient pursuing an enhanced role in the community after treatment. It also might include improved global physical and psychological health. Our model, as depicted in Figure 1, assumes that changes at the impact level are mediated by changes at the outcome level. Of course, this is always an empirical question to be tested. It is conceivable that a treatment might increase community role functioning without improving the patients' status on either the causal mechanism constructs or diagnosis. The important point here is that in addition to the fact that the structural causal mechanism variables represent mediating constructs, outcome changes will mediate impact level changes. This leads us to the consideration of gathering multiple indicators for these two classes of variables.

The Importance of Multiple Indicators of Outcome Constructs

Advances in confirmatory factor analysis and the theory of measurement models in recent years has led to a critically important observation: No measurement is ever error-free (Turner, 1994). This is particularly true for psychological measures of abstract constructs such as depression or personality status. However, even in the physical sciences, the use of a simple balance to measure mass, for example, may be affected by friction, imperfections in the mechanism, and errors in reading the scale, among others.

Thus, there is no simple distinction between perfectly reliable and unreliable measures; it is the degree of unreliability that distinguishes indicators. Random measurement error in therapy outcome assessment can emanate from any number of sources that are too numerous to list. Unreliability is not limited to self-report measures and may also be a factor in the type of data typically gathered by independent assessors. The important characteristic of these errors of measurement is that they are totally unsystematic. However, if this error loses its random nature, the problem is no longer one of reliability but validity. The validity of a measure, or indicator, is simply the extent to which it measures what the researcher claims it does: the theoretical concept. As soon as the error in one's measures becomes systematic, some variation in the indicators is related to theoretical, or practical, concepts other than the one it was designed to measure. Put another way, a measure may be reliable, but measuring, completely or in part, concepts other than what investigators intend it to measure. Thus, it is still an error-laden measure.

Recognition of these two sources of measurement error are important because of their consequences in research design and statistical analysis (Turner, 1994b). This issue becomes more important because of the mediating nature of many of the outcome variables, as described earlier. The analysis of mediation involves analysis of partial variance (APV). The techniques of APV, which include the related methods of simultaneous and hierarchical multiple regression and analysis of covariance, are used extensively in the identification of mediators in experimental and correlational research.

Unfortunately, the usefulness of APV procedures is compromised by the assumption that each partialed variable, or covariate, must be measured without error (Arbuckle, 1988; Bentler, 1980; Bentler & Woodward, 1979; Cohen & Cohen, 1983; Hoyle, 1991; Kenny, 1979; Loehlin, 1987; Sorbom, 1978; Sullivan & Feldman, 1979). The method of APV makes other assumptions as well (e.g., homogeneity of within-groups regression), but the assumption of infallible partialed variables is the most critical and debilitating assumption (Arbuckle, 1988). More unfortunate still is that researchers often are unaware that partialed variables are assumed to be measured without error and that if this assumption is violated, misleading conclusions may be drawn (Arbuckle, 1988; Bentler & Woodward, 1978; Cohen & Cohen, 1983; Cook & Campbell, 1979; Kenny, 1979; Loehlin, 1987; Sorbom, 1978).

The impact of violating this assumption is serious because the effect can be to either under- or overestimate the relationship between the research variable of interest and the dependent variable or even to change the sign of that relationship. That measurement error may increase or decrease or even change the sign of a partial relationship has been demonstrated empirically by Cohen and Cohen (1983). In a simulation study, Cohen and Cohen compared the attenuation-corrected and attenuation-uncorrected values of partial regression coefficients between one independent variable and one dependent variable with one other independent variable partialed out. For the simulation, the reliability of the partialed variable was set to .7, which reflects standard situations in clinical research. In one solution they obtained an estimated partial correlation coefficient of zero when the true coefficient was $-.23$. A second solution led to an observed partial correlation of .24 when the true coefficient was zero. Most alarmingly, they obtained an estimated partial coefficient of .14 when the true coefficient was $-.26$. Based on their findings, Cohen and Cohen (1983) concluded that unreliability in a partialed variable may yield grossly inaccurate results in APV applications.

The problem of distortion attributable to fallible partialed variables arises because the operation of random and nonrandom measurement error in variables acts to attenuate the simple correlation between them (Cohen & Cohen, 1983; Cronbach, 1970; Kenny, 1979; Lord & Novick, 1968; Nunnally, 1967). The difficulty is straightforward in the bivariate case because the estimated correlation between two variables always will be less than the true correlation and a formula for correction of attenuation exists. However, when there are two or more independent variables measured with error, and partialing is conducted, the effects of measurement error are difficult to predict, as demonstrated empirically by Cohen and Cohen (1983). In the multivariate case, correcting the correlations for attenuation and then conducting an APV does not solve the problem because there is no formula for the standard error, which means that neither formal hypothesis testing nor power analysis is possible (Cohen & Cohen, 1983; Kenny, 1979; Lord, 1974). The more mediating variables involved in an analysis the worse the problem becomes. Measurement error in one of the partialed variables can distort the partial regression coefficients of all the other independent variables with which it is correlated. This can lead to the contamination of the results involving the impact of the research factor being studied, the other mediators, and the interaction terms that are used to determine regression homogeneity. Thus, using fallible variables as mediators can lead to the erroneous conclusion that a treatment has an effect when it does not or that a treatment has no effect when it really does. Unreliable mediator variables can even make a treatment look like it does harm when it is actually beneficial (Bentler & Woodward, 1979).

Some principles developed in structural equation modeling with latent variables, however, provide a methodology for solving the problem. The principal avenue by which this technique resolves the problem of less than perfectly reliable independent variables is in the creation of latent variables. Latent variables are hypothetical constructs clinical investigators create instead of using a single measure as the operational definition of a construct. A latent variable may be thought of as a common factor that explains the correlations between two indicators or among three or more indicators of the construct. Thus, the collection of data from clinical participants on multiple measures, or indicators, of the relevant research constructs is necessary to the latent variable approach. The main virtue of latent variables is that they reflect purely the construct of interest and separate random error variance and other irrelevancies from the meaningful effects of the psychological construct (Bentler, 1980). This is accomplished by establishing the latent variable as a cause of the indicators and allowing the instruments to also have components that are unique. These unique components may be made up of random measurement error, irrelevancies such as method variance and aspects of other constructs incidentally measured by the instruments, or construct-specific variance not related to the problem at hand. The unique factor components permit the segregation of true score variance, in Cronbach, Gleser, Nanda, and Rajaratnam's (1972) sense of maximum generalizability to the research context, from the error and unique variance (Arbuckle, 1988; Bentler, 1980; Hoyle, 1991; Kenny, 1979; Loehlin, 1987).

Consequently, a vital component of a core outcome battery is to identify multiple indicators of the outcome constructs to be measured (Turner, 1978, 1994) and to incorporate measurement model assessment into the treatment outcome study. Realization of the need for contemporaneous measurement model assessment and the inclusion of multiple indicators for the causal mechanism and specifying levels of the core outcome battery is critical for the successful application of the core battery.

RECOMMENDATIONS FOR MEASURES

Based on our previous discussion, we first recommend that the core battery avoid prescribing measures for the structural causal mechanism level of outcome. Measures for this level of outcome analysis are best left to the individual investigators. In addition, because of the extensive controversy over the validity of the *DSM–IV* diagnostic system, we also avoid making recommendations for the measurement of the presence or absence of a PD within the specifying outcome level. However, we do feel comfortable making recommendations for the measurement of problem severity within the specifying level and a number of variables measured at the impact level.

Specifying Outcome Level

Daily Diary Cards (Linehan, 1987) are used daily as a self-monitoring log by patients. Patients record daily alcohol consumption, medications taken, illicit drugs used, instances of parasuicide, and ratings of suicide ideation, parasuicidal urges, daily misery, and efforts at coping. The latter ratings are made on 5-point scales. *Misery* refers to average dysphoria, anxiety, guilt, anger, shame, and so on. Cards are handed in at each session to the therapists. Linehan, Armstrong, Suarez, Allmon, and Heard (1991) reported excellent compliance with this self-recording model.

Target behavior and symptoms rating scales (Mintz & Kiesler, 1982; Turner, 1993a) have been used in numerous psychotherapy outcome studies and were a component of the original National Institute of Mental Health Core Battery (Waskow & Parloff, 1975). Interrater reliabilities are good, particularly when assessors have gone through training. We recommend using the target ratings in the manner described Mintz and Kiesler (1982). Patients and assessors arrive at three problems the patient wants to work on during treatment or are specified as specific targets by the investigators. These problems then are coded and rated at all assessment sessions. In a previous study (Turner, 1993b), target behavior ratings were developed especially for patients with BPD for the problems of anger, impulsive behavior, and frequency of self-harm. The target behavior ratings for self-harm, anger, and impulsive behavior were made on a 0–8 scale

(0 = *no symptoms,* 8 = *severe symptoms*). The Pearson product–moment correlations between two independent assessors were .75 for the ratings of anger, .80 for the ratings of impulsive behavior, and .84 for the ratings of self-harm. This suggests that the target behavior rating strategy is worth pursuing as a model for outcome evaluation with patients with BPD and the PDs in general. In addition, the current version of the target rating forms includes a 0–8 dimensional rating for all nine DSM–IV BPD criteria. On the basis of the Structured Clinical Interview for DSM–III (Spitzer & Williams, 1985), the evaluators make dimensional target ratings for the participants based on the most recent 4-week period. This methodology is particularly amenable to the multiple perspectives format because the therapist, patient, and significant others all can rate the patient on the problems and symptoms.

Impact Outcome Level

Measures of Social Role Functioning

The Social Adjustment Scale–LIFE (SAS-L; Linehan, Heard, & Armstrong, 1993; Weissman & Paykel, 1974) interview was adapted and modified from the psychosocial functioning portion of both the Social Adjustment Scale–Self Report (SAS-SR) and the Longitudinal Interview Follow-up Evaluation (LIFE) Base Schedule to assess the variability and frequent change typical in BPD. Events (e.g., jobs, moves, relationships ending) are documented since the last assessment. Using the SAS-L, functioning is rated in each of 10 areas (i.e., work; household; social interpersonal relations with partner, children, parents, friends, and others; global social adjustment; and Global Assessment Scale scores) for the worst week in each preceding month and for the best week overall. Self-report ratings in these areas using the SAS-SR (Weissman & Bothwell, 1976) have been used to corroborate the interview ratings. Average interrater reliabilities on the LIFE combined over 4-month periods in the Linehan et al. (1993) study ranged from .59 to .91, with an overall average of .80.

The Social Behavior Assessment Schedule (Platt, Hirsch, & Knights, 1981) is used to evaluate a patient's disturbed behavior, social functioning, and the impact that this behavior has had on significant others based on

22 problem areas commonly associated with psychiatric disorders. The Social Behavior Assessment Schedule is a standardized, multiple item, semistructured interview that is conducted with significant others in the patient's current life. It does not evaluate the behavior against an ideal but with the expectations and norms of the patient's environment. In this way, greater ecological validity is achieved than would be using an ideal standard of functioning. Specific guidelines are provided for coding the informant's responses on several scales that evaluate the presence of disturbance, the severity of disturbance, the informant's distress level, as well as various ratings on the patient's social performance and a measure of distress caused to others. In the assessment of interrater reliability, Platt et al. (1980) reported intraclass correlation coefficients exceeding .95. In addition, Platt et al. reported that 80% of the individual items reached or exceeded a weighted kappa of .7.

Measures of Alcohol and Drug Abuse

The Addiction Severity Index (McLellan, Luborsky, Woody, & O'Brien, 1980) is a comprehensive measure of the severity of problem areas associated with substance abuse. The Addiction Severity Index is a structured interview covering seven areas: medical condition, employment, drug use, alcohol use, illegal activity, familial relations, and psychiatric conditions. Objective questions are used to assess the number, duration, and extent of problems over the patient's lifetime and within the past 30 days. Patients also provide a subjective report of the problem severity in the past 30 days and the importance of each problem area. Each problem area receives an interviewer rating of problem severity on a 10-point scale (0–9). Additionally, a composite score is derived from interrelated items within each problem area, which are standardized and summed to attain an estimate of a patient's severity level in each area. Interrater reliability was estimated to be .89.

Measures of Global Psychological Functioning

The SCL–90–R (Derogatis, 1977) is a self-report measure designed to assess psychological symptom patterns across a broad range of symptoms and across a broad spectrum of individuals, ranging from nonpatients to psychiatric patients. It yields three global scales (i.e., the Global Severity Index, Positive Symptom Distress Index, and Positive Symptom Total) as well as nine primary symptoms (i.e., somatization, obsessive–compulsive, interpersonal sensitivity, depression, anxiety, hostility, phobic anxiety, paranoid ideation, and psychoticism). It has shown excellent reliability and validity. Additionally, it has demonstrated sensitivity to change in a broad variety of contexts, including interventions and stressful life circumstances.

Measures of Legal Episodes, Hospital Episodes, and Service Utilization Costs

Measures of legal episodes, hospital episodes, and service utilization costs all provide important impact assessments of the results of treatment. This area of measurement involves complexities that are beyond the scope of this chapter, but one easy-to-administer instrument stands out as useful for PD treatment research: the Treatment History Inventory.

The Treatment History Interview (Linehan, 1987b) measures types of treatment received during the target period, such as (a) a description of the hour of professional psychotherapy and counseling; (b) an estimated number of telephone calls to psychotherapists; (c) the hours of nonprofessional treatment (e.g., co-counseling, Alcoholics Anonymous, Narcotics Anonymous, etc.); (d) the hours of formal drug and alcohol program; (e) the days and circumstances of hospitalization; (f) the reasons for stopping psychotherapy or counseling; (g) nonpsychiatric medical problems and treatments, including emergency room and physician visits; and (h) medications prescribed and patterns of use. Previous research on parasuicidal women with BPD by Linehan et al. (1991) has shown the interview to have excellent reliability. Patients' self-reports about psychiatric admissions and days were compared by Linehan et al. with hospital records for patients who reported that they had been admitted to a psychiatric hospital at least once during the past year. Analyses revealed 90% agreement between patients' reports and hospital records for number of admissions per patient and 80% agreement for number of days per patient ($r = .99$). All reports of individual psychotherapy were verified by calling psychotherapists for interviews. There were no false-positives. Additional counts of patients' legal episodes can be made by reviewing agency records.

CONCLUSIONS

In this chapter, we have discussed the value of developing a core outcome battery for treatment research on PDs and the obstacles to developing such a battery. On the basis of this discussion, we have concluded that it is worthwhile to begin developing a minimal core battery. We then suggested a number of criteria to be used when evaluating measures for inclusion and proposed a structure for conceptualizing a core battery. Finally, we recommended seven instruments for inclusion in the battery.

Importantly, we have recommended that a PD core outcome battery avoid including theoretically based instruments at what we term the *structural causal mechanism level of analysis*. We did so because this level of outcome assessment has generated significant controversy and is one of the primary reasons the original Waskow and Parloff (1975) battery ended up being neglected.

Our principal recommendations for indicators are at the specifying and impact levels of measurement. Here, we suggest instruments with substantial reliability and validity evidence and that focus on problems and symptoms, life role functioning deficits, and social costs of PDs. We reiterate that this is simply a first minimalist attempt at specifying a core battery for PD research.

REFERENCES

American Psychiatric Association. (1994). *Diagnostic and statistical manual of mental disorders* (4th ed.). Washington, DC: Author.

Arbuckle, J. (1996). *AMOS users guide.* Chicago: Small Waters Corporation.

Bentler, P. M. (1980). Multivariate analysis with latent variables: Causal modeling. *Annual Review of Psychology, 31,* 419–456.

Bentler, P. M., & Woodward, J. A. (1979). Nonexperimental evaluation research: Contributions of causal modeling. In L. Datta & R. Perloff (Eds.), *Improving evaluation* (pp. 419–456). Beverly Hills, CA: Sage.

Bergin, A. E., & Lambert, M. J. (1978). The evaluation of therapeutic outcomes. In S. L. Garfield & A. E. Bergin (Eds.), *Handbook of psychotherapy and behavior change: An empirical analysis* (2nd ed., pp. 139–190). New York: Wiley.

Blashfield, R. K., & McElroy, R. A. (1995). Confusions in terminology used for classificatory systems. In W. J. Livesley (Ed.), *The DSM–IV personality disorders* (pp. 407–416). New York: Guilford Press.

Clark, L. A. (1995). The challenge of alternative perspectives in classification: A discussion of the basic issues. In W. J. Livesley (Ed.), *The DSM–IV personality disorders* (pp. 482–496). New York: Guilford Press.

Clarkin, J. F., Koenigsberg, H., Yoemans, F., Selzer, M., Kernberg, P., & Kernberg, O. F. (1992). Psychodynamic psychotherapy of the borderline patients. In J. F. Clarkin, E. Marziali, & H. Munroe-Blum (Eds.), *Borderline personality disorder: Clinical and empirical perspectives* (pp. 268–287). New York: Guilford Press.

Cohen, J., & Cohen, P. (1983). *Applied multiple regression/correlation analysis for the behavioral sciences.* Hillsdale, NJ: Erlbaum.

Cook, T. D., & Campbell, D. T. (1979). *Quasi-experimentation: Design and analysis issues for field settings.* Chicago: Rand McNally.

Cronbach, L. J. (1970). *Essentials of psychological testing* (3rd ed.). New York: Harper & Row.

Cronbach, L. J., Gleser, G. C., Nanda, H., & Rajaratnam, N. (1972). *The dependability of behavioral measurements.* New York: Wiley.

Davis, R., & Millon, T. (1995). On the importance of theory to a taxonomy of personality disorders. In W. J. Livesley (Ed.), *The DSM-IV personality disorders* (pp. 377–398). New York: Guilford Press.

Derogatis, L. R. (1977). *SCL–90–R: Administration, scoring, and procedures manual.* Baltimore: Clinical Psychometrics Research.

Hoyle, R. H. (1991). Evaluating measurement models in clinical research: Covariance structure analysis of latent variable models of self conception. *Journal of Consulting and Clinical Psychology, 59,* 67–76.

Hurt, S. W., Clarkin, J. F., Munroe-Blum, H., & Marziali, E. (1992). Borderline behavioral clusters and different treatment approaches. In J. F. Clarkin, E. Marziali, & H. Munroe-Blum (Eds.), *Borderline personality disorder: Clinical and empirical perspectives* (pp. 199–219). New York: Guilford Press.

Jackson, D. N., & Livesley, W. J. (1995). Possible contributions from personality assessment to the classification of personality disorders. In W. J. Livesley (Ed.), *The DSM-IV personality disorders* (pp. 459–481). New York: Guilford Press.

Kendall, P. C., & Norton-Ford, J. D. (1982). Therapy outcome research methods. In P. C. Kendall & J. N. Butcher (Eds.), *Handbook of research methods in clinical psychology* (pp. 429–460). New York: Wiley.

Kenny, D. A. (1979). *Correlation and causality.* New York: Wiley.

Koenigsberg, H., Kaplan, R., Gilmore, M., & Cooper, A. M. (1985). The relationship between syndrome and personality disorder in DSM–III: Experience with 2,462 patients. *American Journal of Psychiatry, 142,* 207–212.

Linehan, M. M. (1987a). *Daily Diary Cards (DDC).* Seattle: University of Washington.

Linehan, M. M. (1987b). *Treatment History Interview (THI).* Seattle: University of Washington.

Linehan, M. M. (1993). *Cognitive-behavioral treatment of borderline personality disorder.* New York: Guilford Press.

Linehan, M. M., Armstrong, H. E., Suarez, A., Allmon, D., & Heard, H. L. (1991). Cognitive-behavioral treatment of chronically parasuicidal borderline patients. *Archives of General Psychiatry, 48,* 1060–1064.

Linehan, M. M., Heard, H. L., & Armstrong, H. E. (1993). Naturalistic follow-up of a behavioral treatment for chronically parasuicidal borderline patients. *Archives of General Psychiatry, 50,* 971–974.

Loehlin, J. C. (1987). *Latent variable models: An introduction to factor, path, and structural analysis.* Hillsdale, NJ: Erlbaum.

Loranger, A. W. (1990). The impact of DSM–III personality disorders on diagnostic practice in a university hospital. *Archives of General Psychiatry, 47,* 672–675.

Lord, F. M. (1974). Significance test for a partial correlation corrected for attenuation. *Educational and Psychological Measurement, 34,* 211–220.

Lord, F. M., & Novick, M. R. (1968). *Statistical theories of mental test scores.* Reading, MA: Addison-Wesley.

McLellan, A. T., Luborsky, L., Woody, G. E., O'Brien, C. P. (1980). An improved diagnostic evaluation instrument for substance abuse patients: The addiction severity index. *Journal of Nervous and Mental Disease, 168,* 26–33.

Messer, S. B., & Warren, S. (1990). Personality change and psychotherapy. In L. A. Pervin (Ed.), *Handbook of personality: Theory and research* (pp. 371–394). New York: Guilford Press.

Platt, S. D., Hirsch, S. R., & Knights, A. C. (1981). Effects of brief hospitalization on psychiatric patients' behavior and social functioning. *Acta Psychiatrica Scandinavia, 63,* 117–128.

Millon, T. (1990). The disorders of personality. In L. a. Pervin (Ed.), *Handbook of personality: Theory and research* (pp. 339–368). New York: Guilford Press.

Mintz, J., & Kiesler, D. J. (1982). Individualized measures of psychotherapy outcome. In P. C. Kendall & J. N. Butcher (Eds.), *Handbook of research methods in clinical psychology* (pp. 535–568). New York: Wiley.

Munroe-Blum, H., & Marziali, E. (1987). *Randomized clinical trial of relationship management time-limited group treatment of borderline personality disorder.* Hamilton, Ontario, Canada: Northern Ontario Mental Health Foundation.

Nunnally, J. C. (1967). *Psychometric theory* (2nd ed.). New York: McGraw-Hill.

Pervin, L. A. (1990). A brief history of modern personality theory. In L. A. Pervin (Ed.), *Handbook of personality: Theory and research* (pp. 3–16). New York: Guilford Press.

Random House Webster's Electronic Dictionary, College Edition (Version 1.0). (1992). New York: Reference Software International.

Reich, J. H. (1989). Prevalence of DSM–III personality disorders in the community. *Social Psychiatry and Psychiatric Epidemiology, 24,* 12–16.

Schwartz, M. A., Wiggins, O. P., & Norko, M. A. (1995). Prototypes, ideal types, and personality disorders: The return to classical phenomenology. In W. J. Livesley (Ed.), *The DSM–IV personality disorders* (pp. 417–432). New York: Guilford Press.

Shea, M. T. (1992). Borderline personality disorder: Research implications. In J. F. Clarkin, E. Marziali, & H. Munroe-Blum (Eds.), *Borderline personality disorder: Clinical and empirical perspectives* (pp. 319–328). New York: The Guilford Press.

Shea, T. (1995). Interrelationships among categories of personality disorders. In W. J. Livesley (Ed.), *The DSM-IV personality disorders* (pp. 397–406). New York: Guilford Press.

Sorbom, D. (1978). An alternative to the methodology of analysis of covariance. *Psychometrika, 43,* 381–396.

Spitzer, R. L., & Williams, J. B. W. (1985). *Structured Clinical Interview for DSM–III Personality Disorders.* New York: New York State Psychiatric Institute, Biometrics Research Department.

Stevenson, J., & Meares, R. (1992). An outcome study of psychotherapy for patients with borderline personality disorder. *American Journal of Psychiatry, 149,* 358–362.

Strupp, H. H., & Hadley, S. W. (1977). A tripartite model of mental health and therapeutic outcomes: With special reference to the negative effects of psychotherapy. *American Psychologist, 32,* 187–196.

Sullivan, J. L., & Feldman, S. (1979). *Multiple indicators: An introduction.* Beverly Hills, CA: Sage.

Turner, R. M. (1978). Multivariate assessment of therapy outcome research. *Journal of Behavior Therapy and Experimental Psychiatry, 9,* 309–314.

Turner, R. M. (1988). The cognitive-behavioral approach to the treatment of borderline personality disorders. *International Journal of Partial Hospitalization, 5,* 279–289.

Turner, R. M. (1989). Case study evaluation of a bio-cognitive-behavioral approach for the treatment of borderline personality disorder. *Behavior Therapy, 20,* 477–489.

Turner, R. M. (1993a). *Target Behaviors and Symptoms Rating Form (TBSR): For the assessment of borderline pathology* (Version 2). Philadelphia: Allegheny University of the Health Sciences.

Turner, R. M. (1993b). Experimental evaluation of the utility of psychodynamic techniques in the practice of cognitive-behavior therapy: Treating borderline personality disorder. *The 26th Annual Meeting of the Association for the Advancement of Behavior Therapy, 1,* 86.

Turner, R. M. (1994a). *Borderline, narcissistic, and histrionic personality disorders.* In M. Hersen & T. Ammerman (Eds.), *Prescriptive treatments for adult disorders* (pp. 393–420). New York: Pergamon Press.

Turner, R. M. (1994b). The utility of structural equation modeling in cognitive behavior therapy research. *Psicologia Conductal, 2,* 23–43.

Turner, R. M., Mukhopadhyay, P., & Dudek, P. (1994). Prototype clusters of borderline personality disorder patients. *The 28th Annual Meeting of the Association for the Advancement of Behavior Therapy, 2,* 117–119.

Waskow, I. E., & Parloff, M. B. (1975). *Psychotherapy change measures.* Rockville, MD: National Institute of Mental Health.

Weissman, M. M. (1993). The epidemiology of personality disorders: A 1990 update. *Journal of Personality Disorders, 7,* 44–62.

Weissman, M. M., & Bothwell, S. (1976). Assessment of social adjustment by patient self-report. *Archives of General Psychiatry, 33,* 1111–1115.

Weissman, M. M., & Paykel, E. S. (1974). *The depressed woman: A study of social relationships.* Chicago: University of Chicago Press.

Widiger, T. A., & Sanderson, C. J. (1995). Toward a dimensional model of personality disorders. In W. J. Livesley (Ed.), *The DSM–IV personality disorders* (pp. 433–458). New York: Guilford Press.

Widiger, T. A., & Weissman, M. M. (1991). Epidemiology of borderline personality disorder. *Hospital and Community Psychiatry, 42,* 1015–1021.

Zimmerman, M., & Coryell, W. (1989). DSM–III personality disorder diagnoses in a nonpatient sample: Demographic correlates and comorbidity. *Archives of General Psychiatry, 46,* 682–689.

18

Conceptual Issues in Measuring Personality Disorder Change

William P. Henry

The measurement of change in Axis II personality disorders is a challenge that may well be unparalleled by any other diagnostic category. These challenges are both pragmatic and theoretical. Although the participants in the American Psychological Association-sponsored conference on measuring change in patients after therapeutic interventions certainly grappled with many abstract conceptual issues, the purpose of the conference was more pragmatic: to make recommendations for specific measurement domains and instruments to make up core assessment batteries. The summary recommendations of the personality disorder advisory group are contained elsewhere in this book. Therefore, in this chapter, I explore in greater depth some of the conceptual issues in Axis II change measurement. I touch on issues involved in the definition of personality disorder (and hence the meaning of change), unique measurement difficulties, the problem of comorbidity, and alternative answers to the broad question, What should be measured? In many cases, the discussion involves casting

I thank my students Ken Critchfield and Tiffini Porter for their thoughtful comments on earlier drafts. I also thank Mike Lambert for his constructive management of our original personality disorder task force meetings and for his considerable patience and encouragement during my writing of this chapter. Finally, I wish to thank Hans Strupp for his inexhaustible curiosity and drive, which have energized the field of psychotherapy research for over four decades.

general taxonomic conundrums into the context of change measurement. I think that it is also important to consider the political and scientific implications of different directions in change assessment. Finally, I propose one specific model, based on interpersonal theory, that I feel coherently addresses these many problems with a unified conceptual and measurement metric encompassing personality theory, a definition of psychopathology, and an explanation of comorbidity.

THE UNIQUE CHALLENGES OF AXIS II CHANGE MEASUREMENT

Measures of change in Axis I symptoms have a longer history than do their Axis II counterparts. However, developing measures of change in personality disorders is not simply a matter of translating similar measurement paradigms into a different content domain. By its nature, Axis II presents several unique problems. I discuss some of these issues, divided along the lines of theoretical versus pragmatic measurement problems, although the two intrinsically interact at times.

Theoretical Issues in Axis II Change Measurement

The obvious first question in change measurement is, Change in what? In this case the "what"—personality disorders—is a theoretically contentious arena in a state of flux. Arguments abound about the specific definitions (i.e., diagnostic descriptors) of each disorder as well as about the most appropriate general taxonomic strategy (i.e., categorical vs. dimensional models). Although it is true that the Axis II diagnoses in the *Diagnostic and Statistical Manual of Mental Disorders (DSM)* are relatively recent additions to the psychiatric nomenclature (the third edition of the *DSM* [*DSM–III*]; American Psychiatric Association, 1980), the reasons behind the unique difficulties in Axis II change measurement run far deeper than their relatively recent emergence. Many of the problems conceptualizing personality disorders and their change are woven into the very form and function of the *DSM* (Henry, 1994).[1]

---

[1] Unless there is a reason to refer to a specific edition of the *Diagnostic and Statistical Manual of Mental Disorders,* I simply refer to it generically for the sake of simplicity.

Intervening Variables and Hypothetical Constructs

In a seminal article, Morey (1991) revisited MacCorquodale and Meehl's (1948) classic distinction between intervening variables and hypothetical constructs as this distinction applies to the classification of mental disorders by the *DSM*. MacCorquodale and Meehl defined an intervening variable as one that is completely reducible to the operational laws that define it, a construct capable of being expressed quantitatively with empirical terms and functions. Intervening variables are variables of convenience, with no necessarily deeper "truth" or factual referent beyond the data they summarize. Hypothetical constructs, on the other hand, are thought to "exist" in some true form and are not exhausted by or reducible to the operations used to measure or represent them. Morey pointed out that although *DSM* diagnoses are intervening variables (reducible to the rules that define them), the underlying hypothetical constructs supposedly tapped by the diagnostic label are not exhausted by the *DSM* criteria. In short, although the operationalized diagnosis should bear some connection to the hypothetical construct in "theoretical space," they are not the same thing. He also lamented the reification of *DSM* diagnoses and suggested that research based solely on *DSM* categorical criteria has created a situation in which the intervening variable has come to be mistaken for or equated with the underlying concepts that truly constitute the mental disorder.

If one accepts this proposition, then Axis II research faces problems not shared to the same degree by research into many Axis I disorders. I suggest that the gap between personality disorders as intervening variables (i.e., *DSM* diagnostic entities) and personality disorders as hypothetical constructs (core dimensions of personality pathology) is far greater than the corresponding gap for Axis I disorders such as depression. Depression has been referred to as a "final common pathway" and represents a reasonably identifiable, stable, and predictable syndrome of surface symptoms (regardless of ideas about etiology or core pathology). As such, the construct of depression *per se* is in some sense more nearly reducible to the *DSM* diagnostic criteria used to define it operationally than are the personality disorders. Minor changes in the criteria for the diagnosis of depression do little to alter the fundamental conception of depression, although changes in the diagnostic criteria for certain personality disorders do seem to alter the basic nature of that disorder.[2]

Why is all of this important to measuring change in personality disorders? The fact is that the dictates of research funding (i.e., the requirement to define specific patient populations diagnostically via structured interviews based on *DSM* criteria) pull for the reification of the diagnostic category. Unfortunately, the formulas for the intervening variables change over time, and the gap between the operational and conceptual constructs is great in many people's minds (see, e.g., Gabbard, 1990, who compares and contrasts the *DSM* definitions of various personality disorders with the more traditional psychodynamic understanding of the core pathologies involved). Since the Axis II diagnosis is by definition *DSM* based, while the underlying theoretical disorder bears a variable relationship to the diagnosis, what is one really measuring change in? Given the initial emphasis on grouping by structured diagnosis, the politics of research pull for measuring changes in the *diagnosis itself* (i.e., changes in criteria with unclear or unknown relationship to the underlying hypothetical constructs, which are themselves often unclear or unknown at this point in time). This situation makes assessing change in personality disorders a far more nebulous affair than assessing change in diagnoses such as depression, specific phobias, eating and substance abuse disorders, and so on.

The Problem of Axis I and Axis II Comorbidity

The term *comorbidity* is a generic term that may actually cover a variety of conceptually distinct relationships among disorders. Typically, the "problem of comorbidity" in Axis II refers either to (a) the high rate of patients receiving multiple Axis II diagnoses or (b) the correlations between various Axis I and Axis II disorders. Tyrer (1995), drawing on Winokur (1990), detailed a more precise list of the possible theoretical relationships among diagnostic entities, with an emphasis on Axis I and Axis II comorbidity. These relationships include two possibilities with particular implications for Axis II change measurement: consanguinity and cosyndromal conditions.

---

[2] For example, in the case of dependent personality disorder, changes from *DSM–III* to *DSM–III–R* to *DSM–IV* change the meaning of dependency variously from a disorder based on perceived instrumental inadequacy to a concept closer to that of self-defeating personality.

The term *consanguinity* refers to the case in which the same "disease process" occurs in different forms across Axes I and II. For example, the high coincidence of substance abuse disorders and Cluster B personality disorders, or between anxiety disorders and Cluster C personality disorders may be explained on the basis that the Axis I and Axis II diagnoses are simply different manifestations of the same underlying pathology. Tyrer et al. (1983) noted that the old term *neuroses* is actually such a consanguineous diagnosis because it refers to a mix of Axis I symptoms (e.g., anxiety, depression, somatization, etc.) and Axis II traits (e.g., dependency, obsessionality, etc.). The idea of consanguinity pulls for a single cross-axis diagnostic category in which features of both axes would be required, explaining much so-called comorbidity. In fact, the "Slater axiom" (Slater, Beard, & Glithero, 1968) states that "when the association of two diagnoses is much greater than expected by chance the two conditions should be regarded as part of the same diagnosis until proved otherwise."

The term *cosyndromal condition* refers to the case in which two or more diagnoses are present, they are not directly related causally (as is the case in consanguinity), but they do not occur together by chance. In terms of Axis II research, this would suggest that certain personality factors serve as a diathesis for the development of certain Axis I conditions (e.g., eating disorders, panic disorders, depression, etc.). That is, a certain personality disorder or cluster may differentially predispose individuals to certain groups of Axis I disorders. For example, Nestadt, Romanoski, Samuels, Folstein, and McHugh (1992) found that higher compulsive personality scores were associated with greater odds of generalized anxiety disorder and simple phobia. Interestingly, some personality traits that may be dysfunctional in some contexts might also serve as *protective* factors against the development of certain Axis I disorders. In the Nestadt et al. study, for instance, higher scores on compulsivity were also correlated with a lower risk for alcohol use disorders.

How do these two instances of comorbidity effect our understanding of the measurement of change in Axis II disorders? In the first case (consanguinity), the idea of change in personality disorder per se would be seen as fallacious along traditional outcome measurement lines. This is so because the "true" disorder is neither a personality nor a symptom disorder but some unidentified core pathology giving rise to both simultaneously. To truly measure change would thus require identifying and operationalizing the coaxial dimension of pathology.

In the second case (cosyndromal conditions) one could, in a strict sense, measure changes in Axis II independently, but this might lead to a variety of potentially false conclusions about therapeutic change in general. For example, it seems possible that a personality diathesis might lead to an Axis I disorder (e.g., panic disorder) and that the secondary sequelae of the Axis I disorder would further entrench the Axis II disorder. Thus, the much-noted difficulty in changing personality disorders might not only be the result of the relative intransigence of the Axis II condition per se but could also reflect the secondary effects of the Axis I disorder. A reverse possibility relates to the known tendency for Axis II assessments to be affected by the presence of Axis I disorders. Change in the Axis I condition may cause what appears to be but is actually artifactual change in Axis II because the assessment of Axis II status was initially colored by the Axis I symptoms.

The Problem of Comorbidity Among Personality Disorders

It has been asked somewhat facetiously, but not without a note of seriousness, If a person has only one personality, can he or she have more than one personality disorder? According to studies based on *DSM* diagnostic criteria, the answer is clearly yes. Two empirical findings are routinely cited to call into question the validity of the current set of Axis II diagnoses. First, if an individual qualifies for an Axis II diagnosis at all, he or she typically qualifies for two to three separate personality disorder diagnoses (see Morey, 1993). Furthermore, the modal Axis II diagnosis is "personality disorder not otherwise specified." These facts suggest a fundamentally flawed nosology.

If the categorical nosology itself is fundamentally flawed,[3] what does this say about change measurement? As in the case of consanguineous Axis I and Axis II diagnoses, Axis II comorbidity suggests that the actual

---

[3] I acknowledge that there is a certain amount of clinical "folk wisdom" in the various Axis II disorders. Clinicians do indeed see patients who resemble avoidant, dependent, or compulsive, personality types. Nonetheless, the empirical data suggest that as a formal nosology proposing distinct syndromes analogous to medical diseases, DSM has not exactly carved nature at its joints.

changes one should be examining if one is to truly understand change processes occur in the more fundamental underlying dimensions of core pathological processes, not in their surface manifestations as highly inter-correlated *DSM* descriptors. There are basically three nonbiological approaches to identifying these underlying dimensions for the purpose of change measurement.[4]

The first method is to formulate the dimensions from within *DSM* itself. This typically involves either factor analysis or multidimensional scaling of (a) the disorders themselves, transformed into continuous variables by creating scale scores for each diagnosis based on the number of criteria met (Zimmerman & Coryell, 1990), or (b) the entire set of Axis II descriptors, treated as separate dichotomous or continuous variables making up one large item pool (Ekselius, Lindstrom, von Knorring, Bodlund, & Kullgren, 1994). Interestingly, these studies typically reveal two to four dimensions with considerable conceptual overlap across methodologies and subject samples.

The second, more purely psychometric method, also based on factor analysis, involves the attempt to delineate the dimensions of normal personality from pools of descriptive but atheoretical items such as trait labels. Personality disorders are conceptualized within the same framework used to define normal personality, with pathology defined quantitatively as extremes on a normally distributed continuum of trait dimensions. The five-factor model (McCrae & Costa, 1987) is clearly the current consensus structure of personality developed with this methodology.

Finally, core dimensions of pathology may be constructed along more theoretical lines. For example, Millon (1996) grouped 15 proposed personality disorders into four main categories, with each category representing a different fundamental dimension of pathology: pleasure-deficient personality, interpersonally imbalanced personality styles, intrapsychically conflicted personalities, and structurally deficient personalities. A simple system was proposed by Henry (1994) based on the Structural Analysis of Social Behavior (SASB; Benjamin, 1974). He defined abnormal personality

---

[4]The biological models of core pathology (e.g., Cloninger, 1987: Eysenck, 1990; Siever & Davis, 1991) offer interesting alternative strategies but are beyond the scope of this chapter.

qualitatively based on attachment theory and the basic drives for bonding (enmeshment) and exploration (differentiation). Individuals with personality disorders were divided into two primary subgroups organized around distinct wish–fear axes as plotted on the SASB circumplex. One group fears being controlled (hostile enmeshment) and wishes for autonomy from others (friendly differentiation), whereas the other group fears hostile differentiation (abandonment) and wishes for loving enmeshment (nurturance and protection).

Clearly, while each of these three strategies do attempt to grapple with the problem of categorical comorbidity, they have different implications for how to define change in Axis II pathology. The dimensions measured may range from the surface, descriptive, atheoretical level to the level of core hypothetical structures and processes (i.e., genotypes) giving rise to the phenotypic regularities. Neither measurement strategy (searching for genotypes by discovering phenotypic regularities or proposing genotypes and searching for the phenotypic invariances) is necessarily correct or incorrect. Most would likely agree that similar underlying pathologies may give rise to varying surface manifestations in different people or in the same person at different times. Likewise, similar descriptive constellations may be the result of much different underlying motivation or pathogenesis. These are fundamental issues in experimental psychopathology and nosology.

I do not, however, typically hear these fundamental issues discussed within the framework of outcome or change assessment. In the long run, how can researchers meaningfully measure change without confronting how the problem is defined to begin with? This is the point at which basic scientific questions, pragmatic measurement issues, and systemic politics[5] square off. I have more to say about these conflicts and their potential resolutions later; for the moment, let me simply acknowledge that it is understandable that for some purposes, one might be interested in measuring Axis II change in terms of tangible results (e.g., substance abuse, lost workdays, etc.) with no concern for underlying dimensions of path-

---

[5] I use the term *systemic politics* to refer to a variety of concerns ranging from the experimental paradigms required for research funding to the economic dictates of managed health care.

ology. On the other hand, the data collected are the basis for our empirical science. In short, in choosing outcome instruments, researchers are also de facto shaping our thinking and the data available for fundamental theoretical questions.

Personality Versus Disorder and the
Variable Meanings of Change Across Disorders

A final area in which a theoretical discussion is crucial to shaping the eventual pragmatics of change measurement is found in the very term *personality disorder*. As commonly used, the term seems to suggest a single "thing," a categorical pathology akin to a disease (e.g., "So and so "*has*" a personality disorder"). For both theoretical and practical measurement reasons, it may be more accurate and profitable to separate the "personality" and the "disorder" components. It is likely the case that the personality component, however defined (except in strict behavioral terms), is more stable across time and contexts than the disorder component, which may manifest itself to a greater or lesser extent depending on current stressors (Rutter, cited in Parker, 1995). Parker (1995) commented on this distinction:

> In addressing the need for a measure of "disorder," there would appear to be distinct advantages to building on such an approach, perhaps by operationalizing such a matrix across intimate and family relationships as well as across work and work relationships, weighted to their expression when the individual is "stressed." . . . Such a measure should allow an individual to reach PD status "at home and/or at work," so respecting a practical reality—that some PD subjects perform adequately (if not prosper) in some environments while creating problems (if not calamities) in other environments. (p. 7)

For most purposes, when it comes to measuring change or outcome following interventions, researchers are usually concerned with changes in the disorder components. Unfortunately, space limitations do not permit an adequate discussion of the differences and interrelationships among the personality and disorder variables. Brief examples of this distinction can be found in the theories of Millon (1996) and Henry (1994), referred to earlier. For example, individuals exhibiting what Millon called the "inter-personally imbalanced pattern" all share a common disorder insofar as disorder is defined in terms of a marked imbalance in self versus other orientation. However, differing personality types (i.e., dependent, narcis-sistic, and antisocial) may be seen to share this "self–other" disorder. Similarly, although those with narcissistic and compulsive personalities may share a common fear of control (hostile enmeshment) and wish for ac-knowledgment (friendly differentiation), their respective underlying per-sonality traits are markedly different (Henry, 1994). In summary, while there are clear correlations between certain personality styles (e.g., border-line personality organization) and certain disorder components (e.g., self-damaging behavioral impulsivity), the two should be seen separately for measurement purposes as well as for the purposes of basic science. Core disorders, such as an inability to internally regulate a coherent self-identity and an inability to adequately differentiate from significant others, vary across the different Axis II diagnoses. This might suggest that for measure-ment and treatment purposes, researchers should construct a problem or disorder taxonomy reflective of interpersonal dysfunctions but distinct from personality types per se. This approach might also aid in understand-ing how basic personality styles serve as diatheses for the development of certain disorder components.

Pragmatic Problems in Axis II Change Measurement

All factors that affect the description of a patient's initial state (whether that description is in the form of formal diagnosis or some other variable) also obviously affect the validity of attempts to measure change in this state. Forget for the moment the larger problems of the questionable va-lidity of the *DSM* categorical personality disorders themselves or the vari-ous theoretical possibilities for identifying underlying core dimensions of pathology. From within the framework of the standard nosology itself, ini-tial measurement and diagnosis are fraught with problems. These prob-lems have been discussed so frequently that I will not belabor the point here (for an excellent review of the issues and empirical research in the area of diagnosing personality disorders, see Zimmerman, 1994). Briefly, however, the major pragmatic difficulties in Axis II assessment, and hence assessment of Axis II change, include the problem of self-report, the level of inference, the effect of Axis I state on Axis II assessment, and reliability versus validity of the measured construct.

Regarding the problem of self-report, Axis II disorders present a number of particular difficulties in assessment via self-report instruments. First, asking an individual to accurately report on his or her own personality processes is more problematic than asking the same individual to report on more objective symptoms such as weight loss. This is particularly true given that the individual is being assessed for a personality disorder, which by definition may limit self-insight. For example, the narcissistic individual does not view himself or herself as grandiose, which is a central diagnostic descriptor. Therefore, in constructing Axis II self-report tests, it is much more difficult to translate the descriptors into items that an individual with that disorder will endorse. Additionally, the potential difficulty in translating a diagnostic descriptor into its underlying phenomenology from the patient's perspective varies greatly across disorders. These problems also hold true to a certain extent in the structured interview. Furthermore, although interview-based data may be superior in some respects (e.g., questions can be clarified, examples elicited, and the patient's interactional style assessed), even highly structured interview formats cannot be standardized to the extent of paper-and-pencil measures. The alternative to self-report is to rely on collateral informants. The evidence to date suggests that the agreement between the two sources is notoriously poor (e.g., Zimmerman, Pfohl, Coryell, Stangl, & Corenthal, 1988, reported a kappa of only .13). In general, informants tend to report more personality pathology than does the patient (Zimmerman, 1994). Is one method more valid than the other? A discussion of this issue is beyond the scope of this chapter, (see Zimmerman, 1994), but suffice it to say that the issue is thorny and attempts to combine sources of information are equally problematic.

Regarding the level of inference, it is well documented that the interrater reliability of diagnosis is lower among the Axis II disorders than the Axis I disorders. This may be due partly to the greater level of inference or clinical judgment required to determine the presence or absence of a given descriptor in many cases. Additionally, the relative level of inference also varies greatly across specific criteria and disorders (Shea, 1992). Examples of low-inference items might include "irritability and aggressiveness, as indicated by repeated physical fights or assaults" (antisocial); "recurrent sucidal behavior, gestures, or threats, or self-mutilating behavior" (borderline); "inappropriate or constricted affect" (schizotypal); or "urgently seeks another relationship as a source of care and support when a close relationship ends" (dependent). Higher inference and clinical judgment may be required to determine the presence of descriptors such as "chronic feelings of emptiness" (borderline); "considers relationships to be more intimate than they actually are" (histrionic); "shows perfectionism that interferes with task completion" (obsessive–compulsive); or "behavior or appearance that is odd, eccentric, or peculiar" (schizotypal). Clearly, if initial judgments are more inferential, estimates of change are more open to the vagaries of interrater differences as well.

Regarding the effect of Axis I state on Axis II assessment, it is likely the case that while conducting initial interviews, most clinicians first assess a patient's Axis I disorder(s) and only secondarily consider additional Axis II diagnoses. This is problematic because an individual's specific Axis I condition may variously color the initial assessment of personality traits and disorder. As a result, changes over time in the Axis I symptom picture may lead to false estimates of personality change because the traits were falsely assessed to begin with (i.e., the so-called "traits" were actually temporary state manifestations of the symptom). For example, Hirschfeld et al. (1983) compared self-report personality inventories of patients while clinically depressed with their scores 1 year later. They found that depression strongly influenced patients' reports of emotional strength, interpersonal dependency, and extraversion but that it did not affect reports of rigidity, activity level, and dominance.

Regarding the reliability versus validity of the measured construct, some of the most psychometrically reliable constructs to measure may also be some of the least important depending on the purpose of change measurement. This is not to denigrate reliable measures. Indeed, I consider a number of the measurement domains recommended by the personality disorder task force to be both relatively reliable *and* important assessments of functional capacities (e.g., social role functioning, health care behaviors, specific behavioral excesses and deficits, symptom status, global life satisfaction, etc.). At a more basic conceptual level, underlying descriptive trait dimensions may also be measured reliably (such as the dimensions of the five-factor model). Although many low-inference, functional measures are important in terms of assessing the practical benefits of intervention, they are not tied to any underlying theory either of disorder or of change. Assessing change for the purpose of basic science research (theory development and confirmation) may require some initial sacrifice in both reliability and perceived relevance. Core theoretical constructs (e.g., prototypic object images related to early social learning, wish–fear conflicts, and defenses) and the internal mechanisms that govern the processes by which these constructs interact to produce dysfunctional patterns of cognition, affect, and behavior may be more important to the ultimate understanding of change and its determinants. Thus, I consider such change data vital, even though it may currently be less psychometrically reliable and of no immediate relevance to sources such as third-party payers. In short, in considering instruments to adopt for a core battery, I believe that it is important to balance atheoretical descriptive measures that serve immediate goals with more theoretical constructs that serve the longer range goal of theory development and testing.

WHAT SHOULD BE MEASURED? PRAGMATIC AND THEORETICAL POSSIBILITIES

The foregoing discussions lead to a crucial distinction: Are researchers to measure changes in personality disorders (as an intervening variable) per se or changes in *individuals* with a personality disorder? This is not an abstract semantic distinction but a central question that guides the entire process of thinking about measuring changes related to Axis II disorders. Because the *DSM* has *defined* personality disorders for the current generation of clinicians and researchers, it is natural to think of change directly in terms of *DSM* diagnoses, criteria, or both. This heuristic structure pulls for conceptualizing change as change in the disorder rather than in the individual with the disorder. Furthermore, the "disorder" is defined descriptively and atheoretically at the level of surface manifestations. This approach has advantages in terms of greater reliability of measurement achieved by lowering the level of inference required. Conversely, it also has drawbacks insofar as it basically ignores underlying mechanisms of the pathology in which change is supposedly being assessed.

Change in the *DSM*-Defined Disorder

Categorical Change

By far, the simplest procedure is simply to conduct repeated structured interviews pre- and postintervention. Does the patient still qualify for the diagnosis? If so, the treatment has not been successful, and if not, the patient has been "cured." The problems with this procedure, which focuses on change in the diagnosis rather than the individual, should be obvious. If a taxonomic syndrome truly exists in nature, there should be a naturally occuring discontinuity in the number of criteria met that clearly separates a normal from a disordered population. In the case of *DSM*-defined personality disorders this is clearly not the case, as the number of descriptors met tends to be normally distributed, with no natural point of rarity (Clark, 1992). The cut points for diagnosis (i.e., five of nine, etc.) are arbitrary. If five of nine criteria are necessary for establishing the presence of a syndrome, and a patient qualifying for the diagnosis on the basis of five criteria drops to four posttreatment, the treatment has succeeded. A patient dropping from nine criteria to five might have actually manifested far greater change but would still be considered a categorical treatment failure.

DSM Descriptors as Continuous Scales

An alternative strategy is to treat the number of criteria met for each diagnosis as a continuous scale tapping the severity of the disorder (Moldin, Rice, Erlenmeyer-Kimling, & Squires-Wheeler, 1994; Widiger, Trull, Hurt, Clarkin, & Frances, 1987; Zimmerman & Coryell, 1990). Although this approach allows for greater gradation in change measurement as opposed to the categorical distinction, it still suffers from numerous conceptual problems. For example, it treats each descriptor equally, as if each descriptor contributes the same "quantity of pathology" to the overall disorder. The empirical data, however, indicate that individual descriptors vary widely in their correlation with the overall presence or absence of the disorder (see Clark, 1992, and Shea, 1992, for excellent overviews of specific problems with *DSM* personality disorder descriptors). In other words, some descriptors (intervening variables) are more central to the core concept of the disorder (the hypothetical construct) than others. An additional problem is raised by disorders that contain distinct underlying components, such as borderline personality disorder which is generally regarded to contain three to four separate dimensions (e.g., intense anger and mood liability; unstable interpersonal relationships; identity disturbance; and an impulsive, self-damaging behavioral style). In this approach to change measurement, changes in descriptors related to each of these dimensions are treated equally when clinically they have quite different meanings and functional implications. Of coarse, this approach, while more dimensional on the surface, also implicitly endorses the validity of the supposed categorical syndrome the descriptive scale measures. Conceptually, this is a highly questionable assumption due to: (a) the high base rate of comorbid Axis II diagnoses; (b) the lack of a naturally occurring point of rarity in the distribution of descriptors for each disorder; and (c) the likelihood that the true underlying constructs are consanguinious, cutting across both axes, as discussed earlier.

DSM Descriptors as Factor-Analytic Dimensions

A final *DSM*-based approach is to combine the entire set of Axis II descriptors, treating them as a large item pool to be reduced through factor analysis in order to establish the underlying core dimensions of pathology (Ekselius et al., 1994). I consider this to be a transitional strategy, occupying a conceptual space somewhere between the purely descriptive, syndromal, or medical approach and purely theoretical dimensional models of core pathology. This methodology has its strengths and weaknesses. On the one hand, the dimensional factors do focus more on the individual rather than on the diagnosis. The factors may have some coherent unidimensional meaning (see Clark & Watson, 1995) and at the least are almost sure to be more conceptually pure than simply treating the descriptors for each disorder as separate scales. The derived factors are based on items that, although technically descriptive and atheoretical, are also the product of a good amount of clinical observation and "folk wisdom." As such, this *DSM*-based factor-analytic approach may help further theory generation.

On the other hand, one cannot escape the constraints of the *DSM* item pool. As discussed earlier, when talking about personality disorders, one is really referring to hypothetical constructs. The *DSM* item pool consists of the intervening variables that are not the same as, nor do they exhaust the meaning of, the underlying constructs. To limit the search for core dimensions of pathology to the *DSM* descriptors is simply a more subtle form of mistakenly equating intervening variables and hypothetical constructs.

Change in Individuals With Personality Disorders

An alternative perspective is to conceptualize change from the standpoint of the individual who *secondarily* belongs to a certain *DSM* diagnostic category. This approach opens up many new possibilities for conceptualizing Axis II change.[6] These possibilities include but are not limited to (a) a more clear separation and hence measurement of the personality versus the disorder components of Axis II pathology; (b) the measurement of increases in positive variables (e.g., self-efficacy, coherence of self-concept, positive states of mind, adaptive role functioning, etc.) as an addition to exclusive focus on reduction in negative variables; (c) changes not just in the problem(s), but also in the coping mechanisms related to these problematic states or traits (e.g., cognitive control processes, maturity of defenses, etc.); and (d) changes in potential cognitive and perceptual distortions that drive (and confirm via self-fulfilling prophecies) prototypic expectations of self and others. In short, focus on the individual, not the descriptive diagnosis, should encourage more theory-driven research into the underlying or core dimensions of personality pathology, how this pathology is manifested as a *process* (not a static description), and how various pathological personality processes serve as diatheses for the development of behavioral disorders or functional problems.

---

[6] I am actually not as "anti-*DSM*" as perhaps my reasoning in this chapter might suggest. I think that *DSM* has performed a vital service by drawing attention to Axis II disorders and has more than fulfilled the mission to stimulate research in this area. Furthermore, clinicians do see patients that certainly fit criteria for various personality disorders, and terms such as "narcissistic," "paranoid," or "avoidant" do quickly convey the "flavor" of the pathology. I would rather have *DSM* to refer to, think about, and react to than not to have it at all. I simply do not believe that it should serve as the basic practical structure or conceptual heuristic to guide assessment, theory generation, or change measurement (or at the least it should not be regarded as the *only* guiding structure).

Levels of Analysis

Eysenck (1990) proposed that models of personality should be hierarchical in nature, incorporating four levels of analysis: singular *behaviors* or cognitions; frequently co-occurring or habitual behaviors and cognitions that constitute *habits;* significantly intercorrelated habitual acts that constitute *traits;* and higher order factors or *dimensions* based on intercorrelated traits. This hierarchical model provides at least one heuristic with which to conceptualize change measurement. What are the pros and cons of each level as they relate to measuring change in individuals with personality disorders? To answer this question, researchers must consider five somewhat interrelated factors: (a) the purpose of content domain of the assessment; (b) the values of the target audience most concerned with the assessment (i.e., the individual, the family, third-party payers, employers, research scientists, or society at large); (c) the definition of personality; (d) the definitions of disorder; and (e) possible relationships between the personality and the disorder. In other words, one cannot, or at least should not, assess change in a vacuum apart from a careful consideration of these five factors.

Assessment Domains and Value Structures

The personality disorders group tried to construct a set of measurement domains that focused on changes in the individual with Axis II pathology that adequately covered the range of possible contents, purposes, and target audiences. For example, possible purposes or contents might include assessment of changes in functional impairment in a specific role context (e.g., employee, parent or spouse), changes in coherence of self-concept, changes in the perceived quality of life, changes directly related to specific treatment target goals (i.e., therapeutic efficacy), changes in comorbid Axis I symptoms, changes in underlying dimensions to assess the relative malleability of proposed genotypic variables (i.e., basic research), and so forth.

Detailing a structure of content domains is just the beginning, however. Target audiences and values must also be considered. While the purpose, the content, the target audience, and related values are related, they are not necessarily isomorphic. For example, the domain of Axis I symptom reduction might be related to much different values if the audience is the individual with the disorder (who is interested in relieving personal distress), an employer (who might be most interested in enhanced productivity and profit), or the third-party payer (who might be most interested in decreased medical utilization). A complete discussion of how domains and values relate to the pros and cons of specific levels of analysis is beyond the scope of this chapter. However, in general, it is likely that patients themselves may often be concerned with broader life changes that may ultimately require changes in the higher order levels of analysis, whereas other sources may have more specific values related to single acts or habits. My point is that when researchers shift away from thinking of change as change in the diagnosis per se, they enter a much more complex arena of possibilities. This shift requires some guiding format for appropriate instrument selection. Such a format should attempt to match the level of analysis of selected measures to the assessment need on the basis of *domain, target audience,* and *value structure.*

Definitions of Personality, Disorder, and Their Relationship

The final layer of complexity regarding Axis II change measurement emerges if one tries to articulate the aforementioned considerations (e.g., domain, values, level of analysis, etc.) with theoretical models of personality, definitions of disorder, and the relationships between the two. However, I believe that such an integration is essential if researchers are to develop a true science of change measurement related to personality disorders. I see this as an enterprise that not only advances basic research but may also significantly improve the ability to measure change for practical reasons that may not be related directly to theoretical concerns.

Once again, unfortunately, a discussion of various models of personality is beyond the scope of this chapter. For the purposes of change measurement, there is one broad distinction that should be mentioned. Is the relationship between "normal" and "abnormal" personality quantitative or qualitative? In other words, does pathological personality represent simply an extreme variant of normal traits that are distributed on a continuum, or can qualitative boundaries be drawn (for an excellent book on this subject, see Strack & Lorr, 1994)? Clearly, this distinction would tend to guide change assessment closer to or farther away from normal models of personality that emphasize measurement along continuously distributed dimensions.

There are many possible nonexclusive ways of defining the disorder component. Disorder may be defined in terms of specific surface or behavioral manifestations (e.g., parasuicidal acts, substance abuse, social withdrawal, etc.) that negatively affect the individual, other people, or both. Disorder can also be located or defined as an underlying trait that presumably drives the surface manifestation (i.e., impulsiveness, harm avoidance, introversion, etc.) or as an underlying cognitive process (e.g., prototypic object images based on early social learning that serve to drive interpersonal expectancies, wishes, and fears). Disorder may also be seen as a qualitative or quantitative deviation from a hypothesized normal structure (e.g., the extremes of a factor-analytic dimension, excesses or deficits in a specific neurochemical system, extreme manifestations of normal traits as measured by the interpersonal circumplex, pathological rigidity of behavior that is not sensitive to context, etc.). How one chooses to define disorder is in some respects arbitrary because the hypothetical constructs of core pathology can doubtless be seen, thought of, and measured in all of these ways. The important point is not the specific definition of disorder per se but the coherence with which a theoretical model of personality is linked with the various possible ways disorder may be manifest and measured at each of the foregoing levels (i.e., behavioral, cognitive, biological, etc.).

This linking involves articulating the various possible relationships between personality and disorder. Morey (1993) listed seven possible relationships:

> (1) Certain personality constellations may *predispose* an individual to certain disorders; (2) personality may *modify* the presentation of certain disorders; (3) certain personality features may be a *complication* of certain disorders; (4) certain personality features may reflect an *attenuated expression* of certain disorders; (5) neither personality features or Axis I disorders have a single specific causal factor, but rather both arise from many *common sources;* . . . (6) certain personality features and certain disorders may be two different manifestations of a *third causal process* (that may be either substantive or stylistic in nature); and (7) the observed co-occurrence may

entirely be an *artifact* of diagnostic strategies and may reflect the poor discriminant validity of our diagnostic techniques.

RECOMMENDATIONS

In this chapter I have attempted to delineate and explore many of the conceptual conundrums that make measuring change in personality disorders such a challenge. The solutions to all of these issues will not come easily or quickly, and some may never come. No doubt the future of Axis II change measurement will be shaped by a variety of interacting forces, including accumulating empirical evidence, advances in theory, the specific focus of researchers who produce the most interesting and compelling data, the politics of science and research funding, the limits of various assessment techniques, and the shifting balance of systemic influence by various special interests (such as managed care, patient consumer groups, etc.). I would like to conclude with some modest personal recommendations that I break down into two categories. The first category includes general strategies to guide the selection of specific measures as well as the more general development of change measurement as a science. I feel that these suggestions are applicable to the field as a whole. I conclude with my own specific, theoretically driven vision of Axis II change.

General Strategies

I do not believe that the process of recommending a core battery for the assessment of change in personality disorders should simply be a matter of selecting a collection of instruments deemed to be the best of their sort at the present time. The recommendation of a comprehensive set of domains to be assessed is an important step beyond the simple listing of instruments, but that too is not enough. I say this because I believe that the purpose of the task force on change measurement should transcend the *content* of assessment and even go beyond providing a coherent structure for the selected content domains. How best to shape the *process* should also be considered carefully. That is, how will current recommendations shape the future development of change measures and indeed the basic science of personality pathology? In this spirit, then, I suggest the following general principles.

1. Do not reify *DSM* diagnoses in thinking or research design. In the long run, it will be more generative to think of change core pathologies or hypothetical constructs as they relate to the individual with a personality disorder, not to think in terms in terms of changes in the *DSM* disorder per se. Following from this is the idea that because of consanguinious and cosyndromal conditions, comprehensive measurement in Axis II change should include measures of Axis I as well. That is, the underlying dysfunctions manifest as Axis II disorders may often be coaxial in nature. Artificially separating the axes for the purpose of change measurement encourages a diagnostic status quo that will work against study of the true genotypes.[7]

2. Pursue a taxonomy of *disorder types* that may cut across various personality styles, traits, and so on. As noted earlier, although the *DSM* tends to categorize dysfunctional personality types (i.e., lumping together the personality and disorder components), individuals with highly different personality traits may share similar disorders. For some purposes of change measurement, it may be the disorder component that is most crucial to isolate and assess directly.[8]

3. Change measurement should encompass more than decreases in identified pathological states and traits. It should be recognized that many manifestations of problematic Axis II personality traits may remain in individuals who have nonetheless changed in important and adaptive ways. These might include measures such as increases in positive states (even though negative states continue); increases in perceived control over problems (although problems remain); changes in coping strategies that have been linked to better long-term adjustment (Vollrath, Alnaes, & Torgersen, 1995); change in the relative balance of optimism–pessimism or percentage of time spent in best versus worst states; and decreases in the prevalence of interpersonal problems across situations (i.e., the ability to engage adaptively in at least some interpersonal contexts).

---

[7] I do not mean to suggest that symptom measures can or should be distinct from interpersonal measures in practice. I do mean to say that insofar as procedures for change measurement affect conceptualizations of core pathology, one would be wise not to focus exclusively on measures directly related to the Axis II descriptors for each disorder.

[8] Bronisch and Klerman (1991) proposed a related idea in that they attempted to separate the concept of personality *functioning* from personality per se and from symptoms.

4. Include measures that promote basic science research (such as those that might identify core coaxial dimensions of pathology). These measures might be aimed primarily at the descriptive understanding of initial pathology and might not be envisioned as change measures per se, at least in the practical sense. However, they might prove valuable in predicting the relative probability of other forms of change. I say this because I have heard increasing concern voiced by researchers that including basic measures that might not be expected to change significantly (at least in the context of brief interventions) is a political risk because third-party payment may be endangered unless all change assessments show large effect sizes. This is an important concern given that managed care agencies are increasingly the main collection source for therapy outcome or change data. Researchers should not compromise the process of basic research for such short-term political agendas.

A Specific Proposal

In conclusion, I would like to briefly outline my own theoretically driven ideas about measuring change in personality disorders. I realize that this is only one of a number of possible valid approaches. I present it as an illustration of the more general principles I feel should ultimately guide the development of thinking about Axis II change and constructing measurement instruments. Specifically, the model I describe links (a) a concrete definition of abnormal personality that is based on basic primate and attachment research; (b) a theory of etiology based on social learning that includes several basic dimensions of pathology; (c) an explanation of how these dimensions account for multiple Axis II diagnoses as well as coaxial consanguinity; and (d) a measurement metric that is uniform across the domains of problem definition, treatment process, and change measurement. For a complete discussion of these principles, see Henry (1994), Henry (1996), and Benjamin (1993a, 1993b).

Early research and writing in the field of motivation emphasized primary biological drives (e.g., hunger, sex, etc.). Bowlby (1977), in proposing his attachment theory, also posited innate interpersonal drives: attachment seeking (bonding or enmeshment) and exploration (or differentiation in interpersonal terms). Early interpersonal transactions with important caretakers, organized around the twin drives of attachment and differentiation, create prototypical cognitive structures or mental representations of the self and others in interaction. These prototypes tend to produce self-confirming expectancies that keep the cognitive structures relatively stable over time. Personality is defined as "the mental operations associated with internal representations of self and others in interaction as made manifest in [observable] interpersonal behavior" (Henry, 1994, p. 324; see also Benjamin, 1994). In other words, personality is defined directly in terms of interpersonal behavior. Normal personality is defined as a base rate of behavior that represents a balance between friendly interpersonal enmeshment and friendly interpersonal differentiation, because these conditions are consistent with successfully fulfilling Bowlby's postulated basic drives of bonding and exploration.

There are hypothesized to be three basic etiological processes through which social learning based on early interpersonal transactions occurs, forming the basis for the interpersonal actions that are labeled *personality* and *personality disorder*. These are *identification* (i.e., directly copying or imitating behavior); *internalization* (i.e., mental representations of the actions of others toward the self, which shape expectancies); and *introjection* (i.e., the process by which one comes to act toward the self as he or she has been treated by others). As these three processes are considered normative, it might be said that the true locus of pathology is the environment—or early social learning. Either normal or pathological patterns are maintained because the prototypical object images create expectancies that drive an individual's actions or reactions toward others. The actions and reactions are entrenched because they pull for complementary actions by others, which tend to confirm the initial expectancy. For example, an individual who sees others as critical expects criticism and behaves in a manner that ultimately "pulls for" criticism. A personality disorder is defined as a baseline of interpersonal behavior that is either overly enmeshed or overly differentiated. The most general principle that guides the development and understanding of a personality disorder is the proposal that the interpersonal dimensionality of early experience (along the axes of affiliation–disaffiliation and dominance–submission or differentiation) matches the interpersonal dimensionality of the adult disorder (regardless of specific behaviors, trait labels, etc.).

Benjamin (1993a) did a masterful job of translating the *DSM* personality disorder descriptors into interpersonal codes based on the fundamental interpersonal circumplex axes as operationalized in the SASB system (Benjamin, 1974). SASB describes behaviors that are either active (focused on others), reactive (focused on self), or introjective (acts by the self toward the self). These behaviors may be affiliative or disaffiliative and are either controlling, submissive, autonomous (granting or taking autonomy), or a simultaneous complex blend of affiliation, interdependence, or both. By examining the way in which various *DSM* personality disorder descriptors translate into specific interpersonal codes in SASB, one can begin to understand the observed comorbidity of Axis II diagnoses. For example, although avoidant and dependent disorders seem to be opposites in that the avoidant may be seen as overly differentiated, while the dependent is overly enmeshed, there is nonetheless a high degree of dual diagnoses of these disorders. An examination of Benjamin's SASB codes for each disorder reveals that they are identical on 50% of their respective interpersonal codes (Benjamin, 1993a, p. 394). Another example is the noted comorbidity of Cluster B disorders (i.e., borderline, antisocial, histrionic, and narcissistic). All Cluster B descriptors together translate into 14 distinct interpersonal SASB codes. Seventy-nine percent of these codes are found in at least two of the four disorders, and about a third of the codes overlap in at least three of the disorders, if not all of them. In short, the interpersonal translation of *dimensionality* of the disorders reveals the similarities and comorbidities among the Axis II diagnoses much more clearly than the *content* of the diagnostic descriptors.

Consanguinity can also be understood by following this procedure of dimensional translation using the interpersonal circumplex. For instance, it has been hypothesized (Benjamin, 1993a) that individuals with borderline personality disorder were routinely subject to harsh criticism and attack followed by periods of total abandonment. The SASB codes for these experiences would be Clusters 1–6 (blame), 1–7 (attack), and 1–8 (ignore). In dimensional terms, these developmental experiences represent exposure to hostile control (overly enmeshed), pure disaffiliation (hate), and hostile autonomy granting (overly differentiated). The internalized image of an abandoning other leads to expectations of being abandoned and hence to perceptual distortions that one is indeed being abandoned. Identification with hostile control and pure disaffiliation explains the rage and desperate attempts of the person with borderline personality disorder to coerce significant others who are perceived as abandoning. The introjection of blame and abandonment can be seen in Axis I symptoms. That is, self-blame and hatred may account for the noted comorbidity with depression, whereas self-abandonment, in dimensional terms, translates into Axis I diagnoses such as substance abuse disorders. In summary, the same interpersonal learning history as copied via identification, internalization, and introjection can be seen to manifest itself interpersonally and intrapsychically in the adult as both Axis I and Axis II symptoms sharing similar dimensionality.

The model I have outlined has clear-cut implications for measuring Axis II change in general. To begin with, personality is defined directly in terms of interpersonal behavior, which suggests that changes in specific interpersonal behaviors (Eysenck's, 1990, Level 1) and patterns of co-occurring behaviors (Eysenck's Level 2: habits, or baseline patterns) should be measured. The advantage of the theoretical model is that behavioral change is not measured in isolation. Rather, there is a framework within which to coherently conceptualize or organize various changes. In broad strokes, changes in specific acts or baseline patterns would be conceptualized as moves away from pathological overenmeshment or hostile differentiation and toward a more balanced and friendly pattern of moderate enmeshment coupled with moderate autonomy. At a more cognitive level, it would also be possible and desirable to measure changes in internalized object images and the distorted or maladaptive expectancies, unfulfilled wishes, and unrealistic fears associated with them that drive the observable interpersonal behaviors.

SUMMARY

I believe that several very basic things happen when individuals with personality disorders change for the better. First, I think that their perceptions and expectancies of others become more benign and realistic. Second, I believe that a general sense of self-efficacy is enhanced. Behaviorally, these changes are manifest as more flexibility, defined as a greater range of inter-personal behaviors that are more context appropriate. Internally, these changes may be reflected in the abandonment of archaic fears of or wishes to please the internalized images of early significant others (see Benjamin, 1993b) and changes in acts by the self toward the self (introject change). These changes are in turn reflected in more adaptive interpersonal strate-gies designed to secure the basic conditions of balanced bonding and au-tonomy from significant others. Although a good case can be made for any number of Axis II change domains (e.g., symptom status, functional ca-pacity related to specific roles, *DSM* descriptors, etc.), I firmly believe that in the long run, researchers must cultivate change measures that are based on observable interpersonal behaviors directly linked to theoretical models of personality, disorder, etiology, and maintenance if they are to measure change for the sake of better understanding change processes.

REFERENCES

American Psychiatric Association. (1980). *Diagnostic and statistical manual of mental disorders* (3rd ed.). Washington, DC: Author.

Benjamin, L. S. (1974). Structural Analysis of Social Behavior. *Psychological Review, 81,* 392–425.

Benjamin, L. S. (1993a). *Interpersonal diagnosis and treatment of personality disorders.* New York: Guilford Press.

Benjamin, L. S. (1993b). Every psychopathology is a gift of love. *Psychotherapy Research, 3,* 1–24.

Benjamin, L. S. (1994). Good defenses make good neighbors. In H. R. Conte & R. Plutchik (Eds.), *Ego defenses: Theory and measurement.* New York: Wiley.

Bowlby, J. (1977). The making and breaking of affectional bonds: 1. Aetiology and psychopathology in the light of attachment theory. *British Journal of Psychiatry, 130,* 201–210.

Bronisch, T., & Klerman, G. L. (1991). Personality functioning: Change and stability in relationship to symptoms and psychopathology. *Journal of Personality Disorders, 5,* 307–317.

Clark, L. A. (1992). Resolving taxonomic issues in personality disorders: The value of large-scale analyses of symptom data. *Journal of Personality Disorders, 4,* 360–376.

Clark, L. A., & Watson, D. (1995). Constructing validity: Issues in objective scale development. *Psychological Assessment, 7,* 309–319.

Cloninger, C. R. (1987). A systematic method for clinical description and classification of personality variants. *Archives of General Psychiatry, 44,* 573–588.

Ekselius, L., Lindstrom, E., von Knorring, L., Bodlund, O., & Kullgren, G. (1994). A principal component analysis of the DSM–IIIR Axis II personality disorders. *Journal of Personality Disorders, 8,* 140–148.

Eysenck, H. J. (1990). Biological dimensions of personality. In L. A. Pervin (Ed.), *Handbook of personality: Theory and research* (pp. 225–243). New York: Guilford Press.

Gabbard, G. O. (1990). *Psychodynamic psychiatry in clinical practice.* Washington, DC: American Psychiatric Press.

Henry, W. P. (1994). Differentiating normal and abnormal personality: An interpersonal approach based on the Structural Analysis of Social Behavior. In S. Strack & M. Lorr (Eds.), *Differentiating normal and abnormal personality.* New York: Springer.

Henry, W. P. (1996). The Structural Analysis of Social Behavior as a common metric for programmatic psychotherapy research. *Journal of Consulting and Clinical Psychology.*

Hirschfeld, R. M. A., Klerman, G. L., Clayton, P. J., Keller, M. B., McDonald-Scott, P., & Larkin, B. H. (1983). Assessing personality: Effects of the depressive state on trait measurement. *American Journal of Psychiatry, 140,* 695–699.

MacCorquodale, K., & Meehl, P. E. (1948). On a distinction between hypothetical constructs and intervening variables. *Psychological Review, 55,* 95–107.

McCrae, R. R., & Costa, P. T. (1987). Validation of the five-factor model of personality across instruments and observers. *Journal of Personality and Social Psychology, 52,* 81–90.

Millon, T. (1996). *Disorders of personality: DSM–IV and beyond.* New York: Wiley.

Moldin, S. O., Rice, J. P., Erlenmeyer-Kimling, L., & Squires-Wheeler, E. (1994). Latent structure of *DSM–III–R* Axis II psychopathology in a normal sample. *Journal of Abnormal Psychology, 103,* 259–266.

Morey, L. C. (1991). Classification of mental disorders as a collection of hypothetical constructs. *Journal of Abnormal Psychology, 100,* 289–293.

Morey, L. C. (1993). Psychological correlates of personality disorders. *Journal of Personality Disorders (7,* Spring Supplement), 149–166.

Nestadt, G., Romanoski, A. J., Samuels, J. F., Folstein, M. F., & McHugh, P. R. (1992). The relationship between personality and DSM–III Axis I disorders in the population: Results from an epidemiological survey. *American Journal of Psychiatry, 149,* 1228–1233.

Parker, G. (1995, October). *The etiology of personality disorders: A review and consideration of research models.* Paper presented at the National Institute of Mental Health conference on personality disorders, Bethesda, MD.

Shea, M. T. (1992). Some characteristics of the Axis II criteria sets and their implications for assessment of personality disorders. *Journal of Personality Disorders, 6,* 377–381.

Siever, L. J., & Davis, K. L. (1991). A psychobiologic perspective on the personality disorders. *American Journal of Psychiatry, 148,* 1647–1658.

Slater, E., Beard, A., & Glithero, E. (1968). Schizophrenia-like psychoses of epilepsy. *British Journal of Psychiatry, 109,* 95–150.

Strack, S., & Lorr, M. (1994). *Differentiating normal and abnormal personality.* New York: Springer.

Tyrer, P. (1995, October). *Comorbidity of Axis I and II disorders.* Paper presented at the National Institute of Mental Health conference on personality disorders, Bethesda, MD.

Tyrer, P., Casey, P., & Gall, J. (1983). The relationship between neuroses and personality disorder. *British Journal of Psychiatry, 142,* 404–408.

Vollrath, M., Alnaes, R., & Torgersen, S. (1995). Coping styles predict change in personality disorders. *Journal of Personality Disorders, 9,* 371–385.

Widiger, T. A., Trull, T. J., Hurt, S. W., Clarkin, J., & Frances, A. (1987). A multidimensional scaling of the DSM–III personality disorders. *Archives of General Psychiatry, 44,* 557–563.

Winokur, G. (1990). The concept of secondary depression and its relationship with comorbidity. *Psychological Clinics of North America, 13,* 567–583.

Zimmerman, M. (1994). Diagnosing personality disorders. *Archives of General Psychiatry, 51,* 225–245.

Zimmerman, M., & Coryell, W. (1990). DSM–III personality disorder dimensions. *Journal of Nervous and Mental Disease, 178,* 686–692.

Zimmerman, M., Pfohl, B., Coryell, W., Stangl, D., & Corenthal, C. (1988). Diagnosing personality disorder in depressed patients: A comparison of patient and informant interviews. *Archives of General Psychiatry, 45,* 733–737.

PART SIX

Afterthoughts

19

Conclusions and
Recommendations

Michael J. Lambert, Leonard M. Horowitz,
and Hans H. Strupp

W hat have these chapters shown us about the state of outcome research? This book and the conference that preceded it have provided a rich source of thoughtful discussion, making explicit the many
nuances involved in assessing the effectiveness of interventions aimed at
helping people overcome their problems. Chapter 2 in this book has provided a list of detailed conclusions from the conference itself. In addition,
each chapter author has provided additional summaries and conclusions
within the area of their expertise and interest. The chapters provide evidence of considerable consensus regarding several major issues:

1. Core batteries are needed to maximize progress toward effective
treatments.

2. Core batteries might best be conceptualized as coming in levels. We
believe that a manual for outcome assessment could be developed in which
a *universal* battery is developed that would be appropriate across all diagnostic categories. Sections within this manual would be devoted to *general*
batteries, appropriate within diagnostic groupings (e.g., mood disorders,
anxiety disorders, etc.). Finally, specific batteries are proposed for disor-

ders within groupings (e.g., some specific measures used only with patients with panic disorder).

3. Several general content domains are essential for a universal battery: the assessment of symptomatic states, social role functioning and interpersonal functioning.

4. The characteristics needed by specific outcome measures can be identified and explicitly stated. These are listed in chapter 2 and are touched on in most of the chapters in this book. The mainstay characteristics of acceptable core batteries include outstanding psychometric properties, multiple data sources, objective referents, pantheoretical assumptions, and sensitivity to change. The latter criterion is essential to outcome measurement, yet it is understudied in the empirical literature because most measures have been developed for other purposes (e.g., diagnosis).

5. There is considerable consensus that the core battery idea must take into account settings in which research is conducted. For example, what is appropriate for a managed care organization is not consistent with clinical trials research in a government-funded protocol. The solution to this problem appears to be the development of necessary but perhaps not sufficient batteries, to which researchers in various settings would add additional measures. Some of the chapters in this book address this issue directly and others provide a more narrow solution of advocating measures that are appropriate for research rather than applied settings.

6. Although agreement on the criteria for selection is nearly universal, little agreement was possible at the level of specific instruments. Individuals carry an allegiance to particular instruments. They also are familiar and comfortable with them. In addition, issues of autonomy loom large when individuals feel they may be "forced" to use an instrument for the sake of uniformity, especially when that instrument is not clearly superior to the alternatives. Furthermore, researchers who study the effects of particular therapies have theoretical interests that may have to be submerged by the need for consensual measures. As these researchers have devoted considerable energy to their work, often developing instrumentation as part of that work, they may lose the subject of their creativity. This is no small loss. It is at this level that the core battery notion becomes difficult to implement.

FUTURE RESEARCH: A MODEL
FOR INSTRUMENT SELECTION

All the authors in this book suggest directions for future research. In particular, chapters 2, 3, and 4 provide general strategies. Obviously, once criteria for ideal instruments have been identified and weighted for importance, it becomes possible to make decisions in a formal way that circumvent, to some degree, the allegiance factor. To foster the development of core batteries, eliminating, as much as possible, purely subjective evaluations of specific measures, we now provide a research strategy that may prove useful in developing core batteries. The research model can be applied to the mood disorders, anxiety disorders, personality disorders, and other general disorder groupings not dealt with in this book (e.g., substance abuse). The model also could be applied to the specific content domains relevant for universal, general, or specific batteries. Here, we present an outline of a specific study to illustrate a strategy we think will advance the field toward the identification of measures that could have widespread use. The model presented is based on an ongoing study by Logan Zemp, a doctoral student at Brigham Young University. His research is concerned specifically with the identification of measures to assess personality functioning. As the reader may recall, the Vanderbilt University conference personality disorder interest group reached consensus on measuring changes in personality functioning involving three areas of concern: maladaptive interpersonal patterns; themes of identity, role, and self-schema; and styles of expression, defense, modes of control, and temperament. Several examples of possible measures for each of these areas are presented in Table 1.

In conjunction with the recommendations of the conference, the proposed research includes several phases: (a) The first phase involves an extensive literature review to identify as many appropriate outcome measures as possible (with available, pertinent data). (b) The second phase of the study summarizes the data on each measure chosen for this study according to the selection criteria established. (c) The next stage of the research asks experts in the area to rank the criteria in order of importance so that weighted score can be provided for each instrument. (d) Other

Table 1

Preliminary Personality Disorders Assessment Measures Requiring Further Investigation

Measure	First author and year	
Structural Analysis of Social Behavior	Benjamin	1972
Schedule for Nonadaptive and Adaptive Personality	Clark	1993
The Wisconsin Personality Disorders Inventory	Klein	1993
Ego Resiliency and Coherence Scale	Block	1965
Defense Style Questionnaire	Bond	1983
Tridimensional Personality Questionnaire	Cloninger	1987
NEO Personality Inventory–Revised	Costa	1992
Diagnostic Interview for Borderlines	Gunderson	1981
Interpersonal Dependency Inventory	Hirschfeld	1977
Positive States of Mind	Horowitz	1988
Personality Diagnostic Questionnaire–Revised	Hyler	1987
Katz Adjustment Scales	Katz	1963
Personality Functioning Scale	Lingiardi	1994
Personality Disorder Examination	Loranger	1987
Standardized Assessment of Personality	Mann	1981
Millon Clinical Multiaxial Inventory	Millon	1983
MMPI Scale for Personality Disorders	Morey	1985
Structured Clinical Interview for *DSM–III* Personality Disorders	Pfohl	1983
Personality Assessment Schedule	Tyrer	1979
Personality Interview Questions	Widiger	1985

NOTE: The first five measures were recommended as examples of appropriate personality functioning measures by the personality disorders group. The first three were listed in the maladaptive interpersonal patterns area. The fourth and fifth measures were assigned the themes of identity and the styles of expression categories, respectively.

experts are asked to rate each of the measures according to the selection criteria, based on the summaries provided. (e) The final phase of the study recommends a core battery for the personality functioning domain of personality disorders that is congruent with the recommendations established by the conference. These five steps are explained further in the following sections.

Literature Review

In a review of the literature, more than 50 possible assessment instruments were identified. Table 1 shows a representative sample of various measures found by Logan Zemp. The measures suggested as possible examples by the conference personality group also are noted at the end of Table 1.

Summarizing Measures According to Criteria

Several lists of selection criteria can be referred to: the six chosen by the conference personality group and the eight produced by the conference as a whole (see chap. 2). The six chosen by the conference personality group are as follows: psychometric adequacy, information source, length and comprehensiveness, breadth of use, ties to the *Diagnostic and Statistical Manual of Mental Disorders* (*DSM*), and sensitivity to change. The group noted the importance of adequate validity and reliability for the six criteria and the need for multiple respondents, involving more than just the client and the clinician. Although the group believed that the measures should be brief, they also held that the assessment be specific and of adequate breadth to effectively gauge the impact of therapy on the client's functioning. The popularity and use of a measure by other researchers was also discussed as an indication of its applicability. The eight selection criteria chosen by the conference as a whole are as follows: clear and standardized procedures for administering and scoring; the availability of norms that discriminate between patient and nonpatient populations; demonstrated reliability; adequate construct and external validity; ease of use, efficiency, and feasibility in clinical settings (i.e., brief and inexpensive); ease of use by the clinician and relevance to clinical needs; not bound to theory; and the possibility of multiple administrations (i.e., before, during, and after treatment). There also was a consensus on the need for selected measures to be sensitive to change and to reflect categorical as well as dimensional information. It was thought that the categorical information would help determine "normalcy" and that the dimensional data would determine the amount of change.

A third set of criteria was reported by Newman and Ciarlo (1994). They listed 11 criteria grouped under five headings that were developed by a panel of experts convened by the National Institute of Mental Health

(NIMH) in 1986. These criteria are finding acceptance among researchers in evaluating outcome instruments (Gunderson, Kolb, & Austin, 1981; Teague, 1993).

There is considerable overlap between the three sets of selection criteria. In the proposed study, the list reported by Newman and Ciarlo (1994) will be used and supplemented with criteria from the American Psychological Association (APA) conference. Criterion 5, "more process-identifying outcome measures," from Newman and Ciarlo's list is not included. The authors commented that this criterion is still controversial given its lack of empirical support and theory-related arguments.

The selection criteria for the Zemp study are as follows.

1. *Relevance to target group.* This criterion notes the importance of using measures that are appropriate for the population being studied and that are congruent with their symptomatology and characteristics. The more heterogeneous a population is, the more complicated and difficult it becomes to measure treatment effects. Therefore, care is needed not only in selecting suitable measures but also in matching them to an appropriate group of participants.

2. *Simple, teachable methods.* This criterion was endorsed strongly by NIMH panelists (Newman & Ciarlo, 1994). It involves the use of clear and adequate instructions and administration manuals. This requirement includes the conference criterion of clear and standardized procedures for administering and scoring.

3. *Use of measures with objective referents.* "An objective referent is one for which concrete examples are given for each level of a measure or at least at key points on the rating scale. A major asset of objective referents is the potential to develop reliable and usable norms for an instrument" (Newman & Ciarlo, 1994, p. 100). The authors in this book note that there is still some controversy over the value of objective referents but believe that measures tied to concrete examples have benefits that need not interfere with individualized treatment.

4. *Use of multiple respondents.* The value of multiple respondents and the different perspectives needed for adequate assessment is readily agreed on by clinicians and researchers (Lambert, 1983; Lambert & Hill, 1994). This criterion also was included by the personality disorders group.

5. *Psychometric strengths and the availability of norms.* The need for adequate reliability, validity, and freedom from bias also was noted in the personality disorders group and the conference criteria lists.

6. *Low measure costs relative to its use.* This is becoming a more serious concern with rising mental health costs and the need to monitor the effectiveness of treatment to meet legal and insurance requirements. Costs involve materials, administering, scoring, processing, and analyzing, reporting, and storing of assessment data.

7. *Understanding by nonprofessional audiences, easy feedback, and uncomplicated interpretation.* The scoring, results, and interpretations of measures should be understood by all parties involved. Terms, explanations, and the presentation of information should be meaningful for those without professional training or who are unfamiliar with the field.

8. *Useful in clinical services.* This criterion emphasizes the importance of measures supporting the process of clinical services with as little interference as possible. Do the measures help in clinical decisions, communications, and providing appropriate treatment? This criterion was also noted by the APA conference.

9. *Compatibility with a variety of clinical theories and practices.* This criterion is similar to the concerns expressed at the conference that a measure not be bound to a particular theory but should be viable for use across a spectrum of theories.

10. *The possibility of multiple administrations.* This refers to a measure having the properties that allow for administration before, during, and after treatment. Properties would include length, costs, resistance to practice effects, and so on.

11. *Comprehensiveness.* The personality disorders group believed it was particularly important for measures in this area to be comprehensive enough to measure the breadth of elements and the change in functioning involved in personality disorders.

12. *Ties to the DSM.* This criterion may not have long-term value as *DSM* categories evolve, but the personality disorders group felt that some relationship to the *DSM* would have theoretical and practical value.

13. *Sensitivity to change.* The personality disorders group considered the need and challenge of finding measures that were sensitive to

change. They noted that measures that assess information that is unlikely to change (i.e., historical information) may negatively bias research attempting to quantify improvement. This criterion is viewed as being central to personality measurement because there is an obvious paradox involved between measuring something as stable as personality while capturing aspects of personality that can and do change as a consequence of interventions.

Sensitivity to change can be estimated by reference to studies that examine specific test items over repeated testing in treated and nontreated samples. Scales that have demonstrated large effect sizes in past psychotherapy and pharmacotherapy research may also be seen as being sensitive to change.

The Rating of Criteria and Measures

We recommend that these 13 criteria be used for selecting measures in future research aimed at evaluating the adequacy of particular measures. The next step in research will involve the weighting of each criterion and the rank ordering of measures identified in the literature search.

Recognized experts will be used for rating the criteria selected. Raters will be given the list of 13 criteria and asked to rank order them according to their importance for evaluating the quality of a treatment outcome measure. Each list sent to the raters would have the 13 criteria independently randomized.

Experts will also be used for rating the different measures. Raters will be given summaries of each of the individual measures with all of the available information pertinent to the criteria. After reviewing the summaries, the raters will be asked to evaluate them by completing a form. The form will use a Likert format for each of the criteria. The number rating system will range from 0 to 5. Zero is selected when there is no available information even though the criterion may be applicable. The rest of the ratings will be as follows: 1 = does not meet the criterion at all, 2 = meets the criterion to a minimal degree, 3 = meets the criterion to a moderate degree, 4 = meets the criterion to a great degree, and 5 = completely meets the criterion.

The raters will be given a description of the three areas listed under personality functioning and asked to report what areas, if any, of the personality functioning domain they believe each measure will be suitable to assess.

Statistical Analysis

The rankings of the criteria will be analyzed to create a weighted criteria list. The ordinal scale rankings will be transformed into standard scores with interval scale properties to develop appropriate weights for the individual criteria. To do this, the method of paired comparison will be used as it relates to an indirect estimate model, the law of comparative judgments (Ghiselli, Campbell, & Zedeck, 1981).

The ratings from the evaluations of the measures will be calculated with the weighted formula of the criteria to produce an overall total score of the instrument's quality based on the study. Tests of statistical significance will be used to determine the confidence that can be placed on the quality scores produced.

Selection of a Core Battery

The final stage of this study would be the recommendation of a core battery for the personality function domain, after the manner suggested by the APA conference. The top scoring measure from each area in the domain will be included in the battery. The core battery will then be assessed in terms of its overall adequacy based on the suggestions generated at the APA conference. The same procedure will be followed for other selection tasks, including the development of a universal battery, a general area battery, or choosing a specific disorder. For example, these same procedures could be applied easily to the task of deciding on a measure or symptomatic distress to be taken by all patients who are undergoing treatment. Because there are a large number of suitable scales for measuring distress, this may be the only way of providing a final "consensus" about which measure to finally recommend.

CONCLUDING REMARKS

We realize that any initial attempt at evolving a procedure has its limitations and flaws. However, the proposed procedure is a beginning attempt to take the next step in the field of outcome research, as suggested by the experts in the area. At the least, the effort will provide additional insights into the factors involved in developing core batteries to measure psychotherapy treatment outcomes. These procedures have the advantage of reducing the subjectivity of instrument choice as well as the likelihood that experts will merely recommend the scales with which they have the greatest familiarity. This will bring researchers closer to the initial goal of the core batteries conference: recommendation of specific measures. The remaining work can be accomplished with the completion of studies on the mood, anxiety, and personality disorders. These studies will provide a tentative battery for each class of disorders. The final step will be to examine the results of the use of the core batteries.

The recommendation of core batteries is an enormously complex task. Outcome assessment is a controversial area of research that is currently receiving attention from government bodies, managed care corporations, as well as traditional scientific organizations (Andrews, 1995; Bologna & Feldman, 1995; Seligman, 1995). We not only hope that some routine methods will emerge, but we also want to be actively involved in determining what these methods are and how they are used. To the extent that the use of particular interventions for treating patients with psychological disorders rests on an empirical foundation, the operationalization of valued outcomes will continue to be a topic of central importance. We look forward to seeing the consequences of more systematically measuring patient change as the treatments themselves evolve in the twenty-first century.

REFERENCES

Andrews, G. (1995). Best practices for implementing outcome management: More science, more art, worldwide. *Behavioral Healthcare Tomorrow, 4*(3), 19–24.

Benjamin, L. (1972). Structural Analysis of Social Behavior. *Psychological Review, 81,* 392–425.

Block, J. (1965). *The challenge of response sets.* New York: Appleton-Century-Crofts.

Bologna, N. C., & Feldman, M. J. (1995). Computer applications for the selection of optimal psych-social therapeutic interventions. *Behavioral Healthcare Tomorrow, 4*(3), 66–70.

Bond, M. P., Gardner, S., Christian, J., & Sigal, J. J. (1983). Empirical study of self-rated defensive styles. *Journal of Personality Disorders, 3,* 101–112.

Clark, L. A. (1993). *Manual for the Schedule for Nonadaptive and Adaptive Personality (SNAP)* Minneapolis: University of Minnesota Press.

Cloninger, C. R. (1987). *The Tridimensional Personality Questionnaire, Version iv.* St. Louis, MO: Washington University School of Medicine, Department of Psychiatry.

Costa, L. A., & McCrae, R. R. (1992). *NEO-PI-R professional manual.* Odessa, FL: Psychological Assessment Resources.

Ghiselli, E. E., Campbell, J. P., & Zedeck, S. (1981). *Measurement theory for the behavioral sciences.* New York: Freeman.

Gunderson, J., Kolb, J., & Austin, V. (1981). The diagnostic interview for borderline disordered patients. *American Journal of Psychiatry, 138,* 896–903.

Hirschfeld, R. M. A., Kierman, G. L., Gough, H. G., Barrett, J., Korchin, S. J., & Chodoff, P. (1977). A measure of interpersonal dependency. *Journal of Personality Assessment, 41,* 610–618.

Horowitz, M., Adler, N., & Kegeles, S. (1988). A scale for measuring the occurrence of positive states of mind. *Psychosomatic Medicine, 50,* 477–483.

Hyler, S. E., & Reider, R. O. (1987). *PDQ-R: Personality Diagnostic Questionnaire-Revised.* New York: New York State Psychiatric Institute.

Katz, M. M., & Lyerly, S. B. (1963). Methods for measuring adjustment and social behavior in the community: 1. Rationale, description, discriminative validity, and scale development. *Psychological Reports, 13,* 503–535.

Klein, M. H., Benjamin, L., Rosenfeldt, R. (1993). The Wisconsin Personality Disorder Inventory. *Journal of Personality Disorders, 7,* 285–303.

Lambert, M. J. (1983). Introduction to assessment in psychotherapy outcome: Historical perspective and current issues. In M. J. Lambert, S. S. DeJulio, & E. R. Christensen (Eds.), *The assessment of psychotherapy outcome* (pp. 3–32). New York: Wiley.

Lambert, M. J., & Hill, C. E. (1994). Assessing psychotherapy outcomes and processes. In A. E. Bergin & S. L. Garfield (Eds.), *Handbook of psychotherapy and behavior change* (4th ed., pp. 143–189). New York: Wiley.

Lingiardi, V., Madeddu, F., Fossati, A., & Massei, C. (1994). Reliability and validity of the Personality Functioning Scale (PFS). *Journal of Personality Disorders, 8,* 111–120.

Loranger, A., Susman, V., Oldham, J., & Russakoff, L. M. (1987). The Personality Disorders Examination: A preliminary report. *Journal of Personality Disorders, 1,* 1–13.

Mann, A., Jenkins, R., Cutting, J., & Cowen, P. (1981). The development and use of a standardized assessment of abnormal personality. *Psychological Medicine, 11,* 839–847.

Millon, T. (1983). *Millon Clinical Multiaxial Inventory manual* (3rd ed.). Minneapolis: Interpretive Scoring Systems.

Morey, L., Waugh, M., & Blashfield, R. (1985). MMPI scales for DSM–III Personality Disorders: Their derivation and correlates. *Journal of Personality Assessments, 49,* 245–251.

Newman, F. L., & Ciarlo, J. A. (1994). Criteria for selecting psychological instruments for treatment outcome assessments. In M. E. Maruish (Ed.), *The use of psychological testing for treatment planning and outcome assessment* (pp. 98–110). Hillside, NJ: Erlbaum.

Pfohl, B., Stangl, D., & Zimmerman, M. (1983). *Structured Interview for DSM–III Personality Disorders, SIDP* (2nd ed.). Unpublished manuscript, University of Iowa, College of Medicine, Iowa City.

Seligman, M. E. P. (1995). The effectiveness of psychotherapy: The *Consumer Reports* study. *American Psychologist, 50,* 965–974.

Teague, G. B. (1993, March). *A review of the Addiction Severity Index using the Newman/Ciarlo criteria for selecting instruments for outcome assessment.* Session handout, National Conference on Mental Health Statistics, Washington, DC.

Tyrer, P., & Alexander, J. (1979). Classification of personality disorder. *British Journal of Psychiatry, 135,* 163–167.

Widiger, T. (1985). *Personality interview questions.* Unpublished manuscript, University of Kentucky, Lexington.

Author Index

Numbers in italics refer to listings in reference sections.

Stroop, J. R., 350, *367*
Strupp, H. H., 16–19, 21, *53,* 58, 59, *80,* 99, 101, *114,* 158, *187,* 250, 254, *262,* 317, *338,* 442, *459*
Stuebing, K. K., 71, *76*
Suarez, A., 452, *458*
Sugahara, C., 408, *430*
Sullivan, J. L., 449, *459*
Susman, V., *502*
Susman, V. L., 372, *386*
Sutherland, G., 360, *367*
Svrakic, D. M., 374, *384*
Swaminathan, H., 383, *385*
Swanson, B. A., *186*
Swinson, R. P., 125, 134, 136, *147*

Talbott, R., 233, *237*
Tamir, L. M., 233, *237*
Tan, L., 276, *281*
Tanaka-Matsumi, J., 162, *188*
Tarika, J., *95*
Tarnowski, K. J., 72, *75*
Tarver, D. J., 122, 128, *151*
Taylor, C. B., 133, *151,* 178, *185*
Taylor, K. L., 27, *51,* 128, *149*
Taylor, S., 170, 172, 175, *188*
Taylor, S. E., 67, *80*
Teague, G. B., 496, *502*
Teasdale, J. D., 81, 83, 84, 86–88, 92, *95, 97, 98,* 350, 353, *367*
Telch, C. F., 322, *337*
Tellegen, A., 29, *53,* 360, *367*
Teti, D. M., 381, *384*
Thase, M., 289, *299*
Thase, M. E., 83, *97,* 308, *338*
Thomas, D., *153*
Thomas, R. E., 69, *77*
Thomas, R. T., 122, 143, *149*
Thompson, C., 356, *367*
Thompson, N. M., 71, *76*
Thompson, W. D., 231, *245*
Todd, T. C., 287, 294, *299*
Tolan, N. T., *241*

Torgersen, S., 125, *152,* 165, *187,* 481, *488*
Torre, M. de la, 344, *367*
Tovey, D. R., 16, *51*
Towle, L. H., *52*
Townsley, R. M., 126, 145, *153*
Trabin, T., 3, *10*
Treece, C., *386, 400*
Treliving, L. R., *184*
Trexler, L., 143, *153,* 227, *238,* 259, *261*
Trivedi, M. H., 206, *244*
Truax, P., 70, 71, *77,* 145, *149,* 274, *279*
Trull, T. J., 71, *79,* 371, 374, *388,* 474, *488*
Tsuang, M. T., 371, *384*
Tuason, V. B., *95*
Tulving, E., 86, *97*
Tunbull, G., *151*
Tunis, S. L., 416, *432*
Tuorila, J., *153*
Turk, C. L., *152*
Turk, D. C., 90, *95*
Turner, M. W., 145, *153*
Turner, R. M., 8, 169, *184,* 433, 438, 448, 449, 451, 452, *459, 460*
Turner, S. M., 126, 133, 135, 142, 145, *146, 153*
Turvey, C., *428*
Tyrer, P., 380, *384, 388,* 464, 465, *488,* 494, *502*

Uhlenhuth, E. H., 215, *239*
Ureño, G., 27, *51,* 164, *185,* 295, *297,* 377, *385,* 423, *429*
Utech, J. E., *334*

Vaillant, G. E., 423, *429, 432*
van Beijsterveldt, B., *383*
VandenBos, G. R., 81, *97*
Van Der Ende, J., 179, *182*
Vanderplas, J. M., 357, 358, *367*

Subject Index

About the Editors

Hans H. Strupp was born in Germany, emigrated to the United States in 1939, and received his PhD in 1954 from the George Washington University. He is a graduate also of the Washington School of Psychiatry. He served on the faculty of the University of North Carolina from 1957 to 1966 and has been at Vanderbilt University since 1966. He is currently Distinguished Professor of Psychology, Emeritus. Dr. Strupp has been engaged in psychotherapy research since 1953 and has authored more than 300 publications dealing with psychotherapy research, practice, and training, primarily from a psychodynamic perspective. He is a past president of the Society for Psychotherapy Research, a recipient of that society's Distinguished Career Contribution Award, and a recipient of the Distinguished Professional Contributions to Knowledge Award of the American Psychological Association (APA). He is also a past president of the APA's Division of Clinical Psychology and holds an honorary degree of Doctor of Medicine from the University of Ulm, Germany.

Leonard M. Horowitz is professor of psychology at Stanford University and co-director of the Terman Gifted Children Project. He received his PhD from the Johns Hopkins University and his clinical training from the Mount Zion Psychiatric Clinic, Mt. Zion Hospital, San Francisco. He has been a Woodrow Wilson Fellow; a Fulbright Fellow at University College, University of London; a Social Science Research Council Fellow; and a Special Fellow of the National Institute of Mental Health. He received a James McKeen Cattell Award in 1986–1987 and was president of the International Society for Psychotherapy Research in 1993. He is on the advisory board of various journals, and his research concerns interpersonal processes that promote or hinder therapeutic change. His test, the Inventory of Interpersonal Problems, is currently being published by the Psychological Corporation.